Optical Interactions in Solids

Optical Interactions in Solids

BALDASSARE DI BARTOLO

Senior Scientist

MITHRAS, a division of Sanders Associates, Inc.

Cambridge, Massachusetts

JOHN WILEY & SONS, INC.

NEW YORK · LONDON · SYDNEY · TORONTO

Library of Congress Catalog Card Number: 67-31206
GB 471 21276 8
Printed in the United States of America

"Il fare un libro è meno che niente,
se il libro fatto non rifà la gente."

To My Parents and to Rita

"Fici 'sti quattru chiacchiri
—e sai comu li fici—
sulu pri fari ridiri
'na pennula d'amici."

Preface

The purpose of this book is to provide physicists working with lasers and absorption and fluorescence spectroscopy of solids with a theoretical background. As one of these workers I have tried to express my understanding of the basic mathematic tools and physics involved in these fields of research: the choice of the different subjects has been determined by the needs that at one time or another have been part of my experience.

This book is not intended to be a work in quantum mechanics or group theory; as a matter of fact it presupposes the equivalent of one year of study of quantum mechanics. No previous knowledge of group theory, however, is required. The content of this work could be the subject of a two-term graduate course in solid-state spectroscopy.

Optical Interactions in Solids is divided into nineteen chapters. In the first chapter quantum mechanics is developed from certain basic postulates, the fundamental concepts are enunciated, and basic tools, such as time-independent and time-dependent perturbation theories, are elaborated.

In the second chapter group theory is developed with particular reference to symmetries in crystals. This treatment does not presuppose any previous knowledge of group theory.

In Chapter 3 the connection between group theory and quantum mechanics is examined. This, I think, may be one of the peculiar aspects of this work, for group theory is introduced from the beginning before any example of physical systems is presented. Quantum mechanics and group theory are then used *at the same time*, and the connections examined are fully exploited throughout the rest of the book.

In Chapter 4 the hydrogen atom is considered, which may seem to be a repetition, for this simple system is covered in many books on quantum mechanics. The introduction of this example will familarize the reader with group theory even in the treatment of simple systems in which no use of it has ever been made. It is important to point out in this context how many group theoretical concepts are unknowingly applied by physicists in the treatment of their problems. The purpose of this chapter is to uncover the group theoretical aspects of some of these treatments so that the reader may become fully conscious of their potentialities.

In Chapter 5 the theory of complex atoms is examined, and here too group theory is used to derive many of the results of atomic spectroscopy.

The basic problems in the evaluation of energy levels of ions in crystals and the role played by crystal symmetries are investigated in Chapter 6. The crystalline hypothesis is introduced and a formal classification of weak, medium, and strong field is introduced. It is pointed out here that, although this classification may resemble different physical situations, the three cases of weak, medium, and strong field may be considered as *schemes* that a worker could choose independently, according to his own particular approach to the problem. These schemes can actually be developed from a purely mathematical point of view.

The three schemes and their relevance to magnetic ions in crystals are examined in Chapters 7, 8, and 9.

In Chapter 10 the effects of covalent bonding on the energy levels of magnetic ions in crystals are studied and a comparison is made between the molecular orbital and crystalline field approaches. The theory of molecular orbitals is then formally established to provide a background for the understanding of some aspects of absorption spectroscopy (charge transfer spectra) described in Chapter 17.

The second part of the book begins with Chapter 11 on the quantum theory of the radiation field. Chapter 12 follows with a formal treatment of molecular vibrations, and Chapter 13 describes a quantum mechanical treatment of thermal vibrations in crystals.

Next, Chapters 14 and 15 deal with the interaction of ionic systems with the radiation field and lattice vibrations, respectively. The basic mechanisms involved in the absorption and emission of radiation are examined and radiationless processes are treated in a similar way. The effects of thermal vibrations of the position and width of sharp lines are also treated in Chapter 15.

Chapter 16 is devoted to the study of vibrational-electronic, or vibronic, transitions of those processes that involve the contemporary emission or absorption of a photon and the absorption or emission of one or more phonons.

Chapter 17 reports the fundamental problems in the evaluation of the absorption spectra of magnetic ions in crystals, as does Chapter 18 with regard to the fluorescence spectra of the same systems.

Finally, in Chapter 19 elements of laser theory are developed without consideration of the technical problems and point mainly to the "lasing" material itself.

I should like to acknowledge the help received from discussions I have had with Professor George Koster, Mr. Roberto Peccei, and Dr. Petros Argyres of M.I.T., with Dr. Perry Miles and Dr. Marvin Weber of the Research Division of the Raytheon Company, with Dr. Charles Naiman, Dr. Mahbub'ul Alam, Mr. Behzad Birang, and Mr. Kenneth Gooen of MITHRAS, and with Dr. Richard Powell and Mr. Carlton Lehr.

The help and the assistance I received from the Research Division of Raytheon, the Quantum Physics Group of Mithras, and Miss Beatrice Shube, Mrs. Aline Walton, Mrs. Charlotte Shelby, and Mr. Kenneth Maddock, editors of John Wiley and Sons, is gratefully acknowledged. I also wish to thank Miss Josephine Silvestro for her help in the bibliographic search, Mrs. Doris Hanson, Mr. Kent Groote, Mr. Raymond Tourtellot, and Mr. Elpidio Silvestri for their assistance at different stages of the work, and Mrs. Norma Osborne of the Osborne Technical Services for her typing of the manuscript.

Baldassare Di Bartolo

Watertown, Massachusetts
June 1967

Contents

Optical Interactions in Solids

1

Elements of Quantum Mechanics

1. REVIEW OF CLASSICAL MECHANICS

Let us assume that we have a system with N degrees of freedom, and represented by N generalized coordinates $q_1, q_2 \cdots q_N$.

In the Lagrangian formulation the equations of motion are given by the following N second-order differential equations:

$$\frac{d}{dt}\frac{\partial L}{\partial \dot{q}_i} - \frac{\partial L}{\partial q_i} = 0. \tag{1.1}$$

The Lagrangian L, for conservative systems, is defined as

$$L(q_i, \dot{q}_i) = T - V, \tag{1.2}$$

where $T =$ kinetic energy and $V =$ potential energy. For a one-coordinate conservative system $q_i = x$ and

$$L = \tfrac{1}{2}m\dot{x}^2 - V(x) \tag{1.3}$$

and (1.1) reduces to

$$m\ddot{x} = -\frac{\partial V}{\partial x} \tag{1.4}$$

An example of a nonconservative system is given by a particle with a charge q in an electromagnetic field. The Lagrangian is given by

$$L = T - q\phi + \frac{q}{c}\mathbf{v} \cdot \mathbf{A}, \tag{1.5}$$

ϕ being the scalar and $\mathbf{A}$ the vector potential of the field. In fact,

$$\frac{d}{dt}\frac{\partial L}{\partial \dot{x}} = m\ddot{x} + \frac{q}{c}\frac{dA_x}{dt}$$

$$\frac{\partial L}{\partial x} = -q\left[\frac{\partial \phi}{\partial x} + \frac{\partial}{\partial x}\left(\frac{1}{c}\mathbf{v} \cdot \mathbf{A}\right)\right].$$

Then we have the vector equation

$$m\ddot{\mathbf{r}} = q\left[-\nabla\phi + \nabla\left(\frac{1}{c}\mathbf{v}\cdot\mathbf{A}\right) - \frac{1}{c}\frac{d\mathbf{A}}{dt}\right]. \tag{1.6}$$

Taking into account

$$\mathbf{v}\times(\nabla\times\mathbf{A}) = \nabla(\mathbf{v}\cdot\mathbf{A}) - (\mathbf{v}\cdot\nabla)\,\mathbf{A}$$

$$\frac{d\mathbf{A}}{dt} = \frac{\partial\mathbf{A}}{\partial t} + (\mathbf{v}\cdot\nabla)\,\mathbf{A},$$

we transform (1.6) into

$$\begin{aligned} m\ddot{\mathbf{r}} &= q\left[-\nabla\phi - \frac{1}{c}\frac{\partial\mathbf{A}}{\partial t} - \frac{1}{c}\mathbf{v}\times(\nabla\times\mathbf{A})\right] \\ &= q\left[\mathbf{E} + \frac{1}{c}(\mathbf{v}\times\mathbf{B})\right], \end{aligned} \tag{1.7}$$

since the fields are expressed by

$$\mathbf{E} = -\nabla\phi - \frac{1}{c}\frac{\partial\mathbf{A}}{\partial t}, \tag{1.8}$$

$$\mathbf{B} = \nabla\times\mathbf{A}.$$

The right side of (1.7) expresses the Lorentz force; (1.5) is then proved.

A different formulation of the equations of motion is given by the Hamilton's equations which are derived in the following way.

We define as *generalized momenta* the quantities

$$p_i = \frac{\partial L}{\partial \dot{q}_i} \tag{1.9}$$

and as Hamiltonian of the system the following function:

$$H = \sum_i (p_i\dot{q}_i - L) = H(p_i, q_i, t). \tag{1.10}$$

Differentiating (1.10), we get

$$\begin{aligned} dH &= \sum_i \left(\frac{\partial H}{\partial q_i}\,dq_i + \frac{\partial H}{\partial p_i}\,dp_i\right) + \frac{\partial H}{\partial t}\,dt \\ &= \sum_i \left(p_i\,d\dot{q}_i + \dot{q}_i\,dp_i - \frac{\partial L}{\partial q_i}\,dq_i - \frac{\partial L}{\partial \dot{q}_i}\,d\dot{q}_i\right) - \frac{\partial L}{\partial t}\,dt \\ &= \sum_i \left(\dot{q}_i\,dp_i - \frac{\partial L}{\partial q_i}\,dq_i\right) - \frac{\partial L}{\partial t}\,dt \\ &= \sum_i (\dot{q}_i\,dp_i - \dot{p}_i\,dq_i) - \frac{\partial L}{\partial t}\,dt. \end{aligned} \tag{1.11}$$

Then we get the canonical or Hamilton's equations

$$\dot{q}_i = \frac{\partial H}{\partial p_i}; \qquad \dot{p}_i = -\frac{\partial H}{\partial q_i}; \qquad \frac{\partial H}{\partial t} = -\frac{\partial L}{\partial t}. \tag{1.12}$$

The kinetic energy is in general given by

$$T = \sum_{ij} \alpha_{ij}\dot{q}_i\dot{q}_j, \qquad (\alpha_{ij} = \alpha_{ji}), \tag{1.13}$$

and

$$\sum_i \dot{q}_i \frac{\partial T}{\partial \dot{q}_i} = 2T. \tag{1.14}$$

If the system is conservative ($L = T - V$) we get

$$p_i = \frac{\partial L}{\partial \dot{q}_i} = \frac{\partial T}{\partial \dot{q}_i}. \tag{1.15}$$

Then

$$H = \sum_i (p_i\dot{q}_i - L) = \sum_i \left(\dot{q}_i \frac{\partial T}{\partial \dot{q}_i} - L\right) = T + V. \tag{1.16}$$

Let us now consider the Hamiltonian of a charged particle in an electromagnetic field. The generalized momentum is given by

$$\begin{aligned} p_i &= \frac{\partial L}{\partial \dot{q}_i} = \frac{\partial T}{\partial \dot{q}_i} + \frac{q}{c}\frac{\partial}{\partial \dot{q}_i}(\mathbf{v}\cdot\mathbf{A}) \\ &= \frac{\partial T}{\partial \dot{q}_i} + \frac{q}{c}A_i = mv_i + \frac{q}{c}A_i. \end{aligned} \tag{1.17}$$

Then from (1.17) and (1.5) we get

$$\begin{aligned} H &= \sum_i (p_i\dot{q}_i - L) = \sum_i \left(\frac{\partial L}{\partial \dot{q}_i}\dot{q}_i\right) - \left(T - q\phi + \frac{q}{c}\mathbf{v}\cdot\mathbf{A}\right) \\ &= \sum_i \left[\left(\frac{\partial T}{\partial \dot{q}_i} + \frac{q}{c}A_i\right)\dot{q}_i\right] - \left(T - q\phi + \frac{q}{c}\mathbf{v}\cdot\mathbf{A}\right) \\ &= \sum_i \left[\frac{\partial T}{\partial \dot{q}_i}\dot{q}_i\right] - T + q\phi \\ &= T + q\phi = \tfrac{1}{2}mv^2 + q\phi. \end{aligned} \tag{1.18}$$

We have

$$\tfrac{1}{2}mv^2 = \frac{1}{2}\frac{(m\mathbf{v})^2}{m} = \frac{1}{2}\frac{[\mathbf{p} - (q/c)\mathbf{A}]^2}{m},$$

and

$$H = \frac{1}{2}\frac{[\mathbf{p} - (q/c)\mathbf{A}]^2}{m} + q\phi. \tag{1.19}$$

We want now to introduce the important concept of *Poisson bracket* of two quantities F and G which is defined by

$$\{F, G\} = \sum_i \left(\frac{\partial F}{\partial q_i}\frac{\partial G}{\partial p_i} - \frac{\partial F}{\partial p_i}\frac{\partial G}{\partial q_i}\right). \tag{1.20}$$

The time dependence of any function of the coordinates, momenta, and time of a system with N degrees of freedom is

$$\begin{aligned}\frac{d}{dt}F(q_1, q_2, \ldots, q_n; p_1, p_2, \ldots, p_N, t) \\ &= \frac{\partial F}{\partial t} + \sum_{i=1}^{N}\left(\frac{\partial F}{\partial q_i}\dot{q}_i + \frac{\partial F}{\partial p_i}\dot{p}_i\right) \\ &= \frac{\partial F}{\partial t} + \sum_{i=1}^{N}\left(\frac{\partial F}{\partial q_i}\frac{\partial H}{\partial p_i} - \frac{\partial F}{\partial p_i}\frac{\partial H}{\partial q_i}\right) \\ &= \frac{\partial F}{\partial t} + \{F, H\},\end{aligned} \tag{1.21}$$

where we have taken advantage of (1.12). If F is a constant of the motion, $dF/dt = 0$ and

$$\frac{\partial F}{\partial t} = -\{F, H\}. \tag{1.22}$$

2. VECTOR SPACES AND LINEAR OPERATORS

A *vector space* is a collection of objects $\mathbf{u}, \mathbf{v}, \ldots,$ which have the following properties:

(a) $\mathbf{u} + (\mathbf{v} + \mathbf{w}) = (\mathbf{u} + \mathbf{v}) + \mathbf{w}$

(b) $\mathbf{u} + \mathbf{v} = \mathbf{v} + \mathbf{u}$ (1.23)

(c) $\mathbf{v} + \mathbf{x} = \mathbf{u}$; given $\mathbf{v}$, there is only one vector $\mathbf{x}$ which summed to it gives $\mathbf{u}$.

The *inner product* of two vectors is a complex number which has the following properties:

(a) $(\mathbf{v}, \mathbf{u}) = (\mathbf{u}, \mathbf{v})^*$

(b) $(\mathbf{u}, \mathbf{u}) =$ real number (1.24)

(c) $(\mathbf{v}, a\mathbf{u}) = a(\mathbf{v}, \mathbf{u})$

(d) $([\mathbf{u} + \mathbf{v}], \mathbf{w}) = (\mathbf{u}, \mathbf{w}) + (\mathbf{v}, \mathbf{w})$.

The length of a vector $\mathbf{u}$ is defined as

$$|\mathbf{u}| = \sqrt{(\mathbf{u}, \mathbf{u})}. \tag{1.25}$$

Two vectors **u**, **v** are *orthogonal* if

$$(\mathbf{u}, \mathbf{v}) = 0. \tag{1.26}$$

n vectors $\mathbf{a}_1, \mathbf{a}_2, \ldots, \mathbf{a}_n$ are *linearly independent*, if there is no ensemble of complex numbers $c_1 c_2, \ldots, c_n$ such that:

$$c_1\mathbf{a}_1 + c_2\mathbf{a}_2 + \cdots + c_n\mathbf{a}_n = 0. \tag{1.27}$$

Given a certain vector space, if it is possible to choose a set of n vectors which are linearly independent, but it is not possible to choose a set of $n + 1$ vectors which are linearly independent, then the vector space is said to be *n-dimensional.*

In an n-dimensional vector space any vector of the space can be expressed as a linear combination of n linearly independent vectors

$$\mathbf{x} = x_1\mathbf{a}_1 + x_2\mathbf{a}_2 + \cdots + x_n\mathbf{a}_n \tag{1.28}$$

and $x_1, x_2, \ldots, x_n$ are the *components* of **x** with respect to the basis vectors $a_1, a_2, \ldots, a_n$. To specify an entire vector space it is enough to specify a certain basis; by allowing the complex numbers x_i to take any value, we can generate the entire vector space.

Once we choose a certain basis we can express a vector **x** in the following matrix form:

$$\mathbf{x} \equiv \begin{pmatrix} x_1 \\ x_2 \\ \cdot \\ \cdot \\ \cdot \\ x_n \end{pmatrix}. \tag{1.29}$$

It is always possible to choose basis vectors which are mutually orthogonal. A basis $\mathbf{a}_1, \mathbf{a}_2, \ldots, \mathbf{a}_n$ is said to be *orthonormal*, if

$$(\mathbf{a}_i, \mathbf{a}_j) = \delta_{ij}. \tag{1.30}$$

In this case, the inner product of two vectors **x**, **y** is given by

$$\begin{aligned}(\mathbf{x}, \mathbf{y}) &= \left(\sum_i x_i\mathbf{a}_i, \sum_j y_j\mathbf{a}_j\right) \\ &= \sum_{ij} x_i^* y_j \delta_{ij} = \sum_i x_i^* y_i.\end{aligned} \tag{1.31}$$

In an n-dimensional vector space there can be at most n mutually orthogonal vectors.

Let us consider a vector space R_n of dimensionality n. An *operator* Q can transform a vector **u** of R_n in another vector **v** of R_n

$$\mathbf{v} = Q\mathbf{u}. \tag{1.32}$$

The operator Q is said to be *linear* if

$$Q(\mathbf{u} + \mathbf{w}) = Q\mathbf{u} + Q\mathbf{w} \tag{1.33}$$
$$Q(c\mathbf{u}) = cQ\mathbf{u} \qquad (c = \text{const})$$

for any $\mathbf{u}$, $\mathbf{w}$, c.

A linear operator Q can be expressed in matrix form in the following way. If the basis vectors are $\mathbf{a}_1, \mathbf{a}_2, \ldots, \mathbf{a}_n$, then

$$Q\mathbf{a}_j = \sum_{i=1}^{n} Q_{ij}\mathbf{a}_i \qquad (j = 1, 2, \ldots, n) \tag{1.34}$$

and Q can be represented by the following matrix[1] which completely defines the effect of operator Q on the basis vectors:

$$\mathbf{Q} = \begin{pmatrix} Q_{11} & Q_{12} & \cdots & Q_{1n} \\ Q_{21} & Q_{22} & \cdots & Q_{2n} \\ \cdots & \cdots & \cdots & \cdots \\ Q_{n1} & Q_{n2} & \cdots & Q_{nn} \end{pmatrix} \tag{1.35}$$

From (1.32) and (1.34)

$$\mathbf{v} = \sum_i v_i\mathbf{a}_i = Q\left(\sum_j u_j\mathbf{a}_j\right)$$
$$= \sum_j u_j(Qa_j) = \sum_{ij} Q_{ij}u_j\mathbf{a}_i,$$

[1] Given a matrix $\mathbf{A}$, we have the following definitions:

Complex matrix: $\mathbf{A}^*:(\mathbf{A}^*)_{ij} = (\mathbf{A})_{ij}^*$

Transpose: $\tilde{\mathbf{A}}:(\tilde{\mathbf{A}})_{ij} = (\mathbf{A})_{ji}$

Adjoint: $\mathbf{A}^+:(\mathbf{A}^+)_{ij} = (\mathbf{A})_{ji}^*$.

A matrix $\mathbf{A}$ is called *nonsingular* if it possesses an inverse $\mathbf{A}^{-1}$:

$$\mathbf{A}\mathbf{A}^{-1} = \mathbf{A}^{-1}\mathbf{A} = \mathbf{1}$$

Hermitian: $\mathbf{A}^+ = \mathbf{A}$

Symmetric: $\tilde{\mathbf{A}} = \mathbf{A}$

Skew symmetric: $\tilde{\mathbf{A}} = -\mathbf{A}$

Orthogonal: $\tilde{\mathbf{A}} = \mathbf{A}^{-1}$ or $\tilde{\mathbf{A}}\mathbf{A} = \mathbf{1}$

Unitary: $\mathbf{A}^+ = \mathbf{A}^{-1}$.

Notice:

$$(\mathbf{ABC})^{-1} = \mathbf{C}^{-1}\mathbf{B}^{-1}\mathbf{A}^{-1}$$
$$(\mathbf{ABC})^+ = \mathbf{C}^+\mathbf{B}^+\mathbf{A}^+.$$

and then

$$v_i = \sum_{j=1}^{n} Q_{ij} u_j \tag{1.36}$$

or, in matrix form,

$$\begin{pmatrix} v_1 \\ v_2 \\ \cdot \\ \cdot \\ \cdot \\ v_n \end{pmatrix} = \begin{pmatrix} Q_{11} & Q_{12} & \cdots & Q_{1n} \\ Q_{21} & Q_{22} & \cdots & Q_{2n} \\ \cdots & \cdots & \cdots & \cdots \\ Q_{n1} & Q_{n2} & \cdots & Q_{nn} \end{pmatrix} \begin{pmatrix} u_1 \\ u_2 \\ \cdot \\ \cdot \\ \cdot \\ u_n \end{pmatrix} \tag{1.37}$$

We shall be dealing with two types of linear transformation:

Linear Unitary Transformation. A linear operator Q is called *unitary* if

$$(Q\mathbf{u}, Q\mathbf{w}) = (\mathbf{u}, \mathbf{w}). \tag{1.38}$$

If, in particular, $\mathbf{u} = \mathbf{a}_i$ and $\mathbf{w} = \mathbf{a}_j$, with $(\mathbf{a}_i, \mathbf{a}_j) = \delta_{ij}$,

$$(Q\mathbf{a}_i, Q\mathbf{a}_j) = \delta_{ij}; \tag{1.39}$$

but

$$Q\mathbf{a}_i = \sum_{l=1}^{n} Q_{li}\mathbf{a}_l$$
$$Q\mathbf{a}_j = \sum_{m=1}^{n} Q_{mj}\mathbf{a}_m. \tag{1.40}$$

Therefore

$$\begin{aligned}(Q\mathbf{a}_i, Q\mathbf{a}_j) &= \sum_{l,m} Q_{li}^* Q_{mj} \delta_{lm} \\ &= \sum_l Q_{li}^* Q_{lj} = \sum_l (\mathbf{Q}^+)_{il} Q_{lj} = (\mathbf{Q}^+\mathbf{Q})_{ij} = \delta_{ij},\end{aligned} \tag{1.41}$$

or

$$\mathbf{Q}^+\mathbf{Q} = \mathbf{1}. \tag{1.42}$$

Then we can say:

"*If the basis vectors of a vector space are orthonormal, the matrix representing a linear unitary operator is unitary.*"

Linear Hermitian Transformation. A linear operator Q is said to be *Hermitian* if

$$(Q\mathbf{u}, \mathbf{w}) = (\mathbf{u}, Q\mathbf{w}). \tag{1.43}$$

If, in particular, $\mathbf{u} = \mathbf{a}_i$ and $\mathbf{w} = \mathbf{a}_j$, with $(\mathbf{a}_i, \mathbf{a}_j) = \delta_{ij}$,

$$(Q\mathbf{a}_i, \mathbf{a}_j) = \sum_{l=1}^{n} Q_{li}^*(\mathbf{a}_l, \mathbf{a}_j) = Q_{ji}^*,$$
$$(\mathbf{a}_i, Q\mathbf{a}_j) = \sum_{m=1}^{n} Q_{mj}(\mathbf{a}_i, \mathbf{a}_m) = Q_{ij}, \tag{1.44}$$

and

$$Q_{ij}^* = (\mathbf{Q}^+)_{ij} = Q_{ij} \tag{1.45}$$

or

$$\mathbf{Q}^+ = \mathbf{Q}. \tag{1.46}$$

We can say then that:

"*If the basis vectors of a vector space are orthonormal, the matrix representing a linear Hermitian operator is Hermitian.*"

We shall be dealing with two types of vector spaces:

Real Vector Space. The *real vector space* is formed by all the spatial vectors of finite dimensions. Since each vector can be expressed as a linear combination of three linearly independent vectors, this space is three dimensional.

Hilbert Space. The *Hilbert space* is a vector space in which the basis vectors are linearly independent functions of one or more variables.

A vector of the Hilbert space is a function $u(x)$ which can be expressed in the following way:

$$\mathbf{u} = u(x) = u_1 f_1(x) + u_2 f_2(x) + \cdots + u_n f_n(x), \tag{1.47}$$

where the basis vectors are given by

$$\mathbf{a}_1 = f_1(x), \quad \mathbf{a}_2 = f_2(x) \cdots \mathbf{a}_n = f_n(x). \tag{1.48}$$

The *inner product* of two vector functions $u(x)$ and $w(x)$ is now defined as

$$(\mathbf{u}, \mathbf{w}) = \int u(x)^* \, w(x) \, dx. \tag{1.49}$$

Two functions $u(x)$, $w(x)$ are *orthogonal*, if their inner product is zero.

A Hilbert space may have infinite dimension; in this case the space is formed by vector-functions of finite length:

$$(\mathbf{u}, \mathbf{u}) = \int |u(x)|^2 \, dx = \text{finite number}. \tag{1.50}$$

The requirement of the finiteness of the vector functions length implies that any inner product is also finite. In fact, because of the Schwarz inequality,

$$|(\mathbf{u}, \mathbf{w})|^2 = \left| \int u(x)^* \, w(x) \, dx \right|^2 \leq \int |u(x)|^2 \, dx \int |w(x)|^2 \, dx$$

$$= (\mathbf{u}, \mathbf{u}) \, (\mathbf{w}, \mathbf{w}) = \text{finite number}. \tag{1.51}$$

Let us assume now that $\mathbf{Q}$ is the matrix representation of an operator Q, in a space V_n defined by a set of basis vectors $\mathbf{a}_1, \mathbf{a}_2, \ldots, \mathbf{a}_n$. Let us choose for the same vector space a different set of basis vectors

$$\mathbf{a}_i' = \sum_{j=1}^{n} S_{ji}\mathbf{a}_j. \tag{1.52}$$

The operator Q, operating on the new basis vectors $\mathbf{a}_i'$ will produce

$$\begin{aligned} Q\mathbf{a}_i' &= \sum_{j=1}^{n} S_{ji} Q\mathbf{a}_j = \sum_{j=1}^{n} S_{ji} \sum_{k=1}^{n} Q_{kj}\mathbf{a}_k \\ &= \sum_{j=1}^{n} S_{ji} \sum_{k=1}^{n} Q_{kj} \sum_{m=1}^{n} (\mathbf{S}^{-1})_{mk}\mathbf{a}_m' = \sum_{m=1}^{n} Q_{mi}'\mathbf{a}_m', \end{aligned} \tag{1.53}$$

and therefore

$$Q_{mi}' = \sum_{kj} (\mathbf{S}^{-1})_{mk} Q_{kj} S_{ji}, \tag{1.54}$$

namely the operator Q in the new basis system is given by

$$\mathbf{Q}' = \mathbf{S}^{-1}\mathbf{Q}\mathbf{S}. \tag{1.55}$$

A transformation of this type is called *similarity transformation.*

Given an n-dimensional vector space V_n, if a vector space W_r of dimension r $(r < n)$ is contained in V_n, we call W_r a *subspace* of V_n.

If an operator Q acting on V_n has the property that for every vector $\mathbf{w}$ of W_r, $Q\mathbf{w}$ is also in W_r, then W_r is said to be an *invariant subspace* of V_n with respect to the operator (or to the transformation) Q.

For example, in a real vector space the subspace that consists of all the vectors in the xy plane is invariant with respect to all rotations about the z-axis. The subspace that consists of all vectors lying along the z-axis is also an invariant subspace with respect to the same rotations.

3. BASIC POSTULATES OF QUANTUM MECHANICS

The essence of quantum mechanics can be expressed in a number of assumptions whose validity is based on the agreement that their logical consequences manifest with the experimental results. This formulation does not necessarily follow the historical development of the subject but it is self-consistent and is justified by the agreement with the experiments.

Postulate 1

A system of particles with f degrees of freedom and coordinates $q_1, q_2, \ldots, q_f$ is described by a state function $\psi(q_i, t)$ which has the property that $\psi^*\psi \, d\tau$ is the probability that the variables lies in the volume $d\tau$ at the time t, namely that q_i has a value in the interval $q_i, q_i + dq_i$ at time t. This function contains all the information available about the system.

Postulate 2

Any physical observable q is represented by a Hermitian differential operator Q; the possible results of an experimental measurement of the observable are the eigenvalues of the differential equation

$$Q\psi_n = q_n\psi_n. \tag{1.56}$$

If, before the measurement, the function ψ is not an eigenfunction of Q then it is impossible to predict with certainty the result of the experiment. If the result of the measurement is q_n, then, by making the measurement, we change the state of the system to a state, which, immediately after the measurement, is described by ψ_n.

A linear operator Q is said to be *Hermitian* if, being $f(x)$ and $g(x)$ any two functions,

$$\int f(x)^* \, Q \, g(x) \, dx = \int [Qf(x)]^* \, g(x) \, dx. \tag{1.57}$$

Let us consider now a Hermitian operator, operating on a vector function ψ. If ψ is such a function that

$$Q\psi = q\psi, \tag{1.58}$$

then ψ and q are said to be respectively an *eigenfunction* and an *eigenvalue* of Q. In general there is a set of possible eigenfunctions and a possible set of eigenvalues for any Hermitian operator. If more than one eigensolutions of (1.58) corresponds to a certain eigenvalue, the eigenvalue is said to be *degenerate*.

A Hermitian operator has real eigenvalues. In fact,

$$\int \psi_n^* Q\psi_n \, d\tau = \int \psi_n^* q_n\psi_n \, d\tau = q_n \int \psi_n^*\psi_n \, d\tau, \tag{1.59}$$

and

$$\int (Q\psi_n)^* \, \psi_n \, d\tau = \int (q_n\psi_n)^* \, \psi_n \, d\tau = q_n^* \int \psi_n^*\psi_n \, d\tau. \tag{1.60}$$

From (1.57)

$$\int \psi_n^* Q\psi_n \, d\tau = \int (Q\psi_n)^* \, \psi_n \, d\tau, \tag{1.61}$$

and then $q_n = q_n^*$. One would expect the eigenvalues of a Hermitian operator to be real, as they represent results of measurements.

Two eigenfunctions of an Hermitian operator are orthogonal to each other if the corresponding eigenvalues are not equal. In fact,

$$\int \psi_n^* Q\psi_m \, d\tau = \int (Q\psi_n)^* \, \psi_m \, d\tau = q_n^* \int \psi_n^*\psi_m \, d\tau = q_n \int \psi_n^*\psi_m \, d\tau, \tag{1.62}$$

and

$$\int \psi_n^* Q \psi_m \, d\tau = q_m \int \psi_n^* \psi_m \, d\tau. \tag{1.63}$$

Then

$$(q_n - q_m) \int \psi_n^* \psi_m = 0 \quad \text{and} \quad \int \psi_n^* \psi_m \, d\tau = 0, \quad \text{if} \quad q_n \neq q_m. \tag{1.64}$$

If $\psi_j (j = 1, 2, \ldots, m)$ are the eigenfunctions of an operator Q, corresponding to an mth degenerate eigenvalue q_n, linear combinations of the ψ_j's can be taken to form a set of m mutually orthogonal functions. These functions are eigenfunctions of Q corresponding to q_n; they are also linearly independent and can be used to expand any other eigenfunction corresponding to the eigenvalue q_n.

Postulate 3

If a function ψ represents a physical system, ψ can be expanded in terms of the eigenfunctions of any operator representing an observable of the system.

The complete set of linearly independent eigenfunctions of an operator may be chosen to be orthogonal. If the eigenfunctions have also been normalized to unity, we have

$$\int \psi_j^* \psi_k \, d\tau = \delta_{jk}. \tag{1.65}$$

If we expand a function ψ in terms of the functions ψ_j of an orthonormal set, we get

$$\psi = \sum_j c_j \psi_j, \tag{1.66}$$

where

$$c_j = \int \psi_j^* \psi \, d\tau. \tag{1.67}$$

Postulate 4

If a function ψ describes a system, the expectation value of an observable q represented by an operator Q is given by

$$\langle q \rangle = \int \psi^* Q \psi \, d\tau. \tag{1.68}$$

Let us expand ψ in terms of the eigenfunctions of Q

$$\psi = \sum_j c_j \psi_j, \tag{1.69}$$

where

$$Q \psi_j = q_j \psi_j. \tag{1.70}$$

Let us assume that ψ is normalized to unity and that the ψ_j's are normalized to unity and have been chosen to be orthogonal. We can write

$$\int \psi^* \psi \, d\tau = \sum_{jk} c_j c_k \int \psi_j \psi_k \, d\tau = \sum_{jk} c_j c_k \delta_{jk} = \sum_j c_j^{\,2} = 1. \tag{1.71}$$

Moreover

$$\int \psi^* Q \psi \, d\tau = \int \left(\sum_j c_j \psi_j\right)^* Q \left(\sum_k c_k \psi_k\right) d\tau$$

$$= \sum_{jk} c_j^* c_k q_k \int \psi_j^* \psi_k \, d\tau = \sum_j |c_j|^2 \, q_j. \tag{1.72}$$

$|c_j|^2$ can be interpreted as the probability of finding the system in the state designated by j; if we make a measurement to determine q, $|c_j|^2$ is the probability of getting the result q_j.

Postulate 5

If a system is at a certain initial time represented by a function ψ, the dependence on time of ψ is given by

$$H\psi = i\hbar \frac{\partial \psi}{\partial t}, \tag{1.73}$$

where H is the operator associated with the Hamiltonian of the system.

Postulate 6

The operators Q and R associated with the dynamical variables q and r must be chosen in such a way that

$$[Q, R] \rightleftharpoons i\hbar\{q, r\}, \tag{1.74}$$

where

$$\{q, r\} = \sum_i \left(\frac{\partial q}{\partial q_i}\frac{\partial r}{\partial p_i} - \frac{\partial q}{\partial p_i}\frac{\partial r}{\partial q_i}\right), \tag{1.75}$$

and

$$[Q, R] = QR - RQ.$$

In case that Q and R represent the coordinate q_k and momentum p_k of a particle in a certain direction

$$\{q_k, p_k\} = \sum_i \left(\frac{\partial q_k}{\partial q_i}\frac{\partial p_k}{\partial p_i} - \frac{\partial q_k}{\partial p_i}\frac{\partial p_k}{\partial q_i}\right) = 1, \tag{1.76}$$

and

$$[q_k, p_j] = i\hbar\delta_{kj}. \tag{1.77}$$

This last equation expresses the so-called *indeterminacy principle.*

4. COMPATIBLE OBSERVABLES AND COMPLETE SET OF COMMUTING OPERATORS

If a complete set of linearly independent functions exists such that each function ψ_i is an eigenfunction of the operators R and S, the corresponding observables are considered *compatible.*

If two observables are compatible, their operators commute. In fact, since

$$\begin{aligned} S\psi_i &= s_i\psi_i, \\ R\psi_i &= r_i\psi_i, \end{aligned} \tag{1.78}$$

we can write

$$(RS - SR)\,\psi_i = 0. \tag{1.79}$$

If the system is represented by a function

$$\psi = \sum_i c_i\psi_i,$$

$$(RS - SR)\sum_i c_i\psi_i = 0 = (RS - SR)\,\psi.$$

Then

$$[R, S] = 0. \tag{1.80}$$

Position and momentum are *not* compatible because of the indeterminacy principle.

If two operators Q and R commute and either Q or R has nondegenerate eigenvalues, its eigenfunctions are also eigenfunctions of the other operator. In fact, if one of the two operators has nondegenerate eigenvalues:

$$Q\psi_i = q_i\psi_i, \qquad (q_i \text{ nondegenerate}), \tag{1.81}$$

and Q and R commute, we get

$$Q(R\psi_i) = R(Q\psi_i) = q_i(R\psi_i). \tag{1.82}$$

$R\psi_i$ is also an eigenfunction of operator Q and can differ from ψ_i only by a multiplicative constant

$$R\psi_i = r_i\psi_i. \tag{1.83}$$

ψ_i is then a simultaneous eigenfunction of Q and R.

An example of two commuting operators, one of which has nondegenerate eigenvalues, is given by L^2 and L_z in a (spinless) hydrogen atom.

In case the Q and R commute and both have degenerate eigenvalues, it can be shown that there exists a complete set of functions which are simultaneous eigenfunctions of Q and R.

A *complete set of commuting operators* is a set of operators all of which commute with one another and are such that, for a given set of eigenvalues (one eigenvalue for each operator of the set), there is only one simultaneous eigenstate. A quantum number corresponds to each operator of the complete set; to individuate a certain state we need then as many quantum numbers as there are operators in the complete set.

5. FORM OF THE OPERATORS

The dynamical variables of a system (position, angular momentum, etc.) are associated in quantum mechanics with linear operator which operate on state eigenfunctions.

The form of the operators cannot be derived unambiguously from the enunciated postulates; we shall adopt the process of association used by Schrödinger. This process consists in associating the operators x, y, z with the dynamical variables x, y, z. Consequently, as we shall see immediately, as a consequence of Postulate 6, the operators $-i\hbar(\partial/\partial x)$, $-i\hbar(\partial/\partial y)$, $-i\hbar(\partial/\partial z)$ will be associated respectively with the cartesian conjugate linear momenta p_x, p_y, p_z.

5.1 Linear Momentum of a Particle

We must have

$$[p_x, x] = i\hbar\{p_x, x\} = i\hbar\left(-\frac{\partial p_x}{\partial p_x}\frac{\partial x}{\partial x}\right) = -i\hbar. \tag{1.84}$$

We propose

$$p_x = -i\hbar\frac{\partial}{\partial x}, \tag{1.85}$$

and we check

$$\left[-i\hbar\frac{\partial}{\partial x}, x\right]f = -i\hbar\frac{\partial}{\partial x}(xf) + i\hbar x\frac{\partial}{\partial x}f = -i\hbar f \tag{1.86}$$

in agreement with (1.84). We can derive the following commutation relations:

$$\begin{aligned} [p_j, x_i] &= -i\hbar\delta_{ij}, \\ [p_i, p_j] &= 0, \\ [x_i, x_j] &= 0. \end{aligned} \tag{1.87}$$

The eigenvalue equation for the momentum operator is

$$p\psi = -i\hbar\,\nabla\psi = \mathbf{p}_0\psi, \qquad (p_0 \text{ is a number}), \tag{1.88}$$

with solutions

$$\psi = A\exp\left(\frac{i\mathbf{p}_0\cdot\mathbf{r}}{\hbar}\right). \tag{1.89}$$

We can then say that the eigenfunctions of the linear momentum operator of a particle are *plane waves*.

5.2 Energy Operator

If a physical system is in a state of definite energy, it is represented by an eigenfunction of the energy operator H with an eigenvalue E:

$$H(q_i, p_i)\,\psi(q_i, t) = E\,\psi(q_i, t). \tag{1.90}$$

Because of Postulate 5, we must have

$$H\,\psi(q_i, t) = i\hbar\,\frac{\partial}{\partial t}\,\psi(q_i, t). \tag{1.91}$$

Then $\psi(q_i, t)$ must be of the form

$$\psi(q_i, t) = u(q_i)e^{-(i/\hbar)Et}, \tag{1.92}$$

where $u(q_i)$ is a solution of

$$H\,u(q_i) = E\,u(q_i). \tag{1.93}$$

The last is the time-independent Schrödinger equation (TISE), which in any system in an energy state gives the eigenvalues (possible values) of the energy.

In the more general case of a system that is not in an energy state its state function is given by a linear combination of eigenfunctions of type (1.92):

$$\psi(q_i, t) = \sum_E c_E e^{-(i/\hbar)Et}\,u_E(q_i). \tag{1.94}$$

Let us assume that ψ and the u's are normalized to unity and that the u's are orthogonal. Then

$$\int \psi^*\psi\,d\tau = \sum_E\sum_{E'} c_E^* c_{E'} \exp\left(i\,\frac{E-E'}{\hbar}\,t\right)\int u_E^* u_{E'}\,d\tau = \sum_E |c_E|^2. \tag{1.95}$$

$|c_E|^2$ is the probability of obtaining the result E if the energy is measured.

Let us go back now to (1.21),

$$\frac{dF(q_i, p_i, t)}{dt} = \frac{\partial F(q_i, p_i, t)}{\partial t} + \{F, H\}, \tag{1.96}$$

where $F = F(q_i, p_i, t)$ is a classical dynamical variable. By using Postulate 6 we can express the quantum mechanical equivalent of (1.96) as follows:

$$\frac{dF}{dt} = \frac{\partial F}{\partial t} + \frac{i}{\hbar}\,[H, F]. \tag{1.97}$$

In this equation F is the operator corresponding to a dynamical variable f and dF/dt is to be understood as the operator whose average value gives the rate of change of the average value of f.

If the Hamiltonian does not depend on time explicitly, then $\partial H/\partial t = 0$ and also $dH/dt = 0$ from (1.97), namely the energy has a constant average value.

If an operator F is independent of time and commutes with the Hamiltonian, then the average value of F will be a constant. In such a case, if the system is in a state of definite energy, f can be measured together with the energy without perturbing the state of the system.

5.3 Angular Momentum Operators

The angular momentum $\mathbf{L}$ of a particle about some point in space is defined by

$$\mathbf{L} = \mathbf{r} \times \mathbf{p} = \begin{vmatrix} \mathbf{i} & \mathbf{j} & \mathbf{k} \\ x & y & z \\ p_x & p_y & p_z \end{vmatrix}, \tag{1.98}$$

where $\mathbf{r}$ is the distance of the particle from that point. The operators which represent the components of the angular momentum are given by

$$\begin{aligned} L_x &= yp_z - zp_y = y\left(-i\hbar\frac{\partial}{\partial z}\right) - z\left(-i\hbar\frac{\partial}{\partial y}\right), \\ L_y &= zp_x - xp_z = z\left(-i\hbar\frac{\partial}{\partial x}\right) - x\left(-i\hbar\frac{\partial}{\partial z}\right), \\ L_z &= xp_y - yp_x = x\left(-i\hbar\frac{\partial}{\partial y}\right) - y\left(-i\hbar\frac{\partial}{\partial x}\right). \end{aligned} \tag{1.99}$$

If we use spherical coordinates

$$\begin{cases} x = r\sin\theta\cos\varphi, \\ y = r\sin\theta\sin\varphi, \\ z = r\cos\theta, \end{cases} \tag{1.100}$$

we get

$$\begin{aligned} L_x &= i\hbar\left(\sin\varphi\frac{\partial}{\partial\theta} + \cot\theta\cos\varphi\frac{\partial}{\partial\varphi}\right) \\ L_y &= i\hbar\left(-\cos\varphi\frac{\partial}{\partial\theta} + \cot\theta\sin\varphi\frac{\partial}{\partial\theta}\right) \\ L_z &= -i\hbar\frac{\partial}{\partial\varphi} \end{aligned} \tag{1.101}$$

and

$$L^2 = -\hbar^2\left\{\frac{1}{\sin\theta}\frac{\partial}{\partial\theta}(\sin\theta)\frac{\partial}{\partial\theta} + \frac{1}{\sin^2\theta}\frac{\partial^2}{\partial\varphi^2}\right\}. \tag{1.102}$$

It is important to investigate the commutation relations among the different components of the angular momentum.

Let us introduce the symbol:

$$\epsilon_{ijk} = \begin{cases} 0 & \text{if two or more indices are equal,} \\ +1 & \text{if } ijk \text{ cyclic permutation of } xyz, \\ -1 & \text{if } ijk \text{ not cyclic permutation of } xyz. \end{cases}$$

By taking into account the commutation relation (1.77) we find

$$\begin{aligned} [L_x, L_y] &= (yp_z - zp_y)(zp_x - xp_z) - (zp_x - xp_z)(yp_z - zp_y) \\ &= -yp_x(zp_z - p_z z) + xp_y(zp_z - p_z z) = i\hbar(xp_y - yp_x) \\ &= i\hbar L_z. \end{aligned} \tag{1.103}$$

In general

$$[L_i, L_j] = i\epsilon_{ijk}\hbar L_k. \tag{1.104}$$

We find also

$$[L^2, L_x] = [L^2, L_y] = [L^2, L_z] = 0. \tag{1.105}$$

These relations could be derived by considering the Poisson brackets and using Postulate 6.

From (1.104) and (1.105) we may see that L^2 and each component of **L** are compatible observables, but any two components of **L** are not compatible.

We can then find simultaneous eigenfunctions for the operators L^2 and L_z. The eigenvalue equations are given by

$$\begin{aligned} L^2\psi &= a^2\psi, \\ L_z\psi &= b\psi, \end{aligned} \tag{1.106}$$

where L^2 is given by (1.102) and L_z by the third of (1.101). The solutions of (1.106) are found to be the so-called *spherical harmonics*, which are functions of the form

$$Y_{lm}(\theta, \varphi) = N_{lm}P_l^m(\cos\theta)\, e^{im\varphi}, \tag{1.107}$$

where

$$N_{lm} = \text{normalizing constant} = \left[\frac{2l+1}{4\pi}\,\frac{(l-|m|)!}{(l+|m|)!}\right]^{1/2}$$

$P_l^m(\cos\theta)$ = associated Legendre functions, polynomials of degree l in $\cos\theta$.

For each value of l there are $2l+1$ values of m ($m = l, l-1, \ldots, -l+1, -l$) and $2l+1$ spherical harmonics. An important property of these functions is their orthogonality

$$\int_0^\pi \int_0^{2\pi} Y^*_{lm}(\theta, \varphi)\, Y_{l'm'}(\theta, \varphi) \sin\theta\, d\theta\, d\varphi = \delta_{ll'}\delta_{mm'}. \tag{1.108}$$

It is also found that the eigenvalues of L^2 and L_z are given, respectively, by $l(l+1)\hbar^2$ and $m\hbar$, where $l = 0, 1, 2, \ldots$ and $m = l, l-1, \ldots, -l$:

$$\begin{aligned} L^2 Y_{lm}(\theta, \varphi) &= l(l+1)\hbar^2 Y_{lm}(\theta, \varphi), \\ L_z Y_{lm}(\theta, \varphi) &= m\hbar Y_{lm}(\theta, \varphi); \end{aligned} \tag{1.109}$$

$2l + 1$ is therefore the degree of degeneracy of L^2. The first four spherical harmonics are given by

$$\begin{aligned} Y_{00} &= \frac{1}{\sqrt{4\pi}}, \\ Y_{11} &= -\frac{3}{\sqrt{8\pi}} \sin\theta e^{i\varphi}, \\ Y_{10} &= \frac{3}{\sqrt{4\pi}} \cos\theta, \\ Y_{1-1} &= \frac{3}{\sqrt{8\pi}} \sin\theta e^{-i\varphi}. \end{aligned} \tag{1.110}$$

5.4 Parity Operator

It has the property

$$P\psi(\mathbf{r}_1, \mathbf{r}_2, \ldots) = \psi(-\mathbf{r}_1, -\mathbf{r}_2, \ldots). \tag{1.111}$$

The eigenvalue equation is

$$P\psi = a\psi. \tag{1.112}$$

If we operate with P again,

$$P^2\psi = a^2\psi = \psi, \tag{1.113}$$

then $a^2 = 1$, $a = \pm 1$. Eigenfunctions corresponding to the eigenvalue 1 are functions of *even* parity; eigenfunctions corresponding to the eigenvalue -1 are functions of *odd* parity.

The spherical harmonics are functions of parity $(-1)^l$.

6. MATRIX FORMALISM AND TRANSFORMATION THEORY

We introduce here the *Dirac notation.* If certain functions u_i represent a complete set and if Q is a certain operator, we may write

$$\langle u_i \mid u_j \rangle = \int u_i^* u_j \, d\tau, \tag{1.114}$$

$$\langle u_i | \, Q \, | u_j \rangle = \int u_i^* Q u_j \, d\tau = Q_{ij}. \tag{1.115}$$

If the u's are orthonormal,

$$\langle u_i \mid u_j \rangle = \delta_{ij}. \tag{1.116}$$

If the u's are eigenfunctions of Q,

$$\langle u_i | Q | u_j \rangle = q_j \langle u_i \mid u_j \rangle = q_j \delta_{ij}. \tag{1.117}$$

6.1 Matrix Representation of Eigenfunctions and Operators

If the functions u_i form a complete orthonormal set, we can expand the state function ψ of a system as follows:

$$\psi = \sum_j a_j u_j, \qquad (a_j = \langle u_j \mid \psi \rangle). \tag{1.118}$$

If the u_j's are eigenfunctions of an operator Q, the numbers a_j's define the state of the system (represented by ψ) in the Q *representation.*

We can identify ψ in the following way:

$$\boldsymbol{\psi} = \begin{pmatrix} a_1 \\ a_2 \\ a_3 \\ \cdot \\ \cdot \\ \cdot \end{pmatrix}. \tag{1.119}$$

If ψ is an eigenstate of Q belonging to an eigenvalue q_i we shall have

$$\boldsymbol{\psi} = \begin{pmatrix} 0 \\ 0 \\ \cdot \\ a_i \\ \cdot \\ \cdot \end{pmatrix}. \tag{1.120}$$

Given an operator R, in general different from Q, we may operate with R on the generic u function

$$Ru_j = \sum_i R_{ij} u_i, \tag{1.121}$$

where

$$R_{ij} = \langle u_i | R | u_j \rangle = \int u_i^* R u_j \, d\tau. \tag{1.122}$$

We may then represent the operator R in the following way:

$$\mathbf{R} = \begin{pmatrix} R_{11} & R_{12} & \cdots \\ R_{21} & R_{22} & \cdots \\ \cdots & \cdots & \cdots \end{pmatrix}. \tag{1.123}$$

We call this matrix the *matrix of the operator R in the Q representation.*

If u_i are eigenfunctions of R, the R matrix is diagonal. If the set of basis functions u_i is orthonormal, for an operator R, to be diagonal in a Q representation means to commute with Q.

The algebraic properties of the operators are mirrored in their matrices:

1. The matrix of a Hermitian operator is Hermitian. (See Section 2 of this chapter for this proof.)
2. The matrix of the product of two operators is the product of the corresponding matrices.
3. The matrices of commuting operators commute.
4. The matrix of an operator which is the inverse of Q is the inverse of the matrix of Q.

Points (2), (3), and (4) are left without proof.

6.2 Different Types of Matrix Representations

The Schrödinger Representation. In a representation of this kind the basis functions are time-independent and the coefficients of the expansion are time-dependent

$$\psi(\mathbf{r}, t) = \sum_j a_j(t)\, u_j(\mathbf{r}), \tag{1.124}$$

where the u_j's form a complete set of time-independent orthonormal functions.

If we use now the time-dependent Schrödinger equation we get

$$\mathbf{H}\psi = i\hbar \frac{\partial}{\partial t} \psi. \tag{1.125}$$

In a Schrödinger representation an operator is time-independent, if the corresponding dynamical variable does not depend on time explicitly.

The Heisenberg Representation. In this representation the basis functions are time-dependent, and the coefficients of the expansion are time-independent. All the basis functions satisfy the time-dependent Schrödinger equation:

$$Hu_n = i\hbar \frac{\partial u_n}{\partial t} \tag{1.126}$$

and form an orthonormal set, at any time. The expansion of a generic state function is given by

$$\psi(\mathbf{r}, t) = \sum_j a_j u_j(\mathbf{r}, t). \tag{1.127}$$

In this representation an operator is generally time-dependent. For a generic matrix element of an operator R we get

$$\begin{aligned}
\dot{R}_{ij} &= \frac{d}{dt}\langle u_i|\, R\, |u_j\rangle \\
&= \left\langle \frac{\partial u_i}{\partial t} \right|\, R\, |u_j\rangle + \langle u_i|\, \frac{\partial R}{\partial t}\, |u_j\rangle + \langle u_i|\, R \left| \frac{\partial u_j}{\partial t} \right\rangle \\
&= i\hbar\, \langle Hu_i|\, R\, |u_j\rangle - \frac{i}{\hbar}\langle u_i|\, R\, |Hu_j\rangle + \langle u_i|\, \frac{\partial R}{\partial t}\, |u_j\rangle \\
&= i\hbar\, \langle u_i|\, HR - RH\, |u_j\rangle + \langle u_i|\, \frac{\partial R}{\partial t}\, |u_j\rangle \\
&= i\hbar\, \langle u_i|\, [H, R]\, |u_j\rangle + \langle u_i|\, \frac{\partial R}{\partial t}\, |u_j\rangle. \qquad (1.128)
\end{aligned}$$

In matrix form

$$\frac{d\mathbf{R}}{dt} = \frac{\partial \mathbf{R}}{\partial t} + \frac{i}{\hbar}\,[\mathbf{H}, \mathbf{R}]. \qquad (1.129)$$

This equation is essentially equal to (1.97). There is no unique Heisenberg (or Schrödinger) representation. It is customary, however, to require that a complete set of commuting operators, including the Hamiltonian, be diagonal in the representation.

The Interaction Representation. In this representation we divide the Hamiltonian in two parts,

$$H = H_0 + H_1, \qquad (1.130)$$

and we take as basis functions the orthonormal set of functions that satisfy the time-dependent Schrödinger equation:

$$H_0 u_n = i\hbar\, \frac{\partial u_n}{\partial t}. \qquad (1.131)$$

The expansion of a generic state function is now given by

$$\psi = \sum_j a_j(t)\, u_j(\mathbf{r}, t) \qquad (1.132)$$

and the time-dependent Schrödinger equation by

$$H \sum_j a_j(t)\, u_j(\mathbf{r}, t) = i\hbar\, \frac{\partial}{\partial t}\left[\sum_j a_j(t)\, u_j(\mathbf{r}, t)\right]. \qquad (1.133)$$

But

$$H \sum_j a_j(t)\, u_j(\mathbf{r}, t) = (H_0 + H_1) \sum_j a_j(t)\, u_j(\mathbf{r}, t)$$

$$= \sum_j a_j(t)\, i\hbar \frac{\partial}{\partial t} u_j(\mathbf{r}, t) + H_1 \sum_j a_j(t)\, u_j(\mathbf{r}, t), \quad (1.134)$$

and

$$i\hbar \frac{\partial}{\partial t}\left[\sum_j a_j(t)\, u_j(\mathbf{r}, t)\right] = i\hbar \sum_j \frac{\partial a_j(t)}{\partial t} u_j(\mathbf{r}, t) + i\hbar \sum_j a_j(t) \frac{\partial u_j(\mathbf{r}, t)}{\partial t}. \quad (1.135)$$

Therefore

$$H_1 \sum_j a_j(t)\, u_j(\mathbf{r}, t) = i\hbar \sum_j \frac{\partial a_j(t)}{\partial t} u_j(\mathbf{r}, t), \quad (1.136)$$

or

$$\mathbf{H}_1 \psi = i\hbar \frac{\partial}{\partial t} \psi. \quad (1.137)$$

If we now consider the generic operator R,

$$\dot{R}_{ij} = \left\langle \frac{\partial u_i}{\partial t} \right| R \left| u_j \right\rangle + \langle u_i | \frac{\partial R}{\partial t} | u_j \rangle + \langle u_i | R \left| \frac{\partial u_j}{\partial t} \right\rangle$$

$$= \langle u_i | \frac{\partial R}{\partial t} | u_j \rangle + \frac{i}{\hbar} \langle u_i | H_0 R - R H_0 | u_j \rangle, \quad (1.138)$$

and in matrix form

$$\frac{d\mathbf{R}}{dt} = \frac{\partial \mathbf{R}}{\partial t} + \frac{i}{\hbar} [\mathbf{H}_0, \mathbf{R}]. \quad (1.139)$$

6.3 Transformation Theory

A state function ψ can be expanded in terms of any set of basis functions.

Consider two sets of basis functions: u_k, v_i, both orthonormal and complete.

We can expand any of the v's in terms of the u's

$$v_j = \sum_k T_{kj} u_k. \quad (1.140)$$

Then

$$v_i^* = \sum_l T_{li}^* u_l^*. \quad (1.141)$$

The inner product of two v functions is given by

$$\langle v_i \mid v_j \rangle = \delta_{ij} = \sum_{lk} T_{li}^* T_{kj} \langle u_l \mid u_k \rangle$$

$$= \sum_{lk} T_{li}^* T_{kj} \delta_{lk} = \sum_k T_{ki}^* T_{kj} = (\mathbf{T}^+ \mathbf{T})_{ij}, \quad (1.142)$$

namely

$$\mathbf{T}^{+}\mathbf{T} = \mathbf{1} \quad \text{or} \quad \mathbf{T}^{+} = \mathbf{T}^{-1}, \tag{1.143}$$

which means that $\mathbf{T}$ is unitary.

A function ψ can be expanded in terms of the v's

$$\psi = \sum_j a'_j v_j, \qquad a'_j = \langle v_j \mid \psi \rangle, \tag{1.144}$$

or in terms of the u's

$$\psi = \sum_k a_k u_k, \qquad a_k = \langle u_k \mid \psi \rangle. \tag{1.145}$$

From (1.140) and (1.145) we now have

$$\begin{aligned} a'_j = \langle v_j \mid \psi \rangle = \sum_k T^*_{kj} \langle u_k \mid \psi \rangle &= \sum_k T^*_{kj} a_k \\ &= \sum_k (\mathbf{T}^{+})_{jk} a_k \end{aligned} \tag{1.146}$$

or

$$\boldsymbol{\psi}' = \mathbf{T}^{+}\boldsymbol{\psi} = \mathbf{T}^{-1}\boldsymbol{\psi}. \tag{1.147}$$

An operator R in the v-based representation will have the matrix elements

$$\begin{aligned} R'_{ij} &= \langle v_i | \, R \, | v_j \rangle = \sum_{lk} T^*_{li} T_{kj} \langle u_l | \, R \, | u_k \rangle \\ &= \sum_{lk} (\mathbf{T}^{+})_{il} T_{kj} R_{lk} = (\mathbf{T}^{+}\mathbf{R}\mathbf{T})_{ij}, \end{aligned} \tag{1.148}$$

or

$$\mathbf{R}' = \mathbf{T}^{+}\mathbf{R}\mathbf{T} = \mathbf{T}^{-1}\mathbf{R}\mathbf{T}, \tag{1.149}$$

where $\mathbf{R}$ is the matrix of R in the u-based representation. A transformation of a matrix in accordance to (1.149) is called *unitary*.

Matrix equations are left invariant by a unitary transformation. In fact, if

$$\mathbf{N} = \mathbf{R}\mathbf{P}, \tag{1.150}$$

we have

$$\begin{aligned} \mathbf{S}^{-1}\mathbf{N}\mathbf{S} &= \mathbf{S}^{-1}\mathbf{R}\mathbf{P}\mathbf{S} \\ &= (\mathbf{S}^{-1}\mathbf{R}\mathbf{S})(\mathbf{S}^{-1}\mathbf{P}\mathbf{S}) = \mathbf{R}'\mathbf{P}', \end{aligned} \tag{1.151}$$

namely,

$$\mathbf{N}' = \mathbf{R}'\mathbf{P}'. \tag{1.152}$$

The Hermitian property is invariant under a unitary transformation. If

$$\mathbf{R}^{+} = \mathbf{R}, \tag{1.153}$$

we have

$$\begin{aligned} \mathbf{R}'^{+} = (\mathbf{S}^{-1}\mathbf{R}\mathbf{S})^{+} &= \mathbf{S}^{+}\mathbf{R}^{+}(\mathbf{S}^{-1})^{+} \\ &= \mathbf{S}^{+}\mathbf{R}\mathbf{S} = \mathbf{R}'. \end{aligned} \tag{1.154}$$

The inner product of two state vectors is invariant under a unitary transformation. If

$$\begin{aligned} \boldsymbol{\psi}' &= \mathbf{S}^{+}\boldsymbol{\psi}, \\ \boldsymbol{\varphi}' &= \mathbf{S}^{+}\boldsymbol{\varphi}, \end{aligned} \tag{1.155}$$

we have

$$\begin{aligned} \boldsymbol{\psi}'^{+}\boldsymbol{\varphi}' = (\mathbf{S}^{+}\boldsymbol{\psi})^{+}\mathbf{S}^{+}\boldsymbol{\varphi} &= \boldsymbol{\psi}^{+}\mathbf{S}\mathbf{S}^{+}\boldsymbol{\varphi} \\ &= \boldsymbol{\psi}^{+}\boldsymbol{\varphi}. \end{aligned} \tag{1.156}$$

6.4 Example of Transformation Theory

Let us assume now that we have expanded a state function in terms of time-independent basis function (eigenfunctions of the Hamiltonian). Let us assume also that the Hamiltonian does not depend on time explicitly. We have

$$\psi(\mathbf{r}, t) = \sum_i a_i^S(t)\, u_i^S(\mathbf{r}), \tag{1.157}$$

where S stays for Schrödinger representation (SR).

If we expand ψ in terms of time-dependent basis functions which are solutions of the time-dependent Schrödinger equation

$$\psi(\mathbf{r}, t) = \sum_j a_j^H u_j^H(\mathbf{r}, t), \tag{1.158}$$

where H stays for Heisenberg representation (HR). The coefficients a_i^S define ψ in the SR; the coefficients a_i^{H} define ψ in the HR.

We have already seen that we can write

$$\psi(\mathbf{r}, t) = \sum_k c_k e^{-i(E_k/\hbar)t} u_k(\mathbf{r}). \tag{1.159}$$

Now $u_k(\mathbf{r})$ follows the TISE, and

$$e^{-i(E_k/\hbar)t} u_k(\mathbf{r})$$

follows the TDSE.

In the Schrödinger representation

$$u_k^S(\mathbf{r}) = u_k(\mathbf{r}); \qquad \boldsymbol{\psi}^S = \begin{pmatrix} c_1 e^{-i(E_1/\hbar)t} \\ c_2 e^{-i(E_2/\hbar)t} \\ \cdots\cdots\cdot \\ \cdots\cdots\cdot \end{pmatrix}. \tag{1.160}$$

In the Heisenberg representation

$$u_k^H(\mathbf{r}, t) = e^{-(i/\hbar)E_k t} u_k(\mathbf{r}); \qquad \boldsymbol{\psi}^H = \begin{pmatrix} c_1 \\ c_2 \\ \cdot \\ \cdot \end{pmatrix}. \tag{1.161}$$

Now

$$\boldsymbol{\psi}^H = \begin{pmatrix} c_1 \\ c_2 \\ \cdot \\ \cdot \end{pmatrix} = \mathbf{S} \begin{pmatrix} c_1 e^{-i(E_1/\hbar)t} \\ c_2 e^{-i(E_2/\hbar)t} \\ \cdots\cdots\cdots \\ \cdots\cdots\cdots \end{pmatrix} = \mathbf{S}\boldsymbol{\psi}^S, \tag{1.162}$$

where

$$\mathbf{S} = \begin{pmatrix} e^{i(E_1/\hbar)t} & 0 & 0 & \cdots \\ 0 & e^{i(E_2/\hbar)t} & 0 & \cdots \\ 0 & 0 & e^{i(E_3/\hbar)t} & \cdots \\ \cdots & \cdots & \cdots & \cdots \end{pmatrix} = \exp\,[i(\mathbf{H}/\hbar)t] \tag{1.163}$$

$\mathbf{S}$ is unitary: $\mathbf{S}^+ = \mathbf{S}^{-1}$. At $t = 0$, $\mathbf{S} = \mathbf{1}$.

We have also for the operators

$$Q^H = e^{i(H/\hbar)t} Q^S e^{-i(H/\hbar)t}. \tag{1.164}$$

6.5 Eigenvalue Equations in Matrix Form

An eigenvalue equation

$$R\psi = r\psi \tag{1.165}$$

can be expressed in matrix form in the following way:

$$\mathbf{R}\boldsymbol{\psi} = r\boldsymbol{\psi}. \tag{1.166}$$

There are as many equations (1.165) as there are eigenfunctions of R belonging to r. These equations have nontrivial solutions only if the determinant of the coefficients is equal to zero:

$$\det\,[\mathbf{R} - r\mathbf{1}] = 0. \tag{1.167}$$

Example

$$\begin{pmatrix} R_{11} & R_{12} \\ R_{21} & R_{22} \end{pmatrix} = \begin{pmatrix} 0 & i \\ -i & 0 \end{pmatrix}$$

is the matrix of an operator in a certain representation.

We want to find

(a) The eigenvalues of this operator (they are independent of the type of representation); (b) the eigenfunctions of the operator in the given representation; and (c) the unitary matrix which makes the matrix of the operator diagonal.

Let us proceed:

1. Let us write down the eigenvalue equation

$$\begin{pmatrix} 0 & i \\ -i & 0 \end{pmatrix} \begin{pmatrix} a_1 \\ a_2 \end{pmatrix} = r \begin{pmatrix} a_1 \\ a_2 \end{pmatrix},$$

or

$$ia_2 = ra_1$$
$$-ia_1 = ra_2.$$

To obtain solutions we must have

$$\begin{pmatrix} -r & i \\ -i & -r \end{pmatrix} = r^2 - 1 = 0, \qquad r = \pm 1.$$

The eigenvalues of the operator are $+1, -1$.

2. Let us find the eigenfunctions. There will be an eigenfunction for $r = 1$ and an eigenfunction for $r = -1$. For $r = 1$

$$-a_1 + ia_2 = 0,$$
$$-ia_1 + a_2 = 0.$$

The eigenfunction will be

$$c\begin{pmatrix} 1 \\ -i \end{pmatrix}.$$

If we normalize

$$c^2 + c^2 = 2c^2 = 1,$$

$$c = \frac{1}{\sqrt{2}};$$

then

$$\psi_1 = \begin{pmatrix} a_1 \\ a_2 \end{pmatrix}_{r_1} = \frac{1}{\sqrt{2}}\begin{pmatrix} 1 \\ -i \end{pmatrix}.$$

For $r = -1$

$$a_1 + ia_2 = 0,$$
$$a_1 = -ia_2.$$

The eigenfunction will be

$$c\begin{pmatrix} 1 \\ i \end{pmatrix}.$$

If we normalize, we get

$$\psi_2 = \begin{pmatrix} a_1 \\ a_2 \end{pmatrix}_{r_2} = \frac{1}{\sqrt{2}}\begin{pmatrix} 1 \\ i \end{pmatrix}.$$

3. Let us find the matrix $\mathbf{S}$ which makes $\mathbf{R}$ diagonal. We build up the following matrix:

$$\mathbf{S} = \left|\begin{pmatrix} a_1 \\ a_2 \end{pmatrix}_{r_1} \begin{pmatrix} a_1 \\ a_2 \end{pmatrix}_{r_2}\right| = \frac{1}{\sqrt{2}}\begin{vmatrix} 1 & 1 \\ -i & i \end{vmatrix}.$$

$\mathbf{S}$ makes $\mathbf{R}$ diagonal:

$$\mathbf{S}^{-1}\begin{pmatrix} 0 & i \\ -i & 0 \end{pmatrix}\mathbf{S} = \frac{1}{2}\begin{pmatrix} 1 & i \\ 1 & -i \end{pmatrix}\begin{pmatrix} 0 & i \\ -i & 0 \end{pmatrix}\begin{pmatrix} 1 & 1 \\ -i & i \end{pmatrix} = \begin{pmatrix} 1 & 0 \\ 0 & -1 \end{pmatrix}.$$

We can write the eigenvalue equation (1.166) in the following way:

$$\mathbf{RS} = \mathbf{Sr}, \tag{1.168}$$

where

$$\mathbf{S} = \left|\begin{pmatrix} a_1 \\ a_2 \end{pmatrix}_{r_1} \quad \begin{pmatrix} a_1 \\ a_2 \end{pmatrix}_{r_2}\right|, \qquad \mathbf{R} = \begin{vmatrix} R_{11} & R_{12} \\ R_{21} & R_{22} \end{vmatrix}, \qquad \mathbf{r} = \begin{vmatrix} r_1 & 0 \\ 0 & r_2 \end{vmatrix},$$

namely,

$$\begin{pmatrix} R_{11} & R_{12} \\ R_{21} & R_{22} \end{pmatrix}\begin{pmatrix} a_1^{r_1} & a_1^{r_2} \\ a_2^{r_1} & a_2^{r_2} \end{pmatrix} = \begin{pmatrix} a_1^{r_1} & a_1^{r_2} \\ a_2^{r_1} & a_2^{r_2} \end{pmatrix}\begin{pmatrix} r_1 & 0 \\ 0 & r_2 \end{pmatrix},$$

or

$$\begin{pmatrix} 0 & i \\ -i & 0 \end{pmatrix}\frac{1}{\sqrt{2}}\begin{pmatrix} 1 & 1 \\ -i & i \end{pmatrix} = \frac{1}{\sqrt{2}}\begin{pmatrix} 1 & 1 \\ -i & i \end{pmatrix}\begin{pmatrix} 1 & 0 \\ 0 & -1 \end{pmatrix}.$$

7. GENERAL THEORY OF ANGULAR MOMENTUM

7.1 Matrix Representation of the Angular Momentum Operators

The angular momentum of a particle, with respect to a certain point, was defined in Sec. 5.3 of this chapter

$$\mathbf{L} = \mathbf{r} \times \mathbf{p}, \tag{1.169}$$

where $\mathbf{r}$ is the distance of the particle from the point.

The following commutation relations were found:

$$[L^2, L_x] = [L^2, L_y] = [L^2, L_z] = 0, \tag{1.170}$$

$$[L_i, L_j] = i\epsilon_{ijk}L_k. \tag{1.171}$$

These relations apply not only to the components of the angular momentum of a particle but also to the total angular momentum of a system of particles, for the $\mathbf{r}$ and $\mathbf{p}$ operators of each particle commute with the same operators of any other particle.

The above commutation relations tell us that we can diagonalize simultaneously the matrix of the operator L^2 and of one of the components of $\mathbf{L}$. We look then for the matrices of L^2, L_x, L_y, L_z in a representation in which both L^2 and L_z are diagonal.

Let us define the following non-Hermitian operators:

$$L_+ = L_x + iL_y = (L_-)^+ \tag{1.172}$$

$$L_- = L_x - iL_y = (L_+)^+. \tag{1.173}$$

By using the relation (1.171) we find

$$[L_z, L_+] = \hbar L_+, \tag{1.174}$$

and

$$[L_z, L_-] = -\hbar L_-. \tag{1.175}$$

We have also

$$L_+L_- = L_x^2 + L_y^2 - i(L_xL_y - L_yL_x)$$
$$= L_x^2 + L_y^2 + \hbar L_z = L^2 - L_z^2 + \hbar L_z. \tag{1.176}$$

Similarly,

$$L_-L_+ = L^2 - L_z^2 - \hbar L_z. \tag{1.177}$$

The eigenvalue $m\hbar$ of L_z specifies an eigenfunction in the L^2 manifold. We have the following diagonal matrix elements:

$$\langle m| L_+L_- |m\rangle = \sum_{m'} \langle m| L_+ |m'\rangle\langle m'| (L_+)^+ |m\rangle$$
$$= \sum_{m'} \langle m| L_+ |m'\rangle(\langle m| L_+ |m'\rangle)^*$$
$$= \sum_{m'} |\langle m| L_+ |m'\rangle|^2 \geq 0. \tag{1.178}$$

Expressing L_+L_- as in (1.176) we find

$$\langle m| L_+L_- |m\rangle = \langle m| L^2 - L_z^2 + \hbar L_z |m\rangle$$
$$= \sum_{m'} |\langle m| L_+ |m'\rangle|^2 = a^2 - m^2\hbar^2 + m\hbar^2 \geq 0, \tag{1.179}$$

where a^2 is the eigenvalue of L^2.

Considering a generic matrix element of both sides of (1.174) we find

$$\langle m| [L_z, L_+] |m'\rangle = \sum_{m''} \langle m| L_z |m''\rangle\langle m''| L_+ |m'\rangle$$
$$- \sum_{m''} \langle m| L_+ |m''\rangle\langle m''| L_z |m'\rangle$$
$$= \sum_{m''} \{\delta_{mm''} m\hbar\langle m''| L_+ |m'\rangle - \langle m| L_+ |m''\rangle m''\hbar\delta_{m''m'}\}$$
$$= (m - m')\hbar\langle m| L_+ |m'\rangle = \hbar\langle m| L_+ |m'\rangle, \tag{1.180}$$

or

$$\hbar(m - m' - 1)\langle m| L_+ |m'\rangle = 0, \tag{1.181}$$

namely,

$$\langle m| L_+ |m'\rangle \neq 0 \qquad \text{only when} \quad m' = m - 1. \tag{1.182}$$

Equation 1.179 then reduces to

$$\langle m| L_+L_- |m\rangle = \sum_{m'} |\langle m| L_+ |m'\rangle|^2$$
$$= |\langle m| L_+ |m - 1\rangle|^2 = a^2 - \hbar^2 m(m - 1) \geq 0. \tag{1.183}$$

If $a^2 \neq \hbar^2 m(m - 1)$ then $\langle m| L_+ |m - 1\rangle$ must be different from zero. On the other hand, $\langle m - 1| L_+ |m'\rangle$ can be different from zero only if $m' = m - 2$. If $a^2 \neq \hbar^2(m - 1)(m - 2)$ then $\langle m - 1| L_+ |m - 2\rangle$ must be different from zero.

We can then have

$$m' = \ldots, m, m-1, m-2, \ldots, \eta, \tag{1.184}$$

where

$$\eta(\eta - 1)\,\hbar^2 = a^2. \tag{1.185}$$

Using a similar procedure, we find the following for the diagonal elements of L_-L_+:

$$\langle m| L_-L_+ |m\rangle = |\langle m| L_- |m+1\rangle|^2 = a^2 - \hbar^2 m(m+1), \tag{1.186}$$

having derived for L_- a relation similar to (1.182),

$$\langle m| L_- |m'\rangle \neq 0 \quad \text{only if} \quad m' = m + 1. \tag{1.187}$$

We now obtain for m' the sequence

$$m' = \ldots, m, m+1, m+2, \ldots, \mu, \tag{1.188}$$

where

$$\mu(\mu + 1)\,\hbar^2 = a^2. \tag{1.189}$$

Equations 1.185 and 1.189 give for the minimum value η and for the maximum value μ of m', respectively;

$$\begin{aligned} \eta &= \frac{1}{2} - \left(\frac{1}{4} + \frac{a^2}{\hbar^2}\right)^{1/2}, \\ \mu &= -\frac{1}{2} + \left(\frac{1}{4} + \frac{a^2}{\hbar^2}\right)^{1/2}, \end{aligned} \tag{1.190}$$

where we have retained only the sign minus in the double solution for η and the sign plus for μ.

The sequence of m values proceeds with integer steps; the difference $\mu - \eta$ is an integer number

$$\mu - \eta = -1 + 2\left(\frac{1}{4} + \frac{a^2}{\hbar^2}\right)^{1/2}, \tag{1.191}$$

or

$$a^2 = \hbar^2 \frac{(\mu - \eta)(\mu - \eta + 2)}{4}. \tag{1.192}$$

Let

$$\frac{\mu - \eta}{2} = j, \qquad (j = 0, \tfrac{1}{2}, 1, \tfrac{3}{2}, 2, \ldots). \tag{1.193}$$

Then the eigenvalues of L^2 are given by

$$a^2 = \hbar^2 j(j+1), \qquad (j = 0, \tfrac{1}{2}, 1, \tfrac{3}{2}, 2, \ldots). \tag{1.194}$$

By replacing a^2 in (1.190) we find

$$\begin{aligned} \eta &= -j, \\ \mu &= j, \end{aligned} \tag{1.195}$$

and then m ranges over

$$m = j, j-1, j-2, \ldots, -j+1, -j. \tag{1.196}$$

Going back to (1.183), taking into account (1.194),

$$\begin{aligned} |\langle m| L_+ |m-1\rangle|^2 &= j(j+1)\,\hbar^2 - m(m-1)\,\hbar^2 \\ &= (j+m)(j-m+1)\,\hbar^2, \end{aligned} \tag{1.197}$$

or

$$\langle m| L_+ |m-1\rangle = \hbar\sqrt{(j+m)(j-m+1)}, \tag{1.198}$$

apart an arbitrary phase factor $e^{i\delta}$ which we put equal to 1. Similarly from (1.186) and (1.194) we derive

$$\langle m| L_- |m+1\rangle = \hbar\sqrt{(j-m)(j+m+1)}. \tag{1.199}$$

We can now derive the matrix elements of L_x, L_y, L_z by using the fact that

$$\begin{aligned} L_x &= \frac{L_+ + L_-}{2}, \\ L_y &= \frac{L_+ - L_-}{2i}, \end{aligned} \tag{1.200}$$

and

$$\langle m| L_z |m'\rangle = m\hbar\delta_{mm'}. \tag{1.201}$$

Let us examine three different cases.

1. $j = 0, \qquad (\mu = \eta = 0;\ m = 0).$

In this case

$$L^2 = L_x = L_y = L_z = 0. \tag{1.202}$$

2. $j = \frac{1}{2} \qquad (\mu = \frac{1}{2};\ \eta = -\frac{1}{2};\ m = \frac{1}{2}, -\frac{1}{2}).$

In the matrix representation, the rows will correspond to $\frac{1}{2}$ and $-\frac{1}{2}$ and the columns to $\frac{1}{2}$ and $-\frac{1}{2}$, in this order. We now get

$$L^2 = \hbar^2 j(j+1)\begin{pmatrix} 1 & 0 \\ 0 & 1 \end{pmatrix} = \tfrac{3}{4}\hbar^2\begin{pmatrix} 1 & 0 \\ 0 & 1 \end{pmatrix}, \tag{1.203}$$

$$L_z = \hbar\begin{pmatrix} \frac{1}{2} & 0 \\ 0 & -\frac{1}{2} \end{pmatrix}. \tag{1.204}$$

Also

$$L_+ = \hbar\begin{pmatrix} 0 & 1 \\ 0 & 0 \end{pmatrix},$$

$$L_- = \hbar\begin{pmatrix} 0 & 0 \\ 1 & 0 \end{pmatrix},$$

and

$$L_x = \frac{\hbar}{2}\begin{pmatrix} 0 & 1 \\ 1 & 0 \end{pmatrix} \tag{1.205}$$

$$L_y = \frac{\hbar}{2}\begin{pmatrix} 0 & -i \\ i & 0 \end{pmatrix}. \tag{1.206}$$

3. $j = 1$ $\quad (\mu = 1, \eta = -1; m = 1, 0, -1)$.

In this case

$$L^2 = j(j+1)\,\hbar^2\begin{pmatrix} 1 & 0 & 0 \\ 0 & 1 & 0 \\ 0 & 0 & 1 \end{pmatrix} = 2\hbar^2\begin{pmatrix} 1 & 0 & 0 \\ 0 & 1 & 0 \\ 0 & 0 & 1 \end{pmatrix}, \tag{1.207}$$

$$L_z = \hbar\begin{pmatrix} 1 & 0 & 0 \\ 0 & 0 & 0 \\ 0 & 0 & -1 \end{pmatrix}, \tag{1.208}$$

$$L_x = \frac{\hbar}{\sqrt{2}}\begin{pmatrix} 0 & 1 & 0 \\ 1 & 0 & 1 \\ 0 & 1 & 0 \end{pmatrix}, \tag{1.209}$$

$$L_y = \frac{\hbar}{\sqrt{2}}\begin{pmatrix} 0 & -i & 0 \\ i & 0 & -i \\ 0 & i & 0 \end{pmatrix}. \tag{1.210}$$

7.2 The Spin of the Electron

Starting from the commutation relations (1.170) and (1.171), we have obtained for L^2 and L_z the eigenvalues $j(j+1)\,\hbar^2$ and $m\hbar$ respectively, with j integer or half-integer. The integer values are the same that we obtain by solving the eigenvalue equations (1.106). The solution of these equations, however, excludes half-integer values: The half-integer j matrices of $\mathbf{L}$ cannot be expressed in terms of $\mathbf{r}$ and $\mathbf{p}$ matrices, and then they have to be excluded as representative of angular momentum components. The difficulty derives from the fact that the relations (1.171) and (1.172) included in our treatment some matrix representations which are not compatible with the definition (1.169) of angular momentum.

However, a particle may present, in principle, an *intrinsic* angular momentum that respects the commutation relations (1.170) and (1.171). (These relations can be considered the most general definition of angular momentum.) In this case new coordinates must be admitted which represent the internal degrees of freedom of the particle. An intrinsic angular momentum which corresponds to $j = \frac{1}{2}$ is the so-called *spin* of the electron, which is indicated by $\mathbf{s}$.

The matrices of the components of $\mathbf{s}$, in a s^2, s_z representation are given by

$$\begin{aligned} s^2 &= \tfrac{3}{4}\hbar^2\begin{pmatrix} 1 & 0 \\ 0 & 1 \end{pmatrix} \\ s_z &= \frac{\hbar}{2}\begin{pmatrix} 1 & 0 \\ 0 & -1 \end{pmatrix} = \tfrac{1}{2}\hbar\sigma_z \\ s_x &= \frac{\hbar}{2}\begin{pmatrix} 0 & 1 \\ 1 & 0 \end{pmatrix} = \tfrac{1}{2}\hbar\sigma_x \\ s_y &= \frac{\hbar}{2}\begin{pmatrix} 0 & -i \\ i & 0 \end{pmatrix} = \tfrac{1}{2}\hbar\sigma_y, \end{aligned} \tag{1.211}$$

where

$$\sigma_x = \begin{pmatrix} 0 & 1 \\ 1 & 0 \end{pmatrix}, \qquad \sigma_y = \begin{pmatrix} 0 & -i \\ i & 0 \end{pmatrix}, \qquad \sigma_z = \begin{pmatrix} 1 & 0 \\ 0 & -1 \end{pmatrix} \tag{1.212}$$

are the so-called *Pauli spin matrices.*

The wavefunctions of s^2, s_z in an s^2, s_z representation are given by

$$\begin{aligned} \alpha &= \begin{pmatrix} 1 \\ 0 \end{pmatrix}, \\ \beta &= \begin{pmatrix} 0 \\ 1 \end{pmatrix}. \end{aligned} \tag{1.213}$$

Since

$$\begin{aligned} s_z\alpha &= \frac{\hbar}{2}\alpha, \\ s_z\beta &= -\frac{\hbar}{2}\beta, \end{aligned} \tag{1.214}$$

α corresponds to the eigenvalue $\hbar/2$ of s_z and β to the eigenvalue $-(\hbar/2)$ of s_z.

8. TIME-INDEPENDENT PERTURBATION THEORY

In some cases the eigenvalue equation cannot be solved exactly; there are really few cases in which an exact solution can be found. Perturbation theory may be used to find approximate solutions.

Let us assume that the Hamiltonian can be written in the form

$$H = H_0 + \epsilon H_1, \tag{1.215}$$

where the energy associated with H_0 is large compared to the energy associated with ϵH_1. We make the following two assumptions: (a) H does not depend on time explicitly, (b) H_0 has a solved eigenvalue equation,

$$H_0 u_i = E_i u_i, \tag{1.216}$$

where the u_i's are orthonormal functions ($\langle u_i \mid u_j \rangle = \delta_{ij}$).

8.1 Nondegenerate Case (E_i's all different)

The eigenvalue equation we have to solve is

$$(H_0 + \epsilon H_1)\psi = E\psi. \tag{1.217}$$

We proceed in the following way. We expand ψ and E in a power series of ϵ:

$$\psi = \psi_0 + \epsilon\psi_1 + \epsilon^2\psi_2 + \epsilon^3\psi_3 + \cdots \tag{1.218}$$

$$E = E_0 + \epsilon E_1 + \epsilon^2 E_2 + \epsilon^3 E_2 + \cdots. \tag{1.219}$$

In the limit $\epsilon \to 0$ (1.217) becomes

$$H_0\psi_0 = E_0\psi_0. \tag{1.220}$$

We must then make the identification

$$\psi_0 = u_i; \qquad E_0 = E_i. \tag{1.221}$$

Plugging (1.218) and (1.219) into (1.217), we get

$$(H_0 + \epsilon H_1)(\psi_0 + \epsilon\psi_1 + \epsilon^2\psi_2 + \cdots)$$
$$= (E_0 + \epsilon E_1 + \epsilon^2 E_2 + \cdots)(\psi_0 + \epsilon\psi_1 + \epsilon^2\psi_2 + \cdots) \tag{1.222}$$

and then

$$H_0\psi_0 + \epsilon(H_1\psi_0 + H_0\psi_1) + \epsilon^2(H_0\psi_2 + H_1\psi_1) + \cdots$$
$$= E_0\psi_0 + \epsilon(E_1\psi_0 + E_0\psi_1) + \epsilon^2(E_2\psi_0 + E_1\psi_1 + E_0\psi_2) + \cdots. \tag{1.223}$$

Equating the coefficients of like powers of ϵ in each side of (1.223), we obtain

$$\begin{aligned} H_0\psi_0 &= E_0\psi_0 \\ H_1\psi_0 + H_0\psi_1 &= E_1\psi_0 + E_0\psi_1 \\ H_0\psi_2 + H_1\psi_1 &= E_2\psi_0 + E_1\psi_1 + E_0\psi_2 \cdots. \end{aligned} \tag{1.224}$$

Let us now expand ψ_1 in terms of the u's:

$$\psi_1 = \sum_k a_k u_k. \tag{1.225}$$

Then from the second of (1.224) we have

$$H_1 u_i + H_0 \sum_k a_k u_k = E_1 u_i + E_i \sum_k a_k u_k, \tag{1.226}$$

namely,

$$H_1 u_i + \sum_k a_k E_k u_k = E_1 u_i + E_i \sum_k a_k u_k. \tag{1.227}$$

We then multiply by u_j^* and integrate over all space

$$\langle u_j| H_1 |u_i\rangle + \sum_k a_k E_k \delta_{jk} = E_1 \delta_{ji} + \sum_k a_k E_i \delta_{jk}. \tag{1.228}$$

Then

$$\langle u_j| H_1 |u_i\rangle + a_j E_j = E_1 \delta_{ji} + a_j E_i. \tag{1.229}$$

If $j = i$,

$$\langle u_i| H_1 |u_i\rangle + a_i E_i = E_1 + a_i E_i. \tag{1.230}$$

Then

$$E_1 = \langle u_i| H_1 |u_i\rangle = (H_1)_{ii}. \tag{1.231}$$

If $j \neq i$,

$$a_j = \frac{\langle u_j| H_1 |u_i\rangle}{E_i - E_j}. \tag{1.232}$$

We have thus obtained a solution to first order in H_1; a_i, however, is still undetermined. This indeterminacy can be removed by using the normalization property of ψ. Since $\psi_0 = u_i$, ψ is normalized to zero-order. We must have

$$\begin{aligned}\langle \psi \mid \psi \rangle = 1 &= \langle \psi_0 + \epsilon\psi_1 + \cdots \mid \psi_0 + \epsilon\psi_1 + \cdots \rangle \\ &= \langle \psi_0 \mid \psi_0 \rangle + \epsilon[\langle \psi_1 \mid \psi_0 \rangle + \langle \psi_0 \mid \psi_1 \rangle] + \cdots.\end{aligned} \tag{1.233}$$

Then

$$\langle \psi_1 \mid \psi_0 \rangle + \langle \psi_0 \mid \psi_1 \rangle = \langle \psi_1 \mid u_i \rangle + \langle u_i \mid \psi_1 \rangle = 0, \tag{1.234}$$

and

$$\left\langle \sum_k a_k u_k \,\middle|\, u_i \right\rangle + \left\langle u_i \,\middle|\, \sum_k a_k u_k \right\rangle = 0 \tag{1.235}$$

or

$$a_i^* + a_i = 0; \qquad a_i = i\gamma, \qquad (\gamma = \text{const}), \tag{1.236}$$

namely,

$$\begin{aligned}\psi = \psi_0 + \epsilon\psi_1 &= u_i + \epsilon \sum_k a_k u_k \\ &= u_i + \epsilon a_i u_i + \epsilon \sum_{k\neq i} a_k u_k \\ &= u_i + i\gamma\epsilon u_i + \epsilon \sum_{k\neq i} a_k u_k \\ &= (1 + i\gamma\epsilon)\, u_i + \epsilon \sum_{k\neq i} a_k u_k \\ &\simeq e^{i\epsilon\gamma} u_i + \epsilon \sum_{k\neq i} a_k u_k,\end{aligned} \tag{1.237}$$

where the a_k's are given by (1.232). a_i in the last equation changes the phase of the original unperturbed wavefunction u_i relative to the phase of the perturbation terms. There is no loss of generality in making this phase equal to zero.

We have then the results

$$E = E_i + \epsilon(H_1)_{ii}, \qquad \text{(to first-order in } \epsilon) \tag{1.238}$$

$$\psi = u_i + \epsilon \sum_{k \neq i} \frac{\langle u_k | H_1 | u_i \rangle}{E_i - E_k}, \qquad \text{(to first-order in } \epsilon). \tag{1.239}$$

By using the third equation of (1.224) and following a similar procedure we get:

$$E = E_i + \epsilon \langle u_i | H_1 | u_i \rangle + \epsilon^2 \sum_{k \neq i} \frac{|\langle u_k | H_1 | u_i \rangle|^2}{E_i - E_k} \tag{1.240}$$

$$\begin{aligned} \psi = u_i &+ \epsilon \sum_{k \neq i} \frac{\langle u_k | H_1 | u_i \rangle}{E_i - E_k} \\ &+ \epsilon^2 \sum_{k \neq i} \left\{ \left[\sum_{m \neq i} \frac{\langle u_k | H_1 | u_m \rangle \langle u_m | H_1 | u_i \rangle}{(E_i - E_k)(E_i - E_m)} - \frac{\langle u_k | H_1 | u_i \rangle \langle u_i | H_1 | u_i \rangle}{(E_i - E_k)^2} \right] u_k \right. \\ &\left. - \frac{1}{2} \frac{|\langle u_k | H_1 | u_i \rangle|^2}{(E_i - E_k)^2} u_i \right\}. \end{aligned} \tag{1.241}$$

8.2 Degenerate Case

A difficulty arises: The energy denominator of (1.232) vanishes when $E_i = E_j$ and $(H_1)_{ij} \neq 0$. The difficulty is overcome when all the matrix elements of the perturbing term in the Hamiltonian between all pairs of degenerate states vanish, namely when the Hamiltonian matrix

$$\mathbf{H} = \mathbf{H}_0 + \mathbf{H}_1 \tag{1.242}$$

is diagonal.

To remove the difficulty of applying perturbation theory to degenerate states we have to diagonalize exactly the appropriate submatrices of the total Hamiltonian. This amounts to finding the proper orthonormal linear combinations v_j of the degenerate eigenfunctions u_i such that the nondiagonal matrix element of H_1 between the states v_j are all zero:

$$\langle v_i | H_1 | v_j \rangle = 0, \qquad \text{if } i \neq j, \tag{1.243}$$

where

$$v_j = \sum_{k=1}^{m} a_{ji} u_i, \qquad (m = \text{degree of degeneracy}). \tag{1.244}$$

The following example will illustrate the procedure that has to be followed.

Example: Stark effect in Hydrogen

The unperturbed Hamiltonian of the hydrogen atom is given by

$$H_0 = \frac{p^2}{2m} - \frac{e^2}{r} = -\frac{\hbar^2}{2m}\nabla^2 - \frac{e^2}{r}. \tag{1.245}$$

The complete set of commuting operators is given by

$$H_0, L_3, L_z, P = \text{parity}. \tag{1.246}$$

The eigenvalue equations are

$$\begin{aligned} H_0\psi_{nlm_l} &= E_n\psi_{nlm_l} && \left(E_n = -\frac{me^4}{2\hbar^2 n^2}\right) \\ L^2\psi_{nlm_l} &= l(l+1)\hbar^2\psi_{nlm_l} && (l = n-1, n-2, \ldots, 0) \\ L_z\psi_{nlm_l} &= m_l\hbar\psi_{nlm_l} && (m_l = l, l-1, \ldots, -l), \end{aligned} \tag{1.247}$$

and the wave functions

$$\psi_{nlm_l} = R_{nl}(r)\, Y_{lm_l}(\theta, \phi). \tag{1.248}$$

The wavefunctions have parity $(-1)^l$ (namely they are odd, if l is odd, even if l is even). The three quantum numbers may have the following values:

$$\begin{aligned} n &= 1, 2, 3, \ldots \\ l &= 0, 1, 2, \ldots, n-1 \\ m_l &= 0, \pm 1, \pm 2, \ldots, \pm l. \end{aligned} \tag{1.249}$$

The states are designated in the following way:

	$l = 0$	$l = 1$	$l = 2$	$l = 3$
$n = 1$	$1s$			
$n = 2$	$2s$	$2p$		
$n = 3$	$3s$	$3p$	$3d$	
$n = 4$	$4s$	$4p$	$4d$	$4f$

For each of the states l there are $2l + 1$ magnetic states m_l.

If an electric field is applied and we take as z-direction the direction of the field, the perturbing energy is represented by

$$H_1 = -eEz = -eEr\cos\theta. \tag{1.250}$$

The complete set of operators commuting with H_1 are

$$H_1, L_z. \tag{1.251}$$

H_1 does not commute with operator P (parity). In fact H_1 is an odd operator. Thus the only matrix elements of H_1 which do not vanish are those between unperturbed states that have opposite parities. Since $\langle\psi|\, H_1\, |\psi\rangle = 0$, all the diagonal elements of H_1 for the unperturbed wave functions are zero.

A nondegenerate state, like $1s$ (ground state), has no first-order Stark-effect.

The first excited state $n = 2$ is fourfold degenerate: the four degenerate states may be indicated as $2s$, $2p_1$, $2p_0$, $2p_{-1}$ (subscripts indicate m_l numbers).

Let us consider the commutator

$$[H_1, L_z] = 0. \tag{1.252}$$

The ks element of this commutator is given by

$$\begin{aligned}\langle k| [H_1, L_z] |s\rangle &= \langle k| H_1 L_z |s\rangle - \langle k| L_z H_1 |s\rangle \\ &= m_s \hbar \langle k| H_1 |s\rangle - m_k \hbar \langle k| H_1 |s\rangle \\ &= (m_s - m_k)\, \hbar \langle k| H_1 |s\rangle = (m_s - m_k)\, \hbar (H_1)_{ks}.\end{aligned} \tag{1.253}$$

Then $(H_1)_{ks} = 0$ unless $m_s = m_k$. This fact expresses a general principle:

Matrix elements of a perturbing Hamiltonian H_1 taken between eigenstates of an operator which commutes with H_1 are zero unless the eigenstates refer to the same eigenvalue of the commuting operator.

In the present case the perturbation connects only states of equal m_l, like $2s$ and $2p_0$. In first approximation

$$\langle 2p_1| eEz |2p_1\rangle = eE \int z \, |\psi_{2p_1}|^2 \, d\tau = 0 \tag{1.254}$$

because z is odd and $|\psi_{2p_1}|^2$ is even. The same happens for $2p_{-1}$. Then $2p_1$ and $2p_{-1}$ are unperturbed in first approximation. We have, on the other hand

$$\begin{aligned}\psi_{2s} &= \frac{1}{\sqrt{32\pi a^3}} \left(2 - \frac{r}{a}\right) e^{-r/2a} \\ \psi_{2p_0} &= \frac{1}{\sqrt{32\pi a^3}} \frac{r}{a} \, e^{-r/2a} \cos\theta,\end{aligned} \tag{1.255}$$

and $\quad \langle 2s| z |2s\rangle = \langle 2p_0| z |2p_0\rangle = 0$

$$\langle 2s| z |2p_0\rangle = \frac{1}{32\pi a^3} \int_0^\infty \int_0^\pi \left(2 - \frac{r}{a}\right) \frac{r}{a} e^{-r/a} r \cos^2\theta 2\pi r^2 \sin\theta \, dr \, d\theta = -3a. \tag{1.256}$$

The perturbation matrix is given by

$$-eE \begin{pmatrix} 0 & -3a \\ -3a & 0 \end{pmatrix} = 3eEa \begin{pmatrix} 0 & 1 \\ 1 & 0 \end{pmatrix}. \tag{1.257}$$

The eigenvalues are given by $\lambda(3eEa)$ where λ is derived as follows:

$$\begin{pmatrix} -\lambda & 1 \\ 1 & -\lambda \end{pmatrix} = \lambda^2 - 1 = 0, \qquad \lambda = \pm 1. \tag{1.258}$$

The energy levels will then be corrected by $\pm 3eEa$. Let us find the new wavefunctions

$$\begin{pmatrix} 0 & 1 \\ 1 & 0 \end{pmatrix} \begin{pmatrix} a_1 \\ a_2 \end{pmatrix} = \lambda \begin{pmatrix} a_1 \\ a_2 \end{pmatrix}; \tag{1.259}$$

then

$$-\lambda a_1 + a_2 = 0. \tag{1.260}$$

If $\lambda = 1$,

$$a_1 = a_2, \qquad \text{and the eigenfunction is } \frac{1}{\sqrt{2}}\begin{pmatrix}1\\1\end{pmatrix};$$

if $\lambda = -1$,

$$a_1 = -a_2, \qquad \text{and the eigenfunction is } \frac{1}{\sqrt{2}}\begin{pmatrix}1\\-1\end{pmatrix}.$$

The eigenfunctions in the new representation are

$$\frac{1}{\sqrt{2}}\begin{pmatrix}1\\1\end{pmatrix}, \quad \frac{1}{\sqrt{2}}\begin{pmatrix}1\\-1\end{pmatrix}. \tag{1.261}$$

We then have

Energy Levels to First Approximation	Eigenfunctions to Zero Approximation
$-\frac{me^4}{2\hbar^2}\frac{1}{4}$	ψ_{2p_1}
$-\frac{me^4}{2\hbar^2}\frac{1}{4}$	$\psi_{2p_{-1}}$
$-\frac{me^4}{2\hbar^2}\frac{1}{4} + 3eEa$	$\frac{1}{\sqrt{2}}(\psi_{2s} + \psi_{2p_0})$
$-\frac{me^4}{2\hbar^2}\frac{1}{4} - 3eEa$	$\frac{1}{\sqrt{2}}(\psi_{2s} - \psi_{2p_0})$

The process of diagonalization of the perturbation matrix gives also the new wave functions in terms of the old ones.

9. TIME-DEPENDENT PERTURBATION THEORY

9.1 Perturbation Acting on a Two-Level System

Let us consider a system represented by a certain Hamiltonian H_0. The time-dependent Schrödinger equation is given by

$$H_0\psi_i = i\hbar\frac{\partial\psi_i}{\partial t}, \tag{1.262}$$

and the time-dependent energy eigenfunctions by

$$\psi_i(t) = e^{-i(E_i/\hbar)t}\psi_i(0), \tag{1.263}$$

where $\psi_i(0)$'s are orthonormal solutions of the eigenvalue equation

$$H_0\,\psi_i(0) = E_i\,\psi_i(0). \tag{1.264}$$

Let us assume now that a time-dependent perturbation, represented by a certain Hamiltonian $H'(t)$ is acting on the system. The time-dependent S.E. of the total system (unperturbed system + perturbation) is given by

$$H\psi(t) = (H_0 + H')\,\psi(t) = i\hbar\,\frac{\partial\psi}{\partial t}, \tag{1.265}$$

and the wavefunction of the total system by

$$\psi(t) = \sum_i c_i(t)\,\psi_i(t). \tag{1.266}$$

In the absence of the perturbation H', the coefficients c_i would be time-independent.

Replacing $\psi(t)$ by the expression given in (1.266), Equation 1.265 becomes:

$$(H_0 + H')\sum_i c_i(t)\,\psi_i(t) = i\hbar\left\{\sum_i c_i(t)\,\frac{\partial\psi_i(t)}{\partial t} + \sum_i \frac{\partial c_i(t)}{\partial t}\,\psi_i(t)\right\}, \tag{1.267}$$

and then

$$\sum_i c_i(t)\,H_0\psi_i(t) + \sum_i c_i(t)\,H'\psi_i(t) = \sum_i c_i(t)\,E_i\psi_i(t) + i\hbar\sum_i \frac{\partial c_i(t)}{\partial t}\,\psi_i(t),$$

and we are left with

$$\sum_i c_i(t)\,H'\psi_i(t) = i\hbar\sum_i \frac{\partial c_i(t)}{\partial t}\,\psi_i(t). \tag{1.268}$$

Multiplying by $\psi_k(t)^*$ and integrating over all space

$$\begin{aligned} i\hbar\,\frac{\partial c_k(t)}{\partial t} &= \sum_i c_i(t)\langle\psi_k(t)|\,H'\,|\,\psi_i(t)\rangle \\ &= \sum_i c_i(t)\langle\psi_k(0)|\,H'\,|\psi_i(0)\rangle\,\exp\left(i\,\frac{E_k - E_i}{\hbar}\,t\right) \\ &= \sum_i c_i(t)\langle\psi_k(0)|\,H'\,|\psi_i(0)\rangle e^{i\omega_{ki}t}, \end{aligned} \tag{1.269}$$

where

$$\omega_{ki} = \frac{E_k - E_i}{\hbar}. \tag{1.270}$$

This is a system of coupled equations. Let us assume that we have only two levels: 0 and k. We have in this case

$$\begin{aligned} i\hbar\,\frac{\partial c_k(t)}{\partial t} &= c_0(t)\langle\psi_k(0)|\,H'\,|\psi_0(0)\rangle e^{i\omega_{k0}t} \\ i\hbar\,\frac{\partial c_0(t)}{\partial t} &= c_k(t)\langle\psi_0(0)|\,H'\,|\psi_k(0)\rangle e^{-i\omega_{0k}t} \end{aligned} \tag{1.271}$$

in the hypothesis that $\langle\psi_k(0)|\,H'\,|\psi_k(0)\rangle = \langle\psi_0(0)|\,H'\,|\psi_0(0)\rangle = 0$.

Let us rewrite the equations in the following way:

$$\dot{c}_k(t) = -\frac{i}{\hbar}\, c_0(t)\, e^{i\omega_{k0}t} M_k$$
$$\dot{c}_0(t) = -\frac{i}{\hbar}\, c_k(t)\, e^{-i\omega_{k0}t} M_k, \tag{1.272}$$

where

$$M_k = \langle \psi_k(0) |\, H' \,| \psi_0(0) \rangle. \tag{1.273}$$

Equations 1.272 can be easily integrated if the perturbation is turned on at the time $t = 0$ and off at a time t and if during the $0 - t$ interval it remains constant. In these conditions M_k is independent of time. We can also assume that the system is in the state ψ_0 at time $t = 0$:

$$c_0(0) = 1,$$
$$c_k(0) = 0. \tag{1.274}$$

We have

$$\ddot{c}_k(t) = -\frac{i}{\hbar}\, \dot{c}_0(t)\, e^{i\omega_{k0}t} M_k - \frac{i}{\hbar}\, c_0(t)(i\omega_{k0})\, M_k e^{i\omega_{k0}t}$$

$$= -\frac{i}{\hbar}\left[-\frac{i}{\hbar}\, c_k(t)\, e^{-i\omega_{k0}t} M_k\right] e^{i\omega_{k0}t} M_k + \frac{\omega_{k0}}{\hbar}\, M_k e^{i\omega_{k0}t}\, \frac{i\hbar \dot{c}_k(t)\, e^{-i\omega_{k0}t}}{M_k},$$

and

$$\ddot{c}_k(t) - i\omega_{k0}\dot{c}_k(t) + \frac{|M_k|^2}{\hbar^2}\, c_k(t) = 0. \tag{1.275}$$

We expect $c_k(t)$ to be of the form:

$$c_k(t) = Ae^{\alpha_1 t} + Be^{\alpha_2 t}, \tag{1.276}$$

where α_1 and α_2 are the two solutions of the following equation:

$$\alpha^2 - i\omega_{k0}\alpha + \frac{|M_k|^2}{\hbar^2} = 0. \tag{1.277}$$

We get

$$\alpha = \frac{i\omega_{k0} \pm [-\omega_{k0}{}^2 - 4(|M_k|^2/\hbar^2)]^{1/2}}{2} = \frac{i}{2}\{\omega_{k0} \pm [\omega_{k0}{}^2 + 4(|M_k|^2/\hbar^2)]^{1/2}\}. \tag{1.278}$$

We take advantage of the initial conditions to determine A and B. Since

$c_k(0) = 0$, we must have $A = -B$; then

$$c_k(t) = A(e^{\alpha_1 t} - e^{\alpha_2 t})$$
$$= A\left(\exp\left\{\frac{i}{2}\,\omega_{k0}t + \frac{i}{2}\,[\omega_{k0}^2 + 4(|M_k|^2/\hbar^2)]^{1/2}t\right\}\right.$$
$$\left. - \exp\left\{\frac{i}{2}\,\omega_{k0}t - \frac{i}{2}\,[\omega_{k0}^2 + 4(|M_k|^2/\hbar^2)]^{1/2}t\right\}\right)$$
$$= 2iA\exp\left(i\,\frac{\omega_{k0}}{2}\,t\right)\sin at = C\exp\left(i\,\frac{\omega_{k0}}{2}\,t\right)\sin at, \tag{1.279}$$

where

$$\begin{aligned} 2iA &= C \\ \tfrac{1}{2}[\omega_{k0}^2 + 4(|M_k|^2/\hbar^2)]^{1/2} &= a. \end{aligned} \tag{1.280}$$

We get then

$$c_0(t) = \frac{i\hbar e^{-i\omega_{k0}t}}{M_k}\,c_k(t)$$
$$= \frac{i\hbar e^{-i\omega_{k0}t}}{M_k}\,C\left[\frac{i\omega_{k0}}{2}\exp(i\omega_{k0}t/2)\sin at + \exp(i\omega_{k0}t/2)a\cos at\right]. \tag{1.281}$$

Then, from the first of (1.272)

$$1 = \frac{i\hbar}{M_k}\,Ca,$$

and

$$C = \frac{M_k}{i\hbar a} = \frac{M_k}{i\,\dfrac{\hbar}{2}\,[\omega_{k0}^2 + 4(|M_k|^2/\hbar^2)]^{1/2}}. \tag{1.282}$$

Therefore

$$c_k(t) = -\frac{2i(M_k/\hbar)}{[\omega_{k0}^2 + 4(|M_k|^2/\hbar^2)]^{1/2}}\sin\tfrac{1}{2}[\omega_{k0}^2 + 4(|M_k|^2/\hbar^2)]^{1/2}t, \tag{1.283}$$

and

$$|c_k(t)|^2 = \frac{4(|M_k|^2/\hbar^2)}{\omega_{k0}^2 + 4(|M_k|^2/\hbar^2)}\sin^2\tfrac{1}{2}[\omega_{k0}^2 + 4(|M_k|^2/\hbar^2)]^{1/2}t, \tag{1.284}$$

where

$$M_k = \langle\psi_k(0)|\,H'\,|\psi_0(0)\rangle. \tag{1.285}$$

$|c_k(t)|^2$ is the probability that, if the system is in a state ψ_0 at the time $t = 0$, it can be found in the state ψ_k at the time t.

9.2 Time Proportional Transition Probability

Let us now consider the case of a multilevel system, under the action of a perturbing Hamiltonian H'. The wavefunction of the system may be expanded as in (1.266) with the coefficients c_i's given by the equations

$$i\hbar \frac{\partial c_k}{\partial t} = \sum_i c_i \langle \psi_k(0)| H' |\psi_i(0)\rangle e^{i\omega_{ki}t}. \tag{1.286}$$

We may replace H' with $\epsilon H'$ and expand the coefficients as follows:

$$c_i = c_i^{(0)} + \epsilon c_i^{(1)} + \epsilon^2 c_i^{(2)} + \cdots. \tag{1.287}$$

Using the above expressions for the coefficients in (1.286), we find

$$i\hbar[\dot{c}_k^{(0)} + \epsilon \dot{c}_k^{(1)} + \epsilon^2 \dot{c}_k^{(2)} + \cdots] = \sum_i [c_i^{(0)} + \epsilon c_i^{(1)} + \epsilon^2 c_i^{(2)} + \cdots]\epsilon\langle \psi_k(0)| H' |\psi_i(0)\rangle e^{i\omega_{ki}t}. \tag{1.288}$$

Equating the coefficient of like powers of ϵ, we obtain

$$\begin{cases} \dot{c}_k^{(0)} = 0 \\ \dot{c}_k^{(s+1)} = \dfrac{1}{i\hbar} \sum_i c_i^{(s)} \langle \psi_k(0)| H' |\psi_i(0)\rangle e^{i\omega_{ki}t} \end{cases} \tag{1.289}$$

These equations can, in principle, be integrated in succession to provide solutions to any degree of approximation. The zero-order coefficients are constant and their values are determined by the initial conditions. Let us assume that at the time $t = 0$ at which the perturbation is applied the system is in a definite state ψ_0; this means that of all the $c_i^{(0)}$'s coefficients only one is different from zero and equal to 1:

$$\begin{aligned} c_o^{(0)} &= 1, \\ c_i^{(0)} &= 0, \qquad i \neq 0. \end{aligned} \tag{1.290}$$

Considering the equations (1.289) to the first order in the perturbation, we obtain:

$$c_k^{(1)}(t) = \frac{1}{i\hbar} \int_0^t \langle \psi_k(0)| H'(t') |\psi_0(0)\rangle e^{\,i\omega_{k0}t'}\, dt' \tag{1.291}$$

If the perturbation H' maintains a constant value after it is applied, (1.291) integrates as follows:

$$c_k^{(1)}(t) = \frac{1}{i\hbar} \langle \psi_k(0)| H' |\psi_0(0)\rangle \left[\frac{e^{i\omega_{k0}t'}}{i\omega_{k0}}\right]_0^t = -\frac{M_k}{\hbar\omega_{k0}} (e^{i\omega_{k0}t} - 1), \tag{1.292}$$

where

$$M_k = \langle \psi_k(0)| H' |\psi_0(0)\rangle \tag{1.293}$$

and the probability of finding the system in a state ψ_k at time t is given by

$$|c_k^{(1)}(t)|^2 = \frac{4\,|M_k|^2}{\hbar^2}\,\frac{\sin^2 \frac{1}{2}\omega_{k0} t}{{\omega_{k0}}^2}. \tag{1.294}$$

It may happen that the final state of the system lies in a "continuum" of energies. In this case we must integrate over the variable energy.

Let us assume that $\rho(E)\,dE$ is the number of states with energy in the interval $(E, E + dE)$. The probability of finding the system, at a time t in the continuum of energies, centered on energy E_k is given by

$$P_k(t) = \int_{-\infty}^{+\infty} |c_k^{(1)}(t)|^2\,\rho(E_k)\,dE_k = \int_{-\infty}^{+\infty} \frac{4\,|M_k|^2}{\hbar^2}\,\frac{\sin^2 \frac{1}{2}\omega_{k0} t}{{\omega_{k0}}^2}\,\rho(E_k)\,dE_k. \tag{1.295}$$

Assuming that M_k and $\rho(E_k)$ are slowly varying functions of k,

$$\begin{aligned} P_k(t) &= \frac{4\,|M_k|^2}{\hbar^2}\,\rho(\omega_k = \omega_0) \int_{-\infty}^{+\infty} \frac{\sin^2 \frac{1}{2}\omega_{k0} t}{{\omega_{k0}}^2}\,d\omega_{k0} \\ &= \frac{4\,|M_k|^2}{\hbar^2}\,\rho(\omega_k = \omega_0)\,\tfrac{1}{2}\pi t. \end{aligned} \tag{1.296}$$

Finally, we find

$$P_k(t) = \frac{2\pi}{\hbar^2}\,|M_k|^2\,\rho(\omega_k = \omega_0)\,t, \tag{1.297}$$

where

$$M_k = \langle \psi_k(0)|\,H'\,|\psi_0(0)\rangle; \tag{1.298}$$

(1.297) expresses the *Golden Rule* and is often used in quantum mechanical problems.

GENERAL REFERENCES

[1] R. H. Dicke and J. P. Wittke, *Introduction to Quantum Mechanics*, Addison-Wesley, Reading, Mass., 1960.

[2] D. Bohm, *Quantum Theory*, Prentice-Hall, Englewood Cliffs, N.J., 1951.

[3] L. I. Schiff, *Quantum Mechanics*, McGraw-Hill, New York, 1955.

2

Elements of Group Theory

1. PROPERTIES OF A GROUP

The elements of a group have the following properties: (a) The product of any two elements is an element of the group; (b) they contain the identity operation E; (c) they have the associative property: $P(QR) = (PQ)R$; and (d) every element has a reciprocal: $RS = SR = E$.

The number of elements in a group is called *order of the group*. Let us consider now an equilateral triangle as in Fig. 2.1 and the following operations that we may perform on it: (a) Identity operation E; (b) Clockwise rotation through 120°: C_3; (c) Counter clockwise rotation through 120°: C_3^2; (d) Reflection about plane ZY: σ_1; (e) Reflection about plane $Z2$: σ_2; (f) Reflection about plane $Z3$: σ_3.

The above operations represent all of the *inequivalent covering operations*

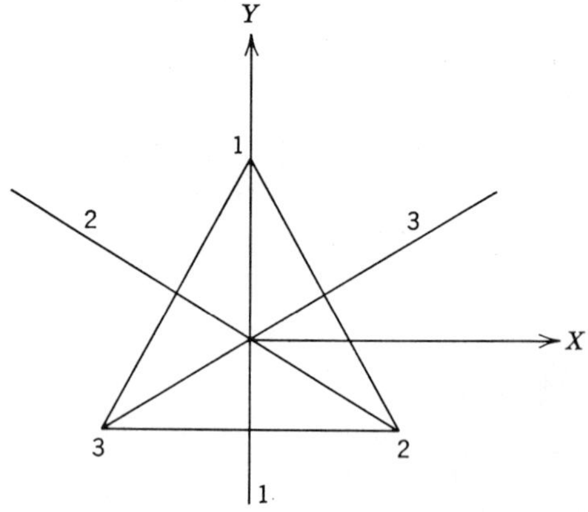

Fig. 2.1. Equilateral triangle with relative axes. The axis Z is perpendicular to the X and Y axes.

which can be performed on an equilateral triangle leaving it unchanged with respect to the axes. The operations can be arranged in the following multiplication table:

	E	C_3	C_3^2	σ_1	σ_2	σ_3
E	E	C_3	C_3^2	σ_1	σ_2	σ_3
C_3	C_3	C_3^2	E	σ_3	σ_1	σ_2
C_3^2	C_3^2	E	C_3	σ_2	σ_3	σ_1
σ_1	σ_1	σ_2	σ_3	E	C_3	C_3^2
σ_2	σ_2	σ_3	σ_1	C_3^2	E	C_3
σ_3	σ_3	σ_1	σ_2	C_3	C_3^2	E

The operations E, C_3, C_3^2, σ_1, σ_2, σ_3, have all the four properties listed above. They form a group which is called the *symmetry group of the equilateral triangle*, or group C_{3v}.

The products C_3A_i, A_i being any element of the group, span over all the elements of the group. The same is true for the sets of products A_iA_j (i = fixed; $j = 1, \ldots, 6$). This is a general property of the elements of a group.

In general, for two elements A, B of a group: $AB \neq BA$. If, for any two elements A, B of a group $AB = BA$, the group is said to be *Abelian*.

A group is called *cyclic* if all the elements of the group are integer powers of a given element. In the group C_{3v} the elements E, C_3, C_3^2 form a cyclic group (which is a *subgroup* of C_{3v}). The elements of this cyclic group are powers of C_3: C_3, C_3^2, $C_3^3 = E$. 3, the first power of C_3 which is equal to the identity, is called the *order* of C_3. The order of C_3^2 is also 3.

Other subgroups of C_{3v} are

$$\{E\}, \{E, \sigma_1\}, \{E, \sigma_2\}, \{E, \sigma_3\}.$$

They are all cyclic. The order of σ_1, σ_2, and σ_3 is 2; the order of E is 1.

The group C_{3v} has then the following subgroups:

$$\{E\}, \{E, \sigma_1\}, \{E, \sigma_2\}, \{E, \sigma_3\}, \{E, C_3, C_3^2\}.$$

We notice that subgroups must not necessarily be all cyclic. An interesting property of groups, which is here left without proof, is that a group whose order is a prime number is cyclic and Abelian.

Let us consider now the subgroup $\{E, \sigma_1\}$ of C_{3v}. We can multiply all the elements of $\{E, \sigma_1\}$ by all the other elements of C_{3v} not in $\{E, \sigma_1\}$. Multiplying from the left, we obtain the following *left cosets*

$$C_3\{E, \sigma_1\} = \{C_3, \sigma_3\}$$

$$C_3^2\{E, \sigma_1\} = \{C_3^2, \sigma_2\}$$

$$\sigma_2\{E, \sigma_1\} = \{\sigma_2, C_3^2\}$$

$$\sigma_3\{E, \sigma_1\} = \{\sigma_3, C_3\}.$$

Multiplying from the right, we obtain the *right cosets*

$$\{E, \sigma_1\}\, C_3 = \{C_3, \sigma_2\}$$

$$\{E, \sigma_1\}\, C_3^2 = \{C_3^2, \sigma_3\}$$

$$\{E, \sigma_1\}\, \sigma_2 = \{\sigma_2, C_3\}$$

$$\{E, \sigma_1\}\, \sigma_3 = \{\sigma_3, C_3^2\}.$$

For each case we have two distinct cosets.

We notice here that the group C_{3v} can be expressed in terms of the subgroup $\{E, \sigma_1\}$ and the corresponding left or right cosets

$$C_{3v}\colon \{E, \sigma_1\} + C_3\{E, \sigma_1\} + C_3^2\{E, \sigma_1\} = \{E, \sigma_1\} + \{C_3, \sigma_3\} + \{C_3^2, \sigma_2\}$$

$$C_{3v}\colon \{E, \sigma_1\} + \{E, \sigma_1\}\, C_3 + \{E, \sigma_1\}\, C_3^2 = \{E, \sigma_1\} + \{C_3, \sigma_2\} + \{C_3^2, \sigma_3\}.$$

This property is of general nature, in the sense that a group may be decomposed into right or left cosets with respect to a definite subgroup.

2. CLASSES

Given a certain element A of a group G, the element $X^{-1}AX$, X being any element of G, is said to be *conjugate of A with respect to X.*

A collection of elements conjugate to each other form a *class.*

Let us consider now the symmetry group of the equilateral triangle. We have for example

$$EC_3E = C_3 \qquad EC_3^2E = C_3^2$$

$$C_3^2C_3C_3 = C_3 \qquad C_3^2C_3^2C_3 = C_3^2$$

$$C_3C_3C_3^2 = C_3 \qquad C_3C_3^2C_3^2 = C_3^2$$

$$\sigma_1C_3\sigma_1 = C_3^2 \qquad \sigma_1C_3^2\sigma_1 = C_3$$

$$\sigma_2C_3\sigma_2 = C_3^2 \qquad \sigma_2C_3^2\sigma_2 = C_3$$

$$\sigma_3C_3\sigma_3 = C_3^2 \qquad \sigma_3C_3^2\sigma_3 = C_3.$$

Then we may say that C_3 and C_3^2 form a *class.* In the same way we could show that σ_1, σ_2, and σ_3 form another class. The classes of the group of the equilateral triangle are

$$\begin{aligned} &\mathcal{C}_1 = E && \text{(Order of element} = 1)\\ &\mathcal{C}_2 = C_3, C_3^2 && \text{(Order of element} = 3)\\ &\mathcal{C}_3 = \sigma_1, \sigma_2, \sigma_3 && \text{(Order of element} = 2).\end{aligned} \tag{2.1}$$

Any group can be decomposed in terms of nonoverlapping classes which cover completely all the elements of the group.

If a group is Abelian, for a generic element A of the group

$$X^{-1}AX = AX^{-1}X = A, \tag{2.2}$$

namely each element of the group forms a class.

If two symmetry operations belong to the same class it is possible to choose a new system of coordinates in which one operation is replaced by the other. In the group C_{3v} we can rotate counterclockwise of 120° the coordinate system; operation σ_1 (defined as a reflection with respect to the plane ZY) in the rotated coordinate system is equal to operation σ_2 in the old coordinate system.

Another property of the operations belonging to the same class is that they have the same order. Take for example two conjugate elements A and B, where

$$B = X^{-1}AX. \tag{2.3}$$

If the order of A is n, namely $A^n = E$, then

$$\begin{aligned} B^n = (X^{-1}AX)^n &= (X^{-1}AX)(X^{-1}AX)\cdots(X^{-1}AX) \\ &= X^{-1}A^nX = X^{-1}EX = E. \end{aligned} \tag{2.4}$$

If in a group G a certain subgroup H is such that, for any X in G

$$X^{-1}HX = H, \tag{2.5}$$

the subgroup is said to be *invariant* or selfconjugate. A subgroup of order $g/2$ of a group G of order g is an invariant subgroup of G. The proof of this last property is left to the reader.

The right and left cosets of a group with respect to an invariant subgroup are the same, because $HX = XH$.

Given a certain group G with an invariant subgroup H, the collection of elements which consists of H and of all the cosets with respect to H form a group which is called the *factor group* and is indicated by G/H.

In the case of the group C_{3v}, an invariant subgroup is given by $H \equiv \{E, C_3, C_3^2\}$. The factor group C_{3v}/H is then given by

$$\{E, C_3, C_3^2\}, \{\sigma_1, \sigma_2, \sigma_3\}$$

and is a group of order 2.

Finally we want to define the *product of two classes* $\mathcal{C}_i$ and $\mathcal{C}_j$ in the following way:

$$\mathcal{C}_i\mathcal{C}_j = \sum_{l=1}^{h_i}\sum_{k=1}^{h_j} R_l^{\,i} R_k^{\,j}, \tag{2.6}$$

where h_i = number of elements in $\mathcal{C}_i$
h_j = number of elements in $\mathcal{C}_j$
R_l^i = generic element in $\mathcal{C}_i$
R_k^j = generic element in $\mathcal{C}_j$.

We notice that

$$X^{-1}\mathcal{C}_i\mathcal{C}_jX = X^{-1}\mathcal{C}_iXX^{-1}\mathcal{C}_jX = \mathcal{C}_i\mathcal{C}_j \tag{2.7}$$

for any element X of the group. Then, if $\mathcal{C}_i\mathcal{C}_j$ contains one element of a class, it must contain all the elements of the same class, and, therefore, $\mathcal{C}_i\mathcal{C}_j$ is a sum of classes:

$$\mathcal{C}_i\mathcal{C}_j = \sum_{k=1}^{r} c_{ijk}\mathcal{C}_k, \tag{2.8}$$

where r = number of classes, c_{ijk} = integer number or zero.

3. THEORY OF REPRESENTATIONS

Any set of elements which can be put in correspondence with the elements of a group in such a way that they multiply according to the same multiplication table is said to be a *representation* of the group.

Let us assume now that we have an n-dimensional vector space V_n, and that we have a collection of linear unitary transformations $A, B, C, \ldots$ on the vectors of V_n, which form a group G. If we choose a set of basis functions for V_n, then each transformation will be represented by a $n \times n$ matrix. The collection of matrices representing the linear transformations will form a *matrix representation of* G, and the basis vectors are said *to form a basis* for this representation. The order of the matrices, which is equal to the dimension n of the vector space V_n, is called the *degree* of the representation.

If the two matrices $\mathbf{\Gamma}(A)$ and $\mathbf{\Gamma}(B)$ correspond respectively to the elements A and B and if $AB = C$, $\mathbf{\Gamma}(C)$ must represent the element C.

The matrix representing A^{-1} is $[\mathbf{\Gamma}(A)]^{-1}$; only nonsingular matrices are then considered. The identity E is represented by a matrix with generic element δ_{ij}.

The elements of the matrices $\mathbf{\Gamma}(A)$, $\mathbf{\Gamma}(B)$, ... depend in general on the basis vectors chosen for V_n. If a new basis is chosen for V_n, this will correspond, as seen in Sec. 2, of Chapter 1, to a similarity transformation for the matrices $\mathbf{\Gamma}(A)$, $\mathbf{\Gamma}(B)$, ... representing the operators $A, B, \ldots$:

$$\mathbf{\Gamma}'(A) = \mathbf{S}^{-1}\,\mathbf{\Gamma}(A)\,\mathbf{S}; \qquad \mathbf{\Gamma}'(B) = \mathbf{S}^{-1}\,\mathbf{\Gamma}(B)\,\mathbf{S}; \ldots, \tag{2.9}$$

where $\mathbf{S}$ is a nonsingular matrix.

The matrices $\mathbf{\Gamma}'(R)$ form also a representation of the group. In fact, for example, if $AB = C$,

$$\mathbf{\Gamma}(A)\,\mathbf{\Gamma}(B) = \mathbf{\Gamma}(C), \tag{2.10}$$

and

$$\mathbf{S}^{-1}\,\mathbf{\Gamma}(A)\,\mathbf{\Gamma}(B)\,\mathbf{S} = \mathbf{S}^{-1}\,\mathbf{\Gamma}(A)\,\mathbf{S}\mathbf{S}^{-1}\,\mathbf{\Gamma}(B)\,\mathbf{S} = \mathbf{S}^{-1}\,\mathbf{\Gamma}(C)\,\mathbf{S}, \tag{2.11}$$

namely,

$$\mathbf{\Gamma}'(A)\,\mathbf{\Gamma}'(B) = \mathbf{\Gamma}'(C). \tag{2.12}$$

Two representations which differ only by a similarity transformation are said to be *equivalent*.

Let us assume that a subspace W_r, spanned by the basis vectors $\mathbf{a}_1, \mathbf{a}_2, \ldots, \mathbf{a}_r$ is an invariant subspace of V_n with respect to all the linear operators $A, B, C, \ldots$. The basis vectors $\mathbf{a}_{r+1}, \mathbf{a}_{r+2}, \ldots, \mathbf{a}_n$ span in this case a subspace Y_{n-r} and the space V_n can be considered as a sum of the two subspaces

$$V_n = W_r + Y_{n-r} \tag{2.13}$$

If $\mathbf{u}$ is a vector of V_n, we can write

$$\mathbf{u} = \mathbf{u}^r + \mathbf{u}^{n-r}, \tag{2.14}$$

where

$$\begin{aligned} \mathbf{u}^r &= u_1\mathbf{a}_1 + u_2\mathbf{a}_2 + \cdots + u_r\mathbf{a}_r \\ \mathbf{u}^{n-r} &= u_{r+1}\mathbf{a}_{r+1} + u_{r+2}\mathbf{a}_{r+2} + \cdots + u_n\mathbf{a}_n. \end{aligned} \tag{2.15}$$

$\mathbf{u}^r$ belongs to the invariant subspace W_r, $\mathbf{u}^{n-r}$ to the subspace Y_{n-r}.

Let us operate on $\mathbf{u}$ with one of the operators $A, B, C, \ldots$. Let this operator be R

$$\mathbf{v} = R\mathbf{u} = R\mathbf{u}^r + R\mathbf{u}^{n-r}. \tag{2.16}$$

Now, since W_r is an invariant subspace, $R\mathbf{u}^r$ too belongs to W_r; $R\mathbf{u}^{n-r}$ will in general lie in the entire space V_n. The components of $\mathbf{v}$ are given by the following expressions:

$$v_i = \sum_{j=1}^{n} \Gamma(R)_{ji}\, u_j, \qquad (i = 1, 2, \ldots, n). \tag{2.17}$$

In particular,

$$v_i = (R\mathbf{u}^r)_i = \sum_{j=1}^{r} p_{ji} u_j, \qquad (i = 1, 2, \ldots, r), \tag{2.18}$$

and

$$\begin{aligned} v_i &= (R\mathbf{u}^{n-r})_i = \sum_{j=r+1}^{n} r_{ji} u_j, \qquad (i = 1, 2, \ldots, r) \\ v_i &= (R\mathbf{u}^{n-r})_i = \sum_{j=r+1}^{n} s_{ji} u_j, \qquad (i = r+1, r+2, \ldots, n). \end{aligned} \tag{2.19}$$

Then $\mathbf{\Gamma}(R)$ is given by

$$\mathbf{\Gamma}(R) = \left(\begin{array}{c|c} \mathbf{\Gamma}_1(R) & 0 \\ \hline \mathbf{Q}(R) & \mathbf{\Gamma}_2(R) \end{array}\right) \tag{2.20}$$

where $\mathbf{\Gamma}_1(R)$ is the $r \times r$ matrix of the elements p_{ij}, $\mathbf{Q}$ the matrix with r columns and $n - r$ rows of the elements r_{ij} and $\mathbf{\Gamma}_2(R)$ the $(n - r) \times (n - r)$ matrix of the elements s_{ij}. All the matrices $\mathbf{\Gamma}(R)$, R being a generic element of the group, have the form (2.20).

A matrix representation of the form (2.20) is said to be *reducible*. It can be shown that the portions $\mathbf{\Gamma}_1(R)$ and $\mathbf{\Gamma}_2(R)$ of $\mathbf{\Gamma}(R)$ form matrix representations of the group.

We have considered the operators $A, B, C, \ldots$ to be unitary. We have not made any hypothesis with regard to the basis vectors. In general, they are not orthonormal, but they may be made orthonormal by means of a similarity transformation. In this case, the matrices $\mathbf{\Gamma}(R)$ representing the unitary operators are unitary. In fact, as we saw in Sec. 2 of Chapter 1 a unitary operator is described by a unitary matrix if the basis vectors are orthonormal. Now, if R is an element of the group,

$$\begin{aligned} \mathbf{\Gamma}(R^{-1}) = [\mathbf{\Gamma}(R)]^{-1} &= [\mathbf{\Gamma}(R)]^{+} \\ &= \left(\begin{array}{c|c} \mathbf{\Gamma}_1(R)^{+} & \mathbf{Q}(R)^{+} \\ \hline 0 & \mathbf{\Gamma}_2(R) \end{array}\right); \end{aligned} \tag{2.21}$$

but $\mathbf{\Gamma}(R^{-1})$, being R^{-1} an element of the group, must also be of the form (2.20); then $Q^{+}(R) = 0$ and $Q(R) = 0$:

$$\mathbf{\Gamma}(R) = \left(\begin{array}{c|c} \mathbf{\Gamma}_1(R) & 0 \\ \hline 0 & \mathbf{\Gamma}_2(R) \end{array}\right). \tag{2.22}$$

A matrix in the form (2.22) is said to be in the *unitary reduced form*. We write (2.22) in the following way:

$$\mathbf{\Gamma}(R) = \mathbf{\Gamma}_1(R) + \mathbf{\Gamma}_2(R). \tag{2.23}$$

$\mathbf{\Gamma}_1(R)$ is a unitary representation of the group G on the invariant subspace W_r, and $\mathbf{\Gamma}_2(R)$ is a unitary representation of the group on the invariant subspace Y_{n-r}. The invariance of the subspace Y_{n-r} derives from the unitarity of the operators and the orthonormality of the basis chosen.

$\mathbf{\Gamma}_1(R)$ and $\mathbf{\Gamma}_2(R)$ are also called *irreducible unitary representations* of the group.

The vector space V_n may have several subspaces invariant with respect to linear unitary operators forming a group. In this case the unitary matrix representation of an operator, in the reduced form, has square matrices along the diagonal and zero elsewhere. Generalizing (2.23) we may then have

$$\mathbf{\Gamma}(R) = \mathbf{\Gamma}_1(R) + \mathbf{\Gamma}_2(R) + \cdots + \mathbf{\Gamma}_s(R), \qquad (s \leq n) \tag{2.24}$$

and $\mathbf{\Gamma}_i(R)$ are the irreducible unitary representations of the group, each of them representing the element R in an invariant subspace.

Example: Group C_{3v}

Let us take as basis vectors the following:

$$\mathbf{a}_1 = \mathbf{i} + c\mathbf{k}$$

$$\mathbf{a}_2 = -\frac{1}{2}\mathbf{i} - \frac{\sqrt{3}}{2}\mathbf{j} + c\mathbf{k}$$

$$\mathbf{a}_3 = -\frac{1}{2}\mathbf{i} + \frac{\sqrt{3}}{2}\mathbf{j} + c\mathbf{k}.$$

In general, for the operations of group C_{3v} we have

$$R\mathbf{a}_i = \sum_j \mathbf{a}_j \Gamma(R)_{ji};$$

for example,

$$C_3\mathbf{a}_1 = \mathbf{a}_2$$
$$C_3\mathbf{a}_2 = \mathbf{a}_3$$
$$C_3\mathbf{a}_3 = \mathbf{a}_1,$$

and then

$$\mathbf{\Gamma}(C_3) = \begin{pmatrix} 0 & 0 & 1 \\ 1 & 0 & 0 \\ 0 & 1 & 0 \end{pmatrix}.$$

Considering in the same way the other operations we get the following representation:

	E	C_3	$C_3{}^2$	σ_1	σ_2	σ_3
$\mathbf{\Gamma}$	$\begin{pmatrix} 1 & 0 & 0 \\ 0 & 1 & 0 \\ 0 & 0 & 1 \end{pmatrix}$	$\begin{pmatrix} 0 & 0 & 1 \\ 1 & 0 & 0 \\ 0 & 1 & 0 \end{pmatrix}$	$\begin{pmatrix} 0 & 1 & 0 \\ 0 & 0 & 1 \\ 1 & 0 & 0 \end{pmatrix}$	$\begin{pmatrix} 1 & 0 & 0 \\ 0 & 0 & 1 \\ 0 & 1 & 0 \end{pmatrix}$	$\begin{pmatrix} 0 & 0 & 1 \\ 0 & 1 & 0 \\ 1 & 0 & 0 \end{pmatrix}$	$\begin{pmatrix} 0 & 1 & 0 \\ 1 & 0 & 0 \\ 0 & 0 & 1 \end{pmatrix}$.

This matrix representation is unitary. Let us find now, by means of a similarity transformation, a new basis system that reduces the above representation:

$$\mathbf{a}'_i = \sum_j \mathbf{a}_j S_{ji}.$$

The new basis vectors are

$$\mathbf{a}_1' = \frac{1}{\sqrt{3}}\mathbf{a}_1 + \frac{1}{\sqrt{3}}\mathbf{a}_2 + \frac{1}{\sqrt{3}}\mathbf{a}_3 = \frac{c}{\sqrt{3}}\mathbf{k}$$

$$\mathbf{a}_2' = \frac{2}{\sqrt{6}}\mathbf{a}_1 - \frac{1}{\sqrt{6}}\mathbf{a}_2 - \frac{1}{\sqrt{6}}\mathbf{a}_3 = \frac{\sqrt{3}}{2}\mathbf{i}$$

$$\mathbf{a}_3' = \qquad -\frac{1}{\sqrt{2}}\mathbf{a}_2 + \frac{1}{\sqrt{2}}\mathbf{a}_3 = \frac{\sqrt{3}}{2}\mathbf{j},$$

with

$$\mathbf{S} = \begin{pmatrix} \frac{1}{\sqrt{3}} & \frac{2}{\sqrt{6}} & 0 \\ \frac{1}{\sqrt{3}} & -\frac{1}{\sqrt{6}} & -\frac{1}{\sqrt{2}} \\ \frac{1}{\sqrt{3}} & -\frac{1}{\sqrt{6}} & \frac{1}{\sqrt{2}} \end{pmatrix}.$$

The representation of the operation C_3 in the new basis system is given by

$$\mathbf{S}^{-1}\mathbf{\Gamma}(C_3)\mathbf{S} = \begin{pmatrix} 1 & 0 & 0 \\ 0 & -\frac{1}{2} & \frac{\sqrt{3}}{2} \\ 0 & -\frac{\sqrt{3}}{2} & -\frac{1}{2} \end{pmatrix}.$$

All the matrices corresponding to the different operations appear to consist of a unit matrix (of order one) and of a matrix of order two. We have actually, by means of a similarity transformation, divided the vector space defined by $\mathbf{a}_1$, $\mathbf{a}_2$, $\mathbf{a}_3$ in 2 invariant subspaces. The same process has given us two irreducible representations of the group C_{3v}:

E	C_3	$C_3{}^2$	σ_1	σ_2	σ_3
1	1	1	1	1	1
$\begin{pmatrix} 1 & 0 \\ 0 & 1 \end{pmatrix}$	$\begin{pmatrix} -\frac{1}{2} & \frac{\sqrt{3}}{2} \\ -\frac{\sqrt{3}}{2} & -\frac{1}{2} \end{pmatrix}$	$\begin{pmatrix} -\frac{1}{2} & -\frac{\sqrt{3}}{2} \\ \frac{\sqrt{3}}{2} & -\frac{1}{2} \end{pmatrix}$	$\begin{pmatrix} 1 & 0 \\ 0 & -1 \end{pmatrix}$	$\begin{pmatrix} -\frac{1}{2} & \frac{\sqrt{3}}{2} \\ \frac{\sqrt{3}}{2} & \frac{1}{2} \end{pmatrix}$	$\begin{pmatrix} -\frac{1}{2} & -\frac{\sqrt{3}}{2} \\ -\frac{\sqrt{3}}{2} & \frac{1}{2} \end{pmatrix}$.

Actually the group C_{3v} has an additional irreducible representation which can be formed by assigning $+1$ to the operations E, C_3, $C_3{}^2$ and -1 to the operations σ_1, σ_2, σ_3.

For the symmetry group of an equilateral triangle C_{3v} the irreducible inequivalent representations are found to be the following:

	E	C_3	$C_3{}^2$	σ_1	σ_2	σ_3
$\mathbf{\Gamma}_1$	1	1	1	1	1	1
$\mathbf{\Gamma}_2$	1	1	1	-1	-1	-1
$\mathbf{\Gamma}_3$	$\begin{pmatrix} 1 & 0 \\ 0 & 1 \end{pmatrix}$	$\begin{pmatrix} -\frac{1}{2} & \frac{\sqrt{3}}{2} \\ -\frac{\sqrt{3}}{2} & -\frac{1}{2} \end{pmatrix}$	$\begin{pmatrix} -\frac{1}{2} & -\frac{\sqrt{3}}{2} \\ \frac{\sqrt{3}}{2} & -\frac{1}{2} \end{pmatrix}$	$\begin{pmatrix} 1 & 0 \\ 0 & -1 \end{pmatrix}$	$\begin{pmatrix} -\frac{1}{2} & \frac{\sqrt{3}}{2} \\ \frac{\sqrt{3}}{2} & \frac{1}{2} \end{pmatrix}$	$\begin{pmatrix} -\frac{1}{2} & -\frac{\sqrt{3}}{2} \\ -\frac{\sqrt{3}}{2} & \frac{1}{2} \end{pmatrix}$.

The theory that we shall develop in the following sections will show that these are the only irreducible representations of the group C_{3v}.

4. SCHUR'S LEMMA AND ORTHOGONALITY RELATIONS

Schur's lemma, which is of great importance in the theory of representations, states:

$\mathbf{\Gamma}_\alpha(R)$ and $\mathbf{\Gamma}_\beta(R)$ are two irreducible representations of a group of dimensions, respectively, n_α and n_β ($n_\beta \leq n_\alpha$) and there exists a matrix $\mathbf{A}$ (of dimensions $n_\alpha \times n_\beta$) such that

$$\mathbf{A}\mathbf{\Gamma}_\alpha(R) = \mathbf{\Gamma}_\beta(R)\,\mathbf{A} \tag{2.25}$$

for all R. Then (a) *if $n_\alpha \neq n_\beta$, $\mathbf{A}$ is a zero $n_\alpha \times n_\beta$ matrix*; (b) *if $n_\alpha = n_\beta$, $\mathbf{A}$ is a square, nonsingular matrix, and $\mathbf{\Gamma}_\alpha$ and $\mathbf{\Gamma}_\beta$ are equivalent.*

A *corollary* of Schur's lemma states:

A matrix that commutes with every matrix of an irreducible representation of some group is a multiple of the unit matrix.

Schur's lemma is reported here without proof. For proof consult Appendix D of [1].

Consider now the matrix

$$\mathbf{A} = \sum_R \mathbf{\Gamma}_\alpha(R)\mathbf{D}\mathbf{\Gamma}_\beta(R^{-1}), \tag{2.26}$$

where $\mathbf{\Gamma}_\alpha$ and $\mathbf{\Gamma}_\beta$ are two irreducible representations of the group, of dimension respectively n_α and n_β, and $\mathbf{D}$ is an arbitrary matrix with n_α rows and n_β columns. The matrix $\mathbf{A}$ has the same dimensions of $\mathbf{D}$.

Let us multiply (2.26) by $\mathbf{\Gamma}_\alpha(S)$

$$\begin{aligned} \mathbf{\Gamma}_\alpha(S)\mathbf{A} &= \sum_R \mathbf{\Gamma}_\alpha(SR)\mathbf{D}\,\mathbf{\Gamma}_\beta(R^{-1}) \\ &= \sum_R \mathbf{\Gamma}_\alpha(SR)\mathbf{D}\,\mathbf{\Gamma}_\beta[(SR)^{-1}]\mathbf{\Gamma}_\beta(S). \end{aligned} \tag{2.27}$$

Since

$$\sum_R \mathbf{\Gamma}_\alpha(SR)\mathbf{D}\ \mathbf{\Gamma}_\beta[(SR)^{-1}] = \mathbf{A}, \tag{2.28}$$

we get from (2.27)

$$\mathbf{\Gamma}_\alpha(S)\mathbf{A} = \mathbf{A}\ \mathbf{\Gamma}_\beta(S). \tag{2.29}$$

Because of Schur's lemma, if $\mathbf{\Gamma}_\alpha$ and $\mathbf{\Gamma}_\beta$ are not equivalent, $\mathbf{A}$ must vanish:

$$\mathbf{A} = \sum_R \mathbf{\Gamma}_\alpha(R)\mathbf{D}\ \mathbf{\Gamma}_\beta(R^{-1}) = 0 \tag{2.30}$$

or for the ijth element

$$\sum_R \sum_{kl} \Gamma_\alpha(R)_{ij}\ D_{kl}\Gamma_\beta(R^{-1})_{lj} = 0. \tag{2.31}$$

Since $\mathbf{D}$ is arbitrary, we can choose it in such a way that all its elements are zero with the exception of $D_{kl} = 1$:

$$\sum_R \Gamma_\alpha(R)_{ik}\,\Gamma_\beta(R^{-1})_{lj} = 0; \tag{2.32}$$

but for unitary representations $\Gamma_\beta(R^{-1})_{lj} = \Gamma_\beta(R)^*_{jl}$. Therefore, for inequivalent representations

$$\sum_R \Gamma_\alpha(R)_{ik}\,\Gamma_\beta(R)_{jl} = 0. \tag{2.33}$$

If $\mathbf{\Gamma}_\alpha$ and $\mathbf{\Gamma}_\beta$ are identical (2.29) becomes

$$\mathbf{\Gamma}_\alpha(S)\ \mathbf{A} = \mathbf{A}\ \mathbf{\Gamma}_\alpha(S), \tag{2.34}$$

and therefore for the corollary to Schur's lemma

$$\mathbf{A} = \sum_R \mathbf{\Gamma}_\alpha(R)\mathbf{D}\ \mathbf{\Gamma}_\alpha(R^{-1}) = c\mathbf{1}, \tag{2.35}$$

where c depends on $\mathbf{D}$. If we choose $\mathbf{D}$ as in the past with only one element different from zero $D_{kl} = 1$,

$$\sum_R \Gamma_\alpha(R)_{ik}\,\Gamma_\alpha(R^{-1})_{lj} = c_{kl}\delta_{ij}. \tag{2.36}$$

Setting $i = j$ and summing over i,

$$\sum_{i=1}^{n_\alpha} \sum_R \Gamma_\alpha(R)_{ik}\,\Gamma_\alpha(R^{-1})_{li} = n_\alpha c_{kl}, \tag{2.37}$$

but

$$\sum_{i=1}^{n_\alpha} \Gamma_\alpha(R)_{ik}\,\Gamma_\alpha(R^{-1})_{li} = \sum_{i=1}^{n_\alpha} \Gamma_\alpha(R^{-1}R)_{lk} = \delta_{lk}. \tag{2.38}$$

Then

$$\sum_R \delta_{kl} = n_\alpha c_{kl} \tag{2.39}$$

If g is the order of the group,

$$c_{kl} = \frac{g}{n_\alpha}\,\delta_{kl}, \tag{2.40}$$

and for unitary representations

$$\sum_R \Gamma_\alpha(R)_{ik}\,\Gamma_\alpha(R)^*_{lj} = \frac{g}{n_\alpha}\,\delta_{kl}\delta_{ij}. \tag{2.41}$$

Combining (2.41) with (2.33), we get the *orthogonality relations*

$$\sum_R \Gamma_\alpha(R)_{ik}\,\Gamma_\beta(R)^*_{lj} = \frac{g}{n_\alpha}\,\delta_{\alpha\beta}\delta_{il}\delta_{kj}. \tag{2.42}$$

5. CHARACTERS OF A GROUP

Each representation of a group is formed by a set of square matrices; the trace (sum of diagonal elements) of a matrix is said to be the *character* of the matrix. A set of characters correspond to each representation. For the group C_{3v} we find

	E	C_3	$C_3{}^2$	σ_1	σ_2	σ_3
$\mathbf{\Gamma}_1$	1	1	1	1	1	1
$\mathbf{\Gamma}_2$	1	1	1	−1	−1	−1
$\mathbf{\Gamma}_3$	2	−1	−1	0	0	0.

The character of a matrix is not changed by a similarity transformation. In fact, if

$$\mathbf{\Gamma}'(R) = \mathbf{S}^{-1}\,\mathbf{\Gamma}(R)\,\mathbf{S}, \tag{2.43}$$

we have

$$\begin{aligned}\chi'(R) &= \sum_j \Gamma'(R)_{jj} = \sum_j (\mathbf{S}^{-1}\,\mathbf{\Gamma}(R)\,\mathbf{S})_{jj}\\ &= \sum_{jmn} (\mathbf{S}^{-1})_{jm}\,\Gamma(R)_{mn}\,S_{nj} = \sum_m [\mathbf{SS}^{-1}]_{nm}\Gamma(R)_{mn}\\ &= \sum_m \delta_{nm}\Gamma(R)_{mn} = \sum_n \Gamma(R)_{nn} = \chi(R).\end{aligned} \tag{2.44}$$

Therefore the characters of a representation form a set which is independent from any similarity transformation. Two nonequivalent representations have, therefore, different character systems.

We can prove now the following *theorem*:

If two elements belong to the same class, the corresponding matrices for a certain representation have the same characters.

If A and B belong to the same class we have for same element X of the group

$$A = X^{-1}BX \tag{2.45}$$

and

$$\mathbf{\Gamma}(A) = \mathbf{\Gamma}(X^{-1})\,\mathbf{\Gamma}(B)\,\mathbf{\Gamma}(X) = [\mathbf{\Gamma}(X)]^{-1}\,\mathbf{\Gamma}(B)\,\mathbf{\Gamma}(X). \tag{2.46}$$

The last expression, being a similarity transformation, bears

$$\chi(A) = \chi(B). \tag{2.47}$$

An orthogonality relation can be derived for the characters by using formula (2.42) in which we make $i = k$, $l = j$

$$\sum_R \Gamma_\alpha(R)^*_{ii}\,\Gamma_\beta(R)_{jj} = \frac{g}{n_\alpha}\,\delta_{\alpha\beta}\delta_{ij}. \tag{2.48}$$

Summing over i and j, we get

$$\sum_R \left\{\left[\sum_{i=1}^{n_\alpha}\Gamma_\alpha(R)^*_{ii}\right]\left[\sum_{j=1}^{n_\beta}\Gamma_\beta(R)_{jj}\right]\right\} = \frac{g}{n_\alpha}\,\delta_{\alpha\beta}\sum_{i=1}^{n_\alpha}\sum_{j=1}^{n_\beta}\delta_{ij} \tag{2.49}$$

and then the orthogonality relation

$$\sum_R \chi_\alpha(R)^*\,\chi_\beta(R) = g\delta_{\alpha\beta}, \tag{2.50}$$

or

$$\sum_{i=1}^{r} h_i\chi_\alpha(\mathcal{C}_i)^*\,\chi_\beta(\mathcal{C}_i) = g\delta_{\alpha\beta}, \tag{2.51}$$

where $\mathcal{C}_i$ is the generic class of the group, h_i is the number of elements in the class, and r is the number of classes in the group.

We have already seen that the characters do not change under a similarity transformation. The characters then specify the representations, independently from any similarity transformation.

For two irreducible representations the equality of the character systems is not only a necessary but also a sufficient condition for their equivalence. In fact, given two irreducible representations Γ_α and Γ_β with equal character systems $[\chi_\alpha(R) = \chi_\beta(R)]$, (2.50) gives, if they are inequivalent,

$$\sum_R \chi_\alpha(R)^*\,\chi_\beta(R) = 0. \tag{2.52}$$

But, for the equality of characters, again from (2.50),

$$\sum_R \chi_\alpha(R)^*\,\chi_\alpha(R) = \sum_R \chi_\alpha(R)^*\,\chi_\beta(R) = g. \tag{2.53}$$

Equation 2.53 contradicts (2.52): therefore Γ_α and Γ_β cannot be inequivalent and have equal character systems at the same time.

The orthogonality relations can provide a means to reduce the reducible representations. Any reducible representation can be reduced to its irreducible representations by a proper similarity transformation. We can write for the character of a matrix R of the reducible representation:

$$\chi(R) = \sum_{j=1}^{K} c_j \chi_j(R), \tag{2.54}$$

where K = number of irreducible representations,
c_j = number of times the jth irreducible representation occurs in the reducible representation:

From (2.54) and (2.50):

$$\begin{aligned}\sum_R \chi(R)^* \chi_i(R) &= \sum_R \sum_j c_j \chi_j(R)^* \chi_i(R) \\ &= \sum_j c_j g \delta_{ij} = g c_i.\end{aligned} \tag{2.55}$$

Then the number of times the irreducible representation Γ_i occurs in the reducible representation is:

$$c_i = \frac{1}{g} \sum_R \chi(R)^* \chi_i(R). \tag{2.56}$$

Let us now consider a reducible representation Γ. By using the orthogonality relation we get

$$\begin{aligned}\sum_R |\chi(R)|^2 &= \sum_R \sum_i c_i \chi_i(R)^* \sum_j c_j \chi_j(R) \\ &= \sum_{ij} c_i c_j \delta_{ij} = g \sum_i c_i^2,\end{aligned} \tag{2.57}$$

where

$$\sum_i c_i^2$$

is the sum of the squares of the number of times all the irreducible representations are contained in Γ. If Γ is irreducible,

$$\sum c_i^2 = 1 \quad \text{and} \quad \sum_R |\chi(R)|^2 = g.$$

Example

A reducible representation Γ of the symmetry group C_{3v} has the following character table:

E	C_3	C_3^2	σ_1	σ_2	σ_3
5	-1	-1	1	1	1

We can write

$$\Gamma = c_1\Gamma_1 + c_2\Gamma_2 + c_3\Gamma_3.$$

We find

$$c_1 = \tfrac{1}{6}\sum_R \chi_1(R)\,\chi(R) = \tfrac{1}{6}(5 - 1 - 1 + 1 + 1 + 1) = 1,$$

$$c_2 = \tfrac{1}{6}\sum_R \chi_2(R)\,\chi(R) = \tfrac{1}{6}(5 - 1 - 1 - 1 - 1 - 1) = 0,$$

$$c_3 = \tfrac{1}{6}\sum_R \chi_3(R)\,\chi(R) = \tfrac{1}{6}(10 + 1 + 1) = 2,$$

and then

$$\Gamma = \Gamma_1 + 2\Gamma_3.$$

We find also

$$\sum_R |\chi(R)|^2 = 25 + 1 + 1 + 1 + 1 + 1 = 30$$

$$g\sum_i c_i^2 = 6 \times (1 + 4) = 30,$$

and

$$\sum_R |\chi(R)|^2 = g\sum c_i^2.$$

6. PROPERTIES OF THE IRREDUCIBLE REPRESENTATIONS OF A GROUP

Consider a g-dimensional vector formed with the ijth elements of the matrices $\mathbf{\Gamma}_\alpha(R)$ of a group. This vector is orthogonal, because of (2.42), to all the vectors formed with the klth elements of the same matrices. There are n_α^2 such orthogonal vectors, and all these vectors are orthogonal to the $n_\beta^2, n_\gamma^2, \ldots$ vectors formed in the same way with the matrices $\mathbf{\Gamma}_\beta(R)$, $\mathbf{\Gamma}_\gamma(R), \ldots$. The total number of orthogonal vectors is

$$\sum_i n_i^2,$$

each of dimension g. But the number of orthogonal vectors of dimension g which can be constructed is g; therefore

$$\sum_i n_i^2 = g. \tag{2.58}$$

But g is also the order of the group. Therefore we can say that:

The sum of the squares of the dimensions of the irreducible representations of a group is equal to the order of the group.

In a similar way we can derive an important property of the irreducible representations of a group from the orthogonality relation (2.51), which can be written as follows:

$$\sum_{i=1}^{r} \chi_\alpha(\mathcal{C}_i)^* \left(\frac{h_i}{g}\right)^{1/2} \chi_\beta(\mathcal{C}_i)\left(\frac{h_i}{g}\right)^{1/2} = \delta_{\alpha\beta}. \tag{2.59}$$

We can consider the set of characters of a certain representation as components of an r-dimensional vector. The vector formed with the characters of a representation Γ_α is orthogonal to the vector formed with the characters of any other representation. There are, altogether, r' such vectors of dimension r, where r' is the number of irreducible representations, but there can be only r orthogonal vectors of dimension r; therefore we must have $r' = r$ and:

The number of irreducible representation of a group is equal to the number of classes.

7. THE DIRECT PRODUCT REPRESENTATION

Let us assume that

$$\begin{gathered} f_1, f_2, \ldots, f_{n_\alpha} \\ g_1, g_2, \ldots, g_{n_\beta} \end{gathered} \tag{2.60}$$

are two sets of functions which form bases for two irreducible representations Γ_α and Γ_β of a group G. The products $f_i g_k$ form a set which is called *direct product* of the sets f_i and g_k. The functions $f_i g_k$ form a basis for a representation of G of order $n_\alpha n_\beta$. In fact,

$$Rf_i = \sum_{j=1}^{n_\alpha} \Gamma_\alpha(R)_{ji}\, f_j \tag{2.61}$$

$$Rg_k = \sum_{l=1}^{n_\beta} \Gamma_\beta(R)_{lk}\, g_l, \tag{2.62}$$

and

$$\begin{aligned} R(f_i g_k) &= \sum_{j=1}^{n_\alpha} \sum_{l=1}^{n_\beta} \Gamma_\alpha(R)_{ji}\, \Gamma_\beta(R)_{lk}\, f_j g_l \\ &= \sum_{j=1}^{n_\alpha} \sum_{l=1}^{n_\beta} \Gamma(R)_{jl,ik}\, f_j g_l. \end{aligned} \tag{2.63}$$

$\mathbf{\Gamma}$ is a matrix of dimensions $n_\alpha n_\beta \times n_\alpha n_\beta$; the element appearing in the jith row and lkth column is

$$\Gamma(R)_{jl,ik} = \Gamma_\alpha(R)_{ji}\, \Gamma_\beta(R)_{lk}. \tag{2.64}$$

The ensemble of these matrices $\mathbf{\Gamma}$ is called the *direct product* of matrices $\mathbf{\Gamma}_\alpha$ and $\mathbf{\Gamma}_\beta$. The relation (2.63) implies that the direct product of two representations forms a representation of the group.

Let us now call $\chi(R)$, $\chi_\alpha(R)$, and $\chi_\beta(R)$, respectively, the characters of $\mathbf{\Gamma}(R)$, $\mathbf{\Gamma}_\alpha(R)$, and $\mathbf{\Gamma}_\beta(R)$. We have

$$\begin{aligned} \chi(R) = \sum_{ik} \Gamma(R)_{ik,ik} &= \sum_{ik} \Gamma_\alpha(R)_{ii}\, \Gamma_\beta(R)_{kk} \\ &= \chi_\alpha(R)\, \chi_\beta(R). \end{aligned} \tag{2.65}$$

Then

The character of the direct product of two representations Γ_α and Γ_β is the product of the characters of Γ_α and Γ_β.

The direct product of two representations is in general a reducible representation of the group:

$$\mathbf{\Gamma}_\alpha(R) \times \mathbf{\Gamma}_\beta(R) = \sum_{j=1}^{r} c_{\alpha\beta\gamma}\, \mathbf{\Gamma}_\gamma(R), \tag{2.66}$$

and

$$\chi(R) = \chi_\alpha(R)\, \chi_\beta(R) = \sum_{\gamma=1}^{r} c_{\alpha\beta\gamma}\, \chi_\gamma(R), \tag{2.67}$$

and from (2.56)

$$c_{\alpha\beta\gamma} = \frac{1}{g} \sum_R \chi_\gamma(R)^*\, \chi_\alpha(R)\, \chi_\beta(R). \tag{2.68}$$

The coefficients $c_{\alpha\beta\gamma}$ have the following properties:

$$\begin{aligned} c_{\alpha\beta\gamma} &= c_{\beta\alpha\gamma} \\ c_{1\beta\gamma} &= c_{\beta 1\gamma} = \delta_{\beta\gamma} \\ c_{\alpha\beta 1} &= c_{\beta\alpha 1} = \begin{cases} 1, & \text{if } \mathbf{\Gamma}_\beta \text{ equivalent to } \mathbf{\Gamma}_\alpha^* \\ 0, & \text{otherwise.} \end{cases} \end{aligned} \tag{2.69}$$

8. PRODUCT GROUPS AND THEIR REPRESENTATIONS

Suppose we are given two groups

$$\begin{aligned} g &= e, a, b, c, \ldots \\ G &= E, A, B, C, \ldots, \end{aligned} \tag{2.70}$$

and suppose that all products between the elements of the two groups are commutative

$$rR = Rr, \tag{2.71}$$

where r = any element of g,
R = any element of G.

If the groups g and G are of order m and M, respectively, and $\boldsymbol{\gamma}(R)$ and $\mathbf{\Gamma}(R)$ are the matrices representing g and G, respectively, it is possible to order the $(m \times M)^2$ numbers $\gamma(R)_{ij} \times \Gamma(R)_{kl}$ in such a way that they form a $mM \times mM$ matrix; for example, the element appearing in the ikth row and jlth column may be

$$\gamma(r)_{ij} \times \Gamma(R)_{kl}. \tag{2.72}$$

This matrix is called the *product group matrix.*

The character $\chi(rR)$ of $\boldsymbol{\gamma}(r) \times \boldsymbol{\Gamma}(R)$ is given by

$$\chi(rR) = \chi(r)\,\chi(R). \tag{2.73}$$

All of the irreducible representations of $g \times G$ can be obtained by forming the direct product representations which have as components the respective irreducible representations of the component groups.

If g has n irreducible representations and G has N irreducible representations, $g \times G$ has nN irreducible representations.

Examples

Let us find the character table of the product group $g \times G$, where

G = symmetry group D_3.

$g = E, \sigma_h$ (This group is called C_{1h}).

The character table of g is the following:

g	E	σ_h
γ_1	1	1
γ_2	1	−1

The character table of G is the following:

G	E	$2C_3$	$3C_2'$
Γ_1	1	1	1
Γ_2	1	1	−1
Γ_3	2	−1	0

The character table of $G \times g$ is given by

$g \times G$	E	$2C_3$	$3C_2'$	$\sigma_h E$	$2\sigma_h C_3$	$3\sigma_h C_2'$
$\gamma_1 \times \Gamma_1$	1	1	1	1	1	1
$\gamma_1 \times \Gamma_2$	1	1	−1	1	1	−1
$\gamma_1 \times \Gamma_3$	2	−1	0	2	−1	0
$\gamma_2 \times \Gamma_1$	1	1	1	−1	−1	−1
$\gamma_2 \times \Gamma_2$	1	1	−1	−1	−1	1
$\gamma_2 \times \Gamma_3$	2	−1	0	−2	1	0

The product group is called D_{3h}:

$$D_{3h} = C_{1h} \times D_3. \tag{2.74}$$

9. SUMMARY OF RULES

1. The elements of unitary irreducible representations form orthogonal vectors

$$\sum_{\alpha} \Gamma_\alpha(R)_{ij}\, \Gamma_\beta(R)^*_{kl} = \frac{g}{n_\alpha}\, \delta_{\alpha\beta}\delta_{ik}\delta_{jl}. \tag{2.75}$$

2. The characters of nonequivalent unitary irreducible representations form orthogonal vectors:

$$\sum_R \chi_\alpha(R)^*\, \chi_\beta(R) = g\delta_{\alpha\beta}, \qquad \left(\sum_R |\chi_\alpha(R)|^2 = g\right), \tag{2.76}$$

$$\sum_i h_i\, \chi_\alpha(\mathfrak{C}_i)^*\, \chi_\beta(\mathfrak{C}_i) = g\delta_{\alpha\beta}.$$

3. A reducible representation $\Gamma(R)$ can be expressed as

$$\Gamma(R) = c_1\, \Gamma_1(R) + c_2\, \Gamma_2(R) + \cdots, \tag{2.77}$$

where

$$\Gamma_1(R),\ \Gamma_2(R), \ldots = \text{irreducible representations}$$

$$c_j = \frac{1}{g} \sum_R \chi(R)^*\, \chi_j(R).$$

Also,

$$\sum_R |\chi(R)|^2 = g \sum_i c_i^2. \tag{2.78}$$

4. Two equivalent representations have equal character systems.

5. The sum of the squares of the dimensions of the irreducible representations is equal to the order of the group

$$\sum_\alpha {n_\alpha}^2 = g. \tag{2.79}$$

Since

$$n_\alpha \equiv \chi_\alpha(E),$$

$$\sum_\alpha |\chi_\alpha(E)|^2 = g. \tag{2.80}$$

6. The number of irreducible representations is equal to the number of classes.

10. GROUPS OF REAL ORTHOGONAL MATRICES

10.1 Linear Orthogonal Transformations in Real Vector Space

If $\mathbf{R}$ is a real 3×3 orthogonal matrix ($\mathbf{RR}^+ = \mathbf{R}\tilde{\mathbf{R}} = \mathbf{1}$), we can define a coordinate transformation from one cartesian system to another by means of the elements of $\mathbf{R}$:

$$\mathbf{x}' = \mathbf{R}\mathbf{x}, \tag{2.81}$$

or

$$\begin{aligned} x_1' &= R_{11}x_1 + R_{12}x_2 + R_{13}x_3, \\ x_2' &= R_{21}x_1 + R_{22}x_2 + R_{23}x_3, \\ x_3' &= R_{31}x_1 + R_{32}x_2 + R_{33}x_3. \end{aligned} \tag{2.82}$$

A real orthogonal transformation leaves the distances between any two points unchanged. In fact the square of the distance between two points $\mathbf{x}$ and $\mathbf{y}$ is given by $\tilde{\mathbf{d}}\mathbf{d}$ where

$$\mathbf{d} = \begin{pmatrix} x_1 - y_1 \\ x_2 - y_2 \\ x_3 - y_3 \end{pmatrix}. \tag{2.83}$$

The square of the distance between the points $\mathbf{x}'$ and $\mathbf{y}'$ is given by

$$\tilde{\mathbf{d}}'\mathbf{d}' = (\widetilde{\mathbf{R}\mathbf{d}})\mathbf{R}\mathbf{d} = \tilde{\mathbf{d}}\tilde{\mathbf{R}}\mathbf{R}\mathbf{d} = \tilde{\mathbf{d}}\mathbf{d}. \tag{2.84}$$

The real orthogonal matrices have determinants equal to ± 1. In fact, if $\mathbf{R}\tilde{\mathbf{R}} = \mathbf{1}$ we must have

$$(\det \mathbf{R})(\det \tilde{\mathbf{R}}) = (\det \mathbf{R})^2 = 1, \tag{2.85}$$

and

$$\det \mathbf{R} = \pm 1. \tag{2.86}$$

The real orthogonal transformations whose matrices have determinant equal to 1 are called *proper rotations*, those whose matrices have determinant equal to -1 are called *improper rotations.*

Any real orthogonal matrix can be diagonalized by means of a unitary transformation. Given the real orthogonal matrix $\mathbf{R}$, a unitary matrix $\mathbf{T}$ can be formed such that

$$\mathbf{T}^{+}\mathbf{R}\mathbf{T} = \mathbf{T}^{-1}\mathbf{R}\mathbf{T} = \mathbf{D}, \tag{2.87}$$

where $\mathbf{D}$ is a diagonal (unitary) matrix. (2.87) can also be written

$$\mathbf{R}\mathbf{T} = \mathbf{T}\mathbf{D}, \tag{2.88}$$

or

$$\sum_k R_{ik}T_{kj} = \sum_k T_{ik}D_{kk}\delta_{kj} = D_{jj}T_{ij}. \tag{2.89}$$

Equation 2.88 represents an eigenvalue equation and is similar to (1.168). The eigenvalues of $\mathbf{R}$ are given by the diagonal elements of $\mathbf{D}$; the corresponding eigenvectors are the columns of T. The eigenvalues of $\mathbf{R}$ are given by

$$\det (\mathbf{R} - \lambda\mathbf{1}) = 0, \tag{2.90}$$

as in (1.167). The above equation is of the third order in λ; the diagonal matrix **D** will, in general, appear in the form

$$\mathbf{D} = \mathbf{T}^{+}\mathbf{R}\mathbf{T} = \begin{pmatrix} \pm 1 & 0 & 0 \\ 0 & e^{i\theta} & 0 \\ 0 & 0 & e^{-i\theta} \end{pmatrix}. \tag{2.91}$$

Let us consider now the matrix

$$\mathbf{T}' = \mathbf{T}\mathbf{V}, \tag{2.92}$$

where **V** is a unitary matrix given by

$$\mathbf{V} = \begin{pmatrix} 1 & 0 & 0 \\ 0 & \frac{1}{\sqrt{2}} & \frac{i}{\sqrt{2}} \\ 0 & \frac{1}{\sqrt{2}} & -\frac{i}{\sqrt{2}} \end{pmatrix}. \tag{2.93}$$

T′ is also a unitary matrix. The matrix **T** may be chosen in such a way that its first column is real and the other two columns are one the complex conjugate of the other; in this case **T**′ is unitary and real.

Let us perform the following transformation

$$\mathbf{R}' = \mathbf{T}'^{+}\mathbf{R}\mathbf{T}' = \mathbf{V}^{+}(\mathbf{T}^{+}\mathbf{R}\mathbf{T})\,\mathbf{V} = \begin{vmatrix} \pm 1 & 0 & 0 \\ 0 & \cos\theta & -\sin\theta \\ 0 & \sin\theta & \cos\theta \end{vmatrix}. \tag{2.94}$$

If we use the matrix **R**′ in a coordinate transformation we get

$$\begin{aligned} x_1' &= x_1 \\ x_2' &= x_2 \cos\theta - x_3 \sin\theta \\ x_3' &= x_2 \sin\theta + x_3 \cos\theta, \end{aligned} \tag{2.95}$$

and

$$\begin{aligned} x_1' &= -x_1 \\ x_2' &= x_2 \cos\theta - x_3 \sin\theta \\ x_3' &= x_2 \sin\theta + x_3 \cos\theta. \end{aligned} \tag{2.96}$$

The matrix **T**′ which brings **R** into the form (2.94) is itself a real orthogonal matrix, with determinant 1,[1] and represents a proper rotation. **T**′ can be thought of as a rotation which brings the axis x_1 in the direction of the axis about which we can perform the **R** rotation.

[1] The determinant may be adjusted to be $+1$ by multiplying it by -1 if it is negative.

The transformation (2.95) corresponds to a pure rotation about the axis x_1; the transformation (2.96) to a pure rotation about the axis x_1 followed by a reflection through the plane x_2x_3. The operation reflection through the plane x_2x_3 is represented by the following matrix:

$$\begin{pmatrix} -1 & 0 & 0 \\ 0 & 1 & 0 \\ 0 & 0 & 1 \end{pmatrix}. \tag{2.97}$$

However the matrix representing the improper rotation (2.96) can be also written in the following way:

$$\begin{pmatrix} -1 & 0 & 0 \\ 0 & \cos\theta & -\sin\theta \\ 0 & \sin\theta & \cos\theta \end{pmatrix} = \begin{pmatrix} -1 & 0 & 0 \\ 0 & -1 & 0 \\ 0 & 0 & -1 \end{pmatrix} \begin{pmatrix} 1 & 0 & 0 \\ 0 & \cos(\pi+\theta) & -\sin(\pi+\theta) \\ 0 & \sin(\pi+\theta) & \cos(\pi+\theta) \end{pmatrix}, \tag{2.98}$$

or as the product of a proper rotation and of an inversion through the origin, this last operation being represented by the matrix

$$\begin{pmatrix} -1 & 0 & 0 \\ 0 & -1 & 0 \\ 0 & 0 & -1 \end{pmatrix}. \tag{2.99}$$

We can then make the following statement:

A proper rotation can be considered as a rotation about some axis; an improper rotation can be considered as a rotation about some axis followed by a reflection through a plane perpendicular to the axis, or as a rotation about some axis followed by an inversion through the origin.

The product of two improper rotations is a proper rotation. The product of a proper rotation and of an improper rotation is an improper rotation.

All real orthogonal transformations form a group which is called the *orthogonal group*.

The orthogonal group has an infinite number of elements. However, we may have subgroups of the orthogonal group with a finite number of elements. If we consider any of these subgroups, or finite groups, we find that it is either composed of all proper rotations or of as many proper as improper rotations. Therefore, the proper rotations either cover the entire finite group or form an invariant subgroup of the entire finite group.

10.2 Groups of Proper and Improper Rotations

The notation we shall use for the operations which form the different groups is the following:

E = identity; leaves each point in its original position;
C_n = rotation about an axis of symmetry by an angle $2\pi/n$;
σ_h = reflection through a plane of symmetry, perpendicular to the principal axis of symmetry (axis with largest n);
σ_v = reflection through a plane which contains the principal axis;
σ_d = reflection through a plane which contains the principal axis and bisects the angle between two twofold axes perpendicular to the principal axis;
S_n = rotation about an axis by $2\pi/n$ followed by a reflection through a plane perpendicular to the axis of rotation.
$I = S_2$ = inversion through the center of symmetry.

We want now to list the possible groups of proper and improper rotations.

GROUPS OF PROPER ROTATIONS

Any proper rotation may be represented by a rotation about some axis. The possible groups of proper rotations are the following:

C_n: Cyclic groups generated by the powers up to n of a certain basic rotation operation. The order of the group is n. There is an axis of symmetry.
D_n: These groups have n twofold axes perpendicular to the main axis. The order of the group is $2n$. Each D_n group contains C_n as invariant subgroup.
T: The group of operations which sends a regular tetrahedron into itself. The order of the group is 12. It has 4 threefold axes and 3 twofold axes.
O: Octahedral or cubic group. The group of operations which send an octahedron or a cube into itself (It contains all the operations of group T). The order of the group is 24. It has 4 threefold axes, 3 fourfold axes and 6 twofold axes.
Ic: Icosahedral group. The group of operations which send an icosahedron or a pentagonal dodecahedron into itself. It has 6 fivefold axes, 10 threefold axes, 15 twofold axes. The order of the group is 60.

GROUPS OF PROPER AND IMPROPER ROTATIONS

In such a group there are as many proper rotations as there are improper. The proper rotations form an invariant subgroup of half the order of the total group.

There are two possibilities. If we call $\mathfrak{F}$ the subgroup of proper rotation and $\mathfrak{J}$ the subgroup of improper rotation:

(a) $\mathfrak{F} = -\mathfrak{J}$;
(b) $\mathfrak{F} + (-\mathfrak{J})$ = group of proper rotations, which contains $\mathfrak{F}$ as an invariant subgroup of $\frac{1}{2}$ order;

where by $-\mathfrak{J}$ we designate the set of matrices obtained by taking the negatives of all the $\mathfrak{J}$ matrices.

We have now the following groups:

C_{nv}: The subgroup of proper rotations is the group C_n. The group of proper rotations $\mathfrak{F} + (-\mathfrak{J})$ is the group D_n. The order of the group is $2n$.

S_{2n}: The subgroup of proper rotations is C_n. If n is even $\mathfrak{F} + (-\mathfrak{J}) = C_{2n}$; if n is odd $\mathfrak{F} = C_n = -\mathfrak{J}$. The order of the group is $2n$. Examples: $S_2 = C_1 \times I$; $S_6 = C_3 \times I$.

C_{nh}: The subgroup of proper rotations is C_n. If n is even $\mathfrak{F} = C_n = -\mathfrak{J}$; if n is odd $\mathfrak{F} + (-\mathfrak{J}) = C_{2n}$. The order of the group is $2n$. Examples: $C_{2h} = C_2 \times I$; $C_{4h} = C_4 \times I$; $C_{6h} = C_6 \times I$.

D_{nh}: The subgroup of proper rotations is D_n. If n is even $\mathfrak{F} = D_n = -\mathfrak{J}$; if n is odd $\mathfrak{F} + (-\mathfrak{J}) = D_{2n}$. The order of the group is $2n$. Examples: $D_{2h} = D_2 \times I$; $D_{4h} = D_4 \times I$; $D_{6h} = D_6 \times I$.

D_{nd}: The subgroup of proper rotations is D_n. If n is even $\mathfrak{F} + (-\mathfrak{J}) = D_{2n}$; if n is odd $\mathfrak{F} = -\mathfrak{J} = D_n$. The order of the group is $2n$. Example: $D_{3d} = D_3 \times I$.

T_h: The subgroup of proper rotations is T. Also $\mathfrak{F} = T = -\mathfrak{J}$ or $T_h = T \times \mathfrak{J}$. The order of the group is 24.

T_d: The subgroup of proper rotations is T. Also $\mathfrak{F} + (-\mathfrak{J}) = 0$. The order of the group is 24.

O_h: The subgroup of proper rotations is O. Also $\mathfrak{F} = -\mathfrak{J} = O$ or $O_h = O \times I$. The order of the group is 48.

I_h: The subgroup of proper rotations is Ic. Also $\mathfrak{F} = -\mathfrak{J} = Ic$ or $I_h = Ic \times I$. The order of the group is 120.

INFINITE GROUPS OF PROPER ROTATIONS

We will consider only the following groups:

C_∞: This group is formed by all the rotations (by any angle) about a certain axis. Any group C_n is a subgroup of C_∞.

D_∞: This group is formed by all the rotations about a certain axis plus all the twofold rotations about any axis in a plane perpendicular to the main rotation axis. Any group D_n is a subgroup of D_∞.

Group of all proper rotations: This group consists of all the proper rotations about any axis in space.

INFINITE GROUPS OF PROPER AND IMPROPER ROTATIONS

We will consider only the following groups:

$C_{\infty v}$: The subgroup of proper rotations is the group C_∞. The improper rotations are all the reflections about planes containing the main axis: $\mathcal{S} + (-\mathfrak{J}) = D_n$. This is the group of the electric field.

$C_{\infty h}$: The subgroup of proper rotations is the group C_∞. The improper rotations are rotations $\times$ reflections through a plane perpendicular to the main axis. This is the group of the magnetic field.

$D_{\infty h}$: The subgroup of proper rotations is D_∞. The improper rotations are reflections through any plane containing the main axis, and rotations about the main axis $\times$ reflections through a plane perpendicular to the main axis.

Group of all proper and improper rotations: It consists of all real orthogonal coordinate transformations.

11. SPACE GROUPS AND SYMMETRY OF CRYSTALLINE SOLIDS [2]

11.1 The Fundamental Operations of a Space Group

The most general operation of a space group can be represented by the following coordinate transformation:

$$\begin{aligned} x_1' &= R_{11}x_1 + R_{12}x_2 + R_{13}x_3 + t_1 \\ x_1' &= R_{21}x_1 + R_{22}x_2 + R_{23}x_3 + t_2 \\ x_3' &= R_{31}x_1 + R_{32}x_2 + R_{33}x_3 + t_3, \end{aligned} \tag{2.100}$$

or, more concisely

$$\mathbf{x}' = \mathbf{R}\mathbf{x} + \mathbf{t}, \tag{2.101}$$

where $\mathbf{R}$ represents a proper or improper rotation.

The fundamental operator corresponding to the above transformation can be represented by the notation $\{\alpha \mid \mathbf{t}\}$ where α stands for the rotation and $\mathbf{t}$ for the translation. A pure rotation is indicated by $\{\alpha \mid 0\}$ and a pure translation by $\{E \mid \mathbf{t}\}$. The identity operator is indicated by $\{E \mid 0\}$.

Let us consider now the product of two operators $\{\alpha \mid \mathbf{t}\}$ and $\{\beta \mid \mathbf{t}'\}$ where α and β are two rotations represented respectively by the two orthogonal matrices $\mathbf{R}$ and $\mathbf{S}$. We first apply $\{\alpha \mid \mathbf{t}\}$

$$\mathbf{x}' = \{\alpha \mid \mathbf{t}\}\,\mathbf{x} = \mathbf{R}\mathbf{x} + \mathbf{t}, \tag{2.102}$$

and then $\{\beta \mid \mathbf{t}'\}$

$$\mathbf{x}'' = \{\beta \mid \mathbf{t}'\}\,\mathbf{x}' = \mathbf{S}\mathbf{x}' + \mathbf{t}' = \mathbf{S}[\mathbf{R}\mathbf{x} + \mathbf{t}] + \mathbf{t}' = \mathbf{S}\mathbf{R}\mathbf{x} + [\mathbf{S}\mathbf{t} + \mathbf{t}'].$$

Therefore

$$\{\beta \mid \mathbf{t}'\}\{\alpha \mid \mathbf{t}\} = \{\beta\alpha \mid \beta\mathbf{t} + \mathbf{t}'\}. \tag{2.103}$$

The inverse of operator $\{\alpha \mid \mathbf{t}\}$ is given by:

$$\{\alpha \mid \mathbf{t}\}^{-1} = \{\alpha^{-1} \mid -\alpha^{-1}\mathbf{t}\} \tag{2.104}$$

In fact, applying (2.103):

$$\{\alpha \mid \mathbf{t}\}\{\alpha^{-1} \mid -\alpha^{-1}\mathbf{t}\} = \{E \mid -\mathbf{t} + \mathbf{t}\} = \{E \mid 0\}. \tag{2.105}$$

From the above derived relations we can see that the collection of all the transformations of the $\{\alpha \mid \mathbf{t}\}$ type form a group. The collection of all pure translations forms an invariant subgroup of this group. In fact, given a certain operation $\{E \mid \mathbf{t}\}$ we obtain:

$$\begin{aligned}\{\alpha^{-1} \mid -\alpha^{-1}\mathbf{t}'\}\{E \mid \mathbf{t}\}\{\alpha \mid \mathbf{t}'\} \\ = \{\alpha^{-1} \mid -\alpha^{-1}\mathbf{t}' + \alpha^{-1}\mathbf{t}\}\{\alpha \mid \mathbf{t}'\} = \{E \mid \alpha^{-1}\mathbf{t}\},\end{aligned} \tag{2.106}$$

which is a pure translation.

A crystalline solid is a periodic structure whose periodicity is expressed by certain *primitive translations*. Any translation by a vector $\mathbf{T}_n$ which sends the solid into itself can be expressed as linear combination of the *basic primitive translations* $\mathbf{a}_1$, $\mathbf{a}_2$, and $\mathbf{a}_3$:

$$\mathbf{T}_n = n_1\mathbf{a}_1 + n_2\mathbf{a}_2 + n_3\mathbf{a}_3, \tag{2.107}$$

where n_1, n_2, and n_3 are integer numbers. The array of points determined by the translations $\{E \mid \mathbf{T}_n\}$ is called *lattice*. In addition to the translations $\{E \mid \mathbf{T}_n\}$, the lattice may be invariant under other operations $\{\alpha \mid \mathbf{t}\}$, where $\mathbf{t}$ may not be a primitive translation.

The ensemble of all possible operations which leave a periodic solid invariant form a group which is called the *space group*.

The ensemble of all primitive translations is an invariant group of the space group. In fact

$$\{\alpha \mid \mathbf{t}\}\{E \mid \mathbf{T}_n\}\{\alpha^{-1} \mid -\alpha^{-1}\mathbf{t}\} = \{E \mid \alpha\mathbf{T}_n\}, \tag{2.108}$$

where $\alpha\mathbf{T}_n$ is also a primitive translation.

11.2 The One-Dimensional Space Groups

A one-dimensional lattice consists of points in a straight line at distances $x_n = na$, where a is the basic primitive translation.

There are two possible unidimensional space groups:

1. The space group consisting of all possible primitive translations $\{E \mid na\}$ with no rotation allowed. A unidimensional array with such a group is represented in Fig. 2.2*a*.

2. The space group which has the group of primitive translations as an invariant subgroup but also contains operations of the type $\{\alpha \mid t\}$, with t not necessarily a primitive translation. A unidimensional array with such a

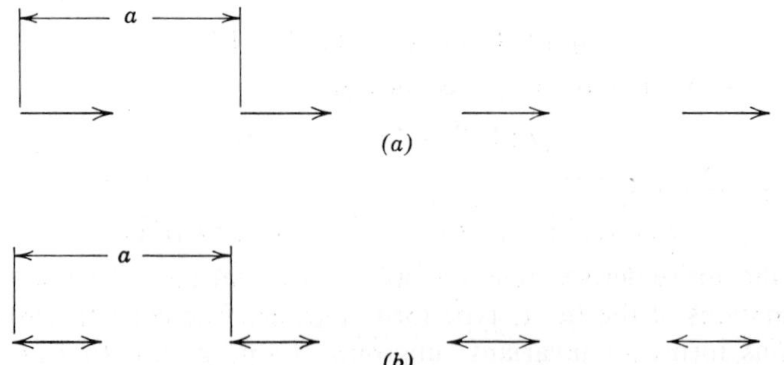

Fig. 2.2. Linear arrays illustrating possible undimensional space groups: (*a*) space group consisting of $\{E \mid na\}$; (*b*) space group consisting of $\{E \mid na\}$ and $\{I \mid na\}$.

group is represented in Fig. 2.2*b*. The most general operation of this group is $\{\alpha \mid t + na\}$.

The only possible α operation is a reflection through the origin which we may indicate by I:

$$x' = \{I \mid t\}\, x = \alpha x + t = -x + t. \tag{2.109}$$

If t is not a primitive translation, it is possible to introduce a coordinate system, such that $t = 0$. In fact let us put

$$\begin{aligned} x &= y + q, \\ x' &= y' + q. \end{aligned} \tag{2.110}$$

Equation 2.109 then becomes

$$y' + q = -y - q + t$$

or

$$y' = -y - 2q + t. \tag{2.111}$$

If we put $q = t/2$, the operation $\{\alpha \mid t\}$ becomes $\{\alpha \mid 0\}$ in the new coordinate system.

This space group may then be considered to consist of all the operators $\{I \mid na\}$ in addition to all the operators $\{E \mid na\}$.

11.3 Bidimensional Space Groups

Bidimensional Point Groups and Bravais Lattices. The most general space group in two dimensions contains as an invariant subgroup the group of all the primitive translations $\{E \mid \mathbf{T}_n\}$, where

$$\mathbf{T}_n = n_1\mathbf{a}_1 + n_2\mathbf{a}_2, \tag{2.112}$$

and, in addition, other operators $\{\alpha \mid \mathbf{t}\}$ where $\mathbf{t}$ is not necessarily a primitive translation and α represents a real orthogonal coordinate transformation.

In analogy to the three-dimensional case discussed in Sec. 10.1 of this chapter, we find that a two-dimensional real orthogonal matrix, when operated on by a similarity transformation, may be put under one of the two forms:

$$\begin{pmatrix} \cos\theta & -\sin\theta \\ \sin\theta & \cos\theta \end{pmatrix} \qquad \begin{pmatrix} -\cos\theta & \sin\theta \\ \sin\theta & \cos\theta \end{pmatrix}. \tag{2.113}$$

In (2.113) the matrix on the left-hand side with a determinant equal to $+1$ represents a *proper* rotation and corresponds to a rotation of the coordinate system; the matrix on the right-hand side with a determinant equal to -1 represents an *improper* rotation and corresponds to a reflection through an axis.

It is clear that in a periodic structure rotational and translational operations must be compatible; this fact puts some restrictions on the possible α's which may appear in the generic operation $\{\alpha \mid \mathbf{t}\}$ of a space group.

Let us call $\mathbf{a}$ the shortest primitive translation in the plane and R a generic rotational operation about an axis perpendicular to the plane. $R\mathbf{a}$ is also a translation in the plane and so are $R\mathbf{a} + \mathbf{a}$ and $R\mathbf{a} - \mathbf{a}$. If α is the angle by which R makes the solid rotate, we must have

$$|R\mathbf{a} - \mathbf{a}| = \left|2a \sin\frac{\alpha}{2}\right| \geq a \quad \text{or} \quad \left|\sin\frac{\alpha}{2}\right| \geq \tfrac{1}{2}, \tag{2.114}$$

which restricts the possible values of α to the interval

$$60^\circ \leq \alpha \leq 300^\circ. \tag{2.115}$$

The relation

$$|R\mathbf{a} + \mathbf{a}| = \left|2a \cos\frac{\alpha}{2}\right| \geq a \quad \text{or} \quad \left|\cos\frac{\alpha}{2}\right| \geq \tfrac{1}{2} \tag{2.116}$$

restricts further the interval of possible α to

$$\alpha \leq 120^\circ, \qquad \alpha \geq 240^\circ. \tag{2.117}$$

The values of α equal to 0 and 180° are, however, still acceptable. We must also have

$$|R\mathbf{a} - R^{-1}\mathbf{a}| = |2a \sin\alpha| \geq a \quad \text{or} \quad |\sin\alpha| \geq \tfrac{1}{2}, \tag{2.118}$$

which gives

$$30^\circ \leq \alpha \leq 150^\circ \quad \text{or} \quad 210^\circ \leq \alpha \leq 330^\circ, \tag{2.119}$$

and

$$|R\mathbf{a} + R^{-1}\mathbf{a}| = |2a \cos\alpha| \geq a \quad \text{or} \quad |\cos\alpha| \geq \tfrac{1}{2}, \tag{2.120}$$

which gives

$$\alpha \leq 60^\circ, \quad 120^\circ \leq \alpha \leq 240^\circ, \quad \alpha \geq 300^\circ. \tag{2.121}$$

We may also have $\alpha = 90$ or 270°. The allowed values of α are then

$$0^\circ, 60^\circ, 120^\circ, 240^\circ, 300^\circ, 90^\circ, 180^\circ, 270^\circ. \tag{2.122}$$

Therefore any rotation through $2\pi/5$ and its powers are excluded in a crystal. The rotations (2.122) can be indicated, respectively, by E, C_6, $C_6{}^2 = C_3$, $C_6{}^4 = C_3^2$, C_6^5, C_4, $C_4^2 = C_6^3 = C_2$, C_4^3.

The possible groups of proper rotations which can be constructed by using these operations are the following:

$$\begin{aligned}
&C_1\colon E,\\
&C_2\colon E, C_2,\\
&C_4\colon E, C_4, C_2 = C_4^2, C_4^3,\\
&C_3\colon C_3, C_3^2,\\
&C_6\colon E, C_6, C_3 = C_6^2, C_2 = C_6^3, C_3^2 = C_6^4, C_6^5.
\end{aligned} \tag{2.123}$$

The other five groups that contain proper and improper rotations in equal number can be formed by the product group of each of the above groups and

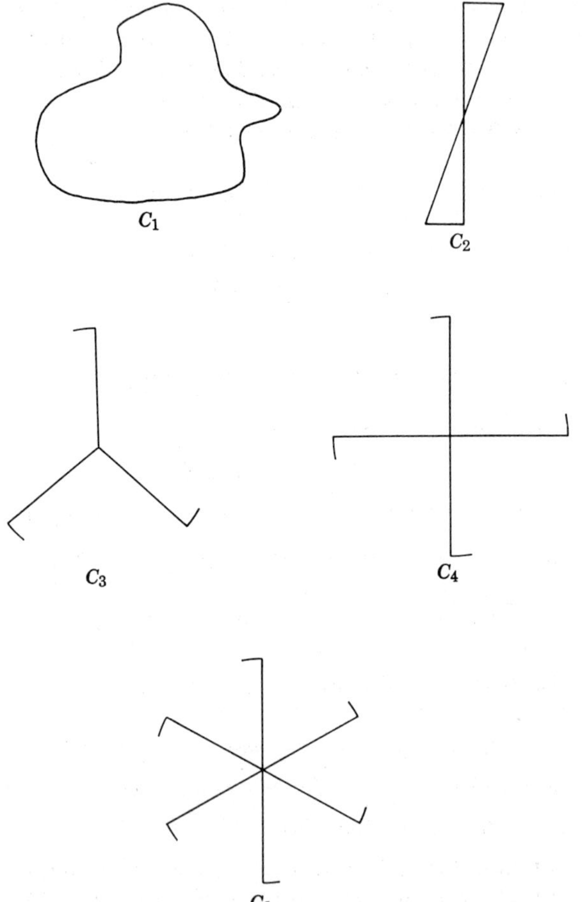

Fig. 2.3. Planar figures illustrating the point groups of proper rotations in two dimensions.

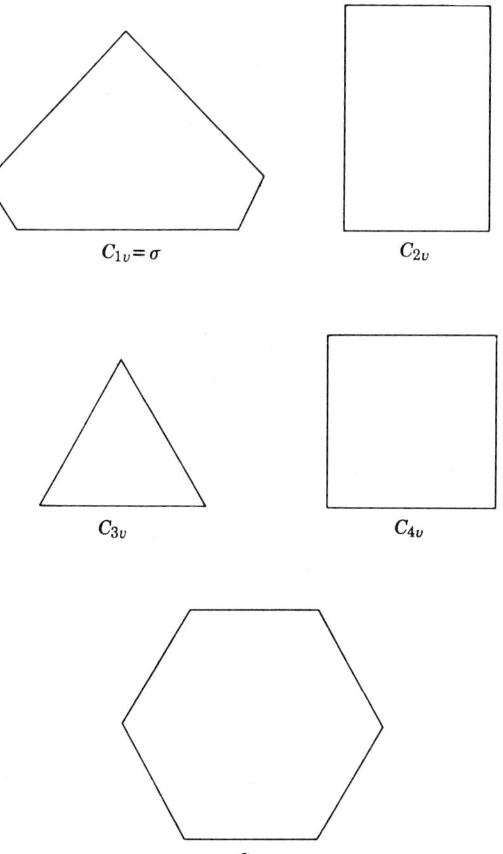

Fig. 2.4. Planar figures illustrating the point groups of proper and improper rotations in two dimensions.

of the group that consists of the operations E and σ. σ here consists of a reflection through some axis. These additional groups are

$$\begin{aligned}
&C_{1v}\colon\ E,\ \sigma, \\
&C_{2v}\colon\ E,\ C_2,\ \sigma,\ \sigma C_2, \\
&C_{4v}\colon\ E,\ C_4,\ C_2,\ C_4^3,\ \sigma,\ \sigma C_4,\ \sigma C_2,\ \sigma C_4^3, \\
&C_{3v}\colon\ E,\ C_3,\ C_3^2,\ \sigma,\ \sigma C_3,\ \sigma C_3^2, \\
&C_{6v}\colon\ E,\ C_6,\ C_3,\ C_2,\ C_3^2,\ C_6^5,\ \sigma,\ \sigma C_6,\ \sigma C_3,\ \sigma C_2,\ \sigma C_3^2,\ \sigma C_6^5.
\end{aligned} \tag{2.124}$$

All can be represented by the planar figures they leave invariant in Figs. 2.3 and 2.4. The 10 rotational groups that we have listed are called *point groups* in two dimensions.

We can summarize our findings up to this point as follows:

1. A space group in two dimensions has an invariant subgroup which consists of the primitive translations $\{E \mid \mathbf{T}_n\}$.
2. The generic operation of the space group is $\{\alpha \mid \mathbf{t}\}$. All the rotational operations α form one of the possible ten-point groups.

If a space group contains a certain point group, the compatibility between rotational and translation operations imposes also some restrictions on the latter.

Let us now examine the ten point groups and see what are the possible groups of primitive translations compatible with them.

C_1: This point group does not put any restriction on the translational group. A generic lattice compatible with it is represented in Fig. 2.5*a*.

C_2: The 180° rotation sends every primitive translation into its negative. This point group does not put any restriction on the translational group and the lattice of Fig. 2.5*a* is also compatible with it.

C_{1v}: We may choose the coordinate system in such a way that σ corresponds to a reflection through the axis x_1:

$$\sigma \equiv \begin{pmatrix} 1 & 0 \\ 0 & -1 \end{pmatrix}. \tag{2.125}$$

Let $\mathbf{a}_1$ be the shortest primitive translation with components a_{11} and a_{12}:

$$\mathbf{a}_1 = \begin{pmatrix} a_{11} \\ a_{12} \end{pmatrix}. \tag{2.126}$$

Let us consider first the case where both a_{11} and a_{12} are different from zero. $\sigma\mathbf{a}_1$ is also a primitive translation, which we call $\mathbf{a}_2$:

$$\sigma\mathbf{a}_1 = \begin{pmatrix} 1 & 0 \\ 0 & -1 \end{pmatrix} \begin{pmatrix} a_{11} \\ a_{12} \end{pmatrix} = \begin{pmatrix} a_{11} \\ -a_{12} \end{pmatrix} = \mathbf{a}_2. \tag{2.127}$$

$\mathbf{a}_2$ has the same length of $\mathbf{a}_1$. A lattice described by $n_1\mathbf{a}_1 + n_2\mathbf{a}_2$ is the lattice Γ_2 represented in Fig. 2.5*b*.

Let us consider next the case in which $a_{12} = 0$. In this case:

$$\mathbf{a}_1 = \begin{pmatrix} a_{11} \\ 0 \end{pmatrix}. \tag{2.128}$$

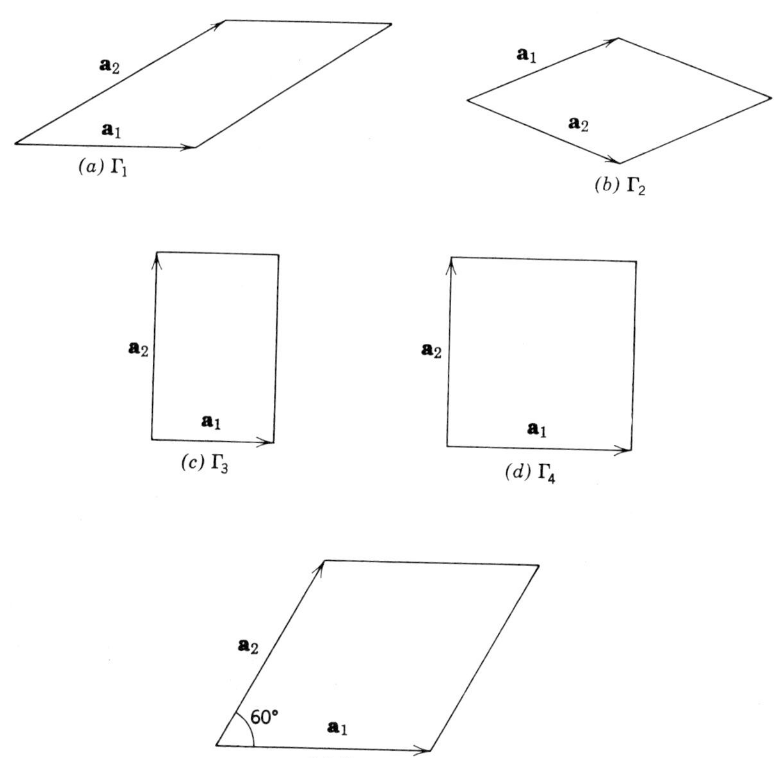

Fig. 2.5. The Bravais lattices in two dimensions:

(*a*) Lattice Γ_1 with

$$\mathbf{a}_1 = \begin{pmatrix} a_{11} \\ a_{12} \end{pmatrix}; \qquad \mathbf{a}_2 = \begin{pmatrix} a_{21} \\ a_{22} \end{pmatrix}.$$

(*b*) Lattice Γ_2 with

$$\mathbf{a}_1 = \begin{pmatrix} a_{11} \\ a_{12} \end{pmatrix}; \qquad \mathbf{a}_2 = \begin{pmatrix} a_{11} \\ -a_{12} \end{pmatrix}.$$

(*c*) Lattice Γ_3 with

$$\mathbf{a}_1 = \begin{pmatrix} a_{11} \\ 0 \end{pmatrix}; \qquad \mathbf{a}_2 = \begin{pmatrix} 0 \\ a_{22} \end{pmatrix}.$$

(*d*) Lattice Γ_4 with

$$\mathbf{a}_1 = \begin{pmatrix} a_{11} \\ 0 \end{pmatrix}; \qquad \mathbf{a}_2 = \begin{pmatrix} 0 \\ a_{11} \end{pmatrix}.$$

(*e*) Lattice Γ_5 with

$$\mathbf{a}_1 = \begin{pmatrix} a_{11} \\ 0 \end{pmatrix}; \qquad \mathbf{a}_2 = \begin{pmatrix} \frac{1}{2} a_{11} \\ \frac{\sqrt{3}}{2} a_{11} \end{pmatrix}.$$

If a_2 is the other basic primitive translation, $\mathbf{a}_2 + \sigma\mathbf{a}_2$ is also a primitive translation:

$$\mathbf{a}_2 + \sigma\mathbf{a}_2 = \begin{pmatrix} a_{21} \\ a_{22} \end{pmatrix} + \begin{pmatrix} 1 & 0 \\ 0 & -1 \end{pmatrix}\begin{pmatrix} a_{21} \\ a_{22} \end{pmatrix}$$

$$= \begin{pmatrix} 2a_{21} \\ 0 \end{pmatrix} = n_1\begin{pmatrix} a_{11} \\ 0 \end{pmatrix} + n_2\begin{pmatrix} a_{21} \\ a_{22} \end{pmatrix}. \qquad (2.129)$$

We must have $n_2 = 0$. If $n_1 = 0$, also $a_{21} = 0$ and

$$\mathbf{a}_1 = \begin{pmatrix} a_{11} \\ 0 \end{pmatrix}, \quad \mathbf{a}_2 = \begin{pmatrix} 0 \\ a_{22} \end{pmatrix}. \qquad (2.130)$$

In this case $\mathbf{a}_2$ and $\sigma\mathbf{a}_2$ could be considered the basic primitive translations; the lattice corresponding to them is the lattice Γ_3 of Fig. 2.5*c*. The reader can verify that for $n_1 = 1$ we again obtain the lattice Γ_2 and that for $n_1 \geq 2$ we obtain nothing new.

C_{2v}: The addition of the operation C_2 to the group C_{1v} does not add any new restriction on the lattices compatible with C_{1v}. Therefore also lattices Γ_2 and Γ_3 are left invariant by C_{2v}.

C_4: The lattice which this group leaves invariant is Γ_4 of Fig. 2.5*d*.

C_{4v}: Lattice Γ_4 left invariant.

C_3, C_{3v}, C_6, C_{6v}: Lattice Γ_5 of Fig. 2.5*e* left invariant.

The bidimensional point groups and the lattices they leave invariant are tabulated in Table 2.1. The five lattices Γ_1 to Γ_5 are called *Bravais lattices* in two dimensions.

Space Groups in Two Dimensions. Space groups may be classified according to the point groups formed by their rotational operations; the ensemble of the space groups which have the same point group form a *class*.

We have not listed all the classes, and we report only a few of the examples.

C_1: This point group contains only the operation identity and does not place any restrictions on the primitive translations. The lattice Γ_1 is left invariant by this group. The only space group belonging to this class may be represented by a pattern like the one in Fig. 2.6.

C_2: This point group contains the operations identity E and the 180° rotation C_2. The lattice Γ_1 is left invariant by this point group. The only space group belonging to this class may be represented by a pattern like the one in Fig. 2.7.

Table 2.1 The Distribution of the 17 Bidimensional Space Groups

System	Bravais Lattices	Point Group	Number of Space Groups	Total Number of Space Groups in the System
1	Γ_1	C_1 C_2	1 1	2
2	Γ_2, Γ_3	C_{1v} C_{2v}	3 4	7
3	Γ_4	C_4 C_{4v}	1 2	3
4	Γ_5	C_3 C_{3v} C_6 C_{6v}	1 2 1 1	5
Total	5	10	17	17

C_{1v}: This point group contains the operation E, C_2, σ, σC_2. Two Bravais lattices (Γ_2 and Γ_3) are left invariant by this group. We may form a space group associating this point group with the lattice Γ_2 (see Fig. 2.8*a*) and two space groups associating this point group with the lattice Γ_3 (see Figs. 2.8*b* and 2.8*c*). We notice here that the space group represented in Fig. 2.8*c* includes the operation $\{\sigma(\mathbf{a}_1/2) + n\mathbf{a}_1\}$. In this case the translational operations associated with σ are *not* primitive translations. We notice also that, in correspondence to this, the crystal presents a glide reflection direction along the direction of the $\mathbf{a}_1$ vector.

Fig. 2.6. Space groups formed by attaching to each point of a Γ_1 lattice a figure of C_1 symmetry.

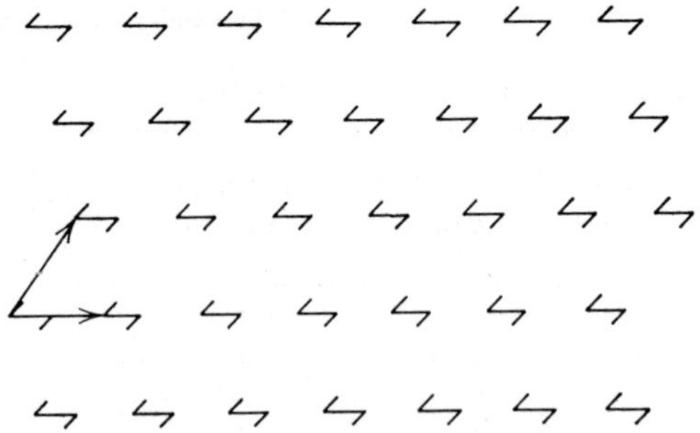

Fig. 2.7. Space group formed by attaching to each point of a Γ_1 lattice a figure of C_2 symmetry.

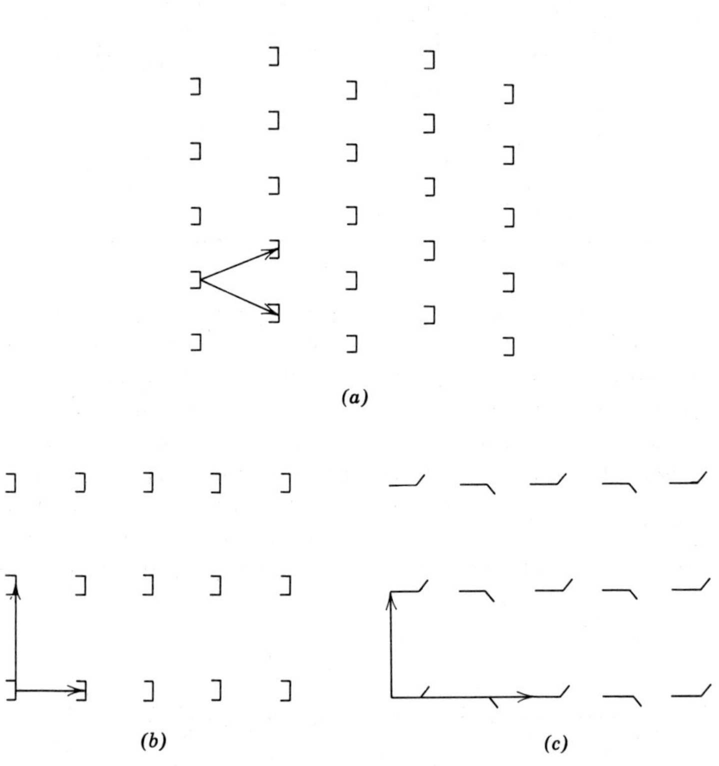

Fig. 2.8. (*a*) space group formed by attaching to each point of a Γ_2 lattice a figure of C_{1v} symmetry; (*b*) space group formed by attaching to each point of a Γ_3 lattice a figure of C_{1v} symmetry; (*c*) space group generated by $\{\sigma \mid \mathbf{v}\}$ with

$$\mathbf{v} = \begin{pmatrix} \frac{1}{2} a_{11} \\ 0 \end{pmatrix}$$

and $\{E \mid \mathbf{T}_n\}$.

Going through the list of all points groups, it turns out that only 17 space groups are possible in two dimensions. The distribution of these groups over the ten possible classes is illustrated in Table 2.1. The same table regroups the classes in *systems*, each system consisting of all the classes which can allow the same Bravais lattices.

11.4 Three-Dimensional Space Groups

The properties of the three-dimensional space groups can be summarized as follows:

1. The generic operation of a space group is $\{\alpha \mid \mathbf{t}\}$, where α indicates a real orthogonal transformation and $\mathbf{t}$ a translation (not necessarily primitive).
2. The primitive translation $\{E \mid \mathbf{T}_n\}$, where

$$\mathbf{T}_n = n_1\mathbf{a}_1 + n_2\mathbf{a}_2 + n_3\mathbf{a}_3 \tag{2.131}$$

and n_1, n_2, n_3 integer numbers, form an invariant subgroup of the space group. The three linearly independent translations $\mathbf{a}_1$, $\mathbf{a}_2$, and $\mathbf{a}_3$ are called *basic primitive translations*. The array of points generated by $\mathbf{T}_n$ is called *lattice*.
3. All the rotational operations α in $\{\alpha \mid \mathbf{t}\}$ form a group which is called the *point group of the crystal*. The fact that the rotational operations have to be compatible with the lattice generated by $\{E \mid \mathbf{T}_n\}$ imposes some restrictions on them. It turns out that the only possible proper rotations are rotations about certain axes through integral multiples of 60 and 90°; the only possible improper rotations are products of the above proper rotations with the inversion operation. The possible point groups in three dimensions are 32 and are listed in Table 2.2. (A correlation of two different types of notation is reported in Table 2.3.)

A space group may be classified according to the point group formed by its rotational operations; for this reason it is said that the space groups can be divided into 32 *classes*.

Table 2.2 Point Groups in Three Dimensions

	C_n	D_n	T	O	C_{nv}	C_{nh}	S_{2n}	D_{nd}	D_{nh}	T_h	T_d	O_h
	$C_1 = E$		T	O		C_{1h}	S_2			T_h	T_d	O_h
	C_2	D_2			C_{2v}	C_{2h}		D_{2d}	D_{2h}			
	C_3	D_3			C_{3v}	C_{3h}		D_{3d}	D_{3h}			
	C_4	D_4			C_{4v}	C_{4h}	S_4		D_{4h}			
	C_6	D_6			C_{6v}	C_{6h}	S_6		D_{6h}			
Total	5	4	1	1	4	5	3	2	4	1	1	1

Table 2.3 Notations for Point Groups[a]

Schoenflies Notation	International Notation	Schoenflies Notation	International Notation
C_1	1	D_2	222
C_2	2	D_3	32
C_3	3	D_4	422
C_4	4	D_5	52
C_5	5	D_6	622
C_6	6	D_{2d}	$\bar{4}2\,m$
C_{2v}	$2\,mm$	D_{3d}	$\bar{3}\,m$
C_{3v}	$3\,m$	D_{2h}	mmm
C_{4v}	$4\,mm$	D_{3h}	$\bar{6}\,m2$
C_{5v}	$5\,m$	D_{4h}	$4/mmm$
C_{6v}	$6\,mm$	D_{5h}	$\overline{10}\,m2$
C_{1h}	m	D_{6h}	$6/mmm$
C_{2h}	$2/m$	T	23
C_{3h}	$\bar{6}$	T_h	$m3$
C_{4h}	$4/m$	O	432
C_{5h}	$\overline{10}$	O_h	$m3m$
C_{6h}	$6/m$	T_d	$\bar{4}3\,m$
S_2	$\bar{1}$	$C_{\infty v}$	∞m
S_4	$\bar{4}$	$D_{\infty h}$	∞/mm
S_6	$\bar{3}$		

[a] This table includes, in addition to the 32 crystal point groups, the five point groups with five-fold rotations and the two point groups $C_{\infty v}$ and $D_{\infty h}$. These seven point groups cannot occur in crystals but may be found in molecules.

4. If $\mathbf{T}_n$ is a primitive translation and $\{\alpha \mid \mathbf{t}\}$ is an operation of the space group, $\alpha\mathbf{T}_n$ is also a primitive translation. Therefore the lattice produced by the primitive translations must be invariant under all the rotation operations of the class (point group). This fact imposes restrictions on the lengths and orientations of the three basic primitive translations $\mathbf{a}_1$, $\mathbf{a}_2$, and $\mathbf{a}_3$. On the basis of these restrictions it is possible to derive 14 *Bravais lattices*. These lattices are reported in Figs. 2.9 to 2.14. A Bravais lattice is an array of points that establishes the skeleton for the space group and represents the possible translations of the space group.

5. The class to which a space group belongs determine the possible Bravais lattices that can be associated with the space group.

6. Several classes may allow the same Bravais lattices. For example, the classes C_2, C_{1h}, and C_{2h} are compatible with the Bravais lattices: simple monoclinic and two face centered monoclinic. They are then said to belong to the same monoclinic *crystal system*.

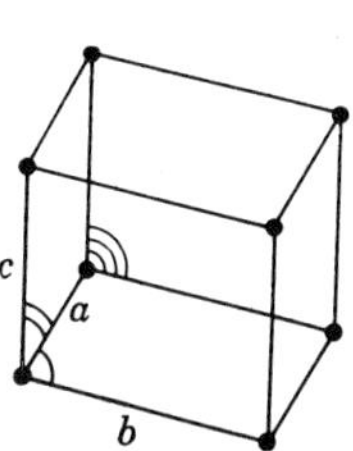

Fig. 2.9. Triclinic bravais lattice (Vector lengths are indicated by letters *a*, *b*, and *c*. Angles different from 90° are indicated by △, △, and △.)

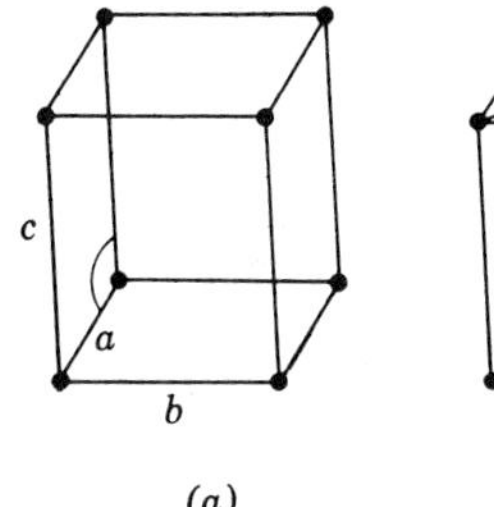

Fig. 2.10. Bravais lattices of the monoclinic system: (*a*) simple monoclinic; (*b*) two face-centered monoclinic.

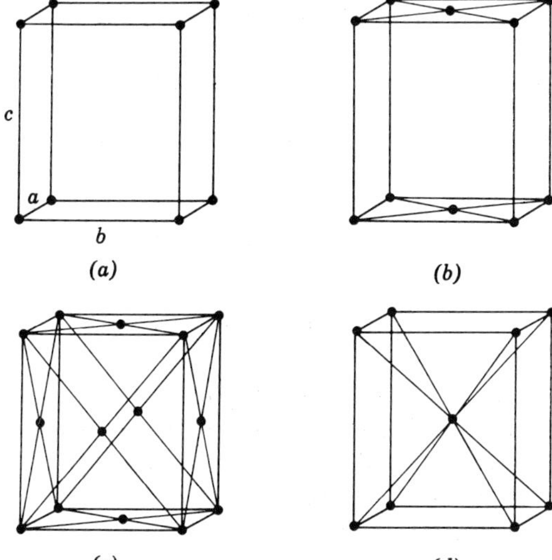

Fig. 2.11. Bravais lattices of the orthorhombic system: (*a*) simple orthorhombic; (*b*) two face-centered orthorhombic; (*c*) all face-centered orthorhombic; (*d*) body-centered orthorhombic.

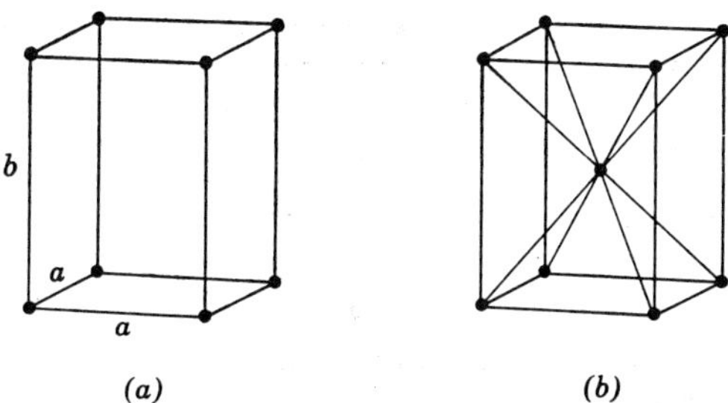

Fig. 2.12. Bravais lattices of the tetragonal system: (*a*) simple tetragonal; (*b*) body-centered tetragonal.

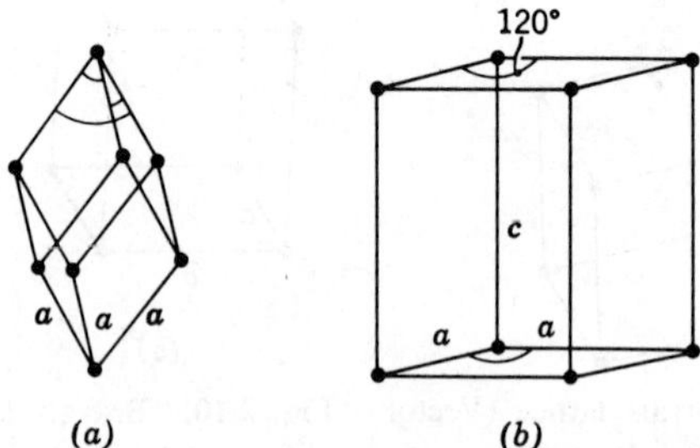

Fig. 2.13. Bravais lattices of the trigonal system: (*a*) trigonal; (*b*) hexagonal.

In Table 2.4 we report the distribution of the 230 space group in the 32 classes. Also the classes are grouped according to the crystal system to which they belong.

7. The most general operator of a space group can be written

$$\{\alpha \mid \mathbf{v}(\alpha) + \mathbf{T}_n\} = \{E \mid \mathbf{T}_n\}\{\alpha \mid \mathbf{v}(\alpha)\}. \tag{2.132}$$

If $\mathbf{v}(\alpha)$ can be taken equal to zero for *all* α's, the space group is called *simple* or *symmorphic*. In such a case for each α there is an operator $\{\alpha \mid 0\}$ of the space group, and since

$$\{\alpha \mid 0\}\{\beta \mid 0\} = \{\alpha\beta \mid 0\} \tag{2.133}$$

the operators $\{\alpha \mid 0\}$ form a group isomorphic[2] with the point group. Therefore the entire point group is contained as a subgroup in a symmorphic space group. For this reason the local symmetry at each lattice point is completely described by the entire point group.

There are 73 symmorphic space groups.

8. If, for at least one α, $\mathbf{v}(\alpha) \neq 0$, the space group is *nonsymmorphic* and does not contain the entire point group as a subgroup. Space group operations $\{\alpha \mid \mathbf{T}_n + \mathbf{v}(\alpha)\}$ correspond to nonprimitive translations associated with

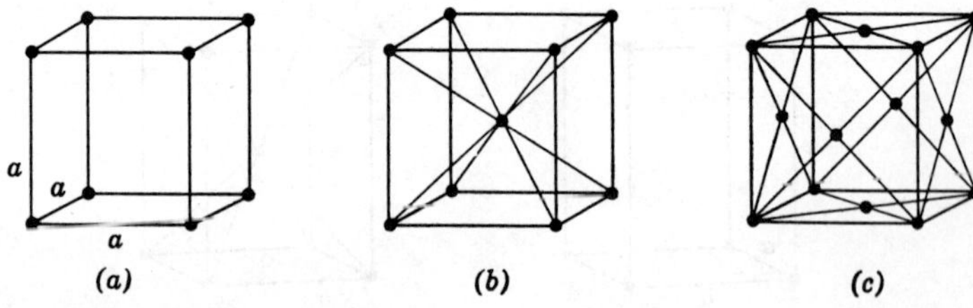

Fig. 2.14. Bravais lattices of the cubic system: (*a*) simple cubic; (*b*) body-centered cubic; (*c*) face-centered cubic.

[2] Two groups are said to be *isomorphic* if their elements are in a one-to-one correspondence.

Table 2.4 The Distribution of the 230 Space Groups

System	Bravais Lattices	Point Group	Number of Space Groups	Total Number of Space Groups in the System
Triclinic	Triclinic	C_1 S_2	1 1	2
Monoclinic	Simple monoclinic Two face-centered monoclinic	C_2 C_{1h} C_{2h}	3 4 6	13
Orthorombic	Simple orthorhombic Two face-centered orthorhombic All face-centered orthorhombic Body-centered orthorhombic	C_{2v} D_2 D_{2h}	22 9 28	59
Tetragonal	Simple tetragonal Body-centered tetragonal	C_4 S_4 C_{4h} C_{4v} D_{2d} D_4 D_{4h}	6 2 6 12 12 10 20	68
Trigonal	Trigonal Hexagonal	C_3 S_6 C_{3v} D_{3d} D_3	4 2 6 6 7	25
Hexagonal	Hexagonal	C_6 C_{3h} C_{6h} C_{6v} D_{3h} D_6 D_{6h}	6 1 2 4 4 6 4	27
Cubic	Simple cubic Face-centered cubic Body-centered cubic	T T_h T_d O O_h	5 7 6 8 10	36
Total	14	32	230	230

proper or improper rotations. The latter correspond in this case to glide planes, the former to screw axes in the crystal.

In a nonsymmorphic space group the local symmetry at a lattice point is described by a point group lower in symmetry than the entire point group.

There are 157 nonsymmorphic space groups.

9. Given a certain space group G, with an invariant subgroup of primitive translations $\mathcal{T}$, the factor group $G/\mathcal{T}$ is isomorphic with the point group of the α rotations.

12. THE IRREDUCIBLE REPRESENTATIONS OF A GROUP OF PRIMITIVE TRANSLATIONS

A group of primitive translations is Abelian, because its operations commute. Therefore the representations of such a group are unidimensional. Let us consider first the translational operations along one basic primitive direction. Since

$$\{E \mid n\mathbf{a}_1\}\{E \mid m\mathbf{a}_1\} = \{E \mid (n + m)\,\mathbf{a}_1\}, \tag{2.134}$$

the representation of the generic operation must be of the type $e^{i\mathbf{k}\cdot n\mathbf{a}}$. The vector **k** may be considered the entity which characterizes the different representations.

In order to make the translational group finite, we may impose the boundary condition:

$$\{E \mid \mathbf{a}_1\}^N = \{E \mid N\mathbf{a}_1\} = \{E \mid 0\}. \tag{2.135}$$

In this case the representation of the operation $\{E \mid \mathbf{a}_1\}$ is given by

$$\exp\left[i\left(\frac{2\pi}{a_1}\frac{s_1}{N}\right)a_1\right], \quad \text{where} \quad s_1 = 0, 1, 2, \ldots, N - 1. \tag{2.136}$$

The generic operation $\{E \mid n\mathbf{a}_1\}$ is represented by

$$\exp\left[i\left(\frac{2\pi}{a_1}\frac{s_1}{N}\right)na_1\right] = \exp\left(i2\pi\frac{s_1}{N}n\right). \tag{2.137}$$

At this point we may define a *reciprocal lattice* with the basic primitive vector

$$\mathbf{b}_1 = \frac{2\pi}{a_1}\mathbf{u}_1, \tag{2.138}$$

where $\mathbf{u}_1$ is the unit vector in the direction of $\mathbf{a}_1$. We can then express the representation (2.137) as follows:

$$\exp\left[i\left(\frac{2\pi}{a_1}\frac{s_1}{N}\right)na_1\right] = e^{ik_1\mathbf{b}_1\cdot n\mathbf{a}_1} = e^{i\mathbf{k}\cdot n\mathbf{a}_1}, \tag{2.139}$$

where

$$\mathbf{k} = k_{1\mathbf{b}1} = \frac{s_1}{N}\frac{2\pi}{a_1}\mathbf{u}_1, \qquad (s_1 = 0, 1, 2, \ldots, N - 1); \tag{2.140}$$

k is defined by the inequalities

$$0 \leq |\mathbf{k}| < \frac{2\pi}{a_1}. \tag{2.141}$$

We notice that for any vector of the reciprocal lattice $\mathbf{K}_q = q_1\mathbf{b}_1$ (q_1 integer number)

$$e^{i\mathbf{K}_q\cdot n\mathbf{a}_1} = e^{iq_1\mathbf{b}_1\cdot n\mathbf{a}_1} = e^{iq_1n2\pi} = 1. \tag{2.142}$$

For this reason we obtain exactly the same representation for $|\mathbf{k}| = 2\pi/a_1$ and for to $|\mathbf{k}| = 0$. Also, the N different values of the $\mathbf{k}$ vector in (2.141) exhaust all the possible distinct representations.

The representations for a unidimensional translational group are reported in Table 2.5.

Now considering the generic translation in three dimensions,

$$\mathbf{T}_n = n_1\mathbf{a}_1 + n_2\mathbf{a}_2 + n_3\mathbf{a}_3, \tag{2.143}$$

we may impose the following periodic boundary conditions:

$$\{E \mid \mathbf{a}_1\}^N = \{E \mid \mathbf{a}_2\}^N = \{E \mid \mathbf{a}_3\}^N = \{E \mid 0\}. \tag{2.144}$$

The group of three-dimensional translations $\{E \mid \mathbf{T}_n\}$ is the direct product of the three translational groups in the directions $\mathbf{a}_1$, $\mathbf{a}_2$, and $\mathbf{a}_3$. The representation of the operation $\{E \mid \mathbf{T}_n\}$ is now given by

$$\exp i\left[\left(\frac{2\pi}{a_1}\frac{s_1}{N}\right)na_1 + \left(\frac{2\pi}{a_2}\frac{s_2}{N}\right)na_2 + \left(\frac{2\pi}{a_3}\frac{s_3}{N}\right)na_3\right] = \exp(i\mathbf{k}\cdot\mathbf{T}_n). \tag{2.145}$$

We may define at this point a *reciprocal lattice* by means of three basic primitive vectors $\mathbf{b}_1$, $\mathbf{b}_2$, and $\mathbf{b}_3$ defined by

$$\mathbf{a}_i \cdot \mathbf{b}_j = 2\pi\delta_{ij}. \tag{2.146}$$

The vector $\mathbf{k}$ may be expressed in the reciprocal space as follows:

$$\mathbf{k} = k_1\mathbf{b}_1 + k_2\mathbf{b}_2 + k_3\mathbf{b}_3.$$

We derive then:

$$\mathbf{k}\cdot\mathbf{a}_1 = (k_1\mathbf{b}_1 + k_2\mathbf{b}_2 + k_3\mathbf{b}_3)\cdot\mathbf{a}_1 = 2\pi k_1. \tag{2.147}$$

Table 2.5 Irreducible Representations of a Group of Unidimensional Translations

s_1	k	$\{E \mid 0\}$	$\{E \mid a\}$	$\{E \mid 2a\}$	$\{E \mid 3a\}$	$\cdots$	$\{E \mid na\}$	$\cdots$
0	0	1	1	1	1	$\cdots$	1	$\cdots$
1	$\frac{2\pi}{aN}$	1	$e^{i(2\pi/N)}$	$e^{i(4\pi/N)}$	$e^{i(6\pi/N)}$	$\cdots$	$e^{i(2\pi n/N)}$	$\cdots$
2	$\frac{4\pi}{aN}$	1	$e^{i(4\pi/N)}$	$e^{i(8\pi/N)}$	$e^{i(12\pi/N)}$	$\cdots$	$e^{i(4\pi n/N)}$	$\cdots$
3	$\frac{6\pi}{aN}$	1	$e^{i(6\pi/N)}$	$e^{i(12\pi/N)}$	$e^{i(18\pi/N)}$	$\cdots$	$e^{i(6\pi n/N)}$	$\cdots$
s_1	$\frac{2\pi s_1}{Na}$	1	$e^{i(2\pi s_1/N)}$	$e^{i(4\pi s_1/N)}$	$e^{i(6\pi s_1/N)}$	$\cdots$	$e^{i(2\pi s_1/N)n}$	$\cdots$

On the other hand, from (2.140)

$$\mathbf{k} \cdot \mathbf{a}_1 = \frac{s_1}{N} 2\pi. \tag{2.148}$$

Therefore

$$k_i = \frac{s_i}{N}, \qquad (s_i = 0, 1, 2, \ldots, N-1, \qquad i = 1, 2, 3) \tag{2.149}$$

The representation of the generic operation $\{E \mid \mathbf{T}_n\}$ is then given by $e^{i\mathbf{k}\cdot\mathbf{T}_n}$ where $\mathbf{k}$ is given by (2.147) with k_i restricted to the values (2.149).

If $\mathbf{K}_q$ is a primitive translation in the reciprocal space, because of (2.146)

$$e^{i\mathbf{K}_q\cdot\mathbf{T}_n} = 1. \tag{2.150}$$

This means that the distinct representations correspond only to the N^3 values of $\mathbf{k}$ as given by (2.149) and that two $\mathbf{k}$ vectors which differ by a primitive vector of the reciprocal space produce the same irreducible representation.

The values of k_i in (2.149): $0 \leq k_1 < 1, 0 \leq k_2 < 1, 0 \leq k_3 < 1$ define a fundamental parallelepiped; each vector $\mathbf{k}$ within this solid in the reciprocal space produces a distinct representation.

Other fundamental solids could be defined in the reciprocal space. In particular we shall define the so-called *Brillouin zone* in the following way. Starting from a point in the reciprocal lattice we draw lines connecting this point with all the other points of the reciprocal lattice; then we intersect each line with a plane perpendicular to it at midpoint between the starting point and the lattice point reached by the line. The volume enclosed by all these planes is the Brillouin zone.

Example

Let us consider the Bravais lattice in two dimensions Γ_5, represented in Fig. 2.15*a*. The basic primitive translations for this lattice are

$$\mathbf{a}_1 = \begin{pmatrix} a \\ 0 \end{pmatrix}; \qquad \mathbf{a}_2 = \begin{pmatrix} \frac{1}{2}a \\ \frac{\sqrt{3}}{2}a \end{pmatrix}.$$

The basic primitive vectors of the reciprocal lattice are given by

$$\mathbf{b}_1 = \frac{4\pi}{\sqrt{3}\,a}\begin{pmatrix} \frac{\sqrt{3}}{2} \\ -\frac{1}{2} \end{pmatrix}; \qquad \mathbf{b}_2 = \frac{4\pi}{\sqrt{3}\,a}\begin{pmatrix} 0 \\ 1 \end{pmatrix}.$$

We can check that

$$\mathbf{b}_i \cdot \mathbf{a}_j = 2\pi\delta_{ij}.$$

Using the $\mathbf{b}_i$ vectors it is possible to construct the reciprocal lattice and the Brillouin zone which is represented by the hexagon in Fig. 2.15*b*. Every point in the interior of the hexagon represents a distinct representation of the group of primitive translations $\{E \mid \mathbf{T}_n\}$.

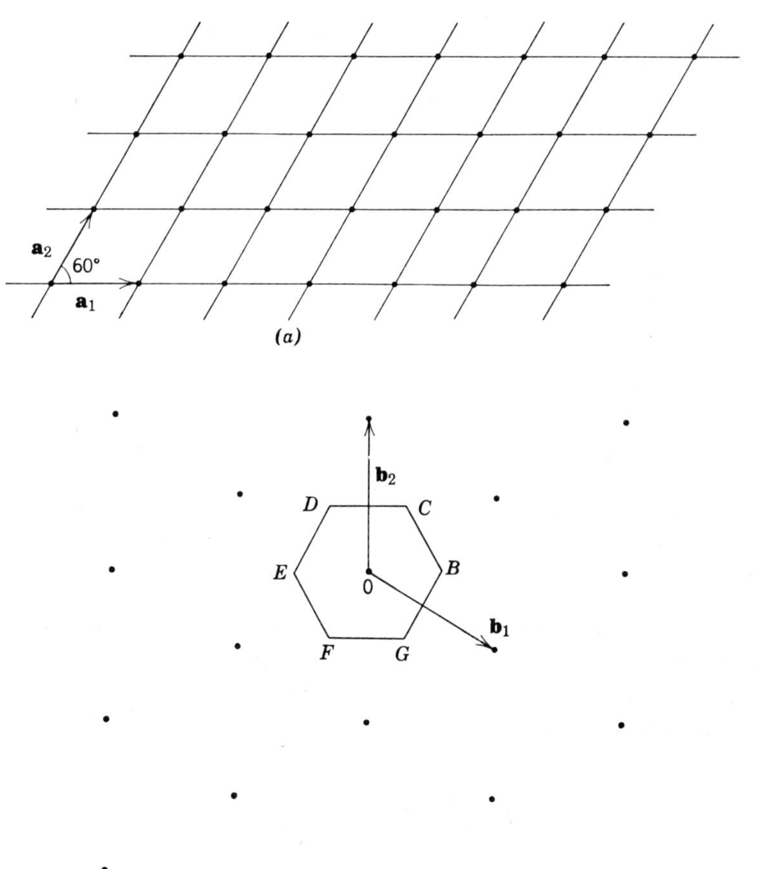

Fig. 2.15. (*a*) Two-dimensional Bravais lattice Γ_5; (*b*) reciprocal lattice and Brillouin zone for the Bravais lattice Γ_5.

The points on the edge of the hexagon from B to C to D to E, but excluding E, correspond also to distinct representations. The points from E to F are to be excluded because they differ from the points on the opposite edge by the vector of the reciprocal lattice $\mathbf{b}_1 + \mathbf{b}_2$; for a similar reason the points on the FG and GB edges are to be excluded.

13. THE IRREDUCIBLE REPRESENTATIONS OF SPACE GROUPS

Let us consider a space group G and let us call $\mathcal{T}$ its invariant subgroup of primitive translations. Let us also call $\{\alpha \mid \mathbf{t}\}$ the generic operation of the space group and G_0 the (point) group of the rotations α.

Let us consider also a unitary irreducible representation of G of dimension n and let us call $\mathbf{D}\{\alpha \mid \mathbf{t}\}$ the matrix of the element $\{\alpha \mid \mathbf{t}\}$ in this representation.

The matrices corresponding to the primitive translations form a (reducible) representation of the group $\mathcal{T}$; we can further assume that in the representation considered these matrices have been put in a diagonal form

$$\mathbf{D}\{E \mid \mathbf{T}_n\} = \begin{pmatrix} e^{i\mathbf{k}_1\cdot\mathbf{T}_n} & & & & & & & 0 \\ & e^{i\mathbf{k}_1\cdot\mathbf{T}_n} & & & & & & \\ & & \cdot & & & & & \\ & & & \cdot & & & & \\ & & & & e^{i\mathbf{k}_i\cdot\mathbf{T}_n} & & & \\ & & & & & e^{i\mathbf{k}_i\cdot\mathbf{T}_n} & & \\ 0 & & & & & & \cdot & \\ & & & & & & & \cdot \\ & & & & & & & \cdot \\ & & & & & & & e^{i\mathbf{k}_q\cdot\mathbf{T}_n} \end{pmatrix}. \quad (2.151)$$

The following treatment follows closely the work by G. K. Koster [2, 3]. Several facts will be stated without proof; for the mathematical details the reader is referred to Koster's work. The following facts are relevant:

1. The elements in the matrix $\mathbf{D}\{E \mid \mathbf{T}_n\}$ are such that every element $e^{i\mathbf{k}_i\cdot\mathbf{T}_n}$ is repeated the same number of times along the diagonal. Let us assume that each element in (2.151) is repeated $d = n/q$ times.
2. The elements of the matrix $\mathbf{D}\{E \mid \mathbf{T}_n\}$ can be arranged in the following way:

$$\mathbf{D}\{E \mid \mathbf{T}_n\} = \begin{pmatrix} \boxed{e^{i\mathbf{k}_1\cdot\mathbf{T}_n}\mathbf{1}} & & & & & 0 \\ & \boxed{e^{i\alpha_2\mathbf{k}_1\cdot\mathbf{T}_n}\mathbf{1}} & & & & \\ & & \boxed{e^{i\alpha_3\mathbf{k}_1\cdot\mathbf{T}_n}\mathbf{1}} & & & \\ & & & \cdot & & \\ & & & & \cdot & \\ & 0 & & & & \cdot \end{pmatrix}. \quad (2.152)$$

Here the matrix has been divided in diagonal blocks of dimensions $d \times d$, with $d = n/q$, and $\mathbf{1}$ is the $d \times d$ unit matrix. $\alpha_1 = E, \alpha_2, \alpha_3, \ldots, \alpha_q$ are elements of the point group G_0 such that

$$\alpha_i\mathbf{k}_1 = \mathbf{k}_i \qquad (i = 1, 2, \ldots, q), \quad (2.153)$$

where $\mathbf{k}_i$ ranges over the different q irreducible representation of $\mathcal{T}$ present in $\mathbf{D}\{E \mid \mathbf{T}_n\}$. The nonequivalent $\mathbf{k}$ vectors produced by the different q rotations α_i are said to form a *star* $\{\mathbf{k}\}$. A star is said to be nondegenerate if the number of $\mathbf{k}$ vectors in $\{\mathbf{k}\}$ is equal to the number of operations in G_0.

3. The matrix for the generic operation $\{\alpha \mid \mathbf{t}\}$ can also be subdivided in blocks of dimensions $d \times d$:

$$\mathbf{D}\{\alpha \mid \mathbf{t}\} = \begin{pmatrix} \mathbf{D}_{11}\{\alpha \mid \mathbf{t}\} & \mathbf{D}_{12}\{\alpha \mid \mathbf{t}\} & \cdots & \mathbf{D}_{1q}\{\alpha \mid \mathbf{t}\} \\ \mathbf{D}_{21}\{\alpha \mid \mathbf{t}\} & \mathbf{D}_{22}\{\alpha \mid \mathbf{t}\} & \cdots & \mathbf{D}_{2q}\{\alpha \mid \mathbf{t}\} \\ \cdots & \cdots & \cdots & \cdots \\ \mathbf{D}_{q1}\{\alpha \mid \mathbf{t}\} & \mathbf{D}_{q2}\{\alpha \mid \mathbf{t}\} & \cdots & \mathbf{D}_{qq}\{\alpha \mid \mathbf{t}\} \end{pmatrix}. \tag{2.154}$$

The ijth block of the $\mathbf{D}\{E \mid \mathbf{T}_n\}$ matrix is given by

$$\mathbf{D}_{ij}\{E \mid \mathbf{T}_n\} = e^{i\alpha \mathbf{k}_i \cdot \mathbf{T}_n} \mathbf{1} \delta_{ij}. \tag{2.155}$$

4. Let us consider the elements $\{\beta \mid \mathbf{b}\}$ of G which have the following property:

$$e^{i\beta \mathbf{k}_1 \cdot \mathbf{T}_n} = e^{\mathbf{k}_1 \cdot \mathbf{T}_n} \tag{2.156}$$

for all $\mathbf{T}_n$. Equation (2.156) implies that

$$\beta \mathbf{k}_1 = \mathbf{k}_1 + \mathbf{K}_j, \tag{2.157}$$

where $\mathbf{K}_j$ is a primitive vector of the reciprocal lattice. The ensemble of all the $\{\beta \mid \mathbf{b}\}$ elements form a group, which is a subgroup of G; this group will be called the group of $\mathbf{k}$ vector and we shall indicate it by the symbol $\mathcal{K}$.

The group $\mathcal{K}$ contains all the $\{E \mid \mathbf{T}_n\}$ elements of G. The rotational operations appearing in the elements $\{\beta \mid \mathbf{b}\}$ of $\mathcal{K}$ form also a point group which we shall call $G_0(\mathbf{k})$.

Those elements β of G_0 which leave $\mathbf{k}_1$ invariant except for a primitive vector of the reciprocal lattice, as in (2.157), form a degenerate star $\{\mathbf{k}\}$.

The matrix $\mathbf{D}\{\beta \mid \mathbf{b}\}$, when blocked off in the form of (2.154), contains only one block different from zero: $\mathbf{D}_{11}\{\beta \mid \mathbf{b}\}$, namely,

$$\mathbf{D}\{\beta \mid \mathbf{b}\} = \left(\begin{array}{c|c} \mathbf{D}_{11}\{\beta \mid \mathbf{b}\} & 0 \\ \hline 0 & 0 \end{array}\right). \tag{2.158}$$

It turns out that the $d \times d$ matrices $\mathbf{D}_{11}\{\beta \mid \mathbf{b}\}$ form an irreducible representation of the group $\mathcal{K}$. The irreducible representations of the group $\mathcal{K}$ are also called the *small representations* of G.

5. The space group G can be decomposed into its left cosets with respect to its subgroup $\mathcal{K}$

$$G = \mathcal{K} + \{\alpha_2 \mid \mathbf{t}_2\}\mathcal{K} + \{\alpha_3 \mid \mathbf{t}_3\}\mathcal{K} + \cdots + \{\alpha_q \mid \mathbf{t}_q\}\mathcal{K}, \tag{2.159}$$

where the $\alpha_2, \alpha_3, \ldots, \alpha_q$ operations have the property (2.153).

6. For any element $\{\alpha \mid \mathbf{t}\}$ of G, and for any α_l we can find an α_m such that

$$e^{i\alpha\alpha_l \mathbf{k} \cdot \mathbf{T}_n} = e^{i\alpha_m \mathbf{k} \cdot \mathbf{T}_n}. \tag{2.160}$$

This implies that

$$\alpha\alpha_l\mathbf{k} = \alpha_m\mathbf{k} + \mathbf{K}_q, \tag{2.161}$$

where $\mathbf{K}_q$ is a primitive vector of the reciprocal lattice, or

$$\alpha_m^{-1}\alpha\alpha_l\mathbf{k} = \mathbf{k} + \alpha_m^{-1}\mathbf{K}_q. \tag{2.162}$$

Namely, $\alpha_m^{-1}\alpha\alpha_l$ must be the rotational part of some element $\{\beta \mid \mathbf{b}\}$ in $\mathcal{K}$:

$$\{\alpha \mid \mathbf{t}\}\{\alpha_l \mid \mathbf{t}_l\} = \{\alpha_m \mid \mathbf{t}_m\}\{\beta \mid \mathbf{b}\}. \tag{2.163}$$

7. The mlth block of the matrix $\mathbf{D}\{\alpha \mid \mathbf{t}\}$ is given by

$$\mathbf{D}_{ml}\{\alpha \mid \mathbf{t}\} = \mathbf{D}_{11}\{\beta \mid \mathbf{b}\}, \tag{2.164}$$

where $\{\beta \mid \mathbf{b}\}$ is the element of $\mathcal{K}$ which respects the relation (2.163).

8. The relevant blocks $\mathbf{D}_{11}\{\beta \mid \mathbf{b}\}$ are given, for any point within the Brillouin zone, by

$$\mathbf{D}_{11}\{\beta \mid \mathbf{b}\} = e^{i\mathbf{k}\cdot\mathbf{b}}\mathbf{\Gamma}_j(\beta), \tag{2.165}$$

where $\{\beta \mid \mathbf{b}\}$ is an element of the $\mathcal{K}$ group and where $\Gamma_j(\beta)$ is an irreducible representation of the group $G_0(\mathbf{k})$. ($G_0(\mathbf{k})$ is one of the 32 possible point groups.) The dimension d of $\mathbf{D}_{11}$ is equal to the dimension of $\Gamma_j(\beta)$. The character of $\mathbf{D}_{11}$ is given by

$$\chi_{\mathbf{k},j}\{\beta \mid \mathbf{b}\} = e^{i\mathbf{k}\cdot\mathbf{b}}\chi_j(\beta). \tag{2.166}$$

The relation (2.165) is also valid for points at the surface of the Brillouin zone for symmorphic space groups. For nonsymmorphic space groups other simplifications can be made; they will not be reported here and the reader is again referred to Koster's work [2, 3].

9. The irreducible representations of the full space group G are specified by the knowledge of: (a) the $\mathbf{k}$ vector which determines the star $\{\mathbf{k}\}$; (b) the label of the representation of the point group $G_0(\mathbf{k})$. The character of an irreducible representation of the full space group G, corresponding to a star $\{\mathbf{k}\}$ is given by

$$\chi_{\{\mathbf{k}\},j}\{\gamma \mid \mathbf{b}\} = \sum_{m=1}^{q} e^{i\mathbf{k}_m\cdot\mathbf{b}}\chi_j(\beta)\delta_{\gamma\mathbf{k}_m,\mathbf{k}_m}. \tag{2.167}$$

Therefore, if the operation $\{\gamma \mid \mathbf{b}\}$ does not belong to the group of the $\mathbf{k}_m$ vector, the corresponding character is zero.

10. The dimension n of a space group representation is equal to the dimension d of the small representation times the number q of arms in the star of the $\mathbf{k}$ vector

$$n = dq. \tag{2.168}$$

11. As we scan through the Brillouin zone, we get all the irreducible representations of the space group G. However, in order to get *distinct* representations, we may limit ourselves to the $\mathbf{k}$ vectors of that part of the Brillouin zone in which no two vectors $\mathbf{k}$ and $\mathbf{k}'$ can be found such that

$$\mathbf{k}' = \alpha\mathbf{k} + \mathbf{K}_j, \tag{2.169}$$

$\mathbf{K}_j$ being a primitive vector of the reciprocal lattice and α any element of the point group.

12. At the point $\mathbf{k} = 0$ the star $\{\mathbf{k}\}$ has the highest possible degeneracy: $q = 1$. The space group G coincides with the group of the $\mathbf{k}$ vector $\mathcal{K}$; also $G_0 \equiv G_0(\mathbf{k})$. The dimensions of the irreducible representations of G are $n = d$, namely they are equal to the dimensions of the representations of $G_0 \equiv G_0(\mathbf{k})$. The characters are given in this case by

$$\begin{aligned} \chi_{\{0\},j}\{E \mid \mathbf{T}_n\} &= d \\ \chi_{\{0\},j}\{\gamma \mid \mathbf{b}\} &= \chi_j(\gamma). \end{aligned} \tag{2.170}$$

13. At a generic point $\mathbf{k}$ within the Brillouin zone each operation of G_0 changes $\mathbf{k}$ to a nonequivalent vector. The star $\{\mathbf{k}\}$ is nondegenerate: the number of $\mathbf{k}$ vectors in $\{\mathbf{k}\}$ is equal to the number of elements in G_0. Also, the point group $G_0(\mathbf{k})$ contains only the element E (identity). Therefore, since $d = 1$ and $q = g_0 =$ order of the point group G_0,

$$n = dq = g_0. \tag{2.171}$$

Example I

Let us consider the two unidimensional space groups, which are represented in Fig. 2.2. The reciprocal lattice is given in Fig. 2.16. The Brillouin zone extends from $k = -\pi/a$ to $k = \pi/a$. Let us consider the two space groups separately.

1. Let us consider first the space group represented in Fig. 2.2*a* and consisting only of the elements $\{E \mid na\}$. In this case the group $\mathcal{C}$ coincides with G. The irreducible representations are all unidimensional and are given by e^{ikna}, where k ranges over the interval $-\pi/a \leq k < \pi/a$.

2. Let us consider next the space group in Fig. 2.2*b*. This group consists of all the $\{E \mid na\}$ and $\{I \mid na\}$ operations.

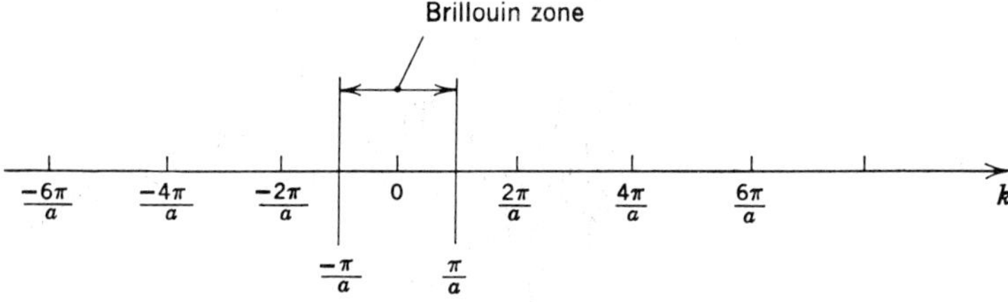

Fig. 2.16. Reciprocal lattice and Brillouin zone for a unidimensional lattice.

We notice that we need consider only the points of the Brillouin zone from 0 to π/a, since the k vectors in the $(0, -\pi/a)$ interval can be obtained by operating on the vectors of the $(0, \pi/a)$ interval with the point group operation I. Let us examine several points over regions in the Brillouin zone.

$k = 0$. At this point the group $\mathcal{K}$ coincides with the entire space group G:

$$G = \{E \mid 0\}\mathcal{K},$$

because

$$e^{ikna} = 1.$$

for all n. The point group $G_0(\mathbf{k})$ coincides with G_0 and consists of the elements: E (identity) and I (inversion). The representations of $G_0(\mathbf{k})$ are given by

G_0	E	I
Γ_1	1	1
Γ_2	1	-1

and

$$\mathbf{D}_{11}\{\beta \mid b\} = \mathbf{\Gamma}_i(\beta).$$

The matrix $\mathbf{D}\{E \mid na\}$ is simply given, because of (2.152) and because the only $\{\alpha_i \mid t_i\}$ operation appearing in the expansion of G in left cosets is $\{E \mid 0\}$, by

$$\mathbf{D}\{E \mid na\} = 1.$$

The matrix $\mathbf{D}\{I \mid na\}$ is given by

$$\mathbf{D}\{I \mid na\} = \mathbf{D}_{11}\{\beta \mid b\},$$

where $\{\beta \mid b\}$ is given, because of (2.163), by

$$\{I \mid na\}\{E \mid 0\} = \{E \mid 0\}\{\beta \mid b\}.$$

We must have $\beta = I$, $b = na$, and

$$\mathbf{D}\{I \mid na\} = \mathbf{D}_{11}\{I \mid na\} = \mathbf{\Gamma}(I).$$

For $k = 0$, we have then the two representations

$k = 0$	$\{E \mid na\}$	$\{I \mid na\}$
Γ_1	1	1
Γ_2	1	-1

$0 < k < \pi/a$. In this region the group $\mathcal{K}$ coincides with the group of primitive translations $\mathcal{T}$. The irreducible representations of $\mathcal{K}$ are given by

$$\mathbf{D}_{11}\{\beta \mid b\} = \mathbf{D}_{11}\{E \mid b\} = e^{ikb},$$

namely, for any b, $\beta = E$.

The space group can be decomposed in left cosets as follows:

$$G = \{E \mid 0\}\mathcal{T} + \{I \mid 0\}\mathcal{T} = \{\alpha_1 \mid 0\}\mathcal{T} + \{\alpha_2 \mid 0\}\mathcal{T},$$

where

$$\alpha_1 = E, \qquad \alpha_2 = I.$$

The matrix $\mathbf{D}\{E \mid na\}$ is simply given by

$$\mathbf{D}\{E \mid na\} = \begin{pmatrix} e^{i\alpha_1 kna} & 0 \\ 0 & e^{i\alpha_2 kna} \end{pmatrix} = \begin{pmatrix} e^{ikna} & 0 \\ 0 & e^{-ikna} \end{pmatrix}.$$

For the matrix $\mathbf{D}\{I \mid na\}$ we have

$$D_{ml}\{I \mid na\} = D_{11}\{\beta \mid b\},$$

where $\{\beta \mid b\}$ is given by

$$\{I \mid na\}\{\alpha_l \mid 0\} = \{\alpha_m \mid 0\}\{\beta \mid b\}.$$

For D_{11}

$$\{I \mid na\}\{\alpha_1 \mid 0\} \neq \{\alpha_1 \mid 0\}\{E \mid b\}$$

for any b, and therefore $D_{11} = 0$.

For D_{12}

$$\{I \mid na\}\{\alpha_2 \mid 0\} = \{\alpha_1 \mid 0\}\{E \mid b\}$$

or

$$\{I \mid na\}\{I \mid 0\} = \{E \mid 0\}\{E \mid b\},$$

which implies $b = na$ and $D_{12} = e^{ikna}$.

For D_{21}

$$\{I \mid na\}\{E \mid 0\} = \{I \mid 0\}\{E \mid b\},$$

or

$$\{I \mid na\} = \{I \mid -b\},$$

which implies $b = -na$ and $D_{21} = e^{-ikna}$.

For D_{22}

$$\{I \mid na\}\{I \mid 0\} \neq \{I \mid 0\}\{E \mid b\}$$

for any b, and therefore $D_{22} = 0$. In this region of the Brillouin zone we have, therefore, one two-dimensional representation for each value of k:

$0 < k < \pi$	$\{E \mid na\}$	$\{I \mid na\}$
Γ	$\begin{pmatrix} e^{ikna} & 0 \\ 0 & e^{-ikna} \end{pmatrix}$	$\begin{pmatrix} 0 & e^{ikna} \\ e^{-ikna} & 0 \end{pmatrix}$

$k = \pi/a$. At this point of the Brillouin zone

$$e^{ikna} = e^{-ikna},$$

and the $\mathcal{K}$ group coincides with the total space group G. Also $G_0(\mathbf{k})$ coincides with G_0 which includes again the operations E and I.

The irreducible representations for $\mathcal{K}$ are given by

$$\mathbf{D}_{11}\{\beta \mid b\} = e^{ikb}\mathbf{\Gamma}_i(\beta) = e^{i(\pi/a)b}\mathbf{\Gamma}_i(\beta),$$

where $\mathbf{\Gamma}_i(\beta)$ is one of the two representations

G_0	E	I
Γ_1	1	1
Γ_2	1	-1

The irreducible representations of G are unidimensional.

For $\mathbf{D}\{E \mid na\}$ we obtain

$$\mathbf{D}\{E \mid na\} = e^{ikna} = e^{i\pi n}.$$

For $\mathbf{D}\{I \mid na\}$:

$$\mathbf{D}\{I \mid na\} = \mathbf{D}_{11}\{\beta \mid b\},$$

where $\{\beta \mid b\}$ is given by

$$\{I \mid na\}\{E \mid 0\} = \{E \mid 0\}\{\beta \mid b\},$$

namely, $\beta = I$, $b = na$. Therefore

$$\mathbf{D}\{I \mid na\} = e^{ikna}\mathbf{\Gamma}_i(\beta).$$

The irreducible representations of G are then given by

$k = \frac{\pi}{a}$	$\{E \mid na\}$	$\{I \mid na\}$
Γ_1	$e^{i\pi n}$	$e^{i\pi n}$
Γ_2	$e^{i\pi n}$	$e^{-i\pi n}$

Example II

Let us now consider the space group of Fig. 2.17*a*. The Bravais lattice for such group is Γ_5, represented in Fig. 2.15*a*; the Brillouin zone is represented in Fig. 2.15*b* and is reproduced in Fig. 2.17*b*.

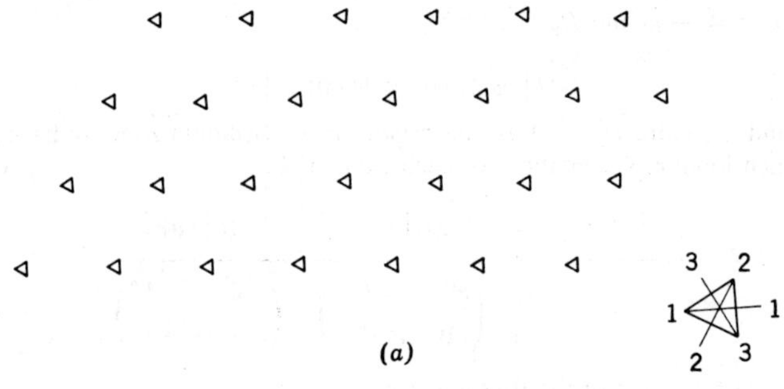

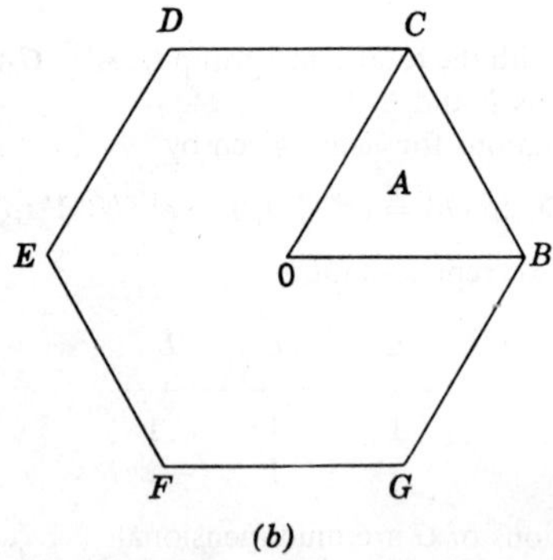

Fig. 2.17. (*a*) Symmorphic group with point group C_{3v} and Bravais lattice Γ_5; (*b*) Brillouin zone for lattice Γ_5.

The point group of this space group is C_{3v} and consists of the following operations:

E: identity
C_3: clockwise rotation through 120°
C_3^2: clockwise rotation through 240°
σ_1: reflection through the 1-1 axis
σ_2: reflection through the 2-2 axis
σ_3: reflection through the 3-3 axis.

The character table for this group is given by

C_{3v}	E	$C_3 C_3^2$	$\sigma_1\sigma_2\sigma_3$
Γ_1	1	1	1
Γ_2	1	1	-1
Γ_3	2	-2	0

In order to find the distinct irreducible representations for the space group, we need to consider only the section OBC of the Brillouin zone in Fig. 2.17*b*. Let us consider different regions in this section separately.

Origin O. At this point the group $\mathcal{K}$ coincides with the entire space group:

$$G = \{E \mid 0\}\mathcal{K},$$

because

$$e^{i\beta\mathbf{k}\cdot\mathbf{T}_n} = e^{i\mathbf{k}\cdot\mathbf{T}_n} = 1$$

for all $\mathbf{T}_n$. The point group $G_0(\mathbf{k})$ coincides with G_0 which is the point group C_{3v}. Also

$$\mathbf{D}\{\beta \mid \mathbf{T}_n\} = \mathbf{D}_{11}\{\beta \mid \mathbf{T}_n\} = \mathbf{\Gamma}_i(\beta),$$

where $\mathbf{\Gamma}_i(\beta)$ is an irreducible representation of C_{3v}. At this point we have therefore two one-dimensional and one two-dimensional irreducible representations.

Points A. For a point A inside the Brillouin zone, the group $\mathcal{K}$ coincides with the group $\mathcal{T}$. This means that $\beta = E$:

$$\mathbf{D}_{11}\{\beta \mid \mathbf{T}_n\} = \mathbf{D}_{11}\{E \mid \mathbf{T}_n\} = e^{i\mathbf{k}\cdot\mathbf{T}_n}.$$

The group G can be divided in left cosets with respect to $\mathcal{K} = \mathcal{T}$:

$$G = \{E \mid 0\}\mathcal{T} + \{C_3 \mid 0\}\mathcal{T} + \{C_3^2 \mid 0\}\mathcal{T} + \{\sigma_1 \mid 0\}\mathcal{T} + \{\sigma_2 \mid 0\}\mathcal{T} + \{\sigma_3 \mid 0\}\mathcal{T} = \sum_{i=1}^{6} \{\alpha_i \mid 0\}\mathcal{T},$$

where

$$\alpha_1 = E,\ \alpha_2 = C_3,\ \alpha_3 = C_3^2,\ \alpha_4 = \sigma_1,\ \alpha_5 = \sigma_2,\ \alpha_6 = \sigma_3.$$

The matrix for a primitive translation is given, according to (2.152), by

$$\mathbf{D}\{E \mid \mathbf{T}_n\} = \begin{pmatrix} e^{i\mathbf{k}\cdot\mathbf{T}_n} & & & & & 0 \\ & e^{i\alpha_2\mathbf{k}\cdot\mathbf{T}_n} & & & & \\ & & e^{i\alpha_3\mathbf{k}\cdot\mathbf{T}_n} & & & \\ & & & e^{i\alpha_4\mathbf{k}\cdot\mathbf{T}_n} & & \\ & & & & e^{i\alpha_5\mathbf{k}\cdot\mathbf{T}_n} & \\ 0 & & & & & e^{i\alpha_6\mathbf{k}\cdot\mathbf{T}_n} \end{pmatrix}.$$

Let us consider now the matrix $\mathbf{D}\{\alpha_i \mid 0\}$. The kjth element of this matrix is given by:

$$D_{kj}\{\alpha_i \mid 0\} = D_{11}\{E \mid 0\} = 1,$$

provided the relation (2.163) is respected:

$$\{\alpha_i \mid 0\}\{\alpha_j \mid 0\} = \{\alpha_k \mid 0\}.$$

This means that the only element in the jth column which is different from zero and equal to 1 is the kth, where k is given by

$$\alpha_i\alpha_j = \alpha_k.$$

The products $\alpha_i\alpha_j$ are now listed:

$$\begin{array}{lll}
\alpha_1\alpha_1 = \alpha_1 & \alpha_2\alpha_1 = \alpha_2 & \alpha_3\alpha_1 = \alpha_3 \\
\alpha_1\alpha_2 = \alpha_2 & \alpha_2\alpha_2 = \alpha_3 & \alpha_3\alpha_2 = \alpha_1 \\
\alpha_1\alpha_3 = \alpha_3 & \alpha_2\alpha_3 = \alpha_1 & \alpha_3\alpha_3 = \alpha_2 \\
\alpha_1\alpha_4 = \alpha_4 & \alpha_2\alpha_4 = \alpha_6 & \alpha_3\alpha_4 = \alpha_5 \\
\alpha_1\alpha_5 = \alpha_5 & \alpha_2\alpha_5 = \alpha_4 & \alpha_3\alpha_5 = \alpha_6 \\
\alpha_1\alpha_6 = \alpha_6 & \alpha_2\alpha_6 = \alpha_5 & \alpha_3\alpha_6 = \alpha_4
\end{array}$$

$$\begin{array}{lll}
\alpha_4\alpha_1 = \alpha_4 & \alpha_5\alpha_1 = \alpha_5 & \alpha_6\alpha_1 = \alpha_6 \\
\alpha_4\alpha_2 = \alpha_5 & \alpha_5\alpha_2 = \alpha_6 & \alpha_6\alpha_2 = \alpha_4 \\
\alpha_4\alpha_3 = \alpha_6 & \alpha_5\alpha_3 = \alpha_4 & \alpha_6\alpha_3 = \alpha_5 \\
\alpha_4\alpha_4 = \alpha_1 & \alpha_5\alpha_4 = \alpha_3 & \alpha_6\alpha_4 = \alpha_2 \\
\alpha_4\alpha_5 = \alpha_2 & \alpha_5\alpha_5 = \alpha_1 & \alpha_6\alpha_5 = \alpha_3 \\
\alpha_4\alpha_6 = \alpha_3 & \alpha_5\alpha_6 = \alpha_2 & \alpha_6\alpha_6 = \alpha_1.
\end{array}$$

The matrices for all the operations $\{\alpha_i \mid 0\}$ are reported in Table 2.6. This representation actually corresponds to the so-called *regular representation* of the point group C_{3v}.

The matrix for the generic operation $\{\alpha \mid \mathbf{T}_n\}$ can be obtained by the product

$$\mathbf{D}\{\alpha \mid \mathbf{T}_n\} = \mathbf{D}\{E \mid \mathbf{T}_n\}\mathbf{D}\{\alpha \mid 0\}.$$

Points in OB. For the points in OB the group $\mathcal{K}$ consists of the operations $\{E \mid \mathbf{T}_n\}$ and $\{\sigma_1 \mid \mathbf{T}_n\}$. The point group $G_0(\mathbf{k})$ consists of the operations E and σ_1; its representations are given by

$G_0(\mathbf{k})$	E	σ_1
Γ_1	1	1
Γ_2	1	-1

We have also

$$\mathbf{D}_{11}\{\beta \mid \mathbf{b}\} = e^{i\mathbf{k}\cdot\mathbf{b}}\Gamma_i(\beta),$$

where $i = 1, 2$ and $\beta = E, \sigma_1$.

The group G can be divided in left cosets with respect to $\mathcal{K}$:

$$\begin{aligned} G &= \{E \mid 0\}\mathcal{K} + \{C_3 \mid 0\}\mathcal{K} + \{C_3{}^2 \mid 0\}\mathcal{K} \\ &= \{\alpha_1 \mid 0\}\mathcal{K} + \{\alpha_2 \mid 0\}\mathcal{K} + \{\alpha_3 \mid 0\}\mathcal{K}. \end{aligned}$$

The matrix for a primitive translation is given, according to (2.152) by

$$\mathbf{D}\{E \mid \mathbf{T}_n\} = \begin{pmatrix} e^{i\mathbf{k}\cdot\mathbf{T}_n} & & 0 \\ & e^{i\alpha_2\mathbf{k}\cdot\mathbf{T}_n} & \\ 0 & & e^{i\alpha_3\mathbf{k}\cdot\mathbf{T}_n} \end{pmatrix}.$$

Table 2.6 Regular Representation for the Point Group C_{3v}

$\{E \mid 0\}$	$\{C_3 \mid 0\}$	$\{C_3^2 \mid 0\}$	$\{\sigma_1 \mid 0\}$	$\{\sigma_2 \mid 0\}$	$\{\sigma_3 \mid 0\}$
$\begin{pmatrix} 1&0&0&0&0&0\\ 0&1&0&0&0&0\\ 0&0&1&0&0&0\\ 0&0&0&1&0&0\\ 0&0&0&0&1&0\\ 0&0&0&0&0&1 \end{pmatrix}$	$\begin{pmatrix} 0&0&1&0&0&0\\ 1&0&0&0&0&0\\ 0&1&0&0&0&0\\ 0&0&0&0&1&0\\ 0&0&0&0&0&1\\ 0&0&0&1&0&0 \end{pmatrix}$	$\begin{pmatrix} 0&1&0&0&0&0\\ 0&0&1&0&0&0\\ 1&0&0&0&0&0\\ 0&0&0&0&0&1\\ 0&0&0&1&0&0\\ 0&0&0&0&1&0 \end{pmatrix}$	$\begin{pmatrix} 0&0&0&1&0&0\\ 0&0&0&0&1&0\\ 0&0&0&0&0&1\\ 1&0&0&0&0&0\\ 0&1&0&0&0&0\\ 0&0&1&0&0&0 \end{pmatrix}$	$\begin{pmatrix} 0&0&0&0&1&0\\ 0&0&0&0&0&1\\ 0&0&0&1&0&0\\ 0&0&1&0&0&0\\ 1&0&0&0&0&0\\ 0&1&0&0&0&0 \end{pmatrix}$	$\begin{pmatrix} 0&0&0&0&0&1\\ 0&0&0&1&0&0\\ 0&0&0&0&1&0\\ 0&1&0&0&0&0\\ 0&0&1&0&0&0\\ 1&0&0&0&0&0 \end{pmatrix}$

Considering the matrix $\mathbf{D}\{\alpha_i \mid 0\}$, the kjth element is given by

$$D_{kj}\{\alpha_i \mid 0\} = D_{11}\{\beta \mid 0\} = \Gamma_i(\beta),$$

where β is given by

$$\{\alpha_i \mid 0\}\{\alpha_j \mid 0\} = \{\alpha_k \mid 0\}\{\beta \mid 0\},$$

namely by

$$\alpha_i\alpha_j = \alpha_k\beta, \qquad (\beta = \alpha_1, \alpha_4).$$

Let us consider $\alpha_4 = \sigma_1$. We obtain

$$\begin{aligned} \alpha_4\alpha_1 &= \alpha_4 = \alpha_1\alpha_4, \\ \alpha_4\alpha_2 &= \alpha_5 = \alpha_3\alpha_4, \qquad \beta = \alpha_4 = \sigma_1. \\ \alpha_4\alpha_3 &= \alpha_6 = \alpha_2\alpha_4, \end{aligned}$$

Therefore the only element different from zero and equal to $\Gamma_i(\sigma_1)$ is in the first column, the first, in the second column, the third and in the third column, the second:

$$\mathbf{D}\{\sigma_1 \mid 0\} = \begin{pmatrix} \pm 1 & 0 & 0 \\ 0 & 0 & \pm 1 \\ 0 & \pm 1 & 0 \end{pmatrix},$$

where the two signs correspond to the two different Γ_i representations.

Let us consider $\alpha_2 = C_3$. We obtain

$$\begin{aligned} \alpha_2\alpha_1 &= \alpha_2 = \alpha_2\alpha_1, \\ \alpha_2\alpha_2 &= \alpha_3 = \alpha_3\alpha_1, \qquad \beta = \alpha_1 = E, \\ \alpha_2\alpha_3 &= \alpha_1 = \alpha_1\alpha_1, \end{aligned}$$

and

$$\mathbf{D}\{C_3 \mid 0\} = \begin{pmatrix} 0 & 0 & 1 \\ 1 & 0 & 0 \\ 0 & 1 & 0 \end{pmatrix}.$$

Let us consider $\alpha_3 = C_3^2$. We obtain

$$\begin{aligned} \alpha_3\alpha_1 &= \alpha_3 = \alpha_3\alpha_1, \\ \alpha_3\alpha_2 &= \alpha_1 = \alpha_1\alpha_1, \qquad \beta = \alpha_1 = E, \\ \alpha_3\alpha_3 &= \alpha_2 = \alpha_2\alpha_1, \end{aligned}$$

and

$$\mathbf{D}\{C_3^2 \mid 0\} = \begin{pmatrix} 0 & 1 & 0 \\ 0 & 0 & 1 \\ 1 & 0 & 0 \end{pmatrix}.$$

For $\alpha_5 = \sigma_2$ we obtain

$$\begin{aligned} \alpha_5\alpha_1 &= \alpha_5 = \alpha_3\alpha_4, \\ \alpha_5\alpha_2 &= \alpha_6 = \alpha_2\alpha_4, \qquad \beta = \alpha_4 = \sigma_1, \\ \alpha_5\alpha_3 &= \alpha_4 = \alpha_1\alpha_4, \end{aligned}$$

and

$$\mathbf{D}\{\sigma_2 \mid 0\} = \begin{pmatrix} 0 & 0 & \pm 1 \\ 0 & \pm 1 & 0 \\ \pm 1 & 0 & 0 \end{pmatrix}.$$

For $\alpha_6 = \sigma_3$ we obtain

$$\alpha_6\alpha_1 = \alpha_6 = \alpha_2\alpha_4,$$

$$\alpha_6\alpha_2 = \alpha_4 = \alpha_1\alpha_4, \qquad \beta = \alpha_4 = \sigma_1,$$

$$\alpha_6\alpha_3 = \alpha_5 = \alpha_3\alpha_4,$$

and

$$\mathbf{D}\{E \mid \sigma_3\} = \begin{pmatrix} 0 & \pm 1 & 0 \\ \pm 1 & 0 & 0 \\ 0 & 0 & \pm 1 \end{pmatrix}.$$

The representations for the space group in this region of the Brillouin zone are reported in Table 2.7.

Points in OC. For the points in OC the group $\mathcal{K}$ consists of the operations $\{E \mid \mathbf{T}_n\}$ and $\{\sigma_2 \mid T_n\}$. The point group $G_0(\mathbf{k})$ consists of the operation E and σ_2:

$$\beta = E, \sigma_2.$$

We can work out the irreducible representations for the points in this region in a very similar way as we did for the points in OB, taking in account the fact that now σ_2 replaces σ_1.

Points in BC. The operation σ_3 sends a point in BC into a point in FE. These points, differing by $\mathbf{b}_1 + \mathbf{b}_2$, a primitive vector of the reciprocal lattice, correspond to the same representation. Therefore the group $\mathcal{K}$ consists now of $\{E \mid \mathbf{T}_n\}$ and $\{\sigma_3 \mid \mathbf{T}_n\}$ and $G_0(\mathbf{k})$ of E and σ_3. The representations can be obtained following the procedure outlined for the points in OB.

Point B. The operations of the C_{3v} group send this point into itself or into another point which differ from B by a primitive vector of the reciprocal lattice. Therefore $\mathcal{K} = G$ and $G_0(\mathbf{k}) = G_0 = C_{3v}$. The irreducible representations are given by

$$\mathbf{D}\{\beta \mid \mathbf{T}_n\} = \mathbf{D}_{11}\{\beta \mid \mathbf{T}_n\} = e^{i\mathbf{k}\cdot\mathbf{T}_n}\mathbf{\Gamma}_i(\beta),$$

where $\mathbf{k}$ is the $\mathbf{k}$ vector corresponding to B and $\mathbf{\Gamma}_i(\beta)$ are the irreducible representations of C_{3v}.

Point C. As for B the irreducible representations are given by

$$\mathbf{D}\{\beta \mid \mathbf{T}_n\} = \mathbf{D}_{11}\{\beta \mid \mathbf{T}_n\} = e^{i\mathbf{k}\cdot\mathbf{T}_n}\mathbf{\Gamma}_i(\beta),$$

where $\mathbf{k}$ is the $\mathbf{k}$ vector corresponding to C and $\mathbf{\Gamma}_i(\beta)$ are the representations of C_{3v}.

The representations for the present example are summarized in Table 2.8.

Table 2.7 Irreducible Representations of the Space Groups of Fig. 2.17*a* in Correspondence to the Points in *OB* of the Brillouin Zone (Fig. 2.17*b*)

	$\{E \mid \mathbf{T}_n\}$	$\{C_3 \mid 0\}$	$\{C_3^2 \mid 0\}$	$\{\sigma_1 \mid 0\}$	$\{\sigma_2 \mid 0\}$	$\{\sigma_3 \mid 0\}$
Γ_1	$\begin{pmatrix} e^{i\mathbf{k}\cdot\mathbf{T}_n} & 0 & 0 \\ 0 & e^{iC_3\mathbf{k}\cdot\mathbf{T}_n} & 0 \\ 0 & 0 & e^{iC_3^2\mathbf{k}\cdot\mathbf{T}_n} \end{pmatrix}$	$\begin{pmatrix} 0 & 0 & 1 \\ 1 & 0 & 0 \\ 0 & 1 & 0 \end{pmatrix}$	$\begin{pmatrix} 0 & 1 & 0 \\ 0 & 0 & 1 \\ 1 & 0 & 0 \end{pmatrix}$	$\begin{pmatrix} 1 & 0 & 0 \\ 0 & 0 & 1 \\ 0 & 1 & 0 \end{pmatrix}$	$\begin{pmatrix} 0 & 0 & 1 \\ 0 & 1 & 0 \\ 1 & 0 & 0 \end{pmatrix}$	$\begin{pmatrix} 0 & 1 & 0 \\ 1 & 0 & 0 \\ 0 & 0 & 1 \end{pmatrix}$
Γ_2	$\begin{pmatrix} e^{i\mathbf{k}\cdot\mathbf{T}_n} & 0 & 0 \\ 0 & e^{iC_3\mathbf{k}\cdot\mathbf{T}_n} & 0 \\ 0 & 0 & e^{iC_3^2\mathbf{k}\cdot\mathbf{T}_n} \end{pmatrix}$	$\begin{pmatrix} 0 & 0 & 1 \\ 1 & 0 & 0 \\ 0 & 1 & 0 \end{pmatrix}$	$\begin{pmatrix} 0 & 1 & 0 \\ 0 & 0 & 1 \\ 1 & 0 & 0 \end{pmatrix}$	$\begin{pmatrix} -1 & 0 & 0 \\ 0 & 0 & -1 \\ 0 & -1 & 0 \end{pmatrix}$	$\begin{pmatrix} 0 & 0 & -1 \\ 0 & -1 & 0 \\ -1 & 0 & 0 \end{pmatrix}$	$\begin{pmatrix} 0 & -1 & 0 \\ -1 & 0 & 0 \\ 0 & 0 & -1 \end{pmatrix}$

Table 2.8 Summary of the Irreducible Representations of the Space Group of Fig. 2.17*a*.

Region	$\mathcal{K}$	$G_0(\mathbf{k})$	Number of Representations	Dimension of Representation	Observations
A	$\mathcal{K} = \mathcal{T}$	$G_0(\mathbf{k}): E$	1	$6\begin{cases} d = 1 \\ q = 6 \end{cases}$	Regular representation for $\{\alpha \mid 0\}$ operations
O, B, C	$\mathcal{K} = G$	$G_0(\mathbf{k}) = G_0 = C_{3v}$	2	$1\begin{cases} d = 1 \\ q = 1 \end{cases}$	$\mathbf{D}\{\beta \mid \mathbf{T}_n\} = e^{i\mathbf{k}\cdot\mathbf{T}_n}\mathbf{\Gamma}_i(\beta)$
			1	$2\begin{cases} d = 2 \\ q = 1 \end{cases}$	$\mathbf{\Gamma}_i(\beta)$ = representations of C_{3v}
OB	$\mathcal{K}: \{E \mid \mathbf{T}_n\}, \{\sigma_1 \mid \mathbf{T}_n\}$	$G_0(\mathbf{k}): E, \sigma_1$	2	$3\begin{cases} d = 1 \\ q = 3 \end{cases}$	
OC	$\mathcal{K}: \{E \mid \mathbf{T}_n\}, \{\sigma_2 \mid \mathbf{T}_n\}$	$G_0(\mathbf{k}): E, \sigma_2$	2	$3\begin{cases} d = 1 \\ q = 3 \end{cases}$	
BC	$\mathcal{K}: \{E \mid \mathbf{T}_n\}, \{\sigma_3 \mid \mathbf{T}_n\}$	$G_0(\mathbf{k}): E, \sigma_3$	2	$3\begin{cases} d = 1 \\ q = 3 \end{cases}$	

REFERENCES

[1] V. Heine, *Group Theory in Quantum Mechanics*, Pergamon Press, New York, 1960.
[2] G. F. Koster, *Notes on Group Theory, Techn. Rep. No. 8*, March 1956, Solid State and Molecular Theory Group, Massachusetts Institute of Technology, Cambridge, Mass.
[3] G. F. Koster, "Space Groups and Their Representations," *Solid State Physics*, Vol. 5, edited by F. Seitz and D. Turnbull, Academic Press, New York, 1957, p. 173.

3

Connection of Quantum Mechanics with Group Theory

1. THE EFFECT OF AN ORTHOGONAL COORDINATE TRANSFORMATION ON THE VECTORS OF A HILBERT SPACE

Given a Hilbert space with a generic vector function $u(\mathbf{x})$, we want to see what is the effect on it of a real orthogonal coordinate transformation $\mathbf{R}$ such as indicated in (2.81) and (2.82).

We know that

$$dx_1'\,dx_2'\,dx_3' = \left| J\left(\frac{x_1', x_2', x_3'}{x_1, x_2, x_3}\right)\right| dx_1\,dx_2\,dx_3, \tag{3.1}$$

where

$$J\left(\frac{x_1', x_2', x_3'}{x_1, x_2, x_3}\right) = \begin{vmatrix} \dfrac{\partial x_1'}{\partial x_1} & \dfrac{\partial x_1'}{\partial x_2} & \dfrac{\partial x_1'}{\partial x_3} \\[2ex] \dfrac{\partial x_2'}{\partial x_1} & \dfrac{\partial x_2'}{\partial x_2} & \dfrac{\partial x_2'}{\partial x_3} \\[2ex] \dfrac{\partial x_3'}{\partial x_1} & \dfrac{\partial x_3'}{\partial x_2} & \dfrac{\partial x_3'}{\partial x_3} \end{vmatrix}, \tag{3.2}$$

and then

$$dx_1'\,dx_2'\,dx_3' = dx_1\,dx_2\,dx_3. \tag{3.3}$$

Let f be a function of x_1, x_2, x_3. This function can be expressed in terms of the transformed coordinates x_1', x_2', x_3':

$$f(x_1, x_2, x_3) = g(x_1', x_2', x_3'). \tag{3.4}$$

We have also:

$$\int f(x_1, x_2, x_3)\,dx_1\,dx_2\,dx_3 = \int g(x_1', x_2', x_3')\,dx_1'\,dx_2'\,dx_3'. \tag{3.5}$$

We can then say that the value of an integral is *invariant* under any real orthogonal coordinate transformation.

If $u(\mathbf{x})$ and $v(\mathbf{x})$ are two vectors of the Hilbert space, their inner product is invariant under any real orthogonal transformation:

$$\begin{aligned}(u, v) &= \int u^*(x_1, x_2, x_3)\, v(x_1, x_2, x_3)\, dx_1\, dx_2\, dx_3 \\ &= \int u^*(x_1', x_2', x_3')\, v(x_1', x_2', x_3')\, dx_1'\, dx_2'\, dx_3' \\ &= \int u^*(x_1', x_2', x_3')\, v(x_1', x_2', x_3')\, dx_1\, dx_2\, dx_3 \\ &= \int [R^{-1}u(x_1, x_2, x_3)]^* R^{-1}v(x_1, x_2, x_3)\, dx_1\, dx_2\, dx_3 \\ &= (R^{-1}u, R^{-1}v), \end{aligned} \tag{3.6}$$

where R^{-1} is an operator, operating on the Hilbert space and defined by

$$R^{-1}u(\mathbf{x}) = u(\mathbf{x}') = u(\mathbf{R}\mathbf{x}). \tag{3.7}$$

The operator R is defined by

$$Ru(\mathbf{x}') = u(\mathbf{R}^{-1}\mathbf{x}') = u(\mathbf{x}). \tag{3.8}$$

The meaning of (3.7) and (3.8) is essentially that a physical rotation through an angle θ is equivalent to a rotation of the coordinate system through an angle $-\theta$.

From (3.6) we can see that the operators corresponding to orthogonal coordinate transformations are *unitary*. It is easy to see that they are also *linear*.

Since R is unitary, its matrix representation, if the basis functions of the Hilbert space are orthonormal, is *unitary*.

Let us see now what is the effect of a transformation like $\mathbf{R}$ on an operator of the Hilbert space. Let this operator be $H(\mathbf{x})$, and let:

$$v(\mathbf{x}) = H(\mathbf{x})\, u(\mathbf{x}). \tag{3.9}$$

Operating a coordinate transformation

$$\begin{aligned} v(\mathbf{x}') = R^{-1}v(\mathbf{x}) &= R^{-1}[H(\mathbf{x})\, u(\mathbf{x})] = H(\mathbf{R}\mathbf{x})\, u(\mathbf{R}\mathbf{x}) \\ &= H(\mathbf{R}\mathbf{x})[R^{-1}u(\mathbf{x})]. \end{aligned} \tag{3.10}$$

Therefore

$$v(\mathbf{x}) = RH(\mathbf{R}\mathbf{x})\, R^{-1}u(\mathbf{x}) = H(\mathbf{x})\, u(\mathbf{x}), \tag{3.11}$$

and then

$$H(\mathbf{x}) = RH(\mathbf{R}\mathbf{x})\, R^{-1}, \tag{3.12}$$

or

$$H(\mathbf{x}') = H(\mathbf{R}\mathbf{x}) = R^{-1}H(\mathbf{x})\, R. \tag{3.13}$$

$R^{-1}H(\mathbf{x})\,R$ is the transformed operator, which operating on the transformed function $R^{-1}u(\mathbf{x})$ gives the transformed product $R^{-1}[H(\mathbf{x})\,u(\mathbf{x})]$.

If

$$H(\mathbf{R}\mathbf{x}) = H(\mathbf{x}), \tag{3.14}$$

we say that the operator H is *invariant under the* **R** *transformation*. In this case from (3.13) and (3.14) we get

$$H(\mathbf{x})\,R = RH(\mathbf{x}), \tag{3.15}$$

and H commutes with R.

2. THE SYMMETRY GROUP OF THE SCHRÖDINGER EQUATION

The eigensolutions of a Schrödinger equation

$$Hu = Eu \tag{3.16}$$

define a Hilbert space. This space consists of subspaces, each of them defined by all the eigenfunctions belonging to the same value of E with dimension equal to the degeneracy of E.

We want to consider now all the transformations under which the Hamiltonian is invariant and examine their effect on the Hilbert space of the eigenfunctions. Let R be the generic coordinate transforming operation under which H is invariant.

It is easily shown that these operations form a group. In fact if

$$H(\mathbf{R}\mathbf{x}) = H(\mathbf{x}) \tag{3.17}$$

$$H(\mathbf{S}\mathbf{x}) = H(\mathbf{x}), \tag{3.18}$$

where R and S are two generic operations, we have

$$H(\mathbf{S}\mathbf{R}\mathbf{x}) = S^{-1}H(\mathbf{R}\mathbf{x})\,S = S^{-1}H(\mathbf{x})\,S = H(\mathbf{S}\mathbf{x}) = H(\mathbf{x}). \tag{3.19}$$

Moreover

$$H(\mathbf{x}) = H(\mathbf{R}\mathbf{R}^{-1}\mathbf{x}) = R^{-1}H(\mathbf{R}^{-1}\mathbf{x})\,R = H(\mathbf{R}^{-1}\mathbf{x}), \tag{3.20}$$

namely, the inverse of transformation **R** leaves the Hamiltonian invariant.

We call the group of these transformations the *group of the Schrödinger equation* and we label it by G.

If we apply R to both sides of (3.16) we get

$$RHu = ERu, \tag{3.21}$$

and, because of the invariance of the Hamiltonian,

$$RH = HR, \tag{3.22}$$

and

$$H(Ru) = E(Ru). \tag{3.23}$$

Ru is a solution of (3.16) belonging to the eigenvalue E. If E is not degenerate,

$$Ru = cu. \tag{3.24}$$

If E is m-fold degenerate:

$$Ru_l = \sum_{i=1}^{m} \Gamma(R)_{il} u_i, \tag{3.25}$$

where the u_i's are the degenerate eigenfunctions belonging to E. If we apply to u_l another operation S belonging to G we get

$$Su_l = \sum_{j=1}^{m} \Gamma(S)_{jl} u_j. \tag{3.26}$$

If we apply $SR = T$ to u_l,

$$Tu_l = SRu_l = \sum_{j=1}^{m} \Gamma(T)_{jl} u_j. \tag{3.27}$$

Since the product SR consists of the operation R followed by the operation S, we have:

$$\begin{aligned}(SR)u_l = S(Ru_l) &= \sum_{i=1}^{m} \Gamma(R)_{il}\, Su_i \\ &= \sum_{i=1}^{m} \Gamma(R)_{il} \sum_{j=1}^{m} \Gamma(S)_{ji}\, u_j = \sum_{i=1}^{m}\sum_{j=1}^{m} \Gamma(R)_{il}\, \Gamma(S)_{ji} u_j.\end{aligned} \tag{3.28}$$

Then

$$\Gamma(T)_{jl} = \sum_{i=1}^{m} \Gamma(S)_{ji}\, \Gamma(R)_{il}, \tag{3.29}$$

or

$$\mathbf{\Gamma}(T) = \mathbf{\Gamma}(S)\, \mathbf{\Gamma}(R). \tag{3.30}$$

By applying all the operations of G to the eigenfunction u_l, we may find a matrix for every element of the group. These matrices form a representation of the group because any relation between operations of the group is mirrored in a relation between these matrices. Therefore the degenerate wavefunctions u_l form a basis for a representation of the group G of the Schrödinger equation.

Let us assume that the basis eigenfunctions belonging to E are orthonormal. In this case for two functions u_j and u_l

$$\begin{aligned}(u_j, u_l) = \delta_{jl} &= (Ru_j, Ru_l) \\ &= \sum_{mn} \Gamma(R)^*_{mj}\, \Gamma(R)_{nl} (u_m, u_n) \\ &= \sum_{m} \Gamma(R)_{mj}\, \Gamma(R)^*_{ml} = \sum_{m} \Gamma(R)^+_{jm}\, \Gamma(R)_{ml},\end{aligned} \tag{3.31}$$

or

$$\mathbf{\Gamma}(R)^+ \mathbf{\Gamma}(R) = \mathbf{1}. \tag{3.32}$$

Therefore, if the basis functions are orthonormal, the matrix representations of the Schrödinger group are unitary.

The particular form of a representation depends on the choice of the basis functions. Given a set of basis functions corresponding to a certain eigenvalue, any other set derived from it by a similarity transformation is rightly a set of basis functions. The representations based on these functions are irreducible. If this were not the case, it could be possible to form sets of functions v_i, linear combinationsof u_l,

$$v_1, v_2, \ldots ; v_i, v_{i+1}, \ldots ; v_j, v_{j+1}, \ldots ; \ \ldots ; \ \ldots, \tag{3.33}$$

such that operations of G would send one of the functions v_i into a linear combination of functions v_j of the same set. In this case, then, the eigenvalues corresponding to the different sets of v_i could be different, which is contrary to our assumption.

We can now enunciate the following rule:

Eigenfunctions belonging to the same eigenvalue form a basis for an irreducible representation of the group of operations which leave the Hamiltonian unchanged. The dimension of this representation is equal to the degree of degeneracy.

There are two exceptions to this rule:

Accidental Degeneracy. In this case only by a fortuitous coincidence is the eigenvalue for two eigenfunctions the same. The eigenfunctions do not belong to the same set of basis functions for a representation of the Schrödinger group. They do not transform into each other under the symmetry operations.

An accidental degeneracy of a system with a Hamiltonian H_0 may, in general, be removed by applying a proper additional term to H_0 which has the same symmetry property of H_0. Examples of accidental degeneracy are presented by the Zeeman levels of atomic systems which may cross for certain values of the magnetic field; by changing the value of the magnetic field the accidental degeneracy is lifted. Atomic hydrogen presents accidental degeneracy for levels with the same principal quantum number n and different angular momentum l have the same energy; this degeneracy is due to the Coulombic nature of the central field and may be lifted by adding a non-Coulombic term to the Hamiltonian. A term of this type is actually present in hydrogen-like atoms like Na.

Excess Degeneracy (Example: Kramers' Degeneracy). This type of degeneracy is due to the fact that the transformation group taken in consideration does not contain all the symmetry operations.

Given a certain system, all the possible eigenfunctions must form basis for some irreducible representation of the Schrödinger group. Therefore by knowing the irreducible representations of the group, we know the possible degrees of degeneracy and the transformation properties of the eigenfunctions under the operations of the Schrödinger group.

Example

Let us assume that a system has the symmetry of the group of operations of the equilateral triangle C_{3v}. The eigenfunctions could then belong to any of the following sets:

A set of eigenfunctions which form bases for the representation Γ_1. These eigenfunctions are nondegenerate and remain unchanged if subjected to any of the operations of the group.

A set of nondegenerate eigenfunctions which form basis for the representation Γ_2. These eigenfunctions remain unchanged if subjected to the operations E, C_3, and $C_3{}^2$, but change sign if subjected to the operations σ_1, σ_2, and σ_3.

A set of doubly degenerate eigenfunctions which form a basis for the irreducible representation Γ_3 and which are bound by the relation

$$R\begin{pmatrix} u_1 \\ u_2 \end{pmatrix} = (u_1, \ u_2)\begin{pmatrix} \Gamma_3(R)_{11} & \Gamma_3(R)_{12} \\ \Gamma_3(R)_{21} & \Gamma_3(R)_{22} \end{pmatrix}. \tag{3.34}$$

Let us see what is the effect of a similarity transformation of the basis functions on the representations of the Schrödinger group. Let us consider the transformation

$$v_j = \sum_{k=1}^{m} T_{kj} u_k, \tag{3.35}$$

and let us operate with R on the functions v_j:

$$\begin{aligned} Rv_j &= \sum_{k=1}^{m} T_{kj} R u_k = \sum_{k=1}^{m} \sum_{p=1}^{m} T_{kj} \Gamma(R)_{pk} \, u_p \\ &= \sum_{k=1}^{m} \sum_{p=1}^{m} \sum_{q=1}^{m} T_{kj} \Gamma(R)_{pk} \, (\mathbf{T}^{-1})_{qp} \, v_q \\ &= \sum_{q=1}^{m} \Gamma'(R)_{qj} \, v_q. \end{aligned} \tag{3.36}$$

Then, if we use the basis functions v_j, the representation is given by

$$\boldsymbol{\Gamma}'(R) = \mathbf{T}^{-1} \boldsymbol{\Gamma}(R) \mathbf{T}. \tag{3.37}$$

3. THE FUNDAMENTAL THEOREM FOR FUNCTIONS AND OPERATORS TRANSFORMING IRREDUCIBLY

A set of n_α functions u_i^α are said *to form a basis* for an irreducible representation Γ_α or *to transform irreducibly* according to the representation Γ_α of a symmetry group G, if

$$R u_i^\alpha = \sum_j \Gamma_\alpha(R)_{ji} \, u_j^\alpha, \tag{3.38}$$

where R is any operation of G. The above relation can be rewritten in the following form:

$$R\begin{pmatrix} u_1^{\alpha} \\ u_2^{\alpha} \\ \cdot \\ u_{n_\alpha}^{\alpha} \end{pmatrix} = (u_1^{\alpha} \quad u_2^{\alpha} \quad \cdots \quad u_{n_\alpha}^{\alpha}) \begin{pmatrix} \Gamma_\alpha(R)_{11} & \Gamma_\alpha(R)_{12} & \cdots & \Gamma_\alpha(R)_{1n_\alpha} \\ \Gamma_\alpha(R)_{21} & \Gamma_\alpha(R)_{22} & \cdots & \Gamma_\alpha(R)_{2n_\alpha} \\ \cdots & \cdots & \cdots & \cdots \\ \Gamma_\alpha(R)_{n_\alpha 1} & \Gamma_\alpha(R)_{n_\alpha 2} & \cdots & \Gamma_\alpha(R)_{n_\alpha n_\alpha} \end{pmatrix}, \tag{3.39}$$

or, more concisely,

$$R\mathbf{u}^{\alpha} = \mathbf{u}^{\alpha}\mathbf{\Gamma}_\alpha(R). \tag{3.40}$$

In (3.38) the ith function u_i is said to transform according to the ith column of the Γ_α representation. If the basis functions are orthonormal, the representations are unitary.

A set of n_α operators Q_i^{α} are said *to transform irreducibly* according to a representation Γ_α of a symmetry group G, if

$$RQ_i^{\alpha}R^{-1} = \sum_j Q_j^{\alpha}\Gamma_\alpha(R)_{ji}, \tag{3.41}$$

where R is any operation of G.

The case of an invariant operator is a particular one in which the operator transforms according to the identity representation Γ_1:

$$Q(\mathbf{x}') = RQ(\mathbf{x})R^{-1} = Q(\mathbf{x}). \tag{3.42}$$

Let us consider a set of u_i^{α} functions transforming irreducibly according to a representation Γ_α and a set of v_j^{α} functions transforming irreducibly according to a representation Γ_β. The product functions $u_i^{\alpha}v_j^{\alpha}$ form basis for the representation $\Gamma_\alpha \times \Gamma_\beta$ which is, in general reducible;

$$\mathbf{\Gamma}_\alpha(R)\,\mathbf{\Gamma}_\beta(R) = \sum_\gamma g_{\alpha\beta\gamma}\,\mathbf{\Gamma}_\gamma(R). \tag{3.43}$$

The representation $\Gamma_\alpha \times \Gamma_\beta$ is brought into a reduced form by a unitary matrix $\mathbf{T}$

$$\mathbf{T}^{\alpha\beta+}[\mathbf{\Gamma}_\alpha(R) \times \mathbf{\Gamma}_\beta(R)]\mathbf{T}^{\alpha\beta} = \mathbf{\Gamma}'(R). \tag{3.44}$$

The generic element of $\mathbf{T}$ may be indicated by $T_{ij,n}^{\alpha\beta,\gamma q}$, where i and j individuate two basis functions respectively in the Γ_α and Γ_β manifolds, Γ_γ is the generic irreducible representation in (3.43) and n individuates a basis function in the Γ_γ manifold. Finally, as Γ_γ may be contained more than once in $\Gamma_\alpha \times \Gamma_\beta$ ($g_{\alpha\beta\gamma}$ may be greater than 1), the index q distinguishes among the different Γ_γ

representations. The indices i and j run over the columns of $\mathbf{T}$, the indices γ, q and n over the rows. We may consider the function

$$w_n^{\gamma,q} = \sum_{i,j} T_{ij,n}^{\alpha\beta,\gamma q} u_i^{\alpha} v_j^{\beta}. \tag{3.45}$$

It is then

$$u_i^{\alpha} v_j^{\beta} = \sum_{\gamma n q} [T_{ij,n}^{\alpha\beta,\gamma q}]^* w_n^{\gamma,q}. \tag{3.46}$$

where $[T_{ij,n}^{\alpha\beta,\gamma q}]^*$ represents the generic element of $\mathbf{T}^+$.

Let us consider now an integral of the following type:

$$(u_i^{\alpha}, Qv_j^{\beta}), \tag{3.47}$$

where Q is an invariant operator. If the representations Γ_α and Γ_β are unitary, besides being irreducible,

$$\begin{aligned}(u_i^{\alpha}, Qv_j^{\beta}) &= (Ru_i^{\alpha}, RQv_j^{\beta}) \\ &= (Ru_i^{\alpha}, QRv_j^{\beta}) = \frac{1}{g}\sum_R (Ru_i^{\alpha}, QRv_j^{\beta}) \\ &= \frac{1}{g}\sum_R \sum_{k,m} \Gamma_\alpha(R)_{ki}^* \, \Gamma_\beta(R)_{mj} (u_k^{\alpha}, Qv_m^{\beta}) \\ &= \frac{1}{n_\alpha} \delta_{\alpha\beta}\delta_{ij} \sum_k (u_k^{\alpha}, Qv_k^{\beta}).\end{aligned} \tag{3.48}$$

We see that the matrix element is different from zero if $\alpha = \beta$, $i = j$ and also is independent of the subscript i. A particular case is given by

$$(u_i^{\alpha}, v_j^{\beta}) = 0 \quad \text{unless} \quad \alpha = \beta, i = j. \tag{3.49}$$

We may now enunciate the first part of what we call the *Fundamental Theorem* [1]:

Matrix elements of invariant operators taken between two given functions vanish unless the two functions transform according to the same column of the same irreducible representation. In the event it does not vanish, the matrix element is independent of the column according to which the two functions transform.

Let us consider, further, an integral of the following type:

$$(f_n^{\gamma}, Q_i^{\alpha} v_j^{\beta}), \tag{3.50}$$

where Q_i^{α} indicate the i component of a set of operators which transform irreducibly according to the ith column of the Γ_α representation. Taking in account (3.46)

$$Q_i^{\alpha} v_j^{\beta} = \sum_{\gamma' n' q'} [T_{ij,n'}^{\alpha\beta,\gamma' q'}]^* w_{n'}^{\gamma' q'}, \tag{3.51}$$

where the $w_{n'}^{\gamma',q'}$ functions transform irreducibly according to the n'th column of the Γ_γ' representation.

The integral (3.50) is then given by

$$(f_n^{\gamma}, Q_i^{\alpha}\, v_j^{\beta}) = \sum_{q=1}^{g_{\alpha\beta\gamma}} c_q [T_{ij,n}^{\alpha\beta,\gamma q}]^*, \tag{3.52}$$

where the coefficients c_q are independent of the indices ijn and depend only on the operators in question and on the indices α, β, γ, q.

If $g_{\alpha\beta\gamma} = 1$,

$$(f_n^{\gamma}, Q_i^{\alpha} v_j^{\beta}) = [T_{ij,n}^{\alpha\beta,\gamma}]^* \times \text{const}, \tag{3.53}$$

where the constant is independent of the subscripts.

If P_i^{α} is the i component of another set of operators which transform irreducibly according to Γ_α, we get also

$$(f_n^{\gamma}, P_i^{\alpha} v_j^{\beta}) = [T_{ij,n}^{\alpha\beta,\gamma}]^* \times \text{const}, \tag{3.54}$$

the constant being different from the one in (3.53) but still independent of subscripts. From (3.53) and (3.54) we get

$$(f_n^{\gamma}, Q_i^{\alpha} v_j^{\beta}) = \text{const}\, (f_n^{\gamma}, P_i^{\alpha} v_j^{\beta}), \tag{3.55}$$

the constant being independent of the subscripts.

We can now enunciate the second part of the *Fundamental Theorem:*

Matrix elements of operators Q_i^{α} transforming irreducibly according to a representation Γ_α, taken between two functions f_n^{γ}, v_j^{β} which transform irreducibly according to columns n and j, respectively of the representations Γ_γ and Γ_β, vanish unless the representation $\Gamma_\alpha \times \Gamma_\beta$ contains the representation Γ_γ. If Γ_γ is contained q times in $\Gamma_\alpha \times \Gamma_\beta$, then the value of the matrix element is uniquely determined by the symmetry property of f_n^{γ}, Q_i^{α}, v_j^{β}, apart of q constants. These constants do not depend on the subscripts n, i, j.

4. THE CONSTRUCTION OF FUNCTIONS TRANSFORMING IRREDUCIBLY [2]

Given a symmetry group G of order g we can define a *projection operator* as follows:

$$\rho_{ij}^{\alpha} = \frac{n_\alpha}{g} \sum_R \Gamma_\alpha(R)_{ij}^* R, \tag{3.56}$$

where Γ_α is an irreducible unitary representation of G, R a generic operation and n_α the dimension of Γ_α.

We want now to consider the n_α functions that we obtain by operating with the operator ρ_{ij}^{α} on an arbitrary function (whose coordinates are affected by ρ_{ij}^{α}), and keeping the index j fixed. These functions are given by

$$f_{ij}^{\alpha} = \rho_{ij}^{\alpha} f = \frac{n_\alpha}{g} \sum_R \Gamma_\alpha(R)_{ij}\, Rf. \tag{3.57}$$

Let us now apply an operation S to f_{ij}^{α}. If $SR = T$,

$$\begin{aligned}
Sf_{ij}^{\alpha} &= \frac{n_\alpha}{g} \sum_R \Gamma_\alpha(R)_{ij}^{*}\, SRf \\
&= \frac{n_\alpha}{g} \sum_R \Gamma_\alpha(R)_{ij}^{*}\, Tf = \frac{n_\alpha}{g} \sum_T \Gamma_\alpha(S^{-1}T)_{ij}^{*}\, Tf \\
&= \frac{n_\alpha}{g} \sum_T \sum_m \Gamma_\alpha(S^{-1})_{im}^{*}\, \Gamma_\alpha(T)_{mj}^{*}\, Tf \\
&= \sum_m \Gamma_\alpha(S)_{mi} \left[\frac{n_\alpha}{g} \sum_T \Gamma_\alpha(T)_{mj}^{*}\, Tf \right] \\
&= \sum_m \Gamma_\alpha(S)_{mi} [\rho_{mj}^{\alpha} f] = \sum_m \Gamma_\alpha(S)_{mi}\, f_{mj}^{\alpha}.
\end{aligned} \tag{3.58}$$

We can now see that the functions f_{ij}^{α} ($i = 1, 2, \ldots, n_\alpha$; j fixed) transform irreducibly according to the representation Γ_α; moreover f_{ij}^{α} transforms according to the ith column of this representation. We can then form basis functions for an irreducible representation Γ_α by applying the projection operator (3.56) to an arbitrary function f.

Some of the properties of these operators are reported here.

1. $$\rho_{ij}^{\alpha} \rho_{kl}^{\beta} = \delta_{\alpha\beta} \delta_{kj} \rho_{il}^{\alpha}. \tag{3.59}$$

The proof follows. If $RS = T$,

$$\begin{aligned}
\rho_{ij}^{\alpha} \rho_{kl}^{\beta} &= \frac{n_\alpha}{g} \frac{n_\beta}{g} \sum_R \sum_S \Gamma_\alpha(R)_{ij}^{*}\, \Gamma_\beta(S)_{kl}^{*}\, RS \\
&= \frac{n_\alpha}{g} \frac{n_\beta}{g} \sum_R \sum_T \Gamma_\alpha(R)_{ij}^{*}\, \Gamma_\beta(R^{-1}T)_{kl}^{*}\, T \\
&= \frac{n_\alpha}{g} \frac{n_\beta}{g} \sum_R \sum_T \Gamma_\alpha(R)_{ij}^{*} \sum_m \Gamma_\beta(R^{-1})_{km}^{*}\, \Gamma_\beta(T)_{ml}^{*}\, T \\
&= \frac{n_\alpha}{g} \sum_R \sum_m \Gamma_\alpha(R)_{ij}^{*}\, \Gamma_\beta(R)_{mk}^{*} \sum_T \frac{n_\beta}{g} \Gamma_\beta(T)_{ml}^{*}\, T \\
&= \frac{n_\alpha}{g} \sum_R \sum_m \Gamma_\alpha(R)_{ij}^{*}\, \Gamma_\beta(R)_{mk}\, \rho_{ml}^{\beta} = \delta_{jk} \delta_{\alpha\beta} \rho_{il}^{\beta}.
\end{aligned}$$

In particular (3.59) gives

$$\rho_{ii}^{\alpha}\rho_{ii}^{\alpha} = [\rho_{ii}^{\alpha}]^2 = \rho_{ii}^{\alpha}. \tag{3.60}$$

2. Because of (3.59) we can derive the following property:

$$\rho_{ij}^{\alpha} f_{jr}^{\alpha} = \rho_{ij}^{\alpha}\rho_{jr}^{\alpha} f = \rho_{ir}^{\alpha} f = f_{ir}^{\alpha}. \tag{3.61}$$

This means that ρ_{ij}^{α}, when applied to a function transforming as the jth column of Γ_α, gives as a result another partner f_{ir}^{α}, transforming as the ith column of the same irreducible representation.

3. If f and g are two arbitrary functions, whose coordinates are affected by the projection operators,

$$(\rho_{ij}^{\alpha} f, \rho_{kl}^{\beta} g) = \delta_{\alpha\beta}\delta_{ki}(f, \rho_{jl}^{\alpha} g). \tag{3.62}$$

In fact, as the generic operator R is unitary,

$$\begin{aligned}
(\rho_{ij}^{\alpha} f, \rho_{kl}^{\beta} g) &= \frac{n_\alpha n_\beta}{g^2} \sum_R \sum_S \Gamma_\alpha(R)_{ij}\, \Gamma_\beta(S)_{kl}^{*}(Rf, Sg) \\
&= \frac{n_\alpha n_\beta}{g^2} \sum_R \sum_S \Gamma_\alpha(R)_{ij}\, \Gamma_\beta(S)_{kl}^{*}(f, R^{-1}Sg) \\
&= \frac{n_\alpha n_\beta}{g^2} \sum_R \sum_S \Gamma_\alpha(R^{-1})_{ij}\, \Gamma_\beta(S)_{kl}^{*}(f, RSg) \\
&= \frac{n_\alpha n_\beta}{g^2} \sum_R \sum_S \Gamma_\alpha(R)_{ji}^{*}\, \Gamma_\beta(S)_{kl}^{*}(f, RSg) \\
&= (f, \rho_{ji}^{\alpha}\rho_{kl}^{\beta} g).
\end{aligned} \tag{3.63}$$

From (3.59) we derive then (3.62).

A consequence of (3.62), if we put $g = f$, regards the functions $\rho_{ij}^{\alpha} f$ that we form by operating with the projection operators; in particular, functions belonging to different representations are orthogonal, and functions belonging to the same representation, but transforming according to different columns, are orthogonal.

4. In order to form the projection operators (3.56) we need to know all the elements of the matrix representation. We may however use other projection operators defined as follows:

$$\eta_\alpha = \sum_\alpha \frac{n_\alpha}{g} \chi_\alpha(R)^* R \tag{3.64}$$

where χ_α is the character of the representation Γ_α. η_α may be rewritten as follows:

$$\eta_\alpha = \sum_\alpha \frac{n_\alpha}{g} \sum_i \Gamma_\alpha(R)_{ii}^{*} R = \sum_i \rho_{ii}^{\alpha}. \tag{3.65}$$

Then

$$\eta_\alpha f = \sum_i \rho_{ii}^\alpha f = \sum_i \sum_R \frac{n_\alpha}{g} \Gamma_\alpha(R)_{ii}^* Rf$$

$$= \sum_R \frac{n_\alpha}{g} \chi_\alpha(R)^* Rf, \tag{3.66}$$

and

$$\sum_\alpha \eta_\alpha f = \sum_\alpha \sum_R \frac{n_\alpha}{g} \chi_\alpha(R)^* Rf = \frac{1}{g} \sum_\alpha \sum_R \chi_\alpha(E)\, \chi_\alpha(R)^* f = f, \tag{3.67}$$

because

$$\sum_\alpha \chi_\alpha(E)\, \chi_\alpha(R)^* = g \quad \text{if} \quad R = E, \text{ zero otherwise.}$$

From (3.67) we can see that $\eta_\alpha f$ contains all the parts of f which transforms irreducibly according to the representation Γ_α. If $\eta_\alpha f = 0$, f does not contain any part which transforms according to Γ_α.

5. THE FULL ROTATIONAL GROUP AND THE QUANTUM THEORY OF ANGULAR MOMENTUM

5.1 The Full Rotational Group

The *full rotational group* consists of all the real orthogonal coordinate transformations, proper and improper. Every proper orthogonal coordinate transformation is equivalent to a rotation of the coordinate system about some axis through an angle θ. Every proper or improper rotation can be put in the form (2.94) by means of a similarity transformation. The matrix which accomplishes this is a real orthogonal matrix (and itself represents a proper rotation). This means that all the rotations through a certain angle, no matter about what axis, belong to the same class. Therefore the proper rotations through a certain angle θ belong to a class; the improper rotations about an angle θ belong to a class. The full rotational group is very important in atomic physics; this group is the symmetry group of the Hamiltonian of atoms in absence of external fields.

The full rotational group may be considered as a product group of the proper coordinate transformations and of the group consisting of the identity and of the inversion operations.

The invariant subgroup of proper rotation is the group composed of all the three-dimensional rotations. This group is not Abelian; the rotation operations do not commute. For example, if we consider a rotation of 90° about the x-axis and a rotation of 90° about the y-axis, we get a result different from the one we get if we perform the operations in the reverse order.

5.2 Proper Rotations and Angular Momentum

Let us consider a rotation operator R which has the property of rotating the coordinate axes through an infinitesimal angle $\delta\alpha$ about the z-axis. We can express this operator as a power series of $\delta\alpha$, namely as

$$R(\delta\alpha) = 1 + \frac{i}{\hbar} J_z \, \delta\alpha, \tag{3.68}$$

where we have retained only the first two terms of the expansion.

A finite rotation about the axis can be expressed as $R(\alpha)$ or R_α. We find:

$$R(\alpha) = \lim_{n\to\infty} \left(1 + \frac{i}{\hbar} J_z \, \delta\alpha\right)^n = e^{(i/\hbar) J_z \alpha}. \tag{3.69}$$

As the operator $R(\delta\alpha)$ is unitary, given two functions f, g:

$$\begin{aligned}(f, g) &= (R(\delta\alpha) f, R(\delta\alpha) g) \\ &= \left(\left(1 + \frac{i}{\hbar} J_z \, \delta\alpha\right) f, \left(1 + \frac{i}{\hbar} J_z \, \delta\alpha\right) g\right) \\ &= (f, g) + \frac{i}{\hbar} \delta\alpha \, [(f, J_z g) - (J_z f, g)],\end{aligned} \tag{3.70}$$

or

$$(f, J_z g) = (J_z f, g); \tag{3.71}$$

namely J_z is a Hermitian operator.

An infinitesimal rotation $\delta\theta$ about a generic axis, whose direction cosines are n_x, n_y, n_z, can be expressed as

$$\begin{aligned}R(\mathbf{n}, \delta\theta) &= \left(1 + \frac{i}{\hbar} J_x n_x \, \delta\theta\right)\left(1 + \frac{i}{\hbar} J_y n_y \, \delta\theta\right)\left(1 + \frac{i}{\hbar} J_z n_z \, \delta\theta\right) \\ &= 1 + \frac{i}{\hbar} (\mathbf{J} \cdot \mathbf{n}) \, \delta\theta.\end{aligned} \tag{3.72}$$

A finite rotation θ about the axis $\mathbf{n}$ is given by

$$R(\mathbf{n}, \theta) = e^{(i/\hbar)(\mathbf{J}\cdot\mathbf{n})\theta}. \tag{3.73}$$

Let us now look for the commutation relation of the components of the operator $\mathbf{J}$. Let us consider a small rotation $\delta\theta$ about an axis in the xy plane, forming an infinitesimal angle $d\varphi$ with the y-axis, namely with direction cosines: $n_x = -d\varphi$, $n_y = 1$, $n_z = 0$. The rotation can be expressed as

$$1 + \frac{i}{\hbar} (J_y - J_x \, d\varphi) \, \delta\theta, \tag{3.74}$$

or, as the product of the three successive rotations

$$\left(1 - \frac{i}{\hbar} J_z \, d\varphi\right)\left(1 + \frac{i}{\hbar} J_y \, \delta\theta\right)\left(1 + \frac{i}{\hbar} J_z \, d\varphi\right). \tag{3.75}$$

Equating the two last expressions we find

$$J_y J_z - J_z J_y = i\hbar J_x, \tag{3.76}$$

or

$$[J_y, J_z] = i\hbar J_x. \tag{3.77}$$

In a similar way we can derive

$$[J_z, J_x] = i\hbar J_y \tag{3.78}$$

$$[J_x, J_y] = i\hbar J_z. \tag{3.79}$$

The last three expressions are equivalent to (1.171) which represent the commutation relations of the angular momentum components. The relation (3.73) can then be considered a general definition of an angular momentum, in the sense that it permits a generalization to systems with many interacting particles and species.

If the system is represented by a Hamiltonian which is invariant with respect to any proper rotation R, then R commutes with H

$$[R, H] = 0. \tag{3.80}$$

This implies that the three components of $\mathbf{J}$ commute with H.

Therefore the rotational invariance implies that the angular momentum is a constant of the motion.

5.3 The Irreducible Representation of the Infinite Group of Proper Rotations

The representations of the group of proper rotations can be found by using as basis functions the eigenfunctions of J^2 and of J_z.

The angular momentum operators operate on the basis functions in the following way:

$$\begin{aligned} J_z \,|jm\rangle &= m\hbar \,|jm\rangle \\ J_+ \,|jm\rangle &= \hbar\sqrt{(j-m)(j+m+1)}\,|j, m+1\rangle \\ J_- \,|jm\rangle &= \hbar\sqrt{(j+m)(j-m+1)}\,|j, m-1\rangle. \end{aligned} \tag{3.81}$$

We can divide the whole Hilbert space in subspaces of dimensions $2j + 1$ defined by the basis functions

$$|j, j\rangle, |j, j-1\rangle, \ldots, |j, -j\rangle. \tag{3.82}$$

These subspaces are invariant with respect to all the proper rotations. Therefore the representations based on these subspaces are all irreducible representations of the group of proper rotations.

Let us evaluate the characters of these representations. Let us operate with a proper rotation R_ω about the z-axis on any basis function of a subspace V_j:

$$R_\omega \,|j, m\rangle = \sum_{m'=-j}^{j} |j, m'\rangle\, D_j(R_\omega)_{m'm}$$
$$= e^{(i/\hbar)\, J_z\omega}\,|jm\rangle = e^{im\omega}\,|jm\rangle. \tag{3.83}$$

The matrix $\mathbf{D}_j(R_\omega)$ is then given by

$$D_j(R_\omega)_{m'm} = \langle jm'|\, R_\omega \,|jm\rangle = e^{im\omega}\delta_{mm'}, \tag{3.84}$$

or

$$\mathbf{D}_j(R_\omega) = \begin{vmatrix} e^{ij\omega} & 0 & \cdots & 0 \\ 0 & e^{i(j-1)\omega} & \cdots & 0 \\ \cdots & \cdots & \cdots & \cdots \\ 0 & 0 & \cdots & e^{-ij\omega} \end{vmatrix}. \tag{3.85}$$

The character of this representation is

$$\chi_j(\omega) = e^{ij\omega} + e^{i(j-1)\omega} + \cdots + e^{-ij\omega} = \frac{\sin\,(j+\frac{1}{2})\,\omega}{\sin\,\frac{1}{2}\omega}. \tag{3.86}$$

As all rotations through an angle ω belong to the same class, (3.86) represents the character of this class of operations.

The dimension of a D_j representation is $2j + 1$. j may be integer or half integer. In the latter case, something peculiar happens. We get in this case

$$\chi_j(2\pi + \omega) = \frac{\sin\,[(j+\frac{1}{2})(2\pi+\omega)]}{\sin\,[\frac{1}{2}(2\pi+\omega)]} = \frac{\sin\,(2\pi n + n\omega)}{\sin\left(\pi + \dfrac{\omega}{2}\right)} = -\chi_j(\omega),$$
$$\chi_j(2\pi - \omega) = \frac{\sin\,[(j+\frac{1}{2})(2\pi-\omega)]}{\sin\,[\frac{1}{2}(2\pi-\omega)]} = \frac{\sin\,(2\pi n - n\omega)}{\sin\left(\pi - \dfrac{\omega}{2}\right)} = -\chi_j(\omega), \tag{3.87}$$

where $n = \text{integer} = j + \frac{1}{2}$. We can rewrite (3.87) as follows:

$$\chi_j(2\pi \pm \omega) = -\chi_j(\omega). \tag{3.88}$$

We also notice

$$\chi_j(\pi) = \chi_j(2\pi - \pi) = -\chi_j(\pi) = 0, \tag{3.89}$$

and

$$\chi_j(4\pi + \omega) = \chi_j[2\pi + (2\pi + \omega)] = -\chi_j(2\pi + \omega) = \chi_j(\omega),$$
$$\chi_j(4\pi - \omega) = \chi_j[2\pi + (2\pi - \omega)] = -\chi_j(2\pi - \omega) = \chi_j(\omega). \tag{3.90}$$

Each character changes sign, as we can see from (3.88), when a rotation of 2π is added to the corresponding operation. For this reason, we say that the character is *double valued.* In the following Table 3.1 we give the characters of the double valued rotation group for certain rotational operations. To take in account the double valued representations the character of the irreducible representations of the full rotation group can be written

$$\chi_j(\omega, \sigma) = (\sigma)^{2j} \frac{\sin (j + \frac{1}{2})\,\omega}{\sin \frac{1}{2}\omega}, \tag{3.91}$$

where σ can be 1 or -1. For single valued representations $2j$ is even and $(\sigma)^{2j} = 1$; for the double valued ones $2j$ is odd and $(\sigma)^{2j} = \sigma$ namely $+1$ or -1.

5.4 The Clebsch-Gordan Coefficients and the Sum of Two Angular Momenta [3]

Given two irreducible representations D_{j_1}, D_{j_2} of the rotational group we can form their direct product representation, which is a representation, in general reducible, of the rotational group. Taking in consideration a generic rotation R_ω about an axis $\mathbf{n}$, we have

$$\mathbf{D}_{j_1}(R_\omega) \times \mathbf{D}_{j_2}(R_\omega) = e^{(i/\hbar)\,\omega(\mathbf{j}_1\cdot\mathbf{n})}e^{(i/\hbar)\,\omega(\mathbf{j}_2\cdot\mathbf{n})} = e^{(i/\hbar)\,\omega[(\mathbf{j}_1+\mathbf{j}_2)\cdot\mathbf{n}]}. \tag{3.92}$$

The problem of reducing the product representation is the same as the problem of adding two angular momenta

$$\mathbf{j} = \mathbf{j}_1 + \mathbf{j}_2. \tag{3.93}$$

The quantum number j indicates the irreducible representations contained in the direct product.

Taking in consideration the characters we have

$$\chi_{j_1}(\omega, \sigma)\,\chi_{j_2}(\omega, \sigma) = \sum_j g_{j_1 j_2 j}\chi_j(\omega, \sigma), \tag{3.94}$$

or, because of (3.91),

$$\sigma^{2(j_1+j_2)} \frac{\sin [(j_1 + \frac{1}{2})\omega] \sin [(j_2 + \frac{1}{2})\,\omega]}{\sin^2 \frac{1}{2}\omega} = \sum_j g_{j_1 j_2 j} \frac{\sin (j + \frac{1}{2})\,\omega}{\sin \frac{1}{2}\omega}. \tag{3.95}$$

From the above relation we can see that j is an integral number if $(j_1 + j_2)$ is integral (namely if j_1 and j_2 are both integral or both half integral), and that j is a half integral number, if $(j_1 + j_2)$ is half integral (namely if either j_1 or j_2 are half integral, the other being integral). On the other hand, from trigonometry we can derive

$$\sin [(j_1 + \tfrac{1}{2})\,\omega] \sin [(j_2 + \tfrac{1}{2})\,\omega] = \sum_{j=|j_1-j_2|}^{j_1+j_2} \sin [(j + \tfrac{1}{2})\,\omega] \sin \omega, \tag{3.96}$$

Table 3.1 Characters of D_j Representations*

j	0 E	360 R	60 C_6	360 + 60 $\bar{C}_6$	90 C_4	360 + 90 $\bar{C}_4$	120 C_3	360 + 120 $\bar{C}_3$	180 C_2	360 + 180 $\bar{C}_2$	260 C_3^2	360 + 260 $\bar{C}_3^2$	270 C_4^3	360 + 270 $\bar{C}_4^3$	300 C_6^5	360 + 300 $\bar{C}_6^5$
0	1	1	1	1	1	1	1	1	1	1	1	1	1	1	1	1
$\frac{1}{2}$	2	−2	$\sqrt{3}$	$-\sqrt{3}$	$\sqrt{2}$	$-\sqrt{2}$	1	−1	0	0	−1	1	$-\sqrt{2}$	$\sqrt{2}$	$-\sqrt{3}$	$\sqrt{3}$
1	3	3	2	2	1	1	0	0	−1	−1	0	0	1	1	2	2
$\frac{3}{2}$	4	−4	$\sqrt{3}$	$-\sqrt{3}$	0	0	−1	1	0	0	1	−1	0	0	$-\sqrt{3}$	$\sqrt{3}$
2	5	5	1	1	−1	−1	−1	−1	1	1	−1	−1	−1	−1	1	1
$\frac{5}{2}$	6	−6	0	0	$-\sqrt{2}$	$\sqrt{2}$	0	0	0	0	0	0	$\sqrt{2}$	$-\sqrt{2}$	0	0
3	7	7	−1	−1	−1	−1	1	1	−1	−1	1	1	−1	−1	−1	−1
$\frac{7}{2}$	8	−8	$-\sqrt{3}$	$\sqrt{3}$	0	0	1	−1	0	0	−1	1	0	0	$\sqrt{3}$	$-\sqrt{3}$
4	9	9	−2	−2	1	1	0	0	1	1	0	0	1	1	−2	−2

* The members above the different operations indicate the degrees of the corresponding angles of rotation.

and therefore

$$\chi_{j_1}\chi_{j_2} = \sum_{j=|j_1-j_2|}^{j_1+j_2} g_{j_1j_2j}\chi_j, \tag{3.97}$$

where j runs over either integral or half integral numbers from $|j_1 - j_2|$ to $j_1 + j_2$ and $g_{j_1j_2j}$ is 1, if j lies in the interval

$$j_1 + j_2, j_1 + j_2 - 1, \ldots, |j_1 - j_2| + 1, \qquad |j_1 - j_2|, \tag{3.98}$$

and zero otherwise.

We can produce the D_{j_1} and D_{j_2} representations by using as basis functions respectively eigenfunctions of j_1, j_{1z} and eigenfunctions of j_2, j_{2z}. The basis functions of the reduced space are then eigenfunctions of j, j_z. An equation similar to (3.45) can now be written:

$$f_m{}^j = \sum_{m_1m_2} T^{j_1j_2j}_{m_1m_2m} f_{m_1}{}^{j_1} f_{m_2}{}^{j_2}. \tag{3.99}$$

where $\mathbf{T}$ can be chosen to be real. In this relation $f_{m_i}{}^{j_i}$ indicates the basis function which transforms as the m_i column of the $\mathbf{D}_j$ matrix; m characterizes a particular basis function of the reduced space. Let us operate with a rotation R_ω on both members of (3.99). We get

$$e^{im\omega} f_m{}^j = \sum_{m_1m_2} T^{j_1j_2j}_{m_1m_2m} f_{m_1}{}^{j_1} f_{m_2}{}^{j_2} e^{i(m_1+m_2)\,\omega}. \tag{3.100}$$

We must then have

$$m = m_1 + m_2. \tag{3.101}$$

Inverting (3.99) we get

$$f_{m_1}{}^{j_1} f_{m_2}{}^{j_2} = \sum_{jm} T^{j_1j_2j}_{m_1m_2m} f_m{}^j, \tag{3.102}$$

where

$$m = m_1 + m_2$$

$$j = j_1 + j_2, j_1 + j_2 - 1, \ldots, |j_1 - j_2|. \tag{3.103}$$

The elements $T^{j_1j_2j}_{m_1m_2m}$ are called *Clebsch-Gordan coefficients*, and may also be written in the following way:

$$T^{j_1j_2j}_{m_1m_2m} = c(j_1j_2j;\, m_1m_2m). \tag{3.104}$$

These coefficients have the following properties:

$$c = 0 \text{ unless } \begin{array}{l} m = m_1 + m_2 \\ j = \text{one of the numbers:} \end{array} \tag{3.105}$$

$$j_1 + j_2, j_1 + j_2 - 1, \ldots, |j_1 - j_2|.$$

These properties are expressed, in short notation, as follows:

$$\Delta(j_1j_2j);\ m = m_1 + m_2. \tag{3.106}$$

5.5 The Wigner-Eckart Theorem [4–6]

A set of operators O_M^K $(M = K, K-1, \ldots, -K)$ may transform irreducibly according to the representation D_K of the full rotation double group

$$RO_M^K R^{-1} = \sum_{M'=-K}^{K} O_{M'}^J D_K(R)_{M'M}. \tag{3.107}$$

Operators of this type are called *irreducible spherical tensor operators of rank J*.

In this case the fundamental theorem's formula (3.53) takes the form

$$(f_{m'}^{\ j'}, O_M^K g_m^{\ j}) = c(jKj'; mMm') \times \text{const.} \tag{3.108}$$

The above formula expresses the *Wigner-Eckart theorem* which can be enunciated as follows:

The dependence of the matrix element $\langle \alpha j'm' |\, O_M^K \,| \alpha jm\rangle$ on quantum numbers m, m', M is contained entirely in the Clebsch-Gordan coefficients

$$\langle \alpha j'm' |\, O_M^K \,| \alpha jm\rangle = c(jKj'; mMm') \langle \alpha j' \|\, O^K \,\| \alpha j\rangle, \tag{3.109}$$

where $\langle \alpha j' \|\, O^K \,\| \alpha j\rangle$ is the so-called reduced *matrix element and depends only on $\alpha\alpha' jj'$ but not on the subscripts m, m', M.*

The reduced matrix element depends only on the radial part of the wave functions and of the operator; it is a measure of the strength of the perturbation and is connected with the physical nature of the perturbation. The Clebsch-Gordan coefficient instead depends only on the angular part of the wave functions and of the operator.

To evaluate the reduced matrix element we may proceed as follows: We calculate the matrix element $\langle \alpha' j'm' |\, O_M^K \,| \alpha jm\rangle$ once, for certain values of m' and m and then we divide the result for the Clebsch-Gordan coefficient $c(jKj'; mMm')$: in general it is advantageous to use $m' = j'$ and $m = j$. The resulting ratio is the reduced matrix element which is independent of m' and m and then can be used for any different couple of mm' numbers.

The relation (3.107) defines a tensor operator, but it is not easy, in general, to use it in order to check if a set of $2K + 1$ operators O_M^K transform irreducibly under rotation. It is entirely equivalent, however, to check the same condition for infinitesimal rotations and this corresponds, according to [4] (page 522), to checking if the operators O_M^K respect the relations

$$\begin{aligned} [J_x \pm iJ_y, O_M^K] &= \hbar\sqrt{(K \mp M)(K \pm M + 1)}\, O_{M\pm1}^K \\ [J_z, O_M^K] &= \hbar M O_M^K. \end{aligned} \tag{3.110}$$

We will give now the following examples of irreducible tensor operators of rank 1:

	$O^1_M(J)$	$O^1_M(r)$
O^1_1	$-\frac{1}{2}J_+ = -\frac{1}{2}(J_x + iJ_y)$	$-\frac{1}{2}(x + iy)$
O^0_1	J_z	z
O^1_{-1}	$\frac{1}{2}J_- = \frac{1}{2}(J_x - iJ_y)$	$\frac{1}{2}(x - iy),$

and the following examples of irreducible tensor operators of rank 2:

	$O^2_M(J)$	$O^2_M(r)$
O^2_2	$J_+{}^2$	$(x + iy)^2$
O^2_1	$-(J_zJ_+ + J_+J_z)$	$-2z(x + iy)$
O^2_0	$\sqrt{\frac{2}{3}}(3J_z{}^2 - J^2)$	$\sqrt{\frac{2}{3}}(3z^2 - r^2)$
O^2_{-1}	$J_zJ_- + J_-J_z$	$2z(x - iy)$
O^2_{-2}	$J_-{}^2$	$(x - iy)^2.$

It is easy to prove that the above operators respect the relations (3.110).

5.6 The Replacement Theorem

Let us assume that P^K_M is some component of a tensor operator P^K and Q^K_M some component of a tensor operator Q^K. From the Wigner-Eckart theorem we have:

$$\langle j'm'|\, Q^K_M \,|jm\rangle = \langle j'm'|\, P^K_M \,|jm\rangle \frac{\langle j'\|\, Q^K \,\|j\rangle}{\langle j'\|\, P^K \,\|j\rangle}. \tag{3.111}$$

If we have the following functions of the components of P^K and Q^K:

$$F(P) = \sum_M a(M)\, P^K_M \tag{3.112}$$

$$F(Q) = \sum_M a(M)\, Q^K_M, \tag{3.113}$$

we get

$$\langle j'm'|\, F(P) \,|jm\rangle = \sum_M a(M)\, c(jKj'; mMm')\, \langle j'\|\, P^K \,\|j\rangle, \tag{3.114}$$

and

$$\langle j'm'|\, F(Q) \,|jm\rangle = \sum_M a(M)\, c(jKj'; mMm')\, \langle j'\|\, Q^K \,\|j\rangle. \tag{3.115}$$

Then we can write

$$\langle j'm'|\, F(Q) \,|jm\rangle = \langle j'm'|\, F(P) \,|jm\rangle \frac{\langle j'\|\, Q^K \,\|j\rangle}{\langle j'\|\, P^K \,|j\rangle}. \tag{3.116}$$

This result expresses the so-called *Replacement theorem*:

If $F(Q)$ is an operator constructed out of components of a certain irreducible tensor operator Q and if $F(P)$ is an operator constructed out of components of another irreducible tensor operator P of the same rank, then the matrices of $F(Q)$ and $F(P)$ between two states jm, and $j'm'$ are identical, except for a multiplicative constant depending only on j, j'.

5.7 A Theorem for Irreducible Tensor Operators of Rank One

We want now to enunciate a theorem for irreducible tensors of rank one which we shall find useful in the future.

Let us consider a tensor operator $\mathbf{O}^1$ of rank one and the tensor operator $\mathbf{J}$ with components

$$
\begin{aligned}
J_1 &= -\frac{1}{\sqrt{2}}(J_x + iJ_y) \\
J_{-1} &= \frac{1}{\sqrt{2}}(J_x - iJ_y) \\
J_0 &= J_z.
\end{aligned}
\tag{3.117}
$$

Because of the Wigner-Eckart theorem,

$$\langle j'j|\, J_z\, |jj\rangle = \hbar j \delta_{jj'} = c(j1j; j0j)\, \langle j'\|\, J\, \|j\rangle. \tag{3.118}$$

From the properties of the Clebsch-Gordan coefficients

$$c(j1j; j0j) = \left(\frac{j}{j+1}\right)^{1/2}. \tag{3.119}$$

Then

$$\langle j'\|\, J\, \|j\rangle = \hbar\sqrt{j(j+1)}\,\delta_{jj'} \tag{3.120}$$

Now, because of the replacement theorem,

$$
\begin{aligned}
\langle jm'|\, O^1_M\, |jm\rangle &= \frac{\langle j\|\, O^1\, \|j\rangle}{\langle j\|\, J\, \|j\rangle}\langle jm'|\, J_M\, |jm\rangle \\
&= \frac{\langle j\|\, O^1\, \|j\rangle}{\hbar\sqrt{j(j+1)}}\langle jm'|\, J_M\, |jm\rangle.
\end{aligned}
\tag{3.121}
$$

But

$$\mathbf{J}\cdot\mathbf{O}^1 = \sum_M J_M O^1_M, \tag{3.122}$$

and

$$
\begin{aligned}
\langle jm'|\, \mathbf{J}\cdot\mathbf{O}^1\, |jm\rangle &= \langle jm'|\sum_M J_M O^1_M\, |jm\rangle \\
&= \text{const}\, \langle j\|\, O^1\, \|j\rangle.
\end{aligned}
\tag{3.123}
$$

If we replace $\mathbf{O}^1$ by $\mathbf{J}$, we find the value of this constant to be $\hbar\sqrt{j(j+1)}\,\delta_{mm'}$. Going now back to (3.121) we get

$$\langle jm'|\, O^1_M\, |jm\rangle = \frac{\langle jm|\, \mathbf{J}\cdot\mathbf{O}^1\, |jm\rangle}{\hbar^2 j(j+1)} \langle jm'|\, J_M\, |jm\rangle. \tag{3.124}$$

This formula expresses the theorem we wanted to prove.

6. THE SPIN OF THE ELECTRON AND THE DOUBLE VALUED REPRESENTATIONS

The eigenfunctions of the spin operator, in a representation in which s^2 and s_z are diagonal are given by

$$\alpha = |\tfrac{1}{2}, \tfrac{1}{2}\rangle = \begin{pmatrix}1\\0\end{pmatrix}$$
$$\beta = |\tfrac{1}{2}, -\tfrac{1}{2}\rangle = \begin{pmatrix}0\\1\end{pmatrix}. \tag{3.125}$$

These functions may be taken as basis functions for the double valued representation $D_{1/2}$ of the proper rotation double group. Let us call $u(R)$ the generic rotation operator which acts on the spinors (3.125):

$$u(R)\,|sm_s\rangle = \sum_{m_s'=-1/2}^{1/2} |sm_s'\rangle\, D_{1/2}(R)_{m_s'm_s}. \tag{3.126}$$

Let us evaluate now the matrix $\mathbf{D}_{1/2}$. For a rotation about the axis z through an angle ϵ we get from (3.85):

$$\mathbf{D}_{1/2}(\epsilon, z) = \begin{vmatrix} e^{i(1/2)\omega} & 0 \\ 0 & e^{-i(1/2)\omega} \end{vmatrix}. \tag{3.127}$$

The basis functions α and β change signs under a rotation of 2π about the z axis. The operator rotation about the axis y, through an angle η can be written

$$\begin{aligned} u(\eta, y) &= \lim_{n\to\infty}\left(1 + \frac{i}{\hbar}\frac{\eta}{n} s_y\right)^n \\ &= \mathbf{1} + \sum_n \frac{\left(\frac{i}{\hbar}\eta s_y\right)^n}{n!} = \mathbf{1} + \sum_{n\,\text{even}} \frac{\left(\frac{i}{\hbar}\eta s_y\right)^n}{n!} + \sum_{n\,\text{odd}} \frac{\left(\frac{i}{\hbar}\eta s_y\right)^n}{n!} \\ &= \mathbf{1} + \sum_{n\,\text{even}} \frac{(\frac{1}{2}i\eta)^n}{n!} + \frac{2}{\hbar} s_y \sum_{n\,\text{odd}} \frac{(\frac{1}{2}i\eta)^n}{n!} \\ &= \mathbf{1}\cos\tfrac{1}{2}\eta + i\frac{2}{\hbar} s_y \sin\tfrac{1}{2}\eta. \end{aligned} \tag{3.128}$$

where $s_y = \frac{\hbar}{2}\begin{pmatrix} 0 & -i \\ i & 0 \end{pmatrix}$ and $\mathbf{1} = \begin{pmatrix} 1 & 0 \\ 0 & 1 \end{pmatrix}$. Therefore

$$\mathbf{D}_{1/2}(\eta, y) = \begin{pmatrix} \cos \frac{1}{2}\eta & \sin \frac{1}{2}\eta \\ -\sin \frac{1}{2}\eta & \cos \frac{1}{2}\eta \end{pmatrix}. \tag{3.129}$$

A physical rotation through an angle ω about a generic axis $\mathbf{n}$ can be expressed as product of rotations through the Euler angles: (a) rotation about the axis z through an angle ϵ; (b) rotation about the new axis y through an angle η, and (c) rotation about the final axis z through an angle θ:

$$\text{Rot}\,(\omega, \mathbf{n}) = \text{Rot}\,(\theta, z)\,\text{Rot}\,(\eta, y)\,\text{Rot}\,(\epsilon, z). \tag{3.130}$$

But a physical rotation through an angle ω is equivalent to a rotation of the coordinate system through an angle $-\omega$:

$$u(-\omega, \mathbf{n}) = u(-\theta, z)\,u(-\eta, y)\,u(-\epsilon, z) \tag{3.131}$$

and

$$u(\omega, \mathbf{n}) = u(\epsilon, z)\,u(\eta, y)\,u(\theta, z). \tag{3.132}$$

Therefore

$$\mathbf{D}_{1/2}(\omega,\mathbf{n}) = \pm\begin{pmatrix} e^{i(1/2)\epsilon} & 0 \\ 0 & e^{-i(1/2)\epsilon} \end{pmatrix}\begin{pmatrix} \cos \frac{1}{2}\eta & \sin \frac{1}{2}\eta \\ -\sin \frac{1}{2}\eta & \cos \frac{1}{2}\eta \end{pmatrix}\begin{pmatrix} e^{i(1/2)\theta} & 0 \\ 0 & e^{-i(1/2)\theta} \end{pmatrix}$$

$$= \pm\begin{pmatrix} e^{(i/2)(\epsilon+\theta)} \cos \frac{1}{2}\eta & e^{(i/2)(\epsilon-\theta)} \sin \frac{1}{2}\eta \\ -e^{-(i/2)(\epsilon-\theta)} \sin \frac{1}{2}\eta & e^{-(i/2)(\epsilon+\theta)} \cos \frac{1}{2}\eta \end{pmatrix}, \tag{3.133}$$

where the $\pm$ sign indicates that an addition of 2π to any of the angles ϵ, η, θ changes the sign of the matrix.

The character of this representation is given by

$$\chi(u) = -\chi(\bar{u}) = 2 \cos \tfrac{1}{2}\eta \cos \tfrac{1}{2}(\epsilon + \theta), \tag{3.134}$$

where u indicates a generic rotation about an axis $\mathbf{n}$ through an angle ω defined by the Euler angles ϵ, η, and θ of the new coordinate system with respect to the old and $\bar{u}$ represents a rotation about the same axis through an angle $2\pi + \omega$.

Since the rotations u and $\bar{u}$ have in general different characters, they belong to different classes. An exception is the case in which $\omega = \pi$. In this case $\chi(u) = \chi(\bar{u}) = 0$.

If we consider a symmetry group g of proper rotations, we can see that any element of g is represented by two matrices (3.133), one with the plus, the other with the minus sign. These matrices satisfy all the group requirements, and form a group G which has twice as many elements as g and is called the *double group* of g. The representations of G represent the *double valued* representations of g.

The irreducible representations of G can be found with the usual method used for any group. If we consider the element $\bar{E}$ of G we find that it commutes with all the other elements of G and therefore is, because of Schur's lemma, represented by the product of a constant by the unit matrix representing E:

$$\bar{E} = cE \tag{3.135}$$

We have also

$$(\bar{E})^2 = E, \tag{3.136}$$

and then

$$c^2 = 1; \qquad c = \pm 1.$$

Namely we can have

$$\bar{E} = E \quad \text{or} \quad \bar{E} = -E. \tag{3.137}$$

Also for a generic rotation,

$$\bar{R} = \bar{E}R = R \quad \text{or} \quad \bar{R} = \bar{E}R = -R, \tag{3.138}$$

and

$$\chi(\bar{R}) = \chi(R) \quad \text{or} \quad \chi(\bar{R}) = -\chi(R). \tag{3.139}$$

The case in which $c = 1$ gives representations of G which are also the single valued representations of g; for these representations $\chi(\bar{R}) = \chi(R)$. The case $c = -1$ gives the double representations of g; for these representations $\chi(\bar{R}) = -\chi(R)$.

The matrices $\mathbf{D}_{1/2}$ given by (3.133) form also a representation of G, reducible or irreducible. The characters of this representation are given by (3.134). Therefore, in general, two rotations R and $\bar{R}$ belong to different classes of G and their characters are opposite in sign. If, however, the rotations are through an angle π, the character (3.134) becomes zero; in this case R and $\bar{R}$ may or may not belong to the same class of G.

Let us consider a rotation through an angle π about the z axis. The matrix (3.133) which represents this rotation is given by:

$$\mathbf{D}_{1/2}(\pi, z) = \begin{pmatrix} i & 0 \\ 0 & -i \end{pmatrix}. \tag{3.140}$$

If R and $\bar{R}$ belong to the same class, then there must exist some element T of G such that

$$T\bar{R}T^{-1} = R, \tag{3.141}$$

or

$$T\begin{pmatrix} -i & 0 \\ 0 & i \end{pmatrix} = \begin{pmatrix} i & 0 \\ 0 & -i \end{pmatrix}T. \tag{3.142}$$

This element is represented by the matrix

$$\begin{pmatrix} 0 & 1 \\ -1 & 0 \end{pmatrix} \tag{3.143}$$

which gives a rotation of 180° about the y axis. Therefore, if R represents a rotation about a certain axis through an angle of 180°, R and $\bar{R}$ belong to the same class, if there is in the group another rotation through 180° about an axis perpendicular to the axis of R.

We have considered until now groups of proper rotations. A group which contains improper rotations is either the product of a group containing only proper rotations by a group formed by the element E (identity) and I (inversion) or is isomorphic with a group containing only proper rotations. In the former case, we can form the double group by using the procedure of Sec. 8 of Ch. 2; in the latter case the double valued representations are given by the double valued representations of the isomorphic group.

Example: Group D_3

The operations of this group consist of

E: identity
C_3, C_3^2: rotations about a threefold axis
$C'_{2,1}, C'_{2,2}, C'_{2,3}$: 180° rotations about three axis at 120° among each other and laying on a plane perpendicular to the threefold axis.

The character table of the single valued representations is given by

	E	$2C_3$	$3C'_2$
Γ_1	1	1	1
Γ_2	1	1	-1
Γ_3	2	-1	0

The identity, the threefold rotations and the 180° rotations belong to three distinct classes.

The elements of the double group are 12. Since the single valued representations are two of order 1 and one of order 2, we expect two double valued representations of order 1 and one of order 2 to fulfill the condition (2.79). In total we shall obtain 6 representations and 6 classes.

In order to regroup the 12 elements of the double group in classes we notice that, among the elements of D_3, there is no 180° rotation about any axis perpendicular to any C'_2 axis. For this reason the operations C'_2 and $\overline{C'_2}$ must belong to two different classes.

The multiplication relations among the different elements of the group help in the calculations of the characters for the double valued representations of order 1. In particular we have

$$(C'_2)^2 = \bar{E},$$

and then

$$\chi(C'_2) = -\chi(\overline{C'_2}) = \pm i.$$

Moreover

$$(C_3)^5 = \overline{C_3{}^2}; \qquad (C_3{}^2)^2 = \overline{C_3};$$

$$(C_3)^3 = \bar{E}; \qquad (\overline{C_3})^3 = C_3{}^6 = E.$$

The characters of the double valued representation of order 2 can be derived from the orthogonality relations. We have then the following character table for the double D_3 group

D_3	E	$\bar{E}$	$C_3, \overline{C_3^2}$	$\overline{C_3}, C_3^2$	$3C_2'$	$\overline{3C_2'}$	
Γ_1	1	1	1	1	1	1	
Γ_2	1	1	1	1	-1	-1	single valued
Γ_3	2	2	-1	-1	0	0	
Γ_4	1	-1	-1	1	i	$-i$	
Γ_5	1	-1	-1	1	$-i$	i	double valued
Γ_6	2	-2	1	-1	0	0	

We notice that the group C_{3v}, which contains three improper rotations, is isomorphic with D_3 and therefore its character table is also given by the above table.

7. THE KRAMERS' DEGENERACY

A *time inversion operation* is an operation which causes the replacement of the time variable by its negative:

$$t \rightarrow -t. \tag{3.144}$$

Let us consider a one-electron system. The eigenfunction of such a system is in general given by

$$\psi(\mathbf{r}, \sigma) = \psi_\alpha(\mathbf{r})\, \alpha + \psi_\beta(\mathbf{r})\, \beta, \tag{3.145}$$

and the Hamiltonian by

$$H(\mathbf{r}, \mathbf{p}, \boldsymbol{\sigma}) = H_0(\mathbf{r}, \mathbf{p}) + H_x(\mathbf{r}, \mathbf{p})\, \sigma_x + H_y(\mathbf{r}, \mathbf{p})\, \sigma_y + H_z(\mathbf{r}, \mathbf{p})\, \sigma_z. \tag{3.146}$$

There will not be higher powers of σ_x, σ_y, and σ_z. Here σ_x, σ_y, and σ_z are given by the *Pauli matrices*

$$\sigma_x = \begin{pmatrix} 0 & 1 \\ 1 & 0 \end{pmatrix}; \quad \sigma_y = \begin{pmatrix} 0 & -i \\ i & 0 \end{pmatrix}; \quad \sigma_z = \begin{pmatrix} 1 & 0 \\ 0 & -1 \end{pmatrix}. \tag{3.147}$$

We claim now that the *time inversion operator* is given by

$$K = i\sigma_y C = \begin{pmatrix} 0 & 1 \\ -1 & 0 \end{pmatrix} C, \tag{3.148}$$

where C is the operator which makes what comes after complex.

We have

$$\begin{aligned} C\psi(\mathbf{r}) &= \psi^*(\mathbf{r}) \\ CHC^{-1} &= H^*. \end{aligned} \tag{3.149}$$

But

$$C^2 = 1; \tag{3.150}$$

then

$$C = C^{-1}. \tag{3.151}$$

Other relations are

$$\begin{aligned} \mathbf{p} &= -i\hbar\nabla \\ C\mathbf{p}C^{-1} &= i\hbar\nabla = -\mathbf{p}, \end{aligned} \tag{3.152}$$

$$\begin{aligned} \mathbf{l} &= \mathbf{r} \times \mathbf{p} \\ C\mathbf{l}C^{-1} &= -\mathbf{l} \end{aligned} \tag{3.153}$$

and

$$\begin{aligned} C\sigma_x C^{-1} &= \sigma_x \\ C\sigma_y C^{-1} &= -\sigma_y \\ C\sigma_z C^{-1} &= \sigma_z. \end{aligned} \tag{3.154}$$

Therefore,

$$CHC^{-1} = H_0(\mathbf{r}, -\mathbf{p}) + H_x(\mathbf{r}, -\mathbf{p})\,\sigma_x + H_z(\mathbf{r}, -p)\,\sigma_z - H_y(\mathbf{r}, -\mathbf{p})\,\sigma_y. \tag{3.155}$$

On the other hand

$$(i\sigma_y)^2 = \begin{pmatrix} 0 & 1 \\ -1 & 0 \end{pmatrix}\begin{pmatrix} 0 & 1 \\ -1 & 0 \end{pmatrix} = \begin{pmatrix} -1 & 0 \\ 0 & -1 \end{pmatrix}, \tag{3.156}$$

and

$$(i\sigma_y)^{-1} = -i\sigma_y. \tag{3.157}$$

Therefore

$$K^{-1} = (i\sigma_y C)^{-1} = C^{-1}(i\sigma_y)^{-1} = -Ci\sigma_y, \tag{3.158}$$

and

$$\begin{aligned} KHK^{-1} &= -i\sigma_y CHC^{-1} i\sigma_y = \sigma_y CHC^{-1}\sigma_y \\ &= H_0(\mathbf{r}, -\mathbf{p}) + H_x(\mathbf{r}, -p)\,\sigma_y\sigma_x\sigma_y \\ &\qquad + H_z(\mathbf{r}, -\mathbf{p})\,\sigma_y\sigma_z\sigma_y - H_y(\mathbf{r}, -\mathbf{p})\,\sigma_y\sigma_y\sigma_y. \end{aligned} \tag{3.159}$$

But

$$\begin{aligned} \sigma_y\sigma_x\sigma_y &= (\sigma_y\sigma_x)\,\sigma_y = -\sigma_x\sigma_y\sigma_y = -\sigma_x \\ \sigma_y\sigma_y\sigma_y &= (\sigma_y)^2\,\sigma_y = \sigma_y \\ \sigma_y\sigma_z\sigma_y &= -\sigma_z(\sigma_y)^2 = -\sigma_z. \end{aligned} \tag{3.160}$$

Then

$$KHK^{-1} = H_0(\mathbf{r}, -\mathbf{p}) - H_x(\mathbf{r}, -\mathbf{p})\,\sigma_x - H_y(\mathbf{r}, -\mathbf{p})\,\sigma_y - H_z(\mathbf{r}, -\mathbf{p})\,\sigma_z. \tag{3.161}$$

With this we have shown that K is in fact the time inversion operator.

We notice that K is not a linear operator. In fact

$$K(a\psi + b\varphi) = a^*K\psi + b^*K\varphi. \tag{3.162}$$

Also, it is not unitary,

$$(K\psi, K\varphi) = (i\sigma_y C\psi, i\sigma_y C\varphi) = (C\psi, C\varphi) = (\psi, \varphi)^*. \tag{3.163}$$

In general, for a system with n electrons, the time inversion operator can be written as follows

$$K = i^n \sigma_{y1}\, \sigma_{y2} \cdots \sigma_{yn} C. \tag{3.164}$$

If the Hamiltonian of the system is time-invariant

$$KHK^{-1} = H \quad \text{or} \quad KH = HK, \tag{3.165}$$

namely K commutes with H. In this case, operating with K on both sides of the Schrödinger equation we get

$$KH\psi = H(K\psi) = E(K\psi). \tag{3.166}$$

$K\psi$ represents an eigenstate of H with the same energy of ψ. $K\psi$ may be a multiple of ψ:

$$K\psi = a\psi. \tag{3.167}$$

In this case ψ and $K\psi$ represent the same state. Also

$$K(K\psi) = K^2\psi = Ka\psi = a^*K\psi = |a|^2\, \psi. \tag{3.168}$$

We have, on the other hand

$$K^2 = (i^n \sigma_{y1}\, \sigma_{y2} \cdots \sigma_{yn})(i^n \sigma_{y1}\, \sigma_{y2} \cdots \sigma_{yn}) = (-1)^n. \tag{3.169}$$

Therefore it is

$$|a|^2 = (-1)^n. \tag{3.170}$$

This relation and (3.167) from which it is derived cannot be valid if n is odd. For n odd then $K\psi \neq a\psi$ and ψ and $K\psi$ represent two different eigenstates corresponding to a degenerate eigenvalue of H.

We can now enunciate the following *Kramers' theorem*:

If the number of electrons of an atomic system is odd, time-invariant perturbations will not remove the degeneracy completely as a twofold degeneracy of each level will remain.

We can recapitulate the situation as follows:

$$K^2 = 1 \qquad n \text{ even} \qquad K\psi = a\psi$$

$$K^2 = -1 \qquad n \text{ odd} \qquad K\psi \neq a\psi.$$

Let us consider more generally the degeneracies brought about by the time inversion symmetry of the Hamiltonian.

If we have a set of wavefunctions ψ_i^α transforming irreducibly according to a certain representation Γ_α of a group G, for the generic operation R of G,

$$R\psi_i^\alpha = \sum_j \psi_j^\alpha \Gamma_\alpha(R)_{ji}. \tag{3.171}$$

We have also:

$$KR\psi_i^\alpha = R(K\psi_i^\alpha) = \sum_j (K\psi_j^\alpha)\,\Gamma_\alpha^*(R)_{ji}, \tag{3.172}$$

if K and R commute. The functions $K\psi_i^\alpha$ form basis for the representation $\Gamma_\alpha^*(R)$. These functions, because of the time inversion symmetry, have the same energy of the functions ψ_i^α. The question is: are the two sets of functions linearly independent? If they are, Kramers' degeneracy is present in the system.

If the representations Γ_α and Γ_α^* are not equivalent

$$\chi_\alpha(R) \neq \chi_\alpha^*(R); \tag{3.173}$$

then the two sets are linearly independent. The representations Γ_α and Γ_α^* occur always together with the same energy giving rise to Kramers' degeneracy. Two complex representations are always degenerate if the Hamiltonian is time-invariant; for this reason they are shown sometimes bracketed together.

If the representations Γ_α and Γ_α^* are equivalent we have to distinguish the case of even number of electrons ($K^2 = 1$) from the case of odd number of electrons ($K^2 = -1$). The following result will be given here without proof [1].

For $K^2 = 1$ (even number of electrons) the sets ψ_i^α and $K\psi_i^\alpha$ are linearly independent, and therefore Kramers' degeneracy is present if Γ_α, Γ_α^* (which are equivalent) *cannot* be made real; for $K^2 = -1$ (odd number of electrons) Kramers' degeneracy is present if Γ_α and Γ_α^* can be made equal to the same *real* representation.

The above result has to be accompanied by a criterion to test the different cases. This criterion was given by Frobenius and Schur [7] and is here stated without proof:

$$\text{If} \quad \sum_R \chi_\alpha(R^2) = \begin{cases} 0, & \Gamma_\alpha, \Gamma_\alpha^* \text{ inequivalent,} \\ g, & \Gamma_\alpha, \Gamma_\alpha^* \text{ equivalent and can be made real,} \\ -g, & \Gamma_\alpha, \Gamma_\alpha^* \text{ equivalent, but cannot be made real.} \end{cases} \tag{3.174}$$

The results of this section are summarized in the following table:

Relation between Γ_α and Γ_α^*	$\sum_R \chi(R^2)$	$K^2 = 1$ (even number of electrons)	$K^2 = -1$ (odd number of electrons)
Γ_α inequivalent to Γ_α^*	0	Doubled degeneracy	Doubled degeneracy
Γ_α, Γ_α^* equivalent, can be made real	g	No extra degeneracy	Doubled degeneracy
Γ_α, Γ_α^* equivalent, cannot be made real	$-g$	Doubled degeneracy	No extra degeneracy

The consequences of the time inversion of the Hamiltonian in the case of point group symmetry are, in brief, the following:

1. States belonging to complex conjugate representations are degenerate. This result is valid for both single valued (even number of electrons) or double valued (odd number of electrons) representations.

2. The double valued representations S_{3g} and S_{3u} of the group S_6 and the double valued representation S_3 of the group C_3 occur always twice.[1] These are the only examples of the case

$$K^2 = -1, \qquad \sum_R \chi(R^2) = g.$$

3. There is no example in the single-valued representations of point groups of a representation equivalent to its complex conjugate but not equivalent to a real representation:

$$K^2 = -1, \qquad \sum_R \chi(R^2) = -g$$

never occurs in point groups.

Let us illustrate what we have found with a couple of examples.

Example: Group C_2

The character table is given by

C_2		E	$\bar{E}$	C_2	$\bar{C}_2$	$\sum_R \chi(R^2)$
$K^2 = 1$	Γ_1	1	1	1	1	4
	Γ_2	1	1	-1	-1	4
$K^2 = -1$	Γ_3	1	-1	$-i$	i	0
	Γ_4	1	-1	i	$-i$	0

[1] A character table for this group, along with character tables for all the point groups, can be found in [8].

where the numbers in the last column are easily calculated by taking the following in account:

$$E^2 = (\bar{E})^2 = E,$$

$$C_2^{\,2} = (\bar{C}_2)^2 = \bar{E}.$$

The four representations can now be placed in the following table which illustrates their properties.

Relation between Γ_α and Γ_α^*	$\sum_R \chi(R^2)$	$k^2 = 1$ (even number of electrons)	$k^2 = -1$ (odd number of electrons)
Γ_α inequivalent to Γ_α^*	0	Doubled degeneracy	Γ_3, Γ_4: doubled degeneracy
Γ_α, Γ_α^* equivalent, can be made real	g	Γ_1, Γ_2: no extra degeneracy	Doubled degeneracy
Γ_α, Γ_α^* equivalent, cannot be made real	$-g$	Doubled degeneracy	No extra degeneracy

No extra degeneracy is introduced by the time invariance in the single-valued representations. On the contrary, if a state is represented by $\Gamma_3(\Gamma_4)$, its time inverse $\Gamma_3^* = \Gamma_4$ $(\Gamma_4^* = \Gamma_3)$ is also present as a degenerate state.

Example: Group D_2

The character table is given by

		E	$\bar{E}$	$C_{2x}, \bar{C}_{2x}$	$C_{2y}, \bar{C}_{2y}$	$C_{2z}, \bar{C}_{2z}$	$\sum_R \chi(R^2)$
$K^2 = 1$	Γ_1	1	1	1	1	1	8
	Γ_2	1	1	1	-1	-1	8
	Γ_3	1	1	-1	1	-1	8
	Γ_4	1	1	-1	-1	1	8
$K^2 = -1$	Γ_5	2	-2	0	0	0	-8

where the numbers of the last column are calculated taking the following in account

$$E^2 = (\bar{E})^2 = E$$

$$C_{2x}^{\;2} = (\bar{C}_{2x})^2 = C_{2y}^{\;2} = (\bar{C}_{2y})^2 = C_{2z}^{\;2} = (\bar{C}_{2z})^2 = \bar{E}.$$

The five representations can now be placed in the following table which illustrates their properties:

Relation between Γ_α and Γ_α^*	$\sum_R \chi(R^2)$	$k^2 = 1$ (even number of electrons)	$k^2 = -1$ (odd number of electrons)
Γ_α inequivalent to Γ_α^*	0	Doubled degeneracy	Doubled degeneracy
Γ_α, Γ_α^* equivalent, can be made real	g	$\Gamma_1, \Gamma_2, \Gamma_3, \Gamma_4$: no extra degeneracy	Doubled degeneracy
Γ_α, Γ_α^* equivalent, cannot be made real	$-g$	Doubled degeneracy	Γ_5: no extra degeneracy

8. THE SYMMETRIC GROUP OF THE HAMILTONIAN AND THE PAULI PRINCIPLE

8.1 The Structure of the Symmetric Groups

Given an ensemble of n numbers, a *permutation* is an operation which rearranges these numbers. The following symbol:

$$P = \begin{pmatrix} 1 & 2 & 3 & \cdots & n \\ a_1 & a_2 & a_3 & \cdots & a_n \end{pmatrix} \tag{3.175}$$

indicates a permutation which replaces 1 by a_1, 2 by a_2 and so on, $a_1, a_2, \ldots, a_n$ being distinct integers taken from the ensemble $1, 2, \ldots, n$.

The operation *identity* is indicated by

$$E = \begin{pmatrix} 1 & 2 & 3 & \cdots & n \\ 1 & 2 & 3 & \cdots & n \end{pmatrix}. \tag{3.176}$$

The operations which produce the $n!$ permutations of the n numbers form a group which is called the *symmetric group of degree n*.

The symmetric groups have the following properties:

1. A generic permutation can be decomposed into *cycles*. A cycle is a permutation in which each element is replaced by the element following it; for example, the permutation

$$P = \begin{pmatrix} 1 & 2 & 3 & 4 & 5 & 6 & 7 \\ 2 & 3 & 5 & 7 & 1 & 6 & 4 \end{pmatrix} \tag{3.177}$$

can be decomposed in three cycles, as follows:

$$P = \begin{pmatrix} 1 & 2 & 3 & 4 & 5 & 6 & 7 \\ 2 & 3 & 5 & 7 & 1 & 6 & 4 \end{pmatrix} = (1 \quad 2 \quad 3 \quad 5)\,(4 \quad 7)\,(6). \qquad (3.178)$$

The decomposition of a permutation into cycles is unique.

2. Permutations with the same cycle structure belong to the same class.

Given a permutation P, the conjugate of P with respect to any other permutation T gives the same cycle structure as P. If T, for example, is

$$T = \begin{pmatrix} 1 & 2 & 3 & 4 & 5 & 6 & 7 \\ 5 & 6 & 1 & 2 & 7 & 3 & 4 \end{pmatrix} \qquad (3.179)$$

and P is given by (3.177), we obtain:

$$T^{-1}PT = \begin{pmatrix} 1 & 2 & 3 & 4 & 5 & 6 & 7 \\ 3 & 4 & 6 & 7 & 1 & 2 & 5 \end{pmatrix}\begin{pmatrix} 1 & 2 & 3 & 4 & 5 & 6 & 7 \\ 2 & 3 & 5 & 7 & 1 & 6 & 4 \end{pmatrix}\begin{pmatrix} 1 & 2 & 3 & 4 & 5 & 6 & 7 \\ 5 & 6 & 1 & 2 & 7 & 3 & 4 \end{pmatrix}$$

$$= \begin{pmatrix} 1 & 2 & 3 & 4 & 5 & 6 & 7 \\ 7 & 4 & 3 & 2 & 6 & 1 & 5 \end{pmatrix} = (1 \quad 7 \quad 5 \quad 6)(2 \quad 4)(3). \qquad (3.180)$$

3. The numbers of different cycle structures is equal to the number of classes. For a symmetric group of degree n, this is the number of ways n can be decomposed in a sum of positive integers; the generic cycle structure may be indicated by the decomposition

$$n = l_1 + 2l_2 + 3l_3 + \cdots + nl_n, \qquad (3.181)$$

where $l_1, l_2, \ldots, l_n$ are respectively the numbers of times the cycles of lengths $1, 2, \ldots, n$ are present in the cycle structure.

The number of elements in a class is given by the number of permutations with a certain cycle structure. For a cycle structure such as (3.181) this number is given by

$$\frac{n!}{1^{l_1}l_1!\,2^{l_2}l_2!\cdots n^{l_n}l_n!}. \qquad (3.182)$$

In case of the group of order 3 we have the following decomposition:

(a) $3 = 3$ No. of elements $= 2$: $(1 \quad 2 \quad 3)$; $(1 \quad 3 \quad 2)$
(b) $3 = 2 + 1$ No. of elements $= 3$: $(2 \quad 3)(1)$; $(1 \quad 3)(2)$; $(1 \quad 2)(3)$
(c) $3 = 1 + 1 + 1$ No. of elements $= 1$: $(1)(2)(3)$.

The second class contains the *transpositions*, namely the permutations which involve the exchange of the positions of two numbers. The total number of elements is $6 = 3!$ The symmetric group of degree 3, is isomorphic with the C_{3v} group of the equilateral triangle. We can establish a one to one correspondence between the symmetry operations of C_{3v} and the permutations of the symmetric group of degree 3, with only one element of a group corresponding to one element of the other group.

Because of this correspondence we may now set up the table for the irreducible representations of the symmetric group 3!, which is essentially equal to the table for the group C_{3v} reported in Sec. 3 of Ch. 2.

	P_1	P_2	P_3	P_4	P_5	P_6
	$\begin{pmatrix}1&2&3\\1&2&3\end{pmatrix}$	$\begin{pmatrix}1&2&3\\2&3&1\end{pmatrix}$	$\begin{pmatrix}1&2&3\\3&1&2\end{pmatrix}$	$\begin{pmatrix}1&2&3\\1&3&2\end{pmatrix}$	$\begin{pmatrix}1&2&3\\3&2&1\end{pmatrix}$	$\begin{pmatrix}1&2&3\\2&1&3\end{pmatrix}$
Γ_1	1	1	1	1	1	1
Γ_2	1	1	1	−1	−1	−1
Γ_3	$\begin{pmatrix}1&0\\0&1\end{pmatrix}$	$\begin{pmatrix}-\frac{1}{2}&\frac{\sqrt{3}}{2}\\-\frac{\sqrt{3}}{2}&-\frac{1}{2}\end{pmatrix}$	$\begin{pmatrix}-\frac{1}{2}&-\frac{\sqrt{3}}{2}\\\frac{\sqrt{3}}{2}&-\frac{1}{2}\end{pmatrix}$	$\begin{pmatrix}1&0\\0&-1\end{pmatrix}$	$\begin{pmatrix}-\frac{1}{2}&\frac{\sqrt{3}}{2}\\\frac{\sqrt{3}}{2}&\frac{1}{2}\end{pmatrix}$	$\begin{pmatrix}-\frac{1}{2}&-\frac{\sqrt{3}}{2}\\-\frac{\sqrt{3}}{2}&\frac{1}{2}\end{pmatrix}$

4. Any cyclic permutation can be decomposed into a product of transpositions; a transposition is a cyclic permutation of length 2:

$$(a_1 a_2 \cdots a_n) = (a_1 a_2)(a_2 a_3)(a_3 a_4) \cdots (a_{n-1} a_n). \tag{3.183}$$

As every permutation can be decomposed in cycles, then any permutation can also be expressed as a product of transpositions.

5. A permutation which can be decomposed in an odd number of transpositions is called *odd*; a permutation which can be decomposed in an even number of transpositions is called *even*. In a symmetric group of order n, the collection of all even permutations is an invariant subgroup of order $n!/2$, which is called *alternating group*.

6. In a symmetric group, one representation, which is called *symmetric*, has all elements equal to 1. Another representation, which is called *antisymmetric*, has 1 in correspondence to the even permutations and -1 in correspondence to the odd permutations. No other one-dimensional representation is present in a symmetric group.

8.2 The Pauli Principle [9]

Let us consider an atomic system with n electrons, whose Hamiltonian H is invariant under the symmetry operations of a group G. The wave functions representing the system are basis functions for the irreducible representations of G. An eigenfunction, belonging to the eigenvalue E_l of the energy, is a solution of the equation

$$H\psi(1, 2, \ldots, n) = E_l\psi(1, 2, \ldots, n) \tag{3.184}$$

where $1, 2, \ldots, n$ stand for all the coordinates (spin included) of respectively electron $1, 2, \ldots, n$.

However, because of the identity of the particles-electrons, the Hamiltonian is also invariant under all the permutations of the symmetric group $\mathcal{S}$ of order n and the eigenfunction must also form basis for the irreducible representations of this group. We can form these basis functions by using the formula

$$\psi_{iq}{}^{\alpha} = \rho_{iq}{}^{\alpha}\psi(1, 2, \ldots, n) = \frac{n_\alpha}{g}\sum_P \Gamma_\alpha(P)^*_{iq}\, P\psi(1, 2, \ldots, n), \tag{3.185}$$

which is equivalent to (3.57).

If we consider, as an example, an atomic system with three electrons, the eigenfunctions must form basis for the representations whose table has been given in page 136. We have, using the same table,

$$\begin{aligned}
\rho_{11}{}^1 &= \tfrac{1}{6}[P_1 + P_2 + P_3 + P_4 + P_5 + P_6] \\
\rho_{11}{}^2 &= \tfrac{1}{6}[P_1 + P_2 + P_3 - P_4 - P_5 - P_6] \\
\rho_{11}{}^3 &= \tfrac{1}{3}[P_1 - \tfrac{1}{2}P_2 - \tfrac{1}{2}P_3 + P_4 - \tfrac{1}{2}P_5 - \tfrac{1}{2}P_6] \\
\rho_{21}{}^3 &= \frac{1}{3}\left[-\frac{\sqrt{3}}{2}P_2 + \frac{\sqrt{3}}{2}P_3 + \frac{\sqrt{3}}{2}P_5 - \frac{\sqrt{3}}{2}P_6\right] \\
\rho_{12}{}^3 &= \frac{1}{3}\left[\frac{\sqrt{3}}{2}P_2 - \frac{\sqrt{3}}{2}P_3 + \frac{\sqrt{3}}{2}P_5 - \frac{\sqrt{3}}{2}P_6\right] \\
\rho_{22}{}^3 &= \tfrac{1}{3}[P_1 - \tfrac{1}{2}P_2 - \tfrac{1}{2}P_3 - P_4 + \tfrac{1}{2}P_5 + \tfrac{1}{2}P_6].
\end{aligned} \tag{3.186}$$

From each solution of (3.184) we may then derive the following possible eigenfunctions:

$$\begin{aligned}
\rho_{11}{}^1\psi(1,2,3) &= \tfrac{1}{6}[\psi(1,2,3) + \psi(2,3,1) + \psi(3,1,2) \\
&\qquad + \psi(1,3,2) + \psi(3,2,1) + \psi(2,1,3)] \\
\rho_{11}{}^2\psi(1,2,3) &= \tfrac{1}{6}[\psi(1,2,3) + \psi(2,3,1) + \psi(3,1,2) \\
&\qquad - \psi(1,3,2) - \psi(3,2,1) - \psi(2,1,3)] \\
\rho_{11}{}^3\psi(1,2,3) &= \tfrac{1}{3}[\psi(1,2,3) - \tfrac{1}{2}\psi(2,3,1) - \tfrac{1}{2}\psi(3,1,2) \\
&\qquad + \psi(1,3,2) - \tfrac{1}{2}\psi(3,2,1) - \tfrac{1}{2}\psi(2,1,3)] \\
\rho_{21}{}^3\psi(1,2,3) &= \frac{1}{3}\left[-\frac{\sqrt{3}}{2}\psi(2,3,1) + \frac{\sqrt{3}}{2}\psi(3,1,2)\right. \\
&\qquad \left. + \frac{\sqrt{3}}{2}\psi(3,2,1) - \frac{\sqrt{3}}{2}\psi(2,1,3)\right] \\
\rho_{12}{}^3\psi(1,2,3) &= \frac{1}{3}\left[\frac{\sqrt{3}}{2}\psi(2,3,1) - \frac{\sqrt{3}}{2}\psi(3,1,2)\right. \\
&\qquad \left. + \frac{\sqrt{3}}{2}\psi(3,2,1) - \frac{\sqrt{3}}{2}\psi(2,1,3)\right] \\
\rho_{22}{}^3\psi(1,2,3) &= \tfrac{1}{3}[\psi(1,2,3) - \tfrac{1}{2}\psi(2,3,1) - \tfrac{1}{2}\psi(3,1,2) \\
&\qquad - \psi(1,3,2) + \tfrac{1}{2}\psi(3,2,1) + \tfrac{1}{2}\psi(2,1,3)].
\end{aligned} \tag{3.187}$$

$\rho_{11}{}^1\psi(1,2,3)$ transforms irreducibly according to the symmetric representation of $\mathfrak{T}$, $\rho_{11}{}^2\psi(1,2,3)$ according to the antisymmetric representation;

$\rho_{11}{}^3\psi(1,2,3)$ and $\rho_{21}{}^3\psi(1,2,3)$ transform according to the representation Γ_3 of $\mathfrak{T}$; the same can be said of $\rho_{12}{}^3\psi(1,2,3)$ and $\rho_{22}{}^3\psi(1,2,3)$.[2]

At this point we can introduce the *Pauli Principle* which states the following:

In nature only antisymmetric states of an electronic systems do really occur.

This means, in other words, that the allowed eigenfunctions must change sign under an odd permutation or that every eigenfunction must be a basis for the antisymmetrical representation of the symmetric group of the Hamiltonian.

In the example of the three electrons system the acceptable eigenfunctions are all of the type $\rho_{11}{}^2\psi(1,2,3)$. All the other possible combinations have to be discarded. In general we can say that, if we indicate by Γ_2 the antisymmetric representation of the symmetric group, only the functions $\rho_{11}{}^2\psi$, ψ being a solution of the Schrödinger equation, are acceptable.

The operator $\rho_{11}{}^2$ can be expressed in the following way:

$$\rho_{11}{}^2 = \frac{1}{n!}\sum_P \Gamma_2(P)_{11}^* P = \frac{1}{n!}\sum_P (-1)^p P, \tag{3.188}$$

where p is the number of different transpositions in which P can be decomposed. If the Hamiltonian can be decomposed in a number of terms, each containing operators acting only on the coordinate of a single electron,

$$H = H(1) + H(2) + \cdots + H(n), \tag{3.189}$$

the typical solution ψ of the Schrödinger equations is given by a product of one-electron wave functions

$$\psi(1, 2, \ldots, n) = \psi_1(1)\psi_2(2) \cdots \psi_n(n).$$

If the ψ_i functions are orthonormal, then the acceptable wave functions take the form of the *Slater determinant*:

$$\sqrt{n!}\,\rho_{11}{}^2\psi = \frac{1}{\sqrt{n!}}\begin{pmatrix} \psi_1(1) & \psi_1(2) & \cdots & \psi_1(n) \\ \psi_2(1) & \psi_2(2) & \cdots & \psi_2(n) \\ \cdots & \cdots & \cdots & \cdots \\ \psi_n(1) & \psi_n(2) & \cdots & \psi_n(n) \end{pmatrix}. \tag{3.190}$$

The factor $\sqrt{n!}$ in the left member of the above equation is introduced for normalization purposes.

[2] The property expressed by (3.61) can be checked here; for example,

$$\rho_{21}{}^3[\rho_{11}{}^3\psi(1,2,3)] = \rho_{21}{}^3\psi(1,2,3).$$

REFERENCES

[1] V. Heine, *Group Theory in Quantum Mechanics*, Pergamon, New York, 1960.
[2] G. F. Koster, Notes on Group Theory, *Techn. Rep. No. 8*, March 1956, Solid State and Molecular Theory Group, Massachusetts Institute of Technology, Cambridge, Mass.
[3] M. E. Rose, *Elementary Theory of Angular Momentum*, Wiley, New York, 1957.
[4] E. Merzbacher, *Quantum Mechanics*, Wiley, New York, 1961.
[5] E. Wigner, *Group Theory and Its Applications to the Quantum Mechanics of Atomic Spectra*, Academic, New York, 1959.
[6] C. Eckart, "The Application of Group Theory to the Quantum Dynamics of Monatomic Systems," *Rev. Mod. Phys.* **2**, 305 (1930).
[7] G. Frobenius and I. Schur, *Sitz. Berichte Preuss. Akad. Wiss.*, 186 (1906).
[8] J. L. Prather, *Atomic Energy Levels in Crystals*, National Bureau of Standards Monograph 19, February 1961.
[9] W. Pauli, in *Handbuch der Physik*, 2d. Ed. Vol. 24, Part I, Springer, Berlin, 1933, pp. 190–191.

4

The Hydrogen Atom

The nonrelativistic Hamiltonian of a hydrogen-like atom is given by

$$H = H_o + H_{so} + H_z + \text{less important terms}, \tag{4.1}$$

where

$$H_o = \frac{p^2}{2m} - \frac{Ze^2}{r} = -\frac{\hbar^2}{2m}\nabla^2 - \frac{Ze^2}{r}$$

$$H_{so} = \text{spin orbit interaction}$$

$$H_z = \text{Zeeman interaction.}$$

In order to solve the Schrödinger equation

$$H\psi = E\psi, \tag{4.2}$$

we shall use perturbation methods. We shall consider the different terms in the Hamiltonian H in order of importance. The results of this treatment, together with the group theoretical properties of the different terms of the Hamiltonian, are summarized in Table 4.1.

1. THE UNPERTURBED HAMILTONIAN

The unperturbed Hamiltonian is given by

$$H_o = \frac{p^2}{2m} - \frac{Ze^2}{r} = -\frac{\hbar^2}{2m}\nabla^2 - \frac{e^2Z}{r}. \tag{4.3}$$

The complete set of commuting operators is given by

$$H_o,\ l^2,\ l_z,\ \text{Parity} = P. \tag{4.4}$$

Table 4.1 Hydrogen Atom (Low H-Field)

	Hamiltonian	Complete Set of Commuting Operators	Properties of the Hamiltonian
H_o	$\frac{p^2}{2m} - \frac{e^2}{r}$	$H_o, l^2, s^2, l_z, s_z, P$ or $H_0, l^2, s^2, j^2, j_z, P$	Degeneracy: $(2l + 1)(2s + 1) = 2(2l + 1)$. $\langle nlsm_lm_s \| H_o \| nlsm_lm_s \rangle = \frac{-me^4}{2\hbar^2 n^2}$. Group: (3$d$ rot for orbital) $\times$ (3d rot for spin). Rep: $D_l \times D_{1/2}$.
H_{so}	$\lambda \mathbf{l} \cdot \mathbf{s}$	$H_{so}, l^2, s^2, j^2, j_z, P$	$[H_{so}, H_o] = 0$. Diagonal in above representation. Does not connect different terms. $\langle lsjm_j \| H_{so} \| lsjm_j \rangle = \lambda \frac{j(j+1) - l(l+1) - \frac{3}{4}}{2}$ Group: (3d rot for orbital) $\times$ (3d rot for spin) referred to same axes. Rep: $D_l \times D_{1/2} = D_{l+1/2} + D_{l-1/2}$.
H_z	$\mu H(l_z + 2s_z)$	$H_z, l^2, s^2, l_z, s_z, P$	$[H_z, H_{so}] \neq 0$. Connects states with equal l, s, m_j, P. $\langle lsjm_j \| H_z \| sjm_j \rangle = g\mu H m_j$, $g = 1 + \frac{j(j+1) + \frac{3}{4} - l(l+1)}{2j(j+1)}$.
		$H_z, l^2, s^2, j^2, l_z, s_z, P$ (Zeeman approximation)	$[H_z, H_{so}] = 0$. Does not connect different j levels (multiplets). Group: $C_{\infty h}$. Rep: $D_j = C_j + C_{j-1} + \cdots + C_{-j}$.

where $\mathbf{l}$ is the angular momentum operator. The eigenvalue equations are[1]

$$\begin{aligned} H_o u_{nlm_l} &= E_n u_{nlm_l} = -\frac{me^4}{2\hbar^2 n^2} \\ l^2 u_{nlm_l} &= l(l+1)\,\hbar^2 u_{nlm_l} \\ l_z u_{nlm_l} &= m_l \hbar u_{nlm_l} \\ P u_{nlm_l} &= (-1)^l\, u_{nlm_l}, \end{aligned} \tag{4.5}$$

and the wave functions

$$|nlm_l\rangle = u_{nlm_l}(r, \theta, \varphi) = R_n(r) y_{lm_l}(\theta, \varphi) \tag{4.6}$$

2. THE SPIN-ORBIT INTERACTION

From electrodynamics, we know that the magnetic moment (in e.m. units) of a current in a single loop is equal to the area A of the loop, times the current (e.s. units) divided by c:

$$\mu = \frac{AI}{c} \tag{4.7}$$

For an electron in an orbit of radius r we have

$$I = \frac{e}{T} = \frac{ev}{2\pi r}, \tag{4.8}$$

where T = period of the orbital motion and v = velocity of the electron. Then

$$\mu = \frac{\pi r^2 e}{Tc} = \frac{\pi r^2 ev}{c^2 \pi r} = \frac{e}{2mc}\, mvr = \frac{e}{2mc}\, l, \tag{4.9}$$

where l = angular momentum. In quantum mechanics μ and l become operators.

At this point, we ought to remember that the electron has a spin. The orbital angular momentum has associated with it a magnetic moment; in the same way a magnetic moment is associated to the spin angular momentum. For the orbital angular momentum, taking the sign of the electron charge in account

$$\boldsymbol{\mu} = -\frac{e}{2mc}\, \mathbf{l}. \tag{4.10}$$

A factor 2 appears in the magnetic moment of the electron

$$\boldsymbol{\mu}_s = -\frac{e}{mc}\, \mathbf{s}. \tag{4.11}$$

[1] The eigenvalue equation for the energy is solved in several books. See [1] and [2].

The *gyromagnetic ratio*, defined by μ/l or μ_s/s, is then $e/2mc$ for the orbital motion and e/mc for the spin.

The electron in the orbit experiences an electric field

$$\mathbf{E} = \frac{Ze}{r^3}\mathbf{r} \tag{4.12}$$

due to the charge Ze of the nucleus. Moving in this field, it also experiences a magnetic field given by

$$\mathbf{H}_{\text{eff}} = \frac{\mathbf{E} \times \mathbf{v}}{c}. \tag{4.13}$$

(In a more formal way this comes out of a Lorentz transformation.) Then, from the last two equations

$$\mathbf{H}_{\text{eff}} = \frac{Ze}{r^3}\mathbf{r} \times \frac{\mathbf{v}}{c} = \frac{Ze}{mcr^3}\mathbf{r} \times m\mathbf{v} = \frac{Ze}{mcr^3}\mathbf{l}. \tag{4.14}$$

The energy of the spin magnetic moment $\boldsymbol{\mu}_s = -(e/mc)\mathbf{s}$ in this field is

$$-\boldsymbol{\mu}_s \cdot \mathbf{H}_{\text{eff}} = \frac{Ze^2}{m^2c^2}\frac{\mathbf{l} \cdot \mathbf{s}}{r^3}. \tag{4.15}$$

The relativistic theory accounts for a factor $\frac{1}{2}$ called *Thomas factor*, which has to be introduced in (4.15). Then we can write the spin-orbit interaction Hamiltonian in the following way:

$$H_{so} = \frac{1}{2}\frac{Ze^2}{(mc)^2}\frac{1}{r^3}\mathbf{l} \cdot \mathbf{s} = \xi(r)\,\mathbf{l} \cdot \mathbf{s}, \tag{4.16}$$

where

$$\xi(r) = \frac{1}{2}\frac{Ze^2}{(mc)^2}\frac{1}{r^3} = \frac{1}{2m^2c^2r}\frac{\partial V(r)}{\partial r}. \tag{4.17}$$

If we introduce the total angular momentum $\mathbf{j}$ as follows:

$$\mathbf{j} = \mathbf{l} + \mathbf{s}, \tag{4.18}$$

we can write

$$\mathbf{l} \cdot \mathbf{s} = \frac{j^2 - l^2 - s^2}{2}, \tag{4.19}$$

and then we can see that $\mathbf{l} \cdot \mathbf{s}$ commutes with j^2, l^2, and s^2. We can also see that $\mathbf{l} \cdot \mathbf{s}$ does not commute with l_z or s_z, but commutes with the z component of the total angular momentum j_z.

The complete set of operators commuting with H_{so} is given by

$$H_{so}, l^2, s^2, j^2, j_z, P. \tag{4.20}$$

The complete set of operators commuting with H_o is

$$H_o, l^2, s^2, l_z, s_z, P. \tag{4.21}$$

Then H_{so} may have matrix elements different from zero between eigenstates of H_o with equal l, s, $m_l + m_s$. We can then diagonalize the energy matrix and find the eigenvalues and the eigenfunctions. But we can immediately find the eigenenergies if instead of representation (4.21) for H_o we use the representation

$$H_o, l^2, s^2, j^2, j_z, P. \tag{4.22}$$

The set (4.22) can also be considered the complete set of commuting operators of the Hamiltonian H_o.

The generic matrix element of the spin-orbit interaction is then given by

$$\begin{aligned}
&\langle nljm_j|\ \xi(r)\,\mathbf{l}\cdot\mathbf{s}\ |n'l'j'm_j'\rangle \\
&\quad = \langle nl|\ \xi(r)\ |n'l'\rangle\,\langle ljm_j|\ \frac{j^2 - l^2 - s^2}{2}\ |l'j'm_j'\rangle \\
&\quad = \zeta_{nl}\frac{j(j+1) - l(l+1) - s(s+1)}{2}\,\delta_{nn'}\delta_{ll'}\delta_{jj'}\delta_{m_jm_j'},
\end{aligned} \tag{4.23}$$

where

$$\begin{aligned}
\zeta_{nl} &= \hbar^2 \int R_{nl}^{\,2}(r)\,\xi(r)\,dr \\
&= \frac{e^2\hbar^2}{2m^2c^2a_0^{\,3}}\,\frac{Z^4}{n^3 l(l+\frac{1}{2})(l+1)}\,.
\end{aligned} \tag{4.24}$$

with a_0 = Bohr radius = $h^2/4\pi^2 me^2$.

If we consider a level nl, the possible values of j are given by

$$j = l + \tfrac{1}{2},\ l - \tfrac{1}{2}. \tag{4.25}$$

Correspondingly we have the following spin-orbit energies

$$j = l + \tfrac{1}{2}, \qquad E_{so} = \frac{\zeta_{nl}}{2}\,l, \tag{4.26}$$

$$j = l + \tfrac{1}{2}, \qquad E_{so} = -\frac{\zeta_{nl}}{2}(l+1), \tag{4.27}$$

where (4.23) has been applied.

3. THE ZEEMAN INTERACTION

The magnetic moment due to the orbital motion $\boldsymbol{\mu} = -(e/2mc)\,\mathbf{l}$ and the magnetic moment due to the spin $\boldsymbol{\mu}_s = -(e/mc)\,\mathbf{s}$ give rise to the following term of the Hamiltonian in the presence of a field **H** in the z direction:

$$H_z = -(\boldsymbol{\mu} + \boldsymbol{\mu}_s) \cdot \mathbf{H} = -(\mu_z + \mu_{sz})\, H = \frac{eH}{2mc}(l_z + 2s_z). \qquad (4.28)$$

The complete set of commuting operators is now

$$H_z, l^2, s^2, l_z, s_z, P. \qquad (4.29)$$

H_z will then have matrix elements different from zero only between eigenstates of $H_o + H_{so}$ corresponding to equal values of $j_z = l_z + s_z$. It may then connect states with different j, but equal l, s, m_j. The so-called *Zeeman approximation* consists in reintroducing j in the complete set (4.29). We can do this if the Zeeman splitting is much smaller than the spin-orbit splitting. Then the approximate complete set is

$$H_z, l^2, s^2, l_z, s_z, j^2, P. \qquad (4.30)$$

The eigenvalues of H_z are found by using the theorem treated in Section 5.7 of Chapter 3:

$$\langle jm_j'|\, \frac{l}{2mc} H(l_z + 2s_z)\, |jm_j\rangle = \frac{eH}{2mc} \langle jm_j'|\, j_z + s_z\, |jm_j\rangle$$

$$= \frac{eH}{2mc} \frac{\langle jm_j'|\, j_z\, |jm_j\rangle \langle j\|\, \mathbf{j} \cdot (\mathbf{j} + \mathbf{s})\, \|j\rangle}{\hbar^2 j(j+1).}. \qquad (4.31)$$

But, since

$$\mathbf{j} - \mathbf{s} = \mathbf{l}, \qquad (4.32)$$

we have

$$\mathbf{j} \cdot \mathbf{s} = \frac{j^2 + s^2 - l^2}{2}, \qquad (4.33)$$

and

$$\mathbf{j} \cdot (\mathbf{j} + \mathbf{s}) = j^2 + \mathbf{j} \cdot \mathbf{s} = j^2 + \frac{j^2 + s^2 - l^2}{2}. \qquad (4.34)$$

Then

$$\langle jm_j'|\, \frac{eH}{2mc} (l_z + 2s_z\, |jm_j\rangle$$

$$= \frac{eH}{2mc} \frac{\langle jm_j'|\, j_z\, |jm_j\rangle \langle j\|\, j^2 + \dfrac{j^2 - l^2 + s^2}{2}\, \|j\rangle}{\hbar^2 j(j+1)}$$

$$= \mu_0 H \delta_{m_j m_j'} m_j \frac{j(j+1) + \dfrac{j(j+1) - l(l+1) + s(s+1)}{2}}{j(j+1)}$$

$$= \mu_0 H m_j g(lsj)\, \delta_{m_j m_j'}, \qquad (4.35)$$

where

$$g = \text{Landé factor} = 1 + \frac{j(j+1) - l(l+1) + s(s+1)}{2j(j+1)} \tag{4.36}$$

$$\mu_0 = \frac{e\hbar}{2mc}. \tag{4.37}$$

The eigenvalues of H_z are then given by

$$\langle n'l'sj'm_j'| H_z |nlsjm_j\rangle = \delta_{nn'}\delta_{ll'}\delta_{jj'}\delta_{m_jm_j'} \frac{e\hbar}{2mc} gm_jH. \tag{4.38}$$

Example: Atomic Hydrogen in State $l = 1$.

Let us now consider together the spin-orbit interaction and the Zeeman term; namely, let us consider the following perturbation:

$$H' = \lambda \mathbf{l} \cdot \mathbf{s} + \frac{eH}{2mc}(l_z + 2s_z). \tag{4.39}$$

To solve the eigenvalue equation for the energy we may start from the lsl_zs_z representation. We have six unperturbed states $|m_lm_s\rangle$:

$$|1, \tfrac{1}{2}\rangle, |1, -\tfrac{1}{2}\rangle, |0, \tfrac{1}{2}\rangle, |0, -\tfrac{1}{2}\rangle, |-1, \tfrac{1}{2}\rangle, |-1, -\tfrac{1}{2}\rangle. \tag{4.40}$$

The matrix of perturbation (4.39) is reported in Table 4.2, where

$$\mu_0 = \frac{e\hbar}{2mc}.$$

We may start from the $lsjj_z$ representation; we have six $| j, m_j >$ states (j may be $\frac{3}{2}$ or $\frac{1}{2}$):

$$| \tfrac{3}{2}, \tfrac{3}{2} > , | \tfrac{3}{2}, \tfrac{1}{2} > , | \tfrac{3}{2} - \tfrac{1}{2} > , | \tfrac{3}{2}, -\tfrac{3}{2} > , | \tfrac{1}{2}, \tfrac{1}{2} > , | \tfrac{1}{2}, -\tfrac{1}{2} > ,$$

and the matrix of the perturbation (4.39) is given by Table 4.3.

Table 4.2 The Matrix Elements of the Spin-Orbit and Zeeman Interactions in Atomic Hydrogen ($l = 1$; Representation lsl_zs_z)

m_l, m_s	$1, \frac{1}{2}$	$1, -\frac{1}{2}$	$0, \frac{1}{2}$	$0, -\frac{1}{2}$	$-1, \frac{1}{2}$	$-1, -\frac{1}{2}$
$1, \frac{1}{2}$	$\lambda/2 + 2\mu_0H$	0	0	0	0	0
$1, -\frac{1}{2}$	0	$-\lambda/2$	$\lambda/\sqrt{2}$	0	0	0
$0, \frac{1}{2}$	0	$\lambda/\sqrt{2}$	μ_0H	0	0	0
$0, -\frac{1}{2}$	0	0	0	$-\mu_0H$	$\lambda/\sqrt{2}$	0
$-1, \frac{1}{2}$	0	0	0	$\lambda/\sqrt{2}$	$-\lambda/2$	0
$-1, -\frac{1}{2}$	0	0	0	0	0	$\lambda/2 - 2\mu_0H$

Table 4.3 The Matrix Elements of the Spin-Orbit and Zeeman Interactions in Atomic Hydrogen ($l = 1$; Representation $lsjj_z$)

j, m_j	$\frac{3}{2}, \frac{3}{2}$	$\frac{3}{2}, \frac{1}{2}$	$\frac{1}{2}, \frac{1}{2}$	$\frac{3}{2}, -\frac{1}{2}$	$\frac{1}{2}, -\frac{1}{2}$	$\frac{3}{2}, -\frac{3}{2}$
$\frac{3}{2}, \frac{3}{2}$	$\lambda/2 + 2\mu_0 H$	0	0	0	0	0
$\frac{3}{2}, \frac{1}{2}$	0	$\lambda/2 + \frac{2}{3}\mu_0 H$	$(\sqrt{2}/3)\mu_0 H$	0	0	0
$\frac{1}{2}, \frac{1}{2}$	0	$(\sqrt{2}/3)\mu_0 H$	$-\lambda + \frac{1}{3}\mu_0 H$	0	0	0
$\frac{3}{2}, -\frac{1}{2}$	0	0	0	$\lambda/2 - \frac{2}{3}\mu_0 H$	$-(\sqrt{2}/3)\mu_0 H$	0
$\frac{1}{2}, -\frac{1}{2}$	0	0	0	$-(\sqrt{2}/3)\mu_0 H$	$-\lambda - \frac{1}{3}\mu_0 H$	0
$\frac{3}{2}, -\frac{3}{2}$	0	0	0	0	0	$\lambda/2 - 2\mu_0 H$

The process of diagonalization of the matrix will give energy eigenvalues which are the corrections to the unperturbed energy levels and new eigenfunctions in terms of the old ones.

We can follow what happens for different values of H in Fig. 4.1.

As we can see m_j is always a good quantum number. The Zeeman approximation, in which the energy is proportional to the magnetic field, is valid only for small values of H. We notice that in the Zeeman approximation we disregard the nondiagonal terms linear in H.

4. GROUP THEORETICAL CONSIDERATIONS FOR THE H ATOM

4.1 The Unperturbed Hamiltonian

The unperturbed Hamiltonian is given by

$$H_o = \frac{p^2}{2m} - \frac{Ze^2}{r}. \tag{4.42}$$

The substitution group is in this case given by the product group

$$R = R_{\text{el}} \times R_{\text{sp}}, \tag{4.43}$$

where

R_{el} = three-dimensional rotation group for orbit;

R_{sp} = three-dimensional rotation group for spin.

The eigenfunctions of H_o are of the type

$$\psi_{nlm_lm_s}(\mathbf{r}, s) = u_{nlm_l}(\mathbf{r})\,\chi_\sigma(s), \tag{4.44}$$

where u_{nlm_l} is the spatial and $\chi_\sigma(s)$ is the spin part. The groups R_{el} and R_{sp} are completely independent; the transformation of the $(2l + 1)$ spatial functions under rotation is completely independent of the transformation of the two spin functions and may be described by using different coordinate axes. The general transformation may be represented by the direct product representation

$$D_l \times D_{1/2}. \tag{4.45}$$

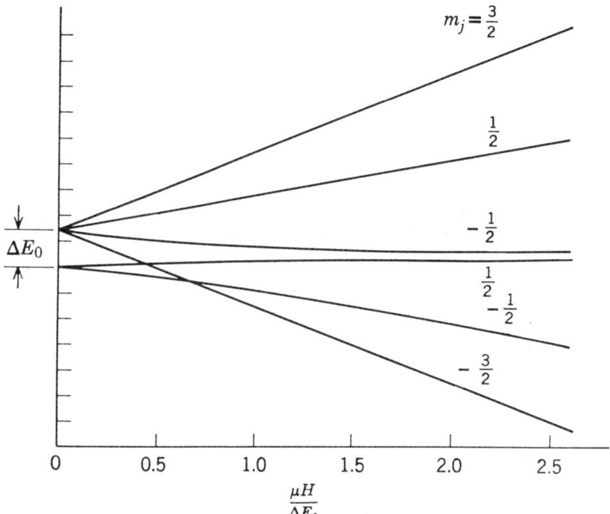

Fig. 4.1 Zeeman levels of Atomic hydrogen in $l = 1$ state. ΔE_0 is the separation of $j = \frac{3}{2}, j = \frac{1}{2}$ levels for zero field and is equal to $\frac{3}{2}\lambda$.

4.2 The Spin-Orbit Interaction

The introduction of this term produces a correlation between rotations in coordinate space and rotations in spin space. The groups R_{el} and R_{sp} are no longer independent and rotational operations on orbits and spins must now be referred to the same axes. The matrices $D_l \times D_{1/2}$ still give a representation of the substitution group, which, however, is no longer irreducible. It splits in the following way

$$D_l \times D_{1/2} = D_{l+1/2} + D_{l-1/2}. \tag{4.46}$$

This corresponds to a new choice of eigenfunctions which are divided in two sets, of degeneracies $2(l + \frac{1}{2}) + 1$ and $2(l - \frac{1}{2}) + 1$. This new choice brings the system from the $m_l m_s$ to the jm_j representation; to operate this choice, we may use the Clebsch-Gordan coefficients.

4.3 The Zeeman Hamiltonian

The introduction of this term changes the symmetry group to $C_{\infty h}$. We have then

$$D_j = C_J + C_{J-1} + \cdots + C_{-J}. \tag{4.47}$$

We must remember that parity is conserved. Then the C representations will be odd if D_j is odd and even if D_j is even.

REFERENCES

[1] H. Eyring, J. Walter, and G. E. Kimball, *Quantum Chemistry* Wiley, New York, 1957.
[2] L. I. Schiff, *Quantum Mechanics*, McGraw-Hill, New York, 1955.

5

The Complex Atom: Multiplet Theory

1. THE HELIUM ATOM

The Hamiltonian of a helium atom is given by

$$H = f_1 + f_2 + g_{12}, \tag{5.1}$$

where

$$f_1 = \frac{p_1^{\,2}}{2m} - \frac{e^2}{r_1},$$

$$f_2 = \frac{p_2^{\,2}}{2m} - \frac{e^2}{r_2},$$

$$g_{12} = \frac{e^2}{r_{12}}.$$

The Schrödinger equation

$$H\psi = E\psi \tag{5.2}$$

is solved by first considering the unperturbed Hamiltonian

$$H_o = f_1 + f_2 \tag{5.3}$$

and solving the corresponding Schrödinger equation and then introducing the perturbation term g_{12}.

When we consider the unperturbed Hamiltonian, the complete set of commuting operators is given by

$$H_o, L_z, S_z, P. \tag{5.4}$$

Let us consider the ground state in which both electrons, with opposite spins, are on the $1s$ level and the first excited state in which one electron is in the $1s$ state and the other in the $2s$ state. We use the following symbols:

$\psi_{\uparrow\downarrow}$ indicates a state function with two electrons in the state $1s$ and antiparallel spins.

$\psi_{\substack{\uparrow \\ \uparrow}}$ indicates a state function with one electron in the state $1s$ and one electron in the state $2s$ and parallel spins up.

$\psi_{\substack{\downarrow \\ \downarrow}}$ indicates a state function with one electron in the state $1s$ and one electron in the state $2s$ and parallel spins down.

$\psi_{\substack{\downarrow \\ \uparrow}}$ indicates a state function with one electron in the state $1s$ and spin up and one electron in the state $2s$ and spin down.

$\psi_{\substack{\uparrow \\ \downarrow}}$ indicates a state function with one electron in the state $1s$ and spin down and one electron in the state $2s$ and spin up.

1.1 The Ground State (degeneracy: 1)

The function representing the ground state is given by

$$\psi_0 = \psi_{\uparrow\downarrow} = \frac{1}{\sqrt{2}} \begin{pmatrix} u_{1s}(1)\,\alpha(1) & u_{1s}(1)\,\beta(1) \\ u_{1s}(2)\,\alpha(2) & u_{1s}(2)\,\beta(2) \end{pmatrix}$$

$$= \frac{1}{\sqrt{2}} u_{1s}(1)\,u_{1s}(2)[\alpha(1)\,\beta(2) - \beta(1)\,\alpha(2)]. \tag{5.5}$$

The matrix element of the Hamiltonian H is given by

$$\begin{aligned}\langle\psi_0|\,H\,|\psi_0\rangle &= \tfrac{1}{2}\{\langle u_{1s}(1)\,u_{1s}(2)\,\alpha(1)\,\beta(2)|\,f_1 + f_2 + g_{12}\,|u_{1s}(1)\,u_{1s}(2)\,\alpha(1)\,\beta(2)\rangle \\ &\quad + \langle u_{1s}(1)\,u_{1s}(2)\,\beta(1)\,\alpha(2)|\,f_1 + f_2 + g_{12}\,|u_{1s}(1)\,u_{1s}(2)\,\beta(1)\,\alpha(2)\rangle\} \\ &= 2\,\langle u_{1s}|\,f\,|u_{1s}\rangle + \langle u_{1s}u_{1s}|\,g_{12}\,|u_{1s}u_{1s}\rangle \\ &= 2E_a + C, \end{aligned} \tag{5.6}$$

where

$$E_a = \langle u_{1s}|\,f\,|u_{1s}\rangle,$$

$$C = \langle u_{1s}u_{1s}|\,g_{12}\,|u_{1s}u_{1s}\rangle.$$

1.2 The First Excited State (degeneracy: 4)

The wavefunctions representing the first excited states are given by

$$
\begin{aligned}
\psi_1 = \psi_{\uparrow\uparrow} &= \frac{1}{\sqrt{2}}\begin{pmatrix} u_{1s}(1)\,\alpha(1) & u_{2s}(1)\,\alpha(1) \\ u_{1s}(2)\,\alpha(2) & u_{2s}(2)\,\alpha(2) \end{pmatrix} \\
&= \frac{1}{\sqrt{2}}\,[u_{1s}(1)\,u_{2s}(2) - u_{2s}(1)\,u_{1s}(2)]\alpha(1)\,\alpha(2), \\
\psi_2 = \psi_{\uparrow\downarrow} &= \frac{1}{\sqrt{2}}\begin{pmatrix} u_{1s}(1)\,\alpha(1) & u_{2s}(1)\,\beta(1) \\ u_{1s}(2)\,\alpha(2) & u_{2s}(2)\,\beta(2) \end{pmatrix} \\
&= \frac{1}{\sqrt{2}}\,[u_{1s}(1)\,\alpha(1)\,u_{2s}(2)\,\beta(2) - u_{2s}(1)\,\beta(1)\,u_{1s}(2)\,\alpha(2)]; \\
\psi_3 = \psi_{\downarrow\uparrow} &= \frac{1}{\sqrt{2}}\begin{pmatrix} u_{1s}(1)\,\beta(1) & u_{2s}(1)\,\alpha(1) \\ u_{1s}(2)\,\beta(2) & u_{2s}(2)\,\alpha(2) \end{pmatrix} \\
&= \frac{1}{\sqrt{2}}\,[u_{1s}(1)\,\beta(1)\,u_{2s}(2)\,\alpha(2) - u_{2s}(1)\,\alpha(1)\,u_{1s}(2)\,\beta(2)], \\
\psi_4 = \psi_{\downarrow\downarrow} &= \frac{1}{\sqrt{2}}\begin{pmatrix} u_{1s}(1)\,\beta(1) & u_{2s}(1)\,\beta(1) \\ u_{1s}(2)\,\beta(2) & u_{2s}(2)\,\beta(2) \end{pmatrix} \\
&= \frac{1}{\sqrt{2}}\,[u_{1s}(1)\,u_{2s}(2) - u_{2s}(1)\,u_{1s}(2)]\beta(1)\,\beta(2).
\end{aligned}
\tag{5.7}
$$

The matrix elements of H are

$$
\begin{aligned}
\langle\psi_1|\,H\,|\psi_1\rangle &= \langle u_{1s}|\,f\,|u_{1s}\rangle + \langle u_{2s}|\,f\,|u_{2s}\rangle + \langle u_{1s}u_{2s}|\,g\,|u_{1s}u_{2s}\rangle - \langle u_{1s}u_{2s}|\,g\,|u_{2s}u_{1s}\rangle, \\
\langle\psi_2|\,H\,|\psi_2\rangle &= \langle u_{1s}|\,f\,|u_{1s}\rangle + \langle u_{2s}|\,f\,|u_{2s}\rangle + \langle u_{1s}u_{2s}|\,g\,|u_{1s}u_{2s}\rangle; \\
\langle\psi_3|\,H\,|\psi_3\rangle &= \langle\psi_2|\,H\,|\psi_2\rangle; \\
\langle\psi_4|\,H\,|\psi_4\rangle &= \langle\psi_1|\,H\,|\psi_1\rangle; \\
\langle\psi_2|\,H\,|\psi_3\rangle &= \langle\psi_3|\,H\,|\psi_2\rangle = -\langle u_{1s}u_{2s}|\,g\,|u_{2s}u_{1s}\rangle.
\end{aligned}
\tag{5.8}
$$

All the other matrix elements are zero. We must remember the following important rule:

Matrix elements of a Hamiltonian taken between eigenstates of a Hermitian operator commuting with it are zero unless the eigenstates refer to the same eigenvalue of the commuting operator.

Now H commutes with L_z, and we cannot have matrix elements different from zero between states with different M_L. Let us proceed as usual by applying perturbation theory to degenerate cases. We begin by diagonalizing the 2×2 matrix:

$$\left| \begin{matrix} \langle u_{1s}| f |u_{1s}\rangle + \langle u_{2s}| f |u_{2s}\rangle + \langle u_{1s}u_{2s}| g |u_{1s}u_{2s}\rangle & -\langle u_{1s}u_{2s}| g |u_{2s}u_{1s}\rangle \\ -\langle u_{1s}u_{2s}| g |u_{2s}u_{1s}\rangle & \langle u_{1s}| f |u_{1s}\rangle + \langle u_{2s}| f |u_{2s}\rangle + \langle u_{1s}u_{2s}| g |u_{1s}u_{2s}\rangle \end{matrix} \right|. \tag{5.9}$$

ψ_1 and ψ_4, not being connected by H to any state, will remain unperturbed. Working out the diagonalization for the 2×2 matrix, we find

$$\begin{aligned} \psi_2' &= \frac{1}{\sqrt{2}}[u_{1s}(1)\, u_{2s}(2) + u_{2s}(1)\, u_{1s}(2)] \frac{1}{\sqrt{2}}[\alpha(1)\, \beta(2) - \alpha(2)\, \beta(1)], \\ \psi_3' &= \frac{1}{\sqrt{2}}[u_{1s}(1)\, u_{2s}(2) - u_{2s}(1)\, u_{1s}(2)] \frac{1}{\sqrt{2}}[\alpha(1)\, \beta(2) + \alpha(2)\, \beta(1)], \end{aligned} \tag{5.10}$$

and the corresponding energy eigenvalues

$$\begin{aligned} \langle \psi_2'| H |\psi_2'\rangle &= \langle u_{1s}| f |u_{1s}\rangle + \langle u_{2s}| f |u_{2s}\rangle \\ &\quad + \langle u_{1s}u_{2s}| g |u_{1s}u_{2s}\rangle + \langle u_{1s}u_{2s}| g |u_{2s}u_{1s}\rangle \\ &= E_a + E_b + A + B, \\ \langle \psi_3'| H |\psi_3'\rangle &= \langle u_{1s}| f |u_{1s}\rangle + \langle u_{2s}| f |u_{2s}\rangle \\ &\quad + \langle u_{1s}u_{2s}| g |u_{1s}u_{2s}\rangle - \langle u_{1s}u_{2s}| g |u_{2s}u_{1s}\rangle \\ &= E_a + E_b + A - B. \end{aligned} \tag{5.11}$$

where

$$\begin{aligned} \langle u_{1s}| f |u_{1s}\rangle &= E_a, \\ \langle u_{2s}| f |u_{2s}\rangle &= E_b, \\ \langle u_{1s}u_{2s}| g |u_{1s}u_{2s}\rangle &= A, \\ \langle u_{1s}u_{2s}| g |u_{2s}u_{1s}\rangle &= B, \end{aligned} \tag{5.12}$$

If we now operate with the operators

$$S^2 = s_1{}^2 + s_2{}^2, \qquad S_z = s_{z_1} + s_{z_2}, \tag{5.13}$$

on the wavefunctions ψ_1, ψ_2', ψ_3', ψ_4, we find that ψ_2' represents an eigenfunction of S^2 and S_z, belonging to $S = 0$, $M_S = 0$ and ψ_1, ψ_3', ψ_4 represent eigenfunctions of S^2 and S_z, belonging respectively to $S = 1$, $M_S = 1$; $S = 1$, $M_S = 0$; $S = 1$, $M_S = -1$.

The energies and the wavefunctions of the ground and excited states of He are then given as follows:

Ground State

$$^1S : E = 2E_a + C, \qquad \psi_0 = \frac{1}{\sqrt{2}} u_{1s}(1)\, u_{1s}(2)\, [\alpha(1)\, \beta(2) - \alpha(2)\, \beta(1)]. \tag{5.14}$$

Excited State

$$^1S: E = E_a + E_b + A + B,$$

$$\psi_2' = \frac{1}{\sqrt{2}} [u_{1s}(1)\, u_{2s}(2) + u_{2s}(1)\, u_{1s}(2)] \frac{1}{\sqrt{2}} [\alpha(1)\, \beta(2) - \alpha(2)\, \beta(1)]; \tag{5.15}$$

$$^3S \begin{cases} M_S = 1 : E = E_a + E_b + A - B, \\ \qquad \psi_1 = \dfrac{1}{\sqrt{2}} [u_{1s}(1)\, u_{2s}(2) - u_{2s}(1)\, u_{1s}(2)]\alpha(1)\, \alpha(2), \\ M_S = 0 : E = E_a + E_b + A - B, \\ \qquad \psi_3' = \dfrac{1}{\sqrt{2}} [u_{1s}(1)\, u_{2s}(2) - u_{2s}(1)\, u_{1s}(2)] \dfrac{1}{\sqrt{2}} [\alpha(1)\, \beta(2) \\ \qquad\qquad + \beta(1)\, \alpha(2)], \\ M_S = -1 : E = E_a + E_b + A - B, \\ \qquad \psi_4 = \dfrac{1}{\sqrt{2}} [u_{1s}(1)\, u_{2s}(2) - u_{2s}(1)\, u_{1s}(2)]\beta(1)\, \beta(2), \end{cases} \tag{5.16}$$

The energy levels are represented in Fig. 5.1.

2. THE MANY ELECTRON ATOM

The Hamiltonian of a many electron atom in a magnetic field H is given by

$$H = H_o + H_{so} + H_z, \tag{5.17}$$

where

$$H_o = \sum_i \frac{p_i^2}{2m} - \sum_i \frac{Ze^2}{r_i} + \sum_{i>j} \frac{e^2}{r_{ij}} = \sum_i f_i + \sum_{i>j} g_{ij},$$

$$H_{so} = \sum_i \xi(r_i)\, \mathbf{l}_i \cdot \mathbf{s}_i, \tag{5.18}$$

$$H_z = \frac{eH}{2mc} (L_z + 2S_z).$$

Other terms of the Hamiltonian, like the diamagnetic term, the spin–spin interaction, the hyperfine interaction, the quadrupole interaction, and the

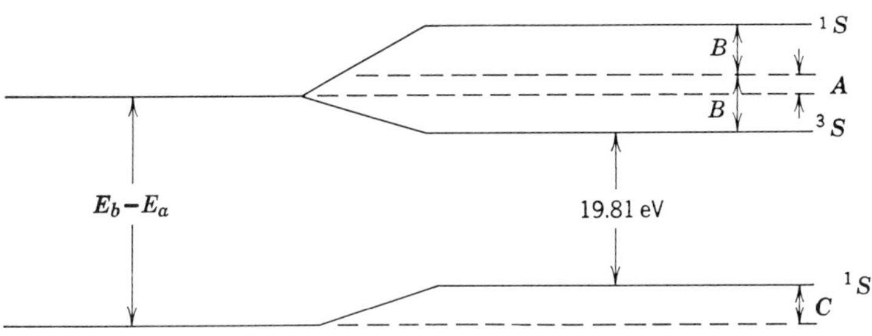

Fig. 5.1. Perturbed energy levels of He.

nuclear Zeeman term are less important and are neglected. In order to solve the Schrödinger equation

$$H\psi = E\psi, \tag{5.19}$$

we use perturbation methods. We shall consider the different terms in the Hamiltonian successively in order of importance. The results of this treatment, together with the group theoretical properties of the Hamiltonian, are shown in Table 5.1.

2.1 The Unperturbed Hamiltonian

The unperturbed Hamiltonian is the Hamiltonian when each electron is considered interacting with the nucleus and with an average charge distribution of all other electrons,

$$H_u = \sum_i \left(-\frac{\hbar^2}{2m} \nabla_i^2 - \frac{Z_{pi}}{r_i} e^2 \right), \tag{5.20}$$

where Z_{pi} = effective nuclear charge seen by electron i.

The solutions of the Schrödinger equation

$$\sum_i \left(-\frac{\hbar^2}{2m} \nabla_i^2 - \frac{Z_{pi}}{r_i} e^2 \right) \psi = E\psi \tag{5.21}$$

are products of elementary functions

$$\psi(\mathbf{r}_i, s_i) = u(\mathbf{r}_i)\, \chi_i(s_i).$$

These u functions can be found by self-consistent methods. Linear combinations of products of elementary ψ functions are also a solution of (5.21).

The Pauli principle, an additional condition independent of the above considerations, must be taken in account; only the antisymmetric combinations of products (determinantal wavefunctions) can be accepted as representative of the physical reality. In order to build up the determinantal

Table 5.1 The Complex Atom

	Hamiltonian	Complete Set of Commuting Operators	Properties of the Hamiltonian
H_u	$\sum_i \left(\frac{p_i^2}{2m} - \frac{Z_{pi}e^2}{r_i}\right)$	H_u, L_z, S_z, P $l_1^2, l_{z_1}, l_2^2, l_{z_2} \cdots$ $s_1^2, s_{z_1}, s_2^2, s_{z_2} \cdots$	Degeneracy: $(2l_1 + 1)(2s_1 + 1)(2l_2 + 1)(2s_2 + 1)$, reduced by Pauli principle. $\langle M_L M_S \| H_u \| M_L M_S \rangle = \sum_i \left(-\frac{me^4 Z_{pi}}{2\hbar^2 n_i}\right)$. Group: $R_{\text{el}_1} \times R_{\text{sp}_1} \times R_{\text{el}_2} \times R_{\text{sp}_2} \times \cdots$. Rep: $d_{l_1} \times d_{s_1} \times d_{l_2} \times d_{s_2} \times \cdots$.
H_o	$\sum \left(\frac{p_i^2}{2m} - \frac{Ze^2}{r_i}\right) + \sum_{i>j} \frac{e^2}{r_{ij}}$	$H_o, L^2, S^2, L_z, S_z, P$	$[H_o, H_u] \neq 0$. May connect states of H_u with equal M_L, M_S, P. May cause configuration interaction between states of equal parities. Group: $R_{\text{el}} \times R_{\text{sp}}$ Rep: $D_L \times D_S \begin{pmatrix} L = l_1 + l_2 + \cdots l_n, l_1 + l_2 + \ldots l_n - 1, \ldots \\ S = s_1 + s_2 + \cdots s_n, s_1 + s_2 + \cdots s_n - 1, \ldots \end{pmatrix}$. Some values of L and S may be excluded by Pauli principle.
H_{so}	$\sum_i \xi_i \mathbf{l}_i \cdot \mathbf{s}_i$	H_{so}, J^2, J_z, P	$[H_{so}, H_o] \neq 0$. May connect states of H_o with equal M_J, P. May cause: term interaction, configuration interaction.
	$\lambda \mathbf{L} \cdot \mathbf{S}$ (Russell-Saunders approximation)	$H_{so}, L^2, S^2, J^2, J_z, P$	$[H_{so}, H_o] \neq 0$. May connect states of H_o with equal $L, S, M_J = M_L + M_S, P$. Splits levels within same terms; lifts J degeneracy. Does not connect different terms. May cause configuration interaction. Group: $R_{\text{el}} \times R_{\text{sp}}$ referred to same axes. Rep: $D_L \times D_S = \sum_J D_S; (J = L + S, L + S - 1, \ldots, \|L - S\|)$.
H_z	$\mu H(L_z + 2S_z)$	H_z, J_z, L^2, S^2, P	$[H_z, H_{so}] \neq 0$. May connect states of H_{so} with equal M_J, P. Splits levels of J manifolds: lifts M_J degeneracy. May cause interaction between different J manifolds, term interaction, configuration interaction.
		H_z, J, J_z, L^2, S^2, P (Zeeman approximation)	$[H_z, H_{so}] = 0$. Diagonal in H_{so}, J^2, J_z, P representation. Splits levels within same J manifold: lifts M_J degeneracy. Group: $C_{\infty h}$. Rep: $D_J = \sum C_{M_J}: (M_J = J, J - 1, \ldots, -J)$.

eigenfunctions, we put the electrons in the different orbits $1s$, $2s$, $2p$, $3s$, $3p$, etc. (no more than two electrons per orbit, because of the Pauli principle). The resulting functions are eigenfunctions of the following commuting operators:

$$H_u, L_z = \sum_i l_{z_i}, S_z = \sum_i s_{z_i}, P = \text{parity}. \tag{5.22}$$

The energy eigenvalues are the sum of the energies of the single electrons. The energy levels are, in general, degenerate. We call every possible distribution of the electrons over the orbits an *electronic configuration*. In the case of a configuration $2p3p$ the degree of degeneracy is

$$(2l_1 + 1) \times (2s_1 + 1) \times (2l_2 + 1) \times (2s_2 + 1) = 36.$$

In the configuration p^2, because of the Pauli principle, the degree of degeneracy is reduced to 15.

2.2 The Electrostatic Interaction

We now apply perturbation theory and find the diagonal and nondiagonal elements of the Hamiltonian

$$H_o = \sum_i \left(-\frac{\hbar^2}{2m} \nabla_i^2 - \frac{Ze^2}{r_i} \right) + \sum_{i>j} \frac{e^2}{r_{ij}} = \sum_i f_i + \sum_{i>j} g_{ij}, \tag{5.23}$$

using the determinantal eigenfunctions. The process of solving the secular equation gives us new energy levels (with the degeneracy partly removed) and new eigenfunctions.

Matrix elements of the Hamiltonian taken between eigenstates of a Hermitian operator commuting with the Hamiltonian are zero unless the eigenstates refer to the same eigenvalue of the commuting operator. The complete set of commuting operators is now

$$H_o, L^2, S^2, L_z, S_z, P. \tag{5.24}$$

The Hamiltonian H_o will not give rise to matrix elements different from zero among states with different quantum numbers M_L, M_S, P. By using this property we can break the secular equation into a number of smaller secular equations.

A convenient procedure consists of building up linear combinations of determinantal functions that diagonalize the operators LS, L_z, S_z and of finding the matrix elements of H_o among the different combinations. Mathematical tools, like projection operators and Clebsch-Gordan coefficients, may be used to find these combinations. Every linear combination of determinantal functions that diagonalizes L, S, L_z, S_z can be labeled by the quantum numbers L, S, M_L, M_S.

There will, in general, be diagonal and off-diagonal matrix elements of H_0 among the various linear combinations. There may be off-diagonal terms of two types:

1. Matrix elements between two eigenstates of L, S, L_z, S_z belonging to the same configuration and labeled by the same quantum numbers L, S, M_L, M_S.
2. Matrix elements between two eigenstates of L, S, L_z, S_z belonging to different configurations and labeled by the same quantum numbers L, S, M_L, M_S.

The latter matrix elements are usually small and can be neglected in a not precise calculation of the energy levels.

The new state functions are eigenfunctions of the operators (5.24). The energy levels are, in general, degenerate, since the electrostatic interaction does not remove the $M_L M_S$ degeneracy, and are known as *spectral terms.*

In the case of the configuration $2p3p$ the electrostatic interaction gives rise to the six terms: ^3D, ^3P, ^3S, ^1D, ^1P, ^1S, with the respective degeneracies 15, 9, 3, 5, 3, 1.

2.3 The Spin-Orbit Interaction

The spin-orbit interaction Hamiltonian is given by

$$H_{so} = \sum_i \xi_i \mathbf{l}_i \cdot \mathbf{s}_i. \tag{5.25}$$

The spin-orbit interaction gives rise to the fine structure of the atomic spectra. The complete set of commuting operators is now

$$H_{so}, J^2 = (\mathbf{L} + \mathbf{S})^2, J_z = L_z + S_z, P. \tag{5.26}$$

The Hamiltonian H_{so} may have matrix elements among eigenstates of H_0 with equal M_j and P quantum numbers.

In order to find the eigenfunctions and the eigenvalues of H_{so}, we can build up linear combinations of eigenfunctions of H_0 that diagonalize the operator J and then find the matrix elements of H_{so} among the different combinations. This procedure breaks the secular equation into smaller secular equations. We may have diagonal matrix elements of H_{so} and off-diagonal elements between eigenstates of J, J_z with equal quantum numbers, J, M_J, P. Energy levels belonging to different spectral terms may be connected by the spin-orbit interaction. There may also be matrix elements different from zero between states with the same J, M_J, P belonging to different electronic configurations.

If, however, the spin-orbit interaction is much smaller than the electrostatic interaction, we can use the so-called *Russell-Saunders approximation.* It consists of disregarding the off-diagonal matrix elements of the H_{so} Hamiltonian among states with the same J but different L, S. In doing so, we consider that L and S are still good quantum numbers and

$$H_{so}, L, S, J, J_z, P. \tag{5.27}$$

as the set of commuting operators. We have in this case

$$\langle LSJM|\, \lambda \mathbf{L}\cdot\mathbf{S}\, |L'S'J'M'_J\rangle = \lambda \frac{J(J+1) - L(L+1) - S(S+1)}{2} \delta_{LL'}\delta_{SS'}\delta_{JJ'}\delta_{M_J M_{J'}}, \tag{5.28}$$

because in this approximation, as we shall see in Section 6 of this chapter,

$$\sum_i \xi_i \mathbf{l}_i \cdot \mathbf{s}_i \rightarrow \lambda \mathbf{L}\cdot\mathbf{S}. \tag{5.29}$$

We have also the *Landé interval rule*:

$$E_J - E_{J-1} = \lambda J. \tag{5.30}$$

The Russell-Saunders approximation breaks down for heavy atoms (λ is approximately proportional to the fourth power of the atomic number). For the rare-earth ions there is evidence in the spectra of a breaking of the Russell-Saunders approximation.

If the spin-orbit interaction is much larger than the electrostatic interaction, we have the so-called *j–j coupling*.

The spin-orbit interaction partly removes the degeneracy of the energy levels, but it leaves a $2J + 1$ degeneracy that can be removed by the application of a magnetic field. Each level, as determined by H_{so}, represents a *multiplet*.

2.4 The Zeeman Hamiltonian

The Zeeman Hamiltonian is given by

$$H_z = \frac{eH}{2mc}(L_z + 2S_z). \tag{5.31}$$

The complete set of commuting operators in this case is

$$H_z, L_z, S_z, L^2, S^2, P. \tag{5.32}$$

We may have diagonal matrix elements and off-diagonal matrix elements between eigenstates of H_{so} with equal quantum numbers M_J, P.

If the Zeeman perturbation is much smaller than the spin-orbit perturbation, we can disregard the off-diagonal matrix elements and consider J as a still good quantum number. If, moreover, we consider the Russell-Saunders approximation valid, we can use the $LSJM$ representation:

$$\langle LSJM_J| \frac{eH}{2mc} (L_z + 2S_z) |LSJM'_J\rangle = \mu_0 gHM_J\delta_{M_JM_J'}, \tag{5.33}$$

where

$$g = 1 + \frac{J(J+1) + S(S+1) - L(L+1)}{2J(J+1)}, \tag{5.34}$$

and

$$\mu_0 = \frac{e\hbar}{2mc}. \tag{5.35}$$

If we cannot disregard the off-diagonal components of the Zeeman interaction, we have to solve secular equations even in the Russell-Saunders approximation (in which we disregard the nondiagonal components of the spin-orbit interaction). We then get a nonlinear magnetic effect which is called the *Paschen-Back effect*. In this case we find deviation of the splitting from the one given by the g factor.

The Zeeman effect removes the M_J degeneracy.

2.5 About Parity

It may be noticed that we have included parity among the operators commuting with the unperturbed Hamiltonian H_u and with all the successive terms of H. The eigenvalue of the operator parity is given by $(-1)^{\sum_i l_i}$, where the sum is extended to the electrons in the atom. The states of the system with an even parity are called *even* or *gerade*; the states with an odd parity are called *odd* or *ungerade*. Gerade and ungerade states are sometimes indicated by subscripts g and u, respectively.

3. GROUP THEORETICAL CONSIDERATIONS FOR A COMPLEX ATOM

3.1 The Unperturbed Hamiltonian

The unperturbed Hamiltonian describes a system in which each electron moves in an independent orbit and has a certain angular momentum, with respect to the nucleus; moreover, each electron has an intrinsic (spin) angular momentum, decoupled from its orbital angular momentum.

In these conditions the group of operations which leave the Hamiltonian invariant is given by the product group

$$R = R_{\text{el}_1} \times R_{\text{sp}_1} \times R_{\text{el}_2} \times R_{\text{sp}_2} \times \cdots \times R_{\text{el}_n} \times R_{\text{sp}_n}, \tag{5.36}$$

where n = number of electrons,

R_{el_i} = three dimensional rotation group for orbital i,

R_{sp_i} = three dimensional rotation group for spin i.

All the transformations on the coordinates and spins of the single electrons are independent. The transformation properties of the eigenfunctions may be represented by the direct product,

$$d_{l_1} \times d_{\mathrm{sp}_1} \times d_{l_2} \times d_{\mathrm{sp}_2} \times \cdots \times d_{l_n} \times d_{\mathrm{sp}_n}. \tag{5.37}$$

We have not, however, taken into account the fact that the Hamiltonian is also invariant with respect to the $n!$ permutation operations of the symmetric group of order n; this property derives from the fact that electrons are indistinguishable particles.

When the symmetric group is taken into account, we can no longer say that electron 1 is in a certain orbit, electron 2 in another orbit, and so on; this corresponds group theoretically to the fact that the state functions must transform irreducibly according to the representations of the symmetric group.

An additional requirement for the eigenfunctions is given by the Pauli principle by which only the antisymmetric representation of the symmetric group of the Hamiltonian can represent an eigenstate of an electronic system. To enforce the Pauli principle we build up determinantal eigenfunctions which are *antisymmetrized* products of one electron functions.

We may define an antisymmetrizing operator A, which, apart from a multiplying constant, is the projection operator $\rho_{11}{}^2$ discussed in Section 8.2 of Chapter 3,

$$A = n!\, \rho_{11}{}^2 = \sum_P (-1)^p P. \tag{5.38}$$

An antisymmetrized (determinantal) eigenfunction can then be expressed in the following way:

$$\psi_{11}{}^2 = \frac{A}{\sqrt{n!}}\, \psi(1, 2, \ldots, n) = \frac{A}{\sqrt{n!}} \prod_{i=1}^{n} \psi_i(i), \tag{5.39}$$

where the coordinate i includes $\mathbf{r}_i$ and spin:

$$\psi(i) = u_i(\mathbf{r}_i)\, \chi_i(s_i). \tag{5.40}$$

If we operate with A on $\psi_{11}{}^2$ we find

$$\begin{aligned} A\psi_{11}{}^2 &= \frac{A^2}{\sqrt{n!}} \prod_{i=1}^{n} \psi_i(i) = \frac{A}{\sqrt{n!}}\, n!\, \rho_{11}{}^2 \prod_{i=1}^{n} \psi_i(i) \\ &= n!\, \frac{n!\,(\rho_{11}{}^2)^2}{\sqrt{n!}} \prod_{i=1}^{n} \psi_i(i) = \frac{(n!)^2}{\sqrt{n!}}\, \rho_{11}{}^2 \prod_{i=1}^{n} \psi_i(i) \\ &= n!\, \frac{A}{\sqrt{n!}} \prod_{i=1}^{n} \psi_i(i) = n!\, \psi_{11}{}^2. \end{aligned} \tag{5.41}$$

3.2 The Electrostatic Interaction

The electrostatic interaction is taken into account by diagonalizing the Hamiltonian H_o given by (5.23).

The introduction of the electrostatic interaction produces a correlation of the following kind. The rotational operations on orbits must now be referred to the same axes and the different three dimensional rotation groups are no longer independent. The direct product 5.37 is still a representation of the symmetry group but is is no longer irreducible. It splits in the following way:

$$d_{l_1} \times d_{l_2} \times \cdots = \sum_L D_L, \tag{5.42}$$

where

$$L = (l_1 + l_2 + \cdots l_n), (l_1 + l_2 + \cdots + l_n - 1), \ldots. \tag{5.43}$$

At this stage the total spin S is introduced as a good quantum number, and this corresponds, group theoretically, to the reduction

$$d_{s_1} \times d_{s_2} \times \cdots = \sum_S D_S, \tag{5.44}$$

where

$$S = (s_1 + s_2 + \cdots s_n), (s_1 + s_2 + \cdots + s_n - 1), \ldots. \tag{5.45}$$

Some of the L and S values are, however, excluded by Pauli principle if we deal with equivalent electrons. We are now at the stage in which terms are formed. Any state function of the system is a product of a basis function for a D_L representation and a basis function for a D_S representation. The total symmetry group is given by

$$R_{\text{el}} \times R_{\text{sp}}, \tag{5.46}$$

where R_{el} = three dimensional rotation group for the orbital part and R_{sp} = three dimensional rotation group for the spin part.

3.3 The Spin Orbit Interaction

The introduction of this term produces a correlation between rotations in coordinate space and in spin space. Operations on orbits and spins must be referred to the same axes. $D_L \times D_S$ is still a representation of the symmetry group, but it is no longer irreducible; it splits in the following way:

$$D_L \times D_S = \sum_J D_J, \tag{5.47}$$

where

$$J = L + S, L + S - 1, \ldots, |L - S|. \tag{5.48}$$

We are now at the stage in which multiplets are formed by the spin orbit interaction. The eigenfunctions are basis for a D_J representation of the symmetry group.

3.4 The Zeeman Hamiltonian

The introduction of this term changes the symmetry group to $C_{\infty h}$. We then have

$$D_J = C_J + C_{J-1} + \cdots + C_J. \tag{5.49}$$

We must remember that parity is conserved. The C representations are odd if D_J is odd and even if D_J is even.

3.5 Observations

In a perturbation calculation the different terms in the Hamiltonian are put in order of decreasing importance for the purpose of getting convergence. The group theoretical treatment does not necessarily have to follow a *parallel* path. It is possible, group theoretically, to consider, for example, the spin-orbit interaction first and then the electrostatic interaction. We would have, in this case, a coupling of individual orbitals of single electrons with respective spins

$$d_{l_i} \times d_{s_i} = d_j, \tag{5.50}$$

where

$$j = l_i + s_i, l_i + s_i - 1, \ldots, |l_i - s_i|, \tag{5.51}$$

and then a coupling of the j orbitals

$$d_{j_1} \times d_{j_2} \times \cdots = \sum_J D_J. \tag{5.52}$$

The representations D_J obtained with this method are exactly the same as those obtained with the method described in Secs. 3.1, 3.2, and 3.3 of this chapter. This alternative method corresponds to the j-j coupling. We may recognize in this possibility of following *different paths* a peculiar aspect of the application of group theory to quantum mechanical problems.

3.6 The "Noncrossing" Rule

Let us assume that the energy values of an atomic system depend only on an external perturbation parameter R (say, magnetic field) and that the system has a total Hamiltonian H. Let us also assume that we know all the eigenfunctions of H but two. Let us then consider two functions ψ_1 and ψ_2 which are orthogonal to all the other eigenfunctions of the system and which are also mutually orthogonal. The two unknown eigenfunctions must be linear combinations of ψ_1 and ψ_2 and the two unknown eigenvalues E_1 and E_2 can be obtained from the secular equation

$$\begin{vmatrix} \langle\psi_1| H |\psi_1\rangle - E & \langle\psi_1| H |\psi_2\rangle \\ \langle\psi_2| H |\psi_1\rangle & \langle\psi_2| H |\psi_2\rangle - E \end{vmatrix} = 0. \tag{5.53}$$

By solving this equation we obtain

$$E = \frac{\langle 1|\ H\ |1\rangle + \langle 2|\ H\ |2\rangle \pm \sqrt{(\langle 1|\ H\ |1\rangle - \langle 2|\ H\ |2\rangle)^2 + 4\ |\langle 1|\ H\ |2\rangle|^2}}{2}. \tag{5.54}$$

There will be a degeneracy ($E_1 = E_2$) if we have, simultaneously,

$$\begin{aligned} \langle 1|\ H\ |1\rangle &= \langle 2|\ H\ |2\rangle, \\ \langle 1|\ H\ |2\rangle &= 0, \end{aligned} \tag{5.55}$$

for the same value of the perturbation parameter R. It is very unlikely that both conditions will be satisfied for one value of R; it is possible, however, that the first condition will be satisfied for a particular value of R if the second condition is satisfied for *any* value of R. When this is the case, ψ_1 and ψ_2 are the basis of two different irreducible representations of the symmetry group of H. We can then state: *Terms of equal symmetry never cross.*

We may apply this rule to the example in Section 8 of Chapter 1 (atomic hydrogen in state $l = 1$, in a homogeneous magnetic field). We then have (see Fig. 1.1): states with equal m_j can never cross.

4. THE ENERGIES OF SPECTRAL TERMS

To find the energies of the spectral terms we must use as unperturbed eigenfunctions the determinant

$$\begin{aligned} \psi &= \frac{1}{\sqrt{n!}} \begin{pmatrix} \psi_1(1) & \psi_2(1) & \cdots & \psi_n(1) \\ \psi_1(2) & \psi_2(2) & \cdots & \psi_n(2) \\ \cdots & \cdots & \cdots & \cdots \\ \psi_1(n) & \psi_2(n) & \cdots & \psi_n(n) \end{pmatrix} \\ &= \frac{1}{\sqrt{n!}} \sum_P (-1)^p\ \psi_1(1)\ \psi_2(2) \cdots \psi_n(n), \end{aligned} \tag{5.56}$$

(where P is any possible permutation of electrons) and look for the matrix elements of

$$H_o = \sum_i \left(-\frac{\hbar^2}{2m} \nabla_i^2 - \frac{Ze^2}{r_i} \right) + \frac{1}{2} \sum_{i \neq j} \frac{e^2}{r_{ij}} = \sum_i f_i + \sum_{\substack{ij \\ (i \neq j)}} g_{ij}, \tag{5.57}$$

where

$$\begin{aligned} f_i &= -\frac{\hbar^2}{2m} \nabla_i^2 - \frac{Ze^2}{r_i} \\ g_{ij} &= \frac{1}{2} \frac{e^2}{r_{ij}}. \end{aligned} \tag{5.58}$$

We can write

$$\psi = D = \frac{A}{\sqrt{n!}}\,\pi, \tag{5.59}$$

where D indicates that ψ is a determinantal function,
A = antisymmetrizing operator,
π = product of elementary functions.

Because of (5.41) we have

$$\begin{aligned}\langle D_j|\, H_o\,|D_i\rangle = \frac{1}{n!}\langle A\pi_j|\, H_o\,|A\pi_i\rangle &= \frac{1}{n!}\langle \pi_j|\, H_o\,|A^2\pi_i\rangle \\ &= \langle \pi_j|\, H_o\,|A\pi_i\rangle.\end{aligned} \tag{5.60}$$

The operator A can be written

$$A = 1 - \sum_{s<t} P_{st} + \sum_{\substack{s<t\\x<y}} P_{st}P_{xy} - \ldots, \tag{5.61}$$

where P_{st} indicates an operation that permutes electrons s and t. The terms $\sum P_{st}P_{xy}$ and the following terms in the sum do not make any contribution to (5.60).

There are three different ways of building up two different elementary functions ψ_a and ψ_a':

$$\begin{aligned}
&\psi_a(1) = u_a(1)\,\chi_a(1); &&\psi_a'(1) = u_a(1)\,\chi_a'(1);\\
&\psi_a(1) = u_a(1)\,\chi_a(1); &&\psi_a'(1) = u_a'(1)\,\chi_a(1);\\
&\psi_a(1) = u_a(1)\,\chi_a(1); &&\psi_a'(1) = u_a'(1)\,\chi_a'(1).
\end{aligned} \tag{5.62}$$

We have the following orthogonality relations:

$$\begin{aligned}&\int u_a^*(1)\,u_b(1)\,d\tau_1 = \delta_{ab};\\ &\sum_{\sigma=-1/2}^{1/2} \chi_{m_s}^*(\sigma)\,\chi_{m_s'}(\sigma) = \delta_{m_s m_s'},\end{aligned} \tag{5.63}$$

where

$$\begin{aligned}&\chi_{1/2}(\tfrac{1}{2}) = \begin{pmatrix}1\\0\end{pmatrix}, &&\chi_{-1/2}(\tfrac{1}{2}) = \begin{pmatrix}0\\0\end{pmatrix},\\ &\chi_{1/2}(-\tfrac{1}{2}) = \begin{pmatrix}0\\0\end{pmatrix}, &&\chi_{-1/2}(-\tfrac{1}{2}) = \begin{pmatrix}0\\1\end{pmatrix}.\end{aligned} \tag{5.64}$$

Let us examine the different ways in which two products π_i and π_j can be different.

π_i ***and*** π_j ***differ by more than two*** ψ***'s***

$$\pi_j = \psi_a(1)\,\psi_b(2)\,\psi_c(3)\,\psi_d(4)\ldots,$$
$$\pi_i = \psi'_a(1)\,\psi'_b(2)\,\psi'_c(3)\,\psi_d(4)\ldots. \tag{5.65}$$

The matrix element of H_0 in this case is zero.

$$\langle D_j|\,H_o\,|D_i\rangle = 0. \tag{5.66}$$

π_i ***and*** π_j ***differ only by two*** ψ***'s***

$$\pi_j = \psi_a(1)\,\psi_b(2)\,\psi_c(3)\ldots,$$
$$\pi_i = \psi'_a(1)\,\psi'_b(2)\,\psi_c(3)\ldots. \tag{5.67}$$

The matrix element of H_0 is given by

$$\langle D_j|\,H_o\,|D_i\rangle = \langle\psi_a(1)\,\psi_b(2)|\,g_{12}\,|\psi'_a(1)\,\psi'_b(2)\rangle - \langle\psi_a(1)\,\psi_b(2)|\,g_{12}\,|\psi'_b(1)\,\psi_a(2)\rangle \tag{5.68}$$

We can write extensively

$$\langle\psi_a(1)\,\psi_b(2)|\,g_{12}\,|\psi'_a(1)\,\psi'_b(2)\rangle = \langle\psi_a(1)\,\psi_b(2)|\,\frac{e^2}{2r_{12}}\,|\psi'_a(1)\,\psi'_b(2)\rangle$$
$$= \sum_{\sigma_1\sigma_2}\iint u_a^*(1)\,\chi_a^*(1)\,u_b^*(2)\,\chi_b^*(2)\,\frac{e^2}{2r_{12}}\,u'_a(1)\,\chi'_a(1)\,u'_b(2)\,\chi'_b(2)\,d\tau_1\,d\tau_2$$
$$= \delta_{m_{s_a}m_{s_a'}}\delta_{m_{s_b}m_{s_b'}}\iint u_a^*(1)\,u_b^*(2)\,\frac{e^2}{2r_{12}}\,u'_a(1)\,u'_b(2)\,d\tau_1\,d\tau_2, \tag{5.69}$$

and

$$\langle\psi_a(1)\,\psi_b(2)|\,g_{12}\,|\psi'_b(1)\,\psi'_a(2)\rangle = \langle\psi_a(1)\,\psi_b(2)|\,\frac{e^2}{2r_{12}}\,|\psi'_b(1)\,\psi'_a(2)\rangle$$
$$= \sum_{\sigma_1\sigma_2}\iint u_a^*(1)\,\chi_a^*(1)\,u_b^*(2)\,\chi_b^*(2)\,\frac{e^2}{2r_{12}}\,u'_b(1)\,\chi'_b(1)\,u'_a(2)\,\chi'_a(2)\,d\tau_1\,d\tau_2$$
$$= \delta_{m_{s_a}m_{s_b'}}\delta_{m_{s_b}m_{s_a'}}\iint u_a(1)\,u_b(2)\,\frac{e^2}{2r_{12}}\,u'_b(1)\,u'_a(2)\,d\tau_1\,d\tau_2. \tag{5.70}$$

More briefly, we can write

$$\langle D_j|\,H_o\,|D_i\rangle = \langle ab|\,g\,|a'b'\rangle_{/\!/} - \langle ab|\,g\,|b'a'\rangle_{/\!/}, \tag{5.71}$$

where $/\!/$ indicates equal spins.

π_i ***and*** π_j ***differ by one*** ψ

In this case

$$\pi_j = \psi_a(1)\,\psi_b(2)\ldots,$$
$$\pi_i = \psi'_a(1)\,\psi_b(2)\ldots, \tag{5.72}$$

and

$$\langle D_j | H_o | D_i \rangle = \langle a | f | a' \rangle_{/\!/} + \sum_{s \neq a} [\langle as | g | a's \rangle_{/\!/} - \langle as | g | sa' \rangle_{/\!/}] \quad (5.73)$$

π_i and π_j are identical

$$\langle D_i | H_o | D_i \rangle = \sum_a \langle a | f | a \rangle + \sum_{a<b} [\langle ab | g | ab \rangle - \langle ab | g | ba \rangle_{/\!/}]. \quad (5.74)$$

The exchange integral term lowers the energy of the system. The electrons that contribute to this effect have parallel spins. The D_i with *more* parallel spins have more exchange integrals and then have lower energy. This is in accord with *Hund's rule* (see Section 5 of this chapter). In other words, we may say that the Pauli principle keeps electrons with parallel spins far apart and then lowers their electrostatic energy.

The situation is represented in the Table 5.2.

Table 5.2 Matrix Elements of the Hamiltonian H_o between States Defined by Determinantal Functions

	$\langle D_j | H_o | D_i \rangle$
$\pi_j \neq \pi_i$ by more than two u's	0
$\pi_j \neq \pi_i$ by two u's	$\langle ab | g | a'b' \rangle_{/\!/} - \langle ab | g | b'a' \rangle_{/\!/}$
$\pi_j \neq \pi_i$ by one u	$\langle a | f | a' \rangle_{/\!/} + \sum_{s \neq a} [\langle as | g | a's \rangle_{/\!/} - \langle as | g | sa' \rangle_{/\!/}]$
$\pi_j = \pi_i$	$\sum_a \langle a | f | a \rangle + \sum_{a<b} [\langle ab | g | ab \rangle - \langle ab | g | ba \rangle_{/\!/}]$

Example: Two Nonequivalent *s* Electrons. Configuration *ss'*

	m_{s_1}	m_{s_2}	M_s	Derived States
I	$\frac{1}{2}$	$\frac{1}{2}$	1	${}^3S(M_S = 1)$
II	$\frac{1}{2}$	$-\frac{1}{2}$	0	${}^3S(M_S = 0)$, ${}^1S(M_S = 0)$
III	$-\frac{1}{2}$	$\frac{1}{2}$	0	
IV	$-\frac{1}{2}$	$-\frac{1}{2}$	-1	${}^3S(M_S = -1)$

The matrix elements of the Hamiltonian H are given by

$$\langle D_{\rm I} | H_o | D_{\rm I} \rangle = \langle 1 | f | 1 \rangle + \langle 2 | f | 2 \rangle + \langle 12 | g | 12 \rangle - \langle 12 | g | 21 \rangle,$$
$$\langle D_{\rm II} | H_o | D_{\rm II} \rangle = \langle 1 | f | 1 \rangle + \langle 2 | f | 2 \rangle + \langle 12 | g | 12 \rangle,$$
$$\langle D_{\rm III} | H_o | D_{\rm III} \rangle = \langle 1 | f | 1 \rangle + \langle 2 | f | s \rangle + \langle 12 | g | 12 \rangle,$$
$$\langle D_{\rm IV} | H_o | D_{\rm IV} \rangle = \langle 1 | f | 1 \rangle + \langle 2 | f | 2 \rangle + \langle 12 | g | 12 \rangle - \langle 12 | g | 21 \rangle.$$

The only nondiagonal matrix element is

$$\langle D_{\text{II}}| H_o |D_{\text{III}}\rangle = -\langle 12| g |21\rangle.$$

Here we need to solve a 2×2 secular equation to find the energies of the levels ^3S and ^1S. We actually need to diagonalize a 2×2 matrix:

$$\begin{pmatrix} \langle D_{\text{II}}| H_o |D_{\text{II}}\rangle & \langle D_{\text{II}}| H_o |D_{\text{III}}\rangle \\ \langle D_{\text{III}}| H_o |D_{\text{II}}\rangle & \langle D_{\text{III}}| H_o |D_{\text{III}}\rangle \end{pmatrix}.$$

The process of diagonalization does not change the trace of this matrix: this property is called the *sum rule*, and can take advantage of this fact.

$$\langle D_{\text{II}}| H_o |D_{\text{II}}\rangle + \langle D_{\text{III}}| H_o |D_{\text{III}}\rangle = \text{energy of } {}^3S + \text{energy of } {}^1S;$$

but the energy of the triplet ^3S is already known. It is given by

$$\langle D_{\text{I}}| H_o |D_{\text{I}}\rangle$$

or

$$\langle D_{\text{IV}}| H_o |D_{\text{IV}}\rangle.$$

The energy of the singlet ^1S is then given by

$$\begin{aligned} \text{energy } {}^1S &= \langle D_{\text{II}}| H_o |D_{\text{II}}\rangle + \langle D_{\text{III}}| H_o |D_{\text{III}}\rangle - \langle D_{\text{I}}| H_o |D_{\text{I}}\rangle \\ &= \langle 1| f |1\rangle + \langle 2| f 2| f |2\rangle + \langle 12| g |12\rangle + \langle 12| g |21\rangle. \end{aligned}$$

Going back to the general case, we shall want to look carefully at the different matrix elements. We have from [1], p. 310,

$$\begin{aligned} &\langle \psi_a(1)\, \psi_b(2)| \, g_{12} \, |\psi'_a(1)\, \psi'_b(2)\rangle \\ &\quad = \delta_{m_{s_a} m_{s_a}'} \delta_{m_{s_b} m_{s_b}'} \delta_{(m_{l_a}+m_{l_b}),(m_{l_a}'+m_{l_b}')} \\ &\qquad \cdot \sum_{k=0}^{\infty} c_k(l_a m_{l_a}; l_{a'} m_{l_{a'}}) c_k(l_{b'} m_{l_{b'}}; l_b m_{l_b}) R^k(ab; a'b'), \end{aligned} \tag{5.75}$$

where

$$\begin{aligned} &R^k(ab; a'b') \\ &= \int_0^\infty \int_0^\infty R^*_{n_a l_a}(r_1)\, R^*_{n_b l_b}(r_2)\, R_{n_{a'} l_{a'}}(r_1)\, R_{n_{b'} l_{b'}}(r_2) \frac{2r(a)^k}{r(b)^{k+1}} r_1^2 r_2^2 \, dr_1 \, dr_2, \end{aligned} \tag{5.76}$$

and $r(a)$ is the smaller and $r(b)$ the larger of r_1, r_2. From these expressions we derive

$$\langle \psi_a(1)\, \psi_b(2)| \, g_{12} \, |\psi_a(1)\, \psi_b(2)\rangle = \sum_{k=0}^{\infty} a^k(l_a m_{l_a}; l_b m_{l_b}) F^k(n_a l_a; n_b l_b), \tag{5.77}$$

where

$$a^k(l_a m_{l_a}; l_b m_{l_b}) = c^k(l_a m_{l_a}; l_a m_{l_a}) c^k(l_b m_{l_b}; l_b l m_{l_b}), \tag{5.78}$$

$$F^k(n_a l_a; n_b l_b) = R^k(ab; ab), \tag{5.79}$$

and

$$\langle \psi_a(1)\, \psi_b(2)|\, g_{12}\, |\psi_b(1)\, \psi_a(2)\rangle = \delta_{m_{s_a} m_{s_b}} \sum_{k=0}^{\infty} b^k(l_a m_{l_a}; l_b m_{l_b}) G^k(n_a l_a; n_b l_b), \tag{5.80}$$

where

$$b^k(l_a m_{l_a}; l_b m_{l_b}) = [c^k(l_a m_{l_a}; l_b m_{l_b})]^2, \tag{5.81}$$

$$G^k(n_a l_a; n_b l_b) = R^k(ab; ba). \tag{5.82}$$

The coefficients a^k, b^k, and c^k can be found in Appendix 20 of [2]. We notice that, for equivalent electrons $n_a = n_b$, $l_a = l_b$ and $F^k = G^k$.

Example: Two Equivalent p Electrons. Configuration p^2

	m_{l_1}	m_{l_2}	m_{s_1}	m_{s_2}	M_L	M_S	M_J	Derived States
1	1	1	$\frac{1}{2}$	$-\frac{1}{2}$	2	0	2	${}^1D_{20}$
2	1	0	$\frac{1}{2}$	$\frac{1}{2}$	1	1	2	${}^3P_{11}$
3	1	0	$\frac{1}{2}$	$-\frac{1}{2}$	1	0	1	${}^3P_{10}\ {}^1D_{10}$
4	0	1	$\frac{1}{2}$	$-\frac{1}{2}$	1	0	1	
5	1	0	$-\frac{1}{2}$	$-\frac{1}{2}$	1	-1	0	${}^3P_{1-1}$
6	1	-1	$\frac{1}{2}$	$\frac{1}{2}$	0	1	1	${}^3P_{01}$
7	1	-1	$\frac{1}{2}$	$-\frac{1}{2}$	0	0	0	${}^3P_{00}\ {}^1D_{00}\ {}^1S_{00}$
8	0	0	$\frac{1}{2}$	$-\frac{1}{2}$	0	0	0	
9	-1	1	$\frac{1}{2}$	$-\frac{1}{2}$	0	0	0	
10	1	-1	$-\frac{1}{2}$	$-\frac{1}{2}$	0	-1	-1	${}^3P_{0-1}$
11	-1	0	$\frac{1}{2}$	$\frac{1}{2}$	-1	1	0	${}^3P_{-11}$
12	-1	0	$\frac{1}{2}$	$-\frac{1}{2}$	-1	0	-1	${}^3P_{-10}\ {}^1D_{-10}$
13	0	-1	$\frac{1}{2}$	$-\frac{1}{2}$	-1	0	-1	
14	-1	0	$-\frac{1}{2}$	$-\frac{1}{2}$	-1	-1	-2	${}^3P_{-1-1}$
15	-1	-1	$-\frac{1}{2}$	$-\frac{1}{2}$	-2	0	-2	${}^1D_{-20}$

We now evaluate the diagonal matrix elements of the Hamiltonian H_0 by making use of (5.74), (5.77), and (5.80). By using the sum rule we then derive the energies of the various terms. We indicate the ith determinantal eigenfunction in the previous table by D_i.

The coefficients k for the electronic configuration p^2 are given by [2]:

m_{l_1}	m_{l_2}	$k = 0$	$k = 2$	$k = 4$	$k = 6$
±1	±1	1	$\frac{1}{25}$	0	0
±1	0	1	$-\frac{2}{25}$	0	0
0	0	1	$\frac{4}{25}$	0	0

The two signs $\pm$ can be combined in any four of the possible ways. The coefficients b^k for p^2 are given by [2]:

m_{l_1}	m_{l_2}	$k = 0$	$k = 2$	$k = 4$	$k = 6$
± 1	± 1	1	$\frac{1}{25}$	0	0
± 1	0	0	$\frac{3}{25}$	0	0
± 1	± 1	0	$\frac{6}{25}$	0	0
0	0	1	$\frac{4}{25}$	0	0

We obtain the following results.

$$\langle D_1 | H_o | D_1 \rangle = \langle 1 | f | 1 \rangle + \langle 2 | f | 2 \rangle + \langle 12 | g | 12 \rangle$$
$$= I + \sum_k F^k(12; 12) = I + F^0(n1; n1) + \tfrac{1}{25}F^2(n1; n1),$$

where $I = \langle 1 | f | 1 \rangle + \langle 2 | f | 2 \rangle$.

Also

$$\langle D_3 | H_o | D_3 \rangle = \langle 1 | f | 1 \rangle + \langle 2 | f | 2 \rangle + \langle 12 | g | 12 \rangle$$
$$= I + \sum_k F^k(12; 12) = I + F^0 - \tfrac{2}{25}F^2$$

$$\langle D_4 | H_o | D_4 \rangle = I + \sum_k F^k(12; 12) = I + F^0 - \tfrac{2}{25}F^2.$$

where $F^0 = F^0(n1; n1)$ and $F^2 = F^2(n1; n1)$. Then,

$$E(^3P + {}^1D) = 2I + 2F^0 - \tfrac{4}{25}F^2,$$

and $E(^3P) = E(^3P + {}^1D) - E(^1D) = I + F^0 - \frac{1}{5}F^2$. Otherwise we can derive $E(^3P)$ directly:

$$E(^3P) = \langle D_2 | H_o | D_2 \rangle = I + \langle 12 | g | 12 \rangle - \langle 12 | g | 21 \rangle$$
$$= I + F^0 - \tfrac{2}{25}F^2 - \tfrac{3}{25}F^2 = I + F^0 - \tfrac{1}{5}F^2.$$

Also

$$E(^3P + {}^1D + {}^1S) = \langle D_7 | H_o | D_7 \rangle + \langle D_8 | H_o | D_8 \rangle + \langle D_9 | H_o | D_9 \rangle$$
$$= 3I + a^0(11; 1\ {-1})F^0 + a^2(11; 1\ {-1})F^2$$
$$+ a^0(10; 10)F^0 + a^2(10; 10)F^2$$
$$+ a^0(1\ {-1}; 11)F^0 + a^2(1\ {-1}; 11)F^2$$
$$= 3I + F^0 + \tfrac{1}{25}F^2 + F^0 + \tfrac{4}{25}F^2 + F^0 + \tfrac{1}{25}F^2$$
$$= 3I + 3F^0 + \tfrac{6}{25}F^2.$$

Therefore

$$E(^1S) = 3I + 3F^0 + \tfrac{6}{25}F^2 - (2I + 2F^0 - \tfrac{4}{25}F^2)$$
$$= I + F^0 + \tfrac{10}{25}F^2.$$

Then, in conclusion, we get

$$E(^3P) = I + F_0 - \tfrac{5}{25}F^2,$$
$$E(^1D) = I + F_0 + \tfrac{1}{25}F^2,$$
$$E(^1S) = I + F_0 + \tfrac{10}{25}F^2.$$

The separations of the term levels depend on the parameter F^2 only.

5. HUND'S RULES AND THE PRINCIPLE OF EQUIVALENCE OF ELECTRONS AND HOLES

5.1 Hund's Rules

Hund's rules are of great help in evaluating the ground state of atomic systems. They can be stated as follows for a given electronic configuration:

1. *Of all the terms allowed by the Pauli principle, the lowest will be one of maximum multiplicity.*
2. *Of these terms with maximum multiplicity that with greatest L value will be lowest.*
3. *For configurations consisting of electrons in a less than half filled shell the spin-orbit splitting is usually normal, that is, the multiplet with the smallest J is lowest; for configurations with a more than half filled shell the multiplets are usually inverted.*

Hund's rules are *not* to be applied to excited states.

A different way of formulating Hund's rules is the following:

Equivalent electrons tend not to share the same orbital and electrons occupying different but equivalent orbitals tend to have their spins parallel.

In Table 5.3 we show some applications of Hund's rules.

5.2 The Principle of Equivalence of Electrons and Holes

We have two results:

1. *The only effect of a closed shell on the calculation of the terms arising from certain electrons in configurations outside the closed shell is to contribute an additive constant to the energy.*
2. *A shell containing $N - n$ electrons has the same term structure as one containing n electrons, where N is the number of electrons in the filled shell. The term separations are the same for a shell lacking n electrons as for a shell with n electrons.*

For proof of these theorems see [1] p. 320. As an example we report the terms produced by equivalent p electrons.

Table 5.3 Ground States of the First Eleven Elements of the Periodic Table

		Configuration	Ground State	L	S	J
1.	H	$2s$ — $2p$ — — — $1s$ ↑	$^2S_{1/2}$	0	$\frac{1}{2}$	$\frac{1}{2}$
2.	He	$2s$ — $2p$ — — — $1s$ ↑↓	$^1S_0$	0	0	0
3.	Li	$2s$ ↑ $2p$ — — — $1s$ ↑↓	$^2S_{1/2}$	0	$\frac{1}{2}$	$\frac{1}{2}$
4.	Be	$2s$ ↑↓ $2p$ — — — $1s$ ↑↓	$^1S_0$	0	0	0
5.	B	$2s$ ↑↓ $2p$ ↑ — — $1s$ ↑↓	$^2P_{1/2}$	1	$\frac{1}{2}$	$\frac{1}{2}$
6.	C	$2s$ ↑↓ $2p$ ↑ ↑ — $1s$ ↑↓	$^3P_0$	1	1	0
7.	N	$2s$ ↑↓ $2p$ ↑ ↑ ↑ $1s$ ↑↓	$^4S_{3/2}$	0	$\frac{3}{2}$	$\frac{3}{2}$
8.	O	$2s$ ↑↓ $2p$ ↑ ↑ ↑↓ $1s$ ↑↓	$^3P_2$	1	1	2
9.	F	$2s$ ↑↓ $2p$ ↑ ↑↓ ↑↓ $1s$ ↑↓	$^2P_{3/2}$	1	$\frac{1}{2}$	$\frac{3}{2}$
10.	Ne	$2s$ ↑↓ $2p$ ↑↓ ↑↓ ↑↓ $1s$ ↑↓	$^1S_0$	0	0	0
11.	Na	$3s$ ↑ $3p$ — — — $2s$ ↑↓ $2p$ ↑↓ ↑↓ ↑↓ $1s$ ↑↓	$^2S_{1/2}$	0	$\frac{1}{2}$	$\frac{1}{2}$

Terms for Equivalent p Electrons

$$p^1, p^5: \quad {}^2P_u;$$

$$p^2, p^4: \quad {}^3P_g, {}^1D_g, {}^1S_g;$$

$$p^3: \quad {}^4S_u, {}^2D_u, {}^2P_u.$$

Every term and every multiplet level deriving from it is a state of definite parity. The subscript u (ungerade) means odd parity. The subscript g (gerade) means even parity.

6. THE SPIN-ORBIT SPLITTING OF TERMS

The spin-orbit Hamiltonian is given by

$$H_{so} = \sum_i \xi(r_i)\mathbf{l}_i \cdot \mathbf{s}_i, \tag{5.83}$$

where the sum extends over all the electrons in the atom.

The spin-orbit Hamiltonian commutes with the total angular momentum **J** and with its component J_z. The generic matrix element is given by

$$\begin{aligned}\langle \alpha' L' S' M_L' M_S' \mid H_{so} \mid \alpha L S M_L M_S \rangle \\ = \sum_{\alpha''} \sum_i \langle \alpha' L' M_L' | \, \xi(r_i)\mathbf{l}_i \, | \alpha'' L M_L \rangle \cdot \langle \alpha'' S' M_S' | \, \mathbf{s}_i \, | \alpha S M_S \rangle. \end{aligned} \tag{5.84}$$

Using the Wigner-Eckart theorem of Section 5.5 of Chapter 3, we find that H_{so} may connect states with $\Delta L = \pm 1, 0$, $\Delta S = \pm 1, 0$. The fact that H_{so} commutes with $\mathbf{J}$, J_z adds the rule $\Delta J = 0$, $\Delta M_J = 0$.

Let us determine the effects of the spin-orbit interaction within the same LS term. The generic matrix element is given by

$$\langle LSM_L'M_S' | \, H_{so} \, | LSM_L M_S \rangle = \sum_i \langle LM_L' | \, \xi(r_i)\mathbf{l}_i \, | LM_L \rangle \cdot \langle SM_S' | \, \mathbf{s}_i \, | SM_S \rangle. \tag{5.85}$$

It is advantageous here to use the result given by (3.116), which allows us to write

$$\begin{aligned}\langle LM_L' | \, \mathbf{l}_i \, | LM_L \rangle &= \langle LM_L' | \, \mathbf{L} \, | LM_L \rangle \frac{\langle L \| \, l_i \, \| L \rangle}{\langle L \| \, L \, \| L \rangle} \\ &= \frac{\langle L \| \, l_i \, \| L \rangle}{\hbar\sqrt{L(L+1)}} \langle LM_L' | \, \mathbf{L} \, | LM_L \rangle, \end{aligned} \tag{5.86}$$

and

$$\langle SM_S' | \, \mathbf{s}_i \, | SM_S \rangle = \frac{\langle S \| \, s_i \, \| S \rangle}{\hbar\sqrt{S(S+1)}} \langle SM_S' | \, \mathbf{S} \, | SM_S \rangle. \tag{5.87}$$

The generic matrix element of H_{so} within the same LS term is then given by

$$\begin{aligned}&\langle LSM_L'M_S' | \, H_{so} \, | LSM_L M_S \rangle \\ &= \frac{\sum_i \langle L \| \, \xi(r_i) l_i \, \| L \rangle \langle S \| \, s_i \, \| S \rangle}{\hbar^2 \sqrt{L(L+1)}\sqrt{S(S+1)}} \langle LSM_L'M_S' | \, \mathbf{L} \cdot \mathbf{S} \, | LSM_L M_S \rangle \\ &= \lambda(L, S) \langle LSM_L'M_S' | \, \mathbf{L} \cdot \mathbf{S} \, | LSM_L M_S \rangle. \end{aligned} \tag{5.88}$$

Therefore the matrix element of $\sum_i \xi(r_i)\,\mathbf{l}_i \cdot \mathbf{s}_i$ and $\lambda\mathbf{L}\cdot\mathbf{S}$ are proportional within the same term. Going from the LSM_LM_S representation to the $LSJM_J$ representation (through a unitary transformation) does not affect their proportionality. For this reason, as

$$\mathbf{L}\cdot\mathbf{S} = \frac{J^2 - S^2 - L^2}{2}, \tag{5.89}$$

the energy of an LSJ level is given by

$$E(L, S, J, M_j) = \lambda(L, S)\,\frac{J(J+1) - S(S+1) - L(L+1)}{2}. \tag{5.90}$$

The separation in energy between levels $J - 1$ and J is given by

$$E(L, S, J) - E(L, S, J-1) = \lambda(L, S)\,J. \tag{5.91}$$

This relation expresses the Landé interval rule.

We now want to find the relation between λ and the one-electron spin-orbit factors:

$$\zeta_{n_il_i} = \hbar^2 \int R^2_{n_il_i}(r)\xi(r)r^2\,dr. \tag{5.92}$$

Let us find the matrix elements of H_{so} by using determinantal wavefunctions. Let us consider only diagonal elements:

$$\langle D_k|\,H_{so}\,|D_k\rangle = \frac{1}{n!}\langle A\pi_k|\,H_{so}\,|A\pi_k\rangle$$

$$= \frac{1}{n!}\langle \pi_k|\,H_{so}\,|A^2\pi_k\rangle = \langle \pi_k|\,H_{so}\,|A\pi_k\rangle.$$

Then

$$\begin{aligned}\langle D_k|\,H_{so}\,|D_k\rangle &= \langle \pi_k|\sum_i \xi(r_i)\mathbf{l}_i\cdot\mathbf{s}_i\,|A\pi_k\rangle \\ &= \sum_i \langle n_il_im_{l_i}m_{s_i}|\,\xi(r_i)\mathbf{l}_i\cdot\mathbf{s}_i\,|n_il_im_{l_i}m_{s_i}\rangle \\ &= \sum_i \langle n_il_i|\,\xi(r_i)\,|n_il_i\rangle m_{l_i}m_{s_i}\hbar^2 \\ &= \sum_i \xi_{n_il_i}m_{l_i}m_{s_i}.\end{aligned} \tag{5.93}$$

The generic diagonal element in the $|LSM_LM_S\rangle$ state is given by

$$\langle LSM_LM_S|\,H_{so}\,|LSM_LM_S\rangle = \lambda M_LM_S. \tag{5.94}$$

The functions $|LSM_LM_S\rangle$ are in general linear combinations of determinantal functions. In particular, certain $|LSM_LM_S\rangle$ functions may be represented by single Slater determinants; for example the determinant D_1, corresponding to $M_L = 2$, $M_S = 0$ in the example in Section 4 of this chapter (which considers the p^2 configuration), represents also the eigenfunction $|L = 2, M_L = 2, S = 0, M_S = 0\rangle$.

If there is only one determinantal function with certain M_L and M_S, we get from (5.93) and (5.94)

$$\lambda = \frac{1}{M_L M_S} \sum_i \zeta_{n_i l_i} m_{l_i} m_{s_i}. \tag{5.95}$$

Let us now consider an atom with an electronic configuration nl^x; in particular, let us examine the ground term. Consistent with Hund's rules, this term has the largest S and L that the Pauli principle allows. For such a state only one determinantal function corresponds to $M_L = L$ and $M_S = S$. We have three cases to explore:

$x < 2l + 1$ SHELL LESS THAN HALF FULL

In this case all the spins are parallel.

$$\lambda = \frac{\zeta_{nl}}{LS} \sum_i m_{l_i} m_{s_i} = \frac{1}{2} \frac{\zeta_{nl}}{LS} \sum_i m_{l_i} = \frac{\zeta_{nl} M_L}{2LS}$$
$$= \frac{\zeta_{nl}}{2S}. \tag{5.96}$$

This is the case for $M_L = 2$, $M_S = 0$ for the configuration p^2 already examined in Section 4 of this chapter:

$$\lambda(^3P) = \frac{1}{M_L M_S} \sum_i \zeta_{n_i l_i} m_{l_i} m_{s_i} = \tfrac{1}{2}\zeta_{np}.$$

$x > 2l + 1$ SHELL MORE THAN HALF FULL

In this case some of the spins are reversed because of the Pauli principle. We have:

$$\lambda = \frac{\zeta_{nl}}{LS} \sum_i m_{l_i} m_{s_i} = \frac{\zeta_{nl}}{LS} \left\{ \tfrac{1}{2} \sum_{k=-l}^{l} m_{l_k} - \tfrac{1}{2} \sum_i m_{l_i} \right\}$$
$$= \frac{\zeta_{nl}}{LS} (-\tfrac{1}{2} M_L) = -\frac{\zeta_{nl}}{2S}. \tag{5.97}$$

$x = 2l + 1$ SHELL HALF FULL

In this case

$$S = \frac{2l+1}{2}, \qquad L = 0, \qquad J = S = \frac{2l+1}{2},$$

and we have no multiplet structure.

7. AN EXAMPLE OF SPIN-ORBIT AND ZEEMAN SPLITTING

Configuration sp + *Closed Shell:*

$$l_1 = 0, \qquad s_1 = \tfrac{1}{2};$$

$$l_2 = 1, \qquad s_2 = \tfrac{1}{2}.$$

We may have the following values of L and S:

$$L = 1, \qquad S = 1, 0.$$

Let us examine the two resulting terms:

$L = 1; S = 1; J = 2, 1, 0$

$J = 2$

$$\frac{J(J+1) - L(L+1) - S(S+1)}{2} = 1;$$

$$g = 1 + \frac{J(J+1) + S(S+1) - L(L+1)}{2J(J+1)} = \frac{3}{2}.$$

Degeneracy: $2J + 1 = 5$; possible values of M_J: $2, 1, 0, -1, -2$.

$J = 1$

$$\frac{J(J+1) - L(L+1) - S(S+1)}{2} = -1;$$

$$g = \tfrac{3}{2}.$$

Degeneracy: $2J + 1 = 3$; possible values of M_J: $1, 0, -1$.

$J = 0$

$$\frac{J(J+1) - L(L+1) - S(S+1)}{2} = -2;$$

$$g = \tfrac{3}{2}.$$

Degeneracy: $2J + 1 = 1$; possible values of M_J:0. The center of gravity remains unchanged: $5 \times 1 + 3 \times (-1) + 1 \times (-2) = 0$.

$L = 1; S = 0; J = 1.$

$J = 1$

$$\frac{J(J+1) - L(L+1) - S(S+1)}{2} = 0;$$

$$g = 1.$$

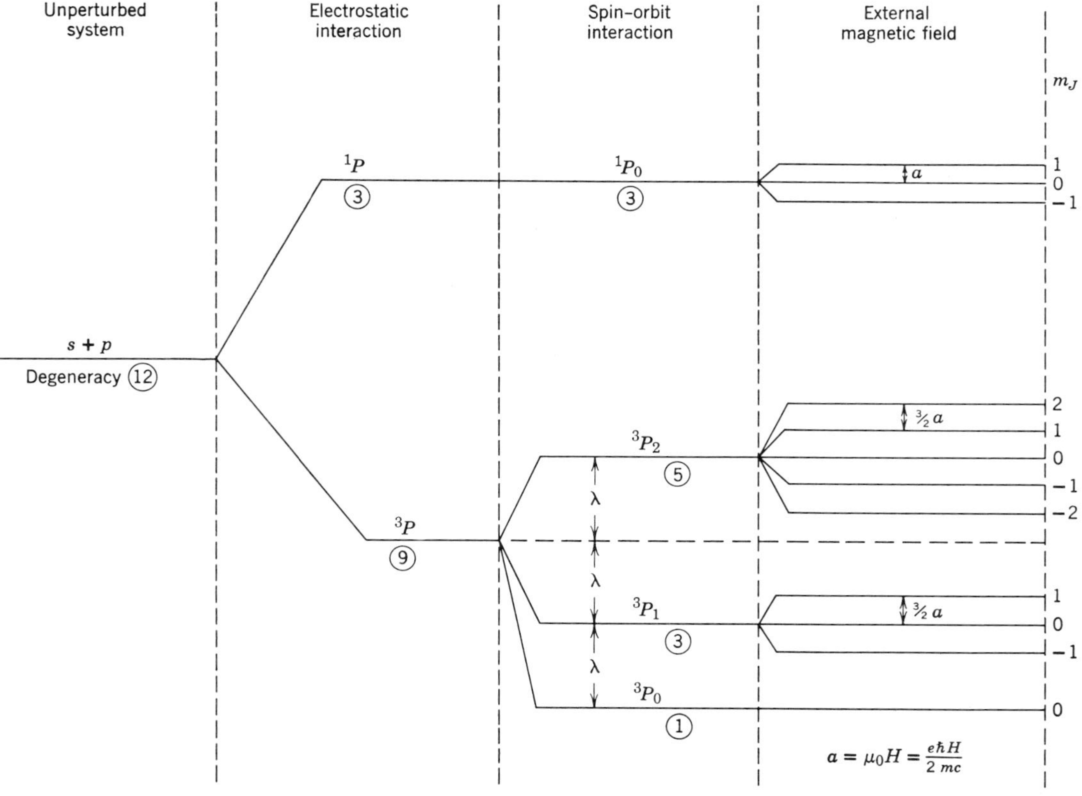

Fig. 5.2. Splitting of the energy levels of an *sp* electronic configuration. Numbers in ○ indicate the degeneracies.

Degeneracy: $2J + 1 = 3$; possible values of M_J:$1, 0, -1$. The different splittings are shown in Fig. 5.2.

REFERENCES

[1] J. C. Slater, *Quantum Theory of Atomic Structure*, Vol. I, McGraw Hill, New York, 1960.

[2] J. C. Slater, *Quantum Theory of Atomic Structure*, Vol. II, McGraw Hill, New York, 1960.

6

The Magnetic Ion in a Crystal: The Role of Symmetry

1. BONDING IN CRYSTALS

A crystal is, in essence, an ensemble of atoms held together by certain *chemical bonds*. These bonds may be of the following types: ionic, covalent, metallic and van der Waals'.

The type and strength of these bonds are of great importance because they may affect such properties of the crystal as hardness, coefficient of thermal expansion, melting point, cleavage, thermal and electrical conductivity. Moreover, they have direct influence on the energy levels of the optically active ions in the crystal.

We can classify the different types of bonding in the following way:

1. *Ionic Bonding*. Atoms with electronic configurations close to those of the rare gases tend to reach such configurations (and to gain stability) by gaining or losing electrons. Typical atoms of this type are on the far right and the far left of the periodic table. An example of the former: Cl; an example of the latter: Na.

2. *Covalent Bonding*. Atoms approaching each other may form a covalent bond by sharing a number of electrons among themselves. In this case the shared electrons are no longer identifiable with a particular nucleus, but they are actually part of an electron cloud that belongs to the bonded atoms.

3. *Metallic Bonding*. This type of bonding is provided by the sharing of electrons of incomplete outer shells by all the atoms in the metal.

4. *Van der Waals Bonding*. This type of bonding is due to the reciprocal perturbations of the electron charges of two atoms. Unlike the covalent

bonding which operates at small distances, the van der Waals bonding may be effective at distances such that no overlap takes place and is associated to smaller energies.

2. THE IONIC BOND IN CRYSTALS

2.1 The Lattice Energy of an Ionic Crystal

The ionic bond is of the greatest importance in crystals. This type of bond is the most common in minerals and in inorganic compounds. It is estimated that about 90% of the natural minerals are mainly ionic; the remaining 10% account for the natural metals, sulfides, and sulfosalts.

We shall now consider a typical case of the formation of a purely ionic crystal such as NaCl. Let us start with one mole of gaseous Na and one mole of gaseous Cl.

First we ionize Na by supplying the system with an amount of energy $I_1 = 118.6$ Kcal:

$$\mathrm{Na} + I_1 \rightarrow \mathrm{Na}^+ + e. \tag{6.1}$$

If we then add one mole of electrons to the Cl atoms, we get the reaction:

$$\mathrm{Cl} + e \rightarrow \mathrm{Cl}^- + EA, \tag{6.2}$$

with a release of energy EA (electron affinity) $= 92.5$ Kcal. The creation of isolated ions then require energy in the amount of $118.6 - 92.5 = 26.1$ Kcal/mole.

Ions of opposite charges, however, gain stability by coming close to one another, due to Coulombic interaction. One mole of Na^+ ions and one of Cl^- will form a mole of Na^+Cl^- pairs with stabilization energy

$$\epsilon_{\mathrm{Coul}} = -\frac{Ne^2}{d} = -\frac{e^2N}{2.814 \times 10^{-8}} = -117.9 \text{ Kcal}, \tag{6.3}$$

where $N =$ Avogadro's number $= 6.025 \times 10^{23}$ and d is the distance between Na^+ and Cl^- in the crystal.

In the actual crystal, however, a given sodium ion has 6 Cl^- ions at distance d, 12 Na^+ ions at distance $d\sqrt{2}$, 8 Cl^- ions at distance $d\sqrt{3}$. The Coulomb interactions will give the energy:

$$-\frac{Ne^2}{d}\left(\frac{6}{\sqrt{1}} - \frac{12}{\sqrt{2}} + \frac{8}{\sqrt{3}} - \frac{6}{\sqrt{4}} + \frac{24}{\sqrt{5}} - \cdots\right) = -NA\frac{e^2}{d}, \tag{6.4}$$

where $A =$ *Madelung constant* $= 1.7476$ for NaCl. Series of the type just reported have been calculated by Madelung, Ewald, and Evjen [1] for the NaCl and other structures.

In addition to the Coulombic attraction created as the ions approach one another, repulsive forces, which become relevant when the electron shells start to overlap, are also present. These forces are associated with the potential energy of each ion produced by the presence of all the other ions:

$$\epsilon_{\text{rep}} = \frac{B}{d^n}, \tag{6.5}$$

where B is a constant and n can be determined by compressibility measurements.

The total binding energy of the crystal, otherwise called *lattice energy*, apart from the energy required by the formation of ions, is given by

$$E_b = \epsilon_{\text{Coul}} + \epsilon_{\text{rep}} = -AN\frac{e^2}{d} + BN\frac{e^2}{d^n}. \tag{6.6}$$

At the equilibrium distance d_0 the energy E_b is a minimum:

$$\frac{\partial E_b}{\partial d} = 0, \tag{6.7}$$

and

$$B = \frac{Ae^2d^{n-1}}{n}. \tag{6.8}$$

Putting the value of B in (6.6),

$$E_b(\text{min}) = -\frac{Ae^2N}{d}\left(1 - \frac{1}{n}\right). \tag{6.9}$$

Since $n = 5 \div 10$, the repulsion energy makes only a small contribution to E_b, and the lattice energy is given mainly by the Coulombic interactions. In the case of NaCl these interactions provide a stabilization energy equal to $117.9 \times 1.7476 = 206$ Kcal per mole.

2.2 The Ionic Radius and the Coordination Number

An ionic radius can be associated with an ion in an ionic crystal. Such a radius can be determined by the use of x-ray diffraction data and by prior knowledge of the ionic radius of another ion; for example, by knowing the ionic radius r_{Br^-} of Br^- from a study of LiBr, one may calculate the ionic radius r_{K^+} of K^+ in KBr by subtracting r_{Br^-} from the K^+–Br^- distance, which can be measured. On the other hand, the prior knowledge of the ionic radius of I^- and the measurement of the distance K^+–I^- in KI can give another value for the ionic radius of K^+. This kind of argument leads to a self-consistent set of averaged ionic radii.

Knowledge of ionic radii may be useful in predicting the crystal structure of a certain compound.

There are certain trends in the ionic radii which are based on the following rules:

1. For ions with the same number of electrons the ionic radius is the smaller, the larger the atomic number. This fact can be explained as due to the greater nuclear attraction for the electron cloud. We have, for example,

$$r_{\mathrm{Mg}^{2+}} < r_{\mathrm{Na}^+} < r_{\mathrm{F}^-} < r_{\mathrm{O}^{2-}}.$$

2. The radii of members of the same family increase as we go down the periodic table (because of the fact that we add more electrons):

$$r_{\mathrm{F}^-} < r_{\mathrm{Cl}^-} < r_{\mathrm{Br}^-} < r_{\mathrm{I}^-}.$$

3. Cations of the same element have smaller radii the lower their ionic charge:

$$r_{\mathrm{Fe}^{2+}} = 0.76\mathrm{A}; \qquad r_{\mathrm{Fe}^{3+}} = 0.64\mathrm{A}.$$

The reverse is true for anions, although ions with various negative charges are rarer.

4. Ionic radii of transition metals, lanthanides, and actinides ions of equal charges present small changes with an increase in atomic number.

In an ionic crystal each ion is surrounded by a number of ions of opposite charge called *ligands*: the number of ligands is called *coordination number* of the ion.

In the NaCl structure, in which ions Na^+ and Cl^- are at the lattice point of a perfectly cubic structure, the coordination number is 6. In the CsCl structure the Cs^+ ion is at the center of a cube and eight Cl^- ions are at the corner of the cube; in this case the coordination number is 8. In the ZnS (zinc blende) structure the Zn^{2+} ion is at the center of a cube and the S^{2-} ions are at the four corners of the cube that form a tetrahedral coordination with coordination number 4.

Most ionic compounds of the type X^+Y^- crystallize in one of the three structures just described. In general a compound chooses the structure that provides the greatest stability brought about by the attractive forces among ions of opposite charges and by the repulsive forces among ions of the same charge. This stability is achieved by allowing ions of opposite charges to come close without any squeezing together of ions of equal charge.

Each structure has a certain range of possible ratios (r_x/r_y) of the cation radius to the anion radius. For each coordination the lowest possible r_x/r_y ratio is given by the condition that positive and negative ions touch each other, allowing also the negative ions to touch each other. Any further decrease of the r_x/r_y ratio implies a squeezing together of the anions and therefore a loss of stability. It is easy to show from geometric considerations that for a cubic coordination, for example, the lowest possible value for r_x/r_y is 0.732; for smaller values of this ratio the octahedral coordination is more stable.

We may then establish the following relation between the r_x/r_y ratio and the coordination number (CN).

$\frac{r_x}{r_y}$	CN	Anion Polyhedron
<0.155	2	
0.155 − 0.225	3	Equilateral triangle
0.225 − 0.414	4	Tetrahedron
0.414 − 0.732	6	Octahedron
0.732 − 1.00	8	Cube
>1.00	12	Close-packed structure of metals

In general, the greater is the ratio of the cation radius to the anion radius the greater is the coordination number.

3. ELECTRONIC CONFIGURATIONS AND PROPERTIES OF MAGNETIC IONS

Several groups of atoms in their ionic states have one or more of their shells only partly filled with electrons. This fact is reflected in some magnetic and optical properties of these ions when they are imbedded in a crystal lattice.

In general, it is found that the electrons of the unfilled shells provide a net magnetic moment that may be oriented by the use of an external magnetic field.

The optical properties of these ions are expressed by the absorption and fluorescence spectra of the crystals of which they are part.

The magnetic ions can be divided into five categories:

1. Transition metal ions of the first series.
2. Transition metal ions of the second series.
3. Transition metal ions of the third series.
4. Lanthanide ions.
5. Actinide ions.

3.1 Transition Metal Ions of the 1st Series (Iron Group) [2]

The electronic configurations of the transition metal atoms of the first series are given by

$$1s^22s^22p^63s^23p^63d^n4s^2 = (\text{Ar core})^{18}\, 3d^n\, 4s^m,$$

where $m = 1, 2$ and $n = 1, 2, \ldots, 10$ and their atomic numbers range from $Z = 21$ (Sc) to $Z = 30$ (Zn).

When in their divalent ionic states, these elements present configurations of the type (Ar core)^{18} $3d^n$ ($n = 1, 2, \ldots, 10$) in which the unfilled $3d$ shell is now the outermost shell. For this reason the orbital motions of the $3d$ electrons are strongly perturbed by the crystalline field and energies of the order of 10,000 cm^{-1} (15,000°K $\equiv$ 1.25 eV $\equiv 2 \times 10^{-12}$ erg) are associated with the coupling of orbitals with this field.

The properties of the ions of this group are summarized in Tables 6.1 to 6.4.

3.2 Transition Metal Ions of the 2nd Series (Palladium Group)

The electronic configurations of the transition metal atoms of the second series are given by

$$1s^2 2s^2 2p^6 3s^2 3p^6 3d^{10} 4s^2 4p^6 4d^n 5s^m = (\text{Kr core})^{36}\, 4d^n\, 5s^m,$$

where $m = 1, 2$ and $n = 1, 2, \ldots, 10$ and their atomic numbers range from $Z = 39$ (Y) to $Z = 48$ (Cd).

When in their divalent ionic states these elements present configurations of the type (Kr core)^{36} $4d^n$, where the unfilled $4d$ shell is the outermost shell.

The properties of these ions are summarized in Tables 6.5 and 6.6.

3.3 Transition Metal Ions of the 3rd Series (Platinum Group)

The electronic configurations of the transition metal atoms of the third series are given by

$$1s^2\, 2s^2\, 2p^6\, 3s^2\, 3p^6\, 3d^{10}\, 4s^2\, 4p^6\, 4d^{10}\, 4f^{14}\, 5s^2\, 5p^6\, 5d^n\, 6s^m$$
$$= (\text{Pd core})^{46}\, 4f^{14}\, 5s^2\, 5p^6\, 5d^n\, 6s^m,$$

where $m = 1, 2$ and $n = 2, 3, 4, 5, 6, 9, 10$ and their atomic numbers range from $Z = 72$ (Hf) to $Z = 80$ (Hg).

The properties and configurations of the ions of these elements are summarized in Table 6.7.

When in their divalent ionic state these elements present configurations of the type (Pd core)^{46} $4f^{14}\, 5s^2\, 5p^6\, 5d^n$ ($n = 2, 3, \ldots, 10$), where the unfilled $4d$ shell is the outermost shell.

3.4 Rare Earth Ions (Group of Lanthanides) [3]

The electronic configurations of the rare earth atoms are given by:

$$1s^2\, 2s^2\, 2p^6\, 3s^2\, 3p^6\, 3d^{10}\, 4s^2\, 4p^6\, 4d^{10}\, 4f^n\, 5s^2\, 5p^6\, 5d^m\, 6s^2$$
$$= (\text{Pd core})^{46}\, 4f^n\, 5s^2\, 5p^6\, 5d^m\, 6s^2,$$

Table 6.1 $3d^n$ Monovalent Transition Metal Ions

Z		Element	Atomic Configuration	Atomic Ground State	X^+ Configuration	X^+ Ground State	X^+ Spin Orbit Parameter (cm^{-1})	X^+ Parameter B(cm^{-1})	X^+ Parameter C(cm^{-1})	X^+ Radius (Å)
20	Ca	Calcium	$3d^0\,4s^2$	$^1S_0$	$3d^0\,4s^1$	^2S				
21	Sc	Scandium	$3d^1\,4s^2$	$^2D_{3/2}$	$3d^1\,4s^1$	^3D	53			
22	Ti	Titanium	$3d^2\,4s^2$	$^3F_2$	$3d^2\,4s^1$	^4F	88	682	2481	
23	V	Vanadium	$3d^3\,4s^2$	$^4F_{3/2}$	$3d^4$	^5D	136	659	2417	
24	Cr	Chromium	$3d^5\,4s^1$	$^7S_3$	$3d^5$	^6S	222	710	2790	
25	Mn	Manganese	$3d^5\,4s^2$	$^6S_{5/2}$	$3d^5\,4s^1$	^7S	254	783	3130	
26	Fe	Iron	$3d^6\,4s^2$	$^5D_4$	$3d^6\,4s^1$	^6D	356	869	3638	
27	Co	Cobalt	$3d^7\,4s^2$	$^4F_{9/2}$	$3d^8$	^3F	456	878	3828	
28	Ni	Nickel	$3d^8\,4s^2$	$^3F_4$	$3d^9$	^2D	603	1037	4314	
29	Cu	Copper	$3d^{10}4s^1$	$^2S_{1/2}$	$3d^{10}$	^1S	828	1216	4745	0.96
30	Zn	Zinc	$3d^{10}4s^2$	$^1S_0$	$3d^{10}4s^1$	^2S				

Table 6.2 $3d^n$ Divalent Transition Metal Ions

Z		Element	X^{2+} Configuration	X^{2+} Ground Term	X^{2+} Spin Orbit Parameter (cm^{-1})	X^{2+} Parameter B (cm^{-1})	X^{2+} Parameter C (cm^{-1})	X^{2+} Radius (Å)
20	Ca	Calcium	$3d^0$	^1S				
21	Sc	Scandium	$3d^1$	^2D	79			
22	Ti	Titanium	$3d^2$	^3F	121	718	2629	0.90
23	V	Vanadium	$3d^3$	^4F	167	766	2855	0.88
24	Cr	Chromium	$3d^4$	^5D	230	830	3430	0.84
25	Mn	Manganese	$3d^5$	^6S	347	960	3325	0.80
26	Fe	Iron	$3d^6$	^5D	410	1058	3901	0.76
27	Co	Cobalt	$3d^7$	^4F	533	1115	4366	0.74
28	Ni	Nickel	$3d^8$	^3F	649	1084	4831	0.74
29	Cu	Copper	$3d^9$	^2D	829	1328	4659	~0.72
30	Zn	Zinc	$3d^{10}$	^1S				0.74

NOTE: The parameters A, B, and C, introduced by Racah, are often used to define the energy levels of d^n ions. They correspond to

$$A = F_0 - 49F_4$$
$$B = F_2 - 5F_4$$
$$C = 35F_4,$$

where

$$F_0 = F^0$$
$$F_0 = \tfrac{1}{49} F^2$$
$$F_4 = \tfrac{1}{441} F^4.$$

Table 6.3 $3d^n$ Trivalent Transition Metal Ions

Z		Element	X^{3+} Configuration	X^{3+} Ground Term	X^{3+} Spin Orbit Parameter (cm^{-1})	X^{3+} Parameter B (cm^{-1})	X^{3+} Parameter C (cm^{-1})	X^{3+} Radius (Å)
21	Sc	Scandium	$3d^0$	^1S				0.81
22	Ti	Titanium	$3d^1$	^2D	154			0.76
23	V	Vanadium	$3d^2$	^3F	209	861	4165	0.74
24	Cr	Chromium	$3d^3$	^4F	273	1030	3850	0.69
25	Mn	Manganese	$3d^4$	^5D	352	1140	3675	0.66
26	Fe	Iron	$3d^5$	^6S				0.64
27	Co	Cobalt	$3d^6$	^5D				0.63
28	Ni	Nickel	$3d^7$	^4F				0.62
29	Cu	Copper	$3d^8$	^3F				
30	Zn	Zinc	$3d^9$	^2D				

Table 6.4 $3d^n$ Tetravalent Transition Metal Ions

Z		Element	X^{4+} Configuration	X^{4+} Ground Term	X^{4+} Spin Orbit Parameter (cm^{-1})	X^{4+} Parameter B (cm^{-1})	X^{4+} Parameter C (cm^{-1})	X^{4+} Radius (Å)
21	Sc	Scandium						
22	Ti	Titanium	$3d^0$	^1S				0.68
23	V	Vanadium	$3d^1$	^2D	248			0.60
24	Cr	Chromium	$3d^2$	^3F	327	1039	4238	0.56
25	Mn	Manganese	$3d^3$	^4F	402			0.34
26	Fe	Iron	$3d^4$	^5D	514	1144	4459	
27	Co	Cobalt	$3d^5$	^6S				
28	Ni	Nickel	$3d^6$	^5D				
29	Cu	Copper	$3d^7$	^4F				
30	Zn	Zinc	$3d^8$	^3F				

Table 6.5 $4d^n$ Monovalent Transition Metal Ions

Z		Element	Atomic Configuration	Atomic Ground State	X^+ Configuration	X^+ Ground Term	X^+ Spin Orbit Parameter (cm^{-1})	X^+ Parameter B (cm^{-1})	X^+ Parameter C (cm^{-1})
38	Sr	Strontium	$5s^2$	$^1S_0$	$5s^1$	^2S			
39	Y	Yttrium	$4d^1\ 5s^2$	$^2D_{3/2}$	$5s^2$	^1S	212	349	1760
40	Zr	Zirconium	$4d^2\ 5s^2$	$^3F_2$	$4d^2\ 5s^1$	^4F	339	454	1765
41	Nb	Niobium	$4d^4\ 5s^1$	$^6D_{1/2}$	$4d^4$	^5D	490	260	1990
42	Mo	Molybdenum	$4d^5\ 5s^1$	$^7S_3$	$4d^5$	^6S	672	440	1987
43	Tc	Technetium	$4d^5\ 5s^2$	$^6S_{5/2}$	$4d^6$	^5D	656		
44	Ru	Ruthenium	$4d^7\ 5s^1$	$^5F_5$	$4d^7$	^4F	887	474	1806
45	Rh	Rhodium	$4d^8\ 5s^1$	$^4F_{9/2}$	$4d^8$	^3F	1212	667	2313
46	Pd	Palladium	$4d^{10}$	$^1S_0$	$4d^9$	^2D	1316		
47	Ag	Silver	$4d^{10}5s^1$	$^2S_{1/2}$	$4d^{10}$	^1S	1830		
48	Cd	Cadmium	$4d^{10}5s^2$	$^1S_0$	$4d^{10}5s^1$	^2S			

Table 6.6 $4d^n$ Divalent Transition Metal Ions

Z		Element	X^{2+} Configuration	X^{2+} Ground State	X^{2+} Spin Orbit Parameter (cm^{-1})	X^{2+} Parameter B (cm^{-1})	X^{2+} Parameter C (cm^{-1})	X^{2+} Radius (Å)
38	Sr	Strontium	$4d^0$	^1S				1.13
39	Y	Yttrium	$4d^1$	^2D	290			
40	Zr	Zirconium	$4d^2$	^3F	403	539	1640	
41	Nb	Niobium	$4d^3$	^4F	554	532	2095	
42	Mo	Molybdenum	$4d^4$	^5D				
43	Tc	Technetium	$4d^5$	^6S				
44	Ru	Ruthenium	$4d^6$	^5D	990			
45	Rh	Rhodium	$4d^7$	^4F	1235	620	4002	
46	Pd	Palladium	$4d^8$	^3F	1615	826	2620	
47	Ag	Silver	$4d^9$	^2D	1844			
48	Cd	Cadmium	$4d^{10}$	^1S				0.97

Table 6.7 $5d^n$ Transition Metal Ions

Z	Element		Atomic Configuration	Atomic Ground State	X^+ Configuration	X^+ Ground Term	X^+ Spin Orbit Parameter (cm^{-1})	X^+ Parameter B (cm^{-1})	X^+ Parameter C (cm^{-1})	X^{2+} Configuration	X^{2+} Ground Term
72	Hf	Hafnium	$5d^2\ 6s^2$	$^3F_2$	$5d\ 6s^2$	^2D	1336	435	1530	$5d^2$	^3F
73	Ta	Tantalum	$5d^3\ 6s^2$	$^4F_{3/2}$	$5d^3\ 6s^1$	^5F	1776	483	1841	$5d^3$	^4F
74	W	Tungsten	$5d^4\ 6s^2$	$^5D_0$	$5d^4\ 6s^1$	^6D	2561			$5d^4$	^5D
75	Re	Rhenium	$5d^5\ 6s^2$	$^6S_{5/2}$	$5d^5\ 6s^1$	^7S				$5d^5$	^6S
76	Os	Osmium	$5d^6\ 6s^2$	$^5D_4$	$5d^6\ 6s^1$	^6D				$5d^6$	^5D
77	Ir	Iridium	$5d^7\ 6s^2$	$^4F_{9/2}$						$5d^7$	^4F
78	Pt	Platinum	$5d^9\ 6s^1$	$^3D_3$	$5d^9$	^2D				$5d^8$	^3F
79	Au	Gold	$5d^{10}\ 6s^1$	$^2S_{1/2}$	$5d^{10}$	^1S				$5d^9$	^2D
80	Hg	Mercury	$5d^{10}\ 6s^2$	$^1S_0$	$5d^{10}\ 6s^1$	^2S				$5d^{10}$	^1S

Table 6.8 $4f^n$ Lanthanides Ions

Z	Element		Atomic Con- figuration	Atomic Ground State	X^{2+} Con- figuration	X^{2+} Ground State	X^{2+} Spin Orbit Parameter (cm^{-1})	X^{3+} Con- figuration	X^{3+} Ground State	X^{3+} Spin Orbit Parameter (cm^{-1})	X^{3+} Radius (Å)[1]
57	La	Lanthanum	$4f^0\ 5d^1\ 6s^2$	$^2D_{3/2}$				$4f^0$	$^1S_0$		1.061
58	Ce	Cerium	$4f^1\ 5d^1\ 6s^2$	$^1G_4$				$4f^1$	$^2F_{5/2}$	643	1.034
59	Pr	Praseodymium	$4f^3\ 5d^0\ 6s^2$	$^4I_{9/2}$	$4f^3$	$^4I_{9/2}$		$4f^2$	$^3H_4$	800	1.013
60	Nd	Neodymium	$4f^4\ 5d^0\ 6s^2$	$^5I_4$				$4f^3$	$^4I_{9/2}$	900	0.995
61	Pm	Promethium	$4f^5\ 5d^0\ 6s^2$	$^6H_{5/2}$				$4f^4$	$^5I_4$		0.979
62	Sm	Samarium	$4f^6\ 5d^0\ 6s^2$	$^7F_0$	$4f^6$	$^7F_0$	1090	$4f^5$	$^6H_{5/2}$	1200	0.964
63	Eu	Europium	$4f^7\ 5d^0\ 6s^2$	$^8S_{7/2}$	$4f^7$	$^8S_{7/2}$		$4f^6$	$^7F_0$	1415	0.950
64	Gd	Gadolinium	$4f^7\ 5d^1\ 6s^2$	$^9D_2$				$4f^7$	$^8S_{7/2}$		0.938
65	Tb	Terbium	$4f^9\ 5d^0\ 6s^2$	$^6H_{15/2}$				$4f^8$	$^7F_6$	1620	0.923
66	Dy	Dysprosium	$4f^{10}\ 5d^0\ 6s^2$	$^5I_8$	$4f^{10}$	$^5I_8$		$4f^9$	$^6H_{15/2}$	1820	0.908
67	Ho	Holmium	$4f^{11}\ 5d^0\ 6s^2$	$^4I_{15/2}$	$4f^{11}$	$^4I_{15/2}$		$4f^{10}$	$^5I_8$	2030	0.894
68	Er	Erbium	$4f^{12}\ 5d^0\ 6s^2$	$^3H_6$	$4f^{12}$	$^3H_6$		$4f^{11}$	$^4I_{15/2}$	2350	0.881
69	Tm	Thulium	$4f^{13}\ 5d^0\ 6s^2$	$^2F_{7/2}$	$4f^{13}$	$^2F_{7/2}$		$4f^{12}$	$^3H_6$	2800	0.869
70	Yb	Ytterbium	$4f^{14}\ 5d^0\ 6s^2$	$^1S_0$	$4f^{14}$	$^1S_0$		$4f^{13}$	$^2F_{7/2}$	2940	0.858
71	Lu	Lutetium	$4f^{14}\ 5d^1\ 6s^2$	$^2D_{3/2}$	$4f^{14}\ 6s^1$	$^2S_{1/2}$		$4f^{14}$	$^1S_0$		0.848

[1] Ionic radii in Å of some cations: Ca^{2+}: 0.99; Ba^{2+}: 1.34; Cd^{2+}: 0.97; Sr^{2+}: 1.12; La^{3+}: 1.14; Pb^{2+}: 1.20

where $m = 1, 2$ and $n = 2, 3, \ldots, 13$ and their atomic numbers range from $Z = 58$ (Ce) and $Z = 70$ (Yb).

When in their trivalent ionic state these elements present configurations of the type (Pd core)^{46} $4f^n\,5s^2\,5p^6$. The unfilled $4f$ shell is now an inner shell screened by the $5s$ and $5p$ shells. The $4f$ electrons have orbital radii of 0.6 to 0.35 Å from Ce to Lu, (for the latter this is less than one half the ionic radius). When these ions are in crystals, the crystal field splitting, because of the screening electrons, is less than 1000 cm^{-1} in most cases. On the other hand, the spin-orbit coupling energy is greater (600–3000 cm^{-1} from Ce to Yb) than in the $3d$ ions.

The properties and configurations of the lanthanide ions are summarized in Table 6.8.

3.5 Actinides Ions [4]

The electronic configurations of the atoms of the actinide group are given by

$$1s^2\,2s^2\,2p^6\,3s^2\,3p^6\,3d^{10}\,4s^2\,4p^6\,4d^{10}\,4f^{14}\,5s^2\,5p^6\,5d^{10}\,5f^n\,6d^m\,7s^2$$
$$= (\text{Pt core})^{78}\,5f^n\,6d^m\,7s^2,$$

where $m = 1, 2$ and $n = 0, 2, 3, \ldots,$ and their atomic numbers range from $Z = 90$ (Th) up.

When in their trivalent ionic state, these elements present configurations of the type (Pt core)^{78} $5f^n\,7s^2$.

The properties and configurations of the actinide ions are summarized in Tables 6.9 and 6.10.

4. THE CRYSTALLINE FIELD HYPOTHESIS

In an ionic crystal the electrons occupy orbitals that are highly localized about the ions in such a way that any electron can still be associated with a particular ion. Each electron, however, feels the influence of the electrons belonging to the other ions (a repulsion) and of the nuclei belonging to the other ions (an attraction). We can take this influence into account by considering that the electrons of the individual ions are subjected to the action of a *crystalline field.*

The crystalline field approximation is not valid in non-ionic crystals. In metals, for example, some electrons escape from the ion into the environment: band theory has to be used. In ferromagnetic materials the exchange interactions (that we disregard in the crystalline field approximation) must be considered. The crystalline field approximation is valid in a magnetically dilute substance in which the magnetic ions are far apart.

Table 6.9 $5f^n$ Trivalent Actinides Ions

Z		Element	Atomic Configuration	Atomic Ground State	X^{3+} Configuration	X^{3+} Spin Orbit Parameter (cm^{-1})	X^{3+} Radius (Å)
89	Ac	Actinium	$5f^0\, 6d^1\, 7s^2$	$^2D_{3/2}$			1.11
90	Th	Thorium	$5f^0\, 6d^2\, 7s^2$	$^3F_2$		1326	1.08
91	Pa	Protactinium	$5f^2\, 6d^1\, 7s^2$	$^4K_{11/2}$			1.05
92	U	Uranium	$5f^3\, 6d^1\, 7s^2$	$^5L_6$	$5f^3$	1700	1.03
93	Np	Neptunium	$5f^4\, 6d^1\, 7s^2$	$^6L_{11/2}$			1.01
94	Pu	Plutonium	$5f^6\, 6d^0\, 7s^2$	$^7F_0$	$5f^5$	2300	1.00
95	Am	Americium	$5f^7\, 6d^0\, 7s^2$	$^8S_{7/2}$	$5f^6$	3500	0.99
96	Cm	Curium	$5f^7\, 6d^1\, 7s^2$	$^9D_2$			

Table 6.10 $5f^n$ Tetravalent and Pentavalent Actinide Ions

Z		Element	X^{4+} Configuration	X^{4+} Spin Orbit Parameter (cm^{-1})	X^{4+} Radius (Å)	X^{5+} Configuration	X^{5+} Spin Orbit Parameter (cm^{-1})	X^{5+} Radius (Å)
89	Ac	Actinium						
90	Th	Thorium			0.99			
91	Pa	Protactinium			0.96			0.90
92	U	Uranium	$5f^2$	1600	0.93			0.87
93	Np	Neptunium	$5f^3$	2100	0.92	$5f^2$	1900	0.88
94	Pu	Plutonium	$5f^4$	2300	0.90	$5f^3$	2700	0.87
95	Am	Americium			0.89	$5f^4$	3000	0.86
96	Cm	Curium						

The crystalline field is completely external to the ion and has a definite symmetry. By knowing this symmetry and by using group theory it is possible to predict the splitting of the energy levels and the transformation properties of the eigenfunctions representing the states. The actual evaluation of the crystal splittings is performed by starting from certain unperturbed eigenfunctions. One has at his disposal three schemes: the weak field, the medium field, and the strong field. Weak, medium, and strong indicate the strength of the crystal field in comparison to the electrostatic interaction between electrons.

Any scheme can, in principle, be used, but the best choice is the one that best resembles the physical situation. For the rare earths the weak field scheme is generally used. For the transition metal ions in a cubic environment the strong field scheme has been used by most workers.

The $3d^n$ transition metals occupy a zone of the periodic table with atomic numbers 21–30. Their electronic configurations are of the type $3d^n4s^2$ or $3d^n4s$. When they enter an ionic crystal as impurities, they lose the electrons of the $4s$ shell and part of the electrons of the $3d$ shell. The partly empty $3d$ shell, responsible for the magnetic properties of the ions, is then the outermost shell and is strongly exposed to the action of the neighboring ions. This fact is the cause of a great difference between the energy levels of the ions in crystals and the energy levels of the free ions. On the other hand, rare earth ions in crystals present spectra which are very similar to free ion spectra, because the $4f$ shell, responsible for their magnetic properties, is shielded from the environment by the outer $5s$ and $5p$ shells.

Now consider an ionic crystal with M nuclei and N electrons. Its Hamiltonian is given by

$$H = \sum_{i=1}^{N} \left(\frac{p_i^2}{2m} - e^2 \sum_{g=1}^{M} \frac{Z_g}{r_{ig}} + e^2 \sum_{j>i} \frac{1}{r_{ij}} \right). \tag{6.10}$$

In the crystalline field approximation the charge of the environment does not penetrate into the region occupied by a certain ion and the perturbing potential satisfies Laplace's equation:

$$\nabla^2 V = 0. \tag{6.11}$$

The solutions of (6.11) are of the type $r^l Y_l^m(\theta, \varphi)$. The general solution is

$$V(r, \theta, \varphi) = \sum_{l,m} A_{lm}\, r^l Y_l^m(\theta, \varphi). \tag{6.12}$$

The Hamiltonian of an ion in a lattice is then given by

$$H = \sum_{i=1}^{n} \left\{ \frac{p_i^2}{2m} - \frac{e^2 Z}{r_i} + e^2 \sum_{j>i} \frac{1}{r_{ij}} + eV(r_i, \theta_i, \varphi_i) \right\} + \lambda \mathbf{L} \cdot \mathbf{S}, \tag{6.13}$$

where n = number of electrons in the ion and

$$V(r_i, \theta_i, \varphi_i) = \sum_{lm} A_{lm} r_i^l Y_e^m(\theta_i, \varphi_i).$$

The crystal field perturbation $e \sum_i V(\mathbf{r}_i)$, caused by the presence of the ligand ions, destroys the spherical symmetry of the environment of a certain ion; therefore L^2 and L_Z no longer commute with the Hamiltonian; after the crystal field perturbation is taken in account, they may be actually replaced by other observables, in dependence of the type of local symmetry. S^2 and S commute with the crystal field perturbation, which does not depend on spin coordinates; they can be considered observables of the ionic system if spin-orbit interaction is disregarded. Finally, parity, which in a free ion is a good quantum number, does or does not remain so if, respectively, the local symmetry does or does not contain a center of inversion.

We want to consider the relative importance of crystal field strength, spin-orbit interaction, and electrostatic interaction. We may distinguish three cases.

Weak Crystal Field. The crystal field potential is small in comparison with the spin-orbit interaction. Here the crystal field splitting is small in comparison with the splitting between multiplets.

Name of Group	*Atomic Numbers*	*Incomplete Shell*
Rare Earth	58 (Ce) to 70 (Yb)	$4f$
Actinide	> 90 (Th)	$5f$–$6d$

In this case we use the $LSJM_J$ representation to take matrix elements of the crystal field perturbation.

Medium Crystal Field. The crystal field potential is small in comparison with the electrostatic interaction but large in comparison with the spin-orbit interaction.

Here the crystal field splitting is large in comparison with the separation of the different multiplets. We say that the crystal field in this case breaks the LS coupling.

Name of Group	*Atomic Numbers*	*Incomplete Shell*
Iron	21 (Sc) to 29 (Cu)	$3d$

In this case we may use the LSM_LM_S representation to take matrix elements of the crystal field perturbation.

Strong Crystal Field. The crystal field potential is large in comparison with the electrostatic interaction. Here the crystal field splitting is large in comparison with the separation of different multiplets. We may say that the crystal field breaks the coupling of the angular momenta of the individual electrons.

Name of Group	*Atomic Numbers*	*Incomplete Shell*
Palladium	40 (Zr) to 47 (Ag)	$4d$
Platinum	72 (Hf) to 79 (Au)	$5d$

In this case we may use determinantal eigenfunctions to evaluate matrix elements of the crystal field perturbation.

There may be an intermediate case in which both electrostatic interaction and crystal field potential are considered simultaneously. In this case one may start with a set of functions which are diagonal either in the electrostatic interaction or in the crystal field perturbation.

In general, it can be said that the crystalline field treatment is more adequate for $4f^n$ ions than for ions with unfilled d shells in crystals. In the latter case more elaborate treatments of the problem, given by the *ligand field theory* and by the *molecular orbital theory* may give more adequate results by properly taking in account the overlapping between central ion and ligands eigenfunctions. However, the crystal field theory, as treated in the following three chapters, continues to maintain its validity for two reasons. First, it may still account for a large part of the optical properties of ions in crystals and second (as we shall see in Chapter 10), it may be considered as a consequence of both ligand field and molecular orbital theories when the ion-ligand overlapping is negligible.

REFERENCES

[1] C. Kittel, *Introduction to Solid State Physics*, Wiley, New York, 1957.

[2] L. E. Orgel, *An Introduction to Transition Metal Chemistry and Ligand Field Theory*, Wiley, New York, 1960.

[3] D. M. Yost, H. Russel and C. S. Garner, *The Rare Earth Elements and Their Compounds*, Wiley, New York, 1947.

[4] G. T. Seaborg and J. J. Katz, eds., *The Actinide Elements*, McGraw-Hill, New York, 1954.

7

The Weak Field Scheme

In this scheme the crystal field term in the total Hamiltonian comes after the spin orbit term. The different terms of the Hamiltonian are reported in Table 7.1, together with their group theoretical properties.

Table 7.1 The Weak Field Scheme

	Hamiltonian	Complete Set of Commuting Operators	Properties of Hamiltonian
H_J	$H_o + H_{so}$	H_J, J^2, J_z, P	Degeneracy: $2J + 1$. Group: $R_{el} \times R_{sp}$ referred to same axes. Rep: D_J.
H_{cryst}	$\sum_i eV(\mathbf{r}_i)$	$H_{\text{cryst}}, \Gamma, \Gamma_z, (P)$	$[H_{\text{cryst}}, H_J] \neq 0$. May connect states of H_J with equal (P). May cause: interaction between different J levels, interaction between different terms, interaction between different configurations. Group: G_c. Rep: $D_J = \sum_i \Gamma_i$.

1. THE HAMILTONIAN OF THE FREE ION

The Hamiltonian of the free ion is given by

$$H_J = H_o + H_{so}. \tag{7.1}$$

The system is defined by the eigenvalues of the operators belonging to the following complete set:

$$H_J, J^2, J_z, P.$$

In the Russel-Saunders approximation also L and S are considered good quantum numbers. The symmetry group of the Hamiltonian H_J is

$$R_{\text{el}} \times R_{\text{sp}},$$

where R_{el} = three dimensional rotation group for the orbital part and R_{sp} = three dimensional rotation group for the spin part. Here R_{el} and R_{sp} are referred to the same axes.

The representation of the state is given by D_J and the degeneracy by $2J + 1$.

2. THE CRYSTAL FIELD PERTURBATION

The crystal field perturbation is expressed by

$$H_{\text{cryst}} = \sum_i eV(\mathbf{r}_i). \tag{7.4}$$

The introduction of the free ion into the crystal results in the splitting of the representation D_J into components, each of which is an irreducible representation of the group of symmetry operations which leave H_{cryst} unchanged. We call this group *crystal group* or G_c. As we said, we have

$$D_J = \sum_i \Gamma_i. \tag{7.5}$$

A state of the system is represented by a representation Γ_i and its degeneracy is given by the dimension of Γ_i.

We may say that, in the same way as M_J specifies a function within the D_J manifold in a free ion, a number M_Γ may specify a function belonging to the Γ representation. In the free ion case J and J_z are operators that indicate constants of the motion; in the present case Γ and Γ_z[1] indicate two constants of the motion. In different words, because of the crystalline field, the ion goes from a $|JJ_z\rangle$ to a $|\Gamma M_\Gamma\rangle$ representation.

The complete set of commuting operators is then given by

$$H_{\text{cryst}},\ \Gamma,\ \Gamma_z,\ (P). \tag{7.6}$$

P (parity) is included in the complete set when the crystal symmetry has a center of symmetry. In this case the operation inversion is an operation of the group G_c which leaves H_{cryst} unchanged and H_{cryst} may connect only states with equal parity.

The state functions, before the application of H_{cryst}, are basis for a D_J representation. We build up the matrix of H_{cryst} by using these functions: by diagonalizing this matrix we get the proper eigenvalues and the proper eigenfunctions.

[1] No significance has to be attached to the subscript z in Γ_z, other than that this operator plays a role equivalent to that of J_z.

By splitting a D_J representation in a number of Γ_i representations of G_c we diagonalize the matrix of $H_{\rm cryst}$ only partially: $H_{\rm cryst}$ may have matrix elements between two states with same numbers Γ, M_Γ, (P), either deriving from the same or from different J manifolds.

3. APPLICATION OF THE WEAK FIELD SCHEME

J may be an integer or half-integer. We must examine the two cases separately.

3.1 J Integer

To illustrate the procedure let us study the following example.

Let us consider an ion in a cubic crystal occupying a site of octahedral symmetry.

The character table of the octahedral group follows:

$G_c \equiv O$		E	$3C_2$	$6C_4$	$6C_2'$	$8C_3$
A_1	Γ_1	1	1	1	1	1
A_2	Γ_2	1	-1	-1	-1	-1
E	Γ_3	2	2	0	0	-1
T_1	Γ_4	3	-1	1	-1	0
T_2	Γ_5	3	-1	-1	1	0

We may find the relevant characters of the D_J representations by using the following formula already derived in Section 5.3 of Chapter 3:

$$\chi_j(\omega) = \frac{\sin\,(j + \frac{1}{2})\,\omega}{\sin\,\frac{1}{2}\omega}\,. \tag{7.7}$$

We find

G_c	E	$3C_2$	$6C_4$	$6C_2'$	$8C_3$
D_0	1	1	1	1	1
D_1	3	-1	1	-1	0
D_2	5	1	-1	1	-1
D_3	7	-1	-1	-1	1
D_4	9	1	1	1	0
D_5	11	-1	1	-1	-1
D_6	13	1	-1	1	1

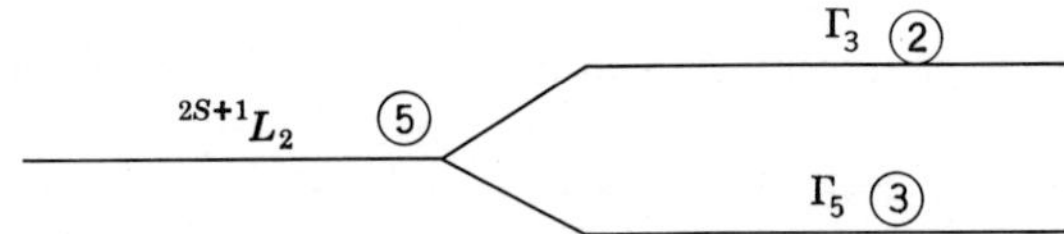

Fig. 7.1. Atom with total angular momentum $J = 2$ in an octahedral field. The numbers in ○ give the total degeneracies of the levels.

Then we take advantage of the following equations:

$$D_J = c_1\Gamma_1 + c_2\Gamma_2 + \cdots$$
$$c_j = \frac{1}{g}\sum_R \chi(R)^* \chi_j(R). \tag{7.8}$$

In the present case g = number of operations = 24. Then

$$\begin{aligned}
D_0 &= \Gamma_1,\\
D_1 &= \Gamma_4,\\
D_2 &= \Gamma_3 + \Gamma_5,\\
D_3 &= \Gamma_2 + \Gamma_4 + \Gamma_5,\\
D_4 &= \Gamma_1 + \Gamma_3 + \Gamma_4 + \Gamma_5,\\
D_5 &= \Gamma_3 + 2\Gamma_4 + \Gamma_5,\\
D_6 &= \Gamma_1 + \Gamma_2 + \Gamma_3 + \Gamma_4 + 2\Gamma_5.
\end{aligned}$$

An atom with $J = 2$ will then be split as in Fig. 7.1 by the crystalline field.

3.2 *J* Half-Integer

If J is a half-integer, the representation D_J is of even degree and then *double-valued.* The double-valued representations of D_J decompose, because of the crystal field perturbation, in terms of the double-valued representations of the symmetry group of the ion in the lattice.

The double-valued representations of the crystal group can be obtained with the method discussed in Section 6 of Chapter 3. Let us consider the octahedral double group O'.

$G_e = O'$		E	$\bar{E}$	$3C_2$	$6C_4$	$\overline{6C_4}$	$6C_2'$	$8C_3$	$\overline{8C_3}$
A_1	Γ_1	1	1	1	1	1	1	1	1
A_2	Γ_2	1	1	1	−1	−1	−1	1	1
E	Γ_3	2	2	2	0	0	0	−1	−1
T_1	Γ_4	3	3	−1	1	1	−1	0	0
T_2	Γ_5	3	3	−1	−1	−1	1	0	0
$E_{1/2}$	Γ_6	2	−2	0	$\sqrt{2}$	$-\sqrt{2}$	0	1	−1
$E_{5/2}$	Γ_7	2	−2	0	$-\sqrt{2}$	$\sqrt{2}$	0	1	−1
G	Γ_8	4	−4	0	0	0	0	−1	1

Let us now find the term splitting of an atom in a cubic lattice in which it has octahedral symmetry. The characters of the reducible D_J representations of even dimensions for the operations of the O' group are given by

	E	$\bar{E}$	$3C_2$	$6C_4$	$\overline{6C_4}$	$6C_2'$	$8C_3$	$\overline{8C_3}$
$D_{1/2}$	2	-2	0	$\sqrt{2}$	$-\sqrt{2}$	0	1	-1
$D_{3/2}$	4	-4	0	0	0	0	-1	1
$D_{5/2}$	6	-6	0	$-\sqrt{2}$	$\sqrt{2}$	0	0	0
$D_{7/2}$	8	-8	0	0	0	0	1	-1
$D_{9/2}$	10	-10	0	$\sqrt{2}$	$-\sqrt{2}$	0	-1	1
$D_{11/2}$	12	-12	0	0	0	0	0	0

In the present case g = number of operations = 48. By applying formulas (7.8) we find

$$\begin{aligned}
D_{3/2} &= \Gamma_8, \\
D_{5/2} &= \Gamma_7 + \Gamma_8, \\
D_{7/2} &= \Gamma_6 + \Gamma_7 + \Gamma_8, \\
D_{9/2} &= \Gamma_6 + 2\Gamma_8, \\
D_{11/2} &= \Gamma_6 + \Gamma_7 + 2\Gamma_8.
\end{aligned}$$

Let us now assume that we have an ion with $L = 3$, $S = \frac{3}{2}$ in a site of octahedral symmetry. Spin orbit coupling gives rise to different J states: ${}^4F_{9/2}$, ${}^4F_{7/2}$, ${}^4F_{5/2}$ and ${}^4F_{3/2}$. The crystalline field produces splittings according to Fig. 7.2. S is no longer a good quantum number after the crystalline field is applied. Actually, even before, S was only a quasi good quantum number, because of the Russell-Saunders approximation.

It has to be noted that no information about the relative position of the different crystal levels arising from an ionic state is given by group theory.

4. SPLITTINGS OF *J* LEVELS IN FIELDS OF DIFFERENT SYMMETRIES

In the following tables we give the degeneracies of crystal levels for different crystal field symmetries.

TERM SPLITTING FOR INTEGRAL *J*

J	0	1	2	3	4	5	6	7	8
Cubic	1	1	2	3	4	4	6	6	7
$n_3n_2n_1$	(001)	(100)	(110)	(201)	(211)	(301)	(312)	(411)	(421)
Hexagonal	1	2	3	5	6	7	9	10	11
Tetragonal	1	2	4	5	7	8	10	11	13
Lower Symmetry	1	3	5	7	9	11	13	15	17

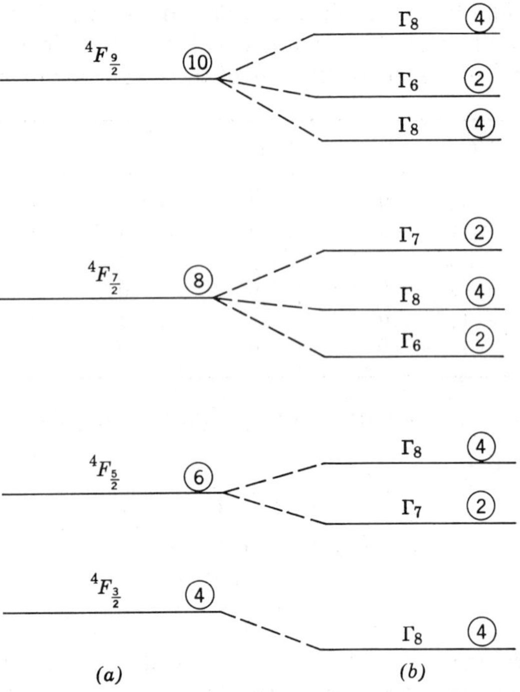

Fig. 7.2. A spectral term ^4F in an octahedral field: (a) free ion multiplets; (b) energy levels of the ion in a weak crystal field.

$n_3n_2n_1$ indicate, respectively, the numbers of triply, doubly, and singly degenerate levels of the cubic symmetries.

TERM SPLITTING FOR HALF-INTEGRAL J

J	$\frac{1}{2}$	$\frac{3}{2}$	$\frac{5}{2}$	$\frac{7}{2}$	$\frac{9}{2}$	$\frac{11}{2}$	$\frac{13}{2}$	$\frac{15}{2}$	$\frac{17}{2}$
Cubic	1	1	2	3	3	4	5	5	6
All Other Groups	1	2	3	4	5	6	7	8	9

We can see that for symmetries other than cubic for J half integer (odd number of electrons) there is splitting into doublets, in agreement with Kramers' theorem.

The type and number of crystal field levels can be found in more detail for all the point groups in [1].

REFERENCE

[1] J. L. Prather, *Atomic Energy Levels in Crystals*, National Bureau of Standards, Monograph 19, February 24, 1961.

8

The Medium Field Scheme

In this scheme the crystal field term in the total Hamiltonian comes after the electrostatic interaction and before the spin-orbit interaction. The different terms of the Hamiltonian are reported in Table 8.1, together with their group theoretical properties.

1. THE HAMILTONIAN OF THE FREE ION

If we disregard the spin-orbit interaction, the Hamiltonian of the free ion is given by

$$H_o = \sum_i \left(\frac{p_i^2}{2m} - \frac{Ze^2}{r_i}\right) + \tfrac{1}{2} \sum_{\substack{ij \\ (i \neq j)}} \frac{e^2}{r_{ij}}. \tag{8.1}$$

The system is defined by the eigenvalues of the operators belonging to the following complete set:

$$H_o, L^2, S^2, L_z, S_z, P. \tag{8.2}$$

The symmetry group of the Hamiltonian H_0 is given by

$$R_{\text{el}} \times R_{\text{sp}}, \tag{8.3}$$

where R_{el} = three dimensional rotation group for the space part and R_{sp} = three dimensional rotation group for the spin part. The representation of the generic state is given by

$$D_L \times D_S. \tag{8.4}$$

2. THE CRYSTAL FIELD PERTURBATION

The Hamiltonian representing the crystal field perturbation is given by

$$H_{\text{cryst}} = \sum_i eV(\mathbf{r}_i). \tag{8.5}$$

Table 8.1 The Medium Field Scheme

	Hamiltonian	Complete Set of Commuting Operators	Properties of Hamiltonian
H_o	$\sum_i \left(\frac{p_i^2}{2m} - \frac{Ze^2}{r_i}\right) + \sum_{i>j} \frac{e^2}{r_{ij}}$	$H_o, L^2, S^2, L_z, S_z, P$	Degeneracy: $(2L + 1)(2S + 1)$. Group: $R_{el} \times R_{sp}$. Rep: $D_L \times D_S$.
H_{cryst}	$\sum_i eV(\mathbf{r}_i)$	$H_{cryst}, S^2, S_z, \Gamma, \Gamma_z, (P)$	$[H_{cryst}, H_o] \neq 0$. May connect states of H_o with equal $S, M_s, (P)$. May cause: term interaction, configuration interaction. Group: $G_c \times R_{sp}$. Rep: $D_L \times D_S = \sum_i \Gamma_i \times D_S$.
H_{so}	$\sum_j \xi_i \mathbf{l}_i \cdot \mathbf{s}_i$	$H_{so}, \Gamma, \Gamma_z, (P)$	$[H_{so}, H_{cryst}] \neq 0$. May connect states of H_{cryst} with equal (P). May cause: interaction between crystal states, term interaction, configuration interaction. Group: G_c. Rep: $\Gamma_i \times D_S = \Gamma_i \times \sum_j \Gamma_j = \sum_k \Gamma_k$.

Placing the ion in the crystal results in the representation $D_L \times D_S$ becoming reducible and being reduced in terms of irreducible representations of the symmetry group G_c which leaves H_{cryst} unchanged. The spin does not appear in H_{cryst} and only D_L is reduced into representations of G_c. The splitting of D_L in components is accomplished in the same way as the splitting of D_J with J integer described in Chapter 7,

$$D_L = \sum_i c_i \Gamma_i. \tag{8.6}$$

The representations of the different states will now be of the type $\Gamma_i \times D_S$. At this stage S is still a good quantum number and we may well use for a state the symbol ${}^{2S+1}\Gamma_i$. The complete set of commuting operators is given by

$$H_{\text{cryst}},\ S^2,\ S_z,\ \Gamma,\ \Gamma_z,\ (P),^1 \tag{8.7}$$

and the total group by

$$G_c \times R_{\text{sp}}, \tag{8.8}$$

where R_{sp} = three dimensional rotation group for the spin part.

H_{cryst} may connect states with equal S, M_S, (P). The state functions, before we apply H_{cryst}, are eigenfunctions of H_0. We build up the matrix of H_{cryst} by using these functions: by diagonalizing this matrix we get the proper eigenvalues and the proper eigenfunctions. By splitting a $D_L \times D_S$ state in a number of ${}^{2S+1}\Gamma_i$ states we diagonalize the matrix H_{cryst} only partly. H_{cryst} may have matrix elements between two states with equal numbers S, M_S, Γ, M_Γ, (P) either deriving from the same term ${}^{2S+1}L$ or from different terms. H_{cryst} may also cause configuration interaction.

If Γ_i is one dimensional, any perturbation on a ${}^{2S+1}\Gamma_i$ state can produce splittings due only to the spin part of the total representation $\Gamma_i \times D_S$ and the orbital angular momentum is said to be *quenched.* The expectation value of the orbital angular momentum is in this case zero. The physical meaning of this result is that the crystalline field fixes the orientation of the angular momentum and prevents other perturbation like spin orbit or magnetic field to influence it. If Γ_i is degenerate but of a degree less than $2L + 1$, the angular momentum is said to be *partially quenched.* If both Γ_i and D_S are non-degenerate, the expectation value of the total angular momentum is zero.

3. THE SPIN-ORBIT INTERACTION

The spin-orbit interaction is given by

$$H_{so} = \sum_i \xi(\mathbf{r}_i)\, \mathbf{l}_i \cdot \mathbf{s}_i \tag{8.9}$$

[1] No significance has to be attached to the subscript z in Γ_z other than that this operator plays a role equivalent to that of L_z.

The introduction of the spin-orbit coupling results in the generic representation $\Gamma_i \times D_S$ becoming reducible and being reduced in terms of irreducible representations of the symmetry group G_c:

$$\Gamma_i \times D_S = \sum_k \Gamma_k. \tag{8.10}$$

When we introduce the spin-orbit interaction, S ceases to be a good quantum number. The complete set of commuting operators is given by

$$H_{so}, \Gamma, \Gamma_z, (P) \tag{8.11}$$

and the total group by G_c.

H_{so} may connect states with equal (P). Before we apply H_{so} the state functions are eigenfunctions of $H_o + H_{\text{cryst}}$. We build up the matrix of H_{so} by using these functions: by diagonalizing this matrix we get the proper eigenvalues and the proper eigenfunctions. By splitting a ${}^{2S+1}\Gamma_i$ state in a number of Γ_k states we diagonalize the matrix of H_{so} only partly; H_{so} may have matrix elements between states with the same numbers Γ, M_Γ, (P), either deriving from the same ${}^{2S+1}\Gamma_i$ state or from different states. H_{cryst} may also cause term interaction and even configuration interaction.

4. AN APPLICATION OF THE MEDIUM FIELD SCHEME

Let us consider an ion in a state ${}^4F$ ($L = 3$, $S = \frac{3}{2}$), as in Co^{2+}. A crystal field of octahedral symmetry will cause the splitting:

$$D_3 = \Gamma_2 + \Gamma_4 + \Gamma_5.$$

The resulting states will then be

$$D_{3/2} \times \Gamma_2; \qquad D_{3/2} \times \Gamma_4; \qquad D_{3/2} \times \Gamma_5,$$

labeled, respectively,

$${}^4\Gamma_2, \qquad {}^4\Gamma_4, \qquad {}^4\Gamma_5,$$

with total degeneracies 4×1, 4×3, and 4×3. The introduction of the spin-orbit coupling will cause the relabeling of $D_{3/2}$ as Γ_8 and

$$D_{3/2} \times \Gamma_2 = \Gamma_8 \times \Gamma_2 = \Gamma_8,$$

$$D_{3/2} \times \Gamma_4 = \Gamma_8 \times \Gamma_4 = \Gamma_6 + \Gamma_7 + 2\Gamma_8,$$

$$D_{3/2} \times \Gamma_5 = \Gamma_8 \times \Gamma_5 = \Gamma_6 + \Gamma_7 + 2\Gamma_8.$$

The splittings are illustrated in Fig. 8.1.

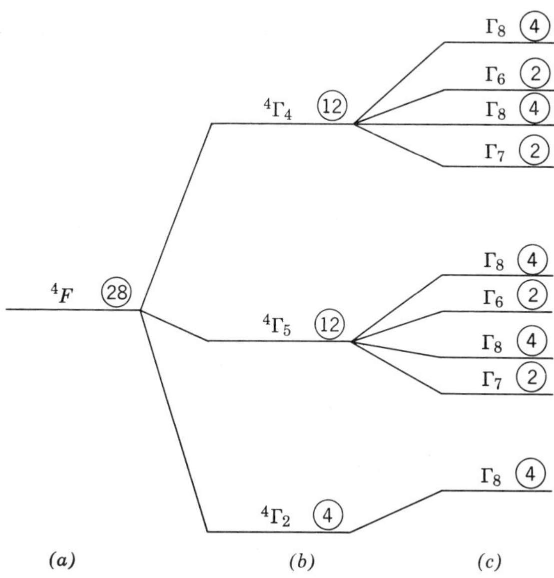

Fig. 8.1. Ion in a ^4F state in an octahedral symmetry: (*a*) free ion's spectral term; (*b*) ion in a medium field (*LS* coupling not included); (*c*) ion in a medium field (*LS* coupling included).

5. THE METHOD OF OPERATOR EQUIVALENTS: THE SPLITTING OF TRANSITION METAL IONS LEVELS IN AN OCTAHEDRAL CRYSTAL FIELD

In the medium field scheme the state functions of the system unperturbed by crystal field or spin-orbit interaction are eigenfunctions of H_0: L and S are good quantum numbers. Transition metal ions have electronic configurations of the type $3d^n$. The ground state may be an S or a D or an F state. We want now to calculate the crystal field splitting of the ground state of these ions. We shall disregard the spin-orbit interaction.

The crystal field Hamiltonian, in case of an octahedral field is given by

$$H_{\text{cryst}} = D \sum_i (x_i^4 + y_i^4 + z_i^4 - \tfrac{3}{5} r_i^4), \tag{8.12}$$

where the sum is extended to all $3d$ electrons and where D, the coefficient that depends on the charge distribution of the ligand ions, is equal to $35e/4R^5$ (R = distance of ion from ligands). We shall consider only what happens *within* the ground term and confine our attention to the evaluation of matrix elements of the type $\langle LM_L | H_{\text{cryst}} | LM_L' \rangle$. The replacement theorem of Section 5.6 of Chapter 3 allows us to express the Hamiltonian given by (8.12) in terms of irreducible tensor operators. The following form for the Hamiltonian (8.12) is given in [1], p. 15:

$$H_{\text{cryst}} = \frac{\beta r^4}{20} DV_z + \frac{\beta r^4}{8} D(V_+ + V_-), \tag{8.13}$$

where

$$\begin{aligned} V_z &= 35L_z^4 - 30L(L+1)L_z^2 + 25L_z^2 - 6L(L+1) + 3L^2(L+1)^2, \\ V_+ &= L_+^4, \\ V_- &= L_-^4. \end{aligned} \tag{8.14}$$

Let us now treat separately the D, F, and S states.

D STATES

For an ion with one electron ($3d^1$) we have the following wavefunctions:

$$\begin{aligned} \psi_2^2 &= R_{32}(r)\, Y_{22}(\theta, \varphi), \\ \psi_2^1 &= R_{32}(r)\, Y_{21}(\theta, \varphi), \\ \psi_2^0 &= R_{32}(r)\, Y_{20}(\theta, \varphi), \\ \psi_2^{-1} &= R_{32}(r)\, Y_{2-1}(\theta, \varphi), \\ \psi_2^{-2} &= R_{32}(r)\, Y_{2-2}(\theta, \varphi). \end{aligned} \tag{8.15}$$

We may use as unperturbed eigenfunctions the following linear combinations of the above functions:

$$\begin{aligned} \varphi_1 &= \psi_2^1, \\ \varphi_2 &= \psi_2^{-1}, \\ \varphi_3 &= \frac{\psi_2^2 - \psi_2^{-2}}{\sqrt{2}}, \\ \varphi_4 &= \psi_2^6 \\ \varphi_5 &= \frac{\psi_2^2 + \psi_2^{-2}}{\sqrt{2}}. \end{aligned} \tag{8.16}$$

We find

$$\begin{aligned} &\langle \varphi_1 | H_{\text{cryst}} | \varphi_1 \rangle \\ &= \frac{D\beta\langle r^4 \rangle}{20} [35 - 30 \times 2 \times 3 + 25 - 6 \times 2 \times 3 + 3 \times 4 \times 9] \\ &= -48 \frac{D\beta\langle r^4 \rangle}{20}. \end{aligned} \tag{8.17}$$

We also find

$$\langle\varphi_2| H_{\text{cryst}} |\varphi_2\rangle = \langle\varphi_3| H_{\text{cryst}} |\varphi_3\rangle = -4D \frac{\beta \langle r^4\rangle 12}{20}, \tag{8.18}$$

and

$$\langle\varphi_4| H_{\text{cryst}} |\varphi_4\rangle = 6D \frac{\beta \langle r^4\rangle 12}{20} = \langle\varphi_5| H_{\text{cryst}} |\varphi_5\rangle. \tag{8.19}$$

We notice that H_{cryst} is diagonal if we use the functions (8.16). Our next task is to evaluate the coefficient β. Let us take for example φ_3. We can write this function as

$$\varphi_3 = \frac{\psi_2{}^2 - \psi_2{}^{-2}}{\sqrt{2}} = iR_{32}(r)\sqrt{\frac{15}{4\pi}}\frac{xy}{r^2}. \tag{8.20}$$

We then evaluate the matrix element,

$$\langle\varphi_3| H_{\text{cryst}} |\varphi_3\rangle = -\frac{15D}{4\pi}\int |R_{32}(r)|^2 r^4 r^2\, dr$$
$$\times \int d\Omega(x^4 + y^4 + z^4 - \tfrac{3}{5}r^4)\frac{(xy)^2}{r^8} = -4D\, \tfrac{2}{105}\langle r^4\rangle. \tag{8.21}$$

Then by comparing (8.18) with (8.21) we get: $\beta = \frac{2}{63}$ for an ion with one electron in the d shell. In a similar way we find that for all D states β is either $+\frac{2}{63}$ or $-\frac{2}{63}$:

1 electron	$\beta = \frac{2}{63}$;
9 electrons	$\beta = -\frac{2}{63}$;
4 electrons	$\beta = -\frac{2}{63}$;
6 electrons	$\beta = \frac{2}{63}$.

F STATES

Let us consider now a transition metal ion with two electrons in the d shell ($3d^2$). We have the state functions:

$$\psi_3{}^3, \psi_3{}^2, \psi_3{}^1, \psi_3{}^0, \psi_3{}^{-1}, \psi_3{}^{-2}, \psi_3{}^{-3}. \tag{8.22}$$

We find the following matrix element of H_{cryst} as given by (8.13):

$$\langle 3M_L| V_z |3M_L\rangle = 60 \times \begin{cases} 6 & \text{for } M_L = 0 \\ 1 & \text{for } M_L = \pm 1 \\ -7 & \text{for } M_L = \pm 2 \\ 3 & \text{for } M_L = \pm 3; \end{cases} \tag{8.23}$$

$$\langle 33| V_{\pm} |3-1\rangle = \langle 3-1| V_{\pm} |33\rangle = 24\sqrt{15}, \tag{8.24}$$

$$\langle 32| V_{\pm} |3-2\rangle = \langle 3-2| V_{\pm} |32\rangle = 24 \times 5, \tag{8.25}$$

and the complete matrix of $H_{cryst}/(3\beta \langle r^4 \rangle D)$ is

M_L	−3	−2	−1	0	1	2	3
−3	3				$\sqrt{15}$		
−2		−7				5	
−1			1				$\sqrt{15}$
0				6			
1	$\sqrt{15}$				1		
2		5				−7	
3			$\sqrt{15}$				3

We reorder the matrix elements in the following way:

M_L	3	−1	−3	1	2	−2	0
3	3	$\sqrt{15}$					
−1	$\sqrt{15}$	1					
−3			3	$\sqrt{15}$			
1			$\sqrt{15}$	1			
2					−7	5	
−2					5	−7	
0							6

Then we get

$$\lambda = 6, 6, 6 \qquad \text{(triple root)},$$
$$\lambda = -2, -2, -2 \qquad \text{(triple root)},$$
$$\lambda = -12 \qquad \text{(single root)};$$

and

$$E_1 = 18\beta \langle r^4 \rangle D \qquad \text{(degeneracy} = 3),$$
$$E_2 = -6\beta \langle r^4 \rangle D \qquad \text{(degeneracy} = 3), \tag{8.26}$$
$$E_3 = -36\beta \langle r^4 \rangle D \qquad \text{(degeneracy} = 1).$$

We have now to evaluate β. Let us choose in general a state which has maximum M_L: $\psi_3{}^3$. This state corresponds to

$$l_1 = 2, \quad m_{l_1} = 2; \quad s_1 = \tfrac{1}{2}, \quad m_{s_1} = \tfrac{1}{2};$$
$$l_2 = 2, \quad m_{l_2} = 1; \quad s_2 = \tfrac{1}{2}, \quad m_{s_2} = \tfrac{1}{2},$$

Table 8.2 Splitting of the Ground Terms of Transition Metal Ions in an Octahedral Field

	Ion	Ground State	β	Orbital Degeneracy of Ground State	Spin Degeneracy of Ground State	Total Degeneracy of Ground State	Energy Levels
$3d^1$	Ti^{3+}	^2D	$\frac{2}{63}$	3	2	6	(2)[a] (3)
$3d^2$	V^{3+}	^3F	$-\frac{2}{315}$	3	3	9	(1) (3) (3)
$3d^3$	Cr^{3+}	^4F	$\frac{2}{315}$	1	4	4	(3) (3) (1)
$3d^4$	Cr^{2+}	^5D	$-\frac{2}{63}$	2	5	10	(3) (2)
$3d^5$	Mn^{2+}, Fe^{3+}	^6S		1	6	6	(1)
$3d^6$	Fe^{2+}	^5D	$\frac{2}{63}$	3	5	15	(2) (3)
$3d^7$	Co^{2+}	^4F	$-\frac{2}{315}$	3	4	12	(1) (3) (3)
$3d^8$	Ni^{2+}	^3F	$\frac{2}{315}$	1	3	3	(3) (3) (1)
$3d^9$	Cu^{2+}	^2D	$-\frac{2}{63}$	2	2	4	(3) (2)

[a] Numbers in ( ) indicate orbital degeneracies.

and is expressed by the determinantal function,

$$\psi({}^3F, M_L = 3, M_S = 1) = \frac{1}{\sqrt{2}} \begin{vmatrix} \psi_2{}^2(\mathbf{r}_1)\,\alpha(1) & \psi_2{}^2(\mathbf{r}_2)\,\alpha(2) \\ \psi_2{}^1(\mathbf{r}_1)\,\alpha(1) & \psi_2{}^1(\mathbf{r}_2)\,\alpha(2) \end{vmatrix}$$
$$= \frac{1}{\sqrt{2}} [\psi_2{}^2(\mathbf{r}_1)\,\psi_2{}^1(\mathbf{r}_2) - \psi_2{}^2(\mathbf{r}_2)\,\psi_2{}^1(\mathbf{r}_1)]\,\alpha(1)\,\alpha(2). \tag{8.27}$$

The Hamiltonian representing the crystal field is given by

$$H_{\text{cryst}} = V_1 + V_2, \tag{8.28}$$

where

$$\begin{aligned} V_1 &= D[x_1{}^4 + y_1{}^4 + z_1{}^4 - \tfrac{3}{5}r_1{}^4], \\ V_2 &= D[x_2{}^4 + y_2{}^4 + z_2{}^4 - \tfrac{3}{5}r_2{}^4]. \end{aligned} \tag{8.29}$$

We find

$$\begin{aligned} \langle {}^3F31|\, H_{\text{cryst}}\, |{}^3F31\rangle &= \tfrac{1}{2} \iint [\psi_2{}^2(\mathbf{r}_1)\,\psi_2{}^1(\mathbf{r}_2) - \psi_2{}^2(\mathbf{r}_2)\,\psi_2{}^1(\mathbf{r}_1)]^*(V_1 + V_2) \\ &\quad \times [\psi_2{}^2(\mathbf{r}_1)\,\psi_2{}^1(\mathbf{r}_2) - \psi_2{}^2(\mathbf{r}_2)\,\psi_2{}^1(\mathbf{r}_1)]\, d\tau_1\, d\tau_2 \\ &= \int \psi_2{}^2(\mathbf{r}_1)\, V_1 \psi_2{}^2(\mathbf{r}_1)\, d\tau_1 + \int \psi_2{}^1(\mathbf{r}_1)\, V_1 \psi_2{}^1(\mathbf{r}_1)\, d\tau_1 \\ &= -\tfrac{8}{7} \langle r^4 \rangle D. \end{aligned} \tag{8.30}$$

On the other hand we have already found in (8.23) the value $60D\beta\,\langle r^4\rangle\, 3$ for this matrix element. Then we have

$$\beta = -\tfrac{2}{315}\,. \tag{8.31}$$

In the same way we may proceed for F states with more than two electrons.

S STATES

We see immediately by just looking at the expression of the equivalent operator (8.13) that the Hamiltonian H_{cryst} will produce no splitting of this state.

We have listed all the results in Table 8.2.

REFERENCE

[1] W. Low, *Paramagnetic Resonance in Solids*, Academic, New York, 1960.

9

The Strong Field Scheme

In this scheme the crystal field term in the total Hamiltonian comes before the electrostatic interaction. The different terms of the Hamiltonian are reported in Table 9.1, together with their group theoretical properties.

1. THE UNPERTURBED HAMILTONIAN

The unperturbed Hamiltonian is given by

$$H_u = \sum_i \left(\frac{p_i^2}{2m} - \frac{Z_{pi}}{r_i} e^2\right), \tag{9.1}$$

where Z_{pi} is the effective nuclear charge seen by electron i. The system is defined by the eigenvalues of the operators belonging to the following complete set:

$$H_u, L_z, S_z, l_1^2, s_1^2, l_{z_1}, s_{z_1}, l_2^2, s_2^2, l_{z_2}, s_{z_2}, \ldots \tag{9.2}$$

The symmetry group of the Hamiltonian H_u is

$$R_{\text{el}_1} \times R_{\text{sp}_1} \times R_{\text{el}_2} \times R_{\text{sp}_2} \times \cdots, \tag{9.3}$$

where R_{el_i} = three-dimensional rotation group for orbital i,

R_{sp_i} = three-dimensional rotation group for spin i.

The representation of a state is given by

$$d_{1_1} \times d_{\text{sp}_1} \times d_{1_2} \times d_{\text{sp}_2} \times \cdots. \tag{9.4}$$

The results of the application of Pauli principle are the determinantal form of the eigenfunctions and a reduction of the possible states.

Table 9.1 The Strong Field Scheme

	Hamiltonian	Complete Set of Commuting Operators	Properties of the Hamiltonian
H_u	$\sum\left(\frac{p_i^2}{2m} - \frac{Z_{pi}e^2}{r_i}\right)$	$H_u, L_z, S_z, P,$ $l_1^2, l_{z_1}, s_1^2, s_{z_1}, \ldots$	Electronic configuration: $1s^2\,2s^2\,2p^6 \ldots.$ Group: $R_{\mathrm{el}_1} \times R_{\mathrm{sp}_1} \times R_{\mathrm{el}_2} \times R_{\mathrm{sp}_2} \times \ldots.$ Rep: $d_{l_1} \times d_{s_1} \times d_{l_2} \times d_{s_2} \times \ldots.$
H_{cryst}	$\sum_i eV(\mathbf{r}_i)$	$H_{\mathrm{cryst}}, S_z, (P),$ $\gamma_1, \gamma_{z_1}, s_1^2, s_{z_1}, \ldots$	$[H_{\mathrm{cryst}}, H_u] \neq 0.$ May connect states of H_u with equal M_s, (P), $s_1, m_{s_1}, s_2, m_{s_2}, \ldots.$ May cause: electronic configuration interaction. Group: $G_{c_1} \times R_{\mathrm{sp}_1} \times G_{c_2} \times R_{\mathrm{sp}_2} \times \ldots.$ Rep: $\gamma_1 \times d_{s_1} \times \gamma_2 \times d_{s_2} \times \ldots; \left(d_{l_i} = \sum \gamma_i\right).$
H_{el}	$H_0 - H_u$	$H_{\mathrm{el}}, S^2, S_z, \Gamma, \Gamma_z, (P)$	$[H_{\mathrm{el}}, H_{\mathrm{cryst}}] \neq 0.$ May connect states of H_{cryst} with equal M_s, (P). May cause: crystal configuration interaction, electronic configuration interaction. Group: $G_c \times R_{\mathrm{sp}}.$ Reps: $\gamma_1 \times d_{s_1} \times \gamma_2 \times d_{s_2} \times \cdots = \left(\sum_i \Gamma_i\right) \times \left(\sum_s D_S\right) = \sum_{is}(\Gamma_i \times D_S).$ Some L and S may be excluded by Pauli principle.
H_{so}	$\sum_i \xi_i \mathbf{l}_i \cdot \mathbf{s}_i$	$H_{so}, \Gamma, \Gamma_z, (P)$	$[H_{so}, H_{\mathrm{el}}] \neq 0.$ May connect states of H_{el} with equal (P). May cause: interaction between ${}^{2S+1}\Gamma$ states, crystal configuration interaction, electronic configuration interaction. Group: G_c. Reps: $\Gamma_i \times D_S = \Gamma_i \times \sum_j \Gamma_j = \sum_k \Gamma_k.$

2. THE CRYSTAL FIELD PERTURBATION

The crystal field perturbation is represented by the Hamiltonian:

$$H_{\text{cryst}} = \sum_i eV(\mathbf{r}_i). \tag{9.5}$$

The crystal field splits the representations of the individual electrons in irreducible representations of the symmetry group of H_{cryst}, but does not act on the spin representations of the individual electrons:

$$d_{l_1} \times d_{s_1} \times d_{l_2} \times d_{s_2} \times \cdots = \left(\sum_i \gamma_i\right) \times d_{s_1} \times \left(\sum_k \gamma_k\right) \times d_{s_2} \times \cdots. \tag{9.6}$$

A state of the system is represented by

$$\gamma_1 \times d_{s_1} \times \gamma_2 \times d_{s_2} \times \cdots, \tag{9.7}$$

and its degeneracy is given by

$$\begin{aligned} r_1 \times (2s_1 + 1) \times r_2 \times (2s_2 + 1) \times \cdots \\ = r_1 \times 2 \times r_2 \times 2 \times \cdots, \end{aligned} \tag{9.8}$$

where r_i is the dimension of the γ_i representation.

We may say that in the same way that m_l specifies a function within a d_l manifold, a number m_γ may specify the eigenfunction of the single electron within the γ manifold. In the former case l, l_z are operators that indicate constants of the motion; in the present case γ, γ_z indicate two constants of the motion.[1] In different words, the single electron, because of the crystalline field, goes from a l, s, m_l, m_s to a γ, s, m_γ, m_s representation. The new elementary eigenfunctions, which we call *crystal eigenfunctions*, are linear combinations of the electronic functions u_{nlm_l} and are basis for the irreducible representations γ_i. We may call every possible distribution of electrons over the crystal orbitals a *crystal configuration*.

The complete set of commuting operators is given by

$$H_{\text{cryst}}, S_z, (P), \gamma_1, s_1, \gamma_{z_1}, s_{z_1}, \gamma_2, s_2, \gamma_{z_2}, s_{z_2}, \ldots, \tag{9.9}$$

and the total group by

$$G_{c_1} \times R_{\text{sp}_1} \times G_{c_2} \times R_{\text{sp}_2} \times \cdots. \tag{9.10}$$

At this point we want to enforce the Pauli principle: we take into account the fact that the total state function of the system must be a basis for the antisymmetrical representation of the symmetric group. We enforce

[1] No significance has to be attached to the subscript z in γ_z other than that this operator plays a role equivalent to that of l_z.

the Pauli principle by building up determinantal functions. H_{cryst} may connect states with equal M_S, (P). The state functions, before we apply H_{cryst}, are eigenfunctions of H_u. When we switch on H_{cryst}, we make linear combinations of the elementary u functions that diagonalize H_{cryst} within the given electronic configuration and find the crystal elementary functions. We then enforce the Pauli principle by building up determinantal functions. By doing so we find functions that are almost diagonal in H_{cryst}: there may be matrix elements of H_{cryst} between states with equal M_S, (P), but belonging to different electronic configurations.

3. THE ELECTROSTATIC INTERACTION

We now have to find the matrix elements of the Hamiltonian

$$H_o = \sum_i \left(-\frac{\hbar}{2m} \nabla_i^2 - \frac{Ze^2}{r_i} \right) + \sum_{i>j} \frac{e^2}{r_{ij}} . \tag{9.11}$$

The electrostatic interaction splits the product representation $\gamma_1 \times \gamma_2 \times \cdots$ into irreducible representations of the crystal group G_c,

$$\gamma_1 \times \gamma_2 \times \cdots = \sum_i \Gamma_i . \tag{9.12}$$

At this stage the total spin S is introduced as a good quantum number and this corresponds group theoretically to

$$d_{s_1} \times d_{s_2} \times \cdots = \sum_S , D_S \tag{9.13}$$

where

$$S = (s_1 + s_2 + \cdots s_n), (s_1 + s_2 + \cdots + s_n - 1), \ldots . \tag{9.14}$$

Some of the L and S representations, however, are excluded by the Pauli principle, if we deal with equivalent electrons. We are now at the stage in which terms ${}^{2S+1}\Gamma$ are formed but still not split. Any state functions of the system is a product of a basis function for a Γ representation and a basis function for a D_S representation.

The total representation of a state of the system is $\Gamma \times D_S$, and its degeneracy is $r \times (2S + 1)$, r being the dimension of the Γ representation.

The complete set of commuting operators is given by

$$H_{\text{el}}, \Gamma, S^2, \Gamma_z, S_z, (P), \tag{9.15}$$

and the total group by $G_c \times R_{\text{sp}}$. Here $H_{\text{el}} = H_0 - H_u$.

H_{el} may connect states with equal M_S, (P). The state functions, before we apply H_{el}, are (if we disregard a possible configuration interaction) determinantal functions built up with crystal functions. By using these functions, we find the matrix of H_{el}, diagonalize it and get the eigenvalues and the eigenfunctions of $H_u + H_{\text{cryst}} + H_{\text{el}}$.

By splitting a state ${}^{2s_1+1}\gamma_1\,{}^{2s_2+1}\gamma_2 \cdots$ in a number of ${}^{2S+1}\Gamma$ states we diagonalize the matrix of H_{el} only partly; H_{el} may have matrix elements between states with equal numbers Γ, S, M_Γ, M_S, (P) and belonging to different crystal configurations or even to different electronic configurations.

4. THE SPIN-ORBIT INTERACTION

The spin-orbit interaction is given by

$$H_{so} = \sum_i \xi(r_i)\,\mathbf{l}_i \cdot \mathbf{s}_i. \tag{9.16}$$

The introduction of this term produces a correlation between rotations in coordinate space and rotations in spin space.

Now operations on crystal orbits and on spins must be referred to the same axes. $\Gamma \times D_S$ is still a representation of the symmetry group, but it is no longer irreducible. It splits in the following way:

$$\Gamma \times D_S = \sum_k \Gamma_k, \tag{9.17}$$

where Γ_k are irreducible representations of G_c.

S ceases to be a good quantum number; the complete set of commuting operators is given by

$$H_{so}, \Gamma, \Gamma_z, (P), \tag{9.18}$$

and the total symmetry group by G_c; H_{so} may connect states with equal (P).

The state functions, before we apply H_{so}, are linear combinations of determinantal functions. We build up the matrix of H_{so} by using these functions: by diagonalizing this matrix we get the proper eigenvalues and the proper eigenfunctions.

By splitting a $\Gamma \times D_S$ state in a number of Γ states we diagonalize the matrix of H_{so} only partially. H_{so} may have matrix elements between states with equal numbers Γ, M_Γ, (P) and belonging to different ${}^{2S+1}\Gamma$ states, or to different crystal configurations or even to different electronic configurations.

10

Covalent Bonding and Its Effect on Magnetic Ions in Crystals

1. THE RELEVANCE OF COVALENT BONDING [1]

The energy level structure of d^n and f^n ions in crystals can be explained, to a large extent, by crystal field theory. This theory is based on the hypothesis that a magnetic ion in a crystal site feels the influence of the ligand ions as an electric field which has the symmetry of the site. In this hypothesis no overlapping of the wavefunctions of the magnetic ion and of the ligands is allowed and the bonding is considered to be of a pure ionic type. A need for extending the crystal field theory arises in several circumstances.

This is the case, for example, when first-principle calculations of the crystal field strength are attempted. The inadequacy of the crystal field theory becomes manifest also when the so-called "transferred hyperfine structure" appears in the spin-resonance spectrum of an ion, due to mixing of the orbitals of the ion with those of the ligands. This phenomenon has been observed in the hyperfine structure of $IrCl_6^{2-}$ and is due to the Cl^- ions [2], and also in systems like Mn^{2+} or Fe^{2+} in ZnF_2 where it is due to orbital mixing of these ions with the F^- ligands [3].

Other spectral parameters, such as Racah's B and C and the spin-orbit interaction, are found to be smaller in the solids than in the free ions; they too are affected by the orbital mixing of ion and ligands.

A modification of the crystal field theory is the *ligand field theory*, which recognizes the presence of overlap between the metal and ligand orbitals, and consequently does not allow first-principle calculations according to point charge or dipole ligand model and pure, metal ion, d wavefunctions. According to this theory, the charge of the ligands, the metal-ligand distance, and the radial parts of the d wavefunctions are considered adjustable. The energy levels are interpreted in terms of B and C coefficients derived from the spectral experimental data; the energy separations of the spectral terms are found in general to be about 75% of those of the free ions.

Both the crystal field theory and the ligand field theory, however, do not predict the occurrence of certain states generally high in energy which produce very strong (charge transfer) absorption transitions of the order of hundreds or thousands times greater than those related to the crystal field spectra.

A way of extending the crystal field theory in order to explain the above phenomena consists of allowing a certain overlapping of the metal ion orbital, and of the ligand orbitals, namely some sharing of the electrons among metal ion and ligands. In this case the bonding in a metal ion complex can be considered covalent to the degree to which the electron sharing is taking place. The complex is then characterized by molecular orbitals which involve both the metal ion and the ligands.

Crystal field theory continues, however, to maintain its validity especially for rare earth ions where the perturbing influence of the environment is much smaller than in d^n ions. In developing a molecular orbital approach to the problem of energy levels of ions in crystals, we shall then limit ourselves to the considerations of ions of this latter type.[1]

2. THE FORMATION OF MOLECULAR ORBITALS

If we consider as an example the molecule H_2, we can imagine that this molecule is formed by moving two H atoms close to each other to a point where a balance is achieved between the attraction of the electrons by both nuclei and the repulsion among the two positively charged nuclei. In this condition the two atoms have achieved a certain stability and the molecule is formed: every electron now moves in the average potential due to the two protons and to the other electron. The electronic wave function that represents the state of an electron is now called a *molecular orbital.* An electron in a molecular orbital does not belong any more to a particular nucleus but it is shared between the two nuclei. This sharing is what chemists call a *covalent bond.*

There are three types of molecular orbital that are relevant in chemistry: the σ *orbitals*, the π *orbitals*, and the δ *orbitals.*

The σ orbitals are by definitions orbitals that do not have any nodal plane containing the internuclear axis. The π orbitals have one nodal plane containing the internuclear axis, and the δ orbitals have two nodal planes containing the internuclear axis.

Before giving some examples of σ, π, and δ orbitals we shall examine the

[1] For the possible effects of covalent bonding on the ligand field parameters of the rare earths, see [4].

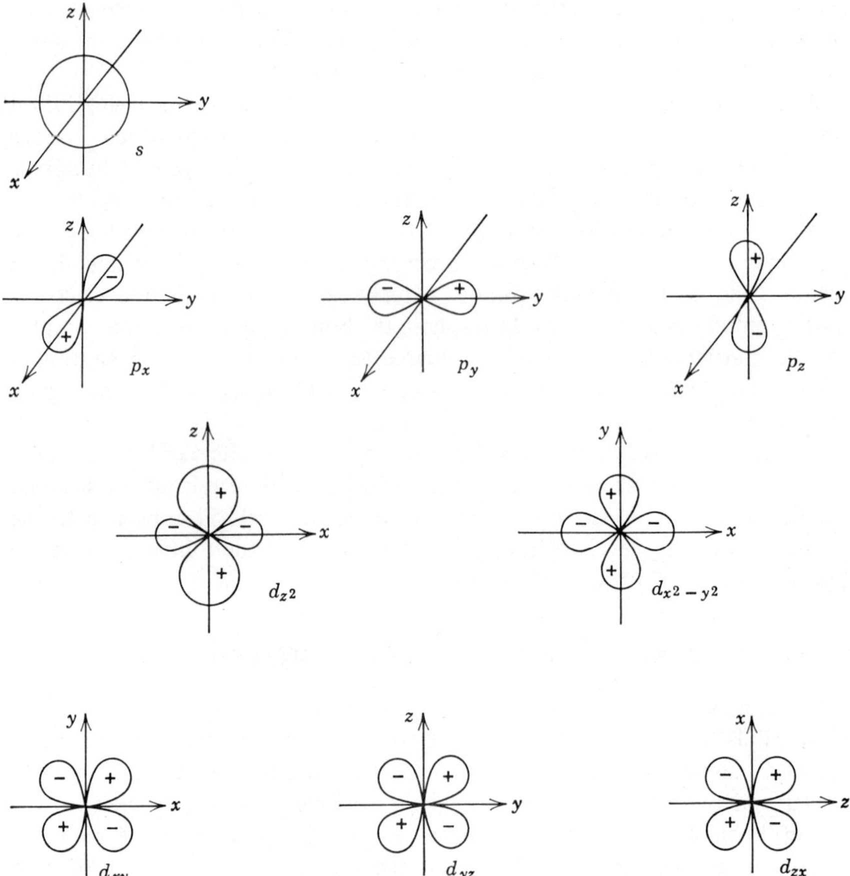

Fig. 10.1. Relevant orbitals for chemical bonding.

atomic orbitals that may be relevant in producing a covalent bond. In Table 10.1 we report the angular parts of the s, p, and d orbitals. The same orbitals are represented in Fig. 10.1.

In general, we can say that a bond is formed by the overlapping of two orbitals which have the same symmetry with respect to the internuclear axis. Let us call this axis the z axis. The σ bonds, symmetric for rotation about the internuclear axis can be produced by overlapping of s—s, s—d_{z^2}, s—p_z, p_z—p_z. π bonds have a nodal plane containing the internuclear axis and can be produced by overlapping of orbitals like p_x—p_x, p_y—p_y. δ bonds have two nodal planes containing the internuclear axis and can be produced by overlapping of orbitals like d_{xy}—d_{xy}, $d_{x^2-y^2}$—$d_{x^2-y^2}$.

Examples of such bonds are given in Figs. 10.2 and 10.3.

Table 10.1 Normalized Angular Parts for s, p, and d Orbitals

Orbital	Normalized Angular Part
s	$\frac{1}{2\sqrt{\pi}}$
p_x	$\frac{\sqrt{3}}{2\sqrt{\pi}} \sin\theta \cos\varphi$
p_y	$\frac{\sqrt{3}}{2\sqrt{\pi}} \sin\theta \sin\varphi$
p_z	$\frac{\sqrt{3}}{2\sqrt{\pi}} \cos\theta$
d_{z^2}	$\frac{\sqrt{5}}{4\sqrt{\pi}} (3\cos^2\theta - 1)$
$d_{x^2-y^2}$	$\frac{\sqrt{15}}{4\sqrt{\pi}} (\sin^2\theta \cos 2\varphi)$
d_{xy}	$\frac{\sqrt{15}}{4\sqrt{\pi}} (\sin^2\theta \sin 2\phi)$
d_{yz}	$\frac{\sqrt{15}}{2\sqrt{\pi}} (\sin\theta \cos\theta \sin\varphi)$
d_{zx}	$\frac{\sqrt{15}}{2\sqrt{\pi}} (\sin\theta \cos\theta \cos\varphi)$

(a)

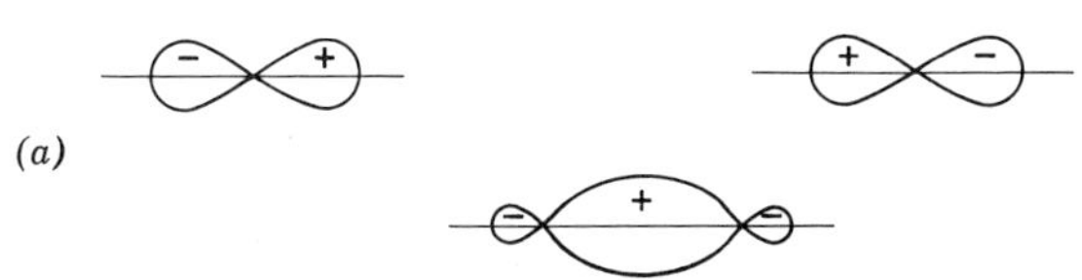

(b)

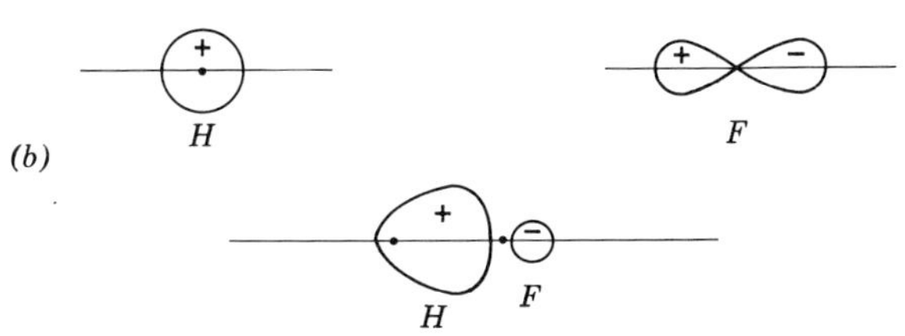

Fig. 10.2. Examples of σ bonds: (a) overlapping of two p orbitals; (b) overlapping of s and p orbitals (molecule HF).

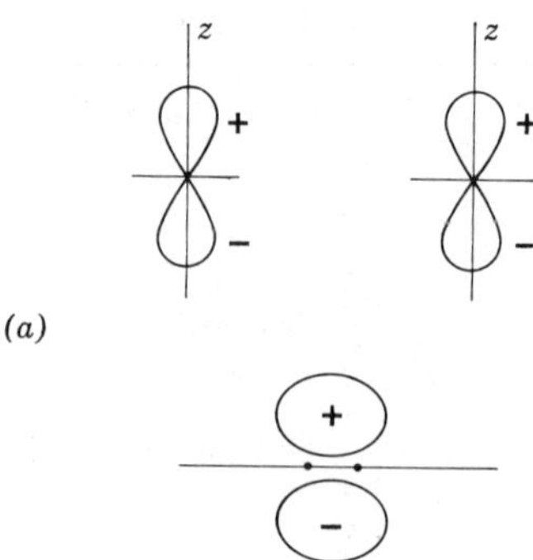

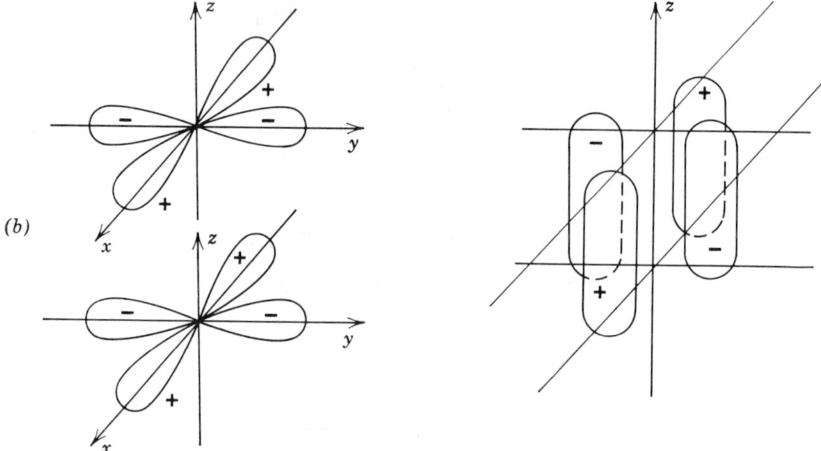

Fig. 10.3. Examples of π and δ bonds: (a) π bond formed by two p_z orbitals; (b) δ bond formed by two $d_{x^2-y^2}$ orbitals.

3. EXAMPLE OF MOLECULAR ORBITALS FORMATION

Let us consider the complex of Fig. 10.4[2] with six equal atoms and assume that each atom has available for π bonding with the other atoms only one p_z atomic orbital. We have then at our disposal six atomic p_z orbitals and want to find six molecular orbitals that transform irreducibly, according to the representations of the symmetry group of the molecule.

[2] This example was presented by Prof. F. A. Cotton in one of his lectures at M.I.T.

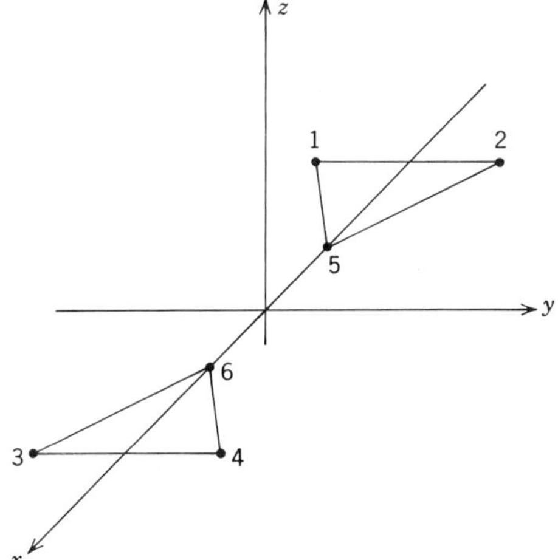

Fig. 10.4. Example of a complex with D_{2h} symmetry.

The symmetry group of the molecule is D_{2h}. The group D_{2h} is the product group $D_2 \times I$ but we restrict ourselves, for the moment, to the group of lower symmetry D_2.

The character table of group D_2 is the following:

	E	$C_2(z)$	$C_2(y)$	$C_2(x)$
A_1	1	1	1	1
B_1	1	1	-1	-1
B_2	1	-1	1	-1
B_3	1	-1	-1	1

In order to find the combinations of atomic orbitals that can establish π bonding between the six atoms, we consider a set of vectors parallel to z and determine how these vectors transform under the operations of the symmetry group D_2. The vectors represent the basis for a (reducible) representation Γ_π of D_2. We find the characters of this representation by using the following rules:

1. Each vector that transforms into itself contributes $+1$ to the character.
2. Each vector that transforms into its opposite contributes -1 to the character.
3. Each vector that does not transform into itself does not contribute to the character.

Taking these rules into account we find

	E	$C_2(z)$	$C_2(y)$	$C_2(x)$
Γ_π	6	0	0	-2

Before reducing this representation we note that the six vectors can be divided in two distinct sets: one consisting of vectors 1, 2, 3, and 4 and the other of vectors 5 and 6. These two sets of vectors are such that no operation of the group can bring a vector of one set into the site of a vector of the other. We then have the following representations for the two sets:

	E	$C_2(z)$	$C_2(y)$	$C_2(x)$
Γ_{1234}	4	0	0	0
Γ_{56}	2	0	0	-2

These two representations can be reduced as follows:

$$\begin{aligned} \Gamma_{1234} &= A_1 + B_1 + B_2 + B_3, \\ \Gamma_{56} &= B_1 + B_2. \end{aligned} \tag{10.1}$$

Let us now form linear combinations of the p_z functions at sites 1, 2, 3, and 4 that transform according to A_1, B_1, B_2, and B_3 and linear combinations of the p_z functions at sites 5 and 6 that transform according to B_1 and B_2. We may proceed in the following way:

Let us call ϕ_i the p_z function at the site i and let us call $\psi(\Gamma_i)$ the molecular orbital which transforms according to the irreducible representation Γ_i.

The different operations of the group have the following effects on the individual functions:

$$\begin{aligned} C_2(z)\,\phi_1 &\to \phi_4, \\ C_2(z)\,\phi_2 &\to \phi_3, \\ C_2(z)\,\phi_3 &\to \phi_2, \\ C_2(z)\,\phi_4 &\to \phi_1. \end{aligned} \tag{10.2}$$

$$\begin{aligned} C_2(y)\,\phi_1 &\to -\phi_3, \\ C_2(y)\,\phi_2 &\to -\phi_4, \\ C_2(y)\,\phi_3 &\to -\phi_1, \\ C_2(y)\,\phi_4 &\to -\phi_2. \end{aligned} \tag{10.3}$$

$$\begin{aligned} C_2(x)\,\phi_1 &\to -\phi_2, \\ C_2(x)\,\phi_2 &\to -\phi_1, \\ C_2(x)\,\phi_3 &\to -\phi_4, \\ C_2(x)\,\phi_4 &\to -\phi_3. \end{aligned} \tag{10.4}$$

We can assume for $\psi(A)$ the form,

$$\psi(A) = a\phi_1 + b\phi_2 + c\phi_3 + d\phi_4.$$

Now we must have

$$C_2(z)\,\psi(A) = a\phi_4 + b\phi_3 + c\phi_2 + d\phi_1 = a\phi_1 + b\phi_2 + c\phi_3 + d\phi_4, \quad (10.5)$$

$$C_2(y)\,\psi(A) = -a\phi_3 - b\phi_4 - c\phi_1 - d\phi_2 = a\phi_1 + b\phi_2 + c\phi_3 + d\phi_4, \quad (10.6)$$

$$C_2(x)\,\psi(A) = -a\phi_2 - b\phi_1 - c\phi_4 - d\phi_3 = a\phi_1 + b\phi_2 + c\phi_3 + d\phi_4. \quad (10.7)$$

From (10.5)

$$a = d; \qquad b = c; \quad (10.8)$$

from (10.6)

$$a = -c; \qquad b = -d; \quad (10.9)$$

and from (10.7)

$$a = -b; \qquad c = -d. \quad (10.10)$$

We can put

$$a = d = 1 = -b = -c; \quad (10.11)$$

then we obtain

$$\psi(A) = \phi_1 - \phi_2 - \phi_3 + \phi_4. \quad (10.12)$$

In order to normalize, we may use the so-called *Hückel approximation.* This rather simple approximation, which gives results with a good accuracy, consists of the following. A molecular orbital is expressed as a linear combination of normalized atomic orbitals,

$$\psi_i = N_i \sum_j c_{ij}\phi_j, \quad (10.13)$$

where N_i is a normalizing factor which is found by assuming that we want ψ_i normalized to unity:

$$\frac{1}{N_i^2} = \int \left(\sum_j c_{ij}\phi_j\right)^2 d\tau = \sum_j c_{ij}^2 \int \phi_j^2\, d\tau + \sum_{\substack{j,k\\ j\neq k}} c_{ij}c_{ik} \int \phi_j\phi_k\, d\tau. \quad (10.14)$$

According to the Hückel approximation, we may neglect in the above calculation the overlap integral, so that N_i reduces to

$$N_i = \left(\sum_j c_{ij}^2\right)^{-1/2}. \quad (10.15)$$

The Hückel approximation comprehends also some assumptions regarding the evaluation of the energies of the molecular orbitals, but we shall consider this point later.

By using the above approximation $\psi(A)$ becomes

$$\psi(A) = \tfrac{1}{2}(\phi_1 - \phi_2 - \phi_3 + \phi_4). \quad (10.16)$$

Using a procedure similar to the one that led us to $\psi(A)$, we can find the five other molecular orbitals. The six molecular orbitals are then given by

$$\begin{aligned}
\psi(A) &= \psi_1 = \tfrac{1}{2}(\phi_1 - \phi_2 - \phi_3 + \phi_4),\\
\psi(B_1) &= \psi_2 = \tfrac{1}{2}(\phi_1 + \phi_2 + \phi_3 + \phi_4),\\
\psi(B_2) &= \psi_3 = \tfrac{1}{2}(\phi_1 + \phi_2 - \phi_3 - \phi_4),\\
\psi(B_3) &= \psi_4 = \tfrac{1}{2}(\phi_1 - \phi_2 + \phi_3 - \phi_4).
\end{aligned} \tag{10.17}$$

$$\begin{aligned}
\psi(B_1) &= \psi_5 = \frac{1}{\sqrt{2}}(\phi_5 + \phi_6),\\
\psi(B_2) &= \psi_6 = \frac{1}{\sqrt{2}}(\phi_5 - \phi_6).
\end{aligned} \tag{10.18}$$

We have classified the atomic orbitals according to the representations of D_2. The real symmetry group of the molecule, however, is $D_{2h} = D_2 \times I$. We have now to classify the wave functions according to D_{2h}; we can do this very easily, considering how the functions change under the inversion operation. We can then make the following assignment:

$$\begin{aligned}
\psi_1 &= \psi(A_{1u}),\\
\psi_2 &= \psi(B_{1u}),\\
\psi_3 &= \psi(B_{2g}),\\
\psi_4 &= \psi(B_{3g}).
\end{aligned} \tag{10.19}$$

$$\begin{aligned}
\psi_5 &= \psi(B_{1u}),\\
\psi_6 &= \psi(B_{2g}).
\end{aligned} \tag{10.20}$$

We now wish to evaluate the energies of the molecular orbitals. Given a molecular orbital, its energy eigenvalue is

$$\begin{aligned}
E_i &= \int \psi_i H \psi_i \, d\tau\\
&= N_i^2 \left\{ \sum_j c_{ij}^2 \int \phi_j H \phi_j \, d\tau + \sum_{\substack{j,k\\ j\neq k}} c_{ij} c_{ik} \int \phi_j H \phi_k \, d\tau \right\}\\
&= \alpha + N_i^2 \sum_{\substack{j,k\\ j\neq k}} c_{ij} c_{ik} \int \phi_j H \phi_k \, d\tau,
\end{aligned} \tag{10.21}$$

where $\alpha = \int \phi_i H \phi_i \, d\tau$ and where we have assumed that the energies of the individual atomic orbitals ϕ_j's are all equal. According to the Hückel approximation, in evaluating E_i we can neglect any integral of the form $\int \phi_j H \phi_k \, d\tau$ in (10.21) if ϕ_j and ϕ_k refer to nonadjacent atoms. If all the ϕ_i's are equivalent, for any two adjacent ϕ_i's we may write

$$\int \phi_j H \phi_k \, d\tau = \beta. \tag{10.22}$$

It can be shown that β is intrinsically negative. Also

$$E_i = \alpha + 2N_i^2 \Big(\sum_{\substack{j,k \\ j=k+1}} c_{ij} c_{ik} \beta \Big). \tag{10.23}$$

Let us evaluate now the energies of the six molecular orbitals (10.17) and (10.18). We may write, for example,

$$H_{11} = \langle \psi_1 | H | \psi_1 \rangle = \tfrac{1}{4} \int (\phi_1 - \phi_2 - \phi_3 + \phi_4) \, H(\phi_1 - \phi_2 - \phi_3 + \phi_4) \, d\tau$$

$$= \tfrac{1}{4}(4\alpha - 4\beta) = \alpha - \beta. \tag{10.24}$$

The diagonal matrix elements of the Hamiltonian are then given by

$$\begin{aligned} E(A_{1u}) &= -\beta = H_{11}, \\ E(B_{1u}) &= \beta = H_{22}, \\ E(B_{2g}) &= \beta = H_{33}, \\ E(B_{3g}) &= -\beta = H_{44}. \end{aligned} \tag{10.25}$$

$$\begin{aligned} E(B_{1u}) &= \beta = H_{55}, \\ E(B_{2g}) &= -\beta = H_{66}, \end{aligned} \tag{10.26}$$

where we have taken $\alpha = 0$. We have also the nondiagonal matrix elements,

$$\begin{aligned} H_{25} &= H_{52} = \frac{1}{2\sqrt{2}}(2\beta + 2\beta) = \sqrt{2}\,\beta, \\ H_{36} &= H_{63} = \sqrt{2}\,\beta; \end{aligned} \tag{10.27}$$

namely we have matrix elements between any two states belonging to the same irreducible representation. This fact gives us two problems to solve: one is to find the actual energies of the two B_{1u} levels and of the two B_{2g} levels by diagonalizing the respective matrices and the other is to find the corrected molecular orbitals. The energies of the B_{1u} levels are given by

$$\begin{pmatrix} \beta - E & \sqrt{2}\,\beta \\ \sqrt{2}\,\beta & \beta - E \end{pmatrix} = 0, \tag{10.28}$$

or

$$E = \beta \pm \sqrt{\beta^2 + \beta^2} = \begin{cases} (1 + \sqrt{2})\,\beta = 2.41\beta \\ (1 - \sqrt{2})\,\beta = -0.41\beta. \end{cases} \tag{10.29}$$

The level with lower energy (2.41β) is called a *bonding level* and the level with higher energy (-0.41β) an *antibonding level.* The antibonding levels are marked with an asterisk: therefore 2.41β is the energy of level B_{1u} and $(-0.41)\,\beta$ the energy of level B_{1u}^*.

The energies of the two B_{2g} levels are given by

$$\begin{pmatrix} \beta - E & \sqrt{2}\,\beta \\ \sqrt{2}\,\beta & -\beta - E \end{pmatrix} = 0, \tag{10.30}$$

or

$$E = \begin{cases} \sqrt{3}\,\beta = 1.73\beta \\ -\sqrt{3}\,\beta = -1.73\beta. \end{cases} \tag{10.31}$$

1.73 is the energy of B_{2g} and $(-1.73)\,\beta$ the energy of B_{2g}^*. The energies of the six orbitals are now reported in Fig. 10.5.

If six electrons are available in the complex for the establishment of the bond, we can put two electrons in each molecular orbital, starting from the

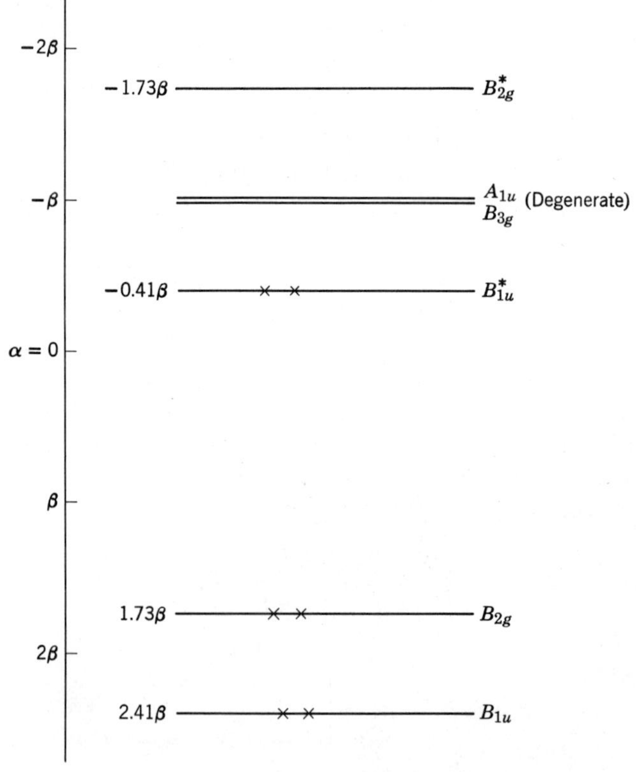

Fig. 10.5. Energy diagram of molecular orbitals of the D_{2h} complex $(\beta < 0)$ of Fig. 10.4.

one lower in energy. The energy of the bond is given by

$$2 \times 2.41\beta + 2 \times 1.73\beta - 2 \times 0.41\beta = 7.46\beta < 0. \tag{10.32}$$

We want now to find the corrected orbitals for the two levels B_{1u} and for the two levels B_{2g}. We can build up new functions for the B_{1u} levels in the following way:

$$\begin{aligned} \psi_2' &= \frac{1}{\sqrt{1+x^2}}(\psi_2 + x\psi_5), \\ \psi_5' &= \frac{1}{\sqrt{1+x^2}}(x\psi_2 - \psi_5). \end{aligned} \tag{10.33}$$

It is easy to verify that, since ψ_2 and ψ_5 are orthonormal,

$$\langle \psi_2' \mid \psi_5' \rangle = \frac{1}{1+x^2}\left\{\langle \psi_2 \mid x\psi_2\rangle - \langle \psi_2 \mid \psi_5\rangle + x^2\langle \psi_5 \mid \psi_2\rangle - x\langle \psi_5 \mid \psi_5\rangle\right\} = 0, \tag{10.34}$$

$$\langle \psi_2' \mid \psi_2' \rangle = \langle \psi_5' \mid \psi_5' \rangle = 1, \tag{10.35}$$

namely the new orbitals also are orthonormal. We can find x by imposing the condition that the eigenvalues of the energies have to be equal to the ones given by (10.29). We have then, for example,

$$\begin{aligned} E(\psi_2') &= \frac{1}{1+x^2}\{\langle(\psi_2 + x\psi_5)|\, H \,|(\psi_2 + x\psi_5)\rangle\} \\ &= \frac{1}{1+x^2}\{\langle\psi_2|\, H \,|\psi_2\rangle + 2x\langle\psi_2|\, H \,|\psi_5\rangle + \langle\psi_5|\, H \,|\psi_5\rangle\} \\ &= \frac{1}{1+x^2}\{\beta + 2\sqrt{2}\,\beta + \beta x^2\} = (1 + \sqrt{2})\,\beta, \end{aligned} \tag{10.36}$$

which gives for x the value 1. It is easy to verify that if we use the same value of x for ψ_5' and evaluate the energy of this function we find

$$E(\psi_5') = (1 - \sqrt{2})\,\beta. \tag{10.37}$$

In the same way we can find the corrected orbitals for the levels B_{2g},

$$\begin{aligned} \psi_3' &= \frac{1}{\sqrt{1+x^2}}(\psi_3 + x\psi_6), \\ \psi_6' &= \frac{1}{\sqrt{1+x^2}}(x\psi_3 - \psi_6). \end{aligned} \tag{10.38}$$

We find x by imposing the condition that

$$\begin{aligned} \langle \psi_3' | H | \psi_3' \rangle &= \sqrt{3}\,\beta, \\ \langle \psi_6' | H | \psi_6' \rangle &= -\sqrt{3}\,\beta. \end{aligned} \tag{10.39}$$

We find that

$$x = \frac{\sqrt{2}}{1+\sqrt{3}}. \tag{10.40}$$

The orbitals are then given by the tabulation on page 233.

We now define as *order of the bond* between two atoms the sum of the products of the coefficients of the atomic orbitals of the two atoms in each of the occupied molecular orbitals, each product multiplied by the number of electrons in the molecular orbital. We have for example for the bond between atoms 1 and 2 and for the bond between atoms 3 and 4,

$$\begin{aligned} 2 \times 0.355 \times 0.355 &= 0.25, \\ 2 \times 0.443 \times 0.443 &= 0.392, \\ 2 \times 0.355 \times 0.355 &= \underline{0.25} \\ & 0.892, \end{aligned}$$

and for the bonds 1—5, 2—5, 4—6, and 3—6,

$$\begin{aligned} 2 \times 0.355 \times 0.5 &= 0.354, \\ 2 \times 0.443 \times 0.326 &= 0.288, \\ 2 \times 0.355 \times (-0.5) &= \underline{-0.354} \\ & 0.288. \end{aligned}$$

This means that the electrons are more localized between atoms 1 and 2 or 3 and 4 than between atoms 1 and 5 or 2 and 5.

In the same way we get for bond 5—6, the order 0.79; for bonds 1—6, 2—6, 4—5, and 3—5 the order −0.288; for bonds 1—4, 1—3, 2—4, and 2—3 the order 0.108.

In summary this example has shown the following:

1. In constructing the molecular orbitals it is sometimes possible to consider a symmetry group of lower symmetry first. The molecular orbitals can then be classified according to the real symmetry group.
2. It is sometimes advantageous to divide the atomic orbitals in two different sets, in such a way that no operation of the group can transform an atomic orbital of one set into an atomic orbital of the other set.
3. The molecular orbitals formed with the atomic orbitals of set 1 have then to be *coupled* with the one formed with the atomic orbitals of set 2. In general molecular orbitals of the two sets with equal symmetry present

	Level	Orbital	Energy
1	A_{1u}	$\psi_1 = \frac{1}{2}(\phi_1 - \phi_2 - \phi_3 + \phi_4) = 0.5(\phi_1 - \phi_2 - \phi_3 + \phi_4)$	$-\beta$
2′	B_{1u}	$\frac{1}{\sqrt{2}}(\psi_2 + \psi_5) = \frac{1}{2\sqrt{2}}(\phi_1 + \phi_2 + \phi_3 + \phi_4) + \frac{1}{2}(\phi_5 + \phi_6)$ $= 0.355(\phi_1 + \phi_2 + \phi_3 + \phi_4) + 0.5(\phi_5 + \phi_6)$	$(1 + \sqrt{2})\beta = 2.41\beta$
3′	B_{2g}	$\left(\frac{2+\sqrt{3}}{3+\sqrt{3}}\right)^{1/2}\left(\psi_2 + \frac{\sqrt{2}}{1+\sqrt{3}}\psi_6\right)$ $= \left(\frac{2+\sqrt{3}}{3+\sqrt{3}}\right)^{1/2}\left[\frac{1}{2}(\phi_1 + \phi_2 - \phi_3 - \phi_4) + \frac{1}{1+\sqrt{3}}(\phi_5 - \phi_6)\right]$ $= 0.443\,(\phi_1 + \phi_2 - \phi_3 - \phi_4) + 0.326(\phi_5 - \phi_6)$	$\sqrt{3}\beta = 1.73\beta$
4	B_{3g}	$\frac{1}{2}(\phi_1 - \phi_2 + \phi_3 - \phi_4) = 0.5(\phi_1 - \phi_2 + \phi_3 - \phi_4)$	$-\beta$
5′	B_{1u}^*	$\frac{1}{\sqrt{2}}(\psi_2 - \psi_5) = \frac{1}{2\sqrt{2}}(\phi_1 + \phi_2 + \phi_3 + \phi_4) - \frac{1}{2}(\phi_5 + \phi_6)$ $= 0.355(\phi_1 + \phi_2 + \phi_3 + \phi_4) - 0.5(\phi_5 + \phi_6)$	$(1 - \sqrt{2})\beta = -0.41\beta$
6′	B_{2g}^*	$\left(\frac{2+\sqrt{3}}{3+\sqrt{3}}\right)^{1/2}\left[\frac{\sqrt{2}}{1+\sqrt{3}}\psi_3 - \psi_6\right]$ $= \left(\frac{2+\sqrt{3}}{3+\sqrt{3}}\right)^{1/2}\left[\frac{1}{\sqrt{2}(1+\sqrt{3})}(\phi_1 + \phi_2 - \phi_3 - \phi_4) - \frac{1}{\sqrt{2}}(\phi_5 - \phi_6)\right]$ $= 0.23(\phi_1 + \phi_2 - \phi_3 - \phi_4) - 0.63(\phi_5 - \phi_6)$	$-\sqrt{3}\beta = -1.73\beta$

off-diagonal matrix element of the Hamiltonian, which require the solution of a secular equation.

4. The final expressions for the molecular orbitals give information about the localization of the electrons in the complex.

4. THE USE OF PROJECTION OPERATORS IN THE CONSTRUCTION OF MOLECULAR ORBITALS

We have already seen in Section 4 of Chapter 3 that, given a symmetry group G of order g, a projection operator is defined as follows:

$$\rho_{ij}^{\alpha} = \frac{n_\alpha}{g} \sum_R \Gamma_\alpha(R)_{ij}^*, \tag{10.41}$$

where Γ_α is an irreducible representation of G, R a generic operation of the group and n_α the dimension of Γ_α.

If f is an arbitrary function whose coordinates are affected by ρ_{ij}^{α}, the n_α functions,

$$f_{ij}^{\alpha} = \rho_{ij}^{\alpha} f = \frac{n_\alpha}{g} \sum_R \Gamma_\alpha(R)_{ij}^* f, \qquad \begin{cases} i = 1, 2, \ldots, n_\alpha, \\ j \text{ fixed}, \end{cases} \tag{10.42}$$

form a basis for the irreducible representation Γ_α.

It is evident from (10.41) that the knowledge of the character table is not enough to form the projection operators, and that a knowledge of the matrices of the representations is needed. This difficulty, however, does not exist for unidimensional representations, where matrices and characters coincide.

Let us take up again the example of the previous section. Consulting the character table for the group D_2 we can construct the following projection operators:

$$\begin{aligned} \rho_{11}^{A} &= \tfrac{1}{4}[E + C_2(z) + C_2(y) + C_2(x)], \\ \rho_{11}^{B_1} &= \tfrac{1}{4}[E + C_2(z) - C_2(y) - C_2(x)], \\ \rho_{11}^{B_2} &= \tfrac{1}{4}[E - C_2(z) + C_2(y) - C_2(x)], \\ \rho_{11}^{B_3} &= \tfrac{1}{4}[E - C_2(z) - C_2(y) + C_2(x)]. \end{aligned} \tag{10.43}$$

Let us apply these operators to the atomic orbital ϕ_1. Since

$$C_2(z)\,\phi_1 \to \phi_4; \qquad C_2(y)\,\phi_1 \to -\phi_3; \qquad C_2(x)\,\phi_1 \to -\phi_2, \tag{10.44}$$

we obtain

$$\begin{aligned}
[\rho_{11}{}^{A}]\,\phi_1 &= \tfrac{1}{4}(\phi_1 + \phi_4 - \phi_3 - \phi_2),\\
[\rho_{11}{}^{B_1}]\,\phi_1 &= \tfrac{1}{4}(\phi_1 + \phi_4 + \phi_3 + \phi_2),\\
[\rho_{11}{}^{B_2}]\,\phi_1 &= \tfrac{1}{4}(\phi_1 - \phi_4 - \phi_3 + \phi_2),\\
[\rho_{11}{}^{B_3}]\,\phi_1 &= \tfrac{1}{4}(\phi_1 - \phi_4 + \phi_3 - \phi_2).
\end{aligned} \tag{10.45}$$

Also, applying $\rho_{11}{}^{B_1}$ and $\rho_{11}{}^{B_2}$ to the atomic orbital ϕ_5, since

$$C_2(z)\,\phi_5 \to \phi_6; \qquad C_2(y)\,\phi_5 \to -\phi_6; \qquad C_2(x)\,\phi_5 \to -\phi_5, \tag{10.46}$$

we obtain

$$\begin{aligned}
[\rho_{11}{}^{B_1}]\,\phi_5 &= \tfrac{1}{4}(\phi_5 + \phi_6 + \phi_6 + \phi_5) = \tfrac{1}{2}(\phi_5 + \phi_6),\\
[\rho_{11}{}^{B_2}]\,\phi_5 &= \tfrac{1}{4}(\phi_5 - \phi_6 - \phi_6 + \phi_5) = \tfrac{1}{2}(\phi_5 - \phi_6).
\end{aligned} \tag{10.47}$$

We can see that, apart from the normalization factors, the linear combinations of atomic orbital (10.45) coincide with the (10.17) already derived and that the (10.47) coincide with the (10.18).

We want now to consider the use of projection operators in the more general case when the representations of the symmetry group which have to be used are not all unidimensional. The best way to illustrate the procedure is to consider another example.

Let us consider a complex of 4 atoms, where each atom has two atomic orbitals (say p_x, p_y) available for bonding with the other three. Such a complex, which has symmetry C_{4v} is represented in Fig. 10.6.

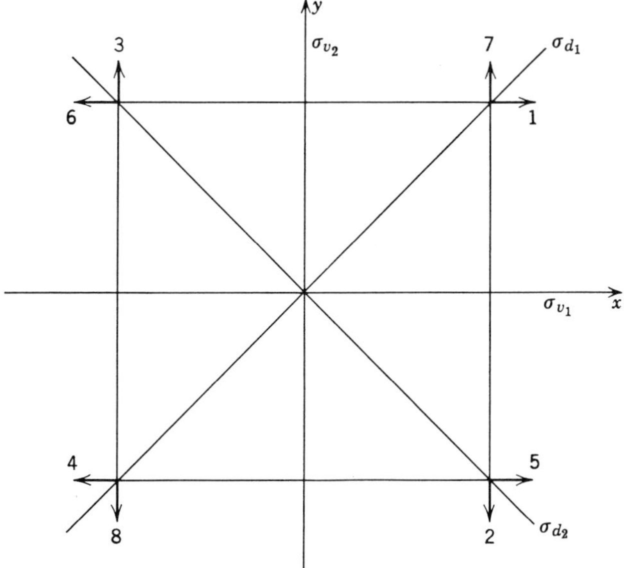

Fig. 10.6. Molecular complex with C_{4v} symmetry.

The first thing we want to do is to report the character table for C_{4v}.

C_{4v}	E	$2C_4$	$C_4^2 \equiv C_2$	$\sigma_{v_1}, \sigma_{v_2}$	$\sigma_{d_1}, \sigma_{d_2}$	Operators Transforming Irreducibly	
A_1	1	1	1	1	1	z	$x^2 + y^2, z^2$
A_2	1	1	1	-1	-1	L_z	
B_1	1	-1	1	1	-1		$x^2 - y^2$
B_2	1	-1	1	-1	1		xy
E	2	0	-2	0	0	$(x, y)(L_x, L_y)$	(xz, yz)

We consider then the vectors in Fig. 10.6 as basis for a representation of C_{4v}. The characters of this representation are given by

E	C_4, C_4^3	C_2	$\sigma_{v_1},\sigma_{v_2}$	$\sigma_{d_1},\sigma_{d_2}$
8	0	0	0	0

and the representation reduces as follows:

$$\Gamma = A_1 + A_2 + B_1 + B_2 + 2E. \qquad (10.48)$$

We have in this case four molecular orbitals belonging each to a different unidimensional representation and two molecular orbitals belonging both to the two-dimensional representation E. In order to construct the projection operators for this representation E we need to know the matrices of the different operations. Since (x, y) transform irreducibly according to E, we can obtain these matrices by considering how x and y transform under the different operations.

C_{4v}	E	C_4	C_4^3	C_2	σ_{v_1}	σ_{v_2}	σ_{d_1}	σ_{d_2}
x	x	$-y$	y	$-x$	x	$-x$	y	$-y$
y	y	x	$-x$	$-y$	$-y$	y	x	$-x$

Taking in account (2.17) the matrices are then given by

C_{4v}	E	C_4	C_4^3	C_2	σ_{v_1}	σ_{v_2}	σ_{d_1}	σ_{d_2}
E	$\begin{pmatrix} 1 & 0 \\ 0 & 1 \end{pmatrix}$	$\begin{pmatrix} 0 & 1 \\ -1 & 0 \end{pmatrix}$	$\begin{pmatrix} 0 & -1 \\ 1 & 0 \end{pmatrix}$	$\begin{pmatrix} -1 & 0 \\ 0 & -1 \end{pmatrix}$	$\begin{pmatrix} 1 & 0 \\ 0 & -1 \end{pmatrix}$	$\begin{pmatrix} -1 & 0 \\ 0 & 1 \end{pmatrix}$	$\begin{pmatrix} 0 & 1 \\ 1 & 0 \end{pmatrix}$	$\begin{pmatrix} 0 & -1 \\ -1 & 0 \end{pmatrix}$

and the projection operators by

$$
\begin{aligned}
\rho_{11}{}^{A_1} &= \tfrac{1}{8}(E + C_4 + C_4{}^3 + C_2 + \sigma_{v_1} + \sigma_{v_2} + \sigma_{d_1} + \sigma_{d_2}),\\
\rho_{11}{}^{A_2} &= \tfrac{1}{8}(E + C_4 + C_4{}^3 + C_2 - \sigma_{v_1} - \sigma_{v_2} - \sigma_{d_1} - \sigma_{d_2}),\\
\rho_{11}{}^{B_1} &= \tfrac{1}{8}(E - C_4 - C_4{}^3 + C_2 + \sigma_{v_1} + \sigma_{v_2} - \sigma_{d_1} - \sigma_{d_2}),\\
\rho_{11}{}^{B_2} &= \tfrac{1}{8}(E - C_4 - C_4{}^3 + C_2 - \sigma_{v_1} - \sigma_{v_2} + \sigma_{d_1} + \sigma_{d_2}),\\
\rho_{11}{}^{E} &= \tfrac{1}{4}(E - C_2 + \sigma_{v_1} - \sigma_{v_2}),\\
\rho_{21}{}^{E} &= \tfrac{1}{4}(- C_4 + C_4{}^3 + \sigma_{d_1} - \sigma_{d_2}),\\
\rho_{12}{}^{B} &= \tfrac{1}{4}(+ C_4 - C_4{}^3 + \sigma_{d_1} - \sigma_{d_2}),\\
\rho_{22}{}^{B} &= \tfrac{1}{4}(E - C_2 - \sigma_{v_1} + \sigma_{v_2}).
\end{aligned}
\tag{10.49}
$$

The function ϕ_1 is transformed as follows:

C_{4v}	E	C_4	$C_4{}^3$	C_2	σ_{v_1}	σ_{v_2}	σ_{d_1}	σ_{d_2}
ϕ_1	ϕ_1	ϕ_2	ϕ_3	ϕ_4	ϕ_5	ϕ_6	ϕ_7	ϕ_8

The molecular orbitals are then given by

$$
\begin{aligned}
[\rho_{11}{}^{A_1}]\,\phi_1 &= \tfrac{1}{8}(\phi_1 + \phi_2 + \phi_3 + \phi_4 + \phi_5 + \phi_6 + \phi_7 + \phi_8),\\
[\rho_{11}{}^{A_2}]\,\phi_1 &= \tfrac{1}{8}(\phi_1 + \phi_2 + \phi_3 + \phi_4 - \phi_5 - \phi_6 - \phi_7 - \phi_8),\\
[\rho_{11}{}^{B_1}]\,\phi_1 &= \tfrac{1}{8}(\phi_1 - \phi_2 - \phi_3 + \phi_4 + \phi_5 + \phi_6 - \phi_7 - \phi_8),\\
[\rho_{11}{}^{B_2}]\,\phi_1 &= \tfrac{1}{8}(\phi_1 - \phi_2 - \phi_3 + \phi_4 - \phi_5 - \phi_6 + \phi_7 + \phi_8),\\
&\left\{\begin{aligned}
[\rho_{11}{}^{E}]\,\phi_1 &= \tfrac{1}{4}(\phi_1 - \phi_4 + \phi_5 - \phi_6),\\
[\rho_{21}{}^{E}]\,\phi_1 &= \tfrac{1}{4}(- \phi_2 + \phi_3 + \phi_7 - \phi_8),
\end{aligned}\right.\\
&\left\{\begin{aligned}
[\rho_{12}{}^{E}]\,\phi_1 &= \tfrac{1}{4}(+ \phi_2 - \phi_3 + \phi_7 - \phi_8),\\
[\rho_{22}{}^{E}]\,\phi_1 &= \tfrac{1}{4}(\phi_1 - \phi_4 - \phi_5 + \phi_6).
\end{aligned}\right.
\end{aligned}
\tag{10.50}
$$

It is easy to show that, in agreement with (3.59),

$$\rho_{21}{}^{E}(\rho_{11}{}^{E}\phi_1) = \rho_{21}{}^{E}\phi_1, \tag{10.51}$$

and

$$\rho_{12}{}^{E}(\rho_{22}{}^{E}\phi_1) = \rho_{12}{}^{E}\phi_1. \tag{10.52}$$

5. THE FORMATION OF HYBRIDS

5.1 Hybrids for σ Bonds

When an atom has to bind itself to other atoms, it may happen that some of its atomic orbitals, which are not very different in energy, combine themselves to produce *hybrid orbitals* that point in the direction of the ligand atoms and establish σ bonds with them. The symmetry properties of the complex are of great help in determining the linear combinations of atomic orbitals which form these hybrid orbitals.

5.2 Hybrids for σ Bonds in a Planar AB_3 Complex

Let us consider the simple case of a planar complex AB_3 when A is the central atom and B the ligand atoms at the vertices of an equilateral triangle (see Fig. 10.7). The symmetry of this complex is D_{3h}. The characters for this group are reported in the following table [5], with the atomic orbitals, which transform irreducibly according to the different representations, in the last two columns.

D_{3h}	E	$2C_3$	$3C_2$	σ_h	$2S_3$	$3\sigma_v$	Atomic Orbitals	
A_1'	1	1	1	1	1	1		s, d_{z^2}
A_2'	1	1	−1	1	1	−1		
E'	2	−1	0	2	−1	0	(p_x, p_y)	$(d_{x^2-y^2}, d_{xy})$
A_1''	1	1	1	−1	−1	−1		
A_2''	1	1	−1	−1	−1	1	p_z	
E''	2	−1	0	−2	1	0		(d_{xz}, d_{yz})

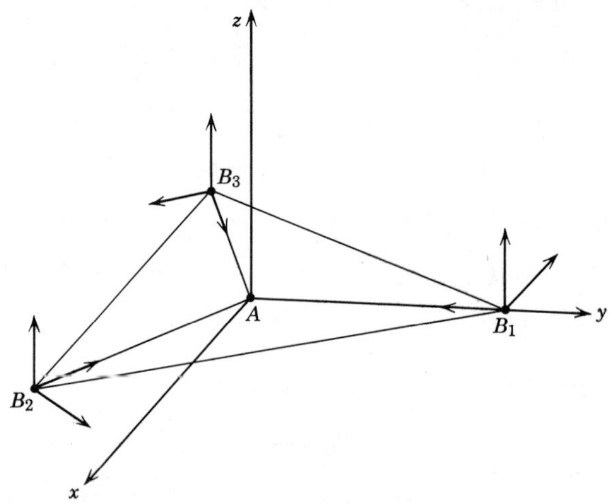

Fig. 10.7. Planar complex with D_{3h} symmetry.

We want now to find out what combinations of atomic orbitals can establish σ bonding between atoms A and B. We consider the set of vectors B_iA and investigate how these vectors transform under the operations of the symmetry group D_{3h}. These vectors represent the basis for a representation Γ_σ of D_{3h} whose characters are given below:

D_{3h}	E	$2C_3$	$3C_2$	σ_h	$2S_3$	$3\sigma_v$	Reduced Γ_σ
Γ_σ	3	0	1	3	0	1	$A_1' + E'$

The available atomic orbitals, which transform according to the above representations, are

$$A_1':s \quad \text{or} \quad d_{z^2}$$
$$E':(p_x, p_y) \quad \text{or} \quad (d_{x^2-y^2}, d_{xy}). \tag{10.53}$$

We may have the following combinations as basis functions for Γ_σ:

$$sp_xp_y; \quad \text{or} \quad sd_{x^2-y^2}d_{xy}; \quad \text{or} \quad d_{z^2}p_xp_y; \quad \text{or} \quad d_{z^2}d_{x^2-y^2}d_{xy}. \tag{10.54}$$

In deciding which of these four combinations the atom uses to form the hybrids for σ bonding, we may use our knowledge of the energies of the various atomic orbitals: if, for example, the available d orbitals have much higher energy than both the s and p available orbitals the atom will choose to hybridize according to the sp^2 combination. In general the hybrids will consist of a mixture of the different combinations with the predominance of one particular combination over all the others.

Let us assume now that in the present case the relevant combination of atomic orbitals is sp^2. The three hybrids that we obtain are

$$\phi_i = a_is + b_ip_x + c_ip_y \qquad (i = 1, 2, 3). \tag{10.55}$$

These hybrids must transform according to the Γ_σ representation of the symmetry group D_{3h}; moreover, they must be orthonormal,

$$a_ia_k + b_ib_k + c_ic_k = \delta_{ik}. \tag{10.56}$$

The three hybrids of the present example will be directed toward the vertices of the equilateral triangle formed by the ligand atoms B. If we take the y axis along the AB_1 direction we can write,

$$\phi_1 = a_1s + c_1p_y,$$
$$\phi_2 = a_2s + b_2p_x - c_2p_y, \tag{10.57}$$
$$\phi_3 = a_3s - b_3p_x - c_3p_y,$$

with all the coefficients intrinsically positive. Because of the symmetry of the complex, we must have for a clockwise C_3 rotation,

$$C_3\phi_1 = \phi_2 \tag{10.58}$$

or

$$\begin{aligned} C_3(a_1 s + c_1 p_y) &= a_1 s + c_1(C_3 p_y) = a_1 s + c_1(p_x \sin 120° + p_y \cos 120°) \\ &= a_1 s + c_1\left(\frac{\sqrt{3}}{2}\, p_x - \tfrac{1}{2} p_y\right) = a_2 s + b_2 p_x - c_2 p_y, \end{aligned} \tag{10.59}$$

which gives

$$\begin{aligned} a_1 &= a_2, \\ b_2 &= \frac{\sqrt{3}}{2}\, c_1, \\ c_2 &= \tfrac{1}{2} c_1; \end{aligned} \tag{10.60}$$

for a clockwise $C_3{}^2$ rotation

$$C_3{}^2\phi_1 = \phi_3, \tag{10.61}$$

or

$$\begin{aligned} C_3{}^2(a_1 s + c_1 p_y) &= a_1 s + c_1(C_3{}^2 p_y) = a_1 s + c_1(p_x \sin 240° + p_y \cos 240°) \\ &= a_1 s + c_1\left(-\frac{\sqrt{3}}{2}\, p_x - \tfrac{1}{2} p_y\right) = a_3 s - b_3 p_x - c_3 p_y\,, \end{aligned} \tag{10.62}$$

which gives

$$\begin{aligned} a_3 &= a_1, \\ b_3 &= \frac{\sqrt{3}}{2}\, c_1, \\ c_3 &= \tfrac{1}{2} c_1. \end{aligned} \tag{10.63}$$

The relations (10.60) and (10.63), together with the orthonormality relations (10.56), determine all the coefficients of (10.57):

$$\begin{aligned} \phi_1 &= \frac{1}{\sqrt{3}}\, s + \frac{2}{\sqrt{6}}\, p_y, \\ \phi_2 &= \frac{1}{\sqrt{3}}\, s + \frac{1}{\sqrt{2}}\, p_x - \frac{1}{\sqrt{6}}\, p_y, \\ \phi_3 &= \frac{1}{\sqrt{3}}\, s - \frac{1}{\sqrt{2}}\, p_x - \frac{1}{\sqrt{6}}\, p_y. \end{aligned} \tag{10.64}$$

5.3 Hybrids for π Bonds

The atomic orbitals of a metal atom in a complex can also combine to establish π bonds with the ligand atoms.

The relevant combinations of orbitals or hybrids may be found by considering a set of vectors, two for each AB_i direction (direction of σ bonds), perpendicular to AB_i. This set of vectors is taken as a basis for the representation Γ_π of the π bonds. This representation is reduced in terms of the irreducible representations of the group and then the hybrids are formed by looking at the available atomic orbitals which transform according to the irreducible representations which are part of Γ_π.

5.4 Hybrids for π Bonds in a Planar AB_3 Complex

Let us now consider how the central ion A in the complex AB_3 of Fig. 10.7 may form hybrids that can establish π bonds with the B ligands.

The six possible π bonds transform under the operations of the group in the same way as the six vectors perpendicular to the AB_i directions. We may take these vectors as the basis for a representation Γ_π of the symmetry group; this representation has the following characters:

D_{3h}	E	$2C_3$	$3C_2$	σ_h	$2S_3$	$3\sigma_v$
Γ_π	6	0	-2	0	0	0

We notice however that this set of vectors can be divided into two subsets, one consisting of the three vectors in the molecular plane and the other of the three vectors perpendicular to the molecular plane. The two sets are such that no operation of the group may bring a vector of one set in coincidence with a vector of the other set. We can then use the vectors in the molecular plane as basis for a $\Gamma_\pi(\|)$ representation and the vectors perpendicular to the molecular plane as basis for a $\Gamma_\pi(\perp)$ representation. These two representations have the following characters:

D_{3h}	E	$2C_3$	$3C_2$	σ_h	$2S_3$	$3\sigma_v$	Reduced reps.
$\Gamma_\pi(\|)$	3	0	-1	3	0	-1	$A_2' + E'$
$\Gamma_\pi(\perp)$	3	0	-1	-3	0	1	$A_2'' + E''$

Notice that

$$\Gamma_\pi = \Gamma_\pi(\|) + \Gamma_\pi(\perp). \tag{10.65}$$

Considering the available atomic orbitals, we could have the following hybrids:

$$\Gamma_\pi(\|) = \begin{cases} A_2' : \text{none} \\ E' : (p_x, p_y) \quad \text{or} \quad (d_{xy}, d_{x^2-y^2}); \end{cases} \tag{10.66}$$

$$\Gamma_\pi(\perp) = \begin{cases} A_2'' : p_z \\ E'' : (d_{xz}, d_{yz}). \end{cases} \tag{10.67}$$

Since no atomic orbital of A_2' symmetry is available, it is not possible to form a complete set of $\pi(\|)$ bonds between A and the B's; this means that we have only two $\pi(\|)$ bonds shared equally among the B ligands.

If we assume that a set of σ bonds has already been established in the complex, we have to make sure that the same atomic orbitals are *not* used for the two types of bond at the same time; for example, if the (p_x, p_y) orbitals are used for the σ bonds, they cannot be used for the $\pi(\|)$ bonds. Because the σ bonds are, in general, stronger, it is safe to consider first the σ bonds and then the π bonds.

6. HYBRIDS OF THE CENTRAL ION IN A TETRAHEDRAL COMPLEX AB_4

A tetrahedral complex AB_4 is represented in Fig. 10.8. The character table and the relevant atomic orbitals for the symmetry group T_d are given below [5]:

T_d	E	$8C_3$	$3C_2$	$6S_4$	$6\sigma_d$	Atomic Orbitals	
A_1	1	1	1	1	1		s
A_2	1	1	1	-1	-1		
E	2	-1	2	0	0		$(d_{x^2-y^2}, d_{z^2})$
T_1	3	0	-1	1	-1		
T_2	3	0	-1	-1	1	(p_x, p_y, p_z)	(d_{xy}, d_{yz}, d_{zx})
						Reduced Reps.	
Γ_σ	4	1	0	0	2	$A_1 + T_2$	
Γ_π	8	-1	0	0	0	$E + T_1 + T_2$	

In the last two rows we have reported the representation Γ_π of the σ bonds, obtained when taking the four B_iA vectors as a basis, and the representation Γ_π for the π bonds. The basis vectors for the latter representation are eight, two for each AB_i direction, perpendicular to each other and perpendicular to AB_i as in Fig. 10.8.

Let us see now what are the atomic orbitals which may form hybrids for the bonds. For the σ bonds,

$$\begin{aligned} &A_1{:}\, s, \\ &T_2{:}\,(p_x, p_y, p_z) \quad \text{or} \quad (d_{xy}, d_{yz}, d_{zx}). \end{aligned} \tag{10.68}$$

The possible hybrids are

$$sp_xp_yp_z; \qquad \text{or} \quad sd_{xy}d_{yz}d_{zx}. \tag{10.69}$$

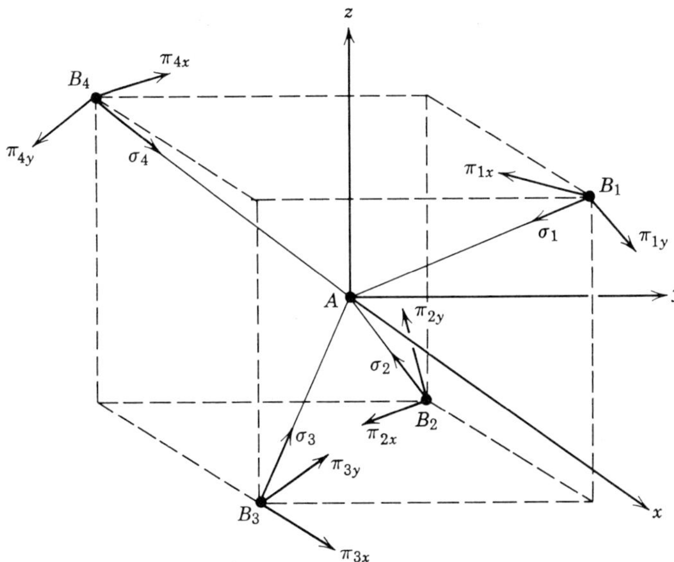

Fig. 10.8. Tetrahedral complex AB_4. The direction cosines of the bonds of the AB_1 pair are the following σ_1: $-1/\sqrt{3}$, $-1/\sqrt{3}$, $-1/\sqrt{3}$, π_{1x}: $1/\sqrt{6}$, $-\sqrt{2/3}$, $1/\sqrt{6}$, π_{1y}: $1/\sqrt{2}$, 0, $-1/\sqrt{2}$. The bonds of the other pairs can be obtained by C_2 rotations about the x, y, and z axes.

If the central ion A is carbon ($1s^22s^22p^2$) the sp^3 hybrids are more probable, because the available $3d$ orbitals are about 230 Kcal/mole higher than the $2p$ orbitals. On the other hand, if the central ion is a transition metal ion, the $3d$ orbitals are lower in energy than the available $4p$ orbitals; in this case the sd^3 hybrids are more probable.

For the π bonds the available atomic orbitals are

$$E: (d_{x^2-y^2}, d_{z^2}),$$

$$T_1: \text{none}, \tag{10.70}$$

$$T_2: (p_x, p_y, p_z) \quad \text{or} \quad (d_{xy}, d_{yz}, d_{zx}).$$

If the σ bonding hybrids are sp^3, the π bonding hybrids are given by

$$d_{x^2-y^2} d_{z^2} d_{xy} d_{yz} d_{zx}. \tag{10.71}$$

On the other hand, if the σ bonding hybrids are sd^3, the π bonding hybrids are given by

$$d_{x^2-y^2} d_{z^2} p_x p_y p_z. \tag{10.72}$$

7. HYBRIDS OF THE CENTRAL ION IN AN OCTAHEDRAL COMPLEX AB_6

An octahedral complex is represented in Fig. 10.9. The character table and the relevant atomic orbitals for the symmetry group O_h are given below [5]:

O_h	E	$8C_3$	$6C_2$	$6C_4$	$3C_2$	I	$6S_4$	$8S_6$	$3\sigma_h$	$6\sigma_d$	Atomic Orbitals
A_{1g}	1	1	1	1	1	1	1	1	1	1	s
A_{2g}	1	1	−1	−1	1	1	−1	1	1	−1	
E_g	2	−1	0	0	2	2	0	−1	2	0	$d_{z^2}, d_{x^2-y^2}$
T_{1g}	3	0	−1	1	−1	3	1	0	−1	−1	
T_{2g}	3	0	1	−1	−1	3	−1	0	−1	1	d_{xy}, d_{yz}, d_{zx}
A_{1u}	1	1	1	1	1	−1	−1	−1	−1	−1	
A_{2u}	1	1	−1	−1	1	−1	1	−1	−1	1	
E_u	2	−1	0	0	2	−2	0	1	−2	0	
T_{1u}	3	0	−1	1	−1	−3	−1	0	1	1	(p_x, p_y, p_z)
T_{2u}	3	0	1	−1	−1	−3	1	0	1	−1	
											Reduced Reps.
Γ_σ	6	0	0	2	2	0	0	0	4	2	$A_{1g} + E_g + T_{1u}$
Γ_π	12	0	0	0	−4	0	0	0	0	0	$T_{1g} + T_{2g} + T_{1u} + T_{2u}$

In the last two rows we have reported the Γ_σ representation, whose basis consists of the six B_iA vectors, and the Γ_π representation whose basis consists of the set of twelve vectors perpendicular to the AB_i directions.

The atomic orbital available for σ bonds are

$$\begin{aligned} A_{1g}&: s, \\ E_g&: (d_{z^2}, d_{x^2-y^2}), \\ T_{1u}&: (p_x, p_y, p_z), \end{aligned} \tag{10.73}$$

and only one type of hybrid is possible:

$$sd_{z^2}d_{x^2-y^2}p_xp_yp_z. \tag{10.74}$$

The atomic orbitals available for π bonds are

$$\begin{aligned} T_{1g}&: \text{none}, \\ T_{2g}&: (d_{xy}, d_{yz}, d_{zx}), \\ T_{1u}&: (p_x, p_y, p_z), \\ T_{2u}&: \text{none}. \end{aligned} \tag{10.75}$$

Since the p^3 orbitals are already taken by the σ hybrids, we are left with the hybrid

$$d_{xy}d_{yz}d_{zx}, \tag{10.76}$$

namely the six ligands will share only three π bonds with the central ion.

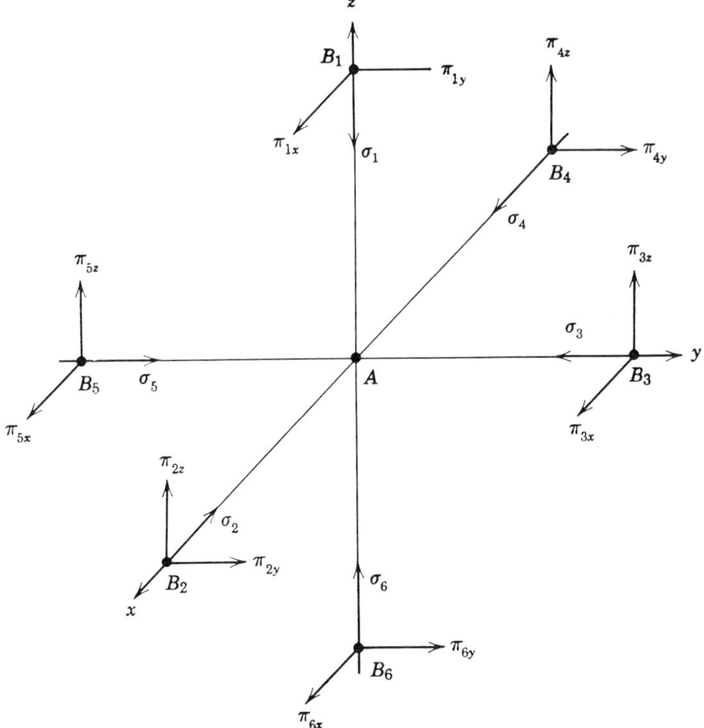

Fig. 10.9. Octahedral complex AB_6.

The hybrids of the central ion in the three complexes considered in this chapter are reported in Table 10.2.

8. THE COMBINATIONS OF LIGAND ORBITALS IN AN AB_n COMPLEX

When considering the problem of molecular bonding in an AB_n complex, we actually take the following steps:

1. Formation of hybrids in the central ion.
2. Formation of proper combinations of ligand orbitals.
3. Consideration of the interaction of the ligand orbitals in combination with the central ion hybrids.

We have already considered the formation of hybrids. In the present section we shall consider the formation of ligand orbital combinations. In the following Sec. 9 we shall address ourselves to the problem of the metal ion-ligand interactions.

Table 10.2 Possible Bonding Orbitals for Molecular Complexes

<table>
<tr><th rowspan="2">Complex</th><th rowspan="2">Symmetry</th><th colspan="2">σ Bonds</th><th colspan="4">π Bonds</th></tr>
<tr><th></th><th></th><th colspan="2"></th><th colspan="2"></th></tr>
<tr><td>Tetrahedral
AB_4</td><td>T_d</td><td>$sp_xp_yp_z$
$sd_{xy}d_{yz}d_{zx}$</td><td>$A_1 + T_2$</td><td colspan="2">$d_{x^2-y^2}d_{z^2}d_{xy}d_{yz}d_{zx}$
$d_{x^2-y^2}d_{z^2}p_xp_yp_z$</td><td colspan="2">$E + T_2$
T_1 (none)</td></tr>
<tr><td>Octahedral
AB_6</td><td>O_h</td><td>$sd_{z^2}d_{x^2-y^2}p_xp_yp_z$</td><td>$A_{1g} + E_g + T_{1u}$</td><td colspan="2">$d_{xy}d_{yz}d_{zx}[p_xp_yp_z]$
[ ] already used in σ bonding</td><td colspan="2">T_{2g}
T_{1u} (used in σ bonding)
T_{1g} (none); T_{2u} (none)</td></tr>
<tr><td rowspan="2">Planar
AB_3</td><td rowspan="2">D_{3h}</td><td rowspan="2">sp_xp_y
$sd_{x^2-y^2}d_{xy}$
$d_{z^2}p_xp_y$
$d_{z^2}d_{x^2-y^2}d_{xy}$</td><td rowspan="2">$A' + E'$</td><td colspan="2">π (‖) Bonds</td><td colspan="2">π (⊥) Bonds</td></tr>
<tr><td>p_xp_y
$d_{xy}d_{x^2-y^2}$</td><td>E'
A_2' (none)</td><td>$p_zd_{xz}d_{yz}$</td><td>$A_2'' + E''$</td></tr>
</table>

8.1 Tetrahedral Complex AB_4

The available atomic orbitals of the four B ligands of a tetrahedral complex establish σ and possibly π bonding with the central atom. The σ and π bonds transform respectively according to the representation Γ_σ and Γ_π already found in Sec. 6 of this chapter.

These representations reduce as follows:

$$\begin{aligned}\Gamma_\sigma &= A_1 + T_2,\\ \Gamma_\pi &= E + T_1 + T_2.\end{aligned} \tag{10.77}$$

In order to find the linear combinations of ligand wavefunctions which transform according to (10.77) we may use the *projection operators*. To construct the projection operators a knowledge of the matrices of all the relevant representations (E, T_1, T_2) is necessary: these matrices can be found by considering how the basis functions listed with the character table transform under the operations of the group.

The combinations of ligand orbitals corresponding to the σ and π bonds are reported in Table 10.3 [6].

Table 10.3 Orbitals for Tetrahedral Complexes[a]

Representation	Metal Orbital	Ligand σ	Ligand π
A_1	s	$\frac{1}{2}(\sigma_1 + \sigma_2 + \sigma_3 + \sigma_4)$	
E	d_{z^2}		$\frac{1}{4}[\pi_{1x} + \pi_{2x} + \pi_{3x} + \pi_{4x}$ $- \sqrt{3}\,(\pi_{1y} + \pi_{2y} + \pi_{3y} + \pi_{4y})]$
	$d_{x^2-y^2}$		$\frac{1}{4}[\pi_{1y} + \pi_{2y} + \pi_{3y} + \pi_{4y}$ $+ \sqrt{3}(\pi_{1x} + \pi_{2x} + \pi_{3x} + \pi_{4x})]$
T_2	p_x, d_{yz}	$\frac{1}{2}(\sigma_1 + \sigma_3 - \sigma_2 - \sigma_4)$	$\frac{1}{4}[\pi_{4x} + \pi_{2x} - \pi_{1x} - \pi_{3x}$ $+ \sqrt{3}\,(\pi_{4y} + \pi_{2y} - \pi_{1y} - \pi_{3y})]$
	p_y, d_{xz}	$\frac{1}{2}(\sigma_1 + \sigma_2 - \sigma_3 - \sigma_4)$	$\frac{1}{2}[\pi_{1x} + \pi_{2x} - \pi_{3x} - \pi_{4x}]$
	p_z, d_{xy}	$\frac{1}{2}(\sigma_1 + \sigma_4 - \sigma_2 - \sigma_3)$	$\frac{1}{4}[\pi_{3x} + \pi_{2x} - \pi_{1x} - \pi_{4x}$ $+ \sqrt{3}\,(\pi_{4y} + \pi_{1y} - \pi_{2y} - \pi_{3y})]$
T_1			$\frac{1}{4}[\pi_{2y} + \pi_{4y} - \pi_{3y} - \pi_{1y}$ $+ \sqrt{3}\,(\pi_{1x} + \pi_{3x} - \pi_{2x} - \pi_{4x})]$
			$\frac{1}{2}[\pi_{1y} + \pi_{2y} - \pi_{3y} - \pi_{4y}]$
			$\frac{1}{4}[\pi_{2y} + \pi_{3y} - \pi_{1y} - \pi_{4y}$ $+ \sqrt{3}\,(\pi_{3x} + \pi_{2x} - \pi_{1x} - \pi_{4x})$

[a] Reproduced from [6] by permission of Prof. L. Helmholz.

8.2 Octahedral Complex AB_6

The available atomic orbitals of the six ligand atoms of an octahedral complex establish σ and possibly π bonding with the central atom. The Γ_σ representation of the σ bonds and the Γ_π representation of the π bonds reduce as follows:

$$\begin{aligned} \Gamma_\sigma &= A_{1g} + E_g + T_{1u}, \\ \Gamma_\pi &= T_{1g} + T_{2g} + T_{1u} + T_{2u}. \end{aligned} \tag{10.78}$$

The combinations of ligand orbitals corresponding to the σ and π bonds for this complex are reported in Table 10.4.

Table 10.4 Orbitals for Octahedral Complexes

Representation	Metal Orbital	Ligand σ	Ligand π
A_{1g}	$4s$	$\frac{1}{\sqrt{6}}(\sigma_1 + \sigma_2 + \sigma_3 + \sigma_4 + \sigma_5 + \sigma_6)$	
E_g	$3d_{z^2}$	$\frac{1}{\sqrt{3}}(2\sigma_1 + 2\sigma_6 - \sigma_2 - \sigma_3 - \sigma_4 - \sigma_5)$	
	$3d_{x^2-y^2}$	$\frac{1}{2}(\sigma_2 - \sigma_3 + \sigma_4 - \sigma_5)$	
T_{1u}	$4p_x$	$\frac{1}{\sqrt{2}}(\sigma_2 - \sigma_4)$	$\frac{1}{2}(\pi_{3x} + \pi_{1x} + \pi_{5x} + \pi_{6x})$
	$4p_y$	$\frac{1}{\sqrt{2}}(\sigma_3 - \sigma_5)$	$\frac{1}{2}(\pi_{2y} + \pi_{1y} + \pi_{4y} + \pi_{6y})$
	$4p_z$	$\frac{1}{\sqrt{2}}(\sigma_1 - \sigma_6)$	$\frac{1}{2}(\pi_{2z} + \pi_{3z} + \pi_{4z} + \pi_{5z})$
T_{2g}	$3d_{xz}$		$\frac{1}{2}(\pi_{2z} + \pi_{1x} - \pi_{4z} - \pi_{6x})$
	$3d_{yz}$		$\frac{1}{2}(\pi_{3z} + \pi_{1y} - \pi_{5z} - \pi_{6y})$
	$3d_{xy}$		$\frac{1}{2}(\pi_{2y} + \pi_{3x} - \pi_{4y} - \pi_{5x})$
T_{1g}			$\frac{1}{2}(\pi_{2z} - \pi_{1x} - \pi_{4z} + \pi_{6x})$
			$\frac{1}{2}(\pi_{3z} - \pi_{1y} - \pi_{5z} + \pi_{6y})$
			$\frac{1}{2}(\pi_{2y} - \pi_{3y} - \pi_{4y} + \pi_{5x})$
T_{2u}			$\frac{1}{2}(\pi_{3x} - \pi_{1x} + \pi_{5x} - \pi_{6x})$
			$\frac{1}{2}(\pi_{2y} - \pi_{1y} + \pi_{4y} - \pi_{6y})$
			$\frac{1}{2}(\pi_{2z} - \pi_{3z} + \pi_{4z} - \pi_{5z})$

9. THE ENERGY LEVELS OF AN AB_n COMPLEX

The energy levels of an AB_n complex derive from the interaction between the central ion hybrids and the combinations of ligand orbitals.

In the present case we may call Γ^M and Γ^L the representations of the metal ion hybrids and of the ligand orbitals respectively. When combining the ion hybrids with the ligand orbitals we may expect the following types of molecular orbitals for the whole complex AB_n:

1. Molecular orbitals with pure metal ion character, arising from hybrids which transform according to a representation Γ_k^M, different from *any* Γ_j^L. The corresponding energy levels are called *nonbonding*.
2. Molecular orbitals with pure ligand character arising from ligand orbital combinations transforming according to a representation Γ_j^L different from *any* Γ_k^M.
3. Molecular orbitals with mixed character arising from interaction of metal ions hybrids transforming according to a representation Γ_k^M with ligand orbitals transforming according to a representation Γ_k^L with $\Gamma_k^M = \Gamma_k^L$. This interaction gives rise to two energy levels, one of lower energy called *bonding* and another of higher energy called *antibonding*. Each resulting molecular orbital includes a greater contribution from the component orbital which is closer in energy to it; therefore, if the ligand orbitals are lower in energy, the bonding orbitals have mainly ligand orbital character and the antibonding orbitals mainly metal ion character.

In the establishment of the energy level scheme for an AB_n complex the *available* atomic orbitals play a very important role. The central ion is in general a transition metal ion of the first (3*d*), second (4*d*), or third (5*d*) series, and it uses *nd*, $(n + 1)\,s$ and $(n + 1)\,p$ atomic orbitals to form its hybrids. The ligands form σ bonding combinations by using either s or p_z orbitals (or any orbital having axial symmetry in the directions of the bond) and a couple of other orbitals, p_x and p_y, to form combinations for π bonding. Double bonding (σ and π) can be established if the ligands have enough available orbitals to establish it.

Consider, for example, the complex $[Co(NH_3)_6]^{3+}$. The electronic configuration of N is $1s^22s^22p^3$; each N atom is using three of the four hybridized 2*s* and 2*p* orbitals to establish bonds with the H atom. Each of the N—H bond contains two electrons, one from N and one from H; the N atom makes then available for the bonding with the ion Co^{3+} a σ oriented orbital and two electrons. Once the energy levels of the σ bonded complex have been established, we have to allocate $6 \times 2 = 12$ electrons from the six N atoms and 6 electrons of the Co^{3+} ion, a total of 18 electrons. No ligand orbital is available for π bonding.

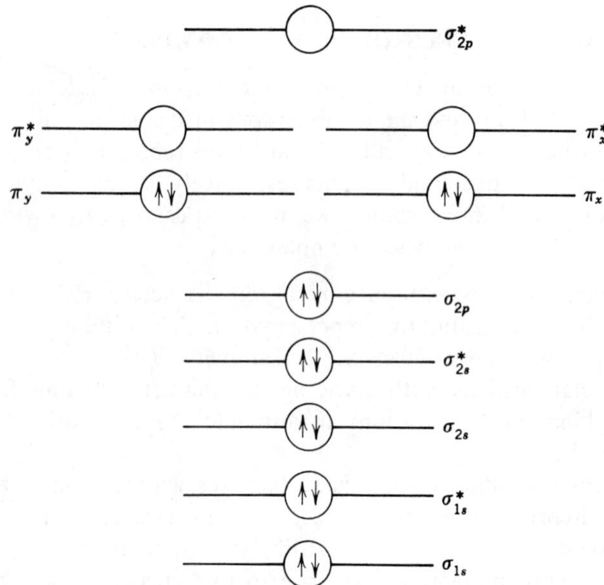

Fig. 10.10. Energy levels of the CN^- ion.

Another interesting example is given by the complex $[Fe(CN)_6]^{3-}$. The electronic configurations of C and N are respectively $1s^22s^22p^2$ and $1s^22s^22p^3$. In the CN^- ion, C and N use their $1s$ and $2s$ orbitals to form σ_s bonds among themselves; they also use one of their p orbitals to form other σ_p bonds and the remaining p orbitals to form π bonds. The energy levels of CN^- are given in Fig. 10.10 where the 14 electrons of the complex have been put in the lowest possible levels. We may assume that the orbitals σ_{2p}, π_x, π_y (and six electrons) are then used by each CN^- ligand to form respectively σ and π bonds with the metal ion Fe^{3+}. The CN^- ligands contribute then 36 electrons to the $[Fe(CN)_6]^{3-}$ complex. We notice however that in the CN^- ion the levels π^*_x, π^*_y, and σ^*_{2p} are unoccupied. This fact is of some interest later.

9.1 The Energy Levels of an Octahedral Complex

Let us first examine the scheme of the σ bonds between the metal ion and the ligands. The six ligand orbitals combinations transform according to A_{1g}, E_g, and T_{1u}. The $3d$ metal ion orbitals transform according to T_{2g} and E_g (with T_{2g} lower in energy), the $4s$ orbital according to A_{1g} and the $4p$ orbitals according to T_{1u}. The A_{1g} metal ion orbital and the A_{1g} ligand orbital interact giving rise to an $A_{1g}(\sigma)$ bonding level and to an $A_{1g}(\sigma^*)$ antibonding level; in the same way the orbitals E_g give rise to levels $e_g(\sigma)$ and $e_g(\sigma^*)$ and the orbitals T_{1u} give rise to the levels $t_{1u}(\sigma)$ and $t_{1u}(\sigma^*)$. On the other hand the three $3d$ metal ion orbitals $3d_{xy}$, $3d_{yz}$, and $3d_{zx}$ transforming according to T_{2g} are left unperturbed by the ligands and may be considered as pure metal ion levels.

The resulting levels of the σ bond formation are shown in Fig. 10.11 where the molecular-orbital energy level diagram for the octahedral complex $[Fe(CN)_6]^{3-}$ is shown. In this complex 12 electrons from the six $(CN)^-$ ligands fill the three lower bonding levels and the five $3d$ electrons of Fe^{3+} occupy the nonbonded t_{2g} level. In the same figure, on the right-hand side the molecular energy diagram of the $[FeF_6]^{3-}$ complex is shown. In this last case the smaller overlap between the F^- ligand σ orbitals and the Fe^{3+} orbitals produce a smaller covalent interaction; consequently, the $e_g(\sigma^*)$ level is closer to the nonbonded t_{2g} level and the value of the crystal field strength 10 Dq is smaller. The highly covalent case can be correlated to the low-spin strong

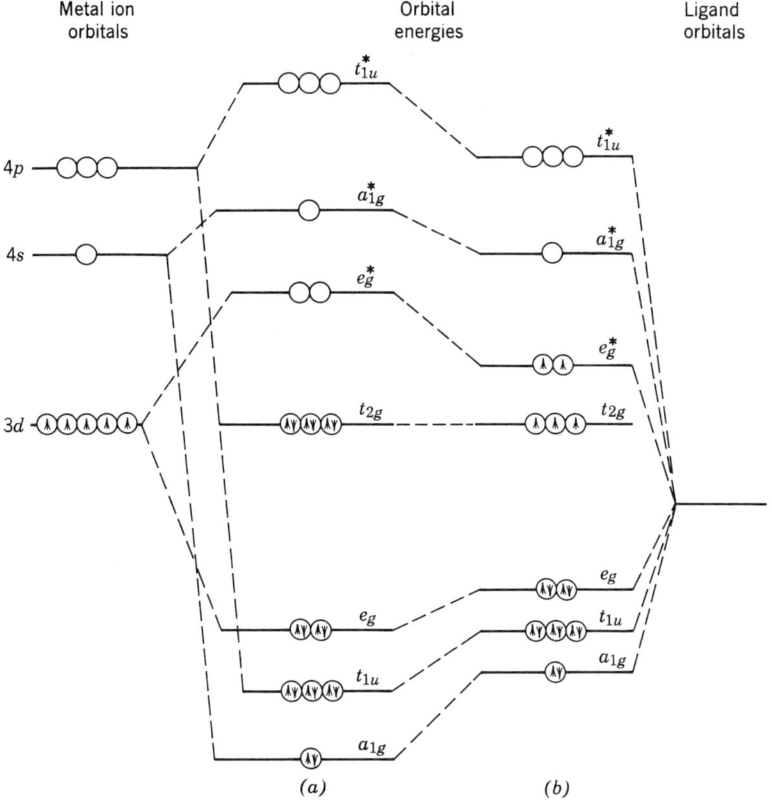

Fig. 10.11. Molecular orbital energy level diagram of (a) $[Fe(CN)_6]^{3-}$, covalent, low spin; (b) $[FeF_6]^{3-}$, ionic, high spin.

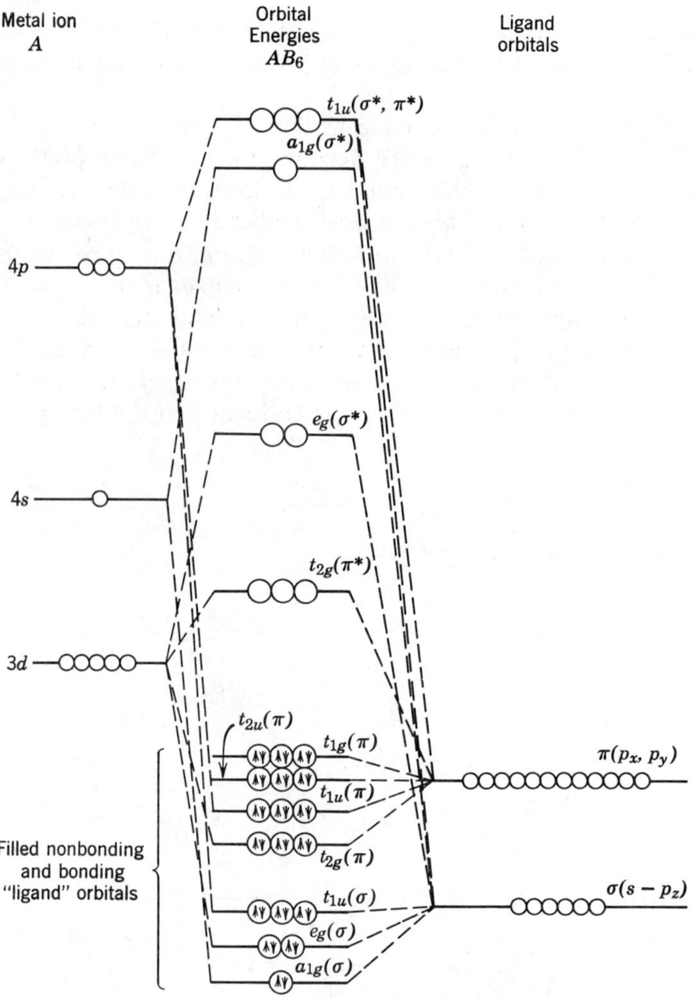

Fig. 10.12. Molecular orbital energy level diagram of an AB_6 octahedral complex with σ and π bonds (reproduced from [8] by permission of the publisher).

field case of crystal field theory; the weakly covalent case can be correlated to thc high-spin weak field case of crystal field theory.

In the present σ-bonding scheme the crystal field strength 10 Dq is the difference in energy between the $e_g(\sigma^*)$ antibonding level and the t_{2g} nonbonding level.[3]

[3] 10 Dq in crystal field theory is the difference in energy between a t_{2g} crystal orbital and an e_g crystal orbital of a d^n ion in an octahedral symmetry site. See for this [7].

Let us examine now the formation of π bonds in an AB_6 complex. The twelve ligand orbital combinations available for π bonding transform according to the representations T_{1u}, T_{2g}, T_{1g}, and T_{2u}. Now the T_{2g} ligand orbitals combine with the previously nonbonding T_{2g} metal ion orbital and form the bonding $t_{2g}(\pi)$ and antibonding $t_{2g}(\pi^*)$ levels. The T_{1g} and T_{2u} ligand orbitals do not interact with any metal ion orbital and therefore preserve their ligand character. The ligand $T_{1u}(\pi)$ combinations interact with the $T_{1u}(4p)$ metal ion orbitals, which are already involved in the σ bonding scheme, and give rise to an additional level $t_{1u}(\pi)$. The t_{1u}^* antibonding level has, in this scheme, only a small ligand π character.

In the σ-π scheme, the crystal field strength 10 Dq is the difference in energy between the $e_g(\sigma^*)$ level and the $t_{2g}(\pi^*)$ level. In Fig. 10.12 the molecular orbital energy level scheme of an AB_6 σ-π bonded complex is shown; it is assumed that each ligand participates in the bonding by using three orbitals and six electrons. The $6 \times 6 = 36$ electrons of the ligands are all located in the bonding and nonbonding levels. The metal ion $3d$ electrons, not shown in the figure, are located in the $t_{2g}(\pi^*)$ and $e_g(\pi^*)$ levels. The considerations made before about the relations between 10 Dq and covalency are still valid. However, it is interesting to consider the influence of π bonding on 10 Dq.

Two different situations may be considered [9], one in which the $T_{2g}\pi$ ligand orbitals are empty and are more energetic than the $T_{2g}d$ metal orbitals and the other when the $T_{2g}\pi$ ligand orbitals are filled with electrons and less energetic than the $T_{2g}d$ orbitals. In the former case the π bonding produces an increase in the value of 10 Dq, in the latter case a decrease in the value of 10 Dq as it is shown in Fig. 10.13. A filled ligand π orbital is called *donor*,

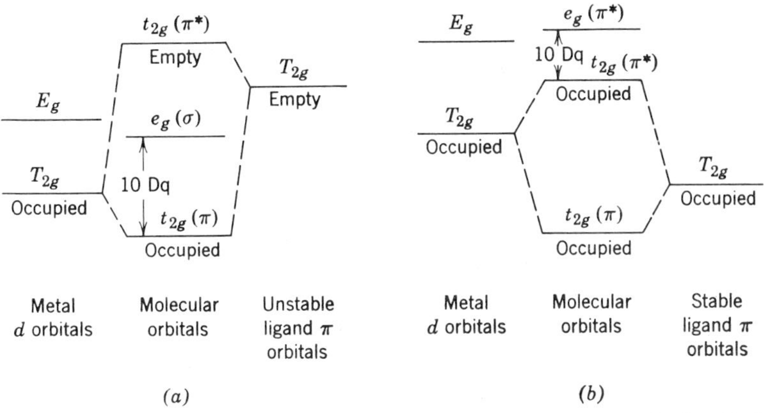

Fig. 10.13. The effect of π bonding on 10 Dq: (a) acceptor ligand orbitals; (b) donor ligand orbital.

and an empty one is an *acceptor*. Take, for example, the Cl^- ion; its electronic configuration is $1s^2 2s^2 2p^6 3s^2 3p^6$ and it participates to the σ-π bonding by using 3 orbitals and 6 electrons. In this case the π ligand orbitals are all occupied and Cl^- acts as a donor, namely electrons from π (bonding) levels can be excited to antibonding levels. On the other hand, the CN^- ion has two π orbitals (and one σ orbital) unoccupied and therefore it acts mainly as an acceptor. The same can be said of the isoelectronic complex CO.

The electronic configuration in the σ-π bonding scheme, when each ligand contributes six electrons and the metal ion has n electrons in the d shell, is given by

$$a_{1g}(\sigma)^2\, e_g(\sigma)^4\, t_{1u}(\sigma)^6\, t_{2g}(\pi)^6\, t_{1u}(\pi)^6\, t_{2u}(\pi)^6\, t_{1g}(\pi)^6\, t_{2g}(\pi^*)^m\, e_g(\pi^*)^{n-m}$$
$$= {}^1A_{1g} t_{2g}(\pi^*)^m\, e_g(\pi^*)^{n-m}, \quad (10.79)$$

where n electrons are distributed on the t_{2g} and e_g levels. An excited configuration is one in which an electron is brought from a lower to an upper level.

9.2 The Energy Levels of a Tetrahedral Complex

The energy level scheme for an AB_4 tetrahedral complex can be worked out by considering Table 10.3. In Fig. 10.14 we have represented the orbital energies of such a complex in which not only the p but also the s atomic ligand orbitals take part in the σ bonding.

The σ ligand orbital combinations transform according to the A_1 and T_2 representations of T_d and include both s and p orbitals. The π ligand orbitals combinations are formed by using two p functions per ligand and transform according to E, T_2, and T_1. The $3d$ metal ion orbitals transform according to E and T_2, the $4s$ orbital according to A_1 and the $4p$ orbitals according to T_2. The A_1 metal ion orbital and the ligand orbitals $A_1(\sigma_s)$ and $A_1(\sigma_p)$ interact giving rise to the three levels $1a_1$, $2a_1$, and $3a_1$. The E metal ion orbitals interact with the $E(\pi)$ ligand orbitals giving rise to levels $1e$ and $2e$. The coupling of the T_2 metal ion and ligand orbitals is complicated by the fact that both the p orbitals and three of the d orbitals of the metal ion transform in the same way. The coupling of the two T_2 metal ion states and of the three T_2 ligand states produces five t_2 levels.

We note also that the T_1 ligand state does not couple to any metal ion hybrid and is left unperturbed by the bonding; therefore, the t_1 level in the complex has a pure ligand character.

In the present scheme the crystal field strength 10 Dq is the energy difference between the $4t_2$ and the $2e$ levels. As expected from crystal field theory, the crystal field strength is smaller in these tetrahedral systems than in the octahedral systems as due to the fact that the interactions between p and d metal ion states and between $T_2(\sigma_p)$ and $T_2(\pi)$ ligand states lower the energy of the $4t_2$ level.

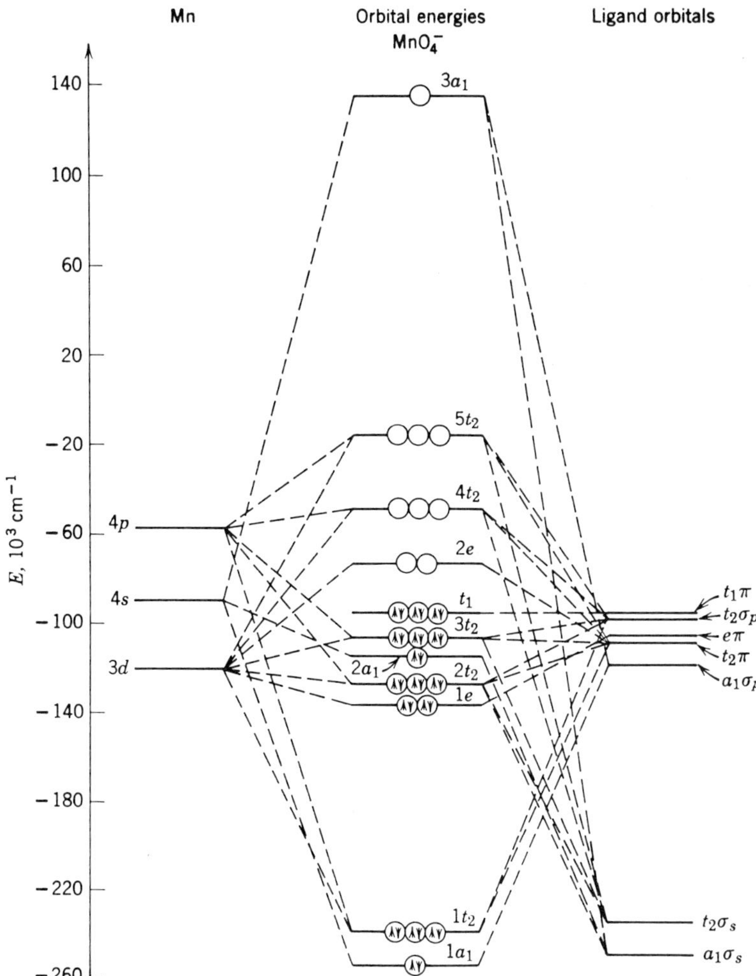

Fig. 10.14. Molecular orbital energy level scheme of the MnO_4^- tetrahedral complex (reproduced from [8] by permission of the publisher).

REFERENCES

[1] A. L. Companion, *Chemical Bonding*, McGraw-Hill, 1964.

[2] K. W. H. Stevens, "On the Magnetic Properties of Covalent XY_6 Complexes," *Proc. Roy. Soc.* (*London*) **A219,** 542 (1953).

[3] M. Tinkham, "Paramagnetic Resonance in Dilute Iron Group Fluorides. I. Fluorine Hyperfine Structure," *Proc. Roy. Soc.* (*London*), **A236,** 535 (1956); "Paramagnetic Resonance in Dilute Iron Group Fluorides. II. Wave Functions of the Magnetic Electrons," *Proc. Roy. Soc.* (*London*), **A236,** 549 (1956).

[4] C. K. Jørgensen, R. Pappalardo and H. H. Schmidtke, "Do the 'Ligand Field' Parameters in Lanthanides Represent Weak Covalent Bonding?," *J. Chem. Phys.* **39**, 1422 (1963).

[5] F. A. Cotton, *Chemical Applications of Group Theory*, Interscience, New York, 1964.

[6] M. Wolfsberg and L. Helmholz, "The Spectra and Electronic Structure of the Tetrahedral Ions MnO_4^-, CrO_4^{--} and ClO_4^-", *J. Chem. Phys.* **20**, 837 (1952); See also M. Wolfsberg, "Studies in Molecular Orbital Theory", Ph.D. Thesis, Washington University, 1951 (unpublished).

[7] D. S. McClure, "Electronic Spectra of Molecules and Ions in Crystals, Part II. Spectra of Ions in Crystals", in *Solid State Physics*, Vol. 9, F. Seitz and D. Turnbull, eds., Academic, New York, 1959.

[8] C. J. Ballhausen and H. B. Gray, *Molecular Orbital Theory*, Benjamin, New York, 1965.

[9] L. E. Orgel, *An Introduction to Transition-Metal Chemistry Ligand-Field Theory*, Wiley, 1960.

11

The Quantum Theory of the Radiation Field

1. THE CLASSICAL ELECTROMAGNETIC FIELD

The electromagnetic field is described classically by the Maxwell equations

$$\nabla \cdot \mathbf{E} = 4\pi\rho, \tag{11.1}$$

$$\nabla \cdot \mathbf{B} = 0, \tag{11.2}$$

$$\nabla \times \mathbf{E} + \frac{1}{c}\frac{\partial \mathbf{B}}{\partial t} = 0, \tag{11.3}$$

$$\nabla \times \mathbf{B} - \frac{1}{c}\frac{\partial \mathbf{E}}{\partial t} = \frac{4\pi}{c}\,\mathbf{j}. \tag{11.4}$$

First let us use the homogeneous Maxwell equations (11.2) and (11.3). Since

$$\nabla \cdot \nabla \times \mathbf{u} = 0, \tag{11.5}$$

we have

$$\mathbf{B} = \nabla \times \mathbf{A}, \tag{11.6}$$

and

$$\nabla \times \mathbf{E} = -\frac{1}{c}\frac{\partial}{\partial t}(\nabla \times \mathbf{A}). \tag{11.7}$$

Also

$$\nabla \times \nabla\varphi = 0 \tag{11.8}$$

gives

$$\mathbf{E} = -\nabla\varphi - \frac{1}{c}\frac{\partial \mathbf{A}}{\partial t}. \tag{11.9}$$

Let us consider now the inhomogeneous Maxwell equations. Replacing the expressions for **E** and **B** in (11.1) and (11.4),

$$\nabla\left(-\nabla\varphi - \frac{1}{c}\frac{\partial \mathbf{A}}{\partial t}\right) = 4\pi\rho,$$

or

$$\nabla^2\varphi + \frac{1}{c}\frac{\partial}{\partial t}(\nabla\cdot\mathbf{A}) = -4\pi\rho. \tag{11.10}$$

Also

$$\nabla\times(\nabla\times\mathbf{A}) - \frac{1}{c}\frac{\partial}{\partial t}\left(-\nabla\varphi - \frac{1}{c}\frac{\partial\mathbf{A}}{\partial t}\right) = \frac{4\pi}{c}\mathbf{j},$$

or

$$\left(\nabla^2\mathbf{A} - \frac{1}{c^2}\frac{\partial^2\mathbf{A}}{\partial t^2}\right) - \nabla\left(\nabla\cdot\mathbf{A} + \frac{1}{c}\frac{\partial\varphi}{\partial t}\right) = -\frac{4\pi}{c}\mathbf{j}. \tag{11.11}$$

φ and **A** are not uniquely defined.

If we make

$$\varphi' = \varphi - \frac{1}{c}\frac{\partial f}{\partial t} \tag{11.12}$$

$$\mathbf{A}' = \mathbf{A} + \nabla f, \tag{11.13}$$

f being any function of coordinates and time, we find:

$$\mathbf{E} = -\frac{1}{c}\frac{\partial\mathbf{A}}{\partial t} - \nabla\varphi = -\frac{1}{c}\frac{\partial\mathbf{A}'}{\partial t} + \frac{1}{c}\frac{\partial}{\partial t}\nabla f - \nabla\varphi' - \frac{1}{c}\frac{\partial}{\partial t}\nabla f$$

$$= -\frac{1}{c}\frac{\partial\mathbf{A}'}{\partial t} - \nabla\varphi'; \tag{11.14}$$

$$\mathbf{B} = \nabla\times\mathbf{A} = \nabla\times(\mathbf{A}' - \nabla f) = \nabla\times\mathbf{A}'. \tag{11.15}$$

There is a basic indeterminacy in φ and **A**. We have to use an additional condition here; and we choose this to be the so-called *Coloumb gauge*,

$$\nabla\cdot\mathbf{A} = 0. \tag{11.16}$$

Taking (11.16) into account Eqs. (11.10) and (11.11) become

$$\nabla^2\varphi = -4\pi\rho, \qquad (\textit{Poisson's equation}), \tag{11.17}$$

$$\nabla^2\mathbf{A} - \frac{1}{c^2}\frac{\partial^2\mathbf{A}}{\partial t^2} = -\frac{4\pi}{c}\mathbf{j} - \frac{1}{c}\frac{\partial(\nabla\varphi)}{\partial t}. \tag{11.18}$$

Poisson's equation may be integrated in the following way. *Green's theorem* states:

$$\int d\tau(G\,\nabla^2\phi - \phi\,\nabla^2 G) = \int dS\left[G\left(\frac{\partial\phi}{\partial n}\right) - \phi\left(\frac{\partial G}{\partial n}\right)\right], \tag{11.19}$$

where the integral in the left member expresses an integral over a volume and the integral in the right member an integral over a surface ($\partial/\partial n$ being a derivative in the direction perpendicular to the surface). Let

$$G(\mathbf{r}, \mathbf{r}') = \frac{1}{|\mathbf{r} - \mathbf{r}'|}. \tag{11.20}$$

We have

$$\nabla_x{}^2 G(\mathbf{r}, \mathbf{r}') = -4\pi\delta(\mathbf{r} - \mathbf{r}'), \tag{11.21}$$

and

$$\int d\mathbf{r}(G\nabla^2\varphi - \varphi\nabla^2 G) = \int d\mathbf{r}'\left[\frac{-4\pi\rho(\mathbf{r}', t)}{|\mathbf{r} - \mathbf{r}'|} + \phi(\mathbf{r}', t)\,4\pi\delta(\mathbf{r} - \mathbf{r}')\right] = 0, \tag{11.22}$$

since

$$\varphi(\infty, t) = G(\infty) = 0.$$

Then

$$\varphi(\mathbf{r}, t) = \int \frac{\rho(\mathbf{r}', t)}{|\mathbf{r} - \mathbf{r}'|}\, d\mathbf{r}'. \tag{11.23}$$

φ is only a function of the distribution of charges; it has no independent existence. If $\rho = 0$, also $\varphi = 0$.

The situation is different for $\mathbf{A}$, which depends on the current density $\mathbf{j}(\mathbf{r}, t)$, but may exist even in the absence of current and charges. If $\rho = \mathbf{j} = 0$ (11.18) becomes the *field equation*

$$\nabla^2\mathbf{A}(\mathbf{r}, t) - \frac{1}{c^2}\frac{\partial^2}{\partial t^2}\mathbf{A}(\mathbf{r}, t) = 0; \tag{11.24}$$

also

$$\mathbf{E} = -\frac{1}{c}\frac{\partial\mathbf{A}}{\partial t}$$

$$\mathbf{B} = \nabla \times \mathbf{A}. \tag{11.25}$$

The field equation for $\mathbf{A}(\mathbf{r}, t)$, together with the expressions (11.25) for $\mathbf{E}$ and $\mathbf{B}$, the condition $\nabla \cdot \mathbf{A} = 0$ and the boundary conditions define the *radiative field*.

2. THE QUANTUM THEORY OF THE ELECTROMAGNETIC FIELD

2.1 The Vector Potential

We want to impose certain boundary conditions. Consider a cubic box of dimensions L_x, L_y, L_z, and impose periodic boundary conditions,

$$\begin{aligned}\mathbf{A}(\mathbf{r} + L_x\mathbf{u}_x) &= \mathbf{A}(\mathbf{r}),\\ \mathbf{A}(\mathbf{r} + L_y\mathbf{u}_y) &= \mathbf{A}(\mathbf{r}),\\ \mathbf{A}(\mathbf{r} + L_z\mathbf{u}_z) &= \mathbf{A}(\mathbf{r}),\end{aligned} \tag{11.26}$$

where $\mathbf{u}_x$, $\mathbf{u}_y$, and $\mathbf{u}_z$ are unit vectors in the x, y, and z directions, respectively. Let us assume that a solution of (11.24) is

$$\mathbf{A}_\alpha(\mathbf{r}, t) = q_\alpha(t)\, \mathcal{A}_\alpha(\mathbf{r}). \tag{11.27}$$

Then, putting $\mathbf{A}_\alpha$ in (11.24), we get

$$q_\alpha \nabla^2 \mathcal{A}_\alpha = \frac{1}{c^2} \ddot{q}_\alpha \mathcal{A}_\alpha. \tag{11.28}$$

We put

$$\frac{c^2 \nabla^2 \mathcal{A}_\alpha}{\mathcal{A}_\alpha} = \frac{\ddot{q}_\alpha}{q_\alpha} = -\omega_\alpha^2. \tag{11.29}$$

This results in

$$\begin{aligned}q_\alpha + \omega_\alpha^2 q_\alpha &= 0,\\ \nabla^2 \mathcal{A}_\alpha + \frac{\omega_\alpha^2}{c^2} \mathcal{A}_\alpha &= 0.\end{aligned} \tag{11.30}$$

The space part of the vector potential can be written

$$\mathcal{A}_\alpha(\mathbf{r}) = \mathbf{a} e^{i\mathbf{k}_\alpha \cdot \mathbf{r}} = \boldsymbol{\pi}_\alpha \left(\frac{4\pi c^2}{V}\right)^{1/2} e^{i\mathbf{k}_\alpha \cdot \mathbf{r}}, \tag{11.31}$$

where

$$k_\alpha = \frac{\omega_\alpha}{c} \quad \text{(dispersion relation for electromagnetic waves)}, \tag{11.32}$$

and

$\boldsymbol{\pi}_\alpha$ = unit vector in the direction of polarization.

The time dependent part of $\mathbf{A}_\alpha$ is given by

$$q_\alpha = |q_\alpha|\, e^{-i\omega_\alpha t}. \tag{11.33}$$

Therefore the complete vector potential is given by

$$\mathbf{A}_\alpha(\mathbf{r}, t) = |q_\alpha| \left(\frac{4\pi c^2}{V}\right)^{1/2} \boldsymbol{\pi}_\alpha e^{i(\mathbf{k}_\alpha \cdot \mathbf{r} - \omega_\alpha t)}, \tag{11.34}$$

where

$$V = L_x L_y L_z.$$

This expression for $\mathbf{A}(\mathbf{r}, t)$ represents a plane wave of wavelength $\lambda_\alpha = 2\pi/k_\alpha$. Because of the Coulomb gauge,

$$\nabla \cdot \mathbf{A}_\alpha(\mathbf{r}, t) = |q_\alpha| \left(\frac{4\pi c^2}{V}\right)^{1/2} (\pi_{\alpha x} k_{\alpha x} + \pi_{\alpha y} k_{\alpha y} + \pi_{\alpha z} k_{\alpha_z}) = 0. \tag{11.35}$$

Then

$$\boldsymbol{\pi}_\alpha \cdot \mathbf{k}_\alpha = 0, \tag{11.36}$$

namely the direction of propagation is perpendicular to the direction of polarization.

Generalizing the expression of $\mathbf{A}_\alpha$ by including negative k_α and ω_α,

$$\mathbf{A}_\alpha(\mathbf{r}, t) = \sum_{\text{Pol}} [q_\alpha(t) \mathcal{A}_\alpha(\mathbf{r}) + q_\alpha^*(t) \mathcal{A}_\alpha^*(\mathbf{r})], \tag{11.37}$$

where the sum is extended to the two independent polarizations. If the vector potential contains more than one Fourier component, the result is

$$\mathbf{A}(\mathbf{r}, t) = \sum_\alpha \sum_{\text{Pol}} [q_\alpha(t) \mathcal{A}_\alpha(\mathbf{r}) + q_\alpha(t) \mathcal{A}_\alpha^*(\mathbf{r})]. \tag{11.38}$$

The values of α can be derived from the boundary condition

$$\begin{aligned} k_{\alpha x} L_x &= 2\pi n_{\alpha x}, \qquad & k_{\alpha x} &= \frac{2\pi}{L_x} n_{\alpha x}, \\ k_{\alpha y} L_y &= 2\pi n_{\alpha y}, \qquad & k_{\alpha y} &= \frac{2\pi}{L_y} n_{\alpha y}, \\ k_{\alpha z} L_z &= 2\pi n_{\alpha z}, \qquad & k_{\alpha z} &= \frac{2\pi}{L_z} n_{\alpha z}. \end{aligned} \tag{11.39}$$

Then we can have

$$\begin{aligned} n_{\alpha x} &= 0, 1, 2, 3, \ldots, \\ n_{\alpha y} &= 0, 1, 2, 3, \ldots, \\ n_{\alpha z} &= 0, 1, 2, 3, \ldots, \end{aligned} \tag{11.40}$$

and α is defined by three numbers:

$$\alpha \equiv (n_{\alpha x}, n_{\alpha y}, n_{\alpha z}). \tag{11.41}$$

When $n_{\alpha x}$, $n_{\alpha y}$, and $n_{\alpha z}$ are specified, we know k_α and ω_α:

$$\mathbf{A}_\alpha(\mathbf{r}, t) = |q_\alpha| \left(\frac{4\pi c^2}{V}\right)^{1/2} \boldsymbol{\pi}_\alpha \times \exp\left\{i\left[\frac{2\pi n_{\alpha x}}{L_x} x + \frac{2\pi n_{\alpha y}}{L_y} y + \frac{2\pi n_{\alpha z}}{L_z} z - \omega_\alpha(n_{\alpha x}, n_{\alpha y}, n_{\alpha z})\, t\right]\right\} + \text{complex conjugate}. \tag{11.42}$$

The sum over the α's is a sum over the n's. We can also see that

$$\mathbf{k}_\alpha = -\mathbf{k}_\alpha; \qquad \mathcal{A}_{-\alpha} = \mathcal{A}_\alpha^*; \qquad \boldsymbol{\pi}_\alpha = \boldsymbol{\pi}_{-\alpha}. \tag{11.43}$$

2.2 The Energy of the Radiation Field

The energy crossing the unit area in the unit time is given by the Poynting vector,

$$\mathbf{S} = \frac{c}{4\pi} \mathbf{E} \times \mathbf{H}. \tag{11.44}$$

Consider a monochromatic wave

$$\begin{aligned} \mathbf{A} = \mathbf{A}_\alpha &= q_\alpha \mathcal{A}_\alpha + q_\alpha^* \mathcal{A}_\alpha^* \\ &= |q_\alpha| \left(\frac{4\pi c^2}{V}\right)^{1/2} \sum_{\text{Pol}} \boldsymbol{\pi}_\alpha [e^{i(\mathbf{k}_\alpha \cdot \mathbf{r} - \omega_\alpha t)} + e^{-i(\mathbf{k}_\alpha \cdot \mathbf{r} - \omega_\alpha t)}]. \end{aligned} \tag{11.45}$$

In case of polarization along z and motion along y,

$$\mathbf{A} = |q_\alpha| \left(\frac{4\pi c^2}{V}\right)^{1/2} \mathbf{u}_z [e^{i(k_{\alpha y} y - \omega_\alpha t)} + e^{-i(k_{\alpha y} y - \omega_\alpha t)}]. \tag{11.46}$$

Then

$$\begin{aligned} \mathbf{E} &= -\frac{1}{c}\frac{\partial \mathbf{A}}{\partial t} = \frac{i\omega_\alpha}{c} (q_\alpha \mathcal{A}_\alpha - q_\alpha^* \mathcal{A}_\alpha^*) \\ &= \frac{i\omega_\alpha}{c} |q_\alpha| \left(\frac{4\pi c^2}{V}\right)^{1/2} \mathbf{u}_z [e^{i(k_{\alpha y} y - \omega_\alpha t} - e^{-i(k_{\alpha y} y - \omega_\alpha t)}] \\ &= -k_{\alpha y} |q_\alpha| \mathbf{u}_z \left(\frac{4\pi c^2}{V}\right)^{1/2} 2 \sin (k_{\alpha y} y - \omega_\alpha t). \end{aligned} \tag{11.47}$$

We also have

$$\begin{aligned} \mathbf{H} = \nabla \times \mathbf{A} &= \begin{vmatrix} \mathbf{u}_x & \mathbf{u}_y & \mathbf{u}_z \\ \dfrac{\partial}{\partial x} & \dfrac{\partial}{\partial y} & \dfrac{\partial}{\partial z} \\ 0 & 0 & A_z \end{vmatrix} = \mathbf{u}_x \frac{\partial A_z}{\partial y} \\ &= \mathbf{u}_x i k_{\alpha y} |q_\alpha| \left(\frac{4\pi c^2}{V}\right)^{1/2} [e^{i(k_{\alpha y} y - \omega_\alpha t)} - e^{-i(k_{\alpha y} y - \omega_\alpha t)}] \\ &= -k_{\alpha y} |q_\alpha| \mathbf{u}_x \left(\frac{4\pi c^2}{V}\right)^{1/2} 2 \sin (k_{\alpha y} y - \omega_\alpha t). \end{aligned} \tag{11.48}$$

E and **H** have the same magnitude and are perpendicular to each other and to **S**. **S** is in the direction of propagation.

2.3 The Hamiltonian of the Radiation Field

The Hamiltonian of the radiation field is given by

$$H = \frac{1}{8\pi}\int (E^2 + H^2)\, d\tau = \frac{1}{4\pi}\int E^2\, d\tau$$

$$= \frac{1}{4\pi}\int\left\{\left[\sum_{\text{Pol}}\sum_{\alpha}\frac{i\omega_\alpha}{c}(q_\alpha \mathcal{A}_\alpha - q_\alpha^* \mathcal{A}_\alpha)\right]\left[\sum_{\text{Pol}'}\sum_{\alpha'}\frac{i\omega_{\alpha'}}{c}(q_{\alpha'}\mathcal{A}_{\alpha'} - q_{\alpha'}\mathcal{A}_{\alpha'}^*)\right]\right\} d\tau; \tag{11.49}$$

but

$$\int \mathcal{A}_\alpha \cdot \mathcal{A}_{\alpha'}\, d\tau = 4\pi c^2 \delta_{\alpha\, -\alpha'},$$

$$\int \mathcal{A}_\alpha \cdot \mathcal{A}_\alpha\, d\tau = 0 = \int \mathcal{A}_\alpha^* \cdot \mathcal{A}_\alpha^*\, d\tau, \tag{11.50}$$

$$\int \mathcal{A}_\alpha^* \cdot \mathcal{A}_\alpha\, d\tau = 4\pi c^2.$$

The classical Hamiltonian of the radiation field is then given by

$$H = -\frac{1}{4\pi c^2}\sum_{\substack{\text{Pol}\\ \text{Pol}'}}\sum_{\alpha\alpha'}\omega_\alpha\omega_{\alpha'}\int [(q_\alpha q_{\alpha'}\mathcal{A}_\alpha \cdot \mathcal{A}_{\alpha'} + q_\alpha^* q_{\alpha'}^* \mathcal{A}_\alpha^* \cdot \mathcal{A}_{\alpha'}^*)$$

$$- (q_\alpha q_{\alpha'}^* \mathcal{A}_\alpha \cdot \mathcal{A}_{\alpha'}^* + q_\alpha^* q_{\alpha'} \mathcal{A}_\alpha^* \cdot \mathcal{A}_{\alpha'})]\, d\tau$$

$$= \frac{1}{4\pi c^2}\sum_{\text{Pol}}\sum_{\alpha}\omega_\alpha{}^2 2 q_\alpha q_\alpha^* 4\pi c^2, \tag{11.51}$$

or

$$H = 2\sum_{\alpha,\lambda}\omega_\alpha{}^2 q_\alpha{}^{\lambda *} q_\alpha{}^\lambda = \sum_{\alpha,\lambda} H_\alpha{}^\lambda, \tag{11.52}$$

where λ ranges over the two possible polarizations.[1] Instead of using q_α, q_α^*, we can use the following coordinates and momenta:

$$Q_\alpha = q_\alpha + q_\alpha^*,$$
$$P_\alpha = \dot{Q}_\alpha = -i\omega_\alpha(q_\alpha - q_\alpha^*). \tag{11.53}$$

[1] In what follows we will drop the superscript λ for simplicity of notation.

Then,

$$
\begin{aligned}
q_\alpha &= \frac{1}{2}\left(Q_\alpha - \frac{1}{i\omega_\alpha} P_\alpha\right), \\
q_\alpha^* &= \frac{1}{2}\left(Q_\alpha + \frac{1}{i\omega_\alpha} P_\alpha\right),
\end{aligned}
\tag{11.54}
$$

$$
\omega_\alpha^2 q_\alpha q_\alpha^* = \frac{1}{4}\left(Q_\alpha^2 + \frac{1}{\omega_\alpha^2} P_\alpha^2\right)\omega_\alpha^2 = \frac{1}{4}(P_\alpha^2 + \omega_\alpha^2 Q_\alpha^2), \tag{11.55}
$$

and

$$
H_\alpha = 2\sum_\alpha \omega_\alpha^2 q_\alpha^* q_\alpha = \frac{1}{2}\sum_\alpha (P_\alpha^2 + \omega_\alpha^2 Q_\alpha^2). \tag{11.56}
$$

It is then possible to consider every Fourier component as represented by a harmonic oscillator whose Hamiltonian is given by H_α. P_α and Q_α satisfy Hamilton's equations:

$$
\frac{\partial H_\alpha}{\partial Q_\alpha} = \omega_\alpha^2 Q_\alpha = -\dot{P}_\alpha, \tag{11.57}
$$

which checks with

$$
\dot{P}_\alpha = \ddot{Q}_\alpha = -\omega_\alpha^2(q_\alpha + q_\alpha^*) = -\omega_\alpha^2 Q_\alpha, \tag{11.58}
$$

and

$$
\frac{\partial H_\alpha}{\partial P_\alpha} = P_\alpha = \dot{Q}_\alpha. \tag{11.59}
$$

It is now time to go into quantum mechanics. We set

$$
\begin{aligned}
&[Q_\alpha, P_{\alpha'}] = i\hbar\delta_{\alpha\alpha'} \\
&[Q_\alpha, Q_{\alpha'}] = [P_\alpha, P_{\alpha'}] = 0.
\end{aligned}
\tag{11.60}
$$

Let us call by q, q^+ the quantum mechanical equivalent of q, q^*, respectively. From (11.54) and (11.60) we derive the following commutation relations:

$$
[q_\alpha, q_{\alpha'}^+] = \frac{\hbar}{2\omega_\alpha}\delta_{\alpha\alpha'}; \qquad [a_\alpha, a_{\alpha'}^+] = \delta_{\alpha\alpha'}, \tag{11.61}
$$

where

$$
\begin{aligned}
a_\alpha &= \left(\frac{2\omega_\alpha}{\hbar}\right)^{1/2} q_\alpha \\
a_\alpha^+ &= \left(\frac{2\omega_\alpha}{\hbar}\right)^{1/2} q_\alpha^+
\end{aligned}
\tag{11.62}
$$

are called respectively the *annihilation* and the *creation* operators. We notice that q and q^+ are not Hermitian.

The vector potential operator can be expressed in terms of q and q^+ as

$$\mathbf{A} = \left(\frac{4\pi c^2}{V}\right)^{1/2} \sum_{\alpha,\lambda} \boldsymbol{\pi}_\alpha^\lambda (q_\alpha^\lambda e^{i\mathbf{k}_\alpha\cdot\mathbf{r}} + q_\alpha^{\lambda+} e^{-i\mathbf{k}_\alpha\cdot\mathbf{r}}), \tag{11.63}$$

where λ indicates the polarization and ranges over 1, 2.

2.4 The Energy Levels of the Radiation Field

The Hamiltonian of the radiation field is given by

$$\begin{aligned} H &= \sum_\alpha \tfrac{1}{2}(P_\alpha^{\ 2} + \omega_\alpha^{\ 2} Q_\alpha^{\ 2}) \\ &= \tfrac{1}{2} \sum_\alpha [-\omega_\alpha^{\ 2}(q_\alpha - q_\alpha^{\ +})^2 + \omega_\alpha^{\ 2}(q_\alpha + q_\alpha^{\ +})^2] \\ &= \sum_\alpha \omega_\alpha^{\ 2}(q_\alpha q_\alpha^{\ +} + q_\alpha^{\ +} q_\alpha). \end{aligned} \tag{11.64}$$

Let us examine a single oscillator, represented by the Hamiltonian

$$H = \omega^2(qq^+ + q^+q). \tag{11.65}$$

Because of the commutation relations,

$$qq^+ = \frac{\hbar}{2\omega} + q^+q, \tag{11.66}$$

and

$$H = \omega^2\left(2q^+q + \frac{\hbar}{2\omega}\right) = 2\omega^2 q^+q + \tfrac{1}{2}\hbar\omega = \hbar\omega(a^+a + \tfrac{1}{2}). \tag{11.67}$$

The commutators of q and q^+ with H are given by

$$\begin{aligned} [H, q] &= 2\omega^2[q^+q, q] = 2\omega^2([q^+, q]q + q^+[q, q]) \\ &= 2\omega^2\left(-\frac{\hbar}{2\omega} q\right) = -\hbar\omega q; \end{aligned} \tag{11.68}$$

$$\begin{aligned} [H, q^+] &= 2\omega^2[q^+q, q^+] = 2\omega^2([q^+, q^+]q + q^+[q, q^+]) \\ &= 2\omega^2\left(\frac{\hbar}{2\omega} q\right) = \hbar\omega q. \end{aligned} \tag{11.69}$$

We have also the following relations:

$$\begin{aligned} \langle m|\,[H, q]\,|n\rangle &= \langle m|\, Hq - qH\,|n\rangle = \langle m|\, Hq\,|n\rangle - \langle m|\, qH\,|n\rangle \\ &= (E_m - E_n)\,\langle m|\, q\,|n\rangle = -\hbar\omega\langle m|\, q\,|n\rangle, \end{aligned}$$

or

$$(E_m - E_n + \hbar\omega)\,\langle m|\, q\,|n\rangle = 0. \tag{11.70}$$

Using the same procedure for $[H, q^+]$, we get

$$(E_m - E_n - \hbar\omega)\langle m| q^+ |n\rangle = 0. \tag{11.71}$$

We also have:

$$q^+q = \frac{1}{2\omega^2}\left(H - \frac{\hbar\omega}{2}\right), \tag{11.72}$$

and

$$(q^+q)_{nn} = \frac{1}{2\omega^2}\left(E_n - \frac{\hbar\omega}{2}\right) = \sum_k q_{nk}{}^+ q_{kn} = \sum_k |q_{nk}{}^+|^2 \geq 0. \tag{11.73}$$

Let us now show that the energy E_0 of the lowest level is $\hbar\omega/2$. First, we can say that, because of (11.73), $E_0 \geq \hbar\omega/2$. If we assume that $E_0 > \hbar\omega/2$,

$$\sum_k |q_{0k}{}^+|^2 = \frac{1}{2\omega^2}\left(E_0 - \frac{\hbar\omega}{2}\right) > 0, \tag{11.74}$$

which implies that there is some k for which q_{0k} is $\neq 0$.

On the other hand, because of (11.71),

$$(E_0 - E_k - \hbar\omega)q_{0k}{}^+ = 0 \tag{11.75}$$

and

$$E_0 = E_k + \hbar\omega, \tag{11.76}$$

which is contrary to our assumption that E_0 was the lowest state. Thus we have proved that the energy of the lowest state is $\hbar\omega/2$.

Let us call E_1 the energy of the first excited state. From (11.73):

$$\sum_k |q_{1k}{}^+|^2 = \frac{1}{2\omega^2}\left(E_1 - \frac{\hbar\omega}{2}\right) > 0, \tag{11.77}$$

which implies that there is at least one k for which $q_{1k}{}^+ \neq 0$; but from (11.71):

$$(E_1 - E_k - \hbar\omega)q_{1k}{}^+ = 0. \tag{11.78}$$

Then

$$E_1 - E_k - \hbar\omega = 0, \tag{11.79}$$

and

$$E_k = E_1 - \hbar\omega. \tag{11.80}$$

E_k can only be $\hbar\omega/2$. Then

$$E_1 = (1 + \tfrac{1}{2})\,\hbar\omega. \tag{11.81}$$

We can show in the same way that

$$E_n = (n + \tfrac{1}{2})\,\hbar\omega. \tag{11.82}$$

If the energy of the oscillator is E_n, we say that the oscillator is excited to the nth level.

From (11.70) we can now derive the fact that $\langle m| q |n\rangle \neq 0$ only when $m = n - 1$ and from (11.71) that $\langle m| q^+ |n\rangle \neq 0$ only when $m = n + 1$. We then have

$$\begin{aligned} E_n &= \langle n| H |n\rangle = (n + \tfrac{1}{2})\hbar\omega \\ &= 2\omega^2\langle n| q^+q |n\rangle + \tfrac{1}{2}\hbar\omega = 2\omega^2 \sum_m \langle n| q^+ |m\rangle\langle m| q |n\rangle + \tfrac{1}{2}\hbar\omega \\ &= 2\omega^2\langle n| q^+|n - 1\rangle\langle n - 1| q |n\rangle + \tfrac{1}{2}\hbar\omega = 2\omega^2 |\langle n - 1| q |n\rangle|^2 + \tfrac{1}{2}\hbar\omega \end{aligned} \tag{11.83}$$

and

$$\begin{aligned} E_{n+1} &= \langle n + 1| H |n + 1\rangle = (n + 1 + \tfrac{1}{2})\hbar\omega \\ &= 2\omega^2\langle n + 1| q^+q |n + 1\rangle + \tfrac{1}{2}\hbar\omega \\ &= 2\omega^2 \sum_m \langle n + 1| q^+ |m\rangle\langle m| q |n + 1\rangle + \tfrac{1}{2}\hbar\omega \\ &= 2\omega^2\langle n + 1| q^+ |n\rangle\langle n| q |n + 1\rangle + \tfrac{1}{2}\hbar\omega \\ &= 2\omega^2 |\langle n + 1| q^+ |n\rangle|^2 + \tfrac{1}{2}\hbar\omega. \end{aligned} \tag{11.84}$$

Then

$$\begin{aligned} \langle n - 1| q |n\rangle &= \left(\frac{n\hbar}{2\omega}\right)^{1/2}, \qquad \langle n - 1| a |n\rangle = \sqrt{n}, \\ \langle n + 1| q^+ |n\rangle &= \left(\frac{(n + 1)\hbar}{2\omega}\right)^{1/2}, \qquad \langle n + 1| a^+ |n\rangle = \sqrt{n + 1} \end{aligned} \tag{11.85}$$

and

$$\begin{aligned} q |n\rangle &= \left(\frac{n\hbar}{2\omega}\right)^{1/2} |n - 1\rangle, \qquad a |n\rangle = \sqrt{n}\, |n - 1\rangle, \\ q^+ |n\rangle &= \left(\frac{(n + 1)\hbar}{2\omega}\right)^{1/2} |n + 1\rangle, \qquad a^+ |n\rangle = \sqrt{n + 1}\, |n + 1\rangle, \end{aligned} \tag{11.86}$$

$$\langle n| q^+q |n\rangle = \frac{n\hbar}{2\omega}, \qquad \langle n| a^+a |n\rangle = n. \tag{11.87}$$

For the whole field the energy levels are given by

$$E_n = \sum_{\alpha,\lambda} [(n_\alpha^\lambda)^2 + \tfrac{1}{2}]\hbar\omega_\alpha. \tag{11.88}$$

12

Molecular Vibrations

1. THE CLASSICAL THEORY OF MOLECULAR VIBRATIONS

Let us consider a molecule with N atoms. This system has $3N$ degrees of freedom.

Let us call the $3N$ cartesian coordinates of the particles $x_i (i = 1, 2, \ldots, 3N)$ and R_i the values that these coordinate have in equilibrium. The general configuration of the system is given by

$$x_i = R_i + u_i. \tag{12.1}$$

If the forces acting among the particles are conservative, we may consider a potential function

$$V = V(u_1, u_2, \ldots, u_{3N}). \tag{12.2}$$

We consider, arbitrarily, the potential equal to zero when the system is in equilibrium. In equilibrium, since all the forces are zero, we have also,

$$\left.\frac{\partial V}{\partial u_i}\right|_{u=0} = 0. \tag{12.3}$$

The potential is then given by

$$\begin{aligned} V &= \frac{1}{2}\sum_{i=1}^{3N}\sum_{j=1}^{3N} \left.\frac{\partial^2 V}{\partial u_i\, \partial u_j}\right|_{u=0} u_i u_j \\ &= \frac{1}{2}\sum_{i=1}^{3N}\sum_{j=1}^{3N} A_{ij} u_i u_j, \end{aligned} \tag{12.4}$$

where

$$A_{ij} = \left.\frac{\partial^2 V}{\partial u_i\, \partial u_j}\right|_{u=0}. \tag{12.5}$$

The quantities A_{ij} form a real symmetrical matrix:

$$A_{ij} = A_{ji} = A_{ij}^*. \tag{12.6}$$

The Lagrangian of the system is given by

$$\begin{aligned} L(u_i, \dot{u}_i) &= T - V \\ &= \frac{1}{2}\sum_{i=1}^{3N} m_i \dot{u}_i^2 - \frac{1}{2}\sum_{i=1}^{3N}\sum_{j=1}^{3N} A_{ij} u_i u_j, \end{aligned} \tag{12.7}$$

where $m_1 = m_2 = m_3$ is the mass of particle 1, $m_4 = m_5 = m_6$ is the mass of particle 2 and so on. The equations of the motion are given by

$$\frac{d}{dt}\frac{\partial L}{\partial \dot{u}_i} - \frac{\partial L}{\partial u_i} = 0, \tag{12.8}$$

which give

$$m_i \ddot{u}_i + \sum_j A_{ij} u_j = 0. \tag{12.9}$$

In the Hamiltonian formulation we have

$$p_i = \frac{\partial L}{\partial \dot{u}_i} = m_i \dot{u}_i, \tag{12.10}$$

and

$$\begin{aligned} H(p_i, u_i) &= \sum_i p_i \dot{u}_i - L \\ &= \sum_i \frac{p_i^2}{2m_i} + \frac{1}{2}\sum_{ij} A_{ij} u_i u_j. \end{aligned} \tag{12.11}$$

The Hamilton's equations, equivalent to (12.9) are given by

$$\begin{aligned} \dot{u}_i &= \frac{\partial H}{\partial p_i} = \frac{p_i}{m_i}, \\ \dot{p}_i &= -\frac{\partial H}{\partial u_i} = -\sum_i A_{ij} u_i. \end{aligned} \tag{12.12}$$

The problem we now face is how to solve either the $3N$ differential equations of the second order (12.9) or the $6N$ first order differential equations (12.12), given the $6N$ initial conditions $u_i(0)$, $\dot{u}_i(0)$. These equations are coupled by the quantities A_{ij}; in order to decouple them, we can make the following transformation in terms of new coordinates:

$$u_i(t) = \sum_{q=1}^{3N} \frac{h_{qi}}{\sqrt{m_i}} e^{-i\omega_q t} C_q. \tag{12.13}$$

If we put (12.13) into (12.9) we get

$$h_{qi}\sqrt{m_i}\,\omega_q^{\ 2} - \sum_j A_{ij}\frac{h_{qj}}{\sqrt{m_j}} = 0 \tag{12.14}$$

or

$$\sum_j B_{ij}h_{qj} = \omega_q^{\ 2}h_{qi}, \tag{12.15}$$

where

$$B_{ij} = \frac{A_{ij}}{\sqrt{m_i m_j}}. \tag{12.16}$$

The quantities B_{ij} define a symmetrical and real matrix which is called *dynamical matrix*. $\omega_q^{\ 2}$ are the eigenvalues and h_{qi} are the eigenvectors of (12.15). We expect $3N$ eigenvalues for ω^2 and $3N$ sets of h_{qi} which define $3N$ eigenvectors. The eigenvalues are found by putting the determinant of the homogeneous equations (12.15) equal to zero:

$$|B_{ij} - \omega^2\delta_{ij}| = 0. \tag{12.17}$$

All the eigenvalues $\omega_q^{\ 2}$ are real (because B is real and symmetric) and nonnegative, since V has a positive quadratic form; ω_q is thus real, as would be expected if (12.13) had to give a bounded motion. We also choose to make ω_q positive.

We notice that some eigenvalues of the dynamical matrix may be zero. In this case, the determinant of the matrix B is zero. If the determinant is of rank $N - n$, there are n eigenfrequencies equal to zero and n corresponding eigenvectors. In case of a molecule with N atoms it can be shown that six of the $3N$ roots of the secular equation (12.17) are zero (see [1], page 22). These roots correspond to the six degrees of freedom (three translational and three rotational), which do not correspond to internal vibrations.

We can choose the $3N - 6$ eigenvectors $h_{\lambda i}$ to be real and orthonormal:

$$\sum_{i=1}^{3N-6} h_{\lambda i}h_{\lambda' i} = \delta_{\lambda\lambda'}. \tag{12.18}$$

They also form a complete set, namely, they completely define the $(3N - 6) \times (3N - 6)$ space, as expressed by the closure relation

$$\sum_{\lambda=1}^{3N-6} h_{\lambda i}h_{\lambda j} = \delta_{ij}. \tag{12.19}$$

In (12.13), then, everything is determined except C_q. These are complex numbers, with their phases and absolute values determined by the initial conditions $u_i(0)$, $\dot{u}_i(0)$.

Another way of solving this dynamical problem is by expressing u_i in terms of *normal coordinates* Q_λ:

$$u_i = \frac{1}{\sqrt{m_i}} \sum_\lambda h_{\lambda i} Q_\lambda, \tag{12.20}$$

where

$$Q_\lambda = \sum_i \sqrt{m_i}\, u_i h_{\lambda i}. \tag{12.21}$$

In this case the kinetic energy, taking (12.18) into account, is given by

$$T = \frac{1}{2} \sum_i m_i \dot{u}_i^2 = \frac{1}{2} \sum_\lambda \sum_{\lambda'} \dot{Q}_\lambda \dot{Q}_{\lambda'} \sum_i h_{\lambda i} h_{\lambda' i} = \frac{1}{2} \sum_\lambda \dot{Q}_\lambda^2, \tag{12.22}$$

and the potential energy, taking into account (12.15) and (12.18), by

$$\begin{aligned} V &= \frac{1}{2} \sum_{ij} A_{ij} u_i u_j = \frac{1}{2} \sum_{ij} B_{ij} \sum_{\lambda\lambda'} h_{\lambda i} h_{\lambda' j} Q_\lambda Q_{\lambda'} \\ &= \sum_{\lambda\lambda'} \frac{1}{2} \sum_i \left(\sum_j B_{ij} h_{\lambda' j} \right) h_{\lambda i} Q_\lambda Q_{\lambda'} \\ &= \sum_{\lambda\lambda'} \left[\frac{1}{2} \left(\sum_i \omega_{\lambda'}^2 h_{\lambda' i} h_{\lambda i} \right) Q_\lambda Q_{\lambda'} \right] = \sum_\lambda \tfrac{1}{2} \omega_\lambda^2 Q_\lambda^2. \end{aligned} \tag{12.23}$$

The Lagrangian is given by

$$L = T - V = \frac{1}{2} \sum_\lambda \dot{Q}_\lambda^2 - \frac{1}{2} \sum_\lambda \omega_\lambda^2 Q_\lambda^2. \tag{12.24}$$

The equation of motion is given for each normal coordinate by

$$\ddot{Q}_\lambda + \omega_\lambda^2 Q_\lambda = 0, \tag{12.25}$$

with the solution

$$Q_\lambda = C_\lambda \cos(\omega_\lambda t + \delta_\lambda). \tag{12.26}$$

From this we derive

$$u_i(t) = \frac{1}{\sqrt{m_i}} \sum_\lambda h_{\lambda i} C_\lambda \cos(\omega_\lambda t + \delta_\lambda), \tag{12.27}$$

where C_λ and δ_λ are derived from the initial conditions and where $h_{\lambda i}$ and ω_q are, respectively, the eigenvectors and the eigenvalues of (12.15).

The Hamiltonian of the system can also be expressed in terms of the normal coordinates. The conjugate momentum of Q_λ is given by

$$P_\lambda = \frac{\partial L}{\partial \dot{Q}_\lambda} = \dot{Q}_\lambda; \tag{12.28}$$

then

$$\begin{aligned} H &= \sum_\lambda P_\lambda \dot{Q}_\lambda - L = \sum_\lambda P_\lambda^2 - \frac{1}{2} \sum_\lambda \dot{Q}_\lambda^2 + \tfrac{1}{2} \omega_\lambda^2 Q_\lambda^2 \\ &= \frac{1}{2} \sum_{\lambda=1}^{3N-6} (P_\lambda^2 + \omega_\lambda^2 Q_\lambda^2). \end{aligned} \tag{12.29}$$

2. THE SYMMETRY OF THE MOLECULES AND THE NORMAL COORDINATES

Most molecules present a symmetry that can be described by a group G of symmetry operations.

The kinetic and the potential energies of the molecule cannot be changed by performing on the molecule a symmetry operation of the group G.

In the general case some eigenvalues ω_λ may be degenerate:

$$\omega_{\lambda 1} = \omega_{\lambda 2} = \cdots = \omega_{\lambda r}. \tag{12.30}$$

T and V are independent of any symmetry operation. Therefore, if r different coordinates Q_λ correspond to the same value of ω_λ, we must have

$$R\omega_{\lambda i} = \sum_{l=1}^{r} a_{li} Q_{\lambda l}, \tag{12.31}$$

where the coefficients a_{li} form an $r \times r$ unitary matrix. If we again operate with an operation S,

$$SRQ_{\lambda i} = \sum_{l=1}^{r} a_{li} SQ_{\lambda l} = \sum_{l=1}^{r} \sum_{m=1}^{r} a_{li} b_{ml} Q_{\lambda m}. \tag{12.32}$$

Also, if $SR = T$,

$$TQ_{\lambda i} = \sum_{m=1}^{r} c_{mi} Q_{\lambda m}. \tag{12.33}$$

From (12.32) and (12.33) we get

$$c_{mi} = \sum_{l=1}^{r} b_{ml} a_{li}, \tag{12.34}$$

which expresses the fact that *the normal coordinates must form a basis for irreducible representations of the symmetry group of the molecule* in the same way as the eigenfunctions of the Hamiltonian.

If an arbitrary set of $3N$ coordinates is used as basis for the symmetry group of a molecular complex, a reducible representation of the group is in general obtained. This representation can be reduced in terms of the irreducible representations of the group. The dimension of each of these representations is equal to the degree of degeneracy of ω_λ; the number of different values of ω_λ is equal to the number of irreducible representations contained in the reducible representation. Also, the normal coordinates corresponding to a certain ω_λ will transform according to the matrices of the relative irreducible representation.

It may happen that the force constants and the masses of the atoms in the molecule have such values that two normal frequencies ω_λ belonging to two distinct representations have the same numerical value. In this case we are in the presence of an *accidental degeneracy*.

3. HOW TO FIND THE NORMAL MODES OF VIBRATION

Let us consider a system of N particles and let us establish a set of $3N$ vectors $\mathbf{x}_i$, $\mathbf{y}_i$ and $\mathbf{z}_i$ attached to each atom and representing the displacements of each atom from its equilibrium position, respectively, in the x, y, and z directions.

Let us consider then these vectors as basis for a representation Γ_m of the symmetry group of the system. This representation is in general reducible and has dimension $3N$. We want now to calculate the characters of Γ_m.

We first observe that only those particles which do not move when the system is subjected to a certain operation R of the group do contribute to the character of R. In fact, in the $3N \times 3N$ matrix representing R, all the 3×3 submatrices corresponding to the particles which change position are displaced from the diagonal; on the other hand for each undisplaced particle there is a 3×3 matrix whose diagonal coincides with the diagonal of the $3N \times 3N$ matrix.

We now consider the coordinates x, y, and z of an undisplaced particle and represent a proper rotation by an angle $2\pi k/n$ about the axis z:

$$C_n^k \begin{pmatrix} x \\ y \\ z \end{pmatrix} = \begin{pmatrix} \cos\dfrac{2\pi k}{n} & -\sin\dfrac{2\pi k}{n} & 0 \\ \sin\dfrac{2\pi k}{n} & \cos\dfrac{2\pi k}{n} & 0 \\ 0 & 0 & 1 \end{pmatrix} \begin{pmatrix} x \\ y \\ z \end{pmatrix}. \tag{12.35}$$

An improper rotation can be represented as

$$S_n^k \begin{pmatrix} x \\ y \\ z \end{pmatrix} = \begin{pmatrix} \cos\dfrac{2\pi k}{n} & -\sin\dfrac{2\pi k}{n} & 0 \\ \sin\dfrac{2\pi k}{n} & \cos\dfrac{2\pi k}{n} & 0 \\ 0 & 0 & -1 \end{pmatrix}. \tag{12.36}$$

We can now ennunciate a general rule by which we can evaluate the characters of the representation Γ_m in the most general case:

1. Only those nuclei contribute to the characters which transformed into themselves.

2. Each nucleus that transforms into itself contributes $\pm 1 + 2\cos(2\pi k/n)$ to the character where + is for proper rotations, − is for improper rotations, n is the order of the rotation, k is the number of units of the rotation.

We list the contributions of each unmoved nucleus to the characters of the different operations:

$$E\colon\ 3,$$

$$C_2\colon\ 1 + 2\cos\frac{2\pi}{2} = -1,$$

$$C_3\colon\ 1 + 2\cos\frac{2\pi}{3} = 0,$$

$$C_3^{\,2}\colon\ 1 + 2\cos\frac{4\pi}{3} = 0,$$

$$C_4 = 1 + 2\cos\frac{2\pi}{4} = 1,$$

$$C_4^{\,3} = 1 + 2\cos\frac{6\pi}{4} = 1,$$

$$C_5 = 1 + 2\cos\frac{2\pi}{5} = 1 + 2\cos 72^\circ = C_5^{\,4},$$

$$C_6 = 1 + 2\cos\frac{2\pi}{6} = 2,$$

$$C_6^{\,5} = 1 + 2\cos\frac{10\pi}{6} = 2.$$

Also,

$$I = \text{Inversion} = -3,$$

$$\sigma = \text{Reflection} = 1,$$

$$S_3 = S_3^{\,2} = -2,$$

$$S_4 = S_4^{\,3} = -1,$$

$$S_5 = S_5^{\,4} = -1 + 2\cos 72^\circ,$$

$$S_5^{\,2} = S_5^{\,3} = -1 + 2\cos 144^\circ,$$

$$S_6 = S_6^{\,5} = 0,$$

$$C_5^{\,2} = 1 + 2\cos\frac{4\pi}{5} = 1 + 2\cos 144^\circ = C_5^{\,3},$$

$$C_5^{\,3} = 1 + 2\cos\frac{6\pi}{5} = 1 + 2\cos 216^\circ = C_5^{\,2},$$

$$C_5^{\,4} = 1 + 2\cos\frac{8\pi}{5} = 1 + 2\cos 288^\circ = C_5^{\,2}.$$

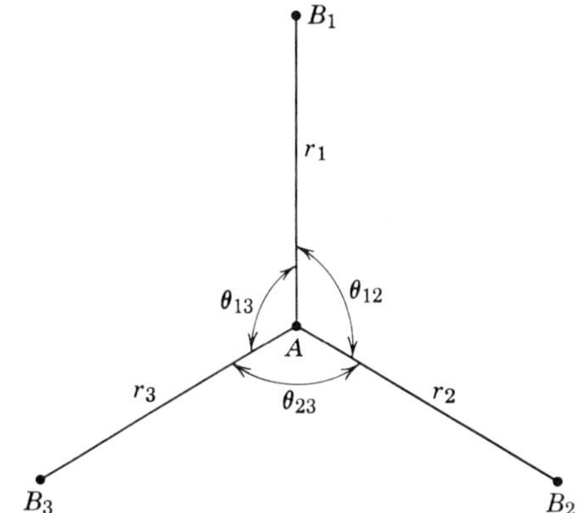

Fig. 12.1. AB_3 planar complex with internal coordinates.

Let us now consider the example represented in Fig. 12.1 of an AB_3 planar complex in which ion A stays at the center of an equilateral triangle and ions B at the vertices. Such a complex has symmetry D_{3h}. The characters for this group are reported in Table 12.1. The same table reports the characters for the representation Γ_m of dimension 12 obtained when taking as basis the 12 vectors $\mathbf{x}_i$, $\mathbf{y}_i$, and $\mathbf{z}_i$ which are attached to the A and B_r ions in Fig. 12.1; Γ_m is reduced as follows, in terms of the irreducible representation of D_{3h}:

$$\Gamma_m = A_1' + A_2' + 3E' + 2A_2'' + E''. \tag{12.37}$$

Three of the 12 degrees of freedom of the complex correspond to translations and three to rotations. Translations transform like x, y, z and rotations like

Table 12.1 Relevant Representations for a Planar AB_3 Complex

D_{3h}	E	$2C_3$	$3C_2$	σ_h	$2S_3$	$3\sigma_v$			
A_1'	1	1	1	1	1	1		x^2+y^2, z^2	Raman active
A_2'	1	1	-1	1	1	-1	L_z		
E'	2	-1	0	2	-1	0	(x, y)	(x^2-y^2, xy)	Raman, *IR* active
A_1''	1	1	1	-1	-1	-1			
A_2''	1	1	-1	-1	-1	1	z		*IR* active
E''	2	-1	0	-2	1	0	(L_x, L_y)	(xz, yz)	
Γ_m	12	0	-2	4	-2	2	$A_1' + A_2' + 3E' + 2A_2'' + E''$		
Γ_T	3	0	-1	1	-2	1	$E' + A_2''$		
Γ_R	3	0	-1	-1	2	-1	$A_2' + E''$		
$\Gamma_T + \Gamma_R$	6	0	-2	0	0	0	$A_2' + A_2'' + E' + E''$		
Γ_V	6	0	0	4	-2	2	$A_1' + 2E' + A_2''$		

L_x, L_y, L_z. The representations Γ_T and Γ_R, corresponding respectively to translations and rotations, reduce as follows

$$\begin{aligned}\Gamma_T &= E' + A_2'' \\ \Gamma_R &= A_2' + E''.\end{aligned} \tag{12.38}$$

The representation corresponding to the six vibrational degrees of freedom is then given by

$$\Gamma_V = \Gamma_m - (\Gamma_T + \Gamma_R) = A_1' + 2E' + A_2''. \tag{12.39}$$

The molecule has therefore four distinct normal modes of vibration (and four distinct vibrational frequencies).

4. THE USE OF SYMMETRY COORDINATES

A displacement pattern of the atoms in a molecule may be expressed in terms of *internal coordinates* such as spacings between atoms and angles between directions of bonds or in terms of *external coordinates*, the cartesian coordinates of the atoms.

We introduce now the new concept of *symmetry coordinates*. These coordinates are linear combinations of the internal coordinates which transform irreducibly according to the representations of the symmetry group of the molecule. These coordinates, in general, may differ from the normal coordinates of the molecule; we shall see the difference between the two types of coordinates by working with the example of the planar molecule AB_3 of Fig. 12.1.

We start by considering the internal coordinates as a basis for two representations $\Gamma(r)$ of the distances and $\Gamma(\theta)$ of the angles. We find the characters of these representations by applying the different operation and simply counting the number of unchanged coordinates (θ_{ij} is unchanged if r_i and r_j are interchanged). We have then

D_{3h}	E	$2C_3$	$3C_2$	σ_h	$2S_3$	$3\sigma_v$	
$\Gamma(r)$	3	0	1	3	0	1	$A_1' + E'$
$\Gamma(\theta)$	3	0	1	3	0	1	$A_1' + E'$.

However, according to our derivation of last section, this complex presents four modes of vibration: two with symmetry E, one with symmetry A_1' and one with symmetry A_2''.

Here we can see that we have one more A_1' representation and that representation A_2'' is missing. The reason for this fact is the following; in taking the internal coordinates we have disregarded including the angle between the plane of the molecule and the direction of the A-B bonds. The inclusion of this angle makes the number of internal coordinates equal to seven, one more than the number of degrees of freedom. This will cause a *redundancy* which is expressed in the presence of the A_1' representation in the reduced $\Gamma(\theta)$. If we now introduce this extra "angle coordinate" as θ_t we have

D_{3h}	E	$2C_3$	$3C_2$	σ_h	$2S_3$	$3\sigma_v$	
$\Gamma(\theta_t)$	1	1	-1	-1	-1	1	A_2''.

We have now to report an important result, whose proof may be found in [1], pages 117–125. The symmetry coordinates are indicated with the symbol $S(\Gamma_\gamma)$ where Γ_γ is the representation according to which S transforms. The result expresses the coordinates S as linear combinations of internal coordinates:

$$S(\Gamma_\gamma) = N \sum_R \chi_\gamma(R) RS_1, \qquad (12.40)$$

where N is a normalization factor, R is the generic symmetry operation, S_1 is *any* internal coordinate and RS_1 stands for the internal coordinate to which S_1 is transferred by the operation R. Relation 12.40 gives only one partner of a degenerate set of symmetry coordinates; the other partners can be found by considering a different coordinate S_1. We shall now illustrate what we have said with the example of the planar AB_3 complex.

Let us choose coordinate $S_1 = r_1$. In the following table we report in the first column the operations of the D_{3h} group; the other three columns indicate the internal coordinates r_i into which r_1 is transformed by a particular operation. For example, operation σ_h transforms r_1 into itself; of the two operations of the $2C_3$ class, one, C_3, transforms r_1 into r_2, the other, $C_3{}^2$, transforms r_1 into r_3. We have then

Table for Rr_1

R	r_1	r_2	r_3	$\chi(A_1')$	$\chi(E')$
E	1	0	0	1	2
$2C_3$	0	1	1	1	-1
$3C_2$	1	1	1	1	0
σ_h	1	0	0	1	2
$2S_3$	0	1	1	1	-1
$3\sigma_v$	1	1	1	1	0

$$\begin{aligned} S(A_{1r}') = N\{&\chi_{A_1'}(E)\, r_1 + \chi_{A_1'}(C_2)\, r_1 + \chi_{A_1'}(\sigma_h)\, r_1 + \chi_{A_1'}(\sigma_v)\, r_1 \\ &+ \chi_{A_1'}(C_3)\, r_2 + \chi_{A_1'}(C_2)\, r_2 + \chi_{A_1'}(S_3)\, r_2 + \chi_{A_1'}(\sigma_v)\, r_2 \\ &+ \chi_{A_1'}(C_3)\, r_3 + \chi_{A_1'}(C_2)\, r_3 + \chi_{A_1'}(S_3)\, r_3 + \chi_{A_1'}(\sigma_v)\, r_3\} \\ = N(4r_1 &+ 4r_2 + 4r_3) = \frac{1}{\sqrt{3}}(r_1 + r_2 + r_3). \end{aligned} \qquad (12.41)$$

Similarly,

$$S_a(E'_r) = N\{2r_1 + 2r_1 - r_2 - r_2 - r_3 - r_3\}$$

$$= N\{4r_1 - 2r_2 - 2r_3\} = \frac{1}{\sqrt{6}}(2r_1 - r_2 - r_3). \qquad (12.42)$$

To find the other partner of $S_a(E'_r)$ we choose now $S_1 = r_2$, we build a table for r_2 with the same method used for r_1 and we find

$$S_b(E'_r) = \frac{1}{\sqrt{6}}(2r_2 - r_1 - r_3). \qquad (12.43)$$

Let us consider now coordinate θ_{12}. The following table elucidates how this coordinate transforms under the operations of the group:

Table for $R\theta_{12}$

R	θ_{12}	θ_{23}	θ_{31}	$\chi(A'_1)$	$\chi(E')$
E	1	0	0	1	2
$2C_3$	0	1	1	1	−1
$3C_2$	1	1	1	1	0
σ_h	1	0	0	1	2
$2S_3$	0	1	1	1	−1
$3\sigma_v$	1	1	1	1	0

We then get

$$S(A'_{1\theta}) = \frac{1}{\sqrt{3}}(\theta_{12} + \theta_{23} + \theta_{31}),$$

$$S_a(E'_\theta) = \frac{1}{\sqrt{6}}(2\theta_{12} - \theta_{23} - \theta_{31}), \qquad (12.44)$$

$$S_b(E'_\theta) = \frac{1}{\sqrt{6}}(2\theta_{23} - \theta_{12} - \theta_{31}).$$

$S(A'_{1\theta})$ implies a change of the angles by the same amount at the same time; this change cannot take place if the vibration is planar. On the other hand, we know that we have only one normal mode A'_1 and this is already represented by the *breathing mode* $S(A_{1r})$. We are then left with the last internal coordinate, the angle between the A-B bonds and the plane of the B_i atoms; this last internal coordinate is a normal coordinate corresponding to the representation A''_2. The symmetry coordinates of the AB_3 planar complex can now be expressed by

$$
\begin{aligned}
A_1(r) &\equiv \frac{1}{\sqrt{3}}(r_1 + r_2 + r_3), \\
E'(r) &\equiv \begin{cases} \dfrac{1}{\sqrt{6}}(2r_1 - r_2 - r_3), \\[2ex] \dfrac{1}{\sqrt{6}}(2r_2 - r_1 - r_3), \end{cases} \\
E'(\theta) &\equiv \begin{cases} \dfrac{1}{\sqrt{6}}(2\theta_{12} - \theta_{23} - \theta_{31}), \\[2ex] \dfrac{1}{\sqrt{6}}(2\theta_{23} - \theta_{12} - \theta_{31}), \end{cases} \\
A_2''(\theta_t) &\equiv \theta_t
\end{aligned}
\tag{12.45}
$$

These symmetry coordinates are not to be confused with the normal coordinates of the molecule; although they transform irreducibly according to the symmetry group of the molecule, they do not allow the complete diagonalization of the secular determinant (12.17). Rather, when kinetic and potential energy of the system are expressed in terms of them this determinant appears in a reduced form which contains a number of blocks, each corresponding to a certain representation and of dimension equal to the number of linearly independent symmetry coordinates associated with that representation.[2] At this stage the problem is not yet completely solved; however, the secular determinant, in its reduced form, is much more manageable. The frequencies of vibrations can be found by breaking up the determinant and solving the eigenvalue problem for each block. The complete diagonalization of the dynamical determinant will give the eigenfrequencies and the eigenvectors that will allow us to express the normal coordinates as linear combinations of the symmetry coordinates.

In the specific example of the AB_3 planar complex the presence of two E' representations requires the solution of a 4×4 secular determinant. The two modes $E'(r)$ and $E'(\theta)$ are actually *mixed* in the sense that the molecule does not vibrate according to the symmetry coordinates corresponding to $E'(r)$ and $E'(\theta)$ but according to a motion that is a linear combination of the two.

5. THE QUANTUM THEORY OF MOLECULAR VIBRATIONS

We have written the Hamiltonian of a molecule of N particles as

$$
H = \frac{1}{2}\sum_q^{3N-6}(P_q^{\,2} + \omega_q^{\,2}Q_q^{\,2}), \tag{12.46}
$$

where

$$Q_q = \sum_i \sqrt{m_i}\, h_{qi} u_i,$$

$$P_q = \dot{Q}_q = \sum_i \frac{h_{qi}}{\sqrt{m_i}} p_i$$

When we go to quantum mechanics, u_i and p_i become operators with the following commutation relations:

$$[u_i, p_i] = i\hbar\delta_{ij}, \qquad [u_i, u_j] = [p_i, p_j] = 0. \tag{12.48}$$

Q_q and P_q also become operators, with commutation relations which we may derive from (12.47) and (12.48):

$$[Q_q, P_{q'}] = i\hbar\delta_{qq'}, \qquad [Q_q, Q_{q'}] = [P_q, P_{q'}] = 0. \tag{12.49}$$

It is possible to consider every term in the Hamiltonian as representing a harmonic oscillator. If we express the operators in an explicit form,

$$Q \rightarrow Q, \qquad P \rightarrow -i\hbar\frac{\partial}{\partial Q}, \tag{12.50}$$

the Hamiltonian of a single oscillator is given by

$$h = \tfrac{1}{2}(P^2 + \omega^2 Q^2) = \frac{1}{2}\left(-\hbar^2\frac{\partial^2}{\partial Q^2} + \omega^2 Q^2\right). \tag{12.51}$$

The eigenvalue equation

$$h\psi_n = E_n\psi_n \tag{12.52}$$

bears [3]:

$$E_n = \hbar\omega(n + \tfrac{1}{2}), \tag{12.53}$$

$$\psi_n(Q) = \mathcal{N}\,[\exp(-\tfrac{1}{2}\alpha^2 Q^2)]H_n(\alpha Q), \tag{12.54}$$

where

$$\mathcal{N} = \left[\frac{(\omega/\hbar)^{1/2}}{2^n n!\,\pi^{1/2}}\right]^{1/2}, \qquad \alpha = \left(\frac{\omega}{\hbar}\right)^{1/2}, \tag{12.55}$$

where H_n is the Hermitian polynomial of order n. The first few polynomials of this type are

$$\begin{aligned} H_0(x) &= 1, \\ H_1(x) &= 2x, \\ H_2(x) &= 4x^2 - 2, \\ H_3(x) &= 8x^3 - 12x. \end{aligned} \tag{12.56}$$

We call the number n the *vibrational quantum number*; this number designates the degree of excitation of a particular oscillator-normal mode. Therefore $n = 0$ designates the ground state, $n = 1$ the first excited state, and so on.

The most general vibrational state of a molecule, with the qth vibrational oscillator in the n_qth excited state, can be expressed by the function

$$\begin{aligned} \psi(n_1, n_2, \ldots) &= \left(\prod_q \mathcal{N}_q\right) \exp\left(-\frac{1}{2}\sum_q \alpha_q^2 Q_q^2\right) \prod_q H_{n_q}(\alpha_q Q_q) \\ &= \prod_q \psi_{n_q}(Q_q). \end{aligned} \tag{12.57}$$

The ground state vibrational function is given by

$$\psi(0_1, 0_2, \ldots) = \left(\prod_q \mathcal{N}_q\right) \exp\left(-\frac{1}{2}\sum_q \alpha_q^2 Q_q^2\right) = \prod_q \psi_0(Q_q). \tag{12.58}$$

In this expression the exponent has the same form as the potential energy and is invariant with respect to all the operations of the symmetry group of the molecule. Therefore the ground state function belongs to the A_1 representation of the molecular symmetry group.

The excited vibrational state with only one oscillator Q_k in its first excited state is represented by

$$\begin{aligned} &\psi(0_1, 0_2, \ldots, 0_{k-1}, 1_k, 0_{k+1}, \ldots) \\ &\quad = \left(\prod_q \mathcal{N}_q\right) \exp\left(-\frac{1}{2}\sum_q \alpha_q^2 Q_q^2\right) H_1(\alpha_k Q_k) \\ &\quad = \left(\prod_q \mathcal{N}_q\right) \exp\left(-\frac{1}{2}\sum_q \alpha_q^2 Q_q^2\right) 2\alpha_k Q_k = \left[\prod_{q \neq k} \psi_{0_q}(Q_q)\right] \psi_{1_k}(Q_k) \end{aligned} \tag{12.59}$$

and transforms like Q_k.

6. THE SELECTION RULES FOR INFRARED AND RAMAN TRANSITIONS. THE FERMI RESONANCE

We are interested mainly in the so-called *fundamental transitions* or *fundamentals* of a molecule. These transitions connect the ground state of the molecule in which all the vibrational oscillators are in their ground states

($n_q = 0$ for all q's) and an excited state of the molecule in which one vibrational oscillator is in its *first* excited state ($n_k = 1$) and all the other oscillators are in their ground states ($n_q = 0$ for $q \neq k$).

The fundamental transitions may be of two different types: *infrared* (*IR*) and *Raman*.

An infrared transition corresponds to the absorption of one photon by the electric dipole mechanism. The energy of the photon excites one vibrational oscillator of frequency equal to the frequency of the incident photon. To evaluate the selection rules for transitions of this type we write down the relevant matrix element (see Section 2 of Chapter 14):

$$\int \psi(0_1, 0_2, \ldots, 0_i, \ldots)\, r_\alpha \psi(0_1, 0_2, \ldots, 1_i, \ldots)\, d\tau, \tag{12.60}$$

where $r_\alpha = x, y, z$. The initial state representation is the perfectly symmetric A_1, the final state representation is $\Gamma(Q_i)$; then the matrix element is different from zero only when $\Gamma(r_\alpha)$ coincides with $\Gamma(Q_i)$. From this we derive the following theorem:

A fundamental transition produces an infrared absorption band if the corresponding normal mode and one or more of the electric dipole coordinates (x, y, z) *belong to the same irreducible representation of the molecular symmetry group.*

A Raman absorption process corresponds to a mechanism by which the energy of an incident photon is used *in part* to excite one of the vibrational oscillators of the molecule. This process produces a *Raman shift* in the frequency of incident photons by an amount $\hbar\omega_i$ where ω_i is the frequency of a Raman active normal mode. To find out what these normal modes are we write down the relevant matrix element,

$$\int \psi(0_1, 0_2, \ldots, 0_i, \ldots)\, P_\alpha \psi(0_1, 0_2, \ldots, 0_i, \ldots)\, d\tau, \tag{12.61}$$

where $P_\alpha = x^2, y^2, z^2, xy, yz, zx$. This matrix element is different from zero only if $\Gamma(P_\alpha)$ and $\Gamma(Q_i)$ coincide. From this we derive the following theorem:

A fundamental transition produces a Raman shift if the corresponding normal mode and one or more of the polarization coordinates $(x^2, y^2, z^2, xy, yz, zx)$ *belong to the same irreducible representation of the symmetry group.*

Let us consider now as an example the case of an AB_3 planar complex with symmetry D_{3h}, which we already examined in Secs. 3 and 4 of this chapter. The characters of the irreducible representations of the D_{3h} group and of other relevant representations for the AB_3 complex are given in Table

12.1. The normal modes of vibration of this molecule are given by

$$\Gamma_V = A_1' + 2E' + A_2''. \tag{12.62}$$

Since x and y transform according to the E' representation and z according to the A_2'' representation, the two E' modes and the A_2'' mode are infrared active. On the other hand, z^2 transforms according to A_1'; also $x^2 - y^2$ and xy transform according to E'. Therefore the normal mode A_1' and the two E' modes are Raman active. In summary we have the following selection rules:

A_1': Raman active,
E': Raman + infrared active,
A_2'': infrared active.

We want to mention the fact that transitions may also take place from the ground state to an excited vibrational state in which one oscillator is in its second, third, . . . ith excited state. Correspondingly, we have what we call *the first, second, . . . , and (i — 1)th overtones*. Selection rules for this type of transition may be worked out by using group theoretical arguments; careful attention has to be given to cases in which degenerate modes are responsible for these transitions. For this the reader may see [1].

Other transitions may take place when two or more vibrational oscillators get excited at the same time; these transitions are called *combination tones*.

Transitions can also take place from an initial state in which the molecule has one or more oscillators in excited states; they can take place when some oscillators are thermally excited. For these reasons they are called *hot transitions*.

The overtones are, in general, an order of magnitude lower in intensity than the fundamentals; this is true especially for the Raman transitions. Circumstances may arise, however, in which an overtone or a combination tone "borrows" some intensity from a fundamental. This happens when an overtone or a combination tone has a frequency close to the frequency of a fundamental and, in addition, both overtone (or combination tone) and fundamental belong to the *same* representation of the symmetry group of the molecule. A mixing of the two modes occurs, the intensity of the overtone is enhanced, and overtone and fundamentals are shifted in energy. This phenomenon is called *Fermi resonance* and is observed, for example, in CO_2 in which the fundamental 1334 cm^{-1} and the first overtone of a 667 cm^{-1} mode interact to produce in the Raman spectrum two bands, one at 1285 and the other at 1388 cm^{-1}.

Molecules in gases or liquids behave as free molecules in the sense that the selection rules determined by the molecular symmetry control the transitions among the different vibrational levels. But a molecule may find itself in an environment where other atoms or other molecules are present, like in a

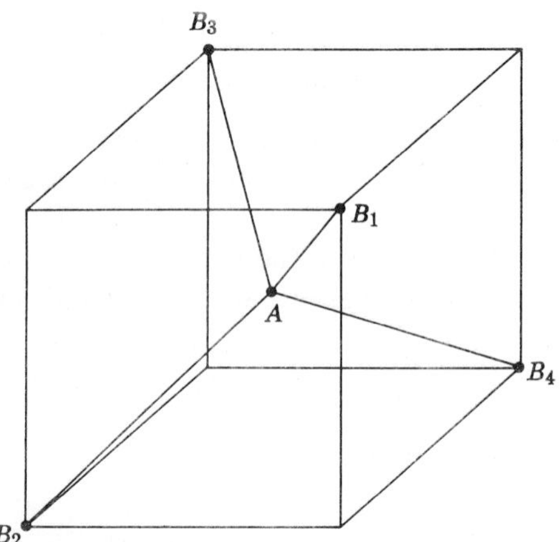

Fig. 12.2. A tetrahedral complex AB_4 (internal coordinates are: r_i = distance between A and B_i, θ_{ij} = angle between $A - B_i$ and $A - B_j$ bonds).

crystal. In this case the proper symmetry that controls the selection rules is the *site symmetry* or the symmetry of the site in which the molecule finds itself. This symmetry is, in general, lower than the molecular symmetry, though occasionally it may be the same. The lowering of the symmetry may cause a change of the selection rules and a lifting of some degeneracies in the vibrational modes.

7. THE NORMAL MODES AND THE SYMMETRY COORDINATES OF A TETRAHEDRAL COMPLEX AB_4

Let us consider now a tetrahedral complex AB_4, as represented in Fig. 12.2. The characters of the irreducible representation of the T_d symmetry group and of other relevant representations for this complex are reported in Table

Table 12.2 Relevant Representations for a Tetrahedral AB_4 Complex

T_d	E	$8C_3$	$3C_2$	$6S_4$	$6\sigma_d$			
A_1	1	1	1	1	1		$x^2+y^2+z^2$	Raman active
A_2	1	1	1	-1	-1			
E	2	-1	2	0	0		$(2z^2-x^2-y^2, x^2-y^2)$	Raman active
T_1	3	0	-1	1	-1	(L_x, L_y, L_z)		
T_2	3	0	-1	-1	1	(x, y, z)	(xy, yz, zx)	Raman, *IR* active
Γ_m	15	0	-1	-1	3	$A_1+E+T_1+3T_2$		
$\Gamma_T+\Gamma_R$	6	0	-2	0	0	T_1+T_2		
Γ_V	9	0	1	-1	3	A_1+E+2T_2		

12.2. The normal modes of vibration of this molecule are given by

$$\Gamma_V = A_1 + E + 2T_2, \tag{12.63}$$

with the following selection rules:

A_1: Raman active,
E: Raman active,
T_2: Raman + infrared active.

We now want to find the symmetry coordinates of this complex in terms of the internal coordinates defined in Fig. 12.2.

We start considering these coordinates as bases for two representations $\Gamma(r)$ of the distances and $\Gamma(\theta)$ of the angles:

T_d	E	C_3	C_2	S_4	σ_d	
$\Gamma(r)$	4	1	0	0	2	$A_1 + T_2$
$\Gamma(\theta)$	6	0	2	0	2	$A_1 + E + T_2$.

We see immediately that one A_1 representation is redundant. Let us proceed as in Section 4 of this chapter by choosing $S_1 = r_1$ and forming the following table:

Table for Rr_1

R	r_1	r_2	r_3	r_4	$\chi(A_1)$	$\chi(T_2)$
E	1	0	0	0	1	3
$8C_3$	2	2	2	2	1	0
$3C_2$	0	1	1	1	1	−1
$6S_4$	0	2	2	2	1	−1
$6\sigma_d$	3	1	1	1	1	1

We have, from (12.40),

$$S(A_{1r}) = N \sum_R \chi_A(R)\, Rr_1 = \tfrac{1}{2}(r_1 + r_2 + r_3 + r_4), \tag{12.64}$$

$$S(T_{2r}) = N \sum_R \chi_{T_1}(R)\, Rr_1 = \frac{1}{2\sqrt{3}}(3r_1 - r_2 - r_3 - r_4). \tag{12.65}$$

Other components of $S(T_{2r})$ are obtained by choosing $S_1 = r_2$ and $S_1 = r_3$.

Let also $S_1 = \theta_{12}$. The corresponding table is given by

Table for $R\theta_{12}$

R	θ_{12}	θ_{13}	θ_{14}	θ_{23}	θ_{24}	θ_{34}	$\chi(A_1)$	$\chi(E)$	$\chi(T_2)$
E	1	0	0	0	0	0	1	2	3
$8C_3$	0	2	2	2	2	0	1	−1	0
$3C_2$	1	0	0	0	0	2	1	2	−1
$6S_4$	0	1	1	1	1	2	1	0	−1
$6\sigma_d$	2	1	1	1	1	0	1	0	1

We have then, from (12.40),

$$S(A_{1\theta}) = N \sum_R \chi_{A_1}(R)\, R\theta_{12}$$

$$= \frac{1}{\sqrt{6}}(\theta_{12} + \theta_{13} + \theta_{14} + \theta_{23} + \theta_{24} + \theta_{34}), \tag{12.66}$$

$$S(E_\theta) = N \sum_R \chi_E(R)\, R\theta_{12}$$

$$= \frac{1}{2\sqrt{3}}(2\theta_{12} - \theta_{13} - \theta_{14} - \theta_{23} - \theta_{24} + 2\theta_{34}), \tag{12.67}$$

$$S(T_{2\theta}) = N \sum_R \chi_{T_2}(R)\, R\theta_{12} = \frac{1}{\sqrt{2}}(\theta_{12} - \theta_{34}). \tag{12.68}$$

Excluding the obviously redundant coordinate $S(A_{1\theta})$, the symmetry coordinates of the tetrahedral complex AB_4 are then given by

$$A_1(r) \equiv \tfrac{1}{2}(r_1 + r_2 + r_3 + r_4);$$

$$T_2(r) \equiv \begin{cases} \dfrac{1}{2\sqrt{3}}(3r_1 - r_2 - r_3 - r_4) \\ \dfrac{1}{2\sqrt{3}}(3r_2 - r_1 - r_3 - r_4) \\ \dfrac{1}{2\sqrt{3}}(3r_3 - r_1 - r_2 - r_4); \end{cases}$$

$$E(\theta) \equiv \begin{cases} \dfrac{1}{2\sqrt{3}}(2\theta_{12} - \theta_{13} - \theta_{14} - \theta_{23} - \theta_{24} + 2\theta_{34}) \\ \dfrac{1}{2\sqrt{3}}(2\theta_{24} - \theta_{12} - \theta_{14} - \theta_{23} - \theta_{34} + 2\theta_{13}); \end{cases} \tag{12.69}$$

$$T_2(\theta) \equiv \begin{cases} \dfrac{1}{\sqrt{2}}(\theta_{12} - \theta_{34}) \\ \dfrac{1}{\sqrt{2}}(\theta_{14} - \theta_{23}) \\ \dfrac{1}{\sqrt{2}}(\theta_{13} - \theta_{24}). \end{cases}$$

8. THE NORMAL MODES AND THE SYMMETRY COORDINATES OF AN OCTAHEDRAL COMPLEX AB_6

Let us consider now an octahedral complex AB_6, as represented in Fig. 12.3. The characters of the irreducible representations of the O_h symmetry group and of other relevant representations for this complex are given in Table 12.3. The normal modes of this molecule are given by

$$\Gamma_V = A_{1g} + E_g + 2T_{1u} + T_{2g} + T_{2u}, \tag{12.70}$$

with the following selection rules:

$$\begin{aligned} A_{1g}&: \text{ Raman active,} \\ E_g&: \text{ Raman active,} \\ T_{1u}&: \text{ infrared active,} \\ T_{2g}&: \text{ Raman active,} \\ T_{2u}&: \text{ inactive.} \end{aligned}$$

We notice that no mode is Raman and infrared-active at the same time, contrary to what was found in preceding examples. We shall see now that this property is common to all complexes with a center of symmetry.

The electric dipole components, being essentially odd functions, must belong to odd (u) representations if the molecule has a center of symmetry (i.e., if the symmetry group contains the operation inversion). On the other hand, the vibrational ground state belongs to the A_{1g} representation; therefore in a molecule with a center of symmetry like the octahedral complex AB_6 the final state of an infrared transition and the normal mode responsible for the transition must belong to the same odd (u) representation of the relevant electric dipole component.

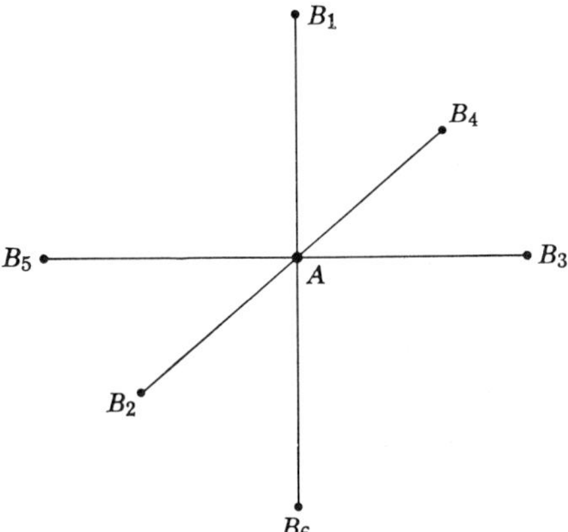

Fig. 12.3. An octahedral complex AB_6 (internal coordinates are: r_i = distance between A and B_i, θ_{ij} = angle between $A - B_i$ and $A - B_j$ bonds).

Table 12.3 Relevant Representations for an Octahedral AB_6 Complex

O_h	E	$6C_4$	$3C_2$ $(=C_4^2)$	$6C_2'$	$8C_3$	I	$6S_4$ $(=6IC_4)$	$3\sigma_h$ $(=3IC_2)$	$6\sigma_h'$ $(=6IC_2')$	$8S_6$ $(=8IC_3)$		
A_{1g}	1	1	1	1	1	1	1	1	1	1	$x^2+y^2+z^2$	Raman active
A_{1u}	1	1	1	1	1	−1	−1	−1	−1	−1		
A_{2g}	1	−1	1	−1	1	1	−1	−1	−1	1		
A_{2u}	1	−1	1	−1	1	−1	1	−1	1	−1		
E_g	2	0	2	0	−1	2	0	2	0	−1	$(2z^2-x^2-y^2, x^2-y^2)$	Raman active
E_u	2	0	2	0	−1	−2	0	−2	0	1		
T_{1g}	3	1	−1	−1	0	3	1	−1	−1	0	(L_x, L_y, L_z)	
T_{1u}	3	1	−1	−1	0	−3	−1	1	1	0	(x, y, z)	*IR* active
T_{2g}	3	−1	−1	1	0	3	−1	−1	1	0	(xy, yz, zx)	Raman active
T_{2u}	3	−1	−1	1	0	−3	1	1	−1	0		Inactive
Γ_m	21	3	−3	−1	0	−3	−1	5	3	0	$A_{1g}+E_g+3T_{1u}+T_{1g}+T_{2g}+T_{2u}$	
$\Gamma_T+\Gamma_R$	6	2	−2	−2	0	0	0	0	0	0	$T_{1g}+T_{1u}$	
Γ_V	15	1	−1	1	0	−3	−1	5	3	0	$A_{1g}+E_g+2T_{1u}+T_{2g}+T_{2u}$	

On the contrary, the polarization components are essentially even functions, and as such belong to even (g) representations of the symmetry group. In a molecule with a center of symmetry the normal mode responsible for a Raman shift must belong to the same even (g) representation of the relevant polarization component.

A consequence of this is the fact that in a molecule with a center of symmetry a normal mode cannot be at the same time infrared and Raman active.

We want now to find the symmetry coordinates of the octahedral complex AB_6 in terms of the internal coordinates defined in Fig. 12.3:

$$\begin{aligned} &\text{6 distances:} \quad r_1, r_2, r_3, r_4, r_5, r_6; \\ &\text{12 angles:} \quad \theta_{12}, \theta_{13}, \theta_{14}, \theta_{15}, \\ &\qquad\qquad\quad \theta_{23}, \theta_{34}, \theta_{45}, \theta_{52}, \\ &\qquad\qquad\quad \theta_{62}, \theta_{63}, \theta_{64}, \theta_{65}. \end{aligned}$$

Since the number of vibrational degrees of freedom is 15, we have a redundancy of 3 coordinates.

We have now to build the character table for the $\Gamma(r)$ and $\Gamma(\theta)$ representations:

O_h	E	$6C_4$	$3C_2$	$6C_2'$	$8C_3$	I	$6S_4$	$3\sigma_h$	$6\sigma_h'$	$8S_6$	
$\Gamma(r)$	6	2	2	2	0	0	0	4	2	0	$A_{1g} + E_g + T_{1u}$
$\Gamma(\theta)$	12	0	0	2	0	0	0	4	2	0	$A_{1g} + E_g + T_{2g} + T_{2u} + T_{1u}$

We can see immediately that we have one A_{1g} and one E_g more than we need.

Let $S_1 = r_1$. We get

Table for Rr_1

R	r_1	r_2	r_3	r_4	r_5	r_6	$\chi(A_{1g})$	$\chi(E_g)$	$\chi(T_{1u})$
E	1	0	0	0	0	0	1	2	3
$6C_4$	2	1	1	1	1	0	1	0	1
$3C_2$	1	0	0	0	0	2	1	2	-1
$6C_2'$	0	1	1	1	1	2	1	0	-1
$8C_3$	0	2	2	2	2	0	1	-1	0
I	0	0	0	0	0	1	1	2	-3
$6S_4$	0	1	1	1	1	2	1	0	-1
$3\sigma_h$	2	0	0	0	0	1	1	2	1
$6\sigma_h'$	2	1	1	1	1	0	1	0	1
$8S_6$	0	2	2	2	2	0	1	-1	0

From the preceding table we obtain

$$S(A_{1gr}) = N \sum_R \chi_{A_{1g}}(R)\, Rr_1$$

$$= \frac{1}{\sqrt{6}}(r_1 + r_2 + r_3 + r_4 + r_5 + r_6); \tag{12.71}$$

$$S(E_{gr}) = N \sum_R \chi_{E_g}(R)\, Rr_1$$

$$= \frac{1}{2\sqrt{3}}(2r_1 - r_2 - r_3 - r_4 - r_5 + 2r_6); \tag{12.72}$$

$$S(T_{1ur}) = N \sum_R \chi_{T_{1u}}(R)\, Rr_1$$

$$= \frac{1}{\sqrt{2}}(r_1 - r_6). \tag{12.73}$$

Let $S_1 = \theta_{12}$. We get the table shown opposite. From this table we derive:

$$S(A_{1g\theta}) = N \sum_R \chi_{A_{1g}}(R)\, R\theta_{12}$$

$$= \frac{1}{2\sqrt{3}}(\theta_{12} + \theta_{13} + \theta_{14} + \theta_{15} + \theta_{23} + \theta_{34} + \theta_{45} + \theta_{52} + \theta_{62} + \theta_{63} + \theta_{64} + \theta_{65}), \tag{12.74}$$

$$S(E_{g\theta}) = N \sum_R \chi_{E_g}(R)\, R\theta_{12}$$

$$= \frac{1}{2\sqrt{6}}[2(\theta_{12} + \theta_{14} + \theta_{62} + \theta_{64}) - (\theta_{13} + \theta_{63} + \theta_{65} + \theta_{51} + \theta_{23} + \theta_{34} + \theta_{45} + \theta_{52})]. \tag{12.75}$$

We can obtain, by analogy, the other normal coordinate of $E_{g\theta}$:

$$N \sum_R \chi_{E_u}(R)\, R\theta_{23} = \frac{1}{2\sqrt{6}}[2(\theta_{23} + \theta_{34} + \theta_{45} + \theta_{52}) - (\theta_{12} + \theta_{14} + \theta_{62} + \theta_{64} + \theta_{13} + \theta_{63} + \theta_{65} + \theta_{51})]. \tag{12.76}$$

It is clear that the normal coordinates (12.74), (12.75), and (12.76) are redundant. Let us proceed now to find the nonredundant normal coordinates,

$$S(T_{2g\theta}) = N \sum_R \chi_{T_{2g}}(R)\, R\theta_{12}$$

$$= \tfrac{1}{2}(\theta_{12} + \theta_{64} - \theta_{14} - \theta_{62}), \tag{12.77}$$

$$S(T_{2u\theta}) = N \sum_R \chi_{T_{2u}}(R)\, R\theta_{12}$$

$$= \frac{1}{2\sqrt{5}}(2\theta_{12} - 2\theta_{14} - 2\theta_{64} + \theta_{34} + \theta_{45} - \theta_{52} - \theta_{23} + \theta_{63} + \theta_{65} - \theta_{13} - \theta_{15}). \tag{12.78}$$

$$S(T_{1u\theta}) = N \sum_R \chi_{T_{1u}}(R)\, R\theta_{12}$$

$$= \tfrac{1}{4}(2\theta_{12} - 2\theta_{64} + \theta_{23} + \theta_{52} - \theta_{45} - \theta_{34} + \theta_{13} + \theta_{15} - \theta_{63} - \theta_{65}). \tag{12.79}$$

Table for $R\theta_{12}$

R	θ_{12}	θ_{13}	θ_{14}	θ_{15}	θ_{23}	θ_{34}	θ_{45}	θ_{52}	θ_{62}	θ_{63}	θ_{64}	θ_{65}	$\chi(A_{1g})$	$\chi(E_g)$	$\chi(T_{2g})$	$\chi(T_{2u})$	$\chi(T_{1u})$
E	1	0	0	0	0	0	0	0	0	0	0	0	1	2	3	3	3
$6C_4$	0	1	1	1	1	0	0	1	1	0	0	0	1	0	−1	−1	1
$3C_2$	0	0	1	0	0	0	0	0	1	0	1	0	1	2	−1	−1	−1
$6C_2'$	1	0	0	0	0	1	1	0	0	1	1	1	1	0	1	1	−1
$8C_3$	0	1	0	1	1	1	1	1	0	1	0	1	1	−1	0	0	0
I	0	0	0	0	0	0	0	0	0	0	1	0	1	2	3	−3	−3
$6S_4$	0	0	1	0	0	1	1	0	1	1	0	1	1	0	−1	1	−1
$3\sigma_h$	1	0	1	0	0	0	0	0	1	0	0	0	1	2	−1	1	1
$6\sigma_h'$	1	1	0	1	1	0	0	1	0	0	1	0	1	0	1	−1	1
$8S_6$	0	1	0	1	1	1	1	1	0	1	0	1	1	−1	0	0	0

The normal coordinates can now be listed:

$$A_{1g} \equiv \left\{ \frac{1}{\sqrt{6}} (r_1 + r_2 + r_3 + r_4 + r_5 + r_6), \right.$$

$$E_g \equiv \begin{cases} \dfrac{1}{2\sqrt{3}} (2r_1 + 2r_6 - r_2 - r_3 - r_4 - r_5) \\ \dfrac{1}{2\sqrt{3}} (2r_2 + 2r_4 - r_1 - r_3 - r_5 - r_6), \end{cases}$$

$$T_{1u} \equiv \begin{cases} \dfrac{1}{\sqrt{2}} (r_1 - r_6) \\ \dfrac{1}{\sqrt{2}} (r_3 - r_5) \\ \dfrac{1}{\sqrt{2}} (r_2 - r_4), \end{cases}$$

$$T_{2g} \equiv \begin{cases} \frac{1}{2}(\theta_{12} + \theta_{64} - \theta_{14} - \theta_{62}) \\ \frac{1}{2}(\theta_{23} + \theta_{45} - \theta_{43} - \theta_{52}) \\ \frac{1}{2}(\theta_{15} + \theta_{63} - \theta_{13} - \theta_{65}), \end{cases} \tag{12.80}$$

$$T_{2u} \equiv \begin{cases} \dfrac{1}{2\sqrt{5}} (2\theta_{12} - 2\theta_{14} - 2\theta_{64} + \theta_{34} + \theta_{45} \\ \qquad - \theta_{52} - \theta_{23} + \theta_{63} + \theta_{65} - \theta_{13} - \theta_{15}) \\ \dfrac{1}{2\sqrt{5}} (2\theta_{23} - 2\theta_{25} - 2\theta_{45} + \theta_{15} + \theta_{56} \\ \qquad - \theta_{63} - \theta_{13} + \theta_{64} + \theta_{41} - \theta_{62} - \theta_{12}) \\ \dfrac{1}{2\sqrt{5}} (2\theta_{63} - 2\theta_{31} - 2\theta_{51} + \theta_{12} + \theta_{14} \\ \qquad - \theta_{62} - \theta_{64} + \theta_{52} + \theta_{54} - \theta_{23} - \theta_{34}), \end{cases}$$

$$T_{1u} \equiv \begin{cases} \frac{1}{4}(2\theta_{12} - 2\theta_{64} + \theta_{23} + \theta_{52} \\ \qquad - \theta_{45} - \theta_{34} + \theta_{13} + \theta_{15} - \theta_{63} - \theta_{65}) \\ \frac{1}{4}(2\theta_{23} - 2\theta_{45} + \theta_{63} + \theta_{13} \\ \qquad - \theta_{65} - \theta_{15} + \theta_{62} + \theta_{12} - \theta_{64} - \theta_{41}) \\ \frac{1}{4}(2\theta_{63} - 2\theta_{51} + \theta_{62} + \theta_{64} \\ \qquad - \theta_{12} - \theta_{14} + \theta_{23} + \theta_{34} - \theta_{52} - \theta_{54}). \end{cases}$$

REFERENCES

[1] E. B. Wilson, J. C. Decius, and P. C. Cross, *Molecular Vibrations*, McGraw-Hill, New York, 1955.
[2] J. E. Rosenthal and G. M. Murphy, "Group Theory and the Vibrations of Polyatomic Molecules," *Rev. Mod. Phys.*, **8**, 377 (1936).
[3] V. Rojansky, *Introduction to Quantum Mechanics*, Prentice-Hall, Englewood Cliffs, N.J., 1938, p. 87.

13

Lattice Vibrations

1. THE GEOMETRY OF CRYSTALLINE SOLIDS

1.1 Crystal Lattice and Reciprocal Lattice

In a periodic lattic the position of a lattice point is represented by a vector,

$$\mathbf{R}_n = n_1\mathbf{a}_1 + n_2\mathbf{a}_2 + n_3\mathbf{a}_3, \tag{13.1}$$

where $\mathbf{a}_1$, $\mathbf{a}_2$, and $\mathbf{a}_3$ are noncoplanar vectors called *basis vectors* and n_1, n_2, and n_3 are positive integers or zero.

The basis vectors define a *unit cell* whose volume is given by

$$\Omega_a = \mathbf{a}_1 \cdot \mathbf{a}_2 \times \mathbf{a}_3. \tag{13.2}$$

We call *primitive unit cell* the smallest unit cell in the lattice. We define also the so-called *Wigner-Seitz unit cell* in the following way. We consider a generic lattice point at the center of the cell and draw lines connecting this point with all the other points of the lattice; then we intersect each line with a plane perpendicular to it at midpoint between the center of the cell and the lattice point reached by the line. The volume enclosed by all these planes is the Wigner-Seitz unit cell.

We want also to define the *reciprocal lattice* as the lattice whose basis vectors $\mathbf{b}_i$ are given by

$$\mathbf{b}_i \cdot \mathbf{a}_j = 2\pi\delta_{ij} \tag{13.3}$$

or

$$\begin{aligned}
\mathbf{b}_1 &= 2\pi \frac{\mathbf{a}_2 \times \mathbf{a}_3}{\mathbf{a}_1 \cdot \mathbf{a}_2 \times \mathbf{a}_3} = \frac{\pi_a}{\Omega_a} \mathbf{a}_2 \times \mathbf{a}_3, \\
\mathbf{b}_2 &= 2\pi \frac{\mathbf{a}_3 \times \mathbf{a}_1}{\mathbf{a}_1 \cdot \mathbf{a}_2 \times \mathbf{a}_3} = \frac{2\pi}{\Omega_a} \mathbf{a}_3 \times \mathbf{a}_1, \\
\mathbf{b}_3 &= 2\pi \frac{\mathbf{a}_1 \times \mathbf{a}_2}{\mathbf{a}_1 \cdot \mathbf{a}_2 \times \mathbf{a}_3} = \frac{2\pi}{\Omega_a} \mathbf{a}_1 \times \mathbf{a}_2.
\end{aligned} \tag{13.4}$$

The volume of the primitive cell of the reciprocal lattice is given by

$$\Omega_b = \mathbf{b}_1 \cdot \mathbf{b}_2 \times \mathbf{b}_3 = \frac{(2\pi)^3}{\Omega_a}. \tag{13.5}$$

The reciprocal lattice is determined by the vectors $\mathbf{b}_i$:

$$\mathbf{k}_\eta = \eta_1 \mathbf{b}_1 + \eta_2 \mathbf{b}_2 + \eta_3 \mathbf{b}_3, \tag{13.6}$$

where η_1, η_2, and η_3 are positive integers or zero. From (13.3) we have

$$\begin{aligned} \mathbf{k}_\eta \cdot \mathbf{R}_n &= (\eta_1 \mathbf{b}_1 + \eta_2 \mathbf{b}_2 + \eta_3 \mathbf{b}_3) \cdot (n_1 \mathbf{a}_1 + n_2 \mathbf{a}_2 + n_3 \mathbf{a}_3) \\ &= 2\pi \sum_i n_i \eta_i = 2\pi \times \text{integer}, \end{aligned} \tag{13.7}$$

and therefore

$$e^{i\mathbf{k}_\eta \cdot \mathbf{R}_n} = 1. \tag{13.8}$$

The functions $e^{i\mathbf{k}_\eta \cdot \mathbf{r}}$, where $\mathbf{r}$ is any vector in space, are periodic in $\mathbf{r}$ with the periodicity of the lattice

$$e^{i\mathbf{k}_\eta \cdot (\mathbf{r} + \mathbf{R}_n)} = e^{i\mathbf{k}_\eta \cdot \mathbf{r}}. \tag{13.9}$$

They define a *complete* set of functions; we can expand any function $f(\mathbf{r})$ with the periodicity of the lattice in terms of this set:

$$f(\mathbf{r} + \mathbf{R}_n) = f(\mathbf{r}) = \sum_\eta e^{i\mathbf{k}_\eta \cdot \mathbf{r}} g(\mathbf{k}_\eta), \tag{13.10}$$

where

$$g(\mathbf{k}_\eta) = \frac{1}{\Omega_a} \int_{\Omega_a} f(\mathbf{r}) e^{-i\mathbf{k}_\eta \cdot \mathbf{r}} \, d\mathbf{r}, \tag{13.11}$$

because

$$\frac{1}{\Omega_a} \int_{\Omega_a} e^{i(\mathbf{k}_\eta - \mathbf{k}_{\eta'}) \cdot \mathbf{r}} \, d\mathbf{r} = \delta_{\eta\eta'}. \tag{13.12}$$

In a similar way we can see that a function $e^{i\mathbf{k} \cdot \mathbf{R}_n}$ is periodic in $\mathbf{k}$ with the periodicity of the reciprocal lattice

$$e^{i(\mathbf{k} + \mathbf{k}_\eta) \cdot \mathbf{R}_n} = e^{i\mathbf{k} \cdot \mathbf{R}_n}. \tag{13.13}$$

Any function of $\mathbf{k}$ with the periodicity of the reciprocal lattice can be expanded in terms of the functions $e^{i\mathbf{k} \cdot \mathbf{R}_n}$:

$$F(\mathbf{k}) = F(\mathbf{k} + \mathbf{k}_\eta) = \sum_n G(\mathbf{R}_n) e^{i\mathbf{k} \cdot \mathbf{R}_n}, \tag{13.14}$$

where

$$G(\mathbf{R}_n) = \frac{1}{\Omega_b} \int_{\Omega_b} d\mathbf{k} \, F(\mathbf{k}) e^{-i\mathbf{k} \cdot \mathbf{R}_n}, \tag{13.15}$$

because

$$\frac{1}{\Omega_b} \int_{\Omega_b} e^{i\mathbf{k} \cdot (\mathbf{R}_n - \mathbf{R}_{n'})} \, d\mathbf{k} = \delta_{nn'}. \tag{13.16}$$

1.2 Brillouin Zone and q-Space

Let us consider now two volumes, one in the crystal lattice and the other in the reciprocal lattice.

We define as *generating volume* [1] a part of the crystal lattice containing N unit cells, N_1 in the direction $\mathbf{a}_1$, N_2 in the direction $\mathbf{a}_2$, and N_3 in the direction $\mathbf{a}_3$ ($N = N_1 \cdot N_2 \cdot N_3$). The volume V of this part of the crystal is given by

$$N_1\mathbf{a}_1 \cdot N_2\mathbf{a}_2 \times N_3\mathbf{a}_3 = N\mathbf{a}_1 \cdot \mathbf{a}_2 \times \mathbf{a}_3 = N\Omega_a = V. \tag{13.17}$$

We define also as *first Brillouin zone* the Wigner-Seitz cell of the reciprocal lattice, namely a part of this lattice enclosed by planes which intersect the distances between the center of the zone and its neighbor lattice points at mid-distances $\pm\frac{1}{2}\mathbf{b}_1$, $\pm\frac{1}{2}\mathbf{b}_2$, $\pm\frac{1}{2}\mathbf{b}_3$. The volume of this zone is Ω_b.

We consider now a class of vectors in the reciprocal space defined by

$$\mathbf{q} = \sum_{i=1}^{3} \frac{h_i}{N_i}\,\mathbf{b}_i = \frac{h_1}{N_1}\,\mathbf{b}_1 + \frac{h_2}{N_2}\,\mathbf{b}_2 + \frac{h_3}{N_3}\,\mathbf{b}_3, \tag{13.18}$$

where h_i are integer numbers which can assume the values in the range

$$-\frac{N_i}{2} \le h_i \le \frac{N_i}{2}, \tag{13.19}$$

and N_i is the number of unit cells in the direction $\mathbf{a}_i$ in the generating volume. These vectors $\mathbf{q}$ are all contained in the first Brillouin zone; they are N in numbers and are symmetrically arranged with respect to the origin (namely each vector $\mathbf{q}$ has a correspondent $-\mathbf{q}$ in the opposite direction).

The density of $\mathbf{q}$ vectors depend on the assumed size of the generating volume,

$$n(\mathbf{q}) = \frac{N}{\Omega_b} = \frac{N\Omega_a}{(2\pi)^3} = \frac{V}{(2\pi)^3}\,. \tag{13.20}$$

We may pass from summation to integration in q space by using the relation,

$$\sum_{q=1}^{N} \rightarrow \frac{V}{(2\pi)^3}\int_{\Omega_b} d\mathbf{q}. \tag{13.21}$$

We notice that a function $e^{i\mathbf{q}\cdot\mathbf{r}}$ is periodic in the generating volume,

$$e^{i\mathbf{q}\cdot(\mathbf{r}+s_1N_1\mathbf{a}_1+s_2N_2\mathbf{a}_2+s_3N_3\mathbf{a}_3)} = e^{i\mathbf{q}\cdot\mathbf{r}}, \tag{13.22}$$

with s_1, s_2, s_3 integer numbers or zero, because

$$\begin{aligned}
&\mathbf{q}\cdot(s_1N_1\mathbf{a}_1 + s_2N_2\mathbf{a}_2 + s_3N_3\mathbf{a}_3)\\
&\quad= \left(\frac{h_1}{N_1}\,\mathbf{b}_1 + \frac{h_2}{N_2}\,\mathbf{b}_2 + \frac{h_3}{N_3}\,\mathbf{b}_3\right)\cdot(s_1N_1\mathbf{a}_1 + s_2N_2\mathbf{a}_2 + s_3N_3\mathbf{a}_3)\\
&\quad= 2\pi\sum_i h_is_i = 2\pi \times \text{integer}.
\end{aligned} \tag{13.23}$$

A function periodic in the generating volume can be expanded in terms of these $e^{i\mathbf{q}\cdot\mathbf{r}}$ functions,

$$\varphi\left(\mathbf{r} + \sum_i s_i N_i \mathbf{a}_i\right) = \varphi(\mathbf{r})$$

$$= \sum_{\mathbf{q}} e^{i\mathbf{q}\cdot\mathbf{r}} \chi(\mathbf{q}), \tag{13.24}$$

where

$$\chi(\mathbf{q}) = \frac{1}{V} \int_V \varphi(\mathbf{r}) e^{-i\mathbf{q}\cdot\mathbf{r}} \, d\mathbf{r}. \tag{13.25}$$

2. LATTICE VIBRATIONS OF AN INFINITE CRYSTAL WITH ONE ATOM PER UNIT CELL

Let us consider an infinite crystal with one atom per unit cell. The position of a generic atom is given by

$$\mathbf{d}_i = \mathbf{R}_i + \mathbf{u}_i, \tag{13.26}$$

where $\mathbf{R}_i$ is the equilibrium position and $\mathbf{u}_i$ is the displacement.

The kinetic energy and the potential energy are given, respectively, by

$$T = \tfrac{1}{2} m \sum_i \dot{\mathbf{u}}_i^2 = \frac{m}{2} \sum_i \sum_{\alpha=1}^{3} \dot{u}_{i\alpha}^2 \tag{13.27}$$

$$V = \tfrac{1}{2} \sum_i \sum_j \sum_{\alpha=1}^{3} \sum_{\beta=1}^{3} A_{i\alpha,j\beta} u_{i\alpha} u_{j\beta}, \tag{13.28}$$

where

$$A_{i\alpha,j\beta} = \left. \frac{\partial^2 V}{\partial u_{i\alpha}\, \partial u_{j\beta}} \right|_{u=0}. \tag{13.29}$$

The matrix **A** has the following properties:

1. It is real and symmetrical

$$A_{i\alpha,j\beta} = A^*_{i\alpha,j\beta} = A_{j\beta,i\alpha}. \tag{13.30}$$

2. The force acting on the ith atom in the α direction is given by

$$F_{i\alpha} = -\frac{\partial V}{\partial u_{i\alpha}} = -\sum_{j\beta} A_{i\alpha,j\beta} u_{j\beta}. \tag{13.31}$$

Then $A_{i\alpha,j\beta}$ represents the α component of the force acting on the atom at the $\mathbf{R}_i$ site, because of a unit displacement of the atom at the $\mathbf{R}_j$ site in the β direction. But the force between two atoms depends only on their *relative* position; therefore we can write

$$A_{i\alpha,j\beta} = A^{i-j}_{\alpha,\beta} = A^{n}_{\alpha,\beta}, \tag{13.32}$$

where

$$\mathbf{R}_n = \mathbf{R}_i - \mathbf{R}_j.$$

3. If we add a constant, arbitrary displacement $\mathbf{c}$ to all the $\mathbf{u}_j$'s in (13.31) we get

$$F_{i\alpha} = -\sum_{j\beta} A_{i\alpha,j\beta}(u_{j\beta} + c_\beta). \tag{13.33}$$

Subtracting (13.31) from (13.33) we find

$$\sum_{j\beta} A_{i\alpha,j\beta} c_\beta = \sum_\beta c_\beta \sum_j A_{i\alpha,j\beta} = 0, \tag{13.34}$$

which implies

$$\sum_j A_{i\alpha,j\beta} = 0. \tag{13.35}$$

4. Since each atom is in a center of symmetry (this is the case for an infinite lattice with one atom per unit cell),

$$A_{i\alpha,j\beta} = A_{i\beta,j\alpha}. \tag{13.36}$$

Let us consider now the equation of motion of the generic atom in the α direction:

$$m\ddot{u}_{i\alpha} = -\sum_{j\beta} A_{i\alpha,j\beta} u_{j\beta}. \tag{13.37}$$

In order to decouple (13.37), we shall look for solutions of the type

$$\mathbf{u}_i(t) = \mathfrak{V}(\mathbf{q})e^{-i\omega t + i\mathbf{q}\cdot\mathbf{R}_i}, \tag{13.38}$$

where $\mathbf{q}$ is an arbitrary vector. By using this expressions in (13.37) we obtain

$$\omega^2(\mathbf{q})\mathfrak{V}_\alpha(\mathbf{q}) = \frac{1}{m}\sum_{j\beta} A_{i\alpha,j\beta} e^{-i\mathbf{q}\cdot(\mathbf{R}_i - \mathbf{R}_j)}\mathfrak{V}_\beta(\mathbf{q})$$

$$= \sum_\beta G_{\alpha\beta}(\mathbf{q})\mathfrak{V}_\beta(\mathbf{q}), \tag{13.39}$$

where

$$G_{\alpha\beta}(\mathbf{q}) = \frac{1}{m}\sum_j A_{i\alpha,j\beta} e^{-i\mathbf{q}\cdot(\mathbf{R}_i - \mathbf{R}_j)}. \tag{13.40}$$

The frequencies $\omega(\mathbf{q})$ are determined by solving the 3×3 determinantal equation,

$$\det\,[G_{\alpha\beta}(\mathbf{q}) - \omega^2(\mathbf{q})\delta_{\alpha\beta}] = 0 \tag{13.41}$$

The (3×3) matrix $\mathbf{G}$ has the following properties:

1. It is Hermitian. In fact, because of (13.32), we can write

$$G^+_{\alpha\beta}(\mathbf{q}) = \frac{1}{m}\sum_n A^n_{\beta\alpha}\; e^{i\mathbf{q}\cdot\mathbf{R}_n}$$

$$= \frac{1}{m}\sum_n A^{-n}_{\alpha\beta}\; e^{-i\mathbf{q}\cdot\mathbf{R}_n} = \frac{1}{m}\sum_n A^n_{\alpha\beta}\; e^{-i\mathbf{q}\cdot\mathbf{R}_n} = G_{\alpha\beta}(\mathbf{q}). \tag{13.42}$$

2. It is periodical in the reciprocal lattice

$$G_{\alpha\beta}(\mathbf{k}_\eta + \mathbf{q}) = \frac{1}{m} \sum_n A^n_{\alpha\beta} e^{-i(\mathbf{q}+\mathbf{k}_\eta)\cdot\mathbf{R}_n}$$

$$= \frac{1}{m} \sum_n A^n_{\alpha\beta}\, e^{-i\mathbf{q}\cdot\mathbf{R}_n} = G_{\alpha\beta}(\mathbf{q}). \tag{13.43}$$

3. It is also

$$G^*_{\alpha\beta}(\mathbf{q}) = G_{\alpha\beta}(-\mathbf{q}). \tag{13.44}$$

In the present case, because of the inversion symmetry presented by the crystal,

$$G^*_{\alpha\beta}(\mathbf{q}) = \frac{1}{m} \sum_n A^n_{\alpha\beta} e^{i\mathbf{q}\cdot\mathbf{R}_n}$$

$$= \frac{1}{m} \sum_n A^{-n}_{\alpha\beta}\, e^{-i\mathbf{q}\cdot\mathbf{R}_n} = \frac{1}{m} \sum_n A^n_{\alpha\beta} e^{-i\mathbf{q}\cdot\mathbf{R}_n} = G_{\alpha\beta}(\mathbf{q}), \tag{13.45}$$

namely, **G** is also real.

From the first property it follows that **G** has three positive eigenvalues $\omega_\lambda{}^2(\mathbf{q})$ where $\lambda = 1, 2, 3$. The values of $\omega_\lambda(\mathbf{q})$ can also be chosen to be positive.

It is also clear that $\omega_\lambda{}^2(\mathbf{q})$ and $\mathfrak{V}^\lambda(\mathbf{q})$ are, like $G_{\alpha\beta}(\mathbf{q})$, periodical in the reciprocal lattice.

The eigenvectors $\mathfrak{V}^\lambda(\mathbf{q})$ can be chosen to be real and orthonormal,

$$\begin{aligned} \mathfrak{V}^\lambda(\mathbf{q}) \cdot \mathfrak{V}^{\lambda'}(\mathbf{q}) &= \sum_\alpha \mathcal{V}_\alpha{}^\lambda(\mathbf{q}) \mathcal{V}_\alpha{}^{\lambda'}(\mathbf{q}) = \delta_{\lambda\lambda'}, \\ \sum_\lambda \mathcal{V}_\alpha{}^\lambda(\mathbf{q}) \mathcal{V}_\beta{}^\lambda(\mathbf{q}) &= \delta_{\alpha\beta}. \end{aligned} \tag{13.46}$$

We can now write down the expression for the generic displacement,

$$\mathbf{u}_i(t) = \int_{BZ} d\mathbf{q} \sum_{\lambda=1}^{3} C^\lambda(\mathbf{q})\, \mathfrak{V}^\lambda(\mathbf{q})\, e^{i\mathbf{q}\cdot\mathbf{R}_i} \cos \omega_\lambda(\mathbf{q})\, t, \tag{13.47}$$

where $C^\lambda(\mathbf{q})$ are complex constants; $\mathfrak{V}^\lambda(\mathbf{q})$ can now be considered as polarization vectors and $\mathbf{q}$, as a wave vector. The integral is extended to the first Brillouin zone, because of the periodicity of $C^\lambda(\mathbf{q})$, $\mathfrak{V}^\lambda(\mathbf{q})$, and $\omega_\lambda(\mathbf{q})$.

Finally, because of (13.35),

$$G_{\alpha\beta}(\mathbf{0}) = \frac{1}{m} \sum_n A^n_{\alpha\beta} = 0 \tag{13.48}$$

and

$$\omega_\lambda(\mathbf{0}) = 0 \qquad (\lambda = 1, 2, 3). \tag{13.49}$$

From (13.47) and (13.49) it can be seen that the three modes of vibration corresponding to $\mathbf{q} = 0$ produce a uniform displacement of all the particles.

3. LATTICE VIBRATIONS OF A FINITE CRYSTAL WITH ONE ATOM PER UNIT CELL

We have considered until now an infinite crystal with one atom per unit cell. The Brillouin zone concept is a *geometrical* concept; this zone is the Wigner-Seitz unit cell of the reciprocal lattice (another *geometrical* concept).

We consider now a finite crystal with N_i unit cells in the direction $\mathbf{a}_i$ and with one atom per unit cell.

1. We identify the equilibrium configuration of the finite crystal with the generating volume of the infinite lattice;
2. We impose the so-called *Born-Von Karman boundary conditions*:

$$\mathbf{u}(\mathbf{R}_i) = u(\mathbf{R}_i + m_1\mathbf{L}_1 + m_2\mathbf{L}_2 + m_3\mathbf{L}_3), \tag{13.50}$$

where m_1, m_2, and m_3 are integer numbers or zero and $\mathbf{L}_j = N_j\mathbf{a}_j$ are the dimensions of the crystal.

Because of the conditions (13.50) we must have, in (13.38),

$$e^{i\mathbf{q}\cdot\left(\mathbf{R}_i+\sum_j m_j\mathbf{L}_j\right)} = e^{i\mathbf{q}\cdot\mathbf{R}_i} \tag{13.51}$$

or

$$e^{i\mathbf{q}\cdot\sum_j m_j\mathbf{L}_j} = 1, \tag{13.52}$$

namely,

$$\mathbf{q}\cdot\sum_j m_j\mathbf{L}_j = 2\pi \times \text{integer}. \tag{13.53}$$

This is the relation that defines the so-called $\mathbf{q}$ space of Section 1.2 in this chapter. Every $\mathbf{q}$ corresponds to a distinct point in the Brillouin zone; the density of these points, as we can see from (13.20), is greater, the greater is the volume of the crystal. For a finite volume the $\mathbf{q}$'s form a *discrete* set.

We can express the $\mathbf{q}$ vectors as in (13.18):

$$\mathbf{q} = \sum_i \frac{h_i}{N_i}\mathbf{b}_i, \tag{13.54}$$

with

$$-\frac{N_i}{2} \leq h_i \leq \frac{N_i}{2}. \tag{13.55}$$

The kinetic energy and the potential energy are given, respectively by

$$T = \frac{m}{2}\sum_i |\dot{\mathbf{u}}_i|^2 = \frac{m}{2}\sum_{i=1}^{N}\sum_{\alpha=1}^{3}\dot{\mathbf{u}}_{i\alpha}^{\,2}, \tag{13.56}$$

$$V = \tfrac{1}{2}\sum_{i=1}^{N}\sum_j\sum_{\alpha=1}^{3}\sum_{\beta=1}^{3} A_{i\alpha,j\beta}u_{i\alpha}u_{j\beta}. \tag{13.57}$$

In (13.57) the sum over j runs over the *infinite* lattice, a part of which, the generating volume, coincides with the real finite crystal. Actually the sum should extend to N, but for a large N, the terms with j outside the generating volume represent only a neglibible fraction of the total, if the forces among the atoms have a finite field of action [2].

The equations of motions are given, as in the previous case, by (13.37) and are now $3N$ in number. Solutions of the type (13.38) lead to the eigenvalue equation

$$\sum_{\beta} G_{\alpha\beta}(\mathbf{q})\, \mathcal{V}_{q\beta} = \omega_q^{\,2} \mathcal{V}_{q\alpha}, \tag{13.58}$$

where now $\mathbf{q}$ ranges over N values within the first Brillouin zone.

The matrix $\mathbf{G}$ is still Hermitian and periodical in the reciprocal lattice. However, in the most general case of absence of inversion symmetry, $G_{\alpha\beta}$ is complex and the eigenvectors $\boldsymbol{\mathcal{V}}_q$ are also complex. They can, however, be chosen to be orthonormal,

$$\begin{aligned} \boldsymbol{\mathcal{V}}_q^{\lambda *} \cdot \boldsymbol{\mathcal{V}}_q^{\lambda'} &= \sum_{\alpha} \mathcal{V}_{q\alpha}^{\lambda *} \mathcal{V}_{q\alpha}^{\lambda'} = \delta_{\lambda\lambda'}; \\ \sum_{\lambda} \mathcal{V}_{q\alpha}^{\lambda *} \mathcal{V}_{q\beta}^{\lambda} &= \delta_{\alpha\beta}. \end{aligned} \tag{13.59}$$

We can also take

$$\begin{aligned} \omega_{-q\lambda} &= \omega^*_{q\lambda} = \omega_{q\lambda}; \\ \boldsymbol{\mathcal{V}}_{-q}^{\lambda} &= \boldsymbol{\mathcal{V}}_q^{\lambda *}. \end{aligned} \tag{13.60}$$

The general expression for the displacement is now given by

$$u_i(t) = \sum_{q}^{N} \sum_{\lambda=1}^{3} C_q^{\lambda} \boldsymbol{\mathcal{V}}_q^{\lambda} e^{i\mathbf{q}\cdot\mathbf{R}_i} \cos \omega_{q\lambda} t, \tag{13.61}$$

where the $3N$ values for $|C_q^{\lambda}|$ and the $3N$ values for the phases of C_q^{λ} are determined by the intial conditions.

Let us introduce now the *complex normal coordinates* in the following way:

$$u_{i\alpha} = \frac{1}{\sqrt{Nm}} \sum_{q\lambda}^{3N} Q_q^{\lambda} \mathcal{V}_{q\alpha}^{\lambda} e^{i\mathbf{q}\cdot\mathbf{R}_i}. \tag{13.62}$$

We can check that $u_{i\alpha}$ satisfies the periodic boundary conditions. The inverse transformation of (13.62) is given by

$$Q_q^{\lambda} = \left(\frac{m}{N}\right)^{1/2} \sum_{i\alpha}^{3N} u_{i\alpha} \mathcal{V}_{q\alpha}^{\lambda *} e^{-i\mathbf{q}\cdot\mathbf{R}_i}. \tag{13.63}$$

In fact, since

$$\frac{1}{N} \sum_{i}^{N} e^{i(\mathbf{q}-\mathbf{q}')\cdot\mathbf{R}_i} = \delta_{\mathbf{q}\mathbf{q}'}, \tag{13.64}$$

and because of (13.59)

$$\left(\frac{m}{N}\right)^{1/2}\sum_{i\alpha}^{3N} u_{i\alpha}\mathcal{V}_{q\alpha}^{\lambda *} e^{-i\mathbf{q}\cdot\mathbf{R}_i} = \frac{1}{N}\sum_{i\alpha}^{3N}\sum_{q'\lambda'}^{3N} Q_{q'}^{\lambda'}\mathcal{V}_{q'\alpha}^{\lambda'} e^{i\mathbf{q}'\cdot\mathbf{R}_i}\mathcal{V}_{q\alpha}^{\lambda *} e^{-i\mathbf{q}\cdot\mathbf{R}_i}$$

$$= \sum_{q'\lambda'}^{3N}\left(\sum_{\alpha}^{3}\mathcal{V}_{q'\alpha}^{\lambda'}\mathcal{V}_{q\alpha}^{\lambda *}\right) Q_{q'}^{\lambda'}\left(\sum_{i}^{N}\frac{1}{N} e^{i(\mathbf{q}-\mathbf{q}_i)\cdot\mathbf{R}_i}\right)$$

$$= \sum_{\lambda'}^{3}\left(\sum_{\alpha}\mathcal{V}_{q\alpha}^{\lambda'}\mathcal{V}_{q\alpha}^{\lambda *}\right) Q_q^{\lambda'} = Q_q^{\lambda}. \tag{13.65}$$

We notice that

$$Q_{-q}^{\lambda} = Q_q^{\lambda *}, \tag{13.66}$$

and therefore the coordinates associated with $\mathbf{q}$ and $-\mathbf{q}$ are not independent; actually we have only $3N$ independent real coordinates. For this reason we can rewrite (13.62) as

$$u_{i\alpha} = \frac{1}{\sqrt{Nm}}\sum_{q>0}^{N/2}\sum_{\alpha=1}^{3}(Q_q^{\lambda}\mathcal{V}_{q\alpha}^{\lambda} e^{i\mathbf{q}\cdot\mathbf{R}_i} + Q_q^{\lambda *}\mathcal{V}_{q\alpha}^{\lambda *} e^{-i\mathbf{q}\cdot\mathbf{R}_i}). \tag{13.67}$$

We want now to express the kinetic and potential energies in terms of the new Q coordinates,

$$T = \frac{m}{2}\sum_{i\alpha}^{3N}\dot{u}_{i\alpha}^{2}$$

$$= \frac{m}{2}\sum_{i\alpha}^{3N}\left\{\frac{1}{Nm}\left(\sum_{q\lambda}^{3N}\dot{Q}_q^{\lambda}\mathcal{V}_{q\alpha}^{\lambda} e^{i\mathbf{q}\cdot\mathbf{R}_i}\right)\left(\sum_{q'\lambda'}^{3N}\dot{Q}_{q'}^{\lambda'}\mathcal{V}_{q'\alpha}^{\lambda'} e^{i\mathbf{q}'\cdot\mathbf{R}_i}\right)\right\}$$

$$= \frac{1}{2N}\sum_{i\alpha}^{3N}\left\{\sum_{q\lambda}^{3N}\sum_{q'\lambda'}^{3N}\dot{Q}_q^{\lambda}\dot{Q}_{q'}^{\lambda'} e^{i(\mathbf{q}+\mathbf{q}')\cdot\mathbf{R}_i}\mathcal{V}_{q\alpha}^{\lambda}\mathcal{V}_{q'\alpha}^{\lambda'}\right\}$$

$$= \frac{1}{2}\sum_{q\lambda}^{3N}\sum_{q'\lambda'}^{3N}\dot{Q}_q^{\lambda}\dot{Q}_{q'}^{\lambda'}\delta_{\mathbf{q}',-\mathbf{q}}\sum_{\alpha}\mathcal{V}_{q\alpha}^{\lambda}\mathcal{V}_{q'\alpha}^{\lambda'}$$

$$= \frac{1}{2}\sum_{q\lambda}^{3N}\sum_{\lambda'}\dot{Q}_q^{\lambda}\dot{Q}_{-q}^{\lambda'}\sum_{\alpha}\mathcal{V}_{q\alpha}^{\lambda}\mathcal{V}_{q\alpha}^{\lambda' *} = \frac{1}{2}\sum_{q\lambda}^{3N}\dot{Q}_q^{\lambda}\dot{Q}_{-q}^{\lambda}; \tag{13.68}$$

$$V = \frac{1}{2}\sum_{i\alpha}^{3N}\sum_{j\beta} A_{i\alpha,j\beta}u_{i\alpha}u_{j\beta}$$

$$= \frac{1}{2}\sum_{i\alpha}^{3N}\sum_{j\beta} A_{i\alpha,j\beta}\frac{1}{Nm}\left(\sum_{q\lambda}^{3N} Q_q^{\lambda}\mathcal{V}_{q\alpha}^{\lambda} e^{i\mathbf{q}\cdot\mathbf{R}_i}\right)\left(\sum_{q'\lambda'}^{3N} Q_{q'}^{\lambda}\mathcal{V}_{q'\alpha}^{\lambda'} e^{i\mathbf{q}'\cdot\mathbf{R}_j}\right)$$

$$= \frac{1}{2}\sum_{i\alpha}^{3N}\sum_{q\lambda}^{3N}\sum_{q'\lambda}^{3N}\frac{1}{Nm}\sum_{\beta}\left(\sum_{j} A_{i\alpha,j\beta} e^{i\mathbf{q}'\cdot\mathbf{R}_j}\right) Q_q^{\lambda} Q_{q'}^{\lambda'}\mathcal{V}_{q\alpha}^{\lambda}\mathcal{V}_{q'\beta}^{\lambda'} e^{i\mathbf{q}\cdot\mathbf{R}_i}. \tag{13.69}$$

But

$$\frac{1}{m}\sum_j A_{i\alpha,j\beta}e^{i\mathbf{q}'\cdot\mathbf{R}_j} = \frac{1}{m}\sum_j A_{i\alpha,j\beta}e^{-i\mathbf{q}'\cdot(\mathbf{R}_i-\mathbf{R}_j)}\,e^{i\mathbf{q}'\cdot\mathbf{R}_i}$$

$$= G_{\alpha\beta}(\mathbf{q}')\,e^{i\mathbf{q}'\cdot\mathbf{R}_i}.$$

Then

$$V = \frac{1}{2}\sum_{i\alpha}^{3N}\sum_{q\lambda}^{3N}\sum_{q'\lambda'}^{3N}\frac{1}{N}\sum_{\beta} G_{\alpha\beta}(\mathbf{q}')\,e^{i(\mathbf{q}'+\mathbf{q})\cdot\mathbf{R}_i}Q_q^{\ \lambda}Q_{q'}^{\ \lambda'}\mho_{q\alpha}^{\ \lambda}\mho_{q'\beta}^{\ \lambda'}$$

$$= \frac{1}{2}\sum_{q\lambda}^{3N}\sum_{q'\lambda'}^{3N}\sum_{\alpha}\sum_{\beta} G_{\alpha\beta}(\mathbf{q}')\left(\sum_i \frac{1}{N}\,e^{i(\mathbf{q}'+\mathbf{q})\cdot\mathbf{R}_i}\right)Q_q^{\ \lambda}Q_{q'}^{\ \lambda'}\mho_{q\alpha}^{\ \lambda}\mho_{q'\beta}^{\ \lambda'}$$

$$= \frac{1}{2}\sum_{q\lambda}^{3N}\sum_{q'\lambda'}^{3N}\sum_{\alpha}^{3}\sum_{\beta}^{3} G_{\alpha\beta}(\mathbf{q}')\,\delta_{\mathbf{q}',-\mathbf{q}}Q_q^{\ \lambda}Q_{q'}^{\ \lambda'}\mho_{q\alpha}^{\ \lambda}\mho_{q'\beta}^{\ \lambda'}$$

$$= \frac{1}{2}\sum_{q\lambda}^{3N}\sum_{\lambda'}^{3}\sum_{\alpha}^{3}\left[\sum_{\beta}^{3} G_{\alpha\beta}(-\mathbf{q})\,\mho_{-q\beta}^{\ \lambda'}\right]\mho_{q\alpha}^{\ \lambda}Q_q^{\ \lambda}Q_{-q}^{\ \lambda'}$$

$$= \frac{1}{2}\sum_{q\lambda}^{3N}\sum_{\lambda'}^{3}\sum_{\alpha}^{3}\omega_{q\lambda'}^2\mho_{-q\alpha}^{\ \lambda'}\mho_{q\alpha}^{\ \lambda}Q_q^{\ \lambda}Q_{-q}^{\ \lambda'}$$

$$= \frac{1}{2}\sum_{q\lambda}^{3N}\sum_{\lambda}\omega_{q\lambda'}^2\delta_{\lambda\lambda'}Q_q^{\ \lambda}Q_{-q}^{\ \lambda'} = \frac{1}{2}\sum_{q\lambda}^{3N}\omega_{q\lambda}^{\ 2}Q_q^{\ \lambda}Q_{-q}^{\ \lambda}. \tag{13.70}$$

In brief,

$$T = \frac{1}{2}\sum_{q\lambda}^{3N}\dot{Q}_q^{\ \lambda}\dot{Q}_{-q}^{\ \lambda},$$
$$V = \frac{1}{2}\sum_{q\lambda}^{3N}\omega_{q\lambda}^{\ 2}Q_q^{\ \lambda}Q_{-q}^{\ \lambda}. \tag{13.71}$$

The momentum conjugate to $Q_q^{\ \lambda}$ is given by

$$P_q^{\ \lambda} = \frac{\partial L}{\partial \dot{Q}_q^{\ \lambda}} = \frac{\partial(T-V)}{\partial \dot{Q}_q^{\ \lambda}} = \dot{Q}_{-q}^{\ \lambda}. \tag{13.72}$$

We have also

$$P_{-q}^{\ \lambda} = \dot{Q}_q^{\ \lambda} = P_q^{\ \lambda *}. \tag{13.73}$$

The Hamiltonian is then given by

$$H = \sum_{q\lambda}^{3N} P_q^{\ \lambda}\dot{Q}_q^{\ \lambda} - L$$

$$= \frac{1}{2}\sum_{q\lambda}^{3N} P_q^{\ \lambda}P_{-q}^{\ \lambda} + \frac{1}{2}\sum_{q\lambda}^{3N}\omega_{q\lambda}^{\ 2}Q_q^{\ \lambda}Q_{-q}^{\ \lambda}, \tag{13.74}$$

and the equations of motion in terms of the new coordinates are:

$$\dot{P}_q^{\lambda} = -\frac{\partial H}{\partial Q_q^{\lambda}} = -\omega_{q\lambda}^2 Q_{-q}^{\lambda},$$
$$\dot{Q}_q^{\lambda} = \frac{\partial H}{\partial P_q^{\lambda}} = P_{-q}^{\lambda}. \tag{13.75}$$

The classical solution of these equations is

$$Q_q^{\lambda}(t) = Q_q^{\lambda}(0) \cos(\omega_{q\lambda} t + \delta_{q\lambda}). \tag{13.76}$$

The replacement of (13.76) in (13.62) gives the classical expression for the displacement. The normal coordinates and momenta are related to the coordinates $u_{i\alpha}$ and momenta $p_{i\alpha}$ by the relations,

$$u_{i\alpha} = \frac{1}{\sqrt{Nm}} \sum_{q\lambda}^{3N} \mho_{q\alpha}^{\lambda} e^{i\mathbf{q}\cdot\mathbf{R}_i} Q_q^{\lambda},$$
$$p_{i\alpha} = m\dot{u}_{i\alpha} = \left(\frac{m}{N}\right)^{1/2} \sum_{q\lambda}^{3N} \mho_{q\alpha}^{\lambda} e^{i\mathbf{q}\cdot\mathbf{R}_i} \dot{Q}_q^{\lambda} \tag{13.77}$$
$$= \left(\frac{m}{N}\right)^{1/2} \sum_{q\lambda}^{3N} \mho_{q\alpha}^{\lambda *} e^{-i\mathbf{q}\cdot\mathbf{R}_i} P_q^{\lambda},$$

or by

$$Q_q^{\lambda} = \left(\frac{m}{N}\right)^{1/2} \sum_{i\alpha}^{3N} u_{i\alpha} \mho_{q\alpha}^{\lambda *} e^{-i\mathbf{q}\cdot\mathbf{R}_i},$$
$$P_q^{\lambda} = \frac{1}{\sqrt{Nm}} \sum_{i\alpha}^{3N} p_{i\alpha} \mho_{q\alpha}^{\lambda} e^{i\mathbf{q}\cdot\mathbf{R}_i}. \tag{13.78}$$

Going to quantum mechanics, $\mathbf{u}_i$ and $\mathbf{p}_i$ become Hermitian operators with the commutation relations,

$$[u_{i\alpha}, p_{j\beta}] = i\hbar \delta_{ij} \delta_{\alpha\beta},$$
$$[u_{i\alpha}, u_{j\beta}] = [p_{i\alpha}, p_{j\beta}] = 0. \tag{13.79}$$

The coordinates Q_q^{λ} and the momenta P_q^{λ} become (non-Hermitian) operators with the commutation relations,

$$[Q_q^{\lambda}, Q_{q'}^{\lambda'}] = [P_q^{\lambda}, P_{q'}^{\lambda'}] = 0,$$
$$[Q_q^{\lambda}, P_{q'}^{\lambda'}] = i\hbar \delta_{qq'} \delta_{\lambda\lambda'}. \tag{13.80}$$

Also, because of (13.66),

$$Q_{-q}^{\lambda} = Q_q^{\lambda +},$$
$$P_{-q}^{\lambda} = P_q^{\lambda +}. \tag{13.81}$$

We can now write the Hamiltonian as

$$H = \frac{1}{2} \sum_{q\lambda}^{3N} (P_q^{\lambda +} P_q^{\lambda} + \omega_{q\lambda}^2 Q_q^{\lambda +} Q_q^{\lambda}). \tag{13.82}$$

At this point, in order to solve the Schrödinger equation and find the energy levels of the system, we introduce the dimensionless operators,

$$\begin{aligned} b_q^{\lambda} &= \left(\frac{\omega_{q\lambda}}{2\hbar}\right)^{1/2} \left(Q_q^{\lambda} + \frac{i}{\omega_{q\lambda}} P_q^{\lambda +}\right), \\ b_q^{\lambda +} &= \left(\frac{\omega_{q\lambda}}{2\hbar}\right)^{1/2} \left(Q_q^{\lambda +} - \frac{i}{\omega_{q\lambda}} P_q^{\lambda}\right). \end{aligned} \tag{13.83}$$

The commutation relations for these operators can be easily found taking in account the relations (13.80) and also the relations

$$\begin{aligned} Q_q^{\lambda} &= \left(\frac{\hbar}{2\omega_{q\lambda}}\right)^{1/2} (b_q^{\lambda} + b_{-q}^{\lambda +}), \\ P_q^{\lambda} &= \left(\frac{\hbar\omega_{q\lambda}}{2}\right)^{1/2} \frac{1}{i} (b_{-q}^{\lambda} - b_q^{\lambda +}). \end{aligned} \tag{13.84}$$

We find

$$\begin{aligned} &[b_q^{\lambda}, b_{q'}^{\lambda'}] = [b_q^{\lambda +}, b_{q'}^{\lambda' +}] = 0, \\ &[b_q^{\lambda}, b_{q'}^{\lambda' +}] = \delta_{qq'}\delta_{\lambda\lambda'}, \end{aligned} \tag{13.85}$$

and also

$$H = \sum_{q\lambda}^{3N} \hbar\omega_{q\lambda}(b_q^{\lambda +} b_q^{\lambda} + \tfrac{1}{2}). \tag{13.86}$$

The system is now equivalent to $3N$ independent harmonic oscillators. The operators b_q^{λ} and $b_q^{\lambda +}$ have the same properties of the operators a_k^{λ} and $a_k^{\lambda +}$ of the radiation field Hamiltonian (Section 2.3 of Chapter 11) and play a similar role,

$$\begin{aligned} b_q^{\lambda} \, |n_q^{\lambda}\rangle &= \sqrt{n_q^{\lambda}} \, |n_q^{\lambda} - 1\rangle, \\ b_q^{\lambda +} \, |n_q^{\lambda}\rangle &= \sqrt{n_q^{\lambda} + 1} \, |n_q^{\lambda} + 1\rangle, \\ b_q^{\lambda +} b_q^{\lambda} \, |n_q^{\lambda}\rangle &= n_q^{\lambda} \, |n_q^{\lambda}\rangle. \end{aligned} \tag{13.87}$$

The energy levels of the system are given by

$$E = \sum_{q\lambda}^{3N} (n_q^{\lambda} + \tfrac{1}{2})\hbar\omega_{q\lambda}. \tag{13.88}$$

The displacement and the moment of the generic atom, in terms of the b operators are given by

$$u_{i\alpha} = \frac{1}{\sqrt{Nm}} \sum_{q\lambda}^{3N} \mathcal{V}_{q\alpha}^{\lambda} e^{i\mathbf{q}\cdot\mathbf{R}_i} Q_q^{\lambda}$$

$$= \left(\frac{\hbar}{2Nm}\right)^{1/2} \sum_{q\lambda}^{3N} \frac{\mathcal{V}_{q\alpha}^{\lambda}}{\sqrt{\omega_{q\lambda}}} e^{i\mathbf{q}\cdot\mathbf{R}_i} (b_q^{\lambda} + b_{-q}^{\lambda+})$$

$$= \frac{1}{\sqrt{Nm}} \sum_{q\lambda}^{3N} \left(\frac{\hbar}{2\omega_{q\lambda}}\right)^{1/2} (\mathcal{V}_{q\alpha}^{\lambda} e^{i\mathbf{q}\cdot\mathbf{R}_i} b_q^{\lambda} + \mathcal{V}_{q\alpha}^{\lambda *} e^{-i\mathbf{q}\cdot\mathbf{R}_i} b_q^{\lambda+}), \tag{13.89}$$

$$p_{i\alpha} = \left(\frac{m}{N}\right)^{1/2} \sum_{q\lambda}^{3N} \mathcal{V}_{q\alpha}^{\lambda *} e^{-i\mathbf{q}\cdot\mathbf{R}_i} P_q^{\lambda}$$

$$= \left(\frac{m}{N}\right)^{1/2} \sum_{q\lambda}^{3N} \mathcal{V}_{q\alpha}^{\lambda *} e^{-i\mathbf{q}\cdot\mathbf{R}_i} \left(\frac{\hbar\omega_{q\lambda}}{2}\right)^{1/2} \frac{1}{i} (b_{-q}^{\lambda} - b_q^{\lambda+})$$

$$= \left(\frac{m}{N}\right)^{1/2} \sum_{q\lambda}^{3N} \left(\frac{\hbar\omega_{q\lambda}}{2}\right)^{1/2} \frac{1}{i} (\mathcal{V}_{q\alpha}^{\lambda} e^{i\mathbf{q}\cdot\mathbf{R}_i} b_q^{\lambda} - \mathcal{V}_{q\alpha}^{\lambda *} e^{-i\mathbf{q}\cdot\mathbf{R}_i} b_q^{\lambda+}). \tag{13.90}$$

4. LATTICE VIBRATIONS OF A CRYSTAL WITH MORE THAN ONE ATOM PER UNIT CELL

Let us consider now a crystal with N unit cells and with J atoms in the unit cell. Let m_ν be the mass of the νth atom ($\nu = 1, 2, \ldots, J$) and $\mathbf{u}_{i\nu}$ the displacement of the νth atom in the unit cell at $\mathbf{R}_i$.

The kinetic and the potential energies are now given by

$$T = \frac{1}{2} \sum_{i}^{N} \sum_{\alpha=1}^{3} \sum_{\nu=1}^{J} m_\nu \dot{u}_{i\alpha\nu}^2,$$

$$V = \frac{1}{2} \sum_{i\alpha}^{3N} \sum_{j\beta} \sum_{\nu}^{J} \sum_{\nu'}^{J} A_{i\alpha,j\beta}(\nu\nu') u_{j\beta\nu'}, \tag{13.91}$$

where

$$A_{i\alpha,j\beta}(\nu\nu') = \left.\frac{\partial^2 V}{\partial u_{i\alpha\nu}\, \partial u_{j\beta\nu'}}\right|_{u=0}. \tag{13.92}$$

As in the case of a crystal with one atom per unit cell the $3JN \times 3JN$ matrix $\mathbf{A}$ is symmetrical and real

$$A_{i\alpha,j\beta}(\nu\nu') = A_{j\beta,i\alpha}(\nu'\nu) = A_{\alpha\beta}^{i-j}(\nu\nu')$$

$$= A_{\alpha\beta}^{n}(\nu\nu'), \tag{13.93}$$

where n is the subscript of $\mathbf{R}_n = \mathbf{R}_i - \mathbf{R}_j$. Similarly to (13.35),

$$\sum_{j\nu'} A_{\alpha\beta}^{i-j}(\nu\nu') = 0. \tag{13.94}$$

The equations of motion ($3NJ$ in number) are given by

$$m_\nu \ddot{u}_{i\alpha\nu} = -\sum_{j\beta\nu'} A_{i\alpha,j\beta}(\nu\nu') u_{j\beta\nu'}. \tag{13.95}$$

In order to decouple these equations, we look for solutions of the type

$$\mathbf{u}_{i\nu} = \frac{1}{\sqrt{m_\nu}} \mathfrak{V}_q^{\ \nu} e^{i\mathbf{q}\cdot\mathbf{R}_i - i\omega t}. \tag{13.96}$$

By using this expression in (13.95) we obtain

$$\sqrt{m_\nu}\, \omega^2 \mathfrak{V}_\alpha^{\ \nu} e^{i\mathbf{q}\cdot\mathbf{R}_i} = \sum_{j\beta\nu'} A_{i\alpha,j\beta}(\nu\nu') \frac{1}{\sqrt{m_{\nu'}}} \mathfrak{V}_\beta^{\ \nu'} e^{i\mathbf{q}\cdot\mathbf{R}_j}, \tag{13.97}$$

or

$$\begin{aligned} \omega^2 \mathfrak{V}_\alpha^{\ \nu} &= \sum_{j\beta\nu'} \frac{1}{\sqrt{m_\nu m_{\nu'}}} A_{i\alpha,j\beta}(\nu\nu')\, \mathfrak{V}_\beta^{\ \nu'} e^{i\mathbf{q}\cdot(\mathbf{R}_j - \mathbf{R}_i)} \\ &= \sum_\beta^3 \sum_{\nu'}^J G_{\alpha\beta}^{\nu\nu'}(\mathbf{q})\, \mathfrak{V}_\beta^{\ \nu'}, \qquad (\nu, \nu' = 1, \ldots, J), \end{aligned} \tag{13.98}$$

where $\mathbf{G}$ is a $3J \times 3J$ matrix given by

$$G_{\alpha\beta}^{\nu\nu'}(\mathbf{q}) = \frac{1}{\sqrt{m_\nu m_{\nu'}}} \sum_j A_{i\alpha,j\beta}(\nu\nu')\, e^{-i\mathbf{q}\cdot(\mathbf{R}_i - \mathbf{R}_j)}. \tag{13.99}$$

$\mathbf{G}$ is a Hermitian matrix, periodical in the reciprocal lattice; also $\mathbf{G}(-\mathbf{q}) = \mathbf{G}(\mathbf{q})^*$. The eigenvalues $\omega_{q\lambda}^2$ are positive and are $3J$ in number for each $\mathbf{q}$. The eigenvectors $\mathfrak{V}_q$ are also $3J$ in number for each $\mathbf{q}$ and can be chosen to be orthonormal,

$$\begin{aligned} \sum_{\alpha=1}^3 \sum_{\nu=1}^J \mathfrak{V}_{q\alpha}^{\ \lambda\nu *} \mathfrak{V}_{q\alpha}^{\ \lambda'\nu} &= \delta_{\lambda\lambda'}, \\ \sum_{\lambda=1}^{3J} \mathfrak{V}_{q\alpha}^{\ \lambda\nu *} \mathfrak{V}_{q\beta}^{\ \lambda\nu'} &= \delta_{\alpha\beta}\delta_{\nu\nu'}. \end{aligned} \tag{13.100}$$

We can also take

$$\begin{aligned} \mathfrak{V}_{-q}^{\ \lambda\nu} &= \mathfrak{V}_q^{\ \lambda\nu *}, \\ \omega_{-q\lambda} &= \omega_{q\lambda}. \end{aligned} \tag{13.101}$$

The complex normal coordinates $Q_q^{\ \lambda}$ ($\lambda = 1, 2, \ldots, 3J$) are now introduced in the following way:

$$u_{i\alpha\nu} = \frac{1}{\sqrt{Nm_\nu}} \sum_q^N \sum_\lambda^{3J} Q_q^{\ \lambda} \mathfrak{V}_q^{\ \lambda\nu} e^{i\mathbf{q}\cdot\mathbf{R}_i}. \tag{13.102}$$

This expression satisfies the periodic boundary conditions and the **q**'s are determined, as usual by (13.52). The kinetic and potential energies in terms of the new coordinates are

$$T = \frac{1}{2}\sum_{q}^{N}\sum_{\lambda}^{3J}\dot{Q}_{-q}{}^{\lambda}\dot{Q}_{q}{}^{\lambda},$$
$$V = \frac{1}{2}\sum_{q}^{N}\sum_{\lambda}^{3J}\omega_{q\lambda}{}^{2}Q_{-q}{}^{\lambda}Q_{q}{}^{\lambda}. \tag{13.103}$$

The number of branches in the vibrational spectrum of a complex (more than one atom per unit cell) crystal is $3J$. All the formulas derived for the case of a crystal with one atom per unit cell apply to the present case with the provision that the polarization index λ now has to run over the $3J$ branches.

Let us examine what happens to these branches for $\mathbf{q} = 0$. The dynamical equation (13.98) for $\mathbf{q} = 0$ becomes

$$\sum_{\beta}^{3}\sum_{\nu'}^{J} G_{\alpha\beta}^{\nu\nu'}(\mathbf{0})\,\mathfrak{V}_{0\beta}{}^{\nu'} = \omega_{0\nu}{}^{2}\mathfrak{V}_{0\alpha}{}^{\nu}, \tag{13.104}$$

or

$$\sum_{j}^{N}\sum_{\beta}^{3}\sum_{\nu'}^{J}\frac{A_{i\alpha,j\beta}(\nu\nu')}{\sqrt{m_\nu m_{\nu'}}}\,\mathfrak{V}_{0\beta}{}^{\nu'} = \omega_{0\nu}{}^{2}\mathfrak{V}_{0\alpha}{}^{\nu}. \tag{13.105}$$

We can try an eigenvector such as

$$\mathfrak{V}_{0}{}^{\nu'} = \sqrt{m_{\nu'}}\,\mathfrak{V}_{0}. \tag{13.106}$$

We then get

$$\sum_{j}^{N}\sum_{\beta}^{3}\sum_{\nu'}^{J}\frac{A_{i\alpha,j\beta}(\nu\nu')}{\sqrt{m_\nu}}\,\mathfrak{V}_{0\beta} = \omega_{0\nu}{}^{2}\sqrt{m_\nu}\,\mathfrak{V}_{0\alpha}, \tag{13.107}$$

or

$$\frac{1}{m_\nu}\sum_{\beta}\left[\sum_{j}^{N}\sum_{\nu'}^{J}A_{i\alpha,j\beta}(\nu\nu')\right]\mathfrak{V}_{0\beta} = \omega_{0\nu}{}^{2}\mathfrak{V}_{0\alpha}. \tag{13.108}$$

Therefore $\omega_{0\nu}{}^{2} = 0$ because of (13.94) and because $\mathfrak{V}_0$ is arbitrary. This means that for zero frequency (13.108) has solutions corresponding to a uniform displacement of all the atoms. Because the direction of the displacement $\mathfrak{V}_0$ is arbitrary, there are three independent solutions of this type; and therefore there are three branches that go to zero at $\mathbf{q} = 0$. We call them the *acoustical branches* of the spectrum and the remaining $3J - 3$ the *optical branches.*

For $\mathbf{q} = 0$ the acoustical branches correspond to a uniform displacement of all the atoms. For $\mathbf{q} = 0$ the optical branches correspond to vibrational modes in which atoms in different cells but corresponding to the same index ν have the same displacements, but atoms with a different index ν within the same cell move relatively one to the other.

We can see that for long wavelengths the motions associated with the acoustical branches are motions of the unit cells, whereas the optical modes are related to motions within the cells.

5. THERMODYNAMICS OF PHONONS

5.1 The Density Matrix of an Ensemble

Before going into the thermodynamics of phonons we introduce the concept of *density matrix*. Let us assume that we have an ensemble containing N systems, each represented by a normalized wavefunction $\psi_i (i = 1, 2, \ldots, N)$. Let us also consider a complete orthonormal set of functions u_m in terms of which we can expand the function ψ_i:

$$\psi_i = \sum_m c_{mi} u_m. \tag{13.109}$$

If Q is an operator representing an observable, its average value in the ith system is given by

$$Q_i = \int \psi_i^* Q \psi_i \, d\tau. \tag{13.110}$$

Its ensemble average is given by

$$\begin{aligned} \langle Q \rangle &= \frac{1}{N} \sum_i Q_i \\ &= \frac{1}{N} \sum_{i=1}^{N} \int \psi_i^* Q \psi_i \, d\tau \\ &= \frac{1}{N} \sum_{i=1}^{N} \sum_{mn} c_{mi}^* c_{ni} Q_{mn}, \end{aligned} \tag{13.111}$$

where

$$Q_{mm} = \int u_m^* Q u_n \, d\tau. \tag{13.112}$$

We now define the *density matrix* as an operator whose matrix elements in the u representation are

$$\rho_{mn} = \frac{1}{N} \sum_i c_{ni} c_{mi}. \tag{13.113}$$

The density matrix has the following properties:

It is Hermitian.

$$\rho_{mn} = \rho_{nm}^*. \tag{13.114}$$

Its trace is equal to 1. In fact, if $\overline{\langle\psi_i\,|\,\psi_i\rangle}$ is the ensemble average of $\langle\psi_i\,|\,\psi_i\rangle$, we have

$$\overline{\langle\psi\,|\,\psi\rangle} = 1 = \frac{1}{N}\sum_i\sum_m\sum_n c_{m}^{*}c_{ni}\langle u_n\,|\,u_m\rangle = \sum_N\left(\frac{1}{N}\sum_i c_{ni}^{*}c_{ni}\right) = \sum_n \rho_{nn} = \text{tr}\ \rho. \tag{13.115}$$

From (13.114) and (13.115) we can see that the values ρ_{nn} are real, less than unity, and represent the probability of finding a system in the ensemble in a state described by u_n.

From (13.113) it follows that

$$\begin{aligned}\langle Q\rangle &= \frac{1}{N}\sum_{i=1}^{N}\sum_m\sum_n c_{mi}^{*}c_{ni}Q_{mn}\\ &= \sum_m\sum_n \rho_{nm}Q_{mn} = \text{tr}\,(\rho Q),\end{aligned} \tag{13.116}$$

which is, as expected, independent of the representation used.

For an ensemble such that the probability of finding a system with energy E is propotional to $e^{-E/kt}$ (k = Boltzmann constant), the density matrix is given by

$$\rho = \frac{e^{-H/kT}}{\text{tr}\ e^{-H/kT}}. \tag{13.117}$$

The internal energy is then given by

$$\langle E\rangle = \text{tr}\,(H\rho) = \frac{\text{tr}\ He^{-H/kT}}{\text{tr}\ e^{-H/kT}}. \tag{13.118}$$

On the other hand, we know from thermodynamics that

$$\langle E\rangle = F + TS = F - T\left(\frac{\partial F}{\partial T}\right)_\Omega, \tag{13.119}$$

where

$$F = \text{Helmholtz free energy},$$

$$S = -\left(\frac{\partial F}{\partial T}\right)_\Omega = \text{entropy},$$

$$\Omega = \text{volume}.$$

Since (13.118) and (13.119) have to bear the same result, we must have

$$F = -kT\ln\,[\text{tr}\ e^{-H/kT}] = -kT\ln Z, \tag{13.120}$$

where

$$Z = \text{partition function} = \text{tr}\ e^{-H/kT} \tag{13.121}$$

We notice that the partition function is a function of T, independent of the particular representation used.

5.2 The Internal Energy of a Phonon Gas

The Hamiltonian of a phonon gas is given by

$$H = \sum_{q}^{3N} \hbar\omega_q(b_q{}^+ b_q + \tfrac{1}{2}). \tag{13.122}$$

The energy eigenvalue equation is given by

$$H\,|n_1, n_2, \ldots, n_{3N}\rangle = E_{n_1, n_2 \ldots, n_{3N}}\,|n_1, n_2, \ldots, n_{3N}\rangle, \tag{13.123}$$

or, using a shorter notation,

$$H\,|\{n_q\}\rangle = E_{\{n_q\}}\,|\{n_q\}\rangle, \tag{13.124}$$

where

$$|\{n_q\}\rangle = |n_1, n_2, \ldots, n_{3N}\rangle,$$
$$E_{\{n_q\}} = \sum_{q}^{3N} (n_q + \tfrac{1}{2})\hbar\omega_q. \tag{13.125}$$

Let us calculate the partition function in the chosen representation:

$$\begin{aligned}
Z &= \operatorname{tr} e^{-H/kT} = \sum_{\{n_q\}} \langle\{n_q\}|\, e^{-H/kT}\,|\{n_q\}\rangle \\
&= \sum_{\{n_q\}} \exp\left(-\frac{E_{\{n_q\}}}{kT}\right) = \sum_{\{n_q\}} \exp\left\{-\frac{1}{kT}\left[\sum_q \hbar\omega_q(n_q + \tfrac{1}{2})\right]\right\} \\
&= \sum_{\{n_q\}} \Pi_q \exp\left\{-\frac{1}{kT}\,[\hbar\omega_q(n_q + \tfrac{1}{2})]\right\} \\
&= \Pi_q \sum_{n_q=0}^{\infty} \exp\left[-\frac{1}{kT}\,\hbar\omega_q(n_q + \tfrac{1}{2})\right] = \Pi_q Z_q,
\end{aligned} \tag{13.126}$$

where

$$\begin{aligned}
Z_q = \sum_{n_q=0}^{\infty} \exp\left[-\frac{\hbar\omega_q}{kT}\,(n_q + \tfrac{1}{2})\right] &= \frac{e^{-\hbar\omega_q/kT}}{1 - e^{-\hbar\omega_q/kT}} \\
&= \left(2 \sinh \frac{\hbar\omega_q}{kT}\right)^{-1}.
\end{aligned} \tag{13.127}$$

From this we can derive

$$F = -kT \ln Z = kT \sum_q \ln\left(2 \sinh \frac{\hbar\omega_q}{2kT}\right), \tag{13.128}$$

$$S = -\frac{\partial F}{\partial T} = \sum_q \left\{kT\,\frac{\hbar\omega_q}{2kT^2} \coth \frac{\hbar\omega_q}{2} - k \ln\left(2 \sinh \frac{\hbar\omega_q}{2kT}\right)\right\}, \tag{13.129}$$

and

$$\langle E\rangle = F + TS = \sum_q \frac{\hbar\omega_q}{2} \coth \frac{\hbar\omega_q}{2kT}$$

$$= \sum_q^{3N} \hbar\omega_q \left(\frac{1}{e^{\hbar\omega_q/kT} - 1} + \frac{1}{2}\right). \tag{13.130}$$

But the internal energy can also be written

$$\langle E\rangle = \sum_q \hbar\omega_q(\langle \mathcal{N}_q\rangle + \tfrac{1}{2}), \tag{13.131}$$

where $\mathcal{N}_q$ is the operator *occupation number of phonons*,

$$\mathcal{N}_q = b_q^{+} b_q. \tag{13.132}$$

Therefore the average value of $\mathcal{N}_q$ is given by

$$\langle \mathcal{N}_q\rangle = \frac{1}{e^{\hbar\omega_q/kT} - 1}. \tag{13.133}$$

We see that for low temperatures $\langle \mathcal{N}_q\rangle$ is equal to $e^{-\hbar\omega_q/kT}$ and for very high that temperature $\langle \mathcal{N}_q\rangle$ is given by $kT/\hbar\omega_q$, giving for the energy the classical result,

$$\langle E\rangle = 3NkT. \tag{13.134}$$

From (13.130) we can find a formula for the specific heat,

$$c_v = \frac{1}{V}\frac{\partial}{\partial T}\langle E\rangle = \frac{1}{V}\sum_q \hbar\omega_q \frac{e^{\hbar\omega_q/kT}}{(e^{\hbar\omega_q/kT} - 1)^2}\frac{\hbar\omega_q}{kT^2}$$

$$= \frac{k}{V}\sum_q \frac{(\hbar\omega_q/2kT)^2}{\sinh^2(\hbar\omega_q/2kT)}. \tag{13.135}$$

From (13.130) and (13.135) we see that to evaluate the energy and the specific heat (and for that matter all the thermodynamical properties) of a phonon gas we need to know the frequency spectrum.

5.3 The Einstein and Debye Approximations of the Density of Phonon States

The density of phonon states is the number of frequencies in the photon spectrum per unit volume of the crystal and per unit frequency range. It can be expressed as

$$g(\omega) = \frac{1}{V}\sum_{q\lambda}^{3N} \delta(\omega - \omega_{q\lambda})$$

$$\simeq \frac{1}{(2\pi)^3}\sum_{\lambda=1}^{3}\int_{BZ} d\mathbf{q}\, \delta[\omega - \omega_\lambda(q)], \tag{13.136}$$

where BZ = Brillouin zone.

We must have

$$V \int_{-\infty}^{+\infty} g(\omega)\, d\omega = 3N. \tag{13.137}$$

In the so-called *Einstein approximation*,

$$g(\omega) = \frac{3N}{V}\, \delta(\omega - \omega_E), \tag{13.138}$$

where ω_E = Einstein frequency. Using (13.138) in (13.130) we get

$$\begin{aligned}
\langle E \rangle &= \sum_{q\lambda} \hbar\omega_{q\lambda}\left(\frac{1}{e^{\hbar\omega_{q\lambda}/kT} - 1} + \frac{1}{2}\right) \\
&= \sum_{\lambda} V \int_0^{\infty} g(\omega_\lambda)\, \hbar\omega_\lambda \left(\frac{1}{e^{\hbar\omega_\lambda/kT} - 1} + \frac{1}{2}\right) d\omega_\lambda \\
&= V \sum_{\lambda} \frac{3N}{V} \int_0^{\infty} \delta(\omega_\lambda - \omega_E)\left(\frac{\hbar\omega_\lambda}{2} + \frac{\hbar\omega_\lambda}{e^{\hbar\omega_\lambda/kT} - 1}\right) d\omega_\lambda \\
&= 3N\left(\frac{\hbar\omega_E}{2} + \frac{\hbar\omega_E}{e^{\hbar\omega_E/kT} - 1}\right).
\end{aligned} \tag{13.139}$$

Therefore the temperature dependent part of the energy is given by

$$E(T) = \frac{3N\hbar\omega_E}{e^{\hbar\omega_E/kT} - 1} = \begin{cases} 3NkT & \text{(high } T) \\ 3N\hbar\omega_E e^{-\hbar\omega_E/kT} & \text{(low } T). \end{cases} \tag{13.140}$$

The specific heat is then given by

$$c_v = \frac{1}{V} \times \begin{cases} 3Nk & \text{(high } T) \\ 3N\,\dfrac{(\hbar\omega_E)^2}{kT^2}\, e^{-\hbar\omega_E/kT} & \text{(low } T). \end{cases} \tag{13.141}$$

In the so-called *Debye approximation* the assumption is made that the lattice waves propagate as if they were in an isotropic elastic medium. Three modes of propagation are present, one longitudinal and two transverse and correspondingly three branches in the dispersion curve. The dispersion relations for these branches are

$$\begin{aligned} \omega_l &= v_l q \\ \omega_t &= v_t q, \end{aligned} \tag{13.142}$$

where l = longitudinal and t = transverse.

Under these conditions the density of phonon states, since

$$V g_l(\mathbf{q})\, d\mathbf{q} = n(\mathbf{q})\, d\mathbf{q} = \frac{V}{8\pi^3}\, dq_x\, dq_y\, dq_z, \tag{13.143}$$

is given by

$$Vg_l(\omega) = \frac{V}{8\pi^3} 4\pi q^2 \frac{dq}{d\omega} = \frac{V}{2\pi^2} q^2 \frac{dq}{d\omega} = \frac{V}{2\pi^2} \frac{\omega^2}{{v_l}^3}. \tag{13.144}$$

Analogously

$$Vg_t(\omega) = \frac{V}{2\pi^2} \frac{\omega^2}{{v_t}^3}. \tag{13.145}$$

We may determine $\omega_{\text{max}} = \omega_D$ by putting the total number of modes equal to $3N$:

$$\begin{aligned} V\int_0^{\omega_{\text{max}}} [g_l(\omega) + 2g_t(\omega)]\, d\omega &= \frac{V}{2\pi^2}\left(\frac{1}{{v_l}^3} + \frac{2}{{v_t}^3}\right)\int_0^{\omega_D} \omega^2\, d\omega \\ &= \frac{V}{2\pi^2}\left(\frac{1}{{v_l}^3} + \frac{2}{{v_t}^3}\right)\frac{{\omega_D}^3}{3} = 3N. \end{aligned} \tag{13.146}$$

Then we can write

$$\begin{aligned} g(\omega) = g_l(\omega) + 2g_t(\omega) &= \frac{1}{2\pi^2}\left(\frac{1}{{v_l}^3} + \frac{2}{{v_t}^3}\right)\omega^2 \\ &= \begin{cases} \dfrac{9N}{V}\dfrac{\omega^2}{{\omega_D}^3}, & 0 \le \omega \le \omega_D, \\ 0, & \text{elsewhere}. \end{cases} \end{aligned} \tag{13.147}$$

We can now evaluate the energy of the system,

$$\begin{aligned} E &= V\int_{-\infty}^{+\infty} g(\omega)\left(\frac{\hbar\omega}{2} + \frac{\hbar\omega}{e^{\hbar\omega/kT} - 1}\right) d\omega \\ &= E_0 + E(T). \end{aligned} \tag{13.148}$$

We find

$$\begin{aligned} E_0 &= V\int_{-\infty}^{+\infty} g(\omega)\frac{\hbar\omega}{2}\, d\omega \\ &= V\int_0^{\omega_D} g\frac{N}{V}\frac{\omega^2}{{\omega_D}^3}\frac{\hbar\omega}{2}\, d\omega = \frac{9NkT_D}{8}, \end{aligned} \tag{13.149}$$

where

$$T_D = \text{Debye temperature} = \frac{\hbar\omega_D}{k}$$

and

$$\begin{aligned} E(T) &= V\frac{9N}{V}\frac{1}{{\omega_D}^3}\int_0^{\omega_D} \frac{\hbar\omega^3}{e^{\hbar\omega/kT} - 1}\, d\omega \\ &= 9NkT\left(\frac{T}{T_D}\right)^3 \int_0^{T_D/T} \frac{x^3}{e^x - 1}\, dx. \end{aligned} \tag{13.150}$$

The specific heat is given by

$$c_v = \frac{1}{V}\frac{\partial E(T)}{\partial T} = \frac{9N}{V{\omega_D}^3}\frac{\partial}{\partial T}\left\{\int_0^{\omega_D}\frac{\hbar\omega^3}{e^{\hbar\omega/kT}-1}\,d\omega\right\}$$

$$= 9\frac{N}{V}k\left(\frac{T}{T_D}\right)^3\int_0^{T_D/T}\frac{x^4e^x}{(e^x-1)^2}\,dx. \tag{13.151}$$

6. PHONONS AND PHOTONS. SIMILARITIES AND DIFFERENCES

A close analogy may be established between lattice vibrations and electromagnetic waves. Classically, both the electromagnetic field and the displacement field in an elastic medium may be described as a superposition of waves which obey a linear differential equation of the second order in the time and space coordinates. There are, however, some differences:

1. The lattice waves have a different dispersion relation (ω/q is not constant in general).
2. A third, longitudinal polarization direction is present for the lattice vibrations.
3. The medium is not isotropic to the lattice waves.
4. The frequency spectrum of the lattice modes has a cutoff.

The two transverse waves have equal frequencies, but the longitudinal wave has a higher frequency.

The concepts of *longitudinal* and *transverse* waves are really valid only in a continuous lattice; in a discrete lattice there is not exactly a longitudinal wave, except for certain directions of propagation. In this case we designate by *longitudinal waves* the waves with the largest frequency for every value of the wave vector $\mathbf{q}$.

From the quantum mechanical point of view we notice that phonons are collective excitations and their properties are derived by the quantum mechanical properties of the vibrating particles (atoms or ions in solids). On the other hand, in order to derive the properties and the existence of photons as particles, an additional quantum mechanical postulate on the commutation relation of the coordinates and momenta of the radiative field has to be introduced [see (11.60)].

The momentum of a photon is actually represented by $\hbar\mathbf{k}$, where $\mathbf{k}$ is the wave vector; on the other hand it cannot be said that the phonon contributes the amount $\hbar\mathbf{q}$ to the total momentum of the crystal. However, since it has some properties which are similar to the properties of a momentum, $\hbar\mathbf{q}$ is called *pseudo-momentum* of the phonon [3].

The similarities between lattice vibrations and electromagnetic waves can, in principle, be extended (and we shall do this in Chapter 15) in order to establish the effects of thermal vibrations on the energy levels and optical properties of an ionic system.

REFERENCES

[1] P. N. Argyres, "On the Theory of Lattice Vibrations," unpublished report, Lincoln Laboratory, Massachusetts Institute of Technology.

[2] W. Ledermann, "Asymptotic Formulae Relating to the Physical Theory of Crystals," *Proc. Roy. Soc.* (*London*), **A182,** 362 (1964).

[3] H. H. Jensen, "Introductory Lectures on the Free Phonon Field" in *Phonons and Phonon Interactions*, edited by T. A. Bak, Benjamin, New York 1964, p. 1.

14

The Ion-Photon Interaction: Absorption and Emission of Radiation

1. THE ION-RADIATION INTERACTION

The Hamiltonian of a system which consists of an ion (with one electron) and of the radiation field is given by[1]

$$H = \frac{1}{2m}\left(\mathbf{p} + \frac{e\mathbf{A}}{c}\right)^2 - e\phi + \frac{1}{8\pi}\int (E^2 + H^2)\, d\tau, \tag{14.1}$$

where $\mathbf{p}$ = momentum of the electron,

$\mathbf{A}(\mathbf{r})$ = vector potential at the electron site[2]

$$= \sum_{k\lambda} \sqrt{\frac{hc^2}{\omega_k V}}\, \boldsymbol{\pi}_k^{\lambda}(a_k^{\lambda} e^{i\mathbf{k}\cdot\mathbf{r}} + a_k^{\lambda+} e^{-i\mathbf{k}\cdot\mathbf{r}})$$

ϕ = potential due to the central charge.

The interaction Hamiltonian is given by

$$H_1 = \frac{e}{2mc}(\mathbf{p}\cdot\mathbf{A} + \mathbf{A}\cdot\mathbf{p}). \tag{14.2}$$

But

$$\mathbf{p}\cdot\mathbf{A} = \mathbf{A}\cdot\mathbf{p} + [\mathbf{p}, \mathbf{A}]. \tag{14.3}$$

Considering the x component of commutator $[\mathbf{p}, \mathbf{A}]$, we obtain

$$\begin{aligned} [p_x, A_x]\psi &= p_x A_x \psi - A_x p_x \psi \\ &= \frac{\hbar}{i}\frac{\partial}{\partial x} A_x\psi - A_x \frac{\hbar}{i}\frac{\partial \psi}{\partial x} \\ &= \frac{\hbar}{i}\left(\frac{\partial A_x}{\partial x}\right)\psi + \frac{\hbar}{i} A_x \frac{\partial \psi}{\partial x} - A_x \frac{\hbar}{i}\frac{\partial \psi}{\partial x} = \frac{\hbar}{i}\left(\frac{\partial A_x}{\partial x}\right)\psi. \end{aligned} \tag{14.4}$$

[1] See (1.19).

[2] See (11.62) and (11.63).

Then, since we are using the Coulomb gauge $\nabla \cdot \mathbf{A} = 0$,

$$\mathbf{p} \cdot \mathbf{A} = \mathbf{A} \cdot \mathbf{p} + \frac{\hbar}{i} \nabla \cdot \mathbf{A} = \mathbf{A} \cdot \mathbf{p}. \tag{14.5}$$

Now the Hamiltonian H can be written

$$H = H_0 + H_1 + H_2, \tag{14.6}$$

where

$$\begin{aligned} H_0 &= \frac{p^2}{2m} - e\phi + \frac{1}{8\pi} \int (E^2 + H^2)\, d\tau \\ &= \frac{p^2}{2m} - e\phi + \sum_{k\lambda} (a_k^{\lambda+} a_k^{\lambda} + \tfrac{1}{2}\hbar\omega_k); \end{aligned} \tag{14.7}$$

$$\begin{aligned} H_1 &= \frac{e}{mc} \mathbf{p} \cdot \mathbf{A} \\ &= \frac{e}{m} \sum_{k\lambda} \left(\frac{h}{\omega_k V}\right)^{1/2} \boldsymbol{\pi}_k^{\lambda} \cdot \mathbf{p}(a_k^{\lambda} e^{i\mathbf{k}\cdot\mathbf{r}} + a_k^{\lambda+} e^{-i\mathbf{k}\cdot\mathbf{r}}); \end{aligned} \tag{14.8}$$

$$\begin{aligned} H_2 &= \frac{e^2}{2mc^2} (\mathbf{A})^2 \\ &= \frac{e^2}{m} \frac{h}{V} \sum_{k\lambda} \sum_{k'\lambda'} \frac{1}{\sqrt{\omega_k \omega_{k'}}} \boldsymbol{\pi}_k^{\lambda} \\ &\quad \cdot \boldsymbol{\pi}_{k'}^{\lambda'} (a_k^{\lambda} e^{i\mathbf{k}\cdot\mathbf{r}} + a_k^{\lambda+} e^{-i\mathbf{k}\cdot\mathbf{r}})(a_{k'}^{\lambda'} e^{i\mathbf{k}'\cdot\mathbf{r}} + a_{k'}^{\lambda'+} e^{-i\mathbf{k}'\cdot\mathbf{r}}). \end{aligned} \tag{14.9}$$

In the case of a multielectron ion we have to sum over all the electron coordinates.

The matrix element involved in the creation of a photon of frequency ω_k and polarization $\boldsymbol{\pi}_k^{\lambda}$ is given by

$$\begin{aligned} M_k &= \langle \psi_f | H_1 | \psi_i \rangle = \langle \psi_f^{el}; n_k + 1 | H_1 | \psi_i^{el}; n_i \rangle \\ &= \frac{e}{m} \langle \psi_f^{el} | \sum_i e^{-i\mathbf{k}\cdot\mathbf{r}_i} \mathbf{p}_i \cdot \boldsymbol{\pi}_k^{\lambda} | \psi_i^{el} \rangle \left[\frac{h}{\omega_k V} (n_k + 1)\right]^{1/2}, \end{aligned} \tag{14.10}$$

and the matrix element involved in the absorption of a photon of frequency ω_k and polarization $\boldsymbol{\pi}_k^{\lambda}$ by

$$\begin{aligned} M_k &= \langle \psi_f | H_1 | \psi_i \rangle = \langle \psi_f^{el}; n_k - 1 | H_1 | \psi_i^{el}; n_k \rangle \\ &= \frac{e}{m} \langle \psi_f^{el} | \sum_i e^{i\mathbf{k}\cdot\mathbf{r}_i} \mathbf{p}_i \cdot \boldsymbol{\pi}_k^{\lambda} | \psi_i^{el} \rangle \left(\frac{h}{V\omega_k} n_k\right)^{1/2}. \end{aligned} \tag{14.11}$$

Here ψ_f and ψ_i represent the final and initial states, respectively, of the total (ion + radiation) system and ψ_f^{el} and ψ_i^{el}, the final and initial state of the ionic system, respectively; the sum over i is extended to all the electrons in the ion.

2. THE EXPANSION OF THE INTERACTION HAMILTONIAN: DIFFERENT TYPES OF RADIATION

The interaction Hamiltonian between an atomic system and the radiation field is given by

$$\begin{aligned} H_1 &= \frac{e}{mc}\,\mathbf{A}\cdot\mathbf{p} \\ &= \frac{e}{mc}\sum_{k,\lambda} c\left(\frac{h}{V\omega_k}\right)^{1/2}(a_k^{\lambda}e^{i\mathbf{k}\cdot\mathbf{r}} + a_k^{\lambda+}e^{-i\mathbf{k}\cdot\mathbf{r}})(\boldsymbol{\pi}_k^{\lambda}\cdot\mathbf{p}). \end{aligned} \tag{14.12}$$

Let us consider the expansion

$$e^{\pm i\mathbf{k}\cdot\mathbf{r}}\mathbf{p} \approx \mathbf{p} \pm i(\mathbf{k}\cdot\mathbf{r})\,\mathbf{p}. \tag{14.13}$$

For any function of momenta and coordinates $F(p_i, q_i)$ we have, classically, by the use of Hamilton's equations:

$$\begin{aligned} \frac{dF(p_i, q_i)}{dt} &= \frac{\partial F}{\partial t} + \sum_i \left(\frac{\partial F}{\partial q_i}\frac{\partial q_i}{\partial t} + \frac{\partial F}{\partial p_i}\frac{\partial p_i}{\partial t}\right) \\ &= \frac{\partial F}{\partial t} + \sum_i \left(\frac{\partial F}{\partial q_i}\frac{\partial H}{\partial p_i} - \frac{\partial F}{\partial p_i}\frac{\partial H}{\partial q_i}\right) \\ &= \frac{\partial F}{\partial t} + \{F, H\}, \end{aligned} \tag{14.14}$$

where the symbol $\{F, H\}$ indicates a Poisson bracket. If F is not an explicit function of time the term $\partial F/\partial t$ is equal to zero.

Going to quantum mechanics we replace the Poisson bracket by $1/i\hbar$ times the commutator $[F, H]$. We get then

$$\frac{dF}{dt} = -\frac{i}{\hbar}[F, H] = \frac{i}{\hbar}[H, F]. \tag{14.15}$$

In our present case, if $F = x$,

$$\dot{x} = \frac{i}{\hbar}[H, x], \tag{14.16}$$

and

$$p_x = m\dot{x} = i\frac{m}{\hbar}[H, x]; \tag{14.17}$$

but

$$\langle\psi_f^{\text{el}}|\,[H, x]\,|\psi_i^{\text{el}}\rangle = \langle\psi_f^{\text{el}}|\,Hx - xH\,|\psi_i^{\text{el}}\rangle$$
$$= (E_f^{\text{el}} - E_i^{\text{el}})\,\langle\psi_f^{\text{el}}|\,x\,|\psi_i^{\text{el}}\rangle = \hbar\omega_k\langle\psi_f^{\text{el}}|\,x\,|\psi_i^{\text{el}}\rangle \quad (14.18)$$

and

$$\langle\psi_f^{\text{el}}|\,\mathbf{p}\,|\psi_i^{\text{el}}\rangle = im\omega_k\langle\psi_f^{\text{el}}|\,\mathbf{r}\,|\psi_i^{\text{el}}\rangle, \quad (14.19)$$

where $\omega_k = (E_f^{\text{el}} - E_i^{\text{el}})/\hbar$. Therefore the first term in the expansion in (14.13) corresponds to the Hamiltonian:

$$H^{E1} = i\sum_{k,\lambda}\left(\frac{h\omega_k}{V}\right)^{1/2} a_k^{\lambda}\boldsymbol{\pi}_k^{\lambda}\cdot\left(\sum_i e\mathbf{r}_i\right) + i\sum_{k,\lambda}\left(\frac{h\omega_k}{V}\right)^{1/2} a_k^{\lambda+}\boldsymbol{\pi}_k^{\lambda}\cdot\left(\sum e\mathbf{r}_i\right). \quad (14.20)$$

In this expression the first term corresponds to absorption, the second, to emission of radiation. A radiative transition produced by the Hamiltonian (14.20) is called an *electric dipole transition.*

The second term in (14.13) can be written

$$(\mathbf{k}\cdot\mathbf{r})\,\mathbf{p} = \tfrac{1}{2}\{(\mathbf{k}\cdot\mathbf{r})\,\mathbf{p} + (\mathbf{k}\cdot\mathbf{p})\,\mathbf{r}\} + \tfrac{1}{2}\{(\mathbf{k}\cdot\mathbf{r})\,\mathbf{p} - (\mathbf{k}\cdot\mathbf{p})\,\mathbf{r}\}. \quad (14.21)$$

Let us consider the second term of the right member in (14.21). We get

$$\tfrac{1}{2}\{(\mathbf{k}\cdot\mathbf{r})\,\mathbf{p} - (\mathbf{k}\cdot\mathbf{p})\,\mathbf{r}\} = -\tfrac{1}{2}\{\mathbf{k}\times(\mathbf{r}\times\mathbf{p})\}$$
$$= -\frac{\omega_k}{2c}(\mathbf{1}_k\times\mathbf{L}). \quad (14.22)$$

This term in the expansion (14.13) produces a *magnetic dipole interaction* represented by the following expression:

$$H^{M1} = -i\sum_{k\lambda}\left(\frac{h\omega_k}{V}\right)^{1/2} a_k^{\lambda}\boldsymbol{\pi}_k^{\lambda}\cdot\left[\mathbf{1}_k\times\frac{e}{2mc}(\mathbf{L}+2\mathbf{S})\right]$$
$$+ i\sum_{k\lambda}\left(\frac{h\omega_k}{V}\right)^{1/2} a_k^{\lambda+}\boldsymbol{\pi}_k^{\lambda}\cdot\left[\mathbf{1}_k\times\frac{e}{2mc}(\mathbf{L}+2\mathbf{S})\right], \quad (14.23)$$

where $\mathbf{L} = \sum_i \mathbf{l}_i$ and $\mathbf{S} = \sum_i \mathbf{s}_i$ and where the first term produces absorption, the second emission of radiation. In this expression we have added to the orbital magnetic moment $(-e/2mc)\,\mathbf{L}$ the spin magnetic moment $(-e/mc)\,\mathbf{S}$. The justification for this addition derives from the fact that the ion-radiation interaction actually includes a term

$$\frac{e}{2mc}2\mathbf{s}\cdot\mathbf{H} = \frac{e}{mc}\mathbf{s}\cdot(\boldsymbol{\nabla}\times\mathbf{A}). \quad (14.24)$$

If we evaluate $\boldsymbol{\nabla}\times\mathbf{A}$ and then put $e^{i\mathbf{k}\cdot\mathbf{r}}\approx 1$, we come up with the term that we add to the H^{M1} Hamiltonian. The mathematical passages are left to the reader.

Let us now consider the first term of the right member of (14.21). We get

$$\tfrac{1}{2}\{(\mathbf{k}\cdot\mathbf{r})\,\mathbf{p}+(\mathbf{k}\cdot\mathbf{p})\,\mathbf{r}\}=\frac{m}{2}\{(\mathbf{k}\cdot\mathbf{r})\,\dot{\mathbf{r}}+(\mathbf{k}\cdot\dot{\mathbf{r}})\,\mathbf{r}\}$$

$$=\frac{m}{2}\frac{d}{dt}[(\mathbf{k}\cdot\mathbf{r})\,\mathbf{r}]=\frac{im\omega_k}{2}[(\mathbf{k}\cdot\mathbf{r})\,\mathbf{r}]. \quad (14.25)$$

This produces an *electric quadrupole interaction* given by

$$H^{E2}=-\sum_{k\lambda}\left(\frac{h\omega_k}{V}\right)^{1/2}a_k^{\lambda}\tfrac{1}{2}(\mathbf{k}\cdot\mathbf{r})\,(e\mathbf{r}\cdot\boldsymbol{\pi}_k^{\lambda})+\sum_{k\lambda}\left(\frac{h\omega_k}{V}\right)^{1/2}a_k^{\lambda+}\tfrac{1}{2}(\mathbf{k}\cdot\mathbf{r})\,(e\mathbf{r}\cdot\boldsymbol{\pi}_k^{\lambda}). \quad (14.26)$$

3. THE DENSITY OF FINAL STATES

We know that the final state of the total system is in a continuum because of the closely spaced values of k:

$$k_x=\frac{2\pi n_x}{L},$$

$$k_y=\frac{2\pi n_y}{L}, \quad (14.27)$$

$$k_z=\frac{2\pi n_z}{L},$$

having considered periodic boundary conditions over a cube of volume $V = L^3$.

The number of final states with wave vector $\mathbf{k}$ in $(\mathbf{k}, \mathbf{k} + d\mathbf{k})$ and a certain polarization of the photon emitted or absorbed is given by

$$g(\mathbf{k})\,d\mathbf{k}=dn_x\,dn_y\,dn_z$$

$$=\frac{V}{8\pi^3}\,dk_x\,dk_y\,dk_z=\frac{V}{8\pi^3}\,k^2\,dk\,d\Omega_k$$

$$=\frac{V}{8\pi^3c^3}\,\omega_k^{\,2}\,d\omega_k\,d\Omega_k=g(\omega_k)\,d\omega_k\,d\Omega_k, \quad (14.28)$$

where $d\Omega_k$ = infinitesimal solid angle in the direction $\mathbf{k}$.

The density of final states for the emission or absorption of a photon of frequency ν_k and a certain polarization, in any direction of space, is given by

$$4\pi g(\nu_k)=g(\omega_k)\,\frac{d\omega_k}{d\nu_k}\,4\pi=\frac{4\pi V}{c^3}\,\nu_k^{\,2}. \quad (14.29)$$

4. THE TRANSITION PROBABILITY PER UNIT TIME

The probability per unit time that a radiative process takes place is given by the formula, already derived in Section 9.2 of Chapter 1,

$$P_k = \frac{2\pi}{\hbar^2} |M_k|^2 g(\omega_k) = \frac{1}{\hbar^2} |M_k|^2 g(\nu_k), \tag{14.30}$$

where $M_k = \langle \psi_f | H_1 | \psi_i \rangle$,
$g(\nu_k) =$ density of final states.

The probability per unit time that the ionic system can be found with one more, or with one less photon of frequency ω_k and polarization $\boldsymbol{\pi}_k^{\lambda}$, in the direction given by $d\Omega_k$, is given by

$$\begin{aligned} P_k^{\lambda}\, d\Omega_k &= \frac{V}{8\pi^3 c^3} \omega_k^2\, d\Omega_k \frac{2\pi}{\hbar^2} |M_k^{\lambda}|^2 \\ &= \frac{V\omega_k^2}{4\pi^2 c^3 \hbar^2} |M_k^{\lambda}|^2\, d\Omega_k \\ &= \frac{V\omega_k^2}{4\pi^2 c^3 \hbar^2} \frac{h}{V} \begin{Bmatrix} n_k \\ n_k + 1 \end{Bmatrix} \frac{e^2}{\omega_k m^2} \left| \left\langle \psi_f^{\text{el}} \left| \begin{matrix} \sum_i e^{i\mathbf{k}\cdot\mathbf{r}_i} \boldsymbol{\pi}_k^{\lambda} \cdot \mathbf{p}_i \\ \sum_i e^{i\mathbf{k}\cdot\mathbf{r}_i} \boldsymbol{\pi}_k^{\lambda} \cdot \mathbf{p}_i \end{matrix} \right| \psi_i^{\text{el}} \right\rangle \right|^2 d\Omega_k \\ &= \frac{\omega_k e^2}{hc^3 m} \begin{Bmatrix} n_k \\ n_k + 1 \end{Bmatrix} \left| \left\langle \psi_f^{\text{el}} \left| \begin{matrix} \sum_i e^{i\mathbf{k}\cdot\mathbf{r}_i} \boldsymbol{\pi}_k^{\lambda} \cdot \mathbf{p}_i \\ \sum_i e^{-i\mathbf{k}\cdot\mathbf{r}_i} \boldsymbol{\pi}_k^{\lambda} \cdot \mathbf{p}_i \end{matrix} \right| \psi_i^{\text{el}} \right\rangle \right|^2 d\Omega_k, \end{aligned} \tag{14.31}$$

where the upper row corresponds to the absorption and the lower row to the emission of a photon.

We want now to show an important result. Let us consider the integral

$$\langle \psi_f^{\text{el}} | e^{-i\mathbf{k}\cdot\mathbf{r}} \boldsymbol{\pi}_k^{\lambda} \cdot \mathbf{p} | \psi_i^{\text{el}} \rangle = \hbar \langle \psi_f^{\text{el}} | e^{-i\mathbf{k}\cdot\mathbf{r}} \boldsymbol{\pi}_k^{\lambda} \cdot (-i\boldsymbol{\nabla}) | \psi_i^{\text{el}} \rangle. \tag{14.32}$$

Because of the orthogonality of $\mathbf{k}$ and $\boldsymbol{\pi}_k^{\lambda}$ we can interchange $\boldsymbol{\pi}_k^{\lambda} \cdot \boldsymbol{\nabla}$ with $e^{-i\mathbf{k}\cdot\mathbf{r}}$. Taking advantage of the hermiticity of the operator $i\boldsymbol{\nabla}$ we then have

$$\begin{aligned} |\langle \psi_f^{\text{el}} | e^{-i\mathbf{k}\cdot\mathbf{r}} \boldsymbol{\pi}_k^{\lambda} \cdot \mathbf{p} | \psi_i^{\text{el}} \rangle|^2 &= \hbar^2 |\langle \psi_f^{\text{el}} | \boldsymbol{\pi}_k^{\lambda} \cdot (-i\boldsymbol{\nabla}) e^{-i\mathbf{k}\cdot\mathbf{r}} | \psi_i^{\text{el}} \rangle|^2 \\ &= \hbar^2 |\langle (-i\boldsymbol{\nabla}) \cdot \boldsymbol{\pi}_k^{\lambda} \psi_f^{\text{el}} | e^{-i\mathbf{k}\cdot\mathbf{r}} | \psi_i^{\text{el}} \rangle|^2 \\ &= \hbar^2 |\langle \psi_i^{\text{el}} | e^{i\mathbf{k}\cdot\mathbf{r}} (-i\boldsymbol{\nabla}) \cdot \boldsymbol{\pi}_k^{\lambda} | \psi_f^{\text{el}} \rangle|^2 \\ &= |\langle \psi_i^{\text{el}} | e^{i\mathbf{k}\cdot\mathbf{r}} \boldsymbol{\pi}_k^{\lambda} \cdot \mathbf{p} | \psi_f^{\text{el}} \rangle|^2. \end{aligned} \tag{14.33}$$

Therefore we can say that the downward (induced emission) and the upward (absorption) transition probabilities are the same. We can write then the *probability per unit time of spontaneous emission of a photon in the solid angle* $d\Omega_k$:

$$P_k^\lambda(\text{sp})\, d\Omega_k = \frac{\omega_k e^2}{hc^3m^2} |\langle \psi_f^{\text{el}}| \sum_i e^{i\mathbf{k}\cdot\mathbf{r}_i} \boldsymbol{\pi}_k^\lambda \cdot \mathbf{p}_i\, |\psi_i^{\text{el}}\rangle|^2\, d\Omega_k; \tag{14.34}$$

and the *probability per unit time of induced emission or absorption in the solid angle* $d\Omega_k$:

$$P_k^\lambda(\text{emi; abs}) = \frac{\omega_k e^2}{hc^3m^2}\, n_k\, |\langle \psi_f^{\text{el}}| \sum_i e^{i\mathbf{k}\cdot\mathbf{r}_i} \boldsymbol{\pi}_k^\lambda \cdot \mathbf{p}_i\, |\psi_i^{\text{el}}\rangle|^2\, d\Omega_k. \tag{14.35}$$

If an atomic system is in an excited state the probability per unit time of the spontaneous emission of a photon of frequency ω_k is then given by

$$\begin{aligned} A &= \sum_\lambda \int P_k^\lambda(\text{sp})\, d\Omega_k \\ &= \frac{\omega_k e^2}{hc^3 m} \sum_\lambda \int d\Omega_k\, |\langle \psi_f^{\text{el}}| \sum_i e^{i\mathbf{k}\cdot\mathbf{r}_i} \boldsymbol{\pi}_k^\lambda \cdot \mathbf{p}_i\, |\psi_i^{\text{el}}\rangle|^2. \end{aligned} \tag{14.36}$$

The probability per unit time of the induced emission of a photon of frequency ω_k is given by

$$B\rho_\nu = An_k, \tag{14.37}$$

where ρ_ν is the energy density of the radiation field. Let us relate ρ_ν to n_k. The energy density is given by

$$\frac{E}{V} = \int \rho_\nu\, d\nu = \sum_{k\lambda} \frac{h\nu_k(n_k^\lambda + \frac{1}{2})}{V} = \frac{2}{V} \int dk\; g(k)\, h\nu_k(n_k + \tfrac{1}{2}), \tag{14.38}$$

where the factor 2 is due to the fact that for any direction of propagation we have two polarizations. From (14.28) and (14.29) we have

$$g(k)\, dk = \frac{V}{8\pi^3}\, 4\pi k^2\, dk = \frac{4\pi V}{c^3}\, \nu^2\, d\nu. \tag{14.39}$$

Then,

$$\frac{E}{V} = \int \frac{8\pi\nu^2}{c^3}\, h\nu(n_\nu + \tfrac{1}{2})\, d\nu = \int \rho_\nu\, d\nu, \tag{14.40}$$

where we have changed notation from n_k to n_ν. We then have

$$\rho_\nu = \frac{8\pi h\nu^3}{c^3} (n_\nu), \tag{14.41}$$

where we have eliminated from $(n_\nu + \frac{1}{2})$ the term $\frac{1}{2}$ which produces a term equal to ∞ in the integration and shifts the zero point energy.

We can now derive the ratio of A and B:

$$\frac{A}{B} = \frac{\rho_\nu}{n_\nu} = \frac{8\pi h\nu^3}{c^3}. \tag{14.42}$$

We can also express the equality of the *absorption* and of the *induced emission* probability in the following way:

$$B_{\text{down}} = B_{\text{up}}. \tag{14.43}$$

The relations (14.42) and (14.43) are called the *Einstein's relations* and A and B the *Einstein's coefficients.*

5. DIPOLE RADIATION

The probability per unit time of dipole absorption of a photon of frequency $\omega_k = (E_f^{\text{el}} - E_i^{\text{el}})/\hbar$ coming to the atom from any direction and with any polarization is given by

$$P_k(\text{abs}) = \frac{\omega_k^{\ 3}}{hc^3}\, n_k \sum_\lambda \int d\Omega_k\, |\langle\psi_f^{\text{el}}|\, \mathbf{M} \qquad {}_k^{\lambda}\, |\psi_i^{\text{el}}\rangle|^2, \tag{14.44}$$

and the probability per unit time of dipole emission of a photon of frequency ω_k in any direction and with any polarization by

$$P_k(\text{emi}) = \frac{\omega_k^{\ 3}}{hc^3}\, (n_k + 1) \sum_\lambda \int d\Omega_k\, |\langle\psi_f^{\text{el}}|\, \mathbf{M} \cdot \boldsymbol{\pi}_k^{\lambda}\, |\psi_i^{\text{el}}\rangle|^2, \tag{14.45}$$

where

$$\mathbf{M} = \sum (e\mathbf{r}_i). \tag{14.46}$$

Let us now consider the probability of spontaneous emission of a photon of frequency ω_k in the direction (θ, φ):

$$dA_k = \sum_\lambda \frac{\omega_k^{\ 3}}{hc^3}\, |\langle\mathbf{M}\rangle_{fi} \cdot \boldsymbol{\pi}_k^{\lambda}|^2\, d\Omega_k, \tag{14.47}$$

where

$$d\Omega_k = \sin\theta\, d\theta\, d\varphi. \tag{14.48}$$

We must have

$$\begin{gathered} \boldsymbol{\pi}_k^{1} \cdot \boldsymbol{\pi}_k^{2} = 0, \\ \boldsymbol{\pi}_k^{1} \cdot \mathbf{k} = \boldsymbol{\pi}_k^{2} \cdot \mathbf{k} = 0. \end{gathered} \tag{14.49}$$

We can then take the unit vectors representing the directions of polarization as Fig. 14.1, where $\mathbf{1}_z$, $\mathbf{k}$, and $\boldsymbol{\pi}_k^{2}$ lie in the same plane yz.

Let us assume now that only the z component of $\mathbf{M}$ has a matrix element between state ψ_f^{el} and ψ_i^{el}; we can see immediately that in this case the system

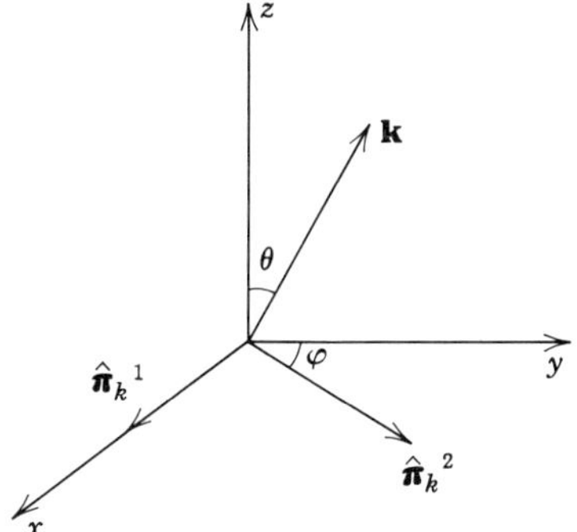

Fig. 14.1. Wave vector **k** and polarization vectors.

can emit photons with polarization $\boldsymbol{\pi}_k^{\ 2}$ only:

$$dA_k = \frac{{\omega_k}^3}{hc^3} |\langle M \rangle_{fi}|^2 \sin^2 \theta \, d\Omega_k. \tag{14.50}$$

If we now integrate over the whole space,

$$A_k = \frac{{\omega_k}^3}{hc^3} |\langle M \rangle_{fi}|^2 \int_0^{\pi} \int_0^{2\pi} \sin^2 \theta \sin \theta \, d\theta \, d\varphi$$

$$= \frac{{\omega_k}^3}{hc^3} |\langle M \rangle_{fi}|^2 \frac{8\pi}{3} = \frac{8\pi{\omega_k}^3}{3hc^3} |\langle M \rangle_{fi}|^2. \tag{14.51}$$

The power irradiated because of such a transition is given by

$$P = \hbar\omega_k A_k = \frac{4{\omega_k}^4}{3c^3} |\langle M \rangle_{fi}|^2. \tag{14.52}$$

In classical electrodynamics the power radiated by an oscillatory electric dipole $M \cos \omega_k t$ is given by

$$P = \frac{{\omega_k}^4}{3c^3} |M|^2, \tag{14.53}$$

where

$$\mathbf{M} = e \int \rho(\mathbf{r})\mathbf{r} \, d\tau, \tag{14.54}$$

and $e\rho(\mathbf{r})$ is the charge density.

By comparing (14.52) and (14.53) we see that M has been replaced by $\langle 2M \rangle_{fi}$. What is the reason for the extra factor 2? The factor 2 is introduced because one classical Fourier component corresponds to two matrix elements. A classical oscillator of amplitude M has two Fourier components,

$$M \cos \omega t = \tfrac{1}{2} M(e^{i\omega t} + e^{-i\omega t}), \tag{14.55}$$

with frequency ω and $-\omega$. From the classical point of view we do not distinguish frequency ω from $-\omega$, namely, photons absorbed from photons emitted. Quantum mechanics, however, allows only one of the two components to enter the matrix element in (14.52).

In a similar way, in the case of a magnetic dipole transition, the probability for spontaneous emission of a photon of frequency ω_k in the direction (θ, φ) is given by

$$dA_k = \sum_\lambda \frac{{\omega_k}^3}{hc^3} |\boldsymbol{\pi}_k{}^\lambda \cdot \mathbf{1}_k \times \langle \mathbf{M} \rangle_{fi}|^2 \, d\Omega_k, \tag{14.47'}$$

where

$$\mathbf{M} = -\frac{e}{2mc} (\mathbf{L} + 2\mathbf{S}). \tag{14.46'}$$

If only the z component of $\mathbf{M}$ is active, the system can emit photons with polarization $\boldsymbol{\pi}_k{}^1$ only:

$$dA_k = \frac{{\omega_k}^3}{hc^3} |\langle M \rangle_{fi}|^2 \sin^2 \theta \, d\Omega_k. \tag{14.50'}$$

Integrating over the whole space we find:

$$A_k = \frac{8\pi {\omega_k}^3}{3hc^3} |\langle M \rangle_{fi}|^2. \tag{14.51'}$$

6. SELECTION RULES FOR RADIATIVE TRANSITIONS

6.1. Selection Rules for Transitions between Eigenstates of Angular Momentum

The relevant types of radiation are represented by the following operators:

Type	Form	Parity	Components Transform as	Rep in a 3d Rotational Symmetry
$E1$	$\sum_i e\mathbf{r}_i$	Odd	x, y, z	D_{1u}
$M1$	$\sum_i \boldsymbol{\mu}_i$	Even	L_x, L_y, L_z	D_{1g}
$E2$	$\frac{1}{2} \sum_i (\mathbf{k} \cdot \mathbf{r}_i)\mathbf{r}_i$	Even	$\begin{Bmatrix} x^2, y^2, z^2 \\ xy, yz, zx \end{Bmatrix}$	D_{2g}

In principle we can have higher orders of multipole radiation. Generally, a 2^l electric pole operator has components which transform under rotation like the spherical harmonics of order l, and a 2^l magnetic pole corresponds to a spherical harmonic of order $l - 1$, multiplied by the operator $\boldsymbol{\mu}$, which carries by itself an angular momentum $\hbar$. Thus *any* 2^l *pole carries an angular momentum* $l\hbar$.

The parity of an lth order spherical harmonic is $(-1)^l$ and that of $\boldsymbol{\mu}$, which is an axial vector, is even. Therefore an electric 2^l-pole has parity $(-1)^l$ and a magnetic 2^l-pole has parity $(-1)^{l-1}$.

No multipole has zero angular momentum. If we call the total angular momentum of the initial and final states $\mathbf{J}_i$ and $\mathbf{J}_f$, respectively, and the angular momentum carried away by the radiation $\mathbf{l}$, we must have

$$\mathbf{J}_f = \mathbf{J}_i + \mathbf{l}. \tag{14.56}$$

Since $l \neq 0$, it follows that a transition from a state with $J_i = 0$ to one with $J_f = 0$ is absolutely forbidden. We shall use the following notation:

	Angular Momentum	Parity
Initial state	J_i	P_i
Final state	J_f	P_f

Let us now examine different cases.

$J_f \neq J_i$ ***and both*** $\neq 0$. (a) If $P_iP_f = (-1)^{J_i - J_f}$ the dominant radiation is electric multipole of order $l = |J_f - J_i|$ and the magnetic multipole radiation which is of order $l = |J_f - J_i| + 1$ is negligible; and (b) If $P_iP_f = (-1)^{J_i - J_f + 1}$, the electric multipole transition of order $l = |J_i - J_f| + 1$ and the magnetic multipole transition of order $l = |J_i - J_f|$ compete. The transition probability is much greater in (a) than in (b).

Example

$$J_i = 1; \qquad J_f = 2; \qquad P_i \neq P_f.$$

Dominant radiation: $l = 1$, electric dipole;

$l = 1$ magnetic dipole forbidden;
$l = 2$ electric quadrupole forbidden;
$l = 2$ magnetic quadrupole not forbidden but negligible.

Example

$$J_i = 1; \qquad J_f = 2; \qquad P_i = P_f.$$

$l = 2$ electric quadrupole
$l = 1$ magnetic dipole
} compete.

$J_i = 0$ ***or*** $J_f = 0$. The transitions with $l = |J_i - J_f| + 1$ are forbidden and only those with $l = |J_i - J_f|$ can occur.

Example

$$J_i = 1; \qquad J_f = 0; \qquad P_i \neq P_f.$$

Dominant radiation: $l = 1$, electric dipole;

$$\left.\begin{array}{l}\text{Magnetic dipole}\\ \text{Electric quadrupole}\\ \text{Magnetic quadrupole}\end{array}\right\}\text{forbidden.}$$

Example

$$J_i = 1; \qquad J_f = 0; \qquad P_i = P_f.$$

Only magnetic dipole allowed.

$J_i = J_f$ ***but both*** $\neq 0$. The transitions with $l = |J_i - J_f|$ cannot occur. Then we have the two cases:

1. $P_i = P_f$.
$$\left.\begin{array}{l}\text{electric quadrupole}\\ \text{magnetic dipole}\end{array}\right\}\text{allowed.}$$
2. $P_i \neq P_f$.
$$\left.\begin{array}{l}\text{electric dipole}\\ \text{magnetic quadrupole}\end{array}\right\}\text{allowed.}$$

We can tabulate our results as follows:

	$J_i, J_f \neq 0$		J_i or $J_f = 0$		$J_i = J_f = 0$
$E1$	$\Delta J = \pm 1, 0;$	yes	$\Delta J = \pm 1;$	yes	
$M1$	$\Delta J = \pm 1, 0;$	no	$\Delta J = \pm 1;$	no	*Absolutely*
$E2$	$\Delta J = \pm 2, \pm 1, 0;$	no	$\Delta J = \pm 2;$	no	*Forbidden*
$M2$	$\Delta J = \pm 2, \pm 1, 0;$	yes	$\Delta J = \pm 2;$	yes	

Yes = change of parity; No = no change of parity.

6.2. Selection Rules for Atomic Systems

Electric Dipole Radiation. If no external field is applied the (degenerate) eigenfunctions of the atom transform according to a representation D_J of the group. Parity is a good quantum number and by using D_{Jg} or D_{Ju} we indicate an even or an odd state, respectively.

The electric dipole operator is given by $\sum_i e\mathbf{r}_i$. The components $\sum_i ex_i$, $\sum_i ey_i$, $\sum_i ez_i$ transform like translations. We may form linear combinations of these components which form an irreducible tensor operator of the first order:

$$
\begin{aligned}
r_1 &= -\sum_i \frac{x_i + iy_i}{\sqrt{2}}, \\
r_0 &= \sum_i z_i \\
r_{-1} &= \sum_i \frac{x_i - iy_i}{\sqrt{2}}.
\end{aligned}
\tag{14.57}
$$

These new components transform like basis functions for the representation D_{1u} of the three-dimensional rotation group (u is for odd).

The spontaneous and induced transitions depend on the matrix elements $\langle \psi_f^{\text{el}} | r_\alpha | \psi_i^{\text{el}} \rangle$. The products $r_\alpha \psi_i^{\text{el}}$ transform according to

$$D_1 \times D_{J_i} = D_{J_i+1} + D_{J_i} + D_{J_i-1} \tag{14.58}$$

if $J_i \geq 1$. If $J_i = 0$ we have

$$D_1 \times D_0 = D_1, \tag{14.59}$$

and then only $J_f = 1$ is allowed, eliminating the transition $J_f = 0 \rightarrow J_i = 0$.

Moreover, since electric dipole is an odd operator, the parity of the final state must be different from the parity of the initial state (*Laporte rule*). We have then these results:

$$
\begin{aligned}
&\Delta J = 0, \pm 1; \qquad J_i = 0 \nleftrightarrow J_f = 0;^3 \\
&P_f \neq P_i.
\end{aligned}
\tag{14.60}
$$

If we apply a magnetic field the eigenfunctions transform according to the representations of the group $C_{\infty h}$. The three components r_1, r_0, and r_{-1} transform respectively according to C_1, C_0, and C_{-1}. The products $r_\alpha \psi_i^{\text{el}}$ transform according to one of the following representations:

$$
\begin{aligned}
C_1 C_{M_{J_i}} &= C_{M_{J_i+1}}, \\
C_0 C_{M_{J_i}} &= C_{M_{J_i}}, \\
C_{-1} C_{M_{J_i}} &= C_{M_{J_i-1}},
\end{aligned}
\tag{14.61}
$$

and then we have the selection rules:

$$
\begin{aligned}
&\Delta M = \pm 1, \qquad \text{for circularly polarized radiation,} \\
&\Delta M = 0, \qquad \text{for linearly polarized radiation,} \\
&P_f \neq P_i.
\end{aligned}
\tag{14.62}
$$

[3] The symbol $\nleftrightarrow$ indicates that a transition is forbidden.

In the Russell-Saunders approximation the approximate eigenfunctions transform like the representation $D_L \times D_S$, whereas the dipole operator components transform like D_1 ($L = 1$, $S = 0$). In this case we then have

$$\begin{aligned} &\Delta L = 0, \pm 1; \qquad L_i = 0 \not\leftrightarrow L_f = 0, \\ &\Delta S = 0, \\ &P_f \neq P_i. \end{aligned} \tag{14.63}$$

These rules are only approximate and allow us to distinguish between large and small matrix elements.

Magnetic Dipole Radiation. This case is similar to the electric dipole case. The magnetic dipole operator for one electron is given by

$$\boldsymbol{\mu} = -\frac{e}{2mc}(\mathbf{L} + 2\mathbf{S}). \tag{14.64}$$

We can form an irreducible tensor operator of the first order,

$$\begin{aligned} \mu_1 &= \frac{e}{2mc}\frac{(L_x + 2S_x) + i(L_y + 2S_y)}{\sqrt{2}}, \\ \mu_0 &= -\frac{e}{2mc}(L_z + 2S_z), \\ \mu_{-1} &= -\frac{e}{2mc}\frac{(L_x + 2S_x) - i(L_y + 2S_y)}{\sqrt{2}}. \end{aligned} \tag{14.65}$$

These new components transform like basis functions for the representation D_{1g} of the three-dimensional rotation group (g is for even). The magnetic dipole operator is, in other words, an even operator.

We have then the following selection rules in the absence of an external field

$$\begin{aligned} &\Delta J = 0, \pm 1; \qquad J_i = 0 \not\leftrightarrow J_f = 0, \\ &P_f = P_i. \end{aligned} \tag{14.66}$$

In the presence of a magnetic field,

$$\begin{aligned} &\Delta M = \pm 1 \qquad \text{for circularly polarized radiation,} \\ &\Delta M = 0 \qquad \text{for linearly polarized radiation,} \\ &P_f = P_i, \end{aligned} \tag{14.67}$$

and, in the case of Russell-Saunders coupling,

$$\begin{aligned} &\Delta L = 0, \pm 1; \qquad L_i = 0 \not\leftrightarrow L_f = 0, \\ &\Delta S = 0, \\ &P_f = P_i. \end{aligned} \tag{14.68}$$

Electric Quadrupole Radiation. The components of this operator are proportional to $\sum_i x_i^2$, $\sum_i y_i^2$, $\sum_i z_i^2$, $\sum_i x_i y_i$, $\sum_i y_i z_i$, $\sum_i z_i x_i$ and transform according to x^2, y^2, z^2, xy, yz, and zx, respectively. Instead of x^2, y^2, and z^2 we may then consider the following linear combinations [1]:

$$\begin{aligned} r^2 &= x^2 + y^2 + z^2, \\ Z^2 &= 2z^2 - x^2 - y^2, \\ \rho^2 &= x^2 - y^2. \end{aligned} \tag{14.69}$$

The inverse relations of (14.69) are given by

$$\begin{aligned} x^2 &= \tfrac{1}{2}\rho^2 + \tfrac{1}{3}r^2 - \tfrac{1}{6}Z^2, \\ y^2 &= \tfrac{1}{3}r^2 - \tfrac{1}{6}Z^2 - \tfrac{1}{2}\rho^2, \\ z^2 &= \tfrac{1}{3}Z^2 + \tfrac{1}{3}r^2. \end{aligned} \tag{14.70}$$

The product $(\mathbf{k}\cdot\mathbf{r})(\mathbf{r}\cdot\boldsymbol{\pi})$, which appears in the term H^{E2} of the interaction Hamiltonian [see (14.26)], can now be expressed as

$$\begin{aligned} (\mathbf{k}\cdot\mathbf{r})(\mathbf{r}\cdot\boldsymbol{\pi}) = {} & \tfrac{1}{3}r^2(\mathbf{k}\cdot\boldsymbol{\pi}) + Z^2(\tfrac{1}{3}k_z\pi_z - \tfrac{1}{6}k_y\pi_y - \tfrac{1}{6}k_x\pi_x) \\ & + \rho^2(\tfrac{1}{2}k_x\pi_x - \tfrac{1}{2}k_y\pi_y) + (k_x\pi_y + k_y\pi_x)\,xy \\ & + (k_z\pi_y + k_y\pi_z)\,yz + (k_x\pi_z + k_z\pi_x)\,xz. \end{aligned} \tag{14.71}$$

The term in (14.71) proportional to r^2 transforms like D_0 and actually does not make any contribution because $\mathbf{K}\cdot\boldsymbol{\pi} = 0$. The other five components, Z^2, ρ^2, xy, yz, and xz, may be combined linearly to form an irreducible tensor operator of the second order:

$$\begin{aligned} &(x + iy)^2, \\ &-2z(x + iy), \\ &\sqrt{\tfrac{2}{3}}(3z^2 - r^2), \\ &2z(x - iy), \\ &(x - iy)^2. \end{aligned} \tag{14.72}$$

The transitions depend on the matrix elements $\langle\psi_f^{\mathrm{el}}|\, Q_\alpha\, |\psi_i^{\mathrm{el}}\rangle$, where Q_α is any of the operator listed in (14.72). The products $Q_\alpha\psi_i^{\mathrm{el}}$ transform according to the representations at the right-hand side of the following reduction:

$$D_2 \times D_{J_i} = D_{J_i+2} + D_{J_i+1} + D_{J_i} + D_{J_i-1} + D_{J_i-2} \tag{14.73}$$

if $J_i \geq 2$. If $J_i = 1$, we have

$$D_2 \times D_1 = D_3 + D_2 + D_1, \tag{14.74}$$

and if $J_i = 0$

$$D_2 \times D_0 = D_2. \tag{14.75}$$

We then have the selection rules

$$\begin{aligned} &\Delta J = \pm 2, \pm 1, 0; \qquad J_i = 1, 0 \not\leftrightarrow J_f = 0; \qquad J_i = 0 \not\leftrightarrow J_f = 0, 1, \\ &P_f = P_i. \end{aligned} \tag{14.76}$$

In the presence of a magnetic field

$$\begin{aligned} \Delta M_J &= \pm 2, \pm 1, 0, \\ P_f &= P_i, \end{aligned} \tag{14.77}$$

and in the case of the Russell-Saunders coupling,

$$\begin{aligned} &\Delta L = \pm 2, \pm 1, 0; \qquad L_i = 1, 0 \not\leftrightarrow L_f = 0; \qquad L_i = 0 \not\leftrightarrow L_f = 0, 1, \\ &\Delta S = 0, \\ &P_f = P_i. \end{aligned} \tag{14.78}$$

6.3. Selection Rules for Ions in Crystals

When considering the energy levels of an ion in a crystal, the representations of the free ion are reduced in terms of the irreducible representations of the symmetry group of the crystal site in which the ion finds itself. In the same way, the representations D_{1u}, D_{1g}, D_{2g} of the electric dipole, magnetic dipole, and electric quadrupole operators, respectively, are reduced in terms of the irreducible representations of this symmetry group. In general, one component may "belong" to a certain representation, another component to another representation and so on.

A transition between two representations is allowed, if the product of the representation of the initial state by the representation of a component of the transition operator contains the representation of the final state. This is strictly related to the polarization of radiation. If, for example, the coordinate z belongs to a certain representation Γ and if the product $\Gamma \times \Gamma_i$, Γ_i being the representation of the initial state, contains the representation Γ_f of the final state, then the correspondent radiation is linearly polarized in the z direction. If $x + iy$ is the active component, the correspondent radiation is right-circularly polarized about the axis z. If $x - iy$ is the active component, the correspondent radiation is left-circularly polarized about the axis z. Essentially, we have a set of selection rules for each symmetry group.

Let us now consider a free ion. Its energy levels in absence of spin-orbit interaction are characterized by different terms ^{2S+1}L. Each term, when spin-orbit interaction is taken in account, produces several multiplets.

Spin-orbit interaction can connect levels with the same J number, belonging to different terms and differing in their S or L numbers by 0 or ± 1. If we disregard the connections between different terms (Russell-Saunders approximation), we can consider L and S as good quantum numbers. In the case of an electric dipole transition we add to the J selection rules the following "almost valid" selection rules for L and S:

$$\Delta L = \pm 1, 0; \qquad \Delta S = 0. \tag{14.79}$$

The validity of these rules is related to the validity of the Russell-Saunders approximation; the appearance of lines which do not respect them is an indication of the presence of strong spin-orbit interaction in the levels connected by the transitions.[4]

The concept of valid and almost valid selection rules can be extended to ions in crystals. Here the valid selection rules are the ones determined by the site symmetry of the emitting center. The approximate selection rules do not rule out the occurrence of transitions; they allow us only to make a distinction between strong (allowed) and weak (forbidden) lines.

For the almost valid selection rules we have to make a distinction between transition metal ions (in which spin-orbit interaction is less important than the crystal field perturbation) and rare earths (in which spin-orbit is more important than the crystal field perturbation).

The energy levels of rare earth ions in crystals correspond rather closely to the energy levels of free ions: each level, however, presents an additional structure due to the crystalline field. The crystal symmetry group is usually C_{3h} or C_{3v}. The energy levels of an f^n configuration in a weak field depends on the F_2, F_4 and F_6 Slater's integrals, on the spin-orbit parameter ζ_{4f} and on the strength of the crystal field.

In a rare earth ion the valid rules are determined by the site symmetry; however, because of the weakness of the crystalline fields the selection rules of the free ion have still some relevance. For magnetic dipole and electric quadrupole radiation we have these approximate rules:

$$\begin{aligned} M1&: \quad J = 0, \pm 1; \qquad && J = 0 \not\leftrightarrow J = 0; \\ E2&: \quad J = 0, \pm 1, \pm 2; \qquad && J = 0 \not\leftrightarrow J = 0, 1. \end{aligned} \tag{14.80}$$

Electric dipole transitions within an f^n configuration are allowed only through environmental perturbation (they would not be allowed in the free ion). Therefore the selection rules which control the electric dipole lines are determined completely by the local field symmetry at the site of the ion.

The energy levels of transition metal ions in crystals are rather different from the energy levels of free ions. The crystal symmetry is often octahedral

[4] An example of intercombination line is the 2537 A line of Hg, corresponding to a transition $^3P_1 \rightarrow {}^1S_0$.

and the energy levels depend on Slater's integrals F_2 and F_4, on the crystal field strength, and on the spin-orbit parameter ζ_{3d}. An approximate description of the state of the system is given in terms of levels ${}^{2S+1}\Gamma$ in which the spin-orbit interaction is neglected and the symmetry is considered purely octahedral; S is a good quantum number, and Γ indicates a representation of the octahedral group. In these conditions only magnetic dipole and electric quadrupole transitions can take place, and the almost valid selection rules are

$$\Delta S = 0; \qquad \Gamma_i \times \Gamma_r \times \Gamma_f = \Gamma_1 + \cdots, \tag{14.81}$$

where Γ_r is the representation to which the transition operator belongs, Γ_i and Γ_f are respectively the representations of the initial and final state, which have the same (even) parity.

If the crystal symmetry is purely octahedral, the radiation is isotropic and its character cannot be recognized by polarization studies. Sometimes polarization studies may still be carried out in cubic crystals if the cubic symmetry is perturbed artificially by means of an external field or by subjecting the crystal to an anisotropic pressure.

In transition metal ions many transitions within the $3d^n$ configuration are of the electric dipole type and therefore occur through perturbation of the environment of the ion. The crystal symmetry of the transition metal ions is in these cases distorted octahedral, a distortion that leaves S as a good quantum number (S is destroyed by the spin-orbit interaction). If the distorting perturbation is greater than the spin-orbit interaction, it is possible to regard S as a "quasi good" quantum number. In this case the almost valid selection rule $\Delta S = 0$ is in order.

Example: Selection Rules in a D_{3h} Symmetry.

We can consider as an example an ion in a D_{3h} symmetry. In Table 14.1 we report the characters of the irreducible representations of this group. If the ion has an even number of electrons only the single valued representations can represent the energy levels of the

Table 14.1 Character Table of Group D_{3h}

		D_{3h}	E		σ_2	$2C_3$		$2S_3$		$3C_2'$	$3\sigma_v$
$2z^2 - x^2 - y^2$		$A_1'(\Gamma_1)$	1		1	1		1		1	1
	L_z	$A_2'(\Gamma_2)$	1		1	1		1		−1	−1
		$A_1''(\Gamma_3)$	1		−1	1		−1		1	−1
	z	$A_2''(\Gamma_4)$	1		−1	1		−1		−1	1
$(x^2 - y^2, xy)$	(x, y)	$E'(\Gamma_5)$	2		2	−1		−1		0	0
(xz, yz)	(L_x, L_y)	$E''(\Gamma_6)$	2		−2	−1		1		0	0
		$D_{1/2}(\Gamma_7)$	2	−2	0	1	−1	$\sqrt{3}$	$-\sqrt{3}$	0	0
		${}_2S_1(\Gamma_8)$	2	−2	0	−2	2	0	0	0	0
		${}_2S_2(\Gamma_9)$	2	−2	0	1	−1	$-\sqrt{3}$	$\sqrt{3}$	0	0

Table 14.2 Electric Dipole Selection rules in a Symmetry D_{3h}

D_{3h}	A_1'	A_2'	A_1''	A_2''	E'	E''	$D_{1/2}$	${}_2S_1$	${}_2S_2$
A_1'				$\parallel$	$\perp$				
A_2'			$\parallel$		$\perp$				
A_1''		$\parallel$				$\perp$			
A_2''	$\parallel$					$\perp$			
E'	$\perp$	$\perp$			$\perp$	$\parallel$			
E''			$\perp$	$\perp$	$\parallel$	$\perp$			
$D_{1/2}$								$\perp$	$\parallel\ \perp$
${}_2S_1$							$\perp$	$\parallel$	$\perp$
${}_2S_2$							$\parallel\ \perp$	$\perp$	

Table 14.3 Magnetic Dipole Selection Rules in a Symmetry D_{3h}

D_{3h}	A_1'	A_2'	A_1''	A_2''	E'	E''	$D_{1/2}$	${}_2S_1$	${}_2S_2$
A_1'		$\parallel$				$\perp$			
A_2'	$\parallel$					$\perp$			
A_1''				$\parallel$	$\perp$				
A_2''			$\parallel$		$\perp$				
E'			$\perp$	$\perp$	$\parallel$	$\perp$			
E''	$\perp$	$\perp$			$\perp$	$\parallel$			
$D_{1/2}$							$\parallel\ \perp$	$\perp$	
${}_2S_1$							$\perp$	$\parallel$	$\perp$
${}_2S_2$								$\perp$	$\parallel\ \perp$

system; if it has an odd number of electrons only the double valued representations have to be considered.

In Table 14.1 we have reported the operators corresponding to electric dipole (x, y, z), magnetic dipole (L_x, L_y, L_z) and electric quadrupole $(2z^2 - x^2 - y^2, x^2 - y^2, xy, yz, zx)$ radiation.

The selection rules can be derived easily; for example, an electric dipole z transition can connect the states A_1'' and A_2' because z transforms according to A_2'' and $A_1'' \times A_2'' = A_2'$.

The selection rules for electric dipole and magnetic dipole transitions are reported in Tables 14.2 and 14.3.

From Tables 14.2 and 14.3 we can see that an ion with an even number of electrons in a D_{3h} symmetry presents *dichroism*, namely one transition is either present in the $\parallel$ or in the $\perp$ polarization. This property is not presented by ions with an odd number of electrons in a D_{3h} symmetry. Dichroism is also presented by ions in other symmetries, such as C_{3h}.

Example: Selection Rules for Cubic Groups.

In the cubic symmetries (groups O, O_h, T, T_h, and T_d) it happens that whenever one component of the electric or magnetic dipole belongs to a representation the other two components belong to the same representation. This causes an absence of polarization effects in the radiation and an isotropic radiation.

7. ABOUT THE INTENSITIES OF RADIATIVE TRANSITIONS

We want now to investigate the order of magnitude of the different radiative transitions.

Let us first consider the situation in the free ions or atoms. The order of magnitude of the ratio of a magnetic dipole transition probability to an electric dipole transition probability is given by

$$\frac{P(M1)}{P(E1)} = \frac{(\mu)^2}{(er)^2} = \frac{(0.927 \times 10^{-20})^2}{(4.8 \times 10^{-10} \times 10^{-8})^2} \approx 3 \times 10^{-6}. \qquad (14.82)$$

The order of magnitude of the ratio of an electric quadrupole transition probability to an electric dipole transition probability is given by

$$\frac{P(E2)}{P(E1)} = \frac{|(\mathbf{k}\cdot\mathbf{r})(\boldsymbol{\pi}\cdot\mathbf{r})|^2}{(\boldsymbol{\pi}\cdot\mathbf{r})^2} \approx (\mathbf{k}\cdot\mathbf{r})^2$$

$$= \frac{\omega^2}{c^2}\,a_0^{\,2} = \left(\frac{2\pi a_0}{\lambda}\right)^2 \approx 10^{-7}. \qquad (14.83)$$

The situation is essentially different for ions in crystals. Here many of the relevant transitions involve levels which belong to the same electronic configuration and which, in free ions, would have the same parity. In these conditions electric dipole transitions may be allowed only by a crystal field perturbation which mixes one of the transition levels with a level of different parity; the actual magnitude of the electric dipole transition depends here on the amount of *parity mixing perturbation.*

In absence of a perturbation of this type the energy levels in the crystal preserve the parity character of the free ion state from which they derive. In these conditions levels belonging to the same electronic configuration may be connected only by magnetic dipole or electric quadrupole transitions. This is true for all site symmetry groups that contain the operation *inversion*, like the cubic groups O_h, T_h, and the groups D_{6h}, D_{4h}, D_{3d}, D_{2h}, C_{6h}, C_{4h}, and S_6.

The selection rules we derived for free atoms may be considered an outcome of the Wigner–Eckart theorem already treated in Section 5.5 of Chapter 3, which may be expressed by

$$\langle J_f M_f|\, T_M^K\, |J_i M_i\rangle = c(J_f K J_i;\, M_f M M_i)\, \langle J_f|\,|T^K|\,|J_i\rangle. \qquad (14.84)$$

Here $|J_f M_f\rangle$ and $|J_i M_i\rangle$ are two eigenstates of angular momentum; T^K is the irreducible tensor operator representing the transition; and T_M^K is its active component. The selection rules are "contained" in the Clebsch-Gordan coefficients $c(J_f K J_i;\, M_f M M_i)$ and may be derived by considering their properties (3.106).

In case of electric dipole transitions the electric dipole operator is represented by a first-rank irreducible tensor of components,

$$T_1^1 = -\frac{x+iy}{\sqrt{2}},$$

$$T_0^1 = z, \tag{14.85}$$

$$T_{-1}^1 = \frac{x-iy}{\sqrt{2}}.$$

Considering $|J_iM_i\rangle$ and $|J_fM_f\rangle$ as the initial and final states, respectively, of an electric dipole transition, we have from (14.84)

$$\langle J_fM_f|\, T_M^1\, |J_iM_i\rangle \propto c(J_f1J_i;\, M_fMM_i). \tag{14.86}$$

The transition probability is then proportional to $|c(J_f1J_i;\, M_fMM_i)|^2$.

Example

Let us consider the coupling of two angular momenta

$$j_1 = 1 \quad \text{and} \quad j_2 = 1.$$

Recall now the properties of the Clebsch-Gordan coefficients.

$$|JM_J\rangle = \sum_{mm'} \langle j_1j_2m_1m_2 \,|\, JM_J\rangle\, |j_1m_1\rangle\, |j_2m_2\rangle\,; \tag{14.87}$$

$$|j_1m_1\rangle\, |j_2m_2\rangle = \sum_{JM_J} \langle j_1j_2m_1m_2 \,|\, JM_J\rangle\, |JM_J\rangle \tag{14.88}$$

We can write the following table for these coefficients (see [2], page 438, and [3], page 76)

j_1m_1	j_2m_2 \ JM_J	22	21	11	20	10	00	2–1	1–1	2–2
11	11	1								
11	10		$\sqrt{\frac{1}{2}}$	$\sqrt{\frac{1}{2}}$						
10	11		$\sqrt{\frac{1}{2}}$	$-\sqrt{\frac{1}{2}}$						
11	1–1				$\sqrt{\frac{1}{6}}$	$\sqrt{\frac{1}{2}}$	$\sqrt{\frac{1}{3}}$			
10	10				$\sqrt{\frac{2}{3}}$	0	$-\sqrt{\frac{1}{3}}$			
1–1	11				$\sqrt{\frac{1}{6}}$	$-\sqrt{\frac{1}{2}}$	$\sqrt{\frac{1}{3}}$			
10	1–1							$\sqrt{\frac{1}{2}}$	$\sqrt{\frac{1}{2}}$	
1–1	10							$\sqrt{\frac{1}{2}}$	$-\sqrt{\frac{1}{2}}$	
1–1	1–1									1

Reading down a column gives the coefficients for the expansion (14.87); reading along a row gives the coefficients in (14.88). Let us examine three types of transition:

$J_i = 1 \to J_f = 1$. The transition probabilities are proportional to

M_i \ M_f	1	0	−1
1	$\frac{1}{2}\parallel$	$\frac{1}{2}\perp$	0
0	$\frac{1}{2}\perp$	0	$\frac{1}{2}\perp$
−1	0	$\frac{1}{2}\perp$	$\frac{1}{2}\parallel$

$J_i = 1 \to J_f = 2$. The transition probabilities are proportional to

M_i \ M_f	2	1	0	−1	−2
1	1	$\frac{1}{2}\parallel$	$\frac{1}{6}\perp$	0	0
0	0	$\frac{1}{2}\perp$	$\frac{2}{3}\parallel$	$\frac{1}{2}\perp$	0
−1	0	0	$\frac{1}{6}\perp$	$\frac{1}{2}\parallel$	$1\perp$

$J_i = 1 \to J_f = 0$. The transition probabilities are proportional to

M_i \ M_f	0
1	$\frac{1}{3}$
0	$\frac{1}{3}$
−1	$\frac{1}{3}$

We now wish to examine a transition of the type $J_i = J \to J_f = J$. We can make use of the theorem (3.116),

$$\langle J_f M_f | \, T^1_\alpha \, | J_i M_i \rangle = c(J_f, J_i) \langle J_f M_f | \, J_\alpha \, | J_i M_i \rangle \, \delta_{J_i J_f}, \tag{14.89}$$

where

$$\langle J, M+1 | \, J_1 \, | JM \rangle = -\frac{\hbar}{\sqrt{2}} \sqrt{J(J+1) - M(M+1)},$$

$$\langle J, M-1 | \, J_{-1} \, | JM \rangle = \frac{\hbar}{\sqrt{2}} \sqrt{J(J+1) - M(M-1)}, \tag{14.90}$$

$$\langle J, M | \, J_0 \, | J, M \rangle = \hbar M.$$

The transition probabilities are then proportional to

$\frac{1}{2}[J(J+1) - M(M+1)]$	$(M+1 \to M)$;	Polarization: $\perp$;	
$\frac{1}{2}[J(J+1) - M(M-1)]$	$(M-1 \to M)$;	Polarization: $\perp$;	(14.91)
M^2	$(M \to M)$;	Polarization: $\parallel$.	

The selection rules for ions in crystals may be considered an outcome of the fundamental theorem for operators transforming irreducibly in its form (3.52) or in the simpler form (3.53) which we write again,

$$\begin{aligned}\langle \Gamma_f M_f | \, T^\gamma_m \, | \Gamma_i M_i \rangle &= c(\Gamma_i \gamma \Gamma_f ; M_i m M_f) \langle \Gamma_f \| \, T^\gamma \, \| \Gamma_i \rangle \\ &= \langle \Gamma_i \gamma M_i m \mid \Gamma_f M_f \rangle \langle \Gamma_f \| \, T^\gamma \, \| \Gamma_i \rangle. \end{aligned} \tag{14.92}$$

Here Γ_i and Γ_f are respectively the representations of the initial and final states, M_i and M_f individuate the relevant functions respectively within the Γ_i and Γ_f manifolds, T^γ is the irreducible operator representing the transition and T^γ_m is its active component.

8. THE STATIC EFFECTS OF THE INTERACTION BETWEEN AN ATOMIC SYSTEM AND THE ELECTROMAGNETIC FIELD

The total Hamiltonian of a one-electron atom plus electromagnetic radiation is given by

$$H = H_0 + H_1 + H_2,$$

where

$$\begin{aligned} H_0 &= \frac{p^2}{2m} + eV + \int \frac{E^2 + H^2}{8\pi} \, d\tau; \\ H_1 &= \frac{e}{mc} \, \mathbf{p} \cdot \mathbf{A}; \\ H_2 &= \frac{e^2}{2mc^2} (\mathbf{A})^2. \end{aligned} \tag{14.93}$$

The eigenfunctions of the unperturbed Hamiltonian H_0 are products of eigenfunctions of the atomic system and eigenfunctions of the radiation field. Let us call:

$$|j\rangle = \text{eigenfunction of} \begin{cases} \text{atom in state } E_j^{\text{el}} \\ \text{one photon of frequency } \omega; \end{cases} \tag{14.94}$$

$$|i\rangle = \text{eigenfunction of} \begin{cases} \text{atom in state } E_i^{\text{el}} \\ \text{no photon.} \end{cases} \tag{14.95}$$

The interaction H_1 does not give any contribution to the energy of the total system (ion plus radiation) in first order. In the second order, however, we have the following correction:

$$(\delta E)_{ii} = (H_2)_{ij} + \sum_{\substack{j \\ (j \neq i)}} \frac{|(H)_{ij}|^2}{E_i - E_j}, \tag{14.96}$$

where

$$E_i = E_i^{\text{el}}$$
$$E_j = E_j^{\text{el}} + \hbar\omega. \tag{14.97}$$

The state j includes the presence of a *virtual* photon and the squared matrix element $|H_{ij}|^2$ may be considered as representing its emission and reabsorption; δE is the contribution of the zero point fluctuations to the energy of the electronic state. It gives rise to the so-called *self-energy* of the electron. The self-energy, in any case, is ∞. However, by subtracting from the theoretical expression for the energy the corresponding expression for a free electron of the same average kinetic energy it is possible to find a finite shift of the electronic energy of the system.

It is found for example in the atom of hydrogen that the state $2s$ has an electromagnetic shift of 1040 Mc, whereas the shift of the $2p$ state is negligible.

The electron may also interact with states: electron plus 2 photons, electron plus 3 photons etc; in these cases higher order perturbation theory should be used.

The probability of finding a bare electron decreases as we consider more divergent terms. The second-order perturbation theory is, however, sufficient in general to account for the electromagnetic (Lamb) shift [4].

REFERENCES

[1] J. L. Prather, *Atomic Energy Levels in Crystals*, National Bureau of Standards Monograph 19, February 1961.

[2] V. Heine, *Group Theory in Quantum Mechanics*, Pergamon, New York, 1960.

[3] E. U. Condon and G. H. Shortley, *The Theory of Atomic Spectra*, Cambridge University Press, Cambridge, 1957.

[4] H. A. Bethe, "The Electromagnetic Shift of Energy Levels," *Phys. Rev.* **72,** 339 (1947).

15

The Ion-Vibration Interaction. Radiationless Processes, Thermal Shift, and Broadening of Sharp Lines

1. THE ION-VIBRATION INTERACTION

Magnetic ions in crystals, besides interacting with the radiative field, may also interact with the thermal vibrations of the lattice in which they are imbedded. The form of this interaction is not well known; however, certain approximations may be made, based mainly on the crystalline field hypothesis, which give reasonable agreement with the experimental results.

The experimental facts which bear information on the ion-vibration interaction are the following:

1. The presence of spectral lines which are allowed by the simultaneous interaction of the ionic system with both thermal vibration and radiative field,
2. The presence of radiationless processes in crystals, by which an ion in an excited state decays by transferring its energy to the lattice vibrations, and
3. The dependence of the width and of the position of spectral lines on the temperature.

The basic mechanism by which the thermal vibrations of the lattice interact with a magnetic ion is due to the modulating effects that the vibrating charges of the ligands produce on the crystalline field and therefore on the energy levels of the system.

The Hamiltonian describing the system (ion and crystal lattice vibrations) is given by:

$$H = H_{\text{latt}} + H_{\text{ion}} + H_{\text{int}}, \tag{15.1}$$

where

$$H_{\text{ion}} = H_o + H_{\text{cryst}} + H_{so},$$
$$H_{\text{latt}} = \sum_k \hbar\omega_k(a_k^+ a_k + \tfrac{1}{2}),$$
$$H_{\text{int}} = \text{interaction Hamiltonian.}$$

The eigenvalue equation,

$$(H_{\text{latt}} + H_{\text{ion}})\,\psi = E\psi \tag{15.2}$$

has the following eigenvalues:

$$E = E_{\text{ion}} + E_{\text{latt}} \tag{15.3}$$

and can be divided in

$$\begin{aligned} H_{\text{ion}}\,\psi_{\text{ion}} &= E_{\text{ion}}\,\psi_{\text{ion}}, \\ H_{\text{latt}}\,\psi_{\text{latt}} &= E_{\text{latt}}\,\psi_{\text{latt}} = \sum_k \hbar\omega_k(n_k + \tfrac{1}{2})\,\psi_{\text{latt}}. \end{aligned} \tag{15.4}$$

The crystalline field is due to the charges of the ligand ions surrounding the magnetic ion; therefore a distortion of the ligand ions affects the crystal field. Such a distortion is a function of the local strain; therefore we can expand the crystal field potential in powers of such a strain.

The local strain is defined by the so-called *strain term* $\epsilon_{\alpha\beta}$:

$$\epsilon_{\alpha\beta} = \frac{1}{2}\left(\frac{\partial u_\alpha}{\partial x_\beta} + \frac{\partial u_\beta}{\partial x_\alpha}\right) \qquad (\alpha, \beta = 1, 2, 3). \tag{15.5}$$

We want to find an expression for this strain when the distortion of the lattice is caused by thermal vibrations. For simplicity we shall assume that

$$\epsilon \approx \left.\frac{\partial u}{\partial x}\right|_{x=0},$$

thus, not taking into any account the anisotropy of the elastic waves. We take as origin for the coordinate axes the point of the lattice in which the nucleus of the ion is located. The displacement u is given by

$$u(x) = \sum_q \left(\frac{\hbar}{2M\omega_q}\right)^{1/2} (e^{iqx} b_q + e^{-iqx} b_q^+), \tag{15.6}$$

where M is the mass of the crystal, b_q and b_q^+ are respectively the annihilation and the creation operators for the qth vibrational oscillator. Then ϵ is given by

$$\epsilon = \left.\frac{\partial u}{\partial x}\right|_{x=0} = i \sum_q \left(\frac{\hbar\omega_q}{2Mv^2}\right)^{1/2} (b_q - b_q^+) \tag{15.7}$$

where v is the average velocity for sound waves in the crystal. The crystal field potential can be expressed as

$$V_{\text{cryst}} = V_0 + V_1\epsilon + V_2\epsilon^2 + \cdots, \tag{15.8}$$

where V_0, the static term, is included in the Hamiltonian H_{ion} as H_{cryst}. V_1 and V_2 are coupling parameters which are functions of the coordinates of the electrons of the magnetic ion and of the static distances between this ion and the ligand charges.

The interaction Hamiltonian can be expressed as

$$H_{\text{int}} = V_1\epsilon + V_2\epsilon^2 + \cdots, \tag{15.9}$$

where

$$\epsilon = i\sum_q \left(\frac{\hbar\omega_q}{2Mv^2}\right)^{1/2}(b_q - b_q^+).$$

2. RADIATIONLESS PROCESSES IN CRYSTALS

2.1 Absorption and Emission of a Phonon

Let us consider first the absorption of a phonon. The initial state of the total system (ion and phonons) is given by

$$\begin{aligned} |i\rangle &= |\psi_i^{\text{el}}; n_1, n_2, n_k, \ldots\rangle \\ &= |\psi_i^{\text{el}}\rangle\,|n_1\rangle\,|n_2\rangle \cdots |n_k\rangle \cdots, \end{aligned} \tag{15.10}$$

where ψ_i^{el} is the wave function of the ion in the initial state and n_i is the occupation numbers of the ith phonon state. The energy of the initial state is given by

$$E_i = E_i^{\text{el}} + \sum_i \hbar\omega_i(n_i + \tfrac{1}{2}), \tag{15.11}$$

where

$$n_i = (e^{\hbar\omega_i/kT} - 1)^{-1}. \tag{15.12}$$

The final state and its energy are given by

$$|f\rangle = |\psi_f^{\text{el}}\rangle\,|n_1\rangle\,|n_2\rangle \cdots |n_k - 1\rangle \cdots, \tag{15.13}$$

$$E_f = E_f^{\text{el}} + \sum_i \hbar\omega_i(n_i + \tfrac{1}{2}) - \hbar\omega_k. \tag{15.14}$$

The relevant matrix element of H_{int} [see (15.9)] connecting the two states is given by

$$\begin{aligned} M &= \langle f|\, H_{\text{int}}\, |i\rangle \\ &= \langle\psi_f^{\text{el}}; n_1, n_2, \ldots n_k - 1, \ldots |H_{\text{int}}\, |\psi_i^{\text{el}}; n_1, n_2, \ldots n_k, \ldots\rangle \\ &= i\langle\psi_f^{\text{el}}|\, V_1\, |\psi_i^{\alpha l}\rangle\langle n_k - 1|\, b_k\, |n_k\rangle\left(\frac{\hbar\omega_k}{2Mv^2}\right)^{1/2} \\ &= i\langle\psi_f^{\text{el}}|\, V_1\, |\psi_i^{\text{el}}\rangle\left(\frac{\hbar\omega_k}{2Mv^2}\right)^{1/2}\sqrt{n_k}. \end{aligned} \tag{15.15}$$

It has to be noted that if the levels i and f are Kramer's degenerate (this is the case of ions with an odd number of electrons) the matrix element $\langle\psi_f^{\text{el}}|\, V_1\, |\psi_i^{\text{el}}\rangle$ is zero. In this case a splitting between the two levels i and f may be produced by the action of a magnetic field and the Zeeman Hamiltonian $g\beta\mathbf{H}\cdot\mathbf{J}$ can admix an upper doublet with the ground state doublet. In such a case $\langle\psi_f^{\text{el}}|\, V_1\, |\psi_i^{\text{el}}\rangle$ has to be replaced by

$$\left(\frac{\beta g}{\Delta_1}\right) \quad (\langle\psi_f^{\text{el}}|\, V_1\, |m\rangle\langle m|\, \mathbf{H}\cdot\mathbf{J}\, |\psi_i^{\text{el}}\rangle + \langle\psi_f^{\text{el}}|\, \mathbf{H}\cdot\mathbf{J}\, |m\rangle\langle m|\, V_1\, |\psi_i^{\text{el}}\rangle), \tag{15.16}$$

where Δ_1 is the energy of the upper doublet.

The probability per unit time that an ion in a state ψ_i^{el} absorbs a phonon jumping to a state ψ_f^{el} is given by

$$W = \frac{2\pi}{\hbar}\,|M|^2\rho(E_f = E_i). \tag{15.17}$$

The density of final states is given by

$$\begin{aligned}\rho(E_f = E_i) &= \rho(E_f)\,\delta(E_f - E_i)\,dE_f\\ &= \rho(E_f^{\text{el}})\,\rho(E_f^{\text{phon}})\,\delta[(E_f^{\text{el}} + E_f^{\text{phon}}) - (E_i^{\text{el}} + E_i^{\text{phon}})]\\ &\qquad\qquad\times dE_f^{\text{el}}\,dE_f^{\text{phon}}\\ &= \frac{1}{\hbar}\,g(\omega_{fi}^{\text{el}} - \omega_r)\,\rho(\omega_k)\,\delta(\omega_{fi}^{\text{el}} - \omega_k)\,d\omega_{fi}^{\text{el}}\,d\omega_k,\end{aligned} \tag{15.18}$$

where

$$\omega_{fi}^{\text{el}} = \frac{E_f^{\text{el}} - E_i^{\text{el}}}{\hbar},$$

$$g(\omega_{fi}^{\text{el}} - \omega_r) = \text{normalized line shape} \simeq \delta(\omega_{fi}^{\text{el}} - \omega_r), \tag{15.19}$$

$$\omega_r = \text{central frequency}.$$

and

$$\begin{aligned}\rho(\omega) &= \frac{3V\omega^2}{2\pi^2 v^3} \qquad \omega \leq \omega_D,\\ \rho(\omega) &= 0 \qquad\qquad \omega > \omega_D.\end{aligned} \tag{15.20}$$

The probability for the absorption of a phonon is now given by

$$\begin{aligned}W_{\text{abs}} &= \frac{2\pi}{\hbar^2}\iint |M|^2\rho(\omega_k)\,\delta(\omega_{fi}^{\text{el}} - \omega_r)\,\delta(\omega_{fi}^{\text{el}} - \omega_k)\,d\omega_{fi}^{\text{el}}\,d\omega_k\\ &= \frac{2\pi}{\hbar^2}\,|M|^2\rho(\omega_r) = \frac{3\omega_r^3}{2\pi\rho v^5\hbar}\,|\langle\psi_f^{\text{el}}|\, V_1\, |\psi_i^{\text{el}}\rangle|^2 n_r,\end{aligned} \tag{15.21}$$

where $\rho = M/V$.

In the same way it is possible to show that the transition probability for the emission of a phonon is given by

$$W_{\text{emi}} = \frac{3\omega_r^{\ 3}}{2\pi\rho v^5\hbar} |\langle\psi_f^{\ \text{el}}|\ V_1\ |\psi_i^{\ \text{el}}\rangle|^2(n_r + 1). \qquad (15.22)$$

As we can see the transition probability for the phonon emission consists of a temperature dependent part which is equal to W_{abs} and of a temperature independent part

$$\frac{3\omega_r^{\ 3}}{2\pi\rho v^5\hbar} |\langle\psi_f^{\ \text{el}}|\ V_1\ |\psi_i^{\ \text{el}}\rangle|^2, \qquad (15.23)$$

which we may call the probability for *spontaneous emission* of one phonon.

Let us consider now a two-level system as given in Fig. 15.1 in which

$$w_{12} = w_{\text{abs}}; \qquad w_{21} = w_{\text{emi}}; \qquad \Delta E_{21} = \hbar\omega_r, \qquad (15.24)$$

and let us see how one phonon processes may bring about the thermal equilibrium to this system.

Let us assume that N_1 and N_2 are respectively the population of the ground state and the population of the excited state. At any time we must have:

$$\begin{aligned} \dot{N}_1 &= N_2 w_{21} - N_1 w_{12}, \\ \dot{N}_2 &= N_1 w_{12} - N_2 w_{21} = -\dot{N}_1. \end{aligned} \qquad (15.25)$$

In equilibrium we have

$$\dot{N}_1 = \dot{N}_2 = 0,$$

and

$$\frac{N_1^{\ \text{e}}}{N_2^{\ \text{e}}} = \frac{w_{21}}{w_{12}} = \frac{n_r + 1}{n_r} = 1 + \frac{1}{n_r} = e^{\hbar\omega_r/kT}. \qquad (15.26)$$

The equilibrium values N_1^{e} and N_2^{e} can be derived from (15.26) and

$$N = N_1(t) + N_2(t). \qquad (15.27)$$

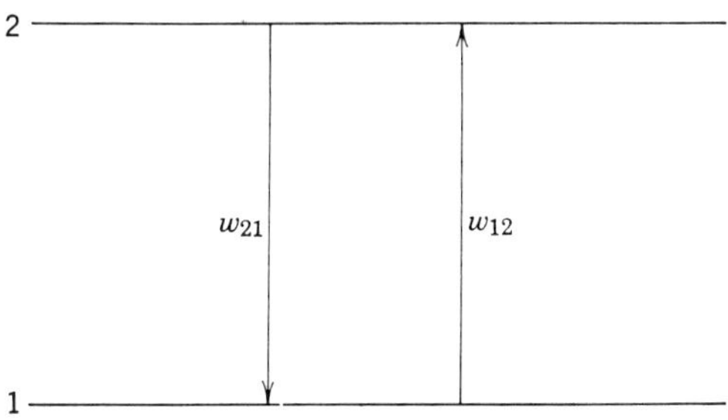

Fig. 15.1. Two level systems with excitation and deexcitation processes.

We fin d

$$N_1^{\rm e} = \frac{N}{1 + e^{-\hbar\omega_r/kT}} = \frac{Nw_{21}}{w_{12} + w_{21}} = Nw_{21}\tau,$$
$$N_2^{\rm e} = N - N_1^{\rm e} = N\,\frac{e^{-\hbar\omega_r/kT}}{1 + e^{-\hbar\omega_r/kT}} = Nw_{12}\tau, \tag{15.28}$$

where

$$\tau^{-1} = w_{12} + w_{21}. \tag{15.29}$$

Starting with a population N_1^0 in level 1 and a population N_2^0 in level 2, let us now see how the system reaches the conditions of equilibrium.

The solutions of (15.25) are given by

$$N_2(t) = N_2^{0}e^{-t/\tau} + Nw_{12}\tau(1 - e^{-t/\tau}),$$
$$N_1(t) = N - N_2(t) = N_1^{0}e^{-t/\tau} + Nw_{21}\tau(1 - e^{-t/\tau}). \tag{15.30}$$

Also,

$$N_2 - N_1 = (N_2^{0} - N_1^{0})e^{-t/\tau} + N(w_{12} - w_{21})\,\tau(1 - e^{-t/\tau})$$
$$= (N_2^{0} - N_1^{0})e^{-t/\tau} + (N_2^{\rm e} - N_1^{\rm e})(1 - e^{-t/\tau}), \tag{15.31}$$

or

$$[N_2(t) - N_1(t)] - [N_2^{\rm e} - N_1^{\rm e}] = [(N_2^{0} - N_1^{0}) - (N_2^{\rm e} - N_1^{\rm e})]\, e^{-t/\tau}. \tag{15.32}$$

The system approaches equilibrium with the characteristic *relaxation time* τ which, taking in account (15.29) and (15.24), is given by

$$\tau^{-1} = w_{12} + w_{21} = \frac{3\omega_r^{\,3}}{2\pi\rho v^5\hbar}\,|\langle\psi_f^{\rm el}|\,V_1\,|\psi_i^{\rm el}\rangle|^2(2n_r + 1)$$
$$= \frac{3\omega_r^{\,3}}{2\pi\rho v^5\hbar}\,|\langle\psi_f^{\rm el}|\,V_1\,|\psi_i^{\rm el}\rangle|^2 \coth\frac{\hbar\omega_r}{2kT}. \tag{15.33}$$

If $\hbar\omega_r \ll kT$,

$$\tau^{-1} = \frac{2kT}{\hbar\omega_r}\,\frac{3\omega_r^{\,3}}{2\pi\rho v^5\hbar}\,|\langle\psi_f^{\rm el}|\,V_1\,|\psi_i^{\rm el}\rangle|^2. \tag{15.34}$$

For non-Kramers levels the inverse of the relaxation time is then proportional to T and to the square of the transition frequency.

For Kramers degenerate states the matrix element in (15.34) has to be replaced by (15.16) which makes the inverse of the relaxation time still proportional to T, but depending on the fourth power of $H(\hbar\omega_r = \beta gH)$.

Summarizing, for one phonon processes, we have:

$$\begin{aligned} \tau_1^{-1} &= a\omega_r^2 T \qquad \text{(non-Kramers levels)}, \\ \tau_1^{-1} &= a' H^4 T \qquad \text{(Kramers levels)}, \end{aligned} \tag{15.35}$$

in the approximation $\hbar\omega_r \ll kT$.

2.2 Raman Processes

In the Debye approximation the density of phonon states, given by (15.20), is proportional to ω^2. We want now to consider the *density of occupied states* as given by

$$n(\omega)\rho(\omega) \propto \frac{\omega^2}{e^{\hbar\omega/kT} - 1}. \tag{15.36}$$

This function is plotted in Fig. 15.2. It has a maximum at $\omega \approx kT/\hbar$. If the energy gap is such that

$$\hbar\omega_r \ll kT, \tag{15.37}$$

the number of phonons available for a single phonon decay is very small compared with the number of phonons available at $\omega \approx kT/\hbar$. In such a case a Raman process may take place; this process involves the absorption of a phonon of frequency ω_a and the emission of a phonon of frequency ω_e such that

$$\omega_e - \omega_a = \omega_r. \tag{15.38}$$

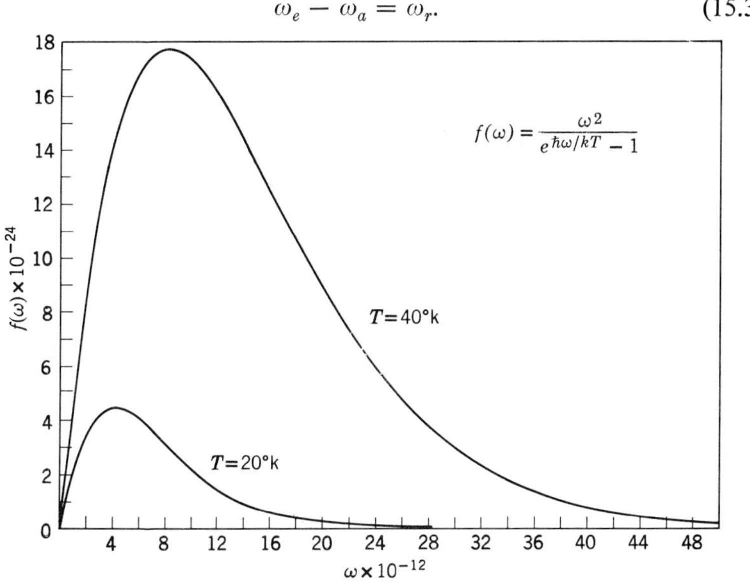

Fig. 15.2. Density of occupied phonon states.

Such a process makes use practically of all the phonons available in the spectrum. Let us calculate now the transition probability for a process of this type.

The initial state of the system is given by

$$|i\rangle = |\psi_i^{\text{el}}; n_1, n_2, \ldots, n_a, n_e, \ldots\rangle \tag{15.39}$$

with energy,

$$E_i = E_i^{\text{el}} + \sum_i \hbar\omega_i(n_i + \tfrac{1}{2}). \tag{15.40}$$

The final state and its energy are given by

$$|f\rangle = |\psi_f^{\text{el}}; n_1, n_2, \ldots n_a - 1, n_e + 1 \cdots\rangle, \tag{15.41}$$

$$E_f = E_f^{\text{el}} + \sum_i \hbar\omega_i(n_i + \tfrac{1}{2}) - \hbar\omega_a + \hbar\omega_e. \tag{15.42}$$

The effective matrix element is given in first order by

$$\begin{aligned}
\langle f| H_{\text{int}} |i\rangle^{\text{I}} &= \langle \psi_f^{\text{el}}, \ldots n_a - 1, n_e + 1, \ldots| H_{\text{int}} |\psi_i^{\text{el}}, \ldots n_a, n_e \cdots\rangle^{\text{I}} \\
&= \langle \psi_f^{\text{el}}| V_2 |\psi_i^{\text{el}}\rangle\langle n_a - 1, n_e + 1| \epsilon^2 |n_a, n_e\rangle \\
&= \frac{\hbar}{2Mv^2}\sqrt{\omega_a\omega_e}\,\langle n_a + 1, n_e + 1| b_a b_e^+ + b_e^+ b_a |n_a, n_e\rangle\langle \psi_f^{\text{el}}| V_2 |\psi_i^{\text{el}}\rangle \\
&= 2\frac{\hbar}{2Mv^2}\langle \psi_f^{\text{el}}| V_2 |\psi_i^{\text{el}}\rangle \sqrt{\omega_a\omega_e}\sqrt{n_a}\sqrt{n_e + 1}.
\end{aligned} \tag{15.43}$$

This matrix element involves only the two states i and f (see Fig. 15.3) and no other upper state. It should be noted that if states i and f are Kramers degenerate (their splitting in this case may be due to the presence of a magnetic field) the matrix element of V_2 in (15.43) is zero and the Raman process requires a higher doublet which the magnetic field may admix with

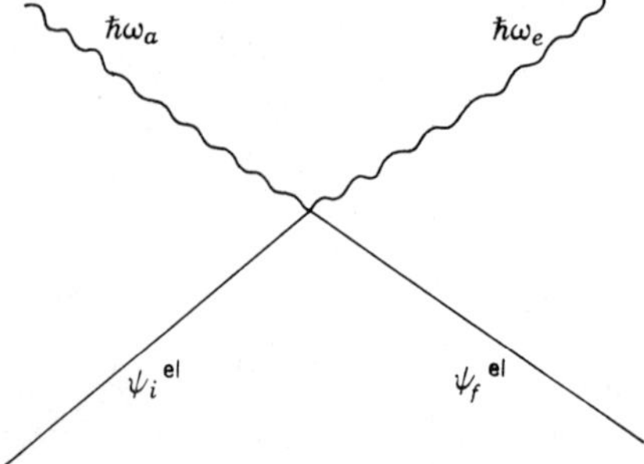

Fig. 15.3. Diagram illustrating the Raman scattering of phonons according to (15.43).

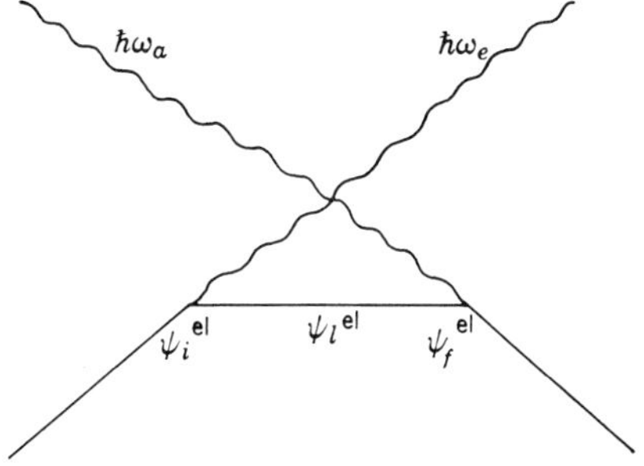

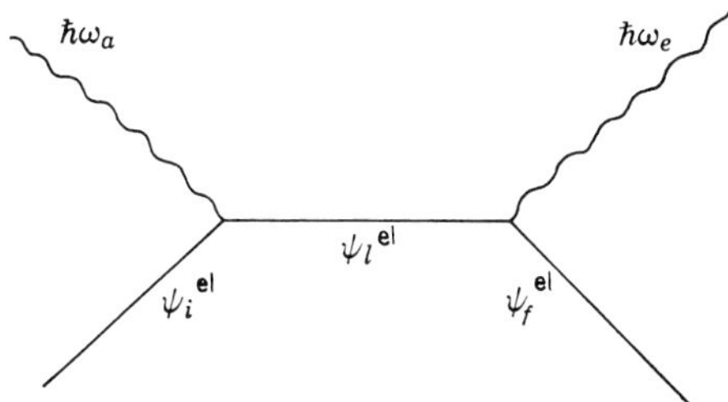

Fig. 15.4. Diagram illustrating the Raman scattering of phonons according to (15.44).

the ground Kramers states. The relevant matrix element in second order (see Fig. 15.4) is given by

$$
\begin{aligned}
&\langle f|\, H_{\text{int}}\,|i\rangle^{\text{II}} \\
&= \langle \psi_f^{\text{el}}, \ldots n_a - 1, n_e + 1 \cdots|\, H_{\text{int}}\,|\psi_i^{\text{el}}, \ldots n_a, n_e \cdots\rangle^{\text{II}} \\
&= \sum_l \left\{ \frac{\langle \psi_f^{\text{el}}; n_a - 1, n_e + 1|\, H_{\text{int}}\,|\psi_l^{\text{el}}; n_a, n_e + 1\rangle \times \langle \psi_l^{\text{el}}; n_a, n_e + 1|\, H_{\text{int}}\,|\psi_i^{\text{el}}; n_a, n_e\rangle}{-\hbar\omega_e - (E_l^{\text{el}} - E_i^{\text{el}})} \right. \\
&\quad \left. + \frac{\langle \psi_f^{\text{el}}; n_a - 1, n_e + 1|\, H_{\text{int}}\,|\psi_l^{\text{el}}; n_a - 1, n_e\rangle \times \langle \psi_l^{\text{el}}; n_a - 1, n_e|\, H_{\text{int}}\,|\psi_i^{\text{el}}; n_a, n_e\rangle}{\hbar\omega_a - (E_l^{\text{el}} - E_i^{\text{el}})} \right\} \\
&\simeq \sum_l \langle \psi_f^{\text{el}}|\, V_1\,|\psi_l^{\text{el}}\rangle\langle \psi_l^{\text{el}}|\, V_1\,|\psi_i^{\text{el}}\rangle \sqrt{n_a}\sqrt{n_e + 1}\, \frac{\hbar}{2Mv^2}\sqrt{\omega_a\omega_e} \\
&\quad \times \left[\frac{1}{-\hbar\omega_e - (E_l^{\text{el}} - E_i^{\text{el}})} + \frac{1}{\hbar\omega_a - (E_l^{\text{el}} - E_i^{\text{el}})}\right]\Bigg\} \\
&\simeq \sum_l \Bigg\{ \langle \psi_f^{\text{el}}|\, V_1\,|\psi_l^{\text{el}}\rangle\langle \psi_l^{\text{el}}|\, V_1\,|\psi_i^{\text{el}}\rangle \sqrt{n_a}\sqrt{n_e + 1}\, \frac{\hbar}{2Mv^2}\sqrt{\omega_a\omega_e}\, \frac{2}{E_i - E_l},
\end{aligned}
\tag{15.44}
$$

where we have disregarded the energy of the phonons in the denominators in comparison to the energy difference $(E_l - E_i)$. This is allowed when $kT \ll |E_l - E_i|$. Here some upper electronic levels are involved, for the total system goes through intermediate virtual states.

Taking (15.43) and (15.44) into account, the relevant matrix element is then given by

$$M = \frac{\hbar}{2Mv^2}\left\{2\langle\psi_f^{\text{el}}|\, V_2\,|\psi_i^{\text{el}}\rangle + 2\sum_l \frac{[\langle\psi_f^{\text{el}}|\, V_1\,|\psi_l^{\text{el}}\rangle\langle\psi_l^{\text{el}}|\, V_1\,|\psi_i^{\text{el}}\rangle]}{E_i^{\text{el}} - E_l^{\text{el}}}\right\} \times \sqrt{\omega_a\omega_e}\sqrt{n_e+1}\sqrt{n_a}. \quad (15.45)$$

In order to evaluate the transition probability for Raman processes, let us consider the density of final states,

$$\begin{aligned}\rho(E_f = E_i) &= \rho(E_f)\,\delta(E_f - E_i)\,dE_f \\ &= \rho(E_f^{\text{el}})\,\rho(E_f^{\text{phon}})\,\delta[(E_f^{\text{el}} + E_f^{\text{phon}}) - (E_i^{\text{el}} + E_i^{\text{phon}})] \\ &\qquad \times dE_f^{\text{el}}\,dE_f^{\text{phon}} \\ &= \frac{1}{\hbar}\,g(\omega_{if}^{\text{el}} - \omega_r)\,\rho(\omega_a)\,\rho(\omega_e)\,\delta[\omega_{if}^{\text{el}} - (\omega_e - \omega_a)] \\ &\qquad \times d\omega_{if}^{\text{el}}\,d\omega_a\,d\omega_e \\ &\simeq \frac{1}{\hbar}\,\delta(\omega_{if}^{\text{el}} - \omega_r)\,\rho(\omega_a)\,\rho(\omega_e)\,\delta[\omega_{if}^{\text{el}} - (\omega_e - \omega_a)] \\ &\qquad \times d\omega_{if}^{\text{el}}\,d\omega_a\,d\omega_e. \end{aligned} \quad (15.46)$$

The transition probability is then given by

$$\begin{aligned} W &= \frac{2\pi}{\hbar^2}\iint |M|^2\,\rho(\omega_a)\,\rho(\omega_e)\,\delta[\omega_r - (\omega_e - \omega_a)]\,d\omega_a\,d\omega_e \\ &\simeq \frac{2\pi}{\hbar^2}\frac{9V^2}{4\pi^4v^6}\iint |M|^2\,\omega_a^2\omega_e^2\delta[\omega_e - \omega_a]\,d\omega_a\,d\omega_e \\ &= \frac{2\pi}{\hbar^2}\frac{9V^2}{4\pi^4v^6}\frac{\hbar^2}{4M^2v^4}\int_0^{\omega_D}\omega^6 n(n+1)\,d\omega \\ &\quad \times \left|2\langle\psi_f^{\text{el}}|\, V_2\,|\psi_i^{\text{el}}\rangle + 2\sum_l\left[\frac{\langle\psi_f^{\text{el}}|\, V_1\,|\psi_l^{\text{el}}\rangle\langle\psi_l^{\text{el}}|\, V_1\,|\psi_i^{\text{el}}\rangle}{E_i^{\text{el}} - E_l^{\text{el}}}\right]\right|^2 \\ &= \frac{9}{\rho^2v^{10}8\pi^3}\left|2\langle\psi_f^{\text{el}}|\, V_2\,|\psi_i^{\text{el}}\rangle + 2\sum_l\left[\frac{\langle\psi_f^{\text{el}}|\, V_1\,|\psi_l^{\text{el}}\rangle\langle\psi_l^{\text{el}}|\, V_1\,|\psi_i^{\text{el}}\rangle}{E_i^{\text{el}} - E_l^{\text{el}}}\right]\right|^2 \\ &\quad \times \int_0^{\omega_D}\frac{\omega^6 e^{\hbar\omega/kT}}{e^{\hbar\omega/kT} - 1}\,d\omega = A\left(\frac{T}{T_D}\right)^7\int_0^{T_D/T}\frac{x^6e^x}{(e^x-1)^2}\,dx, \end{aligned} \quad (15.47)$$

where $T_D = \hbar\omega_D/k$ and

$$A = \frac{9}{\rho^2 v^{10} 8\pi^3}\left|2\langle\psi_f^{\text{el}}|\, V_2\, |\psi_i^{\text{el}}\rangle + 2\sum_l \left[\frac{\langle\psi_f^{\text{el}}|\, V_1\, |\psi_l^{\text{el}}\rangle\langle\psi_l^{\text{el}}|\, V_1\, |\psi_i^{\text{el}}\rangle}{E_i^{\text{el}} - E_l^{\text{el}}}\right]\right|^2. \tag{15.48}$$

A can be considered to be a *coupling coefficient* between the energy levels of the ion and the lattice vibrations.

The values of the expression

$$f\left(\frac{T}{T_D}\right) = \left(\frac{T}{T_D}\right)^7 \int^{T_D/T} \frac{x^6 e^x}{(e^x - 1)^2}\, dx \tag{15.49}$$

for different T/T_D are reported in Table 15.1.

Let us determine how a two-level system with populations different from the equilibrium values can reach equilibrium when Raman processes are active among the two levels. Considering the approximations made in (15.47), we see that the probability for a Raman decay $w_{21}{}^R$ is equal to the probability for a Raman excitation $w_{12}{}^R$. Therefore the relaxation time is given by

$$\begin{aligned}\tau_R{}^{-1} &= w_{21}{}^R + w_{12}{}^R \simeq 2w_{21}{}^R \\ &= \frac{9}{\rho^2 v^{10} 4\pi^3}\left|2\langle\psi_f^{\text{el}}|\, V_2\, |\psi_i^{\text{el}}\rangle - \sum_l \frac{2}{\Delta_l}\left[\langle\psi_f^{\text{el}}|\, V_1\, |\psi_l^{\text{el}}\rangle\langle\psi_l^{\text{el}}|\, V_1\, |\psi_f^{\text{el}}\rangle\right]\right|^2 \\ &\quad\times \int_0^{\omega_D} \frac{\omega^6 e^{\hbar\omega/kT}}{(e^{\hbar\omega/kT} - 1)}\, d\omega,\end{aligned} \tag{15.50}$$

where $\Delta_l = E_l^{\text{el}} - E_i^{\text{el}}$. In case $T_D = \hbar\omega_D/k \gg T$, the integral has the approximate value $6!(kT/\hbar)^7$ and then

$$\begin{aligned}\tau_R{}^{-1} = \frac{9 \times 6!}{\rho^2 v^{10} 4\pi^3}\left(\frac{kT}{\hbar}\right)^7 \bigg|2\langle\psi_f^{\text{el}}|\, V_2\, |\psi_i^{\text{el}}\rangle \\ - \sum_l \frac{2}{\Delta_l}\left[\langle\psi_f^{\text{el}}|\, V_1\, |\psi_l^{\text{el}}\rangle\langle\psi_l^{\text{el}}|\, V_1\, |\psi_f^{\text{el}}\rangle\right]\bigg|^2 = bT^7,\end{aligned} \tag{15.51}$$

which yields a T^{-7} dependence of τ_R for non-Kramers levels.

For Kramers levels the matrix element $\langle\psi_f^{\text{el}}|\, V_2\, |\psi_i^{\text{el}}\rangle$ vanishes. In this case, however, there will be some upper doublet which a magnetic field may admix to the ground state doublet. This will not change the T^7 dependence but will introduce an H^2 dependence in $\tau_R{}^{-1}$. Also, the second term in the squared matrix element of (15.51) is replaced by an expression that introduces a T^9 dependence in $\tau_R{}^{-1}$ with no dependence on H. For detailed calculations of this relaxation time the reader is referred to [1] and to the references therein.

Table 15.1 The Values of

$$\left(\frac{T}{T_D}\right)^7 \int_0^{T_D/T} \frac{x^6 e^x}{(e^x - 1)^2}\, dx$$

		0.1	0.2	0.3	0.4	0.5	0.6	0.7	0.8	0.9
0		19988.1×10^{-3}	4988.1×10^{-3}	2210.3×10^{-3}	1238.1×10^{-3}	788.2×10^{-3}	543.8×10^{-3}	396.4×10^{-3}	300.8×10^{-3}	235.3×10^{-3}
1	188.5×10^{-3}	153.9×10^{-3}	127.6×10^{-3}	107.1×10^{-3}	90.98×10^{-3}	77.95×10^{-3}	67.31×10^{-3}	58.52×10^{-3}	51.18×10^{-3}	44.99×10^{-3}
2	39.73×10^{-3}	35.23×10^{-3}	31.35×10^{-3}	27.99×10^{-3}	25.06×10^{-3}	22.49×10^{-3}	20.24×10^{-3}	18.25×10^{-3}	16.48×10^{-3}	14.92×10^{-3}
3	13.52×10^{-3}	12.28×10^{-3}	11.16×10^{-3}	10.16×10^{-3}	9.26×10^{-3}	8.44×10^{-3}	7.71×10^{-3}	7.05×10^{-3}	6.44×10^{-3}	5.90×10^{-3}
4	5.40×10^{-3}	4.95×10^{-3}	4.54×10^{-3}	4.17×10^{-3}	3.83×10^{-3}	3.52×10^{-3}	3.24×10^{-3}	2.98×10^{-3}	2.74×10^{-3}	2.53×10^{-3}
5	2.33×10^{-3}	2.15×10^{-3}	1.98×10^{-3}	1.83×10^{-3}	1.69×10^{-3}	1.56×10^{-3}	1.44×10^{-3}	1.33×10^{-3}	1.23×10^{-3}	1.14×10^{-3}
6	1.05×10^{-3}	9.77×10^{-4}	9.05×10^{-4}	8.38×10^{-4}	7.77×10^{-4}	7.20×10^{-4}	6.68×10^{-4}	6.19×10^{-4}	5.75×10^{-4}	5.34×10^{-4}
7	4.96×10^{-4}	4.60×10^{-4}	4.28×10^{-4}	3.98×10^{-4}	3.70×10^{-4}	3.45×10^{-4}	3.21×10^{-4}	2.98×10^{-4}	2.78×10^{-4}	2.59×10^{-4}
8	2.41×10^{-4}	2.25×10^{-4}	2.10×10^{-4}	1.96×10^{-4}	1.83×10^{-4}	1.71×10^{-4}	1.59×10^{-4}	1.49×10^{-4}	1.39×10^{-4}	1.30×10^{-4}
9	1.22×10^{-4}	1.14×10^{-4}	1.07×10^{-4}	1.00×10^{-4}	9.37×10^{-5}	8.79×10^{-5}	8.24×10^{-5}	7.73×10^{-5}	7.25×10^{-5}	6.80×10^{-5}
10	6.39×10^{-5}	6.00×10^{-5}	5.63×10^{-5}	5.30×10^{-5}	4.98×10^{-5}	4.68×10^{-5}	4.41×10^{-5}	4.15×10^{-5}	3.90×10^{-5}	3.68×10^{-5}
11	3.47×10^{-5}	3.27×10^{-5}	3.08×10^{-5}	2.91×10^{-5}	2.74×10^{-5}	2.59×10^{-5}	2.44×10^{-5}	2.31×10^{-5}	2.18×10^{-5}	2.06×10^{-5}
12	1.95×10^{-5}	1.84×10^{-5}	1.75×10^{-5}	1.65×10^{-5}	1.56×10^{-5}	1.48×10^{-5}	1.40×10^{-5}	1.33×10^{-5}	1.26×10^{-5}	1.19×10^{-5}
13	1.13×10^{-5}	1.08×10^{-5}	1.03×10^{-5}	9.73×10^{-6}	9.25×10^{-6}	8.79×10^{-6}	8.36×10^{-6}	7.95×10^{-6}	7.56×10^{-6}	7.20×10^{-6}
14	6.85×10^{-6}	6.52×10^{-6}	6.21×10^{-6}	5.92×10^{-6}	5.64×10^{-6}	5.37×10^{-6}	5.12×10^{-6}	4.89×10^{-6}	4.67×10^{-6}	4.46×10^{-6}
15	4.25×10^{-6}	4.06×10^{-6}	3.88×10^{-6}	3.71×10^{-6}	3.55×10^{-6}	3.39×10^{-6}	3.24×10^{-6}	3.10×10^{-6}	2.97×10^{-6}	2.84×10^{-6}
16	2.72×10^{-6}	2.60×10^{-6}	2.49×10^{-6}	2.39×10^{-6}	2.29×10^{-6}	2.19×10^{-6}	2.10×10^{-6}	2.02×10^{-6}	1.93×10^{-6}	1.86×10^{-6}
17	1.78×10^{-6}	1.71×10^{-6}	1.64×10^{-6}	1.58×10^{-6}	1.51×10^{-6}	1.46×10^{-6}	1.40×10^{-6}	1.34×10^{-6}	1.29×10^{-6}	1.24×10^{-6}
18	1.20×10^{-6}	1.15×10^{-6}	1.11×10^{-6}	1.06×10^{-6}	1.03×10^{-6}	9.87×10^{-7}	9.50×10^{-7}	9.15×10^{-7}	8.82×10^{-7}	8.50×10^{-7}
19	8.19×10^{-7}	7.90×10^{-7}	7.61×10^{-7}	7.34×10^{-7}	7.08×10^{-7}	6.83×10^{-7}	6.59×10^{-7}	6.36×10^{-7}	6.14×10^{-7}	5.93×10^{-7}
20	5.72×10^{-7}	5.52×10^{-7}	5.34×10^{-7}	5.16×10^{-7}	4.98×10^{-7}	4.81×10^{-7}	4.65×10^{-7}	4.50×10^{-7}	4.35×10^{-7}	4.20×10^{-7}

Summarizing, for Raman processes, we have

$$\begin{aligned} \tau_R^{-1} &= bT^7 && \text{(non-Kramers levels)}, \\ \tau_R^{-1} &= b'T^9 + b''H^2T^7 && \text{(Kramers levels)}, \end{aligned} \tag{15.52}$$

in the approximation $\hbar\omega_r \ll kT$.

2.3 Orbach Processes

Let us now consider the three-level system represented in Fig. 15.5 in which

$$\begin{aligned} \delta &= E_2 - E_1, \\ \Delta &= E_3 - E_2, \end{aligned} \tag{15.53}$$

and let us assume that

$$\begin{aligned} &\delta \ll \Delta, \\ &\Delta < \hbar\omega_D. \end{aligned} \tag{15.54}$$

Moreover, let us assume that direct processes between levels 2 and 1 are inactive.

The dynamical equations for the populations in the lower two levels are given by

$$\begin{aligned} \frac{dN_2}{dt} &= -N_2 w_{23} + N_3 w_{32}, \\ \frac{dN_1}{dt} &= -N_1 w_{13} + N_3 w_{31}, \end{aligned} \tag{15.55}$$

where the probabilities w_{ij} are one phonon absorption and emission probabilities as given by (15.21) and (15.22),

$$\begin{aligned} w_{13} &= B_1 n(\Delta + \delta), \\ w_{31} &= B_1[n(\Delta + \delta) + 1], \end{aligned} \tag{15.56}$$

$$\begin{aligned} w_{23} &= B_2 n(\Delta), \\ w_{32} &= B_2[n(\Delta) + 1], \end{aligned} \tag{15.57}$$

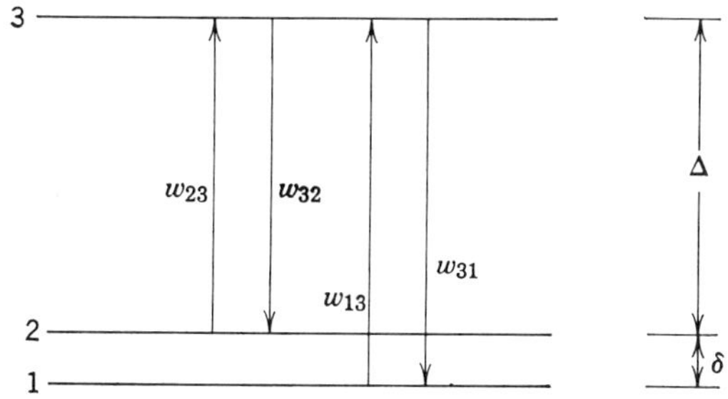

Fig. 15.5. Three level system presenting Orbach processes.

where

$$n(E) = \frac{1}{e^{E/kT} - 1}. \tag{15.58}$$

Taking $B_1 \approx B_2 = B$, (15.55) become

$$\begin{aligned} \frac{dN_2}{dt} &= B\{N_3[n(\Delta) + 1] - N_2 n(\Delta)\}, \\ \frac{dN_1}{dt} &= B\{N_3[n(\Delta + \delta) + 1] - N_1 n(\Delta + \delta)\}. \end{aligned} \tag{15.59}$$

If $kT \ll \Delta$, we can neglect N_3 in comparison to N_1 and N_2. This yields

$$\frac{d(N_2 - N_1)}{dt} = Be^{-\Delta/kT}\{N_1 e^{-\delta/kT} - N_2\}. \tag{15.60}$$

This equation gives the equilibrium value

$$\frac{N_2^{\text{e}}}{N_1^{\text{e}}} = e^{-\delta/kT}, \tag{15.61}$$

which, in turn, since $N_1 + N_2 = N$, gives

$$\begin{aligned} N_2^{\text{e}} &= \frac{Ne^{-\delta/kT}}{1 + e^{-\delta/kT}}, \\ N_1^{\text{e}} &= \frac{N}{1 + e^{-\delta/kT}}. \end{aligned} \tag{15.62}$$

Now (15.59) have the solutions

$$\begin{aligned} N_2(t) &= N_2^{\text{e}} - [N_1(0) - N_1^{\text{e}}]e^{-t/\tau}, \\ N_1(t) &= N_1^{\text{e}} + [N_1(0) - N_1^{\text{e}}]e^{-t/\tau}, \end{aligned} \tag{15.63}$$

where

$$\tau^{-1} = \frac{Be^{-\Delta/kT}}{2}(1 + e^{-\delta/kT}) \approx Be^{-\Delta/kT}. \tag{15.64}$$

The relaxation time related to an Orbach process is therefore proportional to the number $n(\Delta) \approx e^{-\Delta/kT}$ of phonons of energy equal to Δ.

We notice that measurements of relaxation times at different temperatures may give the value of B, which is the probability for spontaneous one-phonon decay (at low temperature) of level 3 in Fig. 15.5. This level may be the final level of a fluorescent line and, as such, its indeterminacy, due to B, may make a known contribution to the width of the fluorescence line. Such a correlation of the Orbach relaxation coefficient with optical linewidths has actually been found in $LaF_3{:}Er^{3+}$ by Yen, Scott, and Scott [2].

We shall now examine the different relaxation processes and compare them.

The direct process gives a relevant contribution to the relaxation time at very low temperatures, because of its dependence on n_r, the number of phonons of frequency equal to that of the transition. At these low temperatures $n_r \approx kT/\delta$ and the Raman and Orbach contributions are very small. The direct processes produce a relaxation time which is proportional to T^{-1} and ω_r^{-2} (ω_r being the frequency of transition) for non-Kramers doublets; for Kramers doublets the relaxation time has the same dependence on T but goes as H^{-4}.

The Orbach process is essentially proportional to the number of phonons present which have energy equal to the crystal field energy Δ. This number is relevant when the Debye temperature T_D is such that $kT_D > \Delta$. We notice that Orbach processes do not introduce any dependence on the field H.

Raman processes make a contribution to the relaxation time, which is essentially independent of the energy of the relaxing level and which involves the whole phonon spectrum. If $kT_D \approx \Delta$ Raman processes may be as relevant as the Orbach processes and may even become dominant.

In summary, for non-Kramers levels

$$\tau^{-1} = \underset{\text{(direct)}}{a\omega_r^2 T} + \underset{\text{(Raman)}}{bT^7} + \underset{\text{(Orbach)}}{ce^{-\Delta/kT}} \tag{15.65}$$

and for Kramers levels

$$\tau^{-1} = \underset{\text{(direct)}}{a'H^4T} + \underset{\text{(Raman)}}{b'T^9 + b''H^2T^7} + \underset{\text{(Orbach)}}{c'e^{-\Delta/kT}}. \tag{15.66}$$

For Kramer's levels in general the Raman and Orbach processes are important at lower temperatures than for non-Kramers levels.

2.4 Multiphonon Processes

Multiphonon relaxation processes can take place between two levels whose energy difference is greater than the greatest energy of the available phonons.

The expression of the ion–phonon interaction Hamiltonian has terms with increasing power in the strain at the ion site. Each term is individually constituted by a part that is a function of the coordinates of the electrons of the unfilled shell and by a part that is a sum of products of creation and annihilation phonon operators. The first term of the expansion corresponds to a first-order process, the second term to a second-order process, and so on; the relative importance of a term decreases as we consider higher order processes.

Straight application of perturbation theory should then provide the probability of a multiphonon decay. The following observations can be made:

1. We assume that the eigenfunctions of the ion in the crystal are determined. By measuring the temperature of the system we know the distribution of phonons on the different frequencies. Therefore the initial state of the total (ion plus phonons) system is determined.
2. The final state of the total system is not determined because its phononic part is not known. The ion may in fact decay by, say, the emission of four phonons or by the emission of five phonons and the absorption of one. All these processes are mutally exclusive, and the relaxation probability must be evaluated by summing over all these possibilities. Besides this, a certain process, say, the emission of 4 phonons, may take place by utilizing any 4 available phonons (provided the sum of their energies is equal to the ionic energy gap). The probability of the process must then be evalulated by summing (eventually integrating) over all the phonon frequencies.
3. The matrix element of the interaction Hamiltonian for a process involving n phonons must be evaluated up to the nth order approximation. A term in the resulting sum may be neglected only if its order of magnitude is very small.
4. A difficult aspect of the calculations derives from the scarcity of data on lattice vibrational frequencies. For large energy gaps phonons belonging to the optical branches of the spectrum may be involved in the decay processes.

The calculations of the transition probabilities of radiationless (multiphonon) processes is extremely complicated. It may, however, be safely assumed with Kiel [3], that these processes are the less probable the larger is the number of emitted phonons, namely, the greater is the energy gap of the two levels involved in the transition. Some experimental evidence [4] confirms this result.

When competing with the radiative decay process the radiationless processes represent a serious loss for a fluorescent system, where a large output of radiation is desired. However, in other instances, they may actually be useful. This is the case of many optically excited fluorescent materials; the exciting light brings a number of ions to an upper excited state from which they quickly decay to a long lived metastable state which becomes the initial state of the fluorescence. This decay, in general, takes place by radiationless processes which dominate over the radiative decay process from the optically excited level to the ground state and increases the population of the metastable level. It is important to note that these processes are extremely fast ($\gtrsim 10^{-7}$ sec) even at very low temperatures and that for this reason it is difficult to measure their temperature dependence.

3. DIFFERENT TYPES OF LINE BROADENING MECHANISMS: LORENTZIAN AND GAUSSIAN LINE SHAPES

3.1 Lifetime Broadening Mechanism and Lorentzian Line Shape

Let us assume that we have a system represented by a Hamiltonian H_0 under the action of a time dependent perturbation H'. From time dependent perturbation theory we know that the total wavefunction of the Hamiltonian

$$H = H_0 + H' \tag{15.67}$$

is given by

$$\psi = \sum_i c_i(t)\, \psi_i(t), \tag{15.68}$$

where $\psi_i(t)$ are eigenfunctions of H_0 and where the time dependent coefficients $c_i(t)$ are given by

$$\begin{aligned} i\hbar \dot{c}_k(t) &= \sum_i c_i(t)\, \langle \psi_k(t)|\, H'\, |\psi_i(t)\rangle \\ &= \sum_i c_i(t)\, \langle \psi_k(0)|\, H'\, |\psi_i(0)\rangle e^{i\omega_{ki}t} \\ &= \sum_i c_i(t)\, H'_{ki} e^{i\omega_{ki}t}, \end{aligned} \tag{15.69}$$

where

$$\omega_{ki} = \frac{E_k - E_i}{\hbar},$$

and

$$H'_{ki} = \langle \psi_k(0)|\, H'\, |\psi_i(0)\rangle.$$

Let us assume now that at time $t = 0$ the system is in a definite eigenstate of H_0;

$$c_n(0) = 1; \qquad c_i(0) = 0 \quad \text{for } i \neq n. \tag{15.70}$$

Let us assume also that there is only one state l to which the system can go:

$$\begin{aligned} &\langle \psi_n(0)|\, H'\, |\psi_l(0)\rangle \neq 0, \\ &\langle \psi_m(0)|\, H'\, |\psi_k(0)\rangle = 0 \quad \text{for } m,\, k \neq n. \end{aligned} \tag{15.71}$$

Equations (15.69) will then reduce to

$$i\hbar \dot{c}_l(t) = c_n \langle \psi_l(0)|\, H'\, |\psi_n(0)\rangle e^{i\omega_{ln}t}, \tag{15.72}$$

$$i\hbar \dot{c}_n(t) = c_l \langle \psi_n(0)|\, H'\, |\psi_l(0)\rangle e^{-i\omega_{ln}t}, \tag{15.73}$$

where

$$\omega_{ln} = \frac{E_l - E_n}{\hbar}.$$

Let us assume that the probability of finding the system in the state n decreases exponentially,

$$c_n = e^{-(\gamma/2)t} \qquad (\gamma = \text{const}). \tag{15.74}$$

We have then from (15.72)

$$i\hbar \dot{c}_l = H'_{ln} e^{[i\omega_{ln}-(\gamma/2)]t}, \tag{15.75}$$

where $H'_{ln} = \langle \psi_l(0)| H' |\psi_n(0)\rangle$. If H'_{ln} is independent of time, integrating from 0 to t we get

$$c_l = -\frac{i}{\hbar} H'_{ln} \frac{e^{[i\omega_{ln}-(\gamma/2)]t} - 1}{i\omega_{ln} - (\gamma/2)}. \tag{15.76}$$

Using the expression found for c_l and taking (15.74) into account, (15.73) gives

$$\gamma = \frac{2}{\hbar^2} |H'_{ln}|^2 \frac{1 - e^{-[i\omega_{ln}-(\gamma/2)]t}}{i\omega_{ln} - (\gamma/2)}; \tag{15.77}$$

γ is not independent of time as we assumed.

We may however proceed in the following way. We can assume that l is actually in a continuum of energies. Equations 15.72 and 15.73, changing the subscript l to λ, become

$$i\hbar \dot{c}_\lambda(t) = c_n H'_{\lambda n} e^{i\omega_{\lambda n} t}, \tag{15.78}$$

$$i\hbar \dot{c}_n(t) = \int c_\lambda H'_{n\lambda} e^{-i\omega_{\lambda n} t}\, d\lambda. \tag{15.79}$$

Using the assumption (15.74) and integrating (15.78) from 0 to t,

$$c_\lambda = -\frac{i}{\hbar} H'_{\lambda n} \frac{e^{[i\omega_{\lambda n}-(\gamma/2)]t} - 1}{i\omega_{\lambda n} - \gamma/2}. \tag{15.80}$$

From (15.79), using (15.80),

$$i\hbar\left(-\frac{\gamma}{2}\right) e^{-(\gamma/2)t} = \frac{i}{\hbar} \int |H'_{\lambda n}|^2 e^{-i\omega_{\lambda n} t} \frac{1 - e^{[i\omega_{\lambda n}-(\gamma/2)]t}}{i\omega_{\lambda n} - (\gamma/2)}\, d\lambda,$$

or

$$\gamma = \int \frac{2i}{\hbar^2} |H'_{\lambda n}|^2 \frac{1 - e^{[i\omega_{n\lambda}+(\gamma/2)]t}}{\omega_{n\lambda} - i\gamma/2}\, d\lambda \tag{15.81}$$

But

$$d\lambda = \frac{d\lambda}{d\omega_{n\lambda}}\, d\omega_{n\lambda} = \rho(\omega_{n\lambda})\, d\omega_{n\lambda}, \tag{15.82}$$

and then,

$$\gamma = \frac{2i}{\hbar^2} \int |H'_{\lambda n}|^2 \rho(\omega_{n\lambda}) \frac{1 - e^{[i\omega_{n\lambda}+(\gamma/2)]t}}{\omega_{n\lambda} - i\gamma/2}\, d\omega_{n\lambda}. \tag{15.83}$$

In evaluating the integral in (15.83), we shall assume γ, which is, in effect, the indeterminacy of the initial level n, very small in comparison to $\omega_{n\lambda}$. We may then write

$$\gamma = \frac{2i}{\hbar^2}\int |H'_{\lambda n}|^2 \rho(\omega_{n\lambda})\,\frac{1 - e^{i\omega_{n\lambda}t}}{\omega_{n\lambda}}\,d\omega_{n\lambda}. \tag{15.84}$$

But

$$\frac{1 - e^{i\omega_{n\lambda}t}}{\omega_{n\lambda}} = \frac{1 - \cos \omega_{n\lambda}t}{\omega_{n\lambda}} - i\,\frac{\sin \omega_{n\lambda}t}{\omega_{n\lambda}}. \tag{15.85}$$

For very large t the first term may be replaced by $1/\omega_{n\lambda}$ for $\omega_n \neq \omega_\lambda$ because the rapidly oscillating $\cos \omega_{n\lambda}t$ does not give any contribution to the integral; at $\omega_{n\lambda} = 0$ this term goes to zero. When it is multiplied by the rest of the integrand and integrated over $\omega_{n\lambda}$, the result is the principal value [5] of the integral.

For very large t the second term in (15.85) can be expressed as $i\pi\delta(\omega_{n\lambda})$. In fact, by definition, the function $\delta(x)$ can be expressed in the following way:

$$\delta(x) = \frac{1}{\pi}\lim_{\alpha\to\infty}\frac{\sin \alpha x}{x}. \tag{15.86}$$

Therefore we may write

$$\lim_{t\to\infty}\frac{1 - e^{i\omega_{n\lambda}t}}{\omega_{n\lambda}} = \frac{\mathfrak{P}}{\omega_{n\lambda}} - i\pi\delta(\omega_{n\lambda}), \tag{15.87}$$

where $\mathfrak{P}$ indicates the principal value. Now γ can be expressed as

$$\begin{aligned}\gamma &= \frac{2i}{\hbar^2}\int |H'_{\lambda n}|^2\rho(\omega_{n\lambda})\left\{\frac{\mathfrak{P}}{\omega_{n\lambda}} - i\pi\delta(\omega_{n\lambda})\right\} d\omega_{n\lambda}\\ &= \frac{2\pi}{\hbar^2}|H'_{\lambda n}|^2\rho(\omega_n = \omega_\lambda) + \frac{2i}{\hbar^2}\mathfrak{P}\int\frac{|H'_{\lambda n}|^2\rho(\omega_{n\lambda})\,d\omega_{n\lambda}}{\omega_{n\lambda}}\\ &= W_{n\lambda} + i\,\frac{2}{\hbar}\mathfrak{P}\int\frac{|H'_{\lambda n}|^2\rho(\omega_{n\lambda})\,d\omega_{n\lambda}}{\hbar\omega_{\lambda n}},\end{aligned} \tag{15.88}$$

where

$$\mathrm{Re}(\gamma) = W_{n\lambda} = \frac{2\pi}{\hbar^2}|H'_{\lambda n}|^2\rho(\omega_n = \omega_\lambda) \tag{15.89}$$

is in effect the transition probability per unit time from state n to state λ. The imaginary part of γ is

$$\mathfrak{I} = \mathrm{Im}\,(\gamma) = \frac{2}{\hbar}\mathfrak{P}\int\frac{|H'_{\lambda n}|^2\rho(\omega_{n\lambda})}{\hbar\omega_{n\lambda}}\,d\omega_{n\lambda}. \tag{15.90}$$

Let us consider now the expression for c_λ after a time $t \gg 1/W_{n\lambda}$:

$$c_\lambda = -\frac{i}{\hbar} H'_{\lambda n} \frac{e^{(i\omega_{\lambda n} - \gamma/2)t} - 1}{i\omega_{\lambda n} - \frac{1}{2}(W + i\mathfrak{J})}$$

$$\xrightarrow[t \gg 1/W]{} \frac{i}{\hbar} H'_{\lambda n} \frac{1}{i(\omega_\lambda - \omega_n - \frac{1}{2}\mathfrak{J}) - \frac{1}{2}W}, \tag{15.91}$$

and

$$|c_\lambda(\infty)|^2 = \frac{1}{\hbar^2} |H'_{\lambda n}|^2 \frac{1}{[(\omega_n + \frac{1}{2}\mathfrak{J}) - \omega_\lambda]^2 + W^2/4}. \tag{15.92}$$

It is interesting to apply the above results to the case of an atom in an excited state interacting with the radiation field. In this case the unperturbed system consists of the atom and the radiation field and the perturbing Hamiltonian H' is given by the interaction between them. The following observations can be made:

1. The real part of γ (equal to the transition probability per unit time) produces a finite width of the transition. In the case of an atom interacting with radiation this width is called the *natural linewidth.* Spectral lines with the shape (15.92) are called *Lorentzian lines.* The appearance of a line breadth derives from the fact that we have allowed the probability $|c_n|^2$ of the atom being in the initial state to decay for a time which is greater than the lifetime of the initial state. For times much shorter than this lifetime, the probability $|c_n|^2$ maintains practically the initial value and the line is very sharp.
2. The imaginary part of γ produces a shift in the energy of the initial level of the transition. This shift is in effect the *Lamb shift.*
3. By the use of the principal value $\mathcal{P}$, (15.90) takes care of the resonances that may occur in correspondence to the emission and reabsorption of virtual photons with energy equal to the energy difference between the initial level and a different level connected to it by H'.

From (15.92) we can see that *the width at half maximum intensity is equal to the total transition probability*,

$$\Delta E = \hbar W. \tag{15.93}$$

We may call W^{-1} the lifetime τ of the state n,

$$(\Delta E)\,\tau = \hbar. \tag{15.94}$$

This is nothing but the uncertainty relation between energy and time which expresses the fact that we may know the energy of a system with an accuracy $\Delta E = \hbar/\tau$ if only the time τ is available to measure it.

Such effects as linewidth and energy shift are a consequence of the interaction between the atomic system and the radiation; similar effects are however found when an atom in a crystal interacts with the thermal vibrations of the lattice. The formalism developed in this section applies whenever an isolated atom interacts with a large number of other degrees of freedom whose density is practically continuous.

Several lifetime shortening mechanisms may be present at the same time; for example, thermal vibrations and radiation damping may be operating at the same time; also several transitions may originate from the same level. In this case the breadth of the level is given by the sum of the breadths due to all these processes,

$$\Delta E = \hbar\left(\sum_{ii} W_{ij}\right). \tag{15.95}$$

We notice also that when a transition connects two excited levels, one with breadth W_i and the other with breadth W_j, the linewidth of the transition is $W_i + W_j$.

In closing this section we want to point out the fact that a Lorentzian profile is due to interactions between the radiative or absorbing systems and some time dependent perturbations; these interactions are *the same* for each atom contributing to the emission or absorption.

3.2 Time-Independent Random Perturbations and Gaussian Line Shape

A Gaussian distribution of frequencies is in general due to a completely different type of mechanism.

An example of Gaussian distribution is presented by the so-called *Doppler broadened lines.* These lines are produced by the fact that atoms or molecules in a container have a Maxwellian distribution of velocities expressed by $\exp(-mv^2/2kT)$. The light emitted by an atom in its excited state is seen in the x direction with the frequency shifted by

$$|\nu - \nu_0| = \frac{\nu_0 |v_x|}{c} \tag{15.96}$$

for $v \ll c$. This fact produces a line with a profile given by

$$\text{const} \times \exp\left[-\frac{mc^2(\nu - \nu_0)^2}{2\nu_0^2 kT}\right], \tag{15.97}$$

which describes a *Gaussian line shape.*

In this case the profile may be considered as the superposition of a great number of independent spectral lines, with each line corresponding to transitions that take place in a certain number of atoms. This fact turns out to be a general propriety of Gaussian lines.

Consider an ensemble of radiating ions in a crystal, in which the influence of the environment on each ion can be thought as due to the presence of a crystalline field. The ions in the crystal may actually see a slightly different crystalline field in dependence of their position; it is a fact that no crystal is perfect and that internal microscopic strains can be present. We may assume that these perturbations of the crystalline field are completely random in space; therefore each ion has an energy that is slightly different from the energy of another ion. The total crystal will then produce a line which is the superposition of many lines of different frequencies.

It is known from the theory of probability that the probability distribution of the sum of a very great number of independent and random variables is a function of the type $Ce^{-\alpha^2x^2}$ (C, α constant); namely, it is a *Gaussian* distribution function. This result is known as the *central limit theorem* [6]. The presence of microscopic random distortions in a crystal will then produce a Gaussian spectral line.

3.3 Probability Densities and Superposition of Probability Densities. The Voigt Profile

The probability dp that a continuous random variable x takes a value in $(x, x + dx)$ can be introduced as follows:

$$dp = p(x)\, dx. \tag{15.98}$$

The function $p(x)$ is said to be a *probability density*. Probability densities respect the normalization condition,

$$\int_{-\infty}^{+\infty} p(x)\, dx = 1. \tag{15.99}$$

The nth moment of the variable x is given by

$$M_n = \overline{x^n} = \int_{-\infty}^{+\infty} x^n p(x)\, dx. \tag{15.100}$$

If $p(x)$ is an even function $\overline{x^n} = 0$, for n odd.

Given a certain probability density $p(x)$, we define as *characteristic function* of $p(x)$ the Fourier transform:

$$s(t) = \int_{-\infty}^{+\infty} p(x)\, e^{-itx}\, dx. \tag{15.101}$$

Given $s(t)$ the density function is given by

$$p(x) = \frac{1}{2\pi} \int_{-\infty}^{+\infty} s(t)\, e^{itx}\, dt. \tag{15.102}$$

We define also the *variance* of x from $\bar{x}$ as follows:

$$\sigma^2 = \int p(x)(x - \bar{x})^2\, dx = \overline{x^2} - 2\bar{x} \int x p(x)\, dx + (\bar{x})^2 = \overline{x^2} - (\bar{x})^2. \tag{15.103}$$

The square root of the variance, σ, is known as the *standard deviation* of x from $\bar{x}$. The above relation expresses the fact that the variance is equal to the second moment minus the squared first moment. If $\bar{x} = 0$, $\sigma^2 = \overline{x^2}$.

Deriving $s(t)$ once and twice we get

$$\begin{aligned} s'(t) &= -\, i \int_{-\infty}^{+\infty} x p(x) e^{-itx}\, dx, \\ s''(t) &= - \int_{-\infty}^{+\infty} x^2 p(x) e^{-itx}\, dx. \end{aligned} \tag{15.104}$$

Also

$$\begin{aligned} s'(0) &= -i\bar{x}, \\ s''(0) &= -\overline{x^2}. \end{aligned} \tag{15.105}$$

Then, replacing these values in (15.103) we find

$$\sigma^2 = -s''(0) + [s'(0)]^2. \tag{15.106}$$

Given two independent probabilities density $p(y)$ and $q(w)$, the probability density of the variable $x = y + w$ is given by the *convolution integral*

$$r(x) = \int_{-\infty}^{+\infty} p(y) q(x - y)\, dy. \tag{15.107}$$

Let us call $s(t)$, $s_p(t)$ and $s_q(t)$, respectively, the characteristic functions of $r(x)$, $p(y)$ and $q(w)$. We have then

$$\begin{aligned} s_p(t) s_q(t) &= \int_{-\infty}^{+\infty} p(y) e^{-ity}\, dy \int_{-\infty}^{+\infty} q(w) e^{-itw}\, dw \\ &= \int_{-\infty}^{+\infty} \int_{-\infty}^{+\infty} p(y) q(w) e^{-it(y+w)}\, dy\, dw \\ &= \int_{-\infty}^{+\infty} \int_{-\infty}^{+\infty} p(y) q(x - y) e^{-itx}\, dx\, dy = s(t). \end{aligned} \tag{15.108}$$

Therefore the characteristic function of the convolution of two probability densities is equal to the product of the characteristic functions of the two probability densities.

A probability density of the form

$$p_L(\nu) = \frac{\Delta\nu_L}{2\pi} \frac{1}{(\nu - \nu_0)^2 + (\Delta\nu_L/2)^2} \tag{15.109}$$

is collect *Lorentzian.* The characteristic function of such a probability density is

$$\begin{aligned} s_L(t) &= \int_{-\infty}^{+\infty} p_L(\nu) e^{-it\nu}\, d\nu \\ &= \frac{\Delta\nu_L}{2\pi} \int_{-\infty}^{+\infty} \frac{e^{-i\nu t}}{(\nu - \nu_0)^2 + (\Delta\nu_L/2)^2}\, d\nu = e^{-(\Delta\nu_L/2)|t|} e^{-i\nu_0 t}. \end{aligned} \tag{15.110}$$

A probability density of the form

$$p_G(\nu) = \frac{1}{\sigma\sqrt{2\pi}} \exp\left(-\frac{(\nu - \nu_0)^2}{2\sigma^2}\right) \tag{15.111}$$

is called *Gaussian.* The characteristic function of such a probability density is given by

$$\begin{aligned} s_G(t) &= \frac{1}{\sigma\sqrt{2\pi}} \int_{-\infty}^{+\infty} e^{-i\nu t} \exp - \frac{(\nu - \nu_0)}{2\sigma^2}\, d\nu \\ &= \frac{1}{\sigma\sqrt{2\pi}} \int_{-\infty}^{+\infty} e^{-i(\nu' + \nu_0)t} e^{-(\nu'^2/2\sigma^2)}\, d\nu' \\ &= \frac{e^{-i\nu_0 t} e^{-(\sigma^2 t^2/2)}}{\sigma\sqrt{2\pi}} \int_{-\infty}^{+\infty} \exp\left(-\left(\frac{\nu'}{\sqrt{2}\sigma} + \frac{i\sigma t}{\sqrt{2}}\right)^2\right) d\nu'. \end{aligned}$$

Putting

$$\frac{\nu'}{\sqrt{2}\sigma} + \frac{i\sigma t}{\sqrt{2}} = y,$$

we get

$$d\nu' = \sqrt{2}\sigma\, dy,$$

and

$$s_G(t) = \frac{e^{-i\nu_0 t} e^{-(\sigma^2 t^2/2)}}{\sigma\sqrt{2\pi}} \sqrt{2}\sigma \int_{-\infty}^{+\infty} e^{-y^2} dy = e^{-i\nu_0 t} e^{-(\sigma^2 t^2/2)}. \tag{15.112}$$

The first and the second derivatives are given by

$$s'_G(t) = -(i\nu_0 + \sigma^2 t) e^{-i\nu_0 t - (\sigma^2 t^2/2)} \tag{15.113}$$

$$s''_G(t) = (i\nu_0 + \sigma^2 t)^2 e^{-i\nu_0 t - (\sigma^2 t^2/2)} - \sigma^2 e^{-i\nu_0 t - (\sigma^2 t^2/2)} \tag{15.114}$$

and

$$s_G'(0) = -i\nu_0 = -i\bar{\nu} \tag{15.115}$$

$$s_G''(0) = -\nu_0^2 - \sigma^2 = -\overline{\nu^2}. \tag{15.116}$$

Therefore the average value of $p_G(\nu)$ is ν_0 and the variance is σ^2.

We may want to express the probability distribution (15.111) in terms of the width at half intensity $\Delta\nu_G$. The following relation between the standard deviation and the halfwidth $\Delta\nu_G$ can be easily derived:

$$\sigma = \frac{\Delta\nu_G}{2\sqrt{2\ln 2}}. \tag{15.117}$$

We can now express a Gaussian probability density in the following way:

$$p_G(\nu) = \frac{2\sqrt{\ln 2}}{\Delta\nu_G\sqrt{\pi}} \cdot \exp\left[-\left(\frac{2(\nu-\nu_0)}{\Delta\nu_G}\sqrt{\ln 2}\right)^2\right]. \tag{15.118}$$

Given now two probability densities $p_L(l)$ and $p_G(\delta)$, let us consider the probability density of the variable $l + \delta = \nu$:

$$\begin{aligned} r_V(\nu) &= \int_{-\infty}^{+\infty} p_G(\delta)p_L(\nu-\delta)\,d\delta \\ &= \frac{2}{\pi\Delta\nu_L}\frac{2\sqrt{\ln 2}}{\Delta\nu_G\sqrt{\pi}}\int_{-\infty}^{+\infty}\frac{\exp\left[-\left(\frac{2\delta}{\Delta\nu_G}\sqrt{\ln 2}\right)^2\right]}{1+\left(\frac{2}{\Delta\nu_L}(\nu-\nu_0-\delta)\right)^2}\,d\delta \\ &= \frac{4\sqrt{\ln 2}}{\pi\sqrt{\pi}}\frac{1}{\Delta\nu_L\Delta\nu_G}\int_{-\infty}^{+\infty}\frac{\exp\left[-\left(\frac{2\delta}{\Delta\nu_G}\sqrt{\ln 2}\right)^2\right]}{1+\left(\frac{2}{\Delta\nu_L}(\nu-\nu_0-\delta)\right)^2}\,d\delta. \end{aligned} \tag{15.119}$$

Let us put

$$\begin{aligned} y &= \frac{2\delta}{\Delta\nu_G}\sqrt{\ln 2}; \qquad d\delta = \frac{\Delta\nu_G}{2\sqrt{\ln 2}}\,dy, \\ \omega &= \frac{2(\nu-\nu_0)\sqrt{\ln 2}}{\Delta\nu_G}, \\ a &= \frac{\Delta\nu_L}{\Delta\nu_G}\sqrt{\ln 2}. \end{aligned} \tag{15.120}$$

With these, $r_V(\nu)$ becomes

$$r_V(\nu) = \frac{4\sqrt{\ln 2}}{\pi\sqrt{\pi}} \frac{1}{\Delta\nu_L \Delta\nu_G} \frac{\Delta\nu_L{}^2\sqrt{\ln 2}}{2\Delta\nu_G} \int_{-\infty}^{+\infty} \frac{e^{-y^2}}{a^2 + (\omega - y)^2}\, dy$$

$$= \frac{2\ln 2}{\pi\sqrt{\pi}} \frac{\Delta\nu_L}{\Delta\nu_G{}^2} \int_{-\infty}^{+\infty} \frac{e^{-y^2}}{a^2 + (\omega - y)^2}\, dy. \qquad (15.121)$$

This probability density (normalized already) is called *Voigt probability density*.

In Fig. 15.6 we report the three shapes of a Gaussian, a Lorentzian and a Voigt profiles with the same half width. The Voigt probability density reduces to a Lorentzian if $\Delta\nu_G = 0$ and to a Gaussian if $\Delta\nu_L = 0$.

Given a Voigt profile, $\Delta\nu_L$ and $\Delta\nu_G$ may be derived in the following way. We may write

$$s_V(t) = s_G(t)s_L(t) = e^{-i\nu_0 t}e^{-(\sigma^2t^2/2)}e^{-i\nu_0 t}e^{-(\Delta\nu/2)|t|}$$

$$= e^{-2i\nu_0 t}e^{-(\sigma^2t^2/2)}e^{-(\Delta\nu_L/2)\,|t|}. \qquad (15.122)$$

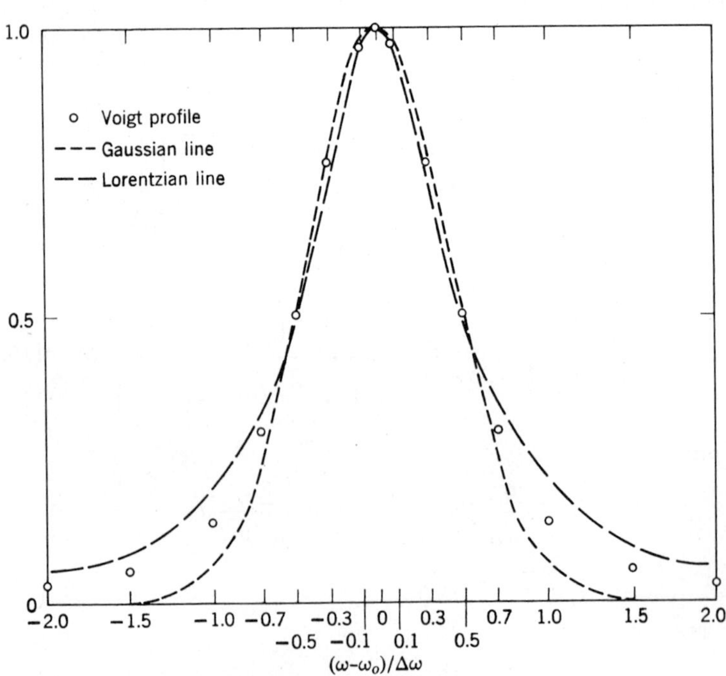

Fig. 15.6. Lorentzian, Gaussian and Voigt line shapes.

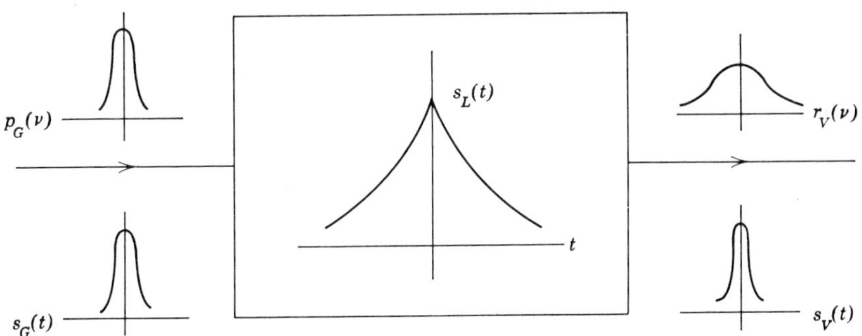

Fig. 15.7. The Voigt profile, as response of a Lorentzian filter to a Gaussian signal.

Putting $\nu_0 = 0$, for $t > 0$, we have

$$\ln s_V(t) = -\frac{\sigma^2 t^2}{2} - \frac{\Delta\nu_L t}{2} = -\left(\frac{\sigma^2}{2}t^2 + \frac{\Delta\nu_L}{2}t\right), \tag{15.123}$$

where the first term predominates for large t's, and the second term for small t's. By plotting $\ln s_V(t)$ in a semilog paper versus t, and versus t^2 we may find σ and $\Delta\nu_L$ respectively for the Gaussian and the Lorentzian contribution [7]. $\Delta\nu_L$ and $\Delta\nu_G$ may also be obtained by using the Posener's tables of [8].

Equation 15.122 lends itself to an interesting interpretation. We can assume that $s_V(t)$ is the Fourier transform of the response of a filter with the characteristic function $s_L(t)$ to an input signal whose transform is $s_G(t)$. We know that the Fourier transform of a Gaussian is a Gaussian; therefore we can represent the situation as in Fig. 15.7.

4. THEORY OF THERMAL BROADENING OF SHARP LINES

We want to examine now the effect of temperature on the shape and width of sharp spectral lines. We restrict ourselves to the case where a purely radiative transition takes place, namely to the so-called *no-phonon lines*; other temperature-dependent lines which are produced by the simultaneously interaction of an ionic system with the thermal vibration and the radiation field, namely the so-called *vibronic lines*, will be considered in the following chapter.

The crystalline field at the ion site, varying in time with the thermal vibrations of the neighboring ions, sets up an interaction between the ionic system and the normal modes of vibrations of the lattice. Such an interaction has been used in the past to explain the temperature dependence of the relaxation time of paramagnetic ions. Kiel [9] has treated the temperature-dependent linewidth of excited states in crystals on the basis of a square law dependence from displacement. A model studied by Silsbee [10] introduces as possible source of broadening of narrow lines the dependence of the lattice vibrations upon the excitation state of the atom; this model, however, has not been applied to any quantitative analysis. Finally, McCumber and Sturge [11] explained the temperature dependence of width and position of the *R* lines in Ruby with a two-phonon Raman-process model, having a single characteristic Debye temperature.

Let us first make the obvious point that the width of a line is the sum of the energy spreads of the two energy levels involved in the transition; the two energy levels may be broadened by the same mechanism or by different mechanisms. It is then proper to start considering the broadening of a single energy level. Consider the *i*th energy level of a multilevel system and the different mechanisms which may produce a broadening in this level. We may list the following processes:

1. Phonon radiationless decay by spontaneous or induced emission of one or more phonons; this process takes place when an ion in an excited state decays to a lower level by transforming its energy into vibrational energy.
2. Phonon excitation of an ion to a more energetic state; this process takes place by the absorption of one or more phonons.
3. Raman relaxation of an ion to a lower state; this process takes place in the following way. The ion in its excited state absorbs a phonon of a certain frequency and re-emits a phonon of higher frequency, the difference between the two frequencies being equal to the frequency difference between the initial and the final states. When the energy of the absorbed phonon is equal to the energy difference between the initial level and an upper level, and the energy of the emitted phonon is equal to the difference in energy between this upper level and the final level of the decay, the process taking place is an Orbach process.
4. Raman excitation of an ion to a higher state. This process takes place in the following way. The ion in a certain state absorbs a phonon of a certain frequency and re-emits a phonon of lower frequency, the difference between the two frequencies being equal to the energy difference between the initial and the final states. A two-phonon excitation may also take place by an inverse Orbach process [12].
5. Vibronic decay of an ion from an excited state. This process involves the emission of a photon and the absorption or emission of one or more phonons.
6. Raman scattering of phonons by an ion in an excited state; this process takes place while the ion *remains* in the same electronic state. The variations of the crystal field due to the lattice vibrations can be considered adiabatic or slow, since for an optical transition the ratio of the maximum lattice

frequency to the optical frequency is much less than one. For this reason, this mechanism can cause relatively slow variations of the energy of the excited state, without affecting its lifetime.

We notice that all these processes, since they involve phonons, are temperature-dependent.

A very important distinction can be made between the first five processes that remove the ion from its electronic state and the last process that leaves it in the same electronic state. The first five processes may affect the linewidth by shortening the lifetime of the state, the last process may affect the width of the level but has no effects on its lifetime. We have already considered the first four processes.

The vibronic decay contributes to the shortening of the lifetime of a metastable state. It has been found [13] that when the energy gap between a metastable state and the lower states is large, this type of decay is mainly responsible for the temperature dependence of the lifetime of the metastable state. However, the contribution of the vibronic decay to the linewidth may be in general considered small.

The linewidth of sharp spectral transitions when seen in fluorescence is in general much greater than the inverse of the fluorescent lifetime. The relation between the lifetime of a level and the energy broadening of the same level can be derived from (15.94):

$$\Delta E(\mathrm{cm}^{-1}) = \frac{5.3 \times 10^{-12}}{\tau(\mathrm{sec})}. \tag{15.124}$$

Take, for example, the R_1 line of ruby which corresponds to a radiative transition to the ground state from a metastable state which has the lifetime of about 3 msec at room temperature. The corresponding lifetime broadening is only $\sim 2 \times 10^{-9}$ cm^{-1}, whereas in effect a linewidth of ~ 10 cm^{-1} is observed. This shows how important are the mechanisms which broaden the energy level without removing the ion from it. We go on now to examine these processes.

4.1 Raman Scattering of Phonons

A Raman scattering process consists of the absorption of a phonon and the emission of another phonon. The ion-vibration interaction Hamiltonian can be written in the following way:

$$H_{\mathrm{int}} = H' + H'', \tag{15.125}$$

where

$$\begin{aligned} H' &= iV_1 \sum_q \left(\frac{\hbar\omega_q}{2Mv^2}\right)^{1/2} (b_q - b_q^{+}), \\ H'' &= -V_2 \frac{\hbar}{2Mv^2} \sum_{qq'} \sqrt{\omega_q \omega_{q'}}\, (b_q - b_q^{+})(b_{q'} - b_{q'}^{+}). \end{aligned} \tag{15.126}$$

The process "absorption of a phonon of frequency ω_k and emission of a phonon of frequency $\omega_{k'}$" is controlled by the following matrix element:

$$
\begin{aligned}
\langle f|\, H_{\text{Raman}}\, |i\rangle &= \langle \psi_i^{\text{el}};\, n_k - 1,\, n_{k'} + 1|\, H_{\text{Raman}}\, |\psi_i^{\text{el}};\, n_k,\, n_{k'}\rangle \\
&= \sum_j \frac{\langle \psi_i^{\text{el}};\, n_k - 1,\, n_{k'} + 1|\, H'\, |\psi_j^{\text{el}};\, n_k - 1,\, n_{k'}\rangle \times \langle \psi_i^{\text{el}};\, n_k - 1,\, n_{k'}|\, H'\, |\psi_i^{\text{el}};\, n_k,\, n_{k'}\rangle}{E_i^{\text{el}} - (E_j^{\text{el}} - \hbar\omega_k)} \\
&+ \frac{\langle \psi_i^{\text{el}};\, n_k - 1,\, n_{k'} + 1|\, H'\, |\psi_j^{\text{el}};\, n_k,\, n_{k'} + 1\rangle \times \langle \psi_j^{\text{el}};\, n_k,\, n_{k'} + 1|\, H'\, |\psi_i^{\text{el}};\, n_k,\, n_k'\rangle}{E_i^{\text{el}} - (E_i^{\text{el}} + \hbar\omega_{k'})} \\
&+ \langle \psi_i^{\text{el}};\, n_k - 1,\, n_{k'} + 1|\, H''\, |\psi_i^{\text{el}};\, n_k,\, n_{k'}\rangle \\
&= \frac{\hbar}{2Mv^2}\sqrt{\omega_k\omega_{k'}}\Bigg\{\sum_j \Bigg[\frac{|\langle \psi_i^{\text{el}}|\, V_1\, |\psi_j^{\text{el}}\rangle|^2}{E_i^{\text{el}} - (E_j^{\text{el}} - \hbar\omega_k)} \\
&\times \langle n_k - 1,\, n_{k'} + 1|\, b_{k'}^{+} b_k\, |n_k,\, n_{k'}\rangle \\
&+ \frac{|\langle \psi_i^{\text{el}}|\, V_1\, |\psi_j^{\text{el}}\rangle|^2}{E_i^{\text{el}} - (E_i^{\text{el}} + \hbar\omega_{k'})} \langle n_k - 1,\, n_{k'} + 1|\, b_k b_{k'}^{+}\, |n_k,\, n_{k'}\rangle\Bigg] \\
&+ \langle \psi_i^{\text{el}}|\, V_2\, |\psi_i^{\text{el}}\rangle\langle n_k - 1,\, n_{k'} + 1|\, 2b_k b_{k'}^{+}\, |n_k,\, n_{k'}\rangle\Bigg\} \\
&\simeq \frac{\hbar}{Mv^2}\sqrt{\omega_k\omega_{k'} n_k(n_{k'} + 1)} \\
&\times \left[\sum_{j\neq i}\frac{|\langle \psi_i^{\text{el}}|\, V_1\, |\psi_j^{\text{el}}\rangle|^2}{E_i^{\text{el}} - E_j^{\text{el}}} + \langle \psi_i^{\text{el}}|\, V_2\, |\psi_i^{\text{el}}\rangle\right].
\end{aligned}
\tag{15.127}
$$

We can write this matrix element in the following way:

$$\langle f|\, H_R\, |i\rangle = \alpha'\sqrt{\omega_k\omega_{k'} n_k(n_{k'} + 1)}, \tag{15.128}$$

where

$$\alpha' = \frac{\hbar}{Mv^2}\left[\sum_{j\neq i}\frac{|\langle \psi_i^{\text{el}}|\, V_1\, |\psi_i^{\text{el}}\rangle|^2}{E_i - E_j} + \langle \psi_i^{\text{el}}|\, V_2\, |\psi_i^{\text{el}}\rangle\right]. \tag{15.129}$$

The probability per unit time of a Raman process is given by

$$W = \frac{2\pi}{\hbar^2}\, |\langle i|\, H_{\text{Raman}}\, |f\rangle|^2 \rho(\omega_f). \tag{15.130}$$

For sharp lines

$$\rho(\omega_f) \simeq \rho(\omega_k)\, \rho(\omega_{k'})\delta(\omega_k - \omega_{k'})\, d\omega_k\, d\omega_{k'}. \tag{15.131}$$

Then the probability per unit time of all Raman processes is given by

$$\begin{aligned}
W &= \frac{2\pi}{\hbar^2}\iint |\langle i|\, H_{\text{Raman}}\, |f\rangle|^2 \rho(\omega_k)\rho(\omega_{k'})\delta(\omega_k - \omega_{k'})\, d\omega_k\, d\omega_{k'} \\
&= \frac{2\pi}{\hbar^2}|\alpha'|^2 \int_0^{\omega_D} [\rho(\omega_k)]^2 \omega_k^{\,2} n_k(n_k + 1)\, d\omega_k \\
&= \frac{2\pi}{\hbar^2}|\alpha'|^2 \frac{9V^2}{4\pi^4 v^6}\int_0^{\omega_D} \frac{\omega_k^{\,6} e^{\hbar\omega_k/kT}}{(e^{\hbar\omega_k/kT} - 1)^2}\, d\omega_k \\
&= \frac{9V^2}{2\pi^3\hbar^2 v^6}|\alpha'|^2 \left(\frac{kT_D}{\hbar}\right)^7 \left(\frac{T}{T_D}\right)^7 \int_0^{T_D/T} \frac{x^6 e^x}{(e^x - 1)^2}\, dx.
\end{aligned} \tag{15.132}$$

Then the contribution of the Raman scattering of phonons to the width of the ionic level is given by

$$\Delta E\ (\text{cm}^{-1}) = \bar{\alpha}\left(\frac{T}{T_D}\right)^7 \int_0^{T_D/T} \frac{x^6 e^x}{(e^x - 1)^2}\, dx \tag{15.133}$$

where

$$\bar{\alpha} = \frac{1}{c}\,\frac{9}{2\pi^3\rho^2 v^{10}}\left(\frac{kT_D}{\hbar}\right)^7 \left[\sum_{j\neq i} \frac{|\langle \psi_i^{\text{el}}|\, V_1\, |\psi_j^{\text{el}}\rangle|^2}{E_i - E_j} + \langle \psi_i^{\text{el}}|\, V_2\, |\psi_i^{\text{el}}\rangle\right]^2. \tag{15.134}$$

$\bar{\alpha}$ is intrinsically positive. Also, the line shape produced by such processes is Lorentzian.

We notice that the Raman processes which make the ion move to an upper or lower level have the same temperature dependence as in (15.47). The values of the expression $\Delta E/\alpha$ are reported in Table 15.1.

Taking into account all the relevant processes, we may express the "thermal" width of an ionic level as follows:

$$\begin{aligned}
\Delta E(\text{cm}^{-1}) &= \bar{\alpha}\left(\frac{T}{T_D}\right)^7 \int_0^{T_D/T} \frac{x^6 e^x}{(e^x - 1)^2}\, dx \\
&\quad + \frac{1}{c}\sum_{j<i} \beta_{ij}\left(\frac{e^{\Delta E_{ij}/kT}}{e^{\Delta E_{ij}/kT} - 1}\right) + \frac{1}{c}\sum_{j>i} \beta_{ji}\left(\frac{1}{e^{\Delta E_{ji}/kT} - 1}\right),
\end{aligned} \tag{15.135}$$

where

$$\beta_{ij} = \frac{3\omega_{ij}^{\,3}}{2\pi\rho v^5\hbar}\, |\langle \psi_i^{\text{el}}|\, V_1\, |\psi_j^{\text{el}}\rangle|^2, \tag{15.136}$$

and $\bar{\alpha}$ is given by (15.134). In (15.135) the first term is related to the Raman scattering process, the second to one phonon excitation and the third to one phonon decay.

5. THEORY OF THERMAL LINE SHIFT

We restrict ourselves again to the case of the no-phonon lines. It has been observed experimentally that sharp spectral lines of magnetic ions in crystals change their position when the temperature of the crystal is changed. Whereas several mechanisms may be responsible for the thermal broadening of spectral lines, one fundamental mechanism is generally responsible for the thermal shift.

The thermal shift of a spectral line is the algebraic sum of the shifts of the two levels involved in the transition. Let us then consider, as before, an ion in the ith state of a multistate system and see what kind of a mechanism may change the energy of this ith state. We may go back to the interaction Hamiltonian between the ionic system and the normal modes of the lattice: this Hamiltonian contains a term which is linear in the strain at the ion site, a term which is quadratic in the strain and terms of increasing power in the strain.

The ion-vibration interaction Hamiltonian is similar in its form to the ion-radiation interaction Hamiltonian, where a term linear in the field and a term proportional to the square of the field appear. As in the radiative case the interaction Hamiltonian is not diagonal in the first order, but gives a contribution to the energy of the system in second order. This contribution can be found by taking the term linear in the displacement and the term quadratic in the displacement and using respectively second order and first order perturbation theory. The result is a temperature-dependent contribution to the energy of the system,

$$\delta E_i = (H'')_{ii} + \sum_j \frac{|(H')_{ij}|^2}{E_i - E_j}, \tag{15.137}$$

where $|i\rangle$ represents a state of the (ion + vibrations) system, and H' and H'' are given by (15.126). Let us now evaluate δE_i:

$$\delta E_i = \sum_j \frac{\langle i|\, H'\,|j\rangle\langle j|\, H'\,|i\rangle}{E_i - E_j} + \langle i|\, H''\,|i\rangle$$

$$= \frac{-\hbar}{2Mv^2} \times \left\{ \sum_{jk} \left[\frac{\langle \psi_i^{\text{el}}; n_k|\, V_1 \sum_l \sqrt{\omega_l}\,(b_l - b_l^+)\, |\psi_j^{\text{el}}; n_k + 1\rangle \times \langle \psi_j^{\text{el}}; n_k + 1|\, V_1 \sum_{l'} \sqrt{\omega_{l'}}(b_{l'} - b_{l'}{}^+)\, |\psi_i^{\text{el}}; n_k\rangle}{E_i^{\text{el}} - (E_j^{\text{el}} + \hbar\omega_k)} \right.\right.$$

$$+ \frac{\langle\psi_i^{\text{el}}; n_k| V_1 \sum_l \sqrt{\omega_l}(b_l - b_l^+) |\psi_j^{\text{el}}; n_k - 1\rangle \times \langle\psi_j^{\text{el}}; n_k - 1| V_1 \sum_{l'} \sqrt{\omega_{l'}}(b_{l'} - b_{l'}^+) |\psi_i^{\text{el}}; n_k\rangle}{E_i^{\text{el}} - (E_j^{\text{el}} - \hbar\omega)}\Bigg]$$

$$+ \langle\psi_i^{\text{el}}; n_k| V_2 \sum_{ll'} \sqrt{\omega_l\omega_{l'}}(b_l - b_l^+)(b_{l'} - b_{l'}^+) |\psi_i^{\text{el}}; n_k\rangle\Bigg\}$$

$$= \frac{\hbar}{2Mv^2}\Bigg\{\sum_{jk} \omega_k\Bigg[\frac{\langle\psi_i^{\text{el}}| V_1 |\psi_j^{\text{el}}\rangle\langle\psi_j^{\text{el}}| V_1 |\psi_i^{\text{el}}\rangle}{E_i^{\text{el}} - (E_j^{\text{el}} + \hbar\omega_k)}\langle n_k| b_k b_k^+ |n_k\rangle$$

$$+ \frac{\langle\psi_i^{\text{el}}| V_1 |\psi_j^{\text{el}}\rangle\langle\psi_j^{\text{el}}| V_1 |\psi_i^{\text{el}}\rangle}{E_i^{\text{el}} - (E_j^{\text{el}} - \hbar\omega_k)}\langle n_k| b_k^+ b_k |n_k\rangle\Bigg]$$

$$+ \sum_k \omega_k\langle\psi_i^{\text{el}}| V_2 |\psi_i^{\text{el}}\rangle\langle n_k| b_k b_k^+ + b_k^+ b_k |n_k\rangle\Bigg\}$$

$$= \frac{\hbar}{2Mv^2}\Bigg\{\sum_{jk} \omega_k |\langle\psi_i^{\text{el}}| V_1 |\psi_j^{\text{el}}\rangle|^2$$

$$\times \left[\frac{n_k + 1}{E_i^{\text{el}} - (E_j^{\text{el}} + \hbar\omega_k)} + \frac{n_k}{E_i^{\text{el}} - (E_j^{\text{el}} - \hbar\omega_k)}\right]$$

$$+ \sum_k \omega_k\langle\psi_i^{\text{el}}| V_2 |\psi_i^{\text{el}}\rangle(1 + 2n_k)\Bigg\}. \tag{15.138}$$

The "zero field" contribution is given by

$$\frac{\hbar}{2Mv^2}\sum_k \omega_k\Bigg\{\sum_j \frac{|\langle\psi_i| V_1 |\psi_j\rangle|^2}{E_i^{\text{el}} - (E_j^{\text{el}} + \hbar\omega_k)} + \langle\psi_i^{\text{el}}| V_2 |\psi_i^{\text{el}}\rangle\Bigg\}. \tag{15.139}$$

This contribution is temperature-independent and produces a static shift similar to the Lamb shift due to the interaction of the atomic systems with the "zero" electromagnetic field [14].

Disregarding the zero field contribution and taking into account the fact that if $j = i$ the two terms in [ ] cancel out, we get

$$\delta E_i = \frac{\hbar}{2Mv^2}\sum_k \omega_k n_k\Bigg\{\sum_{j\neq i} |\langle\psi_i^{\text{el}}| V_1 |\psi_j^{\text{el}}\rangle|^2$$

$$\times \left[\frac{1}{E_i^{\text{el}} - E_j^{\text{el}} - \hbar\omega_k} + \frac{1}{E_i^{\text{el}} - E_j^{\text{el}} + \hbar\omega_k}\right] + 2\langle\psi_i^{\text{el}}| V_2 |\psi_i^{\text{el}}\rangle\Bigg\}. \tag{15.140}$$

We may distinguish two cases, one in which $|E_i - E_j| \gg \hbar\omega_D$ and the other in which $|E_i - E_j| \lessdot \hbar\omega_D$.

When $|E_i - E_i| \gg \hbar\omega_D$,

$$\delta E_i \simeq \frac{\hbar}{Mv^2}\sum_k \omega_k n_k\left[\sum_{j\neq i}\frac{|\langle\psi_i^{\text{el}}|\,V_1\,|\psi_j^{\text{el}}\rangle|^2}{E_i^{\text{el}} - E_j^{\text{el}}} + \langle\psi_i^{\text{el}}|\,V_2\,|\psi_i^{\text{el}}\rangle\right] = \alpha \sum_k n_k\omega_k, \tag{15.141}$$

where:

$$\alpha' = \frac{\hbar}{Mv^2}\left[\sum_{j\neq i}\frac{|\langle\psi_i^{\text{el}}|\,V_1\,|\psi_j^{\text{el}}\rangle|^2}{E_i^{\text{el}} - E_j^{\text{el}}} + \langle\psi_i^{\text{el}}|\,V_2\,|\psi_i^{\text{el}}\rangle\right]. \tag{15.142}$$

But we can write

$$\sum_k n_k\omega_k \to \int_0^{\omega_D}\frac{\rho(\omega_k)\omega_k}{e^{\hbar\omega_k/kT}-1}\,d\omega_k = \frac{3V}{2\pi^2v^3}\int_0^{\omega_D}\frac{\omega_k^{\,3}\,d\omega_k}{e^{\hbar\omega_k/kT}-1}$$
$$= \frac{3V}{2\pi^2v^3}\left(\frac{kT}{\hbar}\right)^4\int_0^{T_D/T}\frac{x^3}{e^x-1}\,dx. \tag{15.143}$$

Therefore the lineshift of the ionic level i in cm^{-1} is given by

$$\delta E\,(\text{cm}^{-1}) = \alpha\left(\frac{T}{T_D}\right)^4\int_0^{T_D/T}\frac{x^3}{e^x-1}\,dx, \tag{15.144}$$

where

$$\alpha = \frac{3}{4\pi^3\rho v^5 c}\left(\frac{kT_D}{\hbar}\right)^4\left[\sum_{j\neq i}\frac{|\langle\psi_i^{\text{el}}|\,V_1\,|\psi_j^{\text{el}}\rangle|^2}{E_i^{\text{el}} - E_j^{\text{el}}} + \langle\psi_i^{\text{el}}|\,V_2\,|\psi_i^{\text{el}}\rangle\right]. \tag{15.145}$$

The values of $\delta E/\alpha$ are reported in Table 15.2.

We notice that in correspondence to the relative importance of the two terms in [ ] and of their sign, the lineshift can, in principle, be either positive or negative.

When $|E_i - E_j| \lessdot \hbar\omega_D$,

$$\delta E_i = \frac{\hbar}{2Mv^2}\left\{\sum_{j\neq i}|\langle\psi_i^{\text{el}}|\,V_1\,|\psi_j^{\text{el}}\rangle|^2\int_0^{\omega_D}\rho(\omega_k)n_k\omega_k\,\frac{2(E_i-E_j)}{(E_i-E_j)^2-(\hbar\omega_k)^2}\,d\omega_k\right\}$$
$$= \frac{\hbar}{Mv^2}\left\{\sum_{j\neq i}\frac{3V}{2\pi^2v^3}\,|\langle\psi_i^{\text{el}}|\,V_1\,|\psi_j^{\text{el}}\rangle|^2\,\frac{(E_i-E_j)^3}{(E_i-E_j)^2}\left(\frac{kT}{\hbar}\right)^4\frac{1}{(kT)^2}\right.$$
$$\left.\times\,\mathcal{P}\int_0^{T_D/T}\frac{x^3}{e^x-1}\,\frac{1}{(T_{ij}^{\,2}/T^2)-x^2}\,dx\right\}$$
$$= \sum_{j\neq i}\left\{\frac{3\omega_{ij}^{\,3}}{\rho v^5 2\pi^2}\,|\langle\psi_i^{\text{el}}|\,V_1\,|\psi_i\rangle|^2\,\frac{T^4}{T_{ij}^{\,2}}\,\mathcal{P}\int_0^{T_D/T}\frac{x^3}{e^x-1}\,\frac{1}{(T_{ij}^{\,2}/T^2)-x^2}\,dx\right\}, \tag{15.146}$$

Table 15.2 The Values of

$$10^5 \times \left(\frac{T}{T_D}\right)^4 \int_0^{T_D/T} \frac{x^3}{e^x - 1}\, dx$$

T_D/T	0.0	0.1	0.2	0.3	0.4	0.5	0.6	0.7	0.8	0.9
0		321000	154499	99110.5	71498.7	54997.5	44051.3	36279.0	30489.9	26022.7
1	22480.5	19610.5	17244.3	15265.4	13590.3	12157.5	10922.3	9848.7	8909.3	8083.1
2	7352.1	6703.8	6124.1	56068.4	5140.7	4722.0	4343.5	4005.4	3690.4	3407.9
3	3150.8	2915.9	2701.9	2505.8	2326.0	2160.9	2009.5	1870.0	1741.8	1623.3
4	1514.4	1413.8	1320.6	1234.4	1154.7	1080.8	1012.3	948.6	889.7	835.6
5	783.9	736.6	692.4	651.1	612.8	577.2	543.8	512.6	483.5	456.0
6	431.0	407.2	385.0	364.2	344.6	326.1	308.9	292.8	277.6	263.4
7	250.0	237.4	225.6	211.4	204.0	194.0	184.6	175.9	167.6	159.7
8	152.3	145.4	139.0	132.7	126.5	120.9	115.6	110.6	105.8	101.3
9	97.0	93.0	89.1	85.3	81.9	78.6	75.4	72.5	69.6	66.9
10	64.3	61.8	59.4	57.1	55.0	53.2	51.1	49.2	47.4	45.7
11	44.2	42.6	41.1	39.7	38.3	37.0	35.7	34.5	33.4	32.2
12	31.3	30.3	29.4	28.4	27.5	26.6	25.7	24.8	24.1	23.4
13	22.6	21.9	21.2	20.6	20.0	19.5	18.9	18.4	17.8	17.3
14	16.7	16.3	15.8	15.4	15.0	14.6	14.2	13.8	13.5	13.1
15	12.8	12.4	12.0	11.7	11.3	11.1	10.8	10.6	10.3	10.1

where $T_{ij} = (E_i - E_j)/k$ and where $\mathcal{P}$ indicates that the principal value of the integral is being taken, in line with the argument we developed in Section 3.1 of this chapter. Taking (15.136) into account, we can write the previous formula as

$$\delta E(\text{cm}^{-1}) = \sum_{j \neq i} \frac{1}{2\pi^2 c} \beta_{ij} \frac{T^2}{T_{ij}^{\ 2}} \mathcal{P} \int_0^{T_D/T} \frac{x^3}{e^x - 1} \frac{1}{\left(\frac{T_{ij}^{\ 2}}{T^2} - x^2\right)^{-1}} dx. \quad (15.147)$$

We notice that if an ionic level of energy E_i has a level of energy E_j close to it it does not necessarily mean that a resonance between $E_j - E_i$ and the energy of an available phonon must occur, the reason being that the matrix element of V_1 between these two levels, and consequently β_{ij}, may be zero. In such a case (15.144) is still valid.

Let us consider this formula again and notice that the total heat of the crystal is given, according to (13.150), by

$$E(T) = 9NkT\left(\frac{T}{T_D}\right)^3 \int_0^{T_D/T} \frac{x^3}{e^x - 1} dx. \quad (15.148)$$

Therefore in many instances we expect the lineshift to be proportional to the total heat; this fact has been confirmed experimentally [15]. If we consider now a grammole

$$R = Nk = 1.9857 \text{ cal/deg}; \quad (15.149)$$

we then have

$$E(T) = 17.871 T_D \frac{\delta E}{\alpha}. \quad (15.150)$$

We can now make the following observations:

1. The energy shift given by the formula (15.139) is the phonon zero point contribution, which is similar to the Lamb shift found in atomic system and is temperature independent. This shift depends on the mass of the ion and may produce the appearance of several peaks in a radiative line if more than one isotope of the ion are present [14].

2. In the Lamb shift case we encounter the problem of an interaction between the atomic system and the oscillators representing the electromagnetic field which are infinite in number, and we obtain a finite shift by actually subtracting two infinite quantities. In the present case, the number of perturbing modes with which the ion interacts is finite and the evaluation of (15.137) gives directly the value of the shift.

3. In the Lamb shift case the assumption is made that all the oscillators are in their ground states, whereas here, when the temperature is different from zero, the phonon oscillators are all in excited states. The analog of the thermal shift in the radiative case would be a Lamb shift which would depend on the intensity of the radiation present at the atomic site. This phenomenon

is certainly present in atomic systems but it cannot be observed experimentally because it is extremely small; the cause of this smallness is the fact that the density of photon oscillators is much lower than the density of phonon oscillators as it can be seen by considering the fact that the velocity of sound is $\sim 10^5$ and the velocity of light is 3×10^{10} cm/sec.

REFERENCES

[1] R. Orbach, "Spin-Lattice Relaxation in Solids," in *Fluctuations, Relaxation and Resonance in Magnetic Systems*, edited by D. ter Haar, Plenum, New York, 1962, p. 219.

[2] W. M. Yen, W. C. Scott and P. L. Scott, "Correlation of the Orbach Relaxation Coefficient with Optical Linewidths: $LaF_3:Er^{3+}$," *Phys. Rev.* **137,** A1109 (1965).

[3] A. Kiel, "Multi-Phonon Spontaneous Emission in Paramagnetic Crystals," in *Quantum Electronics Proceedings of the Third International Congress*, edited by P. Givet and N. Bloembergen, Columbia, New York, 1964, p. 765.

[4] M. J. Weber, "Radiative and Non-Radiative Transitions of Rare Earth Ions: Er^{3+} in LaF_3," in *Physics of Quantum Electronics*, edited by P. L. Kelley, B. Lax and P. E. Tannenwald, McGraw-Hill, New York, 1966, p. 350.

[5] F. B. Hildebrand, *Advanced Calculus for Engineers*, Prentice-Hall, Englewood Cliffs, N.J., 1948, p. 532.

[6] H. Cramer, *Mathematical Methods of Statistics*, Princeton, Princeton, N.J., 1946, p. 213.

[7] W. M. Yen, R. L. Greene, W. C. Scott, and D. L. Huber, "Optical Linewidth and Line-Shape Studies of Energy Transfer Mechanism between Rare-Earth Impurity Ions," *Phys. Rev.* **140,** A1188 (1965).

[8] D. W. Posener, "The Shape of Spectrai Lines: Tables of the Voigt Profile," *Austral. J. Phys.* **12,** 184 (1959).

[9] A. Kiel, "The Interaction of Paramagnetic Ions with Lattice Vibrations," The John Hopkins University Radiation Laboratory, Baltimore, Maryland, Technical Report No. AF-93, unpublished; also "Temperature Dependent Linewidth of Excited States in Crystals: I. Line Broadening due to Adiabatic Variation of the Local Fields," *Phys. Rev.* **126,** 1292 (1962).

[10] R. H. Silsbee, "Thermal Broadening of the Mössbauer Line and of Narrow Line Electronic Spectra in Solids," *Phys. Rev.* **128,** 1726 (1962); also, "Phonon Broadening of Narrow Line Spectra," in *Quantum Electronics Proceedings of the Third International Congress*, edited by P. Grivet and N. Bloembergen, Columbia, New York, 1964, p. 774.

[11] D. E. McCumber and M. D. Sturge, "Linewidth and Temperature Shift of the *R* Lines in Ruby," *J. Appl. Phys.* **34,** 1682 (1963).

[12] J. C. Gill, "Spin-Lattice Relaxation of Chromium Ions in Ruby," *Proc. Phys. Soc. (London)* **79,** 58 (1962).

[13] B. Di Bartolo and R. Peccei, "Thermal Effects of the Fluorescence Lifetime and Spectrum of $MgO:V^{2+}$," *Phys. Rev.* **137,** A1770 (1965).

[14] G. F. Imbusch, W. M. Yen, A. L. Schawlow, G. E. Devlin and J. P. Remeika, "Isotope Shift in the *R* Lines of Chromium in Ruby and MgO," *Phys. Rev.* **136,** A481 (1964).

[15] G. F. Imbusch, W. M. Yen, A. L. Schawlow, D. E. McCumber and M. D. Sturge, "Temperature Dependence of the Width and Position of the ${}^2E \rightarrow {}^4A_2$ Fluorescence Lines of Cr^{3+} and V^{2+} in MgO," *Phys. Rev.* **133,** A1029 (1964).

16

Vibrational-Electronic Interaction and Spectra

1. INTRODUCTION

Magnetic ions in crystals often present, in their absorption or fluorescence spectra, lines that are strongly dependent on temperature and whose frequencies do not correspond to any energy gap in the energy level scheme. These lines correspond to transitions that involve two simultaneous events: a change in the electronic state of the ion and a change in the excitation state of a vibrational crystal mode. Such transitions are called *vibrational-electronic or vibronic.*

Vibronic transitions may accompany purely electronic transitions which are allowed by the selection rules and are often undesired sources of confusion in the understanding of the spectral structure.

In an ion in a center of inversion all the electric dipole transitions are forbidden by the Laporte rule. The selection rules may, however, be released by the presence of the thermal vibrations of the lattice through the intervention of an ion-phonon interaction. In this case the lines of electric dipole nature are all vibronic.

2. ION-VIBRATION INTERACTION IN MOLECULAR COMPLEXES

If the crystalline field hypothesis is valid, the vibrational frequencies which affect the spectra of an optically active center are due to the modulating effects of the ligands' motion. When examining the case in which the localized vibrational modes are most relevant, we may then restrict ourselves to the consideration of the cluster (or molecule) which consists of the central (magnetic) ion and of the coordinating ligands.

Because the motion of the ligands affects the central ion through the time-dependent coulombic interaction, we consider the system that consists of the central ion plus the molecular vibrations. The Hamiltonian for such a system is given by

$$H = H_{\text{ion}} + H_v + H_{\text{int}}, \tag{16.1}$$

where

$$\begin{aligned} H_{\text{ion}} &= H_o + H_{\text{cryst}} + H_{so}, \\ H_v &= \frac{1}{2}\sum_q (P_q^{\,2} + \omega_q^{\,2}Q_q^{\,2}) = \sum_q (n_q + \tfrac{1}{2})\,\hbar\omega_q. \end{aligned} \tag{16.2}$$

The eigenvalue equation,

$$(H_{\text{ion}} + H_v)\psi = E\psi, \tag{16.3}$$

has the following eigenvalues,

$$E = E_{\text{ion}} + \sum_q (n_q + \tfrac{1}{2})\,\hbar\omega_q, \tag{16.4}$$

and can be divided into

$$\begin{aligned} H_{\text{ion}}\psi_{\text{ion}} &= E_{\text{ion}}\psi_{\text{ion}}, \\ H_v\psi_v &= E_v\psi_v \end{aligned} \tag{16.5}$$

We shall assume that we know how to solve (16.5).

To find an expression for the interaction Hamiltonian we take as origin for the coordinate axes the nucleus of the central ion and expand the crystalline potential in terms of the normal displacements of the molecule:

$$\begin{aligned} V_{\text{cryst}} &= V_0 + \sum_q \frac{\partial V}{\partial Q_q}\bigg|_0 Q_q + \frac{1}{2!}\sum_{qq'} \frac{\partial^2 V}{\partial Q_q\,\partial Q_{q'}}\bigg|_0 Q_qQ_{q'} + \cdots \\ &= V_0 + \sum_q V_qQ_q + \sum_{qq'} V_{qq'}Q_qQ_{q'} + \cdots, \end{aligned} \tag{16.6}$$

where each normal coordinate Q_q is a linear combination of the displacements of the ions. We notice that V_q and $V_{qq'}$ are functions of the coordinates of the electrons of the central ion.

The term V_0 in (16.6) is the time-independent, static perturbation that produces the splitting of the free ion levels. We can then write

$$H_{\text{int}} = \sum_q V_qQ_q + \sum_{qq'} V_{qq'}Q_qQ_{q'} + \cdots. \tag{16.7}$$

The normal modes displacements are linear combinations of the displacements of the ions in the molecule; they transform irreducibly as the representations of the local symmetry (point) group. We notice here an important difference between a static perturbation of definite symmetry and a vibrational perturbation. A static term may produce a change of the symmetry group: in ruby the trigonal perturbation reduces the symmetry group from O_h to C_{3v}. A static perturbation changes the symmetry of a complex and is diagonal in the new, perturbed, wavefunctions; that is, it belongs to the representation A_1 of the symmetry group it establishes. On the other hand, a vibrational perturbation does not produce any change in the symmetry of the complex, but it may transform, in principle, as any of the representations of the symmetry group.

To evaluate a matrix element of vibrational perturbation we can make use of the Wigner-Eckart's theorem as we did for the static term.

The quantities V_q, $V_{qq'}$ contain the coordinates of the electrons of the ionic system, H_{int} is left invariant by any operation of the symmetry group; because each symmetry operation operates on the Q_q and on the electrons, the V_q's must have the same symmetry of the Q_q's. This means that the V_q's must transform irreducibly according to the representation $\Gamma(Q_q)^*$ and that the $V_{qq'}$ must transform according to $\Gamma(Q_q)^* \times \Gamma(Q_{q'})^*$.

We have therefore selection rules for the matrix element of the vibrational perturbation. Two states Γ and Γ' may be connected by V_q if $\Gamma \times \Gamma_q^* \times \Gamma'$ contains the representation A_1 and by $V_{qq'}$ if the product $\Gamma \times \Gamma_q^* \times \Gamma_{q'}^* \times \Gamma'$ contains the representation A_1.

3. VIBRONIC SPECTRA OF MOLECULAR COMPLEXES

We shall now examine the case in which an optically active ion interacts concurrently with the radiation field and with the thermal vibration of the molecular complex, undergoing a change in its electronic state (with emission or absorption of photons) and also producing a change in the vibrational state of a mode of the complex.

We consider the "total system," which consists of the ion, the electromagnetic field and the modes of vibrations of the complex and is represented by

$$H = H_{\text{ion}} + H_v + H_{\text{em}} + H_{\text{int}}^v + H_{\text{int}}^{\text{em}}, \tag{16.8}$$

where

$$H_{\text{ion}} = H_o + H_{\text{cryst}} + H_{so},$$

$$H_v = \tfrac{1}{2}\sum_q (P_q^2 + \omega_q^2 Q_q^2) = \text{Hamiltonian of the vibrational modes}, \tag{16.9}$$

$$H_{\text{em}} = \tfrac{1}{2}\sum_{k\lambda} [(P_k^\lambda)^2 + \omega_k^2 (Q_k^\lambda)^2] = \text{Hamiltonian of the radiative field},$$

and where λ ranges over the two polarizations corresponding to each $\mathbf{k}$. Also

$$\begin{aligned} H_{\text{int}}^{v} &= \sum_{q} V_q Q_q + \sum_{qq'} V_{qq'} Q_q Q_{q'}, \\ H_{\text{int}}^{\text{em}} &= -\frac{e}{mc} \sum_{i} \mathbf{p}_i \cdot \mathbf{A}, \end{aligned} \tag{16.10}$$

where $\mathbf{A}$ is the vector potential at the ion site and the sum over i extends to all the electrons in the ion.

The most general state function of the unperturbed total system in which the radiation field oscillators and the vibrational oscillators have different degrees of excitation is given by

$$\begin{aligned} \psi &= |\psi^{\text{el}}; \underbrace{n_1, n_2, \ldots, n_q, \ldots}_{\text{phonon part}}; \underbrace{n_1, n_2, \ldots, n_k, \ldots}_{\text{photon part}} \rangle \\ &= |\psi^{\text{el}}\rangle\, |n_1\rangle\, |n_2\rangle, \ldots, |n_q\rangle \cdots |n_1\rangle\, |n_2\rangle, \ldots, |n_k\rangle \cdots. \end{aligned} \tag{16.11}$$

Let us now determine how the operators (16.9) and (16.10) operate on such functions.

The operators H_v and H_{int}^{v} can be expressed in terms of the non-Hermitian operators

$$\begin{aligned} b_q &= \left(\frac{\omega_q}{2\hbar}\right)^{1/2} \left(Q_q + \frac{i}{\omega_q} P_q\right), \\ b_q^{+} &= \left(\frac{\omega_q}{2\hbar}\right)^{1/2} \left(Q_q - \frac{i}{\omega_q} P_q\right). \end{aligned} \tag{16.12}$$

The commutation relations of these operators are:

$$\begin{aligned} [b_q, b_{q'}] &= [b_q^{+}, b_{q'}^{+}] = 0, \\ [b_q, b_{q'}^{+}] &= \delta_{qq'}. \end{aligned} \tag{16.13}$$

The operators Q_q and P_q can be expressed as

$$\begin{aligned} Q_q &= \left(\frac{\hbar}{2\omega_q}\right)^{1/2} (b_q + b_q^{+}) \\ P_q &= \frac{1}{i}\left(\frac{\hbar\omega_q}{2}\right)^{1/2} (b_q - b_q^{+}) \end{aligned} \tag{16.14}$$

The Hamiltonian of the vibrational modes can now be written

$$H_v = \sum_{q} \hbar\omega_q (b_q^{+} b_q + \tfrac{1}{2}) \tag{16.15}$$

The operators b_q and b_q^+ have the following properties:

$$\begin{aligned} b_q |n_q\rangle &= \sqrt{n_q}\, |n_q - 1\rangle, \\ b_q^+ |n_q\rangle &= \sqrt{n_q + 1}\, |n_q + 1\rangle, \\ b_q^+ b_q |n_q\rangle &= n_q \mid n_q. \end{aligned} \tag{16.16}$$

Taking (16.16) into account, we find also

$$\langle n_q - 1|\, Q_p \,|n_q\rangle = \langle n_q|\, Q_p \,|n_q - 1\rangle = \left(\frac{n_p \hbar}{2\omega_p}\right)^{1/2} \delta_{pq}, \tag{16.17}$$

which defines the way H_{int}^{v} acts on the functions (16.11).

In a similar way the operators H_{em} and $H_{\text{int}}^{\text{em}}$ can be expressed in terms of annihilation and creation photon operators:

$$\begin{aligned} a_k^{\lambda} &= \left(\frac{\omega_k}{2\hbar}\right)^{1/2} \left(Q_k^{\lambda} + \frac{i}{\omega_k} P_k^{\lambda}\right), \\ a_k^{\lambda+} &= \left(\frac{\omega_k}{2\hbar}\right)^{1/2} \left(Q_k^{\lambda} - \frac{i}{\omega_k} P_k^{\lambda}\right). \end{aligned} \tag{16.18}$$

The commutation relations of these operators are similar to (16.13). The Hamiltonian of the radiative field is then given by

$$H_{\text{em}} = \sum_{k\lambda} \hbar\omega_k (a_k^{\lambda+} a_k^{\lambda} + \tfrac{1}{2}). \tag{16.19}$$

The operators a_k^{λ}, $a_k^{\lambda+}$ also have the properties

$$\begin{aligned} a_k^{\lambda} |n_k^{\lambda}\rangle &= \sqrt{n_k^{\lambda}}\, |n_k^{\lambda} - 1\rangle, \\ a_k^{\lambda+} |n_k^{\lambda}\rangle &= \sqrt{n_k^{\lambda} + 1}\, |n_k^{\lambda} + 1\rangle, \\ a_k^{\lambda+} a_k^{\lambda} |n_k^{+}\rangle &= n_k^{\lambda} |n_k^{\lambda}\rangle. \end{aligned} \tag{16.20}$$

The vector potential can be expressed in terms of a_k^{λ} and $a_k^{\lambda+}$ as

$$\mathbf{A} = \sum_{k\lambda} \left(\frac{hc^2}{\omega_k V}\right)^{1/2} \boldsymbol{\pi}_k^{\lambda} (a_k^{\lambda} e^{i\mathbf{k}\cdot\mathbf{r}} + a_k^{\lambda+} e^{-i\mathbf{k}\cdot\mathbf{r}}). \tag{16.21}$$

The expression (16.21), together with the properties in (16.20), defines the way $H_{\text{int}}^{\text{em}}$ acts on the functions (16.11).

3.1 Vibronic Lines in Emission

The matrix element involved in the creation of a photon of frequency ν_k and polarization $\boldsymbol{\pi}_k^\lambda$ and of a phonon of frequency ν_p is given by

$$M = \sum_j \frac{\langle\psi_f^{\text{el}}; n_p + 1; n_k + 1|\, H_{\text{int}}\,|\psi_j\rangle\langle\psi_j|\, H_{\text{int}}\,|\psi_i^{\text{el}}; n_p; n_k\rangle}{E_i - E_j}$$

$$= \sum_j \left[\frac{\langle\psi_f^{\text{el}}; n_p + 1; n_k + 1|\, H_{\text{int}}^{\text{em}}\,|\psi_j^{\text{el}}; n_p + 1; n_k\rangle \times \langle\psi_j^{\text{el}}; n_p + 1; n_k|\, H_{\text{int}}^{v}\,|\psi_i^{\text{el}}; n_p; n_k\rangle}{E_i^{\text{el}} - (E_j^{\text{el}} + \hbar\omega_p)} \right.$$

$$\left. + \frac{\langle\psi_f^{\text{el}}; n_p + 1; n_k + 1|\, H_{\text{int}}^{v}\,|\psi_j^{\text{el}}; n_p; n_k + 1\rangle \times \langle\psi_j^{\text{el}}; n_p; n_k + 1|\, H_{\text{int}}^{\text{em}}\,|\psi_i^{\text{el}}; n_p; n_k\rangle}{E_i^{\text{el}} - (E_j^{\text{el}} + \hbar\omega_k)} \right]$$

$$= \sum_j \left[\frac{\langle\psi_f^{\text{el}}; n_k + 1|\, H_{\text{int}}^{\text{em}}\,|\psi_j^{\text{el}}; n_k\rangle\langle\psi_j^{\text{el}}|\, V_p\,|\psi_i^{\text{el}}\rangle\sqrt{n_p + 1}}{E_i^{\text{el}} - (E_j^{\text{el}} + \hbar\omega_p)} \right.$$

$$\left. + \frac{\langle\psi_f^{\text{el}}|\, V_p\,|\psi_j^{\text{el}}\rangle\langle\psi_j^{\text{el}}; n_k + 1|\, H_{\text{int}}^{\text{em}}\,|\psi_i^{\text{el}}; n_k\rangle\sqrt{n_p + 1}}{E_i^{\text{el}} - (E_j^{\text{el}} + \hbar\omega_k)} \right] \left(\frac{\hbar}{2\omega_p}\right)^{1/2}$$

$$\simeq \frac{e}{m}\left(\frac{\hbar}{2\omega_p}\right)^{1/2}\left(\frac{2\pi\hbar}{\omega_k V}\right)^{1/2}\sqrt{n_k + 1}\sqrt{n_p + 1}$$

$$\times \left[\sum_j \frac{\langle\psi_f^{\text{el}}|\sum e^{-i\mathbf{k}\cdot\mathbf{r}}\,\mathbf{p}\cdot\boldsymbol{\pi}_k^\lambda\,|\psi_j^{\text{el}}\rangle\langle\psi_j^{\text{el}}|\, V_p\,|\psi_i^{\text{el}}\rangle}{E_i^{\text{el}} - (E_j^{\text{el}} + \hbar\omega_p)}\right], \tag{16.22}$$

where we have neglected the second term in [ ], since $\omega_k \gg \omega_p$ and where the sum $\sum$ extends to all the electrons in the ion. Therefore we have the following:

Matrix element for the process: creation of a photon plus creation of a phonon (emission in the low energy band):

$$M = \frac{e}{m}\left(\frac{\hbar}{2\omega_p}\right)^{1/2}\left(\frac{2\pi\hbar}{\omega_k V}\right)^{1/2}\left[\sum_j \frac{\langle\psi_f^{\text{el}}|\sum e^{-i\mathbf{k}\cdot\mathbf{r}}\,\mathbf{p}\cdot\boldsymbol{\pi}_k^\lambda\,|\psi_j\rangle\langle\psi_j^{\text{el}}|\, V_p\,|\psi_i^{\text{el}}\rangle}{E_i^{\text{el}} - (E_j^{\text{el}} + \hbar\omega_p)}\right]$$
$$\times \sqrt{n_k + 1}\sqrt{n_p + 1}. \tag{16.23}$$

Matrix element for the process: creation of a photon plus absorption of a phonon (emission in the high energy band):

$$M = \frac{e}{m}\left(\frac{\hbar}{2\omega_p}\right)^{1/2}\left(\frac{2\pi\hbar}{\omega_k V}\right)^{1/2}\left[\sum_j \frac{\langle\psi_f^{\text{el}}|\sum e^{-i\mathbf{k}\cdot\mathbf{r}}\,\mathbf{p}\cdot\boldsymbol{\pi}_k^\lambda\,|\psi_j^{\text{el}}\rangle\langle\psi_j^{\text{el}}|\, V_p\,|\psi_i^{\text{el}}\rangle}{E_i^{\text{el}} - (E_j^{\text{el}} - \hbar\omega_p)}\right]$$
$$\times \sqrt{n_k + 1}\sqrt{n_p}. \tag{16.24}$$

The temperature dependence of the process is contained in

$$n_p = \frac{1}{e^{\hbar\omega_p/kT} - 1}. \qquad (16.25)$$

Because $n_p = 0$ at $T = 0$, we expect the persistence of the process (16.23) and the disappearance of process (16.24) at low temperatures.

3.2 Vibronic Lines in Absorption

The matrix elements involved in the vibronic processes in absorption are given by the following:

Matrix elements for the process: absorption of a photon plus creation of a phonon (absorption in the high energy band):

$$M = \frac{e}{m}\left(\frac{\hbar}{2\omega_p}\right)^{1/2}\left(\frac{2\pi\hbar}{\omega_k V}\right)^{1/2}\left[\sum_j \frac{\langle\psi_f^{\text{el}}|\sum e^{i\mathbf{k}\cdot\mathbf{r}}\mathbf{p}\cdot\boldsymbol{\pi}_k^{\lambda}|\psi_j^{\text{el}}\rangle\langle\psi_j^{\text{el}}|V_p|\psi_i^{\text{el}}\rangle}{E_i^{\text{el}} - (E_j^{\text{el}} + \hbar\omega_p)}\right] \times \sqrt{n_k}\sqrt{n_p + 1}. \qquad (16.26)$$

Matrix element for the process: absorption of a photon plus absorption of a phonon (absorption in the low energy band):

$$M = \frac{e}{m}\left(\frac{\hbar}{2\omega_p}\right)^{1/2}\left(\frac{2\pi\hbar}{\omega_k V}\right)^{1/2}\left[\sum_j \frac{\langle\psi_f^{\text{el}}|\sum e^{i\mathbf{k}\cdot\mathbf{r}}\mathbf{p}\cdot\boldsymbol{\pi}_k^{\lambda}|\psi_j^{\text{el}}\rangle\langle\psi_j^{\text{el}}|V_p|\psi_i^{\text{el}}\rangle}{E_i^{\text{el}} - (E_j^{\text{el}} - \hbar\omega_p)}\right] \times \sqrt{n_k}\sqrt{n_p}. \qquad (16.27)$$

Because $n_p = 0$ at $T = 0$, we expect the persistence of process (16.26) and the disappearance of process (16.27) at low temperatures.

3.3 Selection Rules for Vibronic Processes [1–3]

Vibronic transitions between two energy levels depend essentially on the matrix element

$$[\langle\psi_f^{\text{el}}|e^{i\mathbf{k}\cdot\mathbf{r}}\mathbf{p}\cdot\boldsymbol{\pi}_k^{\lambda}|\psi_j^{\text{el}}\rangle][\langle\psi_j^{\text{el}}|V_p|\psi_i^{\text{el}}\rangle]. \qquad (16.28)$$

We can make the following points:

1. The wavefunctions ψ_i^{el}, ψ_f^{el} and ψ_j^{el} belong to irreducible representations of the symmetry group of the complex.
2. The factor $e^{i\mathbf{k}\cdot\mathbf{r}}$ in the first bracket in (16.28) may be expanded in series, as in (14.13), and will result in electric dipole, magnetic dipole, and electric quadrupole radiation. The three components of the electric dipole operator transform as x, y, and z, the three components of the magnetic operator as L_x, L_y, and L_z. The latter is an even operator, the former an odd operator.

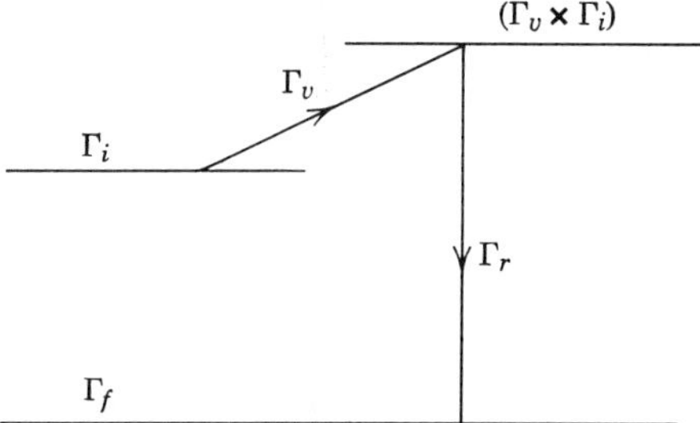

Fig. 16.1. Mechanism for vibronic transitions.

3. The operator V_p represents one of the possible modes of vibration of the complex.
4. If the complex has a center of inversion and ψ_i^{el} and ψ_f^{el} belongs to the same electronic configuration (i.e., have the same parity), V_p must represent an odd mode for electric dipole transitions and an even mode for magnetic dipole transitions.
5. If the complex has a center of inversion and ψ_i^{el} and ψ_f^{el} are states of different parities, V_p must represent an even mode for electric dipole transitions and an odd mode for magnetic dipole transitions.

The selection rules can be illustrated by considering Fig. 16.1, in which Γ_i and Γ_f are, respectively, the initial and the final state of the vibronic transition; Γ_v is the representation of an active vibrational mode and Γ_r is the representation of the radiation operator. The selection rules may be stated simply by saying that a transition is allowed if the direct product representation $\Gamma_i \times \Gamma_v \times \Gamma_r$ contains Γ_f.

We shall show, with a couple of examples, how the selection rules may be worked out in specific cases.

Example 1. Octahedral Complex AB_6 [2, 3]

Let us consider the case in which an optically active ion A is surrounded by six ligands B to form a complex of symmetry O_h. Let us also assume that the ion A has an even number of electrons.

Table 12.3 reports the single-valued representations of the point group O_h. Also, according to (12.70), the vibrational modes of such a complex consist of the three even modes

$$A_{1g},\, E_g,\, T_{2g}$$

and of the three odd modes

$$T_{1u},\, T_{1u},\, T_{2u}.$$

We shall limit ourselves to a consideration of the selection rules for vibronic transitions that are electric dipole in nature. The electric dipole operator transforms according to the T_{1u} representation.

In order to work out the selection rules, the following multiplication table is relevant:

$A_{1g} \times T_{1u} = T_{1u}$	$A_{1u} \times T_{1u} = T_{1g}$
$A_{2g} \times T_{1u} = T_{2u}$	$A_{2u} \times T_{1u} = T_{2g}$
$E_g \times T_{1u} = T_{1u} + T_{2u}$	$E_u \times T_{1u} = T_{1g} + T_{2g}$
$T_{1g} \times T_{1u} = A_{1u} + E_u + T_{1u} + T_{2u}$	$T_{1u} \times T_{1u} = A_{1g} + E_g + T_{1g} + T_{2g}$
$T_{2g} \times T_{1u} = A_{2u} + E_u + T_{1u} + T_{2u}$	$T_{2u} \times T_{1u} = A_{2g} + E_g + T_{1g} + T_{2g}$

$A_{1g} \times T_{2u} = T_{2u}$	$A_{1u} \times T_{2u} = T_{2g}$
$A_{2g} \times T_{2u} = T_{1u}$	$A_{2u} \times T_{2u} = T_{1g}$
$E_g \times T_{2u} = T_{1u} + T_{2u}$	$E_u \times T_{2u} = T_{1g} + T_{2g}$
$T_{1g} \times T_{2u} = A_{2u} + E_u + T_{1u} + T_{2u}$	$T_{1u} \times T_{2u} = A_{2g} + E_g + T_{1g} + T_{2g}$
$T_{2g} \times T_{2u} = A_{1u} + E_u + T_{1u} + T_{2u}$	$T_{2u} \times T_{2u} = A_{1g} + E_g + T_{1g} + T_{2g}$

Selection rules can be derived from this table. Let us consider the two different odd modes T_{1u} and T_{2u} separately.

Mode T_{1u} active. If the initial state is A_{1g}, the vibrational mode T_{1u} may connect it with a state of different parity T_{1u} [state j in (16.28)]. Because

$$T_{1u} \times T_{1u} = A_{1g} + E_g + T_{1g} + T_{2g},$$

this state can be connected by the electric dipole operator (T_{1u}) to states A_{1g}, E_g, T_{1g} and T_{2g}. Therefore the only vibronic transition not allowed is the one from the state A_{1g} to the state A_{2g}. Similarly, if the initial state is A_{1u}, the only forbidden transition is from A_{1u} to A_{2u}.

If the initial state is A_{2g}, the vibrational mode T_{1u} connects it with a state T_{2u}. This state can be connected by the electric dipole operator (T_{1u}) to all the states given by the following product:

$$T_{2u} \times T_{1u} = A_{2g} + E_g + T_{1g} + T_{2g}.$$

The only forbidden transition is from A_{2g} to A_{1g}. Similarly, if the initial state is A_{2u}, the only forbidden transition is from A_{2u} to A_{1u}.

If the initial state is $E_g(E_u)$ or $T_{1g}(T_{1u})$ or $T_{2g}(T_{2u})$ it may be easily verified that all transitions to any $g(u)$ state are allowed.

Mode T_{2u} active. If the initial state is A_{1g}, the vibrational mode T_{2u} connects it with the state T_{2u}. This state may be connected by the electric dipole operator (T_{1u}) to states A_{2g}, E_g, T_{1g}, and T_{2g}. The only vibronic transition not allowed is from A_{1g} to A_{1g}. Similarly if the initial state is A_{1u}, the only forbidden vibronic transition is from A_{1u} to A_{1u}.

If the initial state is A_{2g}, the T_{2u} mode connects it with the state T_{1u}. This state may be connected by the electric dipole operator (T_{1u}) to states A_{1g}, E_g, T_{1g}, and T_{2g}. The only forbidden vibronic transition is from A_{2g} to A_{2g}. Similarly we find $A_{2u} \nrightarrow A_{2u}$.

Table 16.1 Electric Dipole Selection Rules and Active Vibrational modes for Vibronic Transitions in Octahedral AB_6 Complexes

	A_1	A_2	E	T_1	T_2
A_1	T_{1u}	T_{2u}	T_{1u}, T_{2u}	T_{1u}, T_{2u}	T_{1u}, T_{2u}
A_2	T_{2u}	T_{1u}	T_{1u}, T_{2u}	T_{1u}, T_{2u}	T_{1u}, T_{2u}
E	T_{1u}, T_{2u}	T_{1u}, T_{2u}	T_{1u}, T_{2u}	T_{1u}, T_{2u}	T_{1u}, T_{2u}
T_1	T_{1u}, T_{2u}	T_{1u}, T_{2u}	T_{1u}, T_{2u}	T_{1u}, T_{2u}	T_{1u}, T_{2u}
T_2	T_{1u}, T_{2u}	T_{1u}, T_{2u}	T_{1u}, T_{2u}	T_{1u}, T_{2u}	T_{1u}, T_{2u}

As before, if the initial state is $E_g(E_u)$, $T_{1g}(T_{1u})$, or $T_{2g}(T_{2u})$, all transitions to any $g(u)$ state are allowed.

These selection rules are summarized in Table 16.1.

It can also be shown that if the central ion has an odd number of electrons all transitions are allowed. The reader may prove this by considering the double-values representations for the octahedral group reported in Section 3.2 of Chapter 7, or by consulting [4].

Example 2. AB_6 Complex of D_{3d} Symmetry

Let us consider the case of an AB_6 complex of trigonal symmetry D_{3d}. The characters of the irreducible representations of such a group are reported in Table 16.2, together with the different components of the electric dipole and magnetic dipole operators.

From this table we may easily derive the selection rules for electric dipole and magnetic dipole transitions; we report them in Table 16.3.

We should now consider the vibrational modes of the complex. An AB_6 octahedral complex has the following modes:

$$A_{1g}, E_g T_{2g}, 2T_{1u}, T_{2u}.$$

Table 16.2 Character Table for the Point Group D_{3d}

D_{3d}	E	$2C_3$	$3C_2'$	I	$2IC_3$	$3IC_2'$	
A_{1g}	1	1	1	1	1	1	
A_{1u}	1	1	1	-1	-1	-1	
A_{2g}	1	1	-1	1	1	-1	L_z
A_{2u}	1	1	-1	-1	-1	1	z
E_g	2	-1	0	2	-1	0	(L_x, L_y)
E_u	2	-1	0	-2	1	0	(x, y)
S_{1g}	$1 \quad -1$	$-1 \quad 1$	$i \quad -i$	$1 \quad -1$	$-1 \quad 1$	$i \quad -i$	
S_{1u}	$1 \quad -1$	$-1 \quad 1$	$i \quad -i$	$-1 \quad 1$	$1 \quad -1$	$-i \quad i$	
S_{3g}	$1 \quad -1$	$-1 \quad 1$	$-i \quad i$	$1 \quad -1$	$-1 \quad 1$	$-i \quad i$	
S_{3u}	$1 \quad -1$	$-1 \quad 1$	$-i \quad i$	$-1 \quad 1$	$1 \quad -1$	$i \quad -i$	
$D_{1/2g}$	$2 \quad -2$	$1 \quad -1$	$0 \quad 0$	$2 \quad -2$	$1 \quad -1$	$0 \quad 0$	
$D_{1/2u}$	$2 \quad -2$	$1 \quad -1$	$0 \quad 0$	$-2 \quad 2$	$-1 \quad 1$	$0 \quad 0$	

Table 16.3 Selection Rules for Electric Dipole and Magnetic Dipole Transitions in Complexes of D_{3d} Symmetry

	x, y	z	L_x, L_y	L_z
A_{1g}	E_u	A_{2u}	E_g	A_{2g}
A_{1u}	E_g	A_{2g}	E_g	A_{2u}
A_{2g}	E_u	A_{1u}	E_g	A_{1g}
A_{2u}	E_g	A_{1g}	E_u	A_{1u}
E_g	$A_{1u}A_{2u}E_u$	E_u	$A_{1g}A_{2g}E_g$	E_g
E_u	$A_{1g}A_{2g}E_g$	E_g	$A_{1u}A_{2u}E_u$	E_u
S_{1g}	$D_{1/2u}$	S_{3u}	$D_{1/2g}$	S_{3g}
S_{1u}	$D_{1/2g}$	S_{3g}	$D_{1/2u}$	S_{3u}
S_{3g}	$D_{1/2u}$	S_{1u}	$D_{1/2g}$	S_{1g}
S_{3u}	$D_{1/2g}$	S_{1g}	$D_{1/2u}$	S_{1u}
$D_{1/2g}$	$S_{1u}S_{3u}D_{1/2u}$	$D_{1/2u}$	$S_{1g}S_{3g}D_{1/2g}$	$D_{1/2g}$
$D_{1/2u}$	$S_{1g}S_{3g}D_{1/2g}$	$D_{1/2g}$	$S_{1u}S_{3u}D_{1/2u}$	$D_{1/2u}$

The single-valued representations of the group O_h reduce in a D_{3d} environment according to the following table:

O_h	D_{3d}
A_1	A_1
A_2	A_2
E	E
T_1	$A_2 + E$
T_2	$A_1 + E$

Therefore the vibrational modes for an AB_6 complex of D_{3d} symmetry are given by

$$2A_{1g}, 2E_g, A_{1u}, 2A_{2u}, 3E_u.$$

Using the same procedure, we can derive the selection rules for the electric dipole vibronic transitions reported in Table 16.4.

4. SPACE GROUPS AND LATTICE VIBRATIONS

4.1 Basis Functions for Space Groups

Some properties of the vibrational modes of a crystal are related to its symmetry. Among these properties are the degeneracies of the different branches of the dispersion curves and the subdivision of modes into longitudinal and transversal for certain direction of the **k** vector.

The normal modes of vibrations can be assigned to irreducible representations of the space group of the crystal in the sense that the normal coordinates

Table 16.4 Selection Rules for Electric Dipole Vibronic Transitions in a Six-Fold Coordinated Complex of D_{3d} Symmetry

(Active modes: A_{1u}, A_{2u}, E_u. Additional selection rule: $g \not\leftrightarrow u$.)

	A_1	A_2	E	S_1	S_3	$D\frac{1}{2}$
A_1	$\pi(A_{2u})$ $\sigma(E_u)$	$\pi(A_{1u})$ $\sigma(E_u)$	$\pi(E_u)$ $\sigma(A_{1u}), \sigma(A_{2u}), \sigma(E_u)$			
A_2	$\pi(A_{1u})$ $\sigma(E_u)$	$\pi(A_{2u})$ $\sigma(E_u)$	$\pi(E_u)$ $\sigma(A_{1u}), \sigma(A_{2u}), \sigma(E_u)$			
E	$\pi(E_u)$ $\sigma(A_{1u}), \sigma(A_{2u}), \sigma(E_u)$	$\pi(E_u)$ $\sigma(A_{1u}), \sigma(A_{2u}), \sigma(E_u)$	$\pi(A_{1u}), \pi(A_{2u}), \pi(E_u)$ $\sigma(A_{1u}), \sigma(A_{2u}), \sigma(E_u)$			
S_1				$\pi(A_{2u})$ $\sigma(E_u)$	$\pi(A_{1u})$ $\sigma(E_u)$	$\pi(E_u)$ $\sigma(A_{1u}), \sigma(A_{2u}), \sigma(E_u)$
S_3				$\pi(A_{1u})$ $\sigma(E_u)$	$\pi(A_{2u})$ $\sigma(E_u)$	$\pi(E_u)$ $\sigma(A_{1u}), \sigma(A_{2u}), \sigma(E_u)$
$D\frac{1}{2}$				$\pi(E_u)$ $\sigma(A_{1u}), \sigma(A_{2u}), \sigma(E_u)$	$\pi(E_u)$ $\sigma(A_{1u}), \sigma(A_{2u}), \sigma(E_u)$	$\pi(A_{1u}), \pi(A_{2u}), \pi(E_u)$ $\sigma(A_{1u}), \sigma(A_{2u}), \sigma(E_u)$

σ indicates transistions in which the (x, y) components of the electric dipole operator are active; π indicates transitions in which the z component is active.

of a degenerate mode transform irreducibly according to one of the irreducible representations of the space group. It is therefore useful to investigate some general properties of functions that may form basis for irreducible representations of a space group.

Let us consider first the translational operations. For a generic operation $\{E \mid \mathbf{T}_n\}$ we must have

$$\{E \mid \mathbf{T}_n\}\psi(\mathbf{x}) = \psi(\mathbf{x} + \mathbf{T}_n) = e^{i\mathbf{k}\cdot\mathbf{T}_n}\psi(\mathbf{x}), \tag{16.29}$$

where $\mathbf{k}$ is one of the possible values in the Brillouin zone.

Equation 16.29 contains the transformation properties that are imposed by the translational symmetry. Any function $\psi(\mathbf{x})$ that satisfies (16.29) can be written

$$\psi(\mathbf{x}) = u(\mathbf{x})e^{i\mathbf{k}\cdot\mathbf{x}}, \tag{16.30}$$

where $u(\mathbf{x})$ is a periodic function in the sense that

$$u(\mathbf{x} + \mathbf{T}_n) = u(\mathbf{x}). \tag{16.31}$$

A function that has the property contained in (16.29) is called a *Bloch function*. If the translational symmetry were the entire symmetry of the crystal (as in the triclinic lattice), the vector $\mathbf{k}$ could completely define the irreducible representations of the space group and the transformation properties of the basis functions ψ.

In what follows we confine ourselves to a consideration of the 73 simple or symmorphic space groups. To generalize the present considerations to nonsymmorphic space groups the reader is referred to [5].

In a symmorphic group G the generic element is of the type $\{\gamma \mid \mathbf{T}_n\}$ (i.e., nonprimitive translations are not present) and may be considered as given by the product of a pure (primitive) translation and a pure rotation:

$$\{\gamma \mid \mathbf{T}_n\} = \{E \mid \mathbf{T}_n\}\{\gamma \mid 0\}. \tag{16.32}$$

The space group in this case can be considered as the direct product of the translational subgroup $\mathcal{T}$ and of the point group G_0, formed by the operations γ.

Let us consider now the effect of a pure rotation on a Bloch function:

$$\begin{aligned}\{\gamma \mid 0\}\psi_{\mathbf{k}}(\mathbf{x}) &= \{\gamma \mid 0\}u_{\mathbf{k}}(\mathbf{x})e^{i\mathbf{k}\cdot\mathbf{x}} \\ &= u_{\mathbf{k}}(\gamma^{-1}\mathbf{x})e^{i\mathbf{k}\cdot\gamma^{-1}\mathbf{x}} = u_{\mathbf{k}}(\gamma^{-1}\mathbf{x})e^{i\gamma\mathbf{k}\cdot\mathbf{x}}.\end{aligned} \tag{16.33}$$

If $u_{\mathbf{k}}(\mathbf{x})$ is periodic, $u_{\mathbf{k}}(\gamma^{-1}\mathbf{x})$ is also periodic because $\gamma^{-1}\mathbf{T}_n$ is a primitive translation.

Let us then put

$$u_{\mathbf{k}}(\gamma^{-1}\mathbf{x}) = u'_{\gamma\mathbf{k}}(\mathbf{x}). \tag{16.34}$$

Equation 16.33 can now be written

$$\begin{aligned}\{\gamma \mid 0\}\psi_{\mathbf{k}}(\mathbf{x}) &= \{\gamma \mid 0\}u_{\mathbf{k}}(\mathbf{x})e^{i\mathbf{k}\cdot\mathbf{x}} \\ &= u'_{\gamma\mathbf{k}}(\mathbf{x})e^{i\gamma\mathbf{k}\cdot\mathbf{x}}.\end{aligned} \tag{16.35}$$

We can then state the following:

"A rotation $\{\gamma \mid 0\}$ operating on a Bloch function $\psi_{\mathbf{k}}$ with a wave vector $\mathbf{k}$ transforms it into a new function $\psi_{\mathbf{k}'}$ with a wave vector $\mathbf{k}' = \gamma\mathbf{k}$."

By operating on a certain vector $\mathbf{k}$ with all the point group operations γ we obtain the star $\{\mathbf{k}\}$. The nonequivalent $\mathbf{k}$ vectors in $\{\mathbf{k}\}$ are otherwise called the *arms of the star.*

If $\mathbf{k}$ is a vector in an arbitrary direction in the Brillouin zone, the star has as many arms as there are point group operations. If the $\mathbf{k}$ vector touches the boundary of the Brillouin zone, the number of arms is reduced. Finally, corresponding to $\mathbf{k} = 0$ (or to other points like B and C in Fig. 2.17*b*), the $\mathbf{k}$ vector is invariant under all the operations of the point group; namely, the star $\{\mathbf{k}\}$ has only one arm.

Those operations of the point group G_0 that leave the $\mathbf{k}$ vector invariant (except possibly for a primitive vector of the reciprocal lattice) form a subgroup of G_0, which, following the notation of Chapter 2, we call $G_0(\mathbf{k})$. According to the same notation, the space group formed by all the $\{\gamma \mid \mathbf{T}_n\}$ operations with γ in $G_0(\mathbf{k})$ is called $\mathcal{K}$.

When acted on by an operation of $G_0(\mathbf{k})$, the basis function $\psi_{\mathbf{k}}(\mathbf{x})$ may be left unchanged or transformed into a function $\psi'_{\mathbf{k}}(\mathbf{x})$ with the same $\mathbf{k}$. Because $\psi_{\mathbf{k}}$ is of the Bloch form, $\psi'_{\mathbf{k}}$ may differ from $\psi_{\mathbf{k}}$ only in its $u_{\mathbf{k}}(\mathbf{x})$ part, which means that when $\psi'_{\mathbf{k}} \neq \psi_{\mathbf{k}}$ there will be more than one function $u_{\mathbf{k}}(\mathbf{x})$ in association with the same exponential $e^{i\mathbf{k}\cdot\mathbf{x}}$. These different $u_{\mathbf{k}}(\mathbf{x})$ functions, when acted on by the operations of $G_0(\mathbf{x})$, will transform among themselves according to an irreducible representation of $G_0(\mathbf{k})$. Therefore the functions $\psi_{\mathbf{k}}$ with the same $\mathbf{k}$ vector are the basis for irreducible representations of the group $\mathcal{K}$ of the vector $\mathbf{k}$.

In conclusion we can say that the transformation properties of a set of functions, which are basis for an irreducible representation of a space group, are determined by the knowledge of two entities:

1. The $\mathbf{k}$ vector, which determines the transformation properties under translation and the star $\{\mathbf{k}\}$.
2. The irreducible representation of $G_0(\mathbf{k})$ to which the $u_{\mathbf{k}}(\mathbf{x})$ functions belong.

4.2 Normal Modes of Vibrations in Crystals

The normal coordinates representing the modes of vibrations of a crystal form basis for irreducible representations of a space group G. Under translation they transform as follows:

$$\{E \mid \mathbf{T}_n\}Q_{\{\mathbf{k}\},j,s} = e^{i\mathbf{k}\cdot\mathbf{T}_n}Q_{\{\ \},j,s}, \tag{16.36}$$

where $\mathbf{k}$ is one of the q vectors in $\{\mathbf{k}\}$, j indicates the irreducible representation of $G_0(\mathbf{k})$, and s, the row of the basis. In what follows we shall limit ourselves to a consideration of symmorphic space groups.

We consider a point defined by a vector $\mathbf{k}$ in the Brillouin zone; the normal coordinates corresponding to $\mathbf{k}$ transform among themselves under the operations of the space group $\mathcal{K}$ according to irreducible representations of $\mathcal{K}$. In particular, for $\mathbf{k} = 0$, the subgroup $G_0(\mathbf{k})$ of $\mathcal{K}$ coincides with the point group G_0 of G (and $\mathcal{K}$ coincides with G).

In order to form the normal coordinates corresponding to a vector $\mathbf{k}$, let us consider the expression for the displacement of an atom occupying the νth position in the ith unit cell, as given by (13.96):

$$\mathbf{u}_{i\nu}(t) = \frac{1}{\sqrt{m_\nu}}\,\mathcal{V}_{\mathbf{k}}^{\nu}e^{i\mathbf{k}\cdot\mathbf{R}_i - i\omega t}, \tag{16.37}$$

where ν ranges over the J atoms in the unit cell.

In treating the lattice vibrations of a crystal with J atoms per unit cell, we found that the equations of motion can be reduced to the set of $3J$ equations (13.98). This means that to find the normal modes of vibration corresponding to a certain vector $\mathbf{k}$, it is sufficient to consider the $3J$ components of the displacements of the atoms in a unit cell. This corresponds also to the group-theoretical fact that the $3J$ displacements form a basis for a representation (in general, reducible) of the group $\mathcal{K}$ of the $\mathbf{k}$ vector. Since the displacements are already in the Bloch form, the functions associated with the exponential $e^{i\mathbf{k}\cdot\mathbf{R}_i}$ must transform among themselves according to some representation (in general, reducible) of the point group $G_0(\mathbf{k})$. The reduction of this representation in terms of the irreducible representations of $G_0(\mathbf{k})$ provides the normal coordinates and the degeneracies corresponding to a particular $\mathbf{k}$.

Let us consider for the moment the point $\mathbf{k} = 0$. For this value of $\mathbf{k}$, $G_0(\mathbf{k}) = G_0$. In order to find the characters of the (reducible) representation set up by the $3J$ displacement coordinates, we attach to each atom in the unit cell three vectors along the three coordinate axes and then use the following rules:

1. Each vector that transforms into itself or into the corresponding vector of an equivalent atom belonging to a neighboring unit cell contributes $+1$ to the character.

2. Each vector that transforms into the opposite of itself or of the corresponding vector of an equivalent atom of a neighboring unit cell contributes -1 to the character.

3. Any other vector does not contribute to the character.

We can illustrate this procedure with an example.

Example: $SrTiO_3$

Strontium titanate has the perovskite structure reported in Fig. 16.2. The space group is the symmorphic O_h^1. Here $G_0(\mathbf{0}) = O_h$. The unit cell contains one molecule: 3 oxygen, 1 strontium, and 1 titanium atoms.

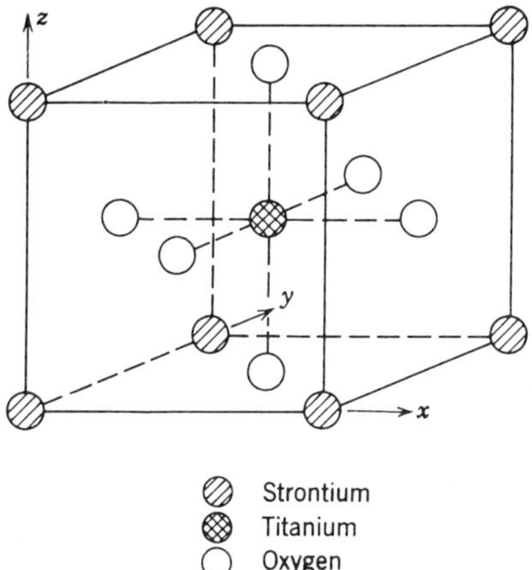

Fig. 16.2. The crystal structure of $SrTiO_3$. The coordinates for the inequivalent sites are: strontium: 0, 0, 0; titanium: $\frac{1}{2}, \frac{1}{2}, \frac{1}{2}$; oxygen: $\frac{1}{2}, \frac{1}{2}, 0$; $\frac{1}{2}, 0, \frac{1}{2}$; $0, \frac{1}{2}, \frac{1}{2}$.

By applying the procedure outlined above we obtain the following characters for the representation set up by the displacement coordinates:

O_h	E	$6C_4$	$3C_2$	$6C_2'$	$8C_3$	I	$6S_4$	$3\sigma_h$	$6\sigma_h'$	$8S_6$
	15	3	-5	-3	0	-15	-3	5	3	0

By consulting Table 12.3 it is easy to see that this representation reduces to $4T_{1u} + T_{2u}$. Since (x, y, z) transform as T_{1u}, the acoustical branch corresponds to T_{1u}. The T_{2u} branch is optically inactive (see Table 12.3) and corresponds to torsional type vibrations. The other three T_{1u} branches are optically active.

The next question we have to ask ourselves is the following: once we have obtained the irreducible representations at $\mathbf{k} = 0$ how can we obtain the same at some other point of the Brillouin zone? The answer is: by using the so called *compatibility relations*.

The concept at the basis of these relations is simply this. If a certain set of functions form a basis for a certain symmetry group A, they must also form a basis for a subgroup B of A. A representation Γ_B of B is compatible with a representation Γ_A of A if the basis for Γ_B is included in the basis for Γ_A. This means that an irreducible representation Γ_B of B is compatible with an irreducible representation Γ_A of A if Γ_A, when reduced in terms of the irreducible representations of B, contains Γ_B. Let us illustrate this point with an example.

Example [6][1]

Let us consider the Brillouin zone of a square lattice as in Fig. 16.3. The point group $G_0(\mathbf{0})$ is given by C_{4v}. In Table 16.5 we report the character tables of the relevant point groups corresponding to some characteristic points in the zone. Let us work out the compatibility relations.

X is a special point at which $G_0(\mathbf{k}) = C_{2v}$ and also a point in the lines Δ and Z. If $\psi(\Delta_2; \mathbf{x})$ is a function belonging to the representation Δ_2 of C_{1h}, this function must change sign under the operation σ_x. When Δ coincides with X, this function must go over a function that still changes sign under the operation σ_x, namely a function that belongs to X_2 or X_3.

Now consider a function $\psi(\Gamma_5, \mathbf{x})$; as we move along the line Δ, the only symmetry operations preserved are E and σ_x and Γ_5 reduces to $\Delta_1 + \Delta_2$.

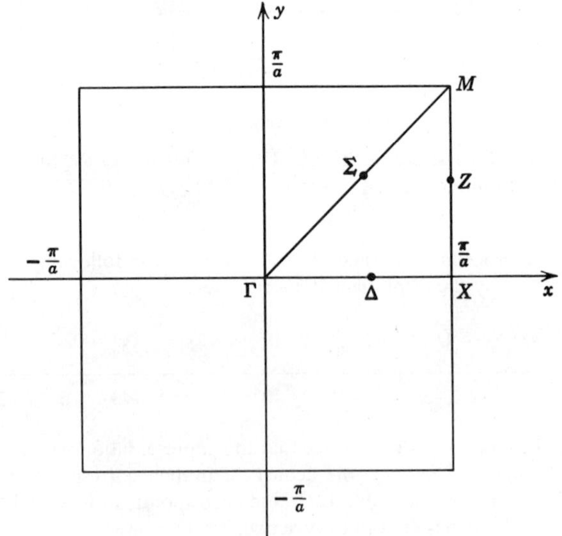

Fig. 16.3. Brillouin zone of a square lattice.

[1] This example and Tables 16.5 and 16.6 are taken from [6] by permission of Dr. V. Heine.

Table 16.5 Relevant Point Groups for Characteristic Points in the Brillouin Zone of a Square Lattice

	C_{4v}	E	$2C_4$	C_2	$2\sigma_v$	$2\sigma_d$
A_1	Γ_1 M_1	1	1	1	1	1
A_2	Γ_2 M_2	1	1	1	−1	−1
B_1	Γ_3 M_3	1	−1	1	1	−1
B_2	Γ_4 M_4	1	−1	1	−1	1
E	Γ_5 M_5	2	0	−2	0	0

	C_{2v}	E	C_2	σ_x	σ_y
A_1	X_1	1	1	1	1
A_2	X_2	1	1	−1	−1
B_1	X_3	1	−1	−1	1
B_2	X_4	1	−1	1	−1

		E	σ_x	Δ
		E	σ_d	Σ
	C_{1h}	E	σ_y	Z
A'	Δ_1 Σ_1 Z_1	1	1	
A''	Δ_2 Σ_2 Z_2	1	−1	

The results of these arguments are reported in Table 16.6.

Table 16.6 Compatibility Relations for Irreducible Representations in a Square Brillouin Zone

Representation	Compatible with
Δ_1	$\Gamma_1, \Gamma_3, \Gamma_5;\ X_1, X_4$
Δ_2	$\Gamma_2, \Gamma_4, \Gamma_5;\ X_2, X_3$
Σ_1	$\Gamma_1, \Gamma_4, \Gamma_5;\ M_1, M_4, M_5$
Σ_2	$\Gamma_2, \Gamma_3, \Gamma_5;\ M_2, M_3, M_5$
Z_1	$X_1, X_3;\ M_1, M_3, M_5$
Z_2	$X_2, X_4;\ M_2, M_4, M_5$

Γ_5 reduces to $\Delta_1 + \Delta_2$, $\Sigma_1 + \Sigma_2$
M_5 reduces to $\Sigma_1 + \Sigma_2$, $Z_1 + Z_2$

Let us get back to the example on $SrTiO_3$.

Example: $SrTiO_3$

The compatibility relations have been worked out by Cowley. [7] We limit ourselves to report the Brillouin zone for the O_h^1 space group in Fig. 16.4 with some typical points. In Table 16.7 we list the irreducible representations of the vibrational modes corresponding to the typical points in Fig. 16.4.

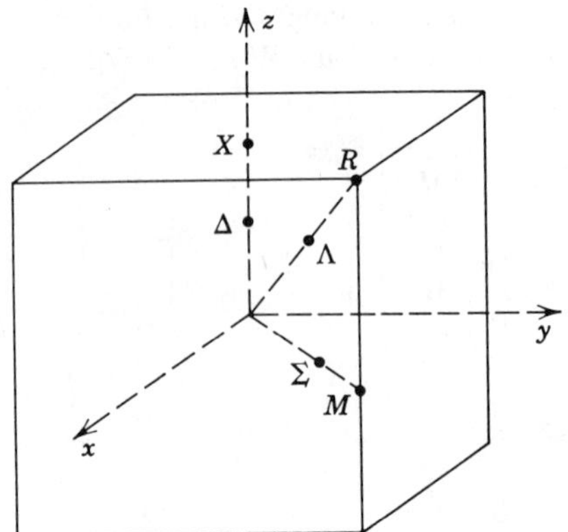

Fig. 16.4. Brillouin zone for the space group O_h^1.

Table 16.7 Irreducible Representations of the Normal Modes of Vibrations of $SrTiO_3$ in Typical Points of the Brillouin Zone [7]

Point	Coordinates	$G_0(\mathbf{k})$	Irreducible Representations of Vibrational Modes
Γ	0, 0, 0	O_h	$4T_{1u} + T_{2u}$
Δ	0, 0, k	C_{4v}	$4A_1 + B_1 + 5E$
X	0, 0, $\frac{1}{2}$	D_{4h}	$2A_{1g} + B_{1g} + 3E_g + 2A_{2u} + 2E_u$
Σ	$k, k, 0$	C_{2v}	$5A_1 + A_2 + 5B_1 + 4B_2$
M	$\frac{1}{2}, \frac{1}{2}, 0$	D_{4h}	$A_{1g} + A_{2g} + B_{1g} + B_{2g} + E_g + A_{2u} + 2B_{1u} + 3E_u$
Λ	k, k, k	C_{3v}	$4A_1 + A_2 + 5E$
R	$\frac{1}{2}, \frac{1}{2}, \frac{1}{2}$	O_h	$T_{2g} + A_{2u} + E_u + 2T_{1u} + T_{2u}$
k	k_1, k_2, k_3	C_1	$15A$

Note. For the characters of the point groups appearing in this table consult [4].

5. LATTICE ABSORPTION IN PERFECT CRYSTALS

The infrared lattice absorption spectra of a perfect crystal are due to processes that consist of the absorption of a photon and the emission of a phonon into the lattice. This process involves the creation of a small electric dipole moment in each unit cell due to the relative displacement of positive and negative ions. The addition of these moments over the whole crystal results in a net observable moment.

The interaction energy of the vibrational degrees of freedom of a crystal with an electromagnetic field is given, according to (14.8) and (14.9), by

$$H_{\text{int}} = \sum_{i,\nu} \frac{e_\nu}{c} [\mathbf{A}(\mathbf{a}_{i\nu}) \cdot \dot{\mathbf{a}}_{i\nu}] + \frac{e^2}{2m_{i\nu}c^2} [\mathbf{A}(\mathbf{a}_{i\nu})]^2, \tag{16.38}$$

where e_ν = charge of the νth ion in the ith cell,

$\mathbf{a}_{i\nu}$ = position of the νth ion in the ith cell,

$\mathbf{A}(\mathbf{a}_{i\nu})$ = vector potential at $\mathbf{a}_{i\nu}$.

The lattice absorption is produced by the term linear in the field. The term in A^2 corresponds to transitions in which the number of photons does not change (scattering of light) or changes by two (Raman processes). By considering only the first term in H_{int}, approximating $\mathbf{a}_{i\nu}$ in $\mathbf{A}(\mathbf{a}_{i\nu})$ by the equilibrium value, and replacing $\dot{\mathbf{a}}_{i\nu}$ with the derivative of the displacement $\mathbf{u}_{i\nu}$ we obtain

$$H_{\text{int}} = \sum_{i,\nu} \frac{e_\nu}{c} \mathbf{A}(\mathbf{R}_i + \mathbf{r}_\nu) \cdot \dot{\mathbf{u}}_{i\nu}. \tag{16.39}$$

From (13.90):

$$\dot{\mathbf{u}}_{i\nu} = \frac{1}{\sqrt{Nm_\nu}} \sum_q^N \sum_\lambda^{3J} \left(\frac{h\omega_{q\lambda}}{2}\right)^{1/2} \frac{1}{i} \left(\mathfrak{V}_q^{\lambda\nu} e^{i\mathbf{q}\cdot\mathbf{R}_i} b_q^{\lambda} - \mathfrak{V}_q^{\lambda\nu *} e^{-i\mathbf{q}\cdot\mathbf{R}_i} b_q^{\lambda+}\right), \tag{16.40}$$

where J = number of ions in the unit cell, N = number of unit cells, and b_q^λ and $b_q^{\lambda+}$ are annihilation and creation phonon operators, respectively.

Also, from (11.63),

$$\mathbf{A}(\mathbf{x}) = \left(\frac{4\pi c^2}{V}\right)^{1/2} \sum_{k,\mu} \left(\frac{\hbar}{2\omega_k}\right)^{1/2} \boldsymbol{\pi}_k^{\mu}\left(a_k^{\mu} e^{i\mathbf{k}\cdot\mathbf{x}} + a_k^{\mu+} e^{-i\mathbf{k}\cdot\mathbf{x}}\right), \tag{16.41}$$

where a_k^μ and $a_k^{\mu+}$ are annihilation and creation photon operators, respectively.

We now consider the absorption transition that consists of the annihilation of a photon of wave vector $\mathbf{k}$ and polarization $\boldsymbol{\pi}$ and the creation of a phonon of wave vector $\mathbf{q}$ and polarization λ. The relevant matrix element is proportional to

$$\sum_\nu e_\nu e^{i\mathbf{k}\cdot\mathbf{r}_\nu} \boldsymbol{\pi} \cdot \mathfrak{V}_q^{\lambda\nu *} \sum_i e^{i(\mathbf{k}-\mathbf{q})\cdot\mathbf{R}_i}. \tag{16.42}$$

The last factor, because of (13.64), is equal to N, the number of unit cells, when

$$\mathbf{k} = \mathbf{q} + \mathbf{K}, \tag{16.43}$$

where $\mathbf{K}$ is a primitive vector of the reciprocal lattice, and zero otherwise. The conservation energy, on the other hand, requires that

$$\omega_{q\lambda} = c\,|\mathbf{k}|. \tag{16.44}$$

The conditions (16.43) and (16.44) are illustrated in Fig. 16.5, in which the intersections of the line ck with the different $\omega_{q\lambda}(k)$ lines give the allowed values of k. Since $c \sim 10^5$ times the velocity of sound, the line representing

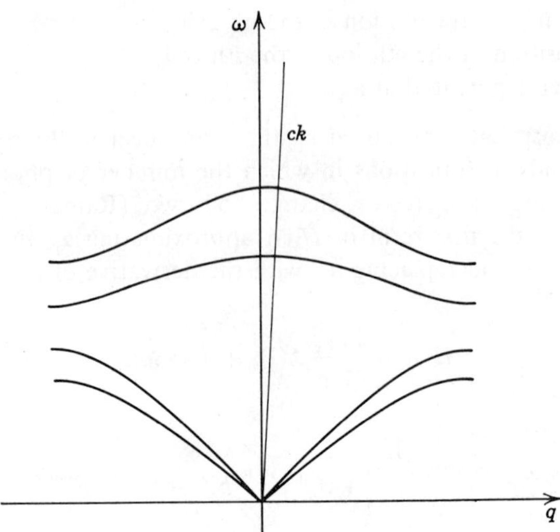

Fig. 16.5. Acoustical and optical branches of a phonon spectrum.

ck is very steep and actually only very small values of k are allowed. It is also evident that $\mathbf{K} = 0$ in (16.43) and that the acoustical branches cannot contribute to the absorption process.

The matrix element is proportional to the product $\boldsymbol{\pi} \cdot \boldsymbol{\mho}$ of the two polarization vectors for the photon and the phonon. For those directions of the wave vector that allow a separation of the vibrational modes into transverse and longitudinal it is clear that only the transverse modes may contribute to the absorption process.

6. PHONON ACTIVATION DUE TO IMPURITY IONS IN PERFECT CRYSTALS

An infrared absorption transition to an allowed optical branch produces the excitation of a single mode corresponding to a definite **k**. The translational invariance in this case imposes the conservation rule that the wave vector of the phonon created must be equal to the wave vector of the photon absorbed. For this reason only phonons with very small wave vectors can be active in the absorption process.

The introduction of impurity ions into the crystal removes the translational invariance and may result in the following:

1. The activation of phonons already present in the perfect crystal and correspondingly an absorption spectrum that resembles, apart from a frequency-dependent weighting function, the phonon density of state.

2. The activation of "localized" modes that produce a sharp line at frequencies higher than the perfect crystal phonons or a broad band at frequencies lower than the perfect crystal phonons. The latter type of absorption corresponds to impurities heavier than the lattice atoms, the former to impurities lighter than the lattice atoms. [8]

The wave vector conservation rule is also broken in vibronic transitions that correspond to the electronic excitation or de-excitation of an impurity ion and to the simultaneous emission (or absorption) of phonons into the lattice. In this case a vibronic transition involves the creation of an electric dipole moment in the single impurity ion, and the absorption (or emission) vibronic spectrum is due to the addition of all the transitions in the individual ions. Because of the removal of the translational invariance, two effects are present:

1. The ion may interact with perfect-lattice phonons that have the correct symmetry, as determined by new "relaxed" selection rules.
2. These selection rules are determined by the transformation properties of the phonons under the operations of the symmetry group which include only those operations that leave the impurity site invariant. This may produce the activation of acoustical and longitudinal branches of the dispersion spectrum.

The normal modes of vibration of a perfect crystal transform according to the irreducible representations of the space group; when the symmetry is reduced because of the presence of an impurity, the new symmetry group includes only those operations of the space group that leave the impurity site invariant. Correspondingly, the space group representations are reduced in terms of the irreducible representations of the impurity site symmetry.

Loudon [8] has carried out such a reduction for three space groups:

1. The face-centered cubic O_h^5 (symmorphic) space group in terms of the irreducible representations of the site group O_h.
2. The zincblend T_d^2 (symmorphic) space group in terms of the irreducible representations of T_d.
3. The diamond O_h^7 (nonsymmorphic) space group in terms of the irreducible representations of the tetrahedral point group T_d.

From Loudon's paper it is possible to derive Table 16.8, in which we report the reduction of the representations of the space group O_h^1 (of $SrTiO_3$) in terms of the irreducible representations of the site symmetry of an impurity.

We notice that for the generic point in the Brillouin zone $[G_0(\mathbf{k}) = C_1]$, the number of times an irreducible representation Γ_i of O_h is contained in the representation of the space group is equal to the dimension n_i of Γ_i. This property is related to the fact already observed in Example II in Section 13

Table 16.8 Reduction of O_h^1 Space Group Representations into O_h Point Group Representations [8]

$G_0(\mathbf{k})$		A_{1g}	A_{2g}	E_g	T_{1g}	T_{2g}	A_{1u}	A_{2u}	E_u	T_{1u}	T_{2u}
	A_{1g}	1		1							
	A_{2g}				1						
	B_{1g}		1	1							
	B_{2g}					1					
	E_g				1	1					
D_{4h}	A_{1u}						1		1		
	A_{2u}									1	
	B_{1u}							1	1		
	B_{2u}										1
	E_u									1	1
	A_1	1		1						1	
	A_2				1		1		1		
C_{4v}	B_1		1	1							1
	B_2					1		1	1		
	E				1	1				1	1
	A_1	1				1		1		1	
C_{3v}	A_2		1		1		1				1
	E			1	1	1			1	1	1
	A_1	1		1		1				1	1
	A_2				1	1	1		1		1
C_{2v}	B_1		1	1	1					1	1
	B_2				1	1		1	1	1	
C_1	A	1	1	2	3	3	1	1	2	3	3

of Chapter 2 (see Table 2.6) that for an arbitrary $\mathbf{k}$ vector the matrices representing the elements $\{\gamma \mid 0\}$ of a symmorphic group form the "regular representation" of the point group G_0. A regular representation, on the other hand, reduces as follows, in terms of the irreducible representations of the point group:

$$\Gamma(\text{regular}) = \sum_i n_i \Gamma_i; \tag{16.45}$$

where i spans over *all* the irreducible representations of the point group, namely, each irreducible representation is contained a number of times equal to its dimensionality in the regular representation.

We notice here that the property of the irreducible representations of the space group for an arbitrary $\mathbf{k}$ described above is of a general nature (i.e., it applies also to nonsymmorphic groups) in the sense that a representation of the space group for an arbitrary **k**, when reduced in terms of their reducible representations of the point group of the crystal G_0, contains all the representations of G_0 as many times as their dimensionalities. [9]

7. SELECTION RULES FOR VIBRONIC TRANSITIONS DUE TO MAGNETIC IMPURITIES IN CRYSTALS

Let us now consider the selection rules that control the vibronic transitions of impurity (magnetic) ions in crystals. In general the magnetic ion, in its initial and final states, occupies electronic levels that belong to an irreducible representation of the site group. The effective interaction Hamiltonian which couples the ion to the phonons present in the crystal is given by

$$H_{\text{int}} = \sum_{\Gamma_s} V_s^{\Gamma} Q_s^{\Gamma}, \tag{16.46}$$

where V_s^{Γ} are functions of the coordinates of the optically active electrons of the ion. Here Q_s^{Γ} span through the irreducible representations of the site symmetry group contained in the reduction of the space group representation exemplified in Table 16.8. The index s individuates the row of the basis. The functions V_s^{Γ} transform as the complex conjugate representations of the representations of the site group spanned by Q_s^{Γ}.

The selection rules can be found easily by group theoretical arguments. Consider Fig. 16.1 in which Γ_i and Γ_f are the initial and final state of the vibronic transition, respectively. Γ_v is the representation of an active vibrational mode, and Γ_r is the representation of the radiation operator (electric dipole or magnetic dipole). Two conclusions can be derived immediately:

1. In centrosymmetric sites, if Γ_i and Γ_f are states with equal parity, only odd vibrational modes can be active in producing electric dipole vibronic transitions and only even modes can be active in producing magnetic dipole vibronic transitions. The contrary is true if Γ_i and Γ_f are states of opposed parities.
2. For an arbitrary direction of the **k** vector the reduction of the space group representation contains *all* the irreducible representations of the site group. Therefore, in principle, there are no selection rules for an arbitrary point in the Brillouin zone.

For special points in the Brillouin zone the situation may be different. Let us illustrate this point with an example.

Example $SrTiO_3$:Eu^{3+} [10]

Let us consider the case of $SrTiO_3$ in which a magnetic impurity (Eu^{3+}) replaces substitutionally for the titanium ion; Eu^{3+} has a $4f^6$ configuration. The lowest spectral term is ^7F which splits, because of spin-orbit interaction, into a manifold of levels $^7F_0$ to $^7F_6$. The first excited spectral term is ^5D which also splits into $^5D_0$ to $^5D_4$. The $^5D_0$ state is the lowest excited state and it transforms as A_{1g} in a site of O_h symmetry. The $^7F_0$ to $^7F_6$ state also splits in terms of the even representations of O_h.

Let us examine the selection rules for the electric dipole vibronic transitions from the $^5D_0$ state to the lower electronic state of the ground state manifold. By considering Fig. 16.1, since $\Gamma_i = A_{1g}$, the selection rules require the following:

1. Γ_v must be an odd mode of vibration.
2. Since $\Gamma_r = \Gamma_{1u}$, $\Gamma_v \times T_{1u}$ must contain Γ_f.

Consider, for example, the normal modes corresponding to $\mathbf{k} = (\frac{1}{2}, \frac{1}{2}, \frac{1}{2})$. Here (see Table 16.7) only the modes A_{2u}, E_u, T_{1u}, and T_{2u} may be active. Since, for example,

$$E_u \times T_{1u} = T_{1g} + T_{2g},$$

the E_u mode can make only the $^5D_0(A_{1g}) \to T_{1g}$, T_{2g} transitions possible. On the other hand, since

$$A_{2u} \times T_{1u} = T_{2g},$$
$$T_{1u} \times T_{1u} = A_{1g} + E_g + T_{1g} + T_{2g},$$
$$T_{2u} \times T_{1u} = A_{2g} + E_g + T_{1g} + T_{2g},$$

Table 16.9 Selection Rules for Electric Dipole Vibronic Transitions from a State of A_{1g} Symmetry in $SrTiO_3{:}Eu^{3+}$ [10][a]

$G_0(\mathbf{k})$	Representation of Vibrational Mode	Final Electronic State				
		A_{1g}	A_{2g}	E_g	T_{1g}	T_{2g}
O_h	A_{2u}					+
	E_u				+	+
	T_{1u}	+		+	+	+
	T_{2u}		+	+	+	+
C_{4v}	A_1	+		+	+	+
	B_1		+	+	+	+
	E	+	+	+	+	+
D_{4h}	A_{2u}	+		+	+	+
	B_{1u}				+	+
	E_u	+	+	+	+	+
C_{2v}	A_1	+	+	+	+	+
	A_2		+	+	+	+
	B_1	+	+	+	+	+
	B_2	+		+	+	+
C_{3v}	A_1	+		+	+	+
	A_2		+	+	+	+
	E	+	+	+	+	+

[a] This table is reproduced from [10] by permission of Dr M. J. Weber.

the transitions $^5D_0(A_{1g}) \to A_{1g}, A_{2g}, E_g, T_{1g}$ cannot be activated by the mode A_{2u}. Also, the transition $^5D_0(A_{1g}) \to A_{2g}$ cannot be activated by the mode T_{1u} and the transition $^5D_0(A_{1g}) \to A_{1g}$ cannot be activated by the mode T_{2u}.

Consider a point $(k, k, 0)$ with C_{2v} symmetry. The representation A_2, according to Table 16.8, reduces to $T_{1g} + T_{2g} + A_{1u} + E_u + T_{2u}$; since

$$
\begin{aligned}
A_{1u} \times T_{1u} &= T_{1g}, \\
E_u \times T_{1u} &= T_{1g} + T_{2g}, \\
T_{2u} \times T_{1u} &= A_{2g} + E_g + T_{1g} + T_{2g},
\end{aligned}
$$

the transition $^5D_0(A_{1g}) \to A_{1g}$, cannot be activated by this mode.

In a similar way selection rules for other special points in the Brillouin zone can be derived. The results are reported in Table 16.9, in which the + sign indicates an allowed transition. Note that, as in the purely electronic case, because of the cubic symmetry, all three components of the electric dipole operator are active.

REFERENCES

[1] R. A. Satten, "Crystalline Field Selection Rules: The Effect of Vibration-Electronic Interaction," *J. Chem. Phys.* **27,** 286 (1957).

[2] R. A. Satten, "On the Theory of Electronic-Vibrational Interaction for Rare Earth and Actinide Series Ions in Crystals II. Octahedral Complexes," *J. Chem. Phys.* **29,** 658 (1958).

[3] R. A. Satten, "Errata: On the Theory of Electronic-Vibrational Interaction for Rare Earths and Actinide Series Ions in Crystals II. Octahedral Complexes," *J. Chem. Phys.* **30,** 590 (1959).

[4] J. L. Prather, *Atomic Energy Levels in Crystals*, National Bureau of Standards Monograph 19, February 1961.

[5] G. K. Koster, "Space Groups and Their Representations" in *Solid State Physics*, edited by F. Seitz and D. Turnbull, Vol. 5, Academic, New York, 1957.

[6] V. Heine, *Group Theory in Quantum Mechanics*, Pergamon, New York, 1960, pp. 277–278.

[7] R. A. Cowley, "Lattice Dynamics and Phase Transitions of Strontium Titanate," *Phys. Rev.* **134,** A981 (1964).

[8] R. Loudon, "Selection Rules for Defect-Activated Lattice Bands and Vibronic Transitions in Face-Centered Cubic, Diamond and Zinc-blend Lattices," *Proc. Phys. Soc.* (London) **84,** 379 (1964).

[9] S. A. Pollack and R. A. Satten, "Electron-Optical Phonon Interaction for Paramagnetic Ions in Crystalline Fields," *J. Chem. Phys.* **36,** 804 (1962).

[10] M. J. Weber and R. F. Schaufele, "Vibronic Spectrum of Eu^{3+} in Strontium Titanate," *Phys. Rev.* **138,** A1544 (1965).

17

Absorption Spectra of Magnetic Ions in Crystals

1. THE A AND B COEFFICIENTS AS RELATED TO MAGNETIC IONS IN CRYSTALS

The probability of spontaneous emission of a photon of frequency ω, as derived in (14.51), is given by

$$A_{21} = \frac{8\pi\omega^3}{3hc^3} |M|^2, \tag{17.1}$$

where $|M|$ is the matrix element of the electric dipole or magnetic dipole operator. The indices indicate that this emission is accompanied by a transition from an upper level 2 to a lower level 1.

This formula has to be transformed somewhat when treating magnetic ions in crystals, because of two effects:

1. For electric dipole transitions the transition probability is proportional to the square of the matrix element of the electric dipole moment and therefore to the square of the electric field at the ion site. The expression (17.1) must be multiplied by a factor $(E_{\text{eff}}/E)^2$, where E_{eff} is the electric field at the ion and E is the field in the vacuum.

2. The transition probability is proportional to the density of final states $k^2\,dk$, where $\mathbf{k}$ is the propagation vector of the photons in the crystal. Since

$$k = \frac{\omega}{v} = \frac{\omega}{c/n} = \frac{n\omega}{c}, \tag{17.2}$$

with n the index of refraction, an extra factor n^3 has to be included in the expression for A. The ratio E_{eff}/E can be expressed as

$$\frac{E_{\text{eff}}}{E} = \frac{E_{\text{eff}}}{E_c}\frac{E_c}{E}, \tag{17.3}$$

where E_c = average value of the electric field in the crystal. E and E_c must correspond to the same photon density. If we indicate the dielectric constant by ϵ,

$$\frac{E^2}{4\pi} = \frac{\epsilon E_c^{\ 2}}{4\pi}, \tag{17.4}$$

or

$$\frac{E_{\text{eff}}}{E} = \frac{E_{\text{eff}}}{E_c}\frac{E_c}{E} = \frac{E_{\text{eff}}}{E}\frac{1}{\sqrt{\epsilon}} = \frac{1}{n}\frac{E_{\text{eff}}}{E_c}, \tag{17.5}$$

where we have used the relation

$$\epsilon = n^2. \tag{17.6}$$

The expression for the spontaneous emission probability, in the case of an electric dipole transition, can now be written

$$A_{21}^{\ E1} = \frac{8\pi\omega^3}{3hc^3}|M|^2\left[\left(\frac{E_{\text{eff}}}{E_c}\right)^2 n\right] \tag{17.7}$$

and for the magnetic dipole case,

$$A_{21}^{\ M1} = \frac{8\pi\omega^3}{3hc^3}|M|^2 n^3. \tag{17.8}$$

We can introduce at this point the adimensional quantity

$$f_{21} = \frac{2m\omega}{3\hbar e^2}|M|^2. \tag{17.9}$$

This quantity is called *f number* or *oscillator strength* of the transition. The probability for spontaneous emission can be expressed in terms of the oscillator strength as

$$A_{21}^{\ E1} = \frac{2e^2\omega^2}{mc^3}\left[\left(\frac{E_{\text{eff}}}{E_c}\right)^2 n\right]f_{21}^{\ E1}, \tag{17.10}$$

$$A_{21}^{\ M1} = \frac{2e^2\omega^2}{mc^3}n^3 f_{21}^{\ M1}. \tag{17.11}$$

A different way of writing the above relation consists of expressing A as $1/\tau_0$ or the inverse of the *radiative lifetime*. We then have for the electric dipole case

$$f_{21}^{\ E1}\tau_0 = \frac{mc^3}{2e^2\omega^2}\left(\frac{E_c}{E_{\text{eff}}}\right)^2\frac{1}{n} = 1.51\left(\frac{E_c}{E_{\text{eff}}}\right)^2\frac{\lambda_0^{\ 2}}{n} \tag{17.12}$$

and for the magnetic dipole case,

$$f_{21}^{\ M1}\tau_0 = \frac{mc^3}{2e^2\omega^2}\frac{1}{n^3} = 1.51\,\frac{\lambda_0^{\ 2}}{n^3}, \tag{17.13}$$

where λ_0 is the wavelength of the radiation in the vacuum.

Let us consider the Einstein coefficient B. The ratio A_{21}/B_{21} is given by [see (14.42)]

$$\frac{A_{21}}{B_{21}} = \frac{8\pi h\nu^3}{c^3/n^3} = \frac{h\omega^3 n^3}{\pi^2 c^3}; \tag{17.14}$$

B_{21} is then given by

$$B_{21}{}^{E1} = \frac{\pi^2 c^3}{h\omega^3 n^2} A_{21}{}^{E1} = \frac{8\pi^3}{3h^2} |M|^2 \left[\left(\frac{E_{\rm eff}}{E_c} \right)^2 \frac{1}{n^2} \right], \tag{17.15}$$

$$B_{21}{}^{M1} = \frac{8\pi^3}{3h^2} |M|^2 \tag{17.16}$$

and can also be expressed in terms of the oscillator strength f_{21}

$$B_{21}{}^{E1} = \frac{2\pi^2 e^2}{mh\omega} \left[\left(\frac{E_{\rm eff}}{E_c} \right)^2 \frac{1}{n^2} \right] f_{21}, \tag{17.17}$$

$$B_{21}{}^{M1} = \frac{2\pi^2 e^2}{mh\omega} f_{21}. \tag{17.18}$$

The coefficient B_{12} is simply related to B_{21} by

$$\frac{B_{12}}{B_{21}} = \frac{g_2}{g_1}, \tag{17.19}$$

where g_1 and g_2 are the statistical weights, respectively, of states 1 and 2. From (17.19) we also derive

$$\frac{f_{21}}{f_{12}} = \frac{g_1}{g_2}. \tag{17.20}$$

The presence of the index of refraction in the expressions of A and B implies that the average properties of the medium may affect the intensity of the radiation.

For the field $E_{\rm eff}$ Dexter [1] suggests that the Lorentz local field expression

$$E_{\rm eff} = E_0(1 + \tfrac{4}{3}\pi\alpha) = E_0\left(\frac{n^2 + 2}{3}\right), \tag{17.21}$$

where α is the electronic polarizability of the atoms, may be used for rare earth impurities in crystals.

2. GENERAL PROPERTIES OF ABSORPTION SPECTRA

2.1 Fundamental Formula

Consider a beam of light, polarized in the direction $\boldsymbol{\pi}$, passing through an absorbing medium with two energy levels, in a direction (θ, φ). Consider also the following notations:

$\rho_\nu(\theta, \varphi, \boldsymbol{\pi})$ = energy density of the beam per unit frequency per unit solid angle (erg sec cm^{-3}),

$A(\theta, \varphi, \boldsymbol{\pi})$ = probability per unit time per unit solid angle of the spontaneous emission of a photon in the (θ, φ) direction with polarization $\boldsymbol{\pi}$ (sec^{-1}),

n_1, n_2 = density of absorbing centers in the ground state and in the excited state, respectively (cm^{-3}),

g_1, g_2 = degeneracy of the ground state and of the excited state, respectively,

$v = c/n$ = velocity of the light in the medium (cm sec^{-1}),

$g(\nu)$ = normalized lineshape of the transition (sec),

$w_{21} = B_{21}\rho_\nu$ = probability for induced emission per unit time (sec^{-1}),

$w_{12} = B_{12}\rho_\nu$ = probability for induced absorption per unit time (sec^{-1}).

The probability for induced emission is given by

$$w_{21} = B_{21}(\theta, \varphi, \boldsymbol{\pi})\rho_\nu(\theta, \varphi, \boldsymbol{\pi}) = \frac{v^3}{h\nu^3} A(\theta, \varphi, \boldsymbol{\pi})\rho_\nu(\theta, \varphi, \boldsymbol{\pi}). \tag{17.22}$$

If the transition is isotropic,

$$A(\theta, \varphi, \boldsymbol{\pi}) = A = \text{const} = \frac{1}{\tau_0}, \tag{17.23}$$

where τ_0 = radiative lifetime and

$$B_{21} = \frac{v^3}{8\pi h\nu^3} A. \tag{17.24}$$

In any case it is

$$\frac{w_{21}}{w_{12}} = \frac{B_{21}}{B_{12}} = \frac{g_1}{g_2}. \tag{17.25}$$

The beam of light passing through the medium experiences a decrease given by

$$\begin{aligned} -\frac{d\rho_\nu}{dt} &= n_1 w_{12} h\nu\, g(\nu) - n_2 w_{21} h\nu\, g(\nu) + n_2 A h\nu\, g(\nu) \\ &= h\nu(B_{12}n_1 - B_{21}n_2)\rho_\nu\, g(\nu) + \frac{n_2 h\nu}{\tau_0}\, g(\nu), \end{aligned} \tag{17.26}$$

where we have considered the case of an isotropic transition. The radiation $(n_2 h\nu/\tau_0)\, g(\nu)$ corresponding to the spontaneous emission will not contribute to the beam energy because it spreads in all directions. Therefore by neglecting this term and taking

$$dx = v\, dt \tag{17.27}$$

we get

$$-d\rho_\nu = \frac{h\nu}{v}(B_{12}n_1 - B_{21}n_2)\rho_\nu\, g(\nu)\, dx$$

$$= \frac{h\nu}{v}\left(\frac{g_2}{g_1}n_1 - n_2\right)B_{21}\rho_\nu\, g(\nu)\, dx. \tag{17.28}$$

We now have to take into account the fact that the populations n_1 and n_2 may actually be functions of the beam energy. If the two energy levels are connected by the natural downward and upward probabilities p_{21} and p_{12}, in absence of radiation the populations are given by

$$\begin{aligned} n_1^{\mathrm{e}} &= \frac{p_{21}n_0}{p_{21} + p_{12}} = p_{21}\tau n_0, \\ n_2^{\mathrm{e}} &= \frac{p_{12}n_0}{p_{21} + p_{12}} = p_{12}\tau n_0, \end{aligned} \tag{17.29}$$

where $\tau = (p_{21} + p_{12})^{-1}$ and $n_0 = n_1^{\mathrm{e}} + n_2^{\mathrm{e}}$. Also,

$$n_1^{\mathrm{e}} - \frac{g_1}{g_2}n_2^{\mathrm{e}} = \left(p_{21} - \frac{g_1}{g_2}p_{12}\right)\tau n_0. \tag{17.30}$$

When radiation is passing through the medium, the populations are given by

$$\begin{aligned} n_1 &= \frac{(p_{21} + w_{21})n_0}{p_{21} + p_{12} + w_{21} + w_{12}}, \\ n_2 &= \frac{(p_{12} + w_{12})n_0}{p_{21} + p_{12} + w_{21} + w_{12}}, \end{aligned} \tag{17.31}$$

and

$$n_1 - \frac{g_1}{g_2}n_2 = \frac{\left(p_{21} - \dfrac{g_1}{g_2}p_{12}\right)n_0}{p_{21} + p_{12} + w_{21} + w_{12}}$$

$$= \frac{n_1^{\mathrm{e}} - \dfrac{g_1}{g_2}n_2^{\mathrm{e}}}{1 + \left(1 + \dfrac{g_1}{g_2}\right)w_{12}\tau}$$

$$= \frac{n_1^{\mathrm{e}} - \dfrac{g_1}{g_2}n_2^{\mathrm{e}}}{1 + \left(1 + \dfrac{g_1}{g_2}\right)B_{12}\rho_\nu\tau}. \tag{17.32}$$

For low intensity beams ($B_{12}\rho_\nu\tau \ll 1$):

$$n_1 - \frac{g_1}{g_2}\, n_2 \approx n_1^{\,e} - \frac{g_1}{g_2}\, n_2^{\,e} \tag{17.33}$$

and (17.28) becomes

$$-\frac{1}{\rho_\nu}\frac{d\rho_\nu}{dx} = \frac{h\nu}{v}\,(B_{12}n_1 - B_{21}n_2)\, g(\nu)$$

$$= \frac{h\nu}{v}\, B_{12}\left(n_1^{\,e} - \frac{g_1}{g_2}\, n_2^{\,e}\right)\, g(\nu), \tag{17.34}$$

and may be integrated as

$$\rho_\nu(x) = \rho_\nu(0)e^{-k_\nu x}, \tag{17.35}$$

where

$$k_\nu = \frac{h\nu}{v}\,(B_{12}n_1 - B_{21}n_2)\, g(\nu)$$

$$= \frac{\lambda^2}{8\pi\tau_0}\frac{g_2}{g_1}\left(n_1^{\,e} - \frac{g_1}{g_2}\, n_2^{\,e}\right)\, g(\nu). \tag{17.36}$$

If we integrate (17.36) over the linewidth, we get

$$\int k_\nu\, d\nu = \frac{\lambda^2}{8\pi\tau_0}\frac{g_2}{g_1}\, n_1^{\,e}\left(1 - \frac{g_1}{g_2}\frac{n_2^{\,e}}{n_1^{\,e}}\right). \tag{17.37}$$

If $\Delta\nu$ is the half linewidth, we have the approximate formula,

$$k_\nu \approx \frac{\lambda^2}{8\pi\tau_0}\frac{g_2}{g_1}\frac{n_1^{\,e}}{\Delta\nu}\left(1 - \frac{g_1}{g_2}\frac{n_1^{\,e}}{n_2^{\,e}}\right). \tag{17.38}$$

If the passing beam is the only cause of atomic excitation for low intensity beams, n_2 is small in comparison to n_1. We can then write

$$\int k_\nu\, d\nu = \frac{\lambda^2}{8\pi}\frac{g_2}{g_1}\frac{n_1^{\,e}}{\tau_0}, \tag{17.39}$$

which may be considered the *fundamental formula of absorption spectroscopy*.

For high intensity beams $\tau B_{12}\rho_\nu \gg 1$,

$$n_1 - \frac{g_1}{g_2}\, n_2 \approx \frac{n_1^{\,e} - (g_1/g_2)n_2^{\,e}}{[1 + (g_1/g_2)]\tau B_{12}\rho_\nu} \tag{17.40}$$

and (17.28) becomes

$$-d\rho_\nu = \frac{h\nu}{v}\left(n_1 - \frac{g_1}{g_2}\, n_2\right)\, B_{12}\rho_\nu\, g(\nu)\, dx$$

$$= \frac{h\nu}{v}\frac{n_1^{\,e} - (g_1/g_2)n_2^{\,e}}{[1 + (g_1/g_2)]\tau}\, g(\nu)\, dx \tag{17.41}$$

and the beam experiences a linear decrease. This condition corresponds to a *saturation* of the absorption line.

2.2 Absorption Cross Section

The absorption cross section of a transition is defined by

$$\sigma(\nu) = \frac{k_\nu}{n_1}, \tag{17.42}$$

where k_ν = absorption coefficient at frequency $\nu(\text{cm}^{-1})$,
n_1 = density of absorbing centers (cm^{-3}).

A general property of the absorption cross section can be derived from (17.39):

$$\int \sigma(\nu)\, d\nu = \frac{\lambda^2}{8\pi} \frac{g_2}{g_1} \frac{1}{\tau_0}, \tag{17.43}$$

where g_1 = statistical weight of the ground state,
g_2 = statistical weight of the excited state,
λ = wavelength of the transition in the medium,
τ_0 = radiative lifetime of the excited state = A_{21}^{-1}.

From (17.43) we can also derive

$$\frac{1}{\tau_0} = A_{21} = \frac{8\pi}{\lambda_0^{\,2}} \frac{g_1}{g_2} n^2 \int \sigma(\nu)\, d\nu. \tag{17.44}$$

This formula relates the radiative lifetime of an excited state to the integrated cross section (obtainable from absorption measurements) of the transition from the ground state to the same excited state.

By using the (17.44) and (17.24) we also get

$$\begin{aligned} B_{21} &= \frac{c}{h\nu n} \frac{g_1}{g_2} \int \sigma(\nu)\, d\nu = B_{12} \frac{g_1}{g_2}, \\ B_{12} &= \frac{c}{h\nu n} \int \sigma(\nu)\, d\nu. \end{aligned} \tag{17.45}$$

Other expressions for the integrated cross section can be derived from (17.43), (17.7), and (17.10) in the electric dipole case,

$$\begin{aligned} \int \sigma(\nu)\, d\nu &= \frac{4\pi^2\omega}{3hc} \frac{g_2}{g_1} |M|^2 \left[\left(\frac{E_{\text{eff}}}{E_c} \right)^2 \frac{1}{n} \right] \\ &= \frac{\pi e^2}{mc} \frac{g_2}{g_1} \left[\left(\frac{E_{\text{eff}}}{E_c} \right)^2 \frac{1}{n} \right] f_{21}^{\,E1} = \frac{\pi e^2}{mc} \left[\left(\frac{E_{\text{eff}}}{E_c} \right)^2 \frac{1}{n} \right] f_{12}^{\,E1}, \end{aligned} \tag{17.46}$$

and from (17.43), (17.8), and (17.11), in the magnetic dipole case,

$$\int \sigma(\nu)\, d\nu = \frac{4\pi^2\omega}{3hc}\frac{g_2}{g_1}|M|^2 n$$

$$= \frac{\pi e^2}{mc}\frac{g_2}{g_1} n f_{21}{}^{M1} = \frac{\pi e^2}{mc} n f_{12}{}^{M1}. \tag{17.47}$$

Let us examine some particular line shapes.

Lorentzian Shape of the Line. When the absorption line has a Lorentzian shape the cross section is given by

$$\sigma(\nu) = \tfrac{1}{2}\pi(\Delta\nu)\,\sigma_0\, g(\nu); \qquad \sigma(\nu_0) = \sigma_0, \tag{17.48}$$

where

$$g(\nu) = \frac{\Delta\nu}{2\pi}\left[(\nu - \nu_0)^2 + \left(\frac{\Delta\nu}{2}\right)^2\right]^{-1}; \qquad \int g(\nu)\, d\nu = 1,$$

$$\Delta\nu = \text{linewidth at half intensity.} \tag{17.49}$$

From (17.43) and (17.48)

$$\int \sigma(\nu)\, d\nu = \tfrac{1}{2}\pi\,\Delta\nu\sigma_0 = \frac{\lambda^2}{8\pi}\frac{g_2}{g_1}\frac{1}{\tau_0} \tag{17.50}$$

and then

$$\sigma_0 = \frac{2}{\pi\,\Delta\nu}\frac{\lambda^2}{8\pi}\frac{g_2}{g_1}\frac{1}{\tau_0}. \tag{17.51}$$

Gaussian Shape of the Line. When the absorption line has a Gaussian shape, the cross section is given by

$$\sigma(\nu) = \sigma_0 \exp\left\{-\left[\frac{2(\nu - \nu_0)}{\Delta\nu}\sqrt{\ln 2}\right]^2\right\}; \qquad \sigma(\nu_0) = \sigma_0. \tag{17.52}$$

From (17.43) and (17.52) we get

$$\int \sigma(\nu)\, d\nu = \frac{1}{2}\left(\frac{\pi}{\ln 2}\right)^{1/2} \sigma_0\,\Delta\nu = \frac{\lambda^2}{8\pi}\frac{g_2}{g_1}\frac{1}{\tau_0}, \tag{17.53}$$

and

$$\sigma_0 = \frac{2}{\Delta\nu}\left(\frac{\ln 2}{\pi}\right)^{1/2}\frac{\lambda^2}{8\pi}\frac{g_2}{g_1}\frac{1}{\tau_0}. \tag{17.54}$$

We note the following properties of a Gaussian line:

1. The points of inflection are at

$$\nu_{\text{inf}} = \nu_0 \pm \frac{\Delta\nu}{2\sqrt{2 \ln 2}}. \tag{17.55}$$

2.

$$\int_{-\infty}^{\infty} \frac{2}{\Delta\nu}\left(\frac{\ln 2}{\pi}\right)^{1/2} \exp\left\{-\left[\frac{2(\nu - \nu_0)}{\Delta\nu}\sqrt{\ln 2}\right]^2\right\} = 1. \tag{17.56}$$

3.

$$\delta = \text{standard deviation}$$

$$= \left[\frac{\int (\nu - \nu_0)^2 \sigma(\nu)\, d\nu}{\int \sigma(\nu)\, d\nu}\right]^{1/2} = \frac{\Delta\nu}{2\sqrt{2 \ln 2}}. \tag{17.57}$$

$\sigma(\nu)$ can be expressed in terms of δ as follows:

$$\sigma(\nu) = \sigma_0 \exp\left[-\frac{(\nu - \nu_0)^2}{2\delta^2}\right]. \tag{17.58}$$

Voigt Shape of the Line. The cross section of a Voigt-shaped line is given by

$$\sigma_V(\nu) = \sigma_0\, r_V(\nu), \tag{17.59}$$

where $r_V(\nu)$ is a *normalized* function of ν given by (15.121):

$$r_V(\nu) = \frac{2 \ln 2}{\pi\sqrt{\pi}} \frac{\Delta\nu_L}{\Delta\nu_G{}^2} \int_{-\infty}^{+\infty} \frac{e^{-y^2}}{a^2 + (\eta - y)^2}\, dy; \qquad \int_{-\infty}^{+\infty} r_V(\nu)\, d\nu = 1, \tag{17.60}$$

where

$$a = \frac{\Delta\nu_L}{\Delta\nu_G}\sqrt{\ln 2},$$

$$\eta = \frac{2(\nu - \nu_0)\sqrt{\ln 2}}{\Delta\nu_G}. \tag{17.61}$$

A line with a Voigt profile may be considered a Gaussian line, broadened by a Lorentzian contribution. This contribution cannot change the integrated intensity of the cross section, but only its shape. Thus the integrated intensity must be the same as that of the pure Gaussian line:

$$\int \sigma_V(\nu)\, d\nu = \frac{\lambda^2}{8\pi} \frac{g_2}{g_1} \frac{1}{\tau_0} = \frac{\Delta\nu_G}{2}\left(\frac{\pi}{\ln 2}\right)^{1/2} \sigma_{0G}, \tag{17.62}$$

where σ_{0G} is the absorption cross section at $\nu = \nu_0$ if $\Delta\nu_L = 0$ (line perfectly

Gaussian). We can express $\sigma_V(\nu)$ as

$$\sigma_V(\nu) = \frac{\Delta\nu_G}{2}\left(\frac{\pi}{\ln 2}\right)^{1/2} \sigma_{0G}\, r_V(\nu)$$
$$= \frac{\Delta\nu_G}{2}\left(\frac{\pi}{\ln 2}\right)^{1/2} \sigma_{0G} \frac{2\ln 2}{\pi\sqrt{\pi}} \frac{\Delta\nu_L}{\Delta\nu_G^{\,2}} \int_{-\infty}^{+\infty} \frac{e^{-y^2}}{a^2 + (\eta - y)^2}\, dy$$
$$= \sigma_{0G} \frac{a}{\pi} \int_{-\infty}^{+\infty} \frac{e^{-y^2}}{a^2 + (\eta - y)^2}\, dy, \tag{17.63}$$

or

$$\sigma_V(\nu) = \sigma_{0G}\, H(a, \eta), \tag{17.64}$$

where

$$H(a, \eta) = \frac{a}{\pi} \int_{-\infty}^{+\infty} \frac{e^{-y^2}}{a^2 + (\eta - y)^2}\, dy. \tag{17.65}$$

This function has been tabulated by Posener [2].

We also have:

$$\sigma_V(\nu_0) = \sigma_{0G} H(a, 0). \tag{17.66}$$

$H(a, 0)$ is equal to 1 for $a = 0$ (Gaussian line) and decreases as a, namely the Lorentzian contribution, increases.

3. ABSORPTION SPECTRA OF MAGNETIC IONS IN CRYSTALS

A large part of the spectra of magnetic ions in crystals can be explained as due to transitions between levels belonging to the *same* electronic configuration, the splitting among the different levels being due to the electrostatic interaction, the spin-orbit coupling, and the crystal field. These transitions are of the type $d^n \rightarrow d^n$ or $f^n \rightarrow f^n$.

In a free ion a transition between intraconfiguration levels can be only magnetic dipole and electric quadrupole in nature. This is so because the final and initial states are characterized by the same parity. On the other hand, in a crystal the different terms of the Hamiltonian representing the influence of the crystalline field may have different inversion symmetries; some terms may be even and others odd. This Hamiltonian does not commute in this case with the operator parity, and it may connect states of the unperturbed system that have different parities. But parity is a characteristic of the electronic configuration and consequently a Hamiltonian of mixed parity may cause interaction between electronic configurations of different parities. Mixing between d^n and $d^{n-1}p$ configurations occurs in transition metal ions and between f^n and $f^{n-1}d$ in rare earth and actinide ions. When such mixing occurs, electric dipole transitions are allowed; as a matter of fact, they represent the overwhelming majority of the transitions in magnetic ionic crystals.

Mixing of states of different parities is also produced by odd lattice vibrations that are coupled to the ionic system. The effect of this mixing is the allowance of certain vibrationally induced electric–dipole transitions. The f numbers of such transitions, which are electronically forbidden but are allowed through lattice–ion interaction, are temperature dependent.

Besides the transitions between intraconfiguration levels, magnetic ions in crystals may also present transitions involving the transfer of an electron from one orbital to another; these transitions are in general electric dipole in nature and produce the strong absorption bands known as *charge transfer spectra.*

Electric and magnetic dipole transitions may be distinguished experimentally. The absorption spectrum can be observed in three ways if the crystal has an optical axis:

1. With propagation vector along the optical axis (axial spectrum),
2. With propagation vector and E field perpendicular to the optical axis (σ spectrum).
3. With propagation vector and H field perpendicular to the optical axis (π spectrum).

If a line appears in the axial and σ spectra, the relative transition is either electric dipole or electric quadrupole.[1] If a line appears in the axial and π spectra, the relative transition is magnetic dipole [3]. On the other hand, a line that appears in the σ spectrum but not in the axial spectrum is magnetic dipole; a line that appears in the π spectrum but not in the axial spectrum is electric dipole.

Electric quadrupole transitions have never been observed with certainty in solids.

3.1 Laporte-forbidden Transitions

The spectral lines arising from transitions between levels belonging to the *same* electronic configuration can be classified as follows:

1. Electric dipole transitions in a crystalline field having no center of symmetry.
2. Electric dipole transitions in a crystalline field having a center of symmetry, vibrationally induced.
3. Magnetic dipole transitions.
4. Magnetic dipole transitions, vibrationally induced.
5. Electric quadrupole transitions.

[1] A distinction between these two could, in principle, be made by examining their different polarizations, but, because of the weakness of the lines, quadrupole transitions are difficult to identify with certainty.

These transitions are said to be *Laporte-forbidden* because they do not respect the Laporte rule [see (14.60)]. Examples of transitions of type 1 are the R lines of ruby; an example of a transition of type 3 is the ${}^4A_2 \rightarrow {}^2E$ line of MgO: Cr^{3+}. MgO:V^{2+} also presents a line that is magnetic dipole in nature.

Transitions of types 2 and 4 are called *vibrational–electronic* or *vibronic*. They take place in the simultaneous absorption of one photon and the emission or absorption of one or several phonons. For this reason the frequency of the optical line is, in general, shifted by the frequency of the emitted or absorbed phonon.

Example of transitions of type 4 are the vibronic transitions presented by Ni^{2+} in MgF_2 [4]. (These transitions have actually been observed in fluorescence.)

In transition metal ions spectra the sharp lines correspond to transitions between two levels belonging to the same $t_{2g}{}^m\, e_g{}^{n-m}$ configuration, whereas the broad bands correspond to transitions between levels belonging to different configurations. Typical values of the f numbers are 10^{-4} for spin-allowed and 10^{-8} for spin-forbidden transitions.

The level structure of trivalent rare earth ions in crystals has been given by Dieke [5]; the levels are actually those of rare earth ions in chlorides, but, apart from the refinements due to the crystalline field and small shifts in energy, they may represent any other rare earth salt. Trivalent rare earths in general present more sharply defined levels than transition metal ions; this fact derives from the weakness of the crystalline field. Parity mixing crystal field perturbations or odd vibrational modes are also shielded by the other electrons and are therefore less effective in producing electric dipole transitions: the f numbers of individual absorption lines in rare earth ions are of the orders of 10^{-6}–10^{-7}.

The absorption spectra of rare earth ions are considerably constant with different salts of the same ion and from solid state to solution. Each spectrum consists of a number of weak and sharp bands that range from the near infrared to the near ultraviolet. It may be difficult sometimes to decide whether a line is due to a pure electronic or to a vibronic transition. Selections rule for vibronic transitions in rare earths have been worked out by Satten [6].

Magnetic dipole transitions have been identified with certainty in rare earth ionic systems, as exemplified by trivalent europium salts [3].

3.2 Charge Transfer Spectra [7–14]

In addition to the Laporte-forbidden transitions, magnetic ions in crystals may present *charge transfer spectra* which can be classified in the following way:

1. *Ligand to metal transfer spectra*, due to a transfer of an electron originally localized in a ligand orbital to the central ion.

2. *Metal oxidation spectra*, due to a transfer of an electron localized in the central ion to an excited ligand orbital that is not much mixed with orbitals of the central ion.

3. *Rydberg spectra*, due to a transfer of an electron localized in the central metal ion to an excited orbital that is not much mixed with the ligand orbitals.

4. *Intraligand spectra*, due to a transfer of an electron from a ligand orbital to another ligand orbital in a polyatomic ligand group. In this process only molecular orbitals of the ligands are involved.

The charge transfer spectra are, in general, Laporte-allowed, and therefore their intensity is much larger than the intensity of the intraconfiguration spectra. Most of the transitions have an f number of $\sim 10^{-1}$.

Ligand to Metal Transfer Spectra. In order to understand how these spectra come about, we refer to Fig. 10.12 in which the molecular orbital energy level diagram of an octahedral AB_6 complex is represented.

A molecular orbital electronic configuration consists of a distribution of electrons on the various molecular orbital levels. Every electronic configuration produces a number of energy levels when the electrostatic interaction is taken into account. If all the bonding and nonbonding levels are filled, the configuration $t_{2g}(\pi^*)^m\ e_g(\sigma^*)^{n-m}$ produces all the energy levels of crystal field theory. Other electronic configurations not predicted by crystal field theory with their accompanying energy levels are now possible. A charge transfer transition involves at least one level not predicted by the crystal field theory. It is possible, for example, in principle to remove an electron from one of the bonding levels or from one of the pure ligand levels $t_{2u}(\pi)$ and $t_{1g}(\pi)$ and bring it to an antibonding level, such as $t_{2g}(\pi^*)$, if this is not completely filled, or to the level $e_g(\sigma^*)$. The ligand to metal transfer spectra are produced by transitions of this type.

We notice that selection rules are at work here, as for any other type of spectrum, and that the particular set of rules given by the specific symmetry of the complex is the valid one. Therefore $t_{2u}(\pi) \rightarrow t_{2g}(\pi^*)$, $e_g(\pi^*)$ transitions are allowed, for they connect states of different parities. If the metal ion contains six $3d$ electrons, the $t_{2g}(\pi^*)$ level is completely occupied, and the first relevant charge transfer transition is

$$\cdots t_{2u}(\pi)^6\, t_{1g}(\pi)^6\, t_{2g}(\pi^*)^6 \rightarrow \cdots t_{2u}(\pi)^5\, t_{1g}(\pi)^6\, t_{2g}(\pi^*)^6\, e_g(\sigma^*)^1.$$

The initial configuration gives a ${}^1A_{1g}$ level. In the final configuration we have to couple the two spins of the nonpaired electrons ($S = 0, 1$) and the two representations t_{2u} and e_g; this produces the energy levels ${}^1T_{1u}$, ${}^1T_{2u}$, ${}^3T_{1u}$, ${}^3T_{2u}$. Because the spin-selection rules are also at work and, for the O_h group, the transitions $A_{1g} \rightarrow T_{1u}$, T_{2u} are both electric–dipole allowed, we expect two strong charge transfer bands due to these transitions. These bands appear in complexes like $[Co(NH_3)_5X]^{2+}$, where $X = F^-, Cl^-, Br^-, I^-$. We find that the energies of these bands decrease as we go from F^- to I^- because it is increasingly easier to remove an electron from the halogen ligand going from F^- to I^- (evidence of this is the decrease of electronegativity). When $X = I^-$, the charge transfer bands become so low that they overlap the crystal field bands.

We notice that the transition $t_{1g}(\pi) \rightarrow e_g(\sigma^*)$ is Laporte-forbidden because it involves two states with the same parity. We expect a weaker band in correspondence to it.

If the metal ion has five electrons, the $t_{2g}(\pi^*)$ level is not completely filled, and Laporte-allowed transitions, such as $t_{2u}(\pi) \rightarrow t_{2g}(\pi^*)$ and $t_{1u}(\pi) \rightarrow t_{2g}(\pi^*)$, can take place; we expect these transitions to produce bands lower in energy than the $t_{2u}(\pi) \rightarrow e_g(\sigma^*)$ transition. It is found experimentally, for example, that the lowest allowed charge transfer band of $IrCl_6^{3-}$ (Ir^{3+} is a $5d^6$ ion) is at about 45,000 cm^{-1} and is due to a $t_{1u}(\pi) \rightarrow e_g(\sigma^*)$ transition, whereas the lowest allowed charge transfer band, due to a $t_{1u}(\pi) \rightarrow t_{2g}(\pi^*)$ transition of $IrCl^{2-}$ (Ir^{2+} is a $5d^5$ ion), is at about 20,000 cm^{-1}. The difference in energy between the lowest allowed bands in the two cases should correspond to the crystal field strength 10 Dq.

For isoelectronic ions of the same series it is generally found that the higher the atomic number, the lower is the energy of the first charge transfer band. For isoelectronic ions of different series the bands are found at higher energies going from the first to the second and third transition metal series; this is related to the fact that, as the principal quantum number of the d shell is increased, the metal ion is less stable towards oxidation; that is, more energy is required to produce a ligand-to-metal transition.

Tetrahedral complexes also present ligand-to-metal charge transfer spectra. The isoelectronic tetrahedral complexes MnO_4^-, CrO_4^{2-}, VO_4^{4-} and TiO_4^{5-} have been examined experimentally by Teltow [12]. The spectra of MnO_4^- and CrO_4^{2-} have also been studied by Wolfsberg and Helmotz, [13] and two strong absorption bands in the visible and near ultraviolet have been attributed to ligand-to-metal electron transfer. As in the octahedral case, the energy of the first charge transfer band decreases with increasing atomic number of the metal ion and increases from the first to the second and third transition metal ion series.

Metal Oxidation Spectra. Spectra of this type may be observed when metal ions in low valence states are coupled with ligands with great electron affinity, as, for example, in the Ru^{2+} ($4d^6$; t_{2g}^6) complex with pyridine as ligands; this complex presents an intense absorption band at $\sim$22,000 cm^{-1}, which is attributed to a transition $t_{2g}^6 \rightarrow t_{2g}^5\pi^*$, where π^* is an antibonding π orbital of the pyridine molecule. (Other lower and weaker bands are observed in this complex and attributed to $d \rightarrow d$ transitions; two very intense bands occurring at 35,000 and 45,000 cm^{-1} are attributed to ligand-to-ligand transitions.)

Similar spectra are observed in the Ru^{2+} complex with phenantroline as the ligand and also in Ir^{3+} ($5d^6$; $t_{2g}{}^6$) complexes with pyridine and phenanthroline as ligands.

Rydberg Spectra. Rydberg spectra are found in lanthanides and actinides and are of the types $4f^n \rightarrow 4f^{n-1}5d$, $5f^n \rightarrow 5f^{n-1}6d$, respectively. Ce^{3+} and Sm^{2+} present spectra of these types. Transition metal ions present $3d^n \rightarrow 3d^{n-1}4p$ spectra in some square complexes such as $(PtCl_4)^{2-}$. The f numbers for these transitions are of the order 10^{-1}.

Divalent rare earth ions present strong absorption bands above groups of sharp lines. Such bands have been found by Butement [14] in divalent samarium, europium, and ytterbium and are explained by him as due to transitions from the $4f^n$ to the $4f^{n-1}5d$ configuration, whereas the sharp lines are assigned to transitions within the $4f^n$ configuration. This interpretation of the spectra is based on the fact that going from trivalent to divalent rare earths a lowering of the $5d$ orbital relative to the $4f$ orbital is expected. The oscillator strengths of the sharp lines are larger than in the trivalent ions, possibly because, of a mixing of the $4f^n$ and $4f^{n-1}5d$ configurations due to asymmetric perturbations; for these transitions oscillator strengths with order of magnitude 10^{-4} have been found in CaF_2:Sm^{2+}.

Intraligand Spectra. If the ligands consist of polyatomic groups, strong absorption bands can be found in the spectra in correspondence to transitions involving only molecular orbitals with ligand character. These transitions are not, in general, affected by the particular metal ion to which the ligands are bounded. For this reason, in interpreting the spectra of metal ion complexes with polyatomic ligands, it is useful to compare them with the spectra of the ligands.

An example of a polyatomic ligand that produces this type of transition is the thiocyanate ion SCN^-.

4. THE EFFECTS OF TEMPERATURE ON ABSORPTION SPECTRA

Atomic and molecular systems generally present spectra of lines or bands that can be resolved. The spectra of solids, instead, consist, in general, of broad bands that cannot be resolved. Crystals containing magnetic ions, however, sometimes present sharp lines in absorption, some of which can also be seen in fluorescence.

Both the broad and the narrow lines widen and shift as the temperature of the crystal is increased. We call a line *broad* when its width is large compared with the typical lattice vibrational frequency and *narrow* when its width is much less than the Debye frequency.

The thermal broadening of the lines in both cases is due to a transfer of energy from the ionic system to the phonon bath, which is accomplished simultaneously by the electronic transition. In broad lines the electronic transition is accompanied by the excitation of several phonons, whereas in narrow lines the number of phonons is unchanged.

It has to be noted that different types of approximation can be used in different cases; for example, the configurational coordinate model examined later in this chapter may be useful as an illustration of the behavior of broad lines but is not of particular advantage in the case of sharp lines when the internuclear distances in the ground aud excited states are practically identical.

4.1 Temperature Effects on Sharp Lines

We have already made a distinction between sharp and broad lines. A line is sharp when its linewidth is small in comparison to the characteristic lattice frequency.

Let us consider the d^n-configuration in an octahedral field. The energy levels are determined mainly by the electrostatic interaction and by the crystal field. The Tanabe and Sugano diagrams [8] give the dependence of the energies of the different levels on the crystal field strength Dq.[2] In these diagrams some of the lines representing the energies of the various states are parallel to the ground line; others vary sharply with Dq.

The energy of a crystal configuration $t_{2g}{}^{m}\, e_g{}^{n-m}$ is given by

$$\begin{aligned} E(m; n-m) &= -4\mathrm{Dq}m + 6\mathrm{Dq}(n-m) \\ &= (6n - 10m)\,\mathrm{Dq}. \end{aligned} \tag{17.67}$$

Then

$$\frac{\partial E}{\partial(\mathrm{Dq})} = 6n - 10m. \tag{17.68}$$

For each configuration we have a certain slope. If the ground and excited states belong to the same $t_{2g}{}^{m}\, e_g{}^{n-m}$ configuration, the lines representing the two states in the Tanabe and Sugano diagrams are parallel, for their separation is due to the electrostatic interaction between the *d* electrons. Thermal fluctuations of the crystal field and therefore of Dq produce fluctuations in the energy of a transition; these fluctuations are large if the energy gap varies strongly with Dq. Sharp lines generally involve an excited level belonging to the same $t_{2g}{}^{m}\, e_g{}^{n-m}$ configuration of the ground level, whereas broad bands involve levels belonging to different configurations.

[2] See footnote, page 252.

The discussion of temperature effects of sharp lines is postponed to Chapter 18, which is concerned with fluorescence.

4.2 Temperature Effects on Bands

The effects of temperature on bands can be classified as follows:

1. Thermal effects on band position.
2. Thermal effects on bandwidth.
3. Thermal effects on band area.

Let us examine these effects separately.

Thermal Effects on Band Position. It has been observed experimentally that the peaks of absorption bands of transition metal ions tend to shift as the temperature of the absorbing material is changed. This effect is certainly expected; the frequency of the transition depends on the strength $\Delta = 10$ Dq of the crystalline field, and the crystalline field is a function of the distance R between the absorbing center and the ligands. The parameter Δ is proportional to R^{-5} in the charge model and to R^{-6} in the dipole model. On the other hand, R is a function of temperature through the expansion coefficient of the material

$$R(T) = R(0)(1 + \alpha T), \tag{17.69}$$

where $\alpha \approx 10^{-5}/°\text{K}$ is the coefficient of linear expansion. Therefore

$$\Delta \propto \frac{c}{R^n} = \frac{c}{R(0)^n\,(1 + \alpha T)^n} \approx \frac{c}{R(0)^n}(1 - n\alpha T). \tag{17.70}$$

An expansion of the crystal reduces the strength of the crystalline field and changes the frequency of the transitions, which therefore depends on the temperature. The law with which the frequency varies depends on the slope $dE/d\Delta$ of the curve of energy versus the parameter Δ (see the Tanabe-Sugano diagrams).

Shifts in wavelength toward the red have been observed by McClure [15] in the ${}^4T_1$ and ${}^4T_2$ bands of Ruby. The bands shift toward the red as the temperature rises from 300 to 700°K by approximately 300 Å ($\sim$900 cm^{-1}). Similarly [16, 17], a shift of $\sim$300 Å toward the red was noticed in the ${}^4T_1$ band of MgO:V^{2+} from 80 to 500°K.

In case of a negative slope $dE/d\Delta$, shifts of the bands toward the blue could be observed.

The type of shift (positive or negative) that is found as a function of temperature may be of some help in the identification of crystal levels.

Temperature Effects on Bandwidths [*18*]. It is a well-known fact in absorption spectroscopy of ionic crystals that the width of a band becomes larger as the temperature increases. The width of a band is, in general, broader than the Debye frequency of the crystal, and therefore the transition involves the excitation of one or more phonons (whereas in a sharp line transition the number of phonons does not change).

The broad widths of the bands produced by ions in crystals can be explained by the use of a *configurational coordinate model.*

In this model each energy state of an ionic center is represented by a wavefunction that consists of the product of an electronic wavefunction and a vibrational wavefunction, according to the *Born-Oppenheimer approximation.* The electronic wavefunctions are expressed in terms of the electrons of the ion; the vibrational wavefunctions are the wavefunctions of the ion in a potential due to the presence of the ligands.

The potential energy of the center depends on the normal coordinates of the neighboring atoms. The most important of these coordinates is the one corresponding to the *breathing* mode, in which all the atoms of the cluster of the nearest neighbors move radially in phase. The other modes, in which part of the ions move onward and part outward, do not influence the potential energy as much as the breathing mode. As a first approximation, it is then possible to use only one configurational coordinate; for small displacements the center ion behaves as a harmonic oscillator.

The configurational coordinate (CC) scheme can explain the following phenomena:

1. *Stokes shift* (difference in energy between absorption and emission).
2. The broadening of the bands (in emission and absorption) with temperature.

A CC scheme is represented in Fig. 17.1. We notice that the minima of the ground and excited states occur at different values of the coordinate. The curve of the excited state has less curvature near the minimum than the curve of the excited state; this is to be expected, for the excited state has a more diffuse charge distribution. The two curves are given by

$$\begin{aligned} V_g(r) &= \tfrac{1}{2}k_g r^2, \\ V_e(r) &= \tfrac{1}{2}k_e(r - r_0)^2 + V_0. \end{aligned} \tag{17.71}$$

The vibrational wavefunctions of the ground and of the excited state are given, respectively, by

$$\begin{aligned} \psi_{ng}(r) &= N_n \exp\left[-\frac{1}{2}\left(\frac{r}{a_g}\right)^2\right] H_n\left(\frac{r}{a_g}\right), \\ \psi_{me}(r) &= N_m \exp\left[-\frac{1}{2}\left(\frac{r - r_0}{a_g}\right)^2\right] H_m\left(\frac{r}{a_g}\right), \end{aligned} \tag{17.72}$$

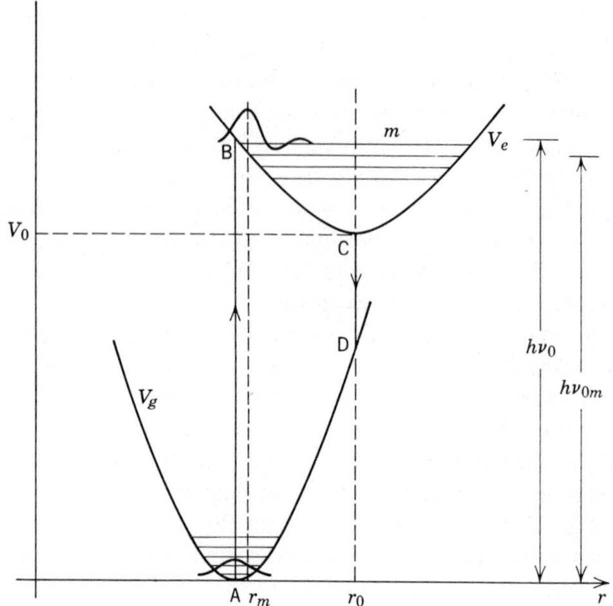

Fig. 17.1. Potential curves of ground and excited states.

where H_n, H_m = Hermitian polynomials,
N_n, N_m = normalizing factors,

and

$$\begin{aligned} a_g^2 &= \frac{\hbar}{\sqrt{k_g M}} = \frac{\hbar}{M\omega_g}, \qquad \omega_g = \left(\frac{k_g}{M}\right)^{1/2}, \\ a_e^2 &= \frac{\hbar}{\sqrt{k_e M}} = \frac{\hbar}{M\omega_e}, \qquad \omega_e = \left(\frac{k_e}{M}\right)^{1/2}, \end{aligned} \tag{17.73}$$

where M = mass of the absorbing center,
$\hbar\omega_g$ = vibrational quantum of the ion in the ground state,
$\hbar\omega_e$ = vibrational quantum of the ion in the excited state.

The absorption and emission processes can be visualized as in Fig. 17.1. At low temperature the optically active center resides in the lowest vibrational state of the lower potential curve (point A). It follows, then:

1. The absorption transition brings the center to an excited state of the upper potential curve (point B).
2. From this vibrational state the center relaxes to the lowest vibrational state of the upper curve (point C) by radiationless process.

3. The center then decays radiatively to an excited vibrational state of the lower curve (point D).
4. Finally, the center decays nonradiatively from D to A.

This representation is based on the assumption that during an electronic transition ($A \to B$ and $C \to D$) the center preserves its configurational coordinate. The assumption expresses the *Franck-Condon principle*. If $\phi_g(\mathbf{x})$, $\phi_e(\mathbf{x})$ are the electronic wavefunctions, respectively, of the ground and of the excited states, the matrix element, because of the Franck-Condon principle,[3] is given by

$$M_{nm} = \int \phi_g^*(\mathbf{x})\, \psi_{ng}^*(r)\, e\mathbf{x}\, \phi_e(\mathbf{x})\, \psi_{me}(r)\, d\mathbf{x}\, dr$$

$$= \mu_{ge} \int \psi_{ng}^*(r)\, \psi_{me}(r)\, dr, \qquad (17.74)$$

where

$$\mu_{ge} = \int \phi_g^*(\mathbf{x})\, e\mathbf{x}\, \phi_e(\mathbf{x})\, d\mathbf{x}. \qquad (17.75)$$

In what follows we shall assume that the initial (ground) state has a very low vibrational number and that the final (excited) state has a high ($n_e \gg 0$) vibrational number. For this reason we shall treat the initial state quantum mechanically and the final state classically:

$$V_e(r_m) - V_0 = \tfrac{1}{2}k_e(r_m - r_0)^2 = (m + \tfrac{1}{2})\, h\nu_e. \qquad (17.76)$$

The function $\psi_{me}(r)$ tends toward a classical distribution for high values of n_e and has a maximum at $r = r_m$.

Let us now consider the low-temperature and high-temperature cases separately.

LOW-TEMPERATURES

At very low temperatures $n_g = 0$, and, because

$$\psi_{me}(r) \propto \delta(r - r_m), \qquad (17.77)$$

we get

$$M_{0m} = \mu_{eg} \int \psi_{0g}^*(r)\, \psi_{me}(r)\, dr \simeq \text{const}\ \psi_{0g}(r_m).$$

Now $|\psi_{0g}|^2$ is a gaussian function and therefore $|M_{0m}|^2$ is also a Gaussian function:

$$|\psi_{0g}|^2 = N_0^2 e^{-(r/a_g)^2}, \qquad (17.78)$$

[3] One way of formulating the Franck-Condon principle is to postulate that the matrix element M is proportional to the overlap integral of the vibrational wavefunctions of the ground and of the excited states.

and

$$|M_{0m}|^2 = \text{const}\ e^{-(r_m/a_g)^2}, \tag{17.79}$$

where a_g is the vibrational amplitude at the zero point energy given by $\sqrt{\hbar/(\omega_g M)}$.

Let us now consider the energy of the excited state harmonic oscillator. Let us differentiate $V_e(r)$ in the region $r \approx 0$:

$$\left.\frac{\partial V_e(r)}{\partial r}\right|_{r=0} = -k_e r_0. \tag{17.80}$$

Therefore

$$V_e(r_m) - V_e(0) = -k_e r_0 r_m = h\nu_{0m} - h\nu_0, \tag{17.81}$$

and

$$r_m = -\frac{h\nu_{0m} - h\nu_0}{k_e r_0}. \tag{17.82}$$

Now (17.79) becomes

$$|M_{0m}|^2 = \text{const}\ \exp\left[-\frac{(h\nu_{0m} - h\nu_0)^2}{k_e^2 r_0^2 a_g^2}\right]. \tag{17.83}$$

The mean square deviation σ_a of the absorption band is given by the expression

$$2\sigma_a^2 = k_e^2 r_0^2 a_g^2. \tag{17.84}$$

In a similar way, if the initial state of the transition is the excited state and the final state is the ground state (case of emission), the mean square deviation of the emission band is given by

$$2\sigma_e^2 = k_g^2 r_0^2 a_e^2. \tag{17.85}$$

We can express (17.84) and (17.85) in a different way. In absorption

$$h\nu_0 = V_0 + n_a h\nu_e, \tag{17.86}$$

where n_a is the number of vibrational quanta emitted after the absorption of a photon and

$$n_a h\nu_e = \tfrac{1}{2} k_e r_0^2. \tag{17.87}$$

Then

$$r_0^2 = \frac{2 n_a h\nu_e}{k_e}, \tag{17.88}$$

and

$$\sigma_a^2 = \frac{k_e^2 r_0^2 a_g^2}{2} = n_a (h\nu_e)\, k_e a_g^2. \tag{17.89}$$

But

$$a_g^2 k_e = \frac{\hbar}{M\omega_g} M\omega_e^2 = \frac{(h\nu_e)^2}{h\nu_g}. \tag{17.90}$$

Therefore

$$\sigma_a^2 = n_a \frac{(h\nu_e)^3}{h\nu_g}. \tag{17.91}$$

In a similar way, in emission,

$$h\nu_0 = V_0 - n_e h\nu_e, \tag{17.92}$$

where ν_0 is the central frequency of the emission band and n_e is the number of vibrational quanta emitted after the emission of a photon. Also,

$$\tfrac{1}{2}k_g r_0^2 = n_e h\nu_g \tag{17.93}$$

and then

$$\sigma_e^2 = n_e \frac{(h\nu_g)^3}{h\nu_e}. \tag{17.94}$$

In case $\nu_g = \nu_e = \nu$,

$$n_a = n_e = n \tag{17.95}$$

and

$$\sigma_a^2 = \sigma_e^2 = n(h\nu)^2. \tag{17.96}$$

HIGH TEMPERATURES

In the low temperature case the mean square deviation of the absorption band is given by (17.84), where a_g is the amplitude of the ion vibration at zero point energy. To find the mean square deviation of the absorption band at any temperature we may replace in (17.84) a_g by the average value of the amplitude:

$$a_g(0) \to [a_g(n)]_{\text{av}} = \sqrt{\sum_{n=0}^{\infty} p_n\, a_g^2(n)}, \tag{17.97}$$

where

$$p_n = \frac{e^{-nh\nu_g/kT}}{\sum_{n=0}^{\infty} e^{-nh\nu_g/kT}} \tag{17.98}$$

and $a_g\,(n)$ is given by

$$\tfrac{1}{2}k_g a_g^2(n) = (n + \tfrac{1}{2})\, h\nu_g. \tag{17.99}$$

Then

$$a_g^2(n) = (2n + 1)\frac{h\nu_g}{k_g} \tag{17.100}$$

and

$$\sum_{n=0}^{\infty} p_n a_g^2(n) = \frac{h\nu_g}{k_g} \frac{\sum_{n=0}^{\infty}(2n + 1)e^{-nh\nu_g/kT}}{\sum_{n=0}^{\infty} e^{-nh\nu_g/kT}}$$

$$= \frac{h\nu_g}{k_g}\left(1 + 2\frac{\sum_{n=0}^{\infty} ne^{-nh\nu_g/kT}}{\sum_{n=0}^{\infty} e^{-nh\nu_g/kT}}\right); \tag{17.101}$$

but

$$\frac{\sum_{n=0}^{\infty} n e^{-nh\nu_g/kT}}{\sum_{n=0}^{\infty} e^{-nh\nu_g/kT}} = \frac{e^{-h\nu_g/kT} + 2e^{-2h\nu_g/kT} + 3e^{-3h\nu_g/kT} + \cdots}{1 + e^{-2h\nu_g/kT} + e^{-3h\nu_g/kT} + \cdots}$$

$$= \frac{d}{d(-h\nu_g/kT)} \ln\left(1 + e^{-h\nu_g/kT} + e^{-2h\nu_g/kT} + \cdots\right)$$

$$= \frac{d}{d(-h\nu_g/kT)} \ln \frac{1}{1 - e^{-h\nu_g/kT}} = \frac{1}{e^{h\nu_g/kT} - 1}. \tag{17.102}$$

Therefore

$$\sum_{n=0}^{\infty} pna_g^2(n) = \frac{h\nu_g}{k_g}\left(1 + \frac{2}{e^{h\nu_g/kT} - 1}\right)$$

$$= \frac{h\nu_g}{k_g} \coth \frac{h\nu_g}{2kT}$$

$$= a_g^2(0) \coth \frac{h\nu_g}{2kT}. \tag{17.103}$$

Then

$$[a_g(n)]_{\text{av}} = a_g(0)\left(\coth \frac{h\nu_g}{2kT}\right)^{1/2} \tag{17.104}$$

and

$$\sigma_a(T) = \sigma_a(0)\left(\coth \frac{h\nu_g}{2kT}\right)^{1/2}. \tag{17.105}$$

Similarly,

$$\sigma_e(T) = \sigma_e(0)\left(\coth \frac{h\nu_e}{2kT}\right)^{1/2}. \tag{17.106}$$

We can now list the following conclusions:

1. The shape of an absorption or emission band at very low temperature is Gaussian.
2. The bandwidth is proportional to the number of phonons emitted after the electronic transition has taken place.
3. The band shape at any temperature is still Gaussian and the bandwidth is proportional to $\sqrt{\coth h\nu/2kT}$, where ν is the frequency of the phonons emitted.

Temperature Effects on Integrated Areas. A transition that is electronically forbidden can sometimes occur because of a vibrational-electronic interaction; in this case the strength of the absorption becomes strongly temperature-dependent. Enhancements of the absorption band areas with temperature were found by McClure [15] in $Al_2O_3:Cr^{3+}$ and by Holmes and McClure [19] in crystalline hydrates such as $NiSO_4 \cdot 7H_2O$ and $KCr(SO_4)_2 \cdot 12H_2O$. By relating fluorescence intensity measurements to the absorption strength of the excitation band, an enhancement of the absorption strength of the $4T_1$ band [16, 17] in $MgO:V^{2+}$ has also been found.

The persistence of absorption at very low temperature is, however, an indication that the transitions are partly electronically allowed.

5. EXCITED STATE ABSORPTION [20–29]

The absorption spectra we have been considering are related to transitions that initiate in the ground state and end in an excited state. The basic assumption in absorption spectroscopy is that during the absorption process a negligible number of ions are in excited states. Situations may arise, however, in which the excited states contain more than a negligible quantity of ions; such a situation may be created by *pumping* enough light into the absorption bands of a crystal. From these bands the excited ions may decay by some rapid (nonradiative) processes to a metastable state. When equilibrium between radiation and crystal is reached, a relevant number of ions may actually find themselves in the metastable state. In these conditions a solid behaves differently (with respect to an incoming beam of light) than an *unpumped* solid, because an absorption may take place from the meta stable level to higher levels.

Let us examine the conditions under which excited-state absorption can be observed. Let us call $I_0(\lambda)$ the intensity of a beam of light at the input of the absorbing material. We have the following equations:

$$\begin{aligned} I_u(\lambda) &= I_0(\lambda) e^{-N_0 \sigma_0(\lambda) L}, \\ I_p(\lambda) &= I_0(\lambda) e^{-N\sigma_0(\lambda) L - n\sigma^*(\lambda) L}, \end{aligned} \tag{17.107}$$

where N_0 = density of absorbing centers (cm^{-3}),
$\sigma_0(\lambda)$ = cross section of a transition originating from the ground state (cm^2),
$\sigma^*(\lambda)$ = cross section of a transition originating from the metastable state,
N = density of absorbing centers in the ground state under pumping conditions (cm^{-3}),
n = density of absorbing centers in the metastable state during pumping (cm^{-3}),
$I_p(\lambda), I_u(\lambda)$ = intensity of the beam output under pumping and normal conditions, respectively,
L = length of the absorbing material.

We notice that

$$N_0 = N + n. \tag{17.108}$$

Then, from (17.107), we can derive

$$\frac{I_p(\lambda)}{I_u(\lambda)} = e^{n[\sigma_0(\lambda)-\sigma^*(\lambda)]L}. \tag{17.109}$$

We can now make the following observations:

1. Any difference of the value of the above ratio from one is evidence of excited state effects.
2. If $\sigma^*(\lambda) = 0$, the presence of ions in the excited state produces a decrease in the absorption coefficient.
3. In order to see excited state absorption we need not only a $\sigma^*(\lambda) \neq 0$, but a population $n \neq 0$.
4. In (17.109) the ratio I_p/I_u is the experimental result; $\sigma_0(\lambda)$ is known from conventional absorption spectroscopy, and n and $\sigma^*(\lambda)$ are two unknown quantities that cannot be determined at the same time. There is a way around this difficulty; there may be a wavelength for which, being the energy level structure of the system known, no excited state absorption is expected, namely, a λ for which $\sigma^*(\lambda) = 0$. In this case the decrease of the absorption coefficient in the pumped crystal gives a value for the excited state population n.
5. From (17.109) we can derive

$$\sigma^*(\lambda) = \sigma_0(\lambda) - \frac{\ln [I_p(\lambda)/I_u(\lambda)]}{nL}. \tag{17.110}$$

The condition $\sigma^* > 0$ imposes a lower limit on n. In Fig. 17.2 some results obtained by Kiang, Stephany, and Unterleitner [23] on the excited state cross section of ruby are reported.

6. Because the metastable state may well be a fluorescent state, we may have, in principle, an indication of the value of n by monitoring the fluorescence.

Excited-state experiments have been done in $Al_2O_3{:}Cr^{3+}$ (ruby) [20–25]. in glasses doped with Gd [26], Ur, and Er [27, 28], and in $SrF_2{:}Sm^{2+}$ [29]. Sometimes a greater cross section can be expected for transitions starting from an excited state than from the ground state; this may be the case in Gd, in which the ground state is ^8S and the excited states are sextets. Excited-state absorption transitions from the resonant level ($^6P_{7/2}$) to other upper sextets respect the spin selection rule $\Delta S = 0$, contrary to what happens in ground-state absorption transitions. Excited-state cross sections stronger than ground-state cross sections can also be expected in a d^5 ion in a O_h symmetry which

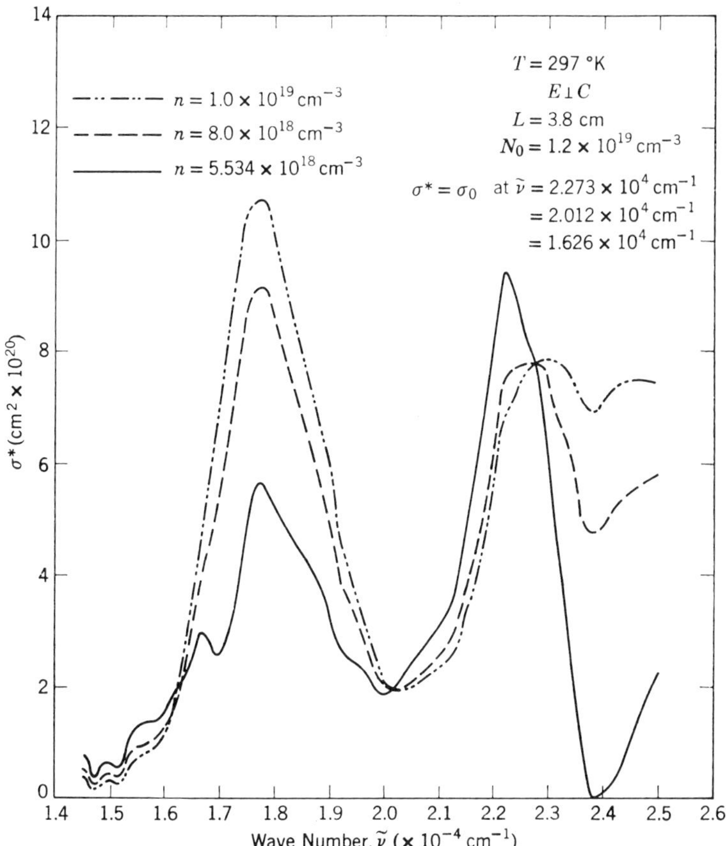

Fig. 17.2. Excited state absorption cross section in ruby (adapted from [23] by permission of Dr. F. Unterleitner and the *IEEE J. Quantum Electron.*)

has in the high-spin configuration a ground state ^6S and a number of quartet excited states.

It is clear therefore that excited-state absorption may represent an important tool for the evaluation of energy levels that are weakly connected to the ground state and that can be seen only in crystals with a high concentration of absorbing centers in conventional absorption.

REFERENCES

[1] D. L. Dexter, "Theory of the Optical Properties of Imperfections in Nonmetals," in *Solid State Physics*, Vol. 6, F. Seitz and D. Turnbull, eds., Academic, New York (1958) p. 353.

[2] D. W. Posener, "The Shape of Spectral Lines: Tables of the Voigt Profile," *Austral. J. Phys.* **12,** 184 (1954).

[3] E. V. Sayre and S. Freed, "Spectra and Quantum States of the Europic Ion in Crystals. II. Fluorescence and Absorption Spectra of Single Crystals of Europic Ethylsulfate Nonahydrate," *J. Chem. Phys.* **24,** 1213 (1956).

[4] L. F. Johnson, R. E. Dietz and H. J. Guggenheim, "Optical Maser Oscillation from Ni^{2+} in MgF_2 Involving Simultaneous Emission of Phonons," *Phys. Rev. Letters* **11,** 318 (1963).

[5] G. H. Dieke, "Spectroscopic Observations in Maser Materials," in *Advances in Quantum Electronics*, J. Singer, ed., Columbia, New York, 1962, p. 164.

[6] R. A. Satten, "Crystalline Field Selection Rules: The Effect of Vibration-Electronic Interactions," *Phys. Rev.* **27,** 286 (1957).

[7] L. E. Orgel, *An Introduction to Transition Metal Chemistry Ligand Field Theory*, Wiley, New York, 1960.

[8] D. S. McClure, "Electronic Spectra of Molecules and Ions in Crystals. Part II. Spectra of Ions in Crystals," in *Solid State Physics*, Vol. 9, F. Seitz and D. Turnbull, eds., Academic, New York, 1959.

[9] T. M. Dunn, "The Visible and Ultra-violet Spectra of Complex Compounds," in *Modern Coordination Chemistry*, J. Lewis and R. G. Wilkins, eds., Interscience, New York, 1964, p. 229.

[10] C. K. Jørgensen, *Absorption Spectra and Chemical Bonding in Complexes*, Pergamon, New York, 1962.

[11] C. K. Jørgensen, *Orbitals in Atoms and Molecules*, Academic, New York, 1962.

[12] J. Teltow, "Das Liniehafte Absorptionsspektrum des Bichromations bei 20°K," *Z. Physik Chem.* **B43,** 375 (1939); also "Die Absorptionsspektrum des Permanganat-chromat-, Vanadat- und Manganations in Kristallen," *Z. Physik Chem.* **B43,** 198 (1939).

[13] M. Wolfsberg and L. Helmhoz, "The Spectra and Electronic Structure of the Tetrahedral Ions MnO_4^-, CrO_4^{--} and ClO_4^-," *J. Chem. Phys.* **20,** 837 (1952).

[14] F. D. S. Butement, "Absorption and Fluorescence Spectra of Bivalent Samarium, Europium and Ytterbium," *Trans. Faraday Soc.* **44,** 617 (1948).

[15] D. S. McClure, "Optical Spectra of Transition Metal Ions in Corundum," *J. Chem. Phys.* **36,** 2657 (1962).

[16] B. Di Bartolo, "Fluorescence of Transition Metal Ions in Crystals," Laboratory for Insulation Research (MIT), Technical Report 190, June 1964, unpublished.

[17] B. Di Bartolo and R. Peccei, "Thermal Effects on the Fluorescence Lifetime and Spectrum of $MgO:V^{2+}$," *Phys. Rev.* **137,** A1770 (1965).

[18] D. Curie, *Luminescence in Crystals*, Methuen, London (1963).

[19] O. Holmes and D. S. McClure, "Optical Spectra of Hydrated Ions of the Transition Metals," *J. Chem. Phys.* **26,** 1686 (1957).

[20] F. Gires and G. Mayer, "Mésures du spectre d'absorption d'un ruby éxcité pour l'étude de son functionnement en maser optique," Comptes Rendues **254,** 659 (1962); "Atténuation et Amplification Optiques du Rubis Fortement Éxcité," in *Quantum Electronics Proceedings of the Third International Congress*, edited by P. Grivet and N. Bloembergen, Columbia, New York, 1964, p. 841.

[21] D. Sheres, "Absorption Spectrum of Excited Ruby," B.S. Thesis, MIT, Physics 1962, unpublished.

[22] G. K. Klauminzer, P. L. Scott and H. W. Moos, "$^2E \rightarrow {}^2T_2$ Absorption Spectrum of Ruby," *Phys. Rev.* **142,** 248 (1966).

[23] Y. C. Kiang, J. F. Stephany and F. C. Unterleitner, "Visible Spectrum Absorption Cross Section of Cr^{3+} in the ^2E State of Pink Ruby," *IEEE J. Quantum Electr.* **QE1,** 295 (1965).

[24] T. Kushida, "Absorption and Emission Properties of Optically Pumped Ruby," *IEEE J. Quantum Electron.* **QE2,** 524 (1966).

[25] C. S. Naiman, B. Di Bartolo and A. Linz, "Effects of Excited State Absorption on a Ruby Light Amplifier," in *Physics of Quantum Electronics*, P. L. Kelley, B. Lax and P. E. Tannenwald, eds., McGraw-Hill, New York, 1966, p. 315.

[26] U.S. Naval Research Laboratory; Memorandum Report 1483.

[27] C. C. Robinson, "Excited State Absorption of Fluorescent Ions in Glasses," *J. Opt. Soc. Am.* **55,** 1576 (1965).

[28] C. C. Robinson, "Excited-State Absorption in Fluorescent Uranium, Erbium and Copper-Tin Glasses," *J. Opt. Soc. Am.* **57,** 4 (1967).

[29] J. W. Huang and H. W. Moos, "Absorption Spectrum of Optically Pumped SrF_2: Sm^{2+}," *Bull. Am. Phys. Soc.* **12,** 1068 (1967).

18

Fluorescence Spectra of Magnetic Ions in Crystals

1. THE FLUORESCENCE EMISSION OF MAGNETIC IONS UNDER CONTINUOUS EXCITATION

The fluorescence of inorganic crystals is in general due to the presence of some magnetic ionic impurity which substitutes for a normal positive ionic constituent. These impurity centers are also, in general, responsible for the absorption spectra of the crystal.

An impurity in a crystal may be represented by a configurational coordinate curve as in Fig. 18.1. Let us assume that the ion is in its ground electronic state and its lowest vibrational state; temperatures below 70°K generally produce such a situation. A transition upward from A to B may be induced by the absorption of a photon of energy $(E_B - E_A)$. The impurity will then be brought to the excited electronic state and to an excited vibrational level of this state. As a consequence of the Franck-Condon principle, which states that atoms do not change their position during an electronic transition, the coordinate of the center, immediately after the absorption has taken place, is the same as the coordinate before the absorption. After the absorption, the center will tend to transfer its vibrational energy to the lattice and to decay to the lowest vibrational level designated by C. From this level the center will further decay to level D of the ground electronic state, giving up the energy $E_C - E_D$ as fluorescent radiation. From D the center will then decay to its lowest vibrational state.

The difference in energy between the energy of the absorbed photon and the energy of the emitted photon is called *Stokes shift*.

We have already found in Section 4.2 of the last chapter that the widths of the emission and of the absorption bands are related to the number n_a and

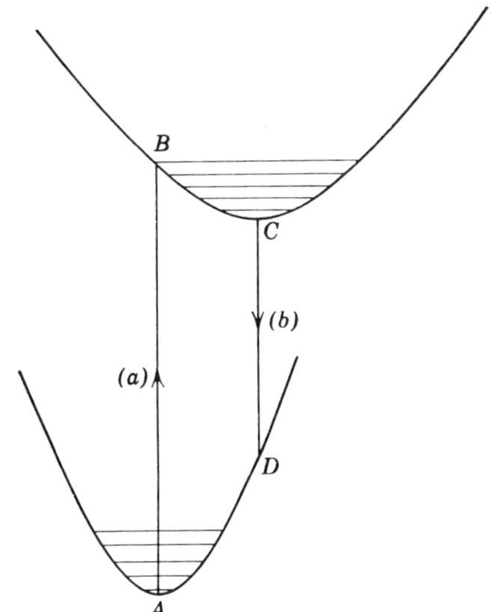

Fig. 18.1. Absorption and fluorescence transitions according to the configurational coordinate model: (*a*) absorption, (*b*) fluorescence.

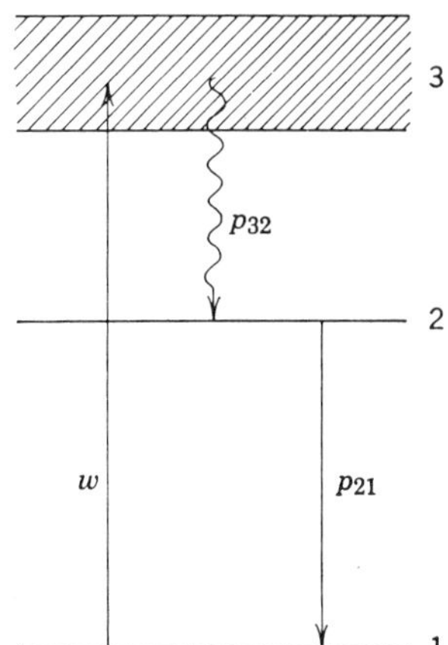

Fig. 18.2. Three-level system with one fluorescent level and quick decay processes between level 3 and level 2.

n_e designating the vibrational levels to which the center is brought, respectively, by absorption and fluorescence transition.

As a consequence, a sharp absorption line implies a very small n_a number; in these conditions the curve representing the excited state must be almost parallel to the curve representing the ground state. If a fluorescence transition can also take place, its energy will then be equal to the energy of the absorption transition. For this reason very sharp lines do not experience any Stokes shift.

Magnetic ions in crystals present sharp lines in absorption, some of which are also seen in fluorescence. They also present absorption bands from which no fluorescence is generally observed. The fluorescence lines originate from long-lived (metastable) states, whose lifetimes are of the order of 10^{-2}–10^{-3} sec; the absorption bands, instead, correspond to short-lived states from which the ions quickly decay to the metastable levels.

The energy level diagram shown in Fig. 18.2 can be used to represent a fluorescent ion in a host lattice. The incident light excites ions from the ground state 1 to an excited state represented by the absorption band 3. The ions then decay by a fast radiationless transition to the metastable state 2. From this fluorescent level the ions decay to the ground state by purely radiative processes and by other processes that we may call *secondary*. The probability per unit time that an ion undergoes a transition from the ground state to the absorption band is given by w. The transition probability per unit time from level 2 to level 1 is p_{21}. We make the simplifying assumption that for an ion in level 3, the probability for decaying to the ground state is negligibly small compared to the probability of a radiationless transition to level 2.

If we let N_0 be the total number of atoms in the system and N_i be the number of atoms in the ith state, the following equations can be written for the system:

$$\frac{dN_3}{dt} = w(N_1 - N_3) - p_{32}N_3,$$

$$\frac{dN_2}{dt} = p_{32}N_3 - p_{21}N_2, \tag{18.1}$$

$$\frac{dN_1}{dt} = -\left(\frac{dN_2}{dt} + \frac{dN_3}{dt}\right),$$

with

$$N_1 + N_2 + N_3 = N_0. \tag{18.2}$$

In equilibrium, under continuous excitation,

$$\begin{aligned} w(N_1 - N_3) - p_{32}N_3 &= 0, \\ p_{32}N_3 - p_{21}N_2 &= 0. \end{aligned} \tag{18.3}$$

Then

$$(w + p_{32})\, N_3 = wN_1. \tag{18.4}$$

Since $p_{32} \gg w$,

$$p_{32}N_3 \approx wN_1, \tag{18.5}$$

and the second of (18.3) becomes

$$wN_1 - p_{21}N_2 = 0. \tag{18.6}$$

Also, $N_3 \approx 0$ and (18.6) can be written

$$w(N_0 - N_2) = p_{21}N_2, \tag{18.7}$$

or

$$N_2 = \frac{wN_0}{w + p_{32}}. \tag{18.8}$$

In (18.8) N_0 and p_{32} are constant, whereas w is a probability proportional to the incoming radiation.

The lifetime of level 2 is the inverse of p_{21} and is called the *fluorescence lifetime*,

$$\tau_F = \frac{1}{p_{21}}. \tag{18.9}$$

We note that the probability p_{21} includes all the decay processes that originate from level 2 and end on level 1. These processes are the purely radiative decay, the vibrationally assisted or vibronic decay, and the radiationless decay.

Substituting (18.9) into (18.8) gives

$$N_2 = \frac{wN_0\tau_F}{1 + \tau_F w}. \qquad (18.10)^1$$

We can also write

$$N_2 - N_1 = N_2 - (N_0 - N_2) = 2N_2 - N_0.$$

With (18.10) this becomes

$$N_2 - N_1 = \frac{2wN_0}{w + p_{21}} - N_0 = N_0 \frac{w - p_{21}}{w + p_{21}}. \qquad (18.11)$$

If $w > p_{21}$, we have $N_2 > N_1$, which indicates a population inversion. This is one of the conditions for achieving laser action. In normal fluorescence measurements $w \ll p_{21}$ or $w^{-1} \gg \tau_f$. Using this in (18.10) gives

$$N_2 \approx wN_0\tau_F. \qquad (18.12)$$

The probability w can be expressed as the product σI_a, where σ is the absorption cross section and I_a the intensity of the exciting (pumping) radiation.

The population in level 2 excited by radiation of frequency in the range ν_a to $\nu_a + d\nu_a$ is then given by

$$dN_2(\nu_a) = N_0 I_a(\nu_a)\, d\nu_a\, \sigma(\nu_a, T)\, \tau_F(T). \qquad (8.13)$$

Therefore in the above approximation dN_2 is linearly proportional to the pumping power.

The intensity of the fluorescence emission is proportional to the population of the fluorescent level and the probability for radiative transition to the ground state:

$$I_f(\nu_a, \nu_f, T)\, d\nu_a\, d\nu_f = dN_2\, w_{21}(\nu_f, T)\, d\nu_f. \qquad (18.14)$$

Using (18.13),

$$I_f(\nu_a, \nu_f, T)\, d\nu_a\, d\nu_f = N_0 I_a(\nu_a)\, \sigma(\nu_a, T)\, \tau_F(T)\, w_{21}(\nu_f, T)\, d\nu_a\, d\nu_f. \qquad (18.15)$$

Here, I_f is the intensity of fluorescence given in number of photons per second in the frequency range $(\nu_f, \nu_f + d\nu_f)$ when pumping in the frequency interval $(\nu_a, \nu_a + d\nu_a)$. This can be put in terms of energy by multiplying I_f by $h\nu_f$.

[1] We notice that in a two level system the denominator is $(1 + 2w\tau_F)$ and for $w \gg \tau_F^{-1}$ the population N_2 can only be $N_0/2$.

Formula 18.15 is fundamental in fluorescence studies. It gives us a general idea about the factors that may affect the fluorescence spectral output.

We can make the following observations:

1. When we sum over ν_a, we obtain the fluorescence output when all the absorption spectrum is used. We may also notice that we can have more than one absorption band accessible to the radiation. One of these bands may belong to an impurity ion present in the crystal, different from the one responsible for the fluorescence: energy transfer may then take place. In this case σ has to take into account the efficiency of this transfer process.

2. By monitoring the fluorescence output at a certain frequency (or, for that matter, the integrated fluorescence output), while varying the frequency of the exciting radiation, the so-called *activation* or *excitation spectrum* is obtained. Such a spectrum can be correlated to the absorption spectrum of the crystal. Measurements of the activation spectrum may uncover the bands responsible for the energy storage and subsequent emission of the radiative energy.

3. The temperature dependence of I_f can be examined by considering the three factors on the right-hand side of (18.15) which are functions of the temperature. In interpreting the temperature-dependence of a fluorescence line, the temperature changes of the absorption band must be considered. The absorption cross section, $\sigma(\nu_a, T)$ may vary with temperature in two ways. There may be a frequency shift and a broadening of the relative transition due to temperature changes; if the spectral output of the exciting source is not uniform in the vicinity of the absorption band, any change in shape or position of the band may cause a change in the amount of energy absorbed. Also, thermal vibrations can sometimes enhance the strength of the absorption, making the cross section depending on T.

Since $w_{21}(\nu_f, T)$ includes both purely radiative transitions and phonon-assisted transitions, it is temperature-dependent. The temperature-dependence of vibronic lines is discussed later. The transition probability of a no phonon line is assumed to be independent of temperature.

4. The fluorescence lifetime is affected by radiative, radiationless, and vibronic decay processes. Its temperature-dependence is a result of the temperature-dependence of the latter two.

We can find the total integrated intensity from (18.15) to be

$$I_f(T) = N_0 I_a \, \sigma_a(T) \, \tau_F(T) \int w_{21}(\nu_f, T) \, d\nu_f \tag{18.16}$$

where

$$I_a \, \sigma_a(T) = \int I_a(\nu_a) \, \sigma_a(\nu_a, T) \, d\nu_a.$$

The temperature-dependence of (18.16) can be determined by examining the experimental data. If it can be explained by the temperature changes in the absorption band (also determined experimentally), this indicates that

$$\tau_F = \frac{1}{\int w_{21}(\nu_f, T)\, d\nu_f}. \tag{18.17}$$

This means that the fluorescence lifetime is affected only by purely radiative and vibronic decay processes and that radiationless processes (or energy transfer to coupled systems) are not effective in depleting the metastable state.

5. In comparing the experimental results with the predictions of (18.15), the data, which are in units of energy, must be renormalized in terms of number of photons, as mentioned before. The frequency-dependence of the whole experimental apparatus must also be accounted for. This includes such things as spectral output of the lamp, frequency response curve of the detector, and efficiency of the dispersing element. A factor $\eta(\nu_f)\, h\nu_f$ can be introduced into (18.15) to account for all this.

2. THE RESPONSE OF FLUORESCENT SYSTEMS TO TRANSIENT EXCITATION

The fluorescence emission of a crystal can also be observed when the exciting energy is turned on only for a time τ. In these conditions the fluorescence signal may give additional information about the system.

2.1 Solution of the Dynamical Equations for a Three-Level System

Let us consider the simple case of a three-level system under pulse excitation. The dynamical equations of the level populations are given by

$$\begin{aligned} \dot{N}_3 &= -(p_{31} + p_{32})\, N_3 + w(t)(N_1 - N_3), \\ \dot{N}_2 &= p_{32}N_3 - p_{21}N_2, \\ N_1 + N_2 + N_3 &= N_0, \end{aligned} \tag{18.18}$$

with $N_2(0) = N_3(0) = 0$. Here $w(t)$ may be considered to be a pulse of height w and length τ,

$$w(t) = w[1(t) - 1(t - \tau)], \tag{18.19}$$

where $1(t)$ is the unit step function.

Let us consider the solutions of (18.18) for $t < \tau$; in this case the above equations reduce to

$$\begin{aligned} \dot{N}_3 &= -[p_3 + 2w1(t)]N_3 - w1(t)\, N_2 + w1(t)\, N_0, \\ \dot{N}_2 &= p_{32}N_3 - p_{21}N_2, \end{aligned} \tag{18.20}$$

where $p_3 = p_{31} + p_{32}$.

Taking the Laplace transforms, we obtain

$$\begin{aligned} (p_3 + 2w)\, \bar{n}_3 + w\bar{n}_2 - \frac{wN_0}{s} &= -s\bar{n}_3, \\ p_{32}\bar{n}_3 - p_{21}\bar{n}_2 &= s\bar{n}_2, \end{aligned} \tag{18.21}$$

where $\bar{n}_i$ is the Laplace transform of N_i.

From the second of these equations

$$\bar{n}_2 = \frac{p_{32}}{p_{21} + s}\, \bar{n}_3, \tag{18.22}$$

which yields

$$\begin{aligned} \bar{n}_3 &= \frac{wN_0}{s}\, \frac{p_{21} + s}{(p_3 + 2w + s)(p_{21} + s) + wp_{32}} = \frac{wN_0}{s}\, \frac{p_{21} + s}{(s - s_1)(s - s_2)}; \\ \bar{n}_2 &= \frac{wN_0}{s}\, \frac{p_{32}}{(p_3 + 2w + s)(p_{21} + s) + wp_{32}} = \frac{wN_0}{s}\, \frac{p_{32}}{(s - s_1)(s - s_2)}, \end{aligned} \tag{18.23}$$

where s_1 and s_2 are the two roots of the equation

$$s^2 + (p_3 + 2w + p_{21})s + p_3p_{21} + 2wp_{21} + wp_{32} = 0. \tag{18.24}$$

They are given by

$$s_{1,2} = \frac{-(p_3 + 2w + p_{21}) \pm \sqrt{(p_3 + 2w - p_{21})^2 - 4wp_{32}}}{2}. \tag{18.25}$$

We can decompose the fractions in (18.23) in the following way:

$$\begin{aligned} \frac{p_{21} + s}{s(s - s_1)(s - s_2)} &= \frac{c_0}{s} + \frac{c_1}{s - s_1} + \frac{c_2}{s - s_2}, \\ \frac{1}{s(s - s_1)(s - s_2)} &= \frac{d_0}{s} + \frac{d_1}{s - s_1} + \frac{d_2}{s - s_2}, \end{aligned} \tag{18.26}$$

where the c_i's and the d_i's are found to be

$$c_0 = \frac{p_{21}}{s_1 s_2},$$
$$c_1 = \frac{1 + p_{21}/s_1}{s_1 - s_2}, \tag{18.27}$$
$$c_2 = \frac{1 + p_{21}/s_2}{s_2 - s_1};$$

$$d_0 = \frac{1}{s_1 s_2},$$
$$d_1 = \frac{1}{s_1(s_1 - s_2)}, \tag{18.28}$$
$$d_2 = \frac{1}{s_2(s_2 - s_1)}.$$

Therefore we get, for $t \leq \tau$:

$$N_3(t) = A + Be^{s_1 t} + Ce^{s_2 t},$$
$$N_2(t) = D + Ee^{s_1 t} + Fe^{s_2 t}, \tag{18.29}$$

where

$$A = \frac{wN_0 p_{21}}{p_3 p_{21} + 2wp_{21} + wp_{32}} = \frac{wN_0 p_{21}}{s_1 s_2},$$
$$B = \frac{wN_0(s_1 + p_{21})}{s_1(s_1 - s_2)}, \tag{18.30}$$
$$C = \frac{wN_0(s_2 + p_{21})}{s_2(s_2 - s_1)},$$

and

$$D = \frac{wN_0 p_{32}}{p_3 p_{21} + 2wp_{21} + wp_{32}} = \frac{wN_0 p_{32}}{s_1 s_2},$$
$$E = \frac{wN_0 p_{32}}{s_1(s_1 - s_2)}, \tag{18.31}$$
$$F = \frac{wN_0 p_{32}}{s_2(s_2 - s_1)}.$$

For the steady-state result of a long pumping pulse we have:

$$N_3(\infty) = \frac{wN_0p_{21}}{p_3p_{21} + 2wp_{21} + wp_{32}},$$
$$N_2(\infty) = \frac{wN_0p_{32}}{p_3p_{21} + 2wp_{21} + wp_{32}} \tag{18.32}$$

and

$$\frac{N_3(\infty)}{N_2(\infty)} = \frac{p_{21}}{p_{32}}. \tag{18.33}$$

The solutions reported in (18.29) are the response to a step-function pumping pulse. The solutions for $t > \tau$ are made trivial because the nonlinearity drops out of the governing equations:

$$\dot{N}_3 = -p_3N_3,$$
$$\dot{N}_2 = p_{32}N_3 - p_{21}N_2. \tag{18.34}$$

The solutions of (18.34) are given by

$$N_3(t) = N_3(\tau)\, e^{-p_3(t-\tau)},$$
$$N_2(t) = \left[N_2(\tau) + \frac{p_{32}}{p_3 - p_{12}}\, N_3(\tau)\right] e^{-p_{21}(t-\tau)} - \frac{p_{32}N_3(\tau)}{p_3 - p_{21}}\, e^{-p_3(t-\tau)}, \tag{18.35}$$

where $N_2(\tau)$ and $N_3(\tau)$ are given by (18.29) for $t = \tau$,

More complicated cases may exist when an ionic system, being first excited to an upper level, decays to the metastable level through n downward jumps. It can be shown that in this case the decay law of the metastable state includes $n + 1$ exponentials, each with a decay constant equal to the lifetime of the corresponding relaxing level.

2.2 The Fluorescence Decay of a Three-Level System

The fluorescence signal of a three-level system actually follows the $N_2(t)$ curve. Such a curve, after the end of the exciting pulse, consists of two exponentials, as in (18.35). Three cases are of interest.

Case I. Pure Exponential Decay. This case takes place under the condition

$$p_3 \gg p_{21}. \tag{18.36}$$

The population $N_2(t)$ consists essentially of an exponential with the decay time equal to p_{21}^{-1}. An example of this case is reported in Fig. 18.3.

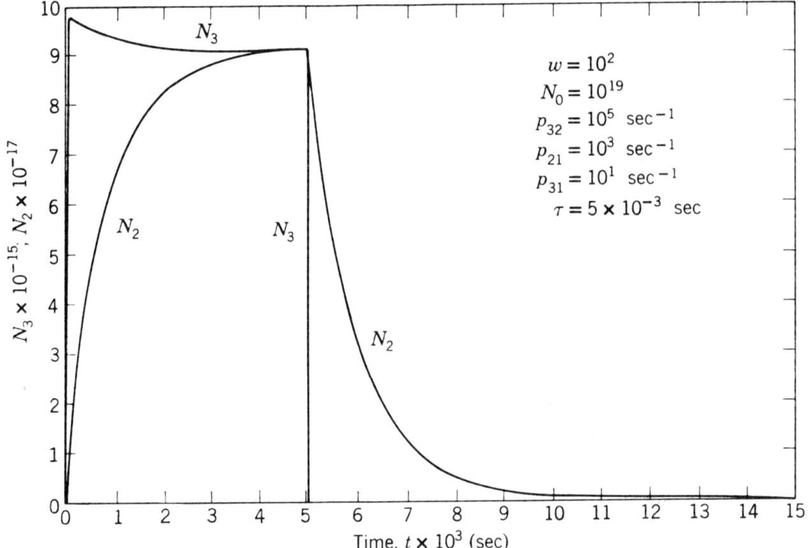

Fig. 18.3. Fluorescence decay of a three-level system.

Case II. Fluorescence Rise. If the exciting pulse is short enough, a maximum can occur for $N_2(t)$ at a time $t_{\max}$ after the end of the pulse given by

$$t_{\max} = \frac{1}{p_{21} - p_3} \ln \left[\frac{p_{21}}{p_3} + \frac{p_{21}(p_3 - p_{21})}{p_3 p_{32}} \frac{N_2(\tau)}{N_3(\tau)}\right]. \tag{18.37}$$

This time is related to the populations and probabilities as follows:

$$t_{\max} \geq 0 \quad \text{for} \quad p_{32} \frac{N_3(\tau)}{N_2(\tau)} \geq p_{21}. \tag{18.38}$$

An example of this type of fluorescence decay is given in Fig. 18.4.

Case III. Double Decay. This case takes place under the conditions

$$\begin{aligned} p_{21} &> p_3, \\ N_2(\tau) &> \frac{p_{32} N_3(\tau)}{p_{21} - p_3}. \end{aligned} \tag{18.39}$$

In this instance (18.35) reduces to the form

$$N_2(t) = Ae^{-p_{21}(t-\tau)} + Be^{-p_3(t-\tau)}. \tag{18.40}$$

It can be shown that the condition (18.39) for $N_2(\tau)$ cannot be realized in a three-level system. The presence of a double decay curve is, in this case,

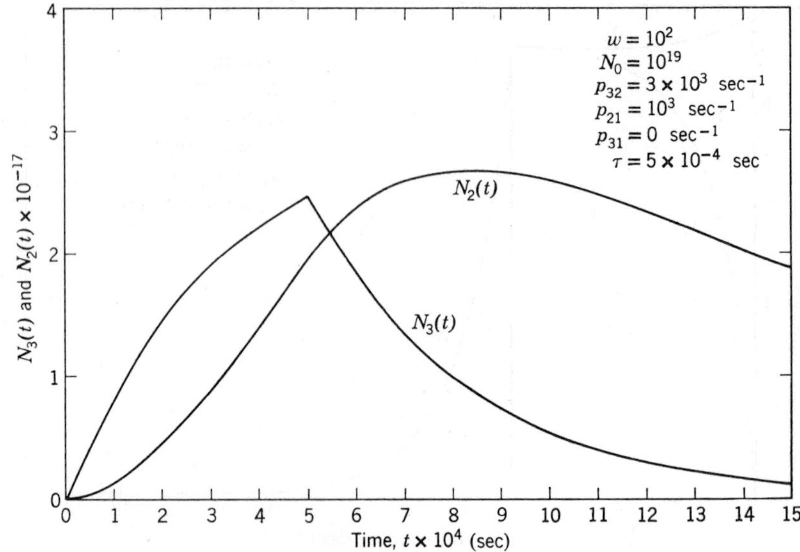

Fig. 18.4. Fluorescence decay of a three-level system.

evidence that level 2 is also pumped directly from some absorption band above level 3 or from some other ion that transfers its excitation energy to the fluorescent ion.

3. GENERAL PROPERTIES OF THE FLUORESCENCE DECAYS IN A MULTILEVEL SYSTEM

In a multilevel system with more than one fluorescent (metastable) state the decays of lines originating from different states may be equal or different, depending on the circumstances.

Let us consider a system with two metastable states, indicated by the indices 3 and 2, and a ground state, 1. Let us assume that levels 2 and 3 are connected by certain probabilities p_{23} and p_{32} which may be due to radiationless processes. The probability p_{31} and p_{21} from the metastable states to the ground state may include radiative, radiationless, and vibronic processes.

The problem we want to examine is the following: starting from a condition in which certain populations $N_3{}^0$ and $N_2{}^0$ have been established in the two levels, how does the system relax to equilibrium with all the population in the ground state? The dynamical equations of the populations are given by

$$\begin{aligned} \dot{N}_3 &= -N_3\beta + N_2 p_{23}, \\ \dot{N}_2 &= N_3 p_{32} - N_2\alpha, \end{aligned} \tag{18.41}$$

where

$$\alpha = p_{23} + p_{21}, \qquad \beta = p_{32} + p_{31}.$$

Taking the Laplace transforms we obtain

$$\begin{aligned} s\bar{n}_3 - N_3^0 &= -\beta\bar{n}_3 + p_{23}\bar{n}_2, \\ s\bar{n}_2 - N_2^0 &= p_{32}\bar{n}_3 - \alpha\bar{n}_2, \end{aligned} \tag{18.42}$$

where $N_2^0 = N_2(0)$ and $N_3^0 = N_3(0)$. From (18.42) we obtain

$$\begin{aligned} \bar{n}_3 &= \frac{N_3^0(s+\alpha) + N_2^0 p_{23}}{(s+\alpha)(s+\beta) - p_{32}p_{23}} = \frac{N_3^0(s+\alpha) + N_2^0 p_{23}}{(s-s_1)(s-s_2)}, \\ \bar{n}_2 &= \frac{N_3^0 p_{32} + N_2^0(s+\beta)}{(s+\alpha)(s+\beta) - p_{32}p_{23}} = \frac{N_3^0 p_{32} + N_2^0(s+\beta)}{(s-s_1)(s-s_2)}, \end{aligned} \tag{18.43}$$

where s_1 and s_2 are given by

$$(s+\alpha)(s+\beta) - p_{32}p_{23} = 0,$$

or

$$s^2 + (\alpha+\beta)\, s + (\alpha\beta - p_{32}p_{23}) = 0, \tag{18.44}$$

which in turn gives

$$s = \frac{-(\alpha+\beta) \pm \sqrt{(\alpha+\beta)^2 - 4(\alpha\beta - p_{32}p_{23})}}{2}. \tag{18.45}$$

The Laplace transforms (18.43) can be rewritten as follows:

$$\begin{aligned} \bar{n}_3 &= \frac{a_1}{s-s_1} + \frac{a_2}{s-s_2}, \\ \bar{n}_2 &= \frac{b_1}{s-s_1} + \frac{b_2}{s-s_2}, \end{aligned} \tag{18.46}$$

with

$$\begin{aligned} a_1 &= \frac{N_3^0(s_1+\alpha) + N_2^0 p_{23}}{s_1 - s_2}, \\ a_2 &= \frac{N_3^0(s_2+\alpha) + N_2^0 p_{23}}{s_2 - s_1}, \\ b_1 &= \frac{N_2^0(s_1+\beta) + N_3^0 p_{32}}{s_1 - s_2}, \\ b_2 &= \frac{N_2^0(s_2+\beta) + N_3^0 p_{32}}{s_2 - s_1}. \end{aligned} \tag{18.47}$$

Going to the time domain, we get

$$N_3(t) = \frac{N_3^0(s_1 + \alpha) + N_2^0 p_{23}}{s_1 - s_2} e^{s_1 t} + \frac{N_3^0(s_2 + \alpha) + N_2^0 p_{23}}{s_2 - s_1} e^{s_2 t}$$
$$N_2(t) = \frac{N_2^0(s_1 + \beta) + N_3^0 p_{32}}{s_1 - s_2} e^{s_1 t} + \frac{N_2^0(s_2 + \beta) + N_3^0 p_{32}}{s_2 - s_1} e^{s_2 t}. \tag{18.48}$$

Having obtained the above general solutions, let us adapt them to some physical situations. In particular, let us consider the case in which radiationless transitions between the two metastable levels are such that

$$p_{32}, p_{23} \gg p_{21}, p_{31}. \tag{18.49}$$

In this case

$$\alpha\beta - p_{32}p_{23} \approx p_{21}p_{32} + p_{31}p_{23}. \tag{18.50}$$

Then,

$$s = \frac{-(\alpha + \beta) \pm \sqrt{(\alpha + \beta)^2 - 4(p_{21}p_{32} + p_{31}p_{23})}}{2}$$
$$\approx -\frac{\alpha + \beta}{2} \pm \frac{(\alpha + \beta)\left[1 - 2\dfrac{p_{21}p_{32} + p_{31}p_{23}}{(\alpha + \beta)^2}\right]}{2} \tag{18.51}$$

and

$$s_1 = -\frac{p_{21}p_{32} + p_{31}p_{23}}{p_{23} + p_{32}},$$
$$s_2 = -\left[(\alpha + \beta) - \frac{p_{21}p_{32} + p_{31}p_{23}}{p_{23} + p_{32}}\right] \approx -(p_{23} + p_{32}). \tag{18.52}$$

Also,

$$s_1 + \alpha \approx p_{23},$$
$$s_1 + \beta \approx p_{32},$$
$$s_2 + \alpha \approx -(p_{23} + p_{32}) + p_{23} = -p_{32}, \tag{18.53}$$
$$s_2 + \beta \approx -(p_{23} + p_{32}) + p_{32} = -p_{23},$$
$$s_2 - s_1 \approx -(p_{32} + p_{23})$$

and

$$N_3(t) = \frac{N_3^0 p_{23} + N_2^0 p_{23}}{p_{32} + p_{23}} e^{-pt} - \frac{N_2^0 p_{23} - N_3^0 p_{32}}{p_{32} + p_{23}} e^{-(p_{32}+p_{23})t},$$
$$N_2(t) = \frac{N_2^0 p_{32} + N_3^0 p_{32}}{p_{32} + p_{23}} e^{-pt} - \frac{N_3^0 p_{32} - N_2^0 p_{23}}{p_{32} + p_{23}} e^{-(p_{32}+p_{23})t}, \tag{18.54}$$

where

$$p = \frac{p_{21}p_{32} + p_{31}p_{23}}{p_{32} + p_{23}}. \tag{18.55}$$

If, at the time $t = 0$, a Boltzmann distribution of populations has already been established in levels 2 and 3,

$$\frac{N_3^{\,0}}{N_2^{\,0}} = \frac{p_{23}}{p_{32}} = e^{-\Delta E_{32}/kT}, \tag{18.56}$$

and (18.55) become

$$\begin{aligned} N_3(t) &= N_3^{\,0} e^{-pt} = N_2^{\,0} \frac{p_{23}}{p_{32}} e^{-pt}, \\ N_2(t) &= N_2^{\,0} e^{-pt}. \end{aligned} \tag{18.57}$$

The common value of the decay time can now be written

$$p = \frac{1}{\tau_F} = \frac{1}{\tau_2}\left(\frac{e^{\Delta E_{32}/kT}}{1 + e^{\Delta E_{32}/kT}}\right) + \frac{1}{\tau_3}\left(\frac{1}{1 + e^{\Delta E_{32}/kT}}\right), \tag{18.58}$$

where $\tau_2 = p_{21}^{\,-1}$ and $\tau_3 = p_{31}^{\,-1}$.

We now examine a different situation, the case in which the radiationless processes between levels 2 and 3 are rather ineffective. In this case

$$p_{23} \approx 0, \tag{18.59}$$

and the equations (18.41) reduce to the equations (18.34), with the solutions

$$\begin{aligned} N_3(t) &= N_3^{\,0} e^{-(p_{32}+p_{31})t}, \\ N_2(t) &= \left(N_2^{\,0} + \frac{p_{32}N_3^{\,0}}{p_{32} + p_{31} - p_{21}}\right) e^{-p_{21}t} - \frac{p_{32}N_3^{\,0}}{p_{32} + p_{31} - p_{21}} e^{-(p_{32}+p_{31})t}. \end{aligned} \tag{18.60}$$

If, further,

$$p_{32} \approx 0, \tag{18.61}$$

we obtain

$$\begin{aligned} N_3(t) &= N_3^{\,0} e^{-p_{31}t}, \\ N_2(t) &= N_2^{\,0} e^{-p_{21}t}. \end{aligned} \tag{18.62}$$

We can now make the following observations:

1. The decay curves of fluorescent lines originating from the same metastable level have the same time-dependence. Fluorescent lines with the same decay curves, however, do not necessarily originate from the same metastable level.

2. If a fluorescent system has two metastable states that are completely disconnected, each line decays with the characteristic time of the level from which it originates [see (18.62)].

3. Consider a fluorescent system that has two metastable states with the higher of the two (level 3) connected by a decay probability p_{32} to the lower level 2. Lines originating from these states have different time decays. A line from level 3 has a pure exponential decay with a decay time $(p_{32} + p_{31})^{-1}$, where p_{31} is the probability connecting level 3 to the ground level. A line from level 2 decays with a time-dependence consisting of the superposition of two exponentials, one with the time constant $(p_{32} + p_{31})^{-1}$ and the other with the time constant p_{21}^{-1} [see (18.60)].

4. If two lines originate from two thermalized metastable levels, they decay with the same time constant that depends [through (18.58)] on the intrinsic decay probabilities of the two levels, the energy separation between the two levels, and the temperature. Also, the statistical weights of the two levels may affect the common value of the decay time.

5. If two fluorescence lines have the same decay, this means either that they originate from the same metastable level or from two levels in thermal equilibrium. A third possibility exists that the two lines originate from two different and nonthermalized levels which accidentally have the same lifetime.

6. If two lines decay with different time-dependence, they originate from different levels which, moreover, are not thermalized.

4. INTERACTIONS OF MAGNETIC IONS AND THEIR EFFECTS ON THE FLUORESCENCE OUTPUT

Enhancement or quenching of the fluorescent output of a crystal containing a certain magnetic ion is often observed when another type of ion is added to the crystal.

If this second ion presents a relevant absorption in a region in which the pumping source is emitting strongly and the energy absorbed by it is transferred by some mechanism to the fluorescent ion, an enhancement of the fluorescence may result.

The opposite effect may take place if, given a certain fluorescent ion, another ion is added to the crystal with no relevant absorption band but with one level coupled to the metastable level of the fluorescent ion. If the additional ion is not fluorescent or is fluorescing with a low efficiency, a reduction of the fluorescence output will result.

4.1 The Different Types of Energy Transfer between Magnetic Ions

Two basic mechanisms may produce energy transfer between two ions:

1. The mechanism by which an energy transfer between an ion S and an ion A takes place may be the *cascade* type, namely by emission of photons by the ion S and reabsorption of photons by the ion A. In this case the ion S must be, by itself, a good emitter of fluorescence in a region in which the ion

A absorbs strongly. In this case the lifetime of the fluorescence of the ion S is not affected by the presence of the ion A and the emission of fluorescence by S shows a decrease only in correspondence to those wavelengths at which A absorbs.

2. Another possible energy transfer mechanism may be the *resonant* type, which produces what is known as *sensitized fluorescence*, wherein the additional doping that provides the enhancement of the absorption features of the compound is called the *sensitizer* and the fluorescent ion is called the *activator*. The sensitizer may not present strong fluorescence, and the activator may not present strong absorption in the fluorescence region of the sensitizer. In the present case the lifetime of the sensitizer, if measurable, is found to decrease in the presence of the activator; correspondingly, *all* the fluorescence emission of the sensitizer originating in the state participating in the energy exchange is quenched in the presence of the activator.

The fluorescence decay of the activator may also be affected by the presence of energy transfer. If a level of the sensitizer is pumping into the fluorescent level of the activator, the populations of the two levels may decay according to (18.35), where N_3 and N_2 indicate the populations of the interacting levels of the sensitizer and of the activator, respectively.

Double doping, when the combination of fluorescent ion and absorption enhancing doping is properly chosen, has been found to increase the efficiency of the fluorescence of a material. Even more efficient coupling may result from triple doping.

4.2 The Basic Mechanisms for Nonradiative Energy Transfer

Nonradiative energy transfer has been examined thoroughly by Dexter [1–4]. In this section we shall refer to his work, reporting only its basic points. The occurrence of a nonradiative energy transfer may be studied by considering a system that consists of ion S (sensitizer) and ion A (activator). This system, if any possible interaction between S and A is disregarded, may be represented by the product of the wavefunction of S and the wavefunction of A.

In particular, two states of the system are of interest:

1. State I with ion S in an excited state $\varphi_S{}^e$ and ion A in the ground state $\varphi_A{}^o$;
2. State F with ion S in the ground state $\varphi_S{}^o$ and ion A in the excited state $\varphi_A{}^e$.

Energy transfer consists of a transition between state I and state F of the S-A system. These two states, if only two electrons are involved in this transition, are given by

$$\psi_I = \frac{1}{\sqrt{2}} [\varphi_S{}^e(\mathbf{r}_1)\, \varphi_A{}^o(\mathbf{r}_2) - \varphi_S{}^e(\mathbf{r}_2)\, \varphi_A{}^o(\mathbf{r}_1)],$$

$$\psi_F = \frac{1}{\sqrt{2}} [\psi_S{}^o(\mathbf{r}_1)\, \varphi_A{}^e(\mathbf{r}_2) - \varphi_S{}^o(\mathbf{r}_2)\, \varphi_A{}^e(\mathbf{r}_1)]. \tag{18.63}$$

An interaction between S and A, such as that due to the Coulomb forces acting between the electrons of the two ions, may be present;

$$H_1 = \frac{1}{2} \sum_i \sum_j \frac{e^2}{|\mathbf{r}_i - \mathbf{r}_j|}, \tag{18.64}$$

where i ranges over the electrons of one ion and j over the electrons of the other. This interaction (18.64), also called *Van der Waals' interaction*, gives rise to Van der Waals' forces in molecular complexes.

The probability per unit time that energy transfer will occur is given by

$$P_{SA} = \frac{2\pi}{\hbar} \left| \int \psi_F^* H_1 \psi_I \, d\tau \right|^2 \rho(E = E_f). \tag{18.65}$$

The Hamiltonian (18.64) may be expanded in a Taylor series about the vector $\mathbf{R}$, which indicates the separation between the nuclei of S and A. This expansion gives rise to the following:

1. A leading term, called electric dipole-dipole interaction, proportional to R^{-3}.
2. A second term, called electric dipole-quadrupole interaction proportional to R^{-4}.
3. A third term, called electric quadrupole-quadrupole interaction proportional to R^{-5} and other terms of negligible importance.
4. An exchange interaction due to the presence in (18.65) of an integral of the type

$$\int [\varphi_A{}^e(\mathbf{r}_1)\, \varphi_S{}^o(\mathbf{r}_2)]^* H_1 [\varphi_A{}^o(\mathbf{r}_2)\, \varphi_S{}^e(\mathbf{r}_1)]\, d\mathbf{r}_1\, d\mathbf{r}_2. \tag{18.66}$$

Here electron 1 is in the sensitizer before the transfer occurs and ends up in the activator; conversely, electron 2 is in the activator before transfer and ends up in the sensitizer.

5. An electric dipole-magnetic dipole interaction, due to the presence of a magnetic field at the ion A, caused by the motion of the electrons of S.

The transfer of energy from S to A is an additional decay path available to an S ion in an excited state. If the presence of the activator does not introduce structural changes in the crystal, the fluorescent lifetime of the sensitizer, in the presence of the activator, is given by

$$\frac{1}{\tau_F} = P_{SA} + \frac{1}{\tau_S}, \tag{18.67}$$

where τ_S is the intrinsic lifetime of the sensitizer. The rate of the energy transfer can then be found experimentally:

$$P_{SA} = \frac{1}{\tau_F} - \frac{1}{\tau_S}. \tag{18.68}$$

The efficiency of the transfer process can be expressed as follows:

$$\eta_T = \frac{P_{SA}}{1/\tau_S + P_{SA}} = 1 - \frac{\tau_F}{\tau_S}. \tag{18.69}$$

The transfer efficiency that is actually measured is an average over space of η_T, weighted by the probability that the nearest activator is in a spherical shell $(v, v + dv)$. This probability is given by

$$w(v)\, dv = Ne^{-Nv}\, dv, \tag{18.70}$$

where N is the density of activator ions and

$$v = \frac{4}{3}\pi R^3. \tag{18.71}$$

The average transfer efficiency is given by

$$\bar{\eta}_T = \int_0^\infty \frac{Ne^{-Nv} P_{SA}}{1/\tau_S + P_{SA}}\, dv. \tag{18.72}$$

We shall find expressions for $\bar{\eta}_T$ corresponding to the various transfer mechanisms. Let us now examine these mechanisms.

Electric Dipole-Electric Dipole Transfer. Disregarding the exchange interactions, which are considered later, the probability for energy transfer is given by

$$P_{SA} = \frac{2\pi}{\hbar^2} \left|\langle S^e A^o| H_1 |S^o A^e\rangle\right|^2 \int f_S(\omega) F_A(\omega)\, d\omega, \tag{18.73}$$

where $f_S(\omega)$ and $F_A(\omega)$ are the normalized line shapes of the relevant transitions, respectively, in the sensitizer and in the activator.

Considering just the interaction between two electrons, one in S and the other in A, the first term in the multipole expansion of the Coulombic interaction gives

$$\frac{e^2}{\epsilon R^3}\left\{\mathbf{r}_S\cdot\mathbf{r}_A - \frac{3(\mathbf{r}_S\cdot\mathbf{R})(\mathbf{r}_A\cdot\mathbf{R})}{R^2}\right\}, \tag{18.74}$$

where ϵ is the dielectric constant of the medium. This is, in effect the interaction energy between two dipoles $e\mathbf{r}_S$ and $e\mathbf{r}_A$, separated by $\mathbf{R}$. If the squared matrix element of (18.65) between initial and final states is averaged over all possible orientations of $\mathbf{R}$, the probability of energy transfer will be proportional to the squares of the following matrix elements:

$$\begin{aligned}\langle\mathbf{r}_S\rangle &= \int \varphi_S{}^e(\mathbf{r}_S)^*\mathbf{r}_S\,\varphi^o(\mathbf{r}_S)\,d\mathbf{r}_S = \langle S^e|\,\mathbf{r}_S\,|S^o\rangle;\\ \langle\mathbf{r}_A\rangle &= \int \varphi_A{}^o(\mathbf{r}_A)^*\mathbf{r}_A\,\varphi_A{}^e(\mathbf{r}_A)\,d\mathbf{r}_A = \langle A^o|\,\mathbf{r}_A\,|A^e\rangle\end{aligned} \tag{18.75}$$

This implies that the present mechanism can be active only if the states S^e and S^o of the sensitizer are connected by an electric dipole transition and if the states A^o and A^e of the activator are similarly connected.

The matrix elements in (18.75) can be related to measurable quantities in S and A, since they determine oscillator strength, absorption cross sections and radiative decay times in these ions. In particular, the matrix element for the sensitizer S can be evaluated from a knowledge of the spontaneous emission probability $A_{21}{}^S$, as expressed in (17.7). In the absence of relevant radiationless or vibronic processes $A_{21}{}^S$ is the inverse of the fluorescence lifetime. The matrix element for the activator can be expressed in terms of the integrated absorption cross section, as in (17.44). The probability for dipole-dipole transfer is then found to be [2]:

$$P_{SA}(dd) = \left(\frac{3\hbar^4c^4}{4\pi}\right)\left(\frac{1}{\tau_S}\right)Q_A\left(\frac{1}{R_{SA}}\right)^6\frac{1}{\epsilon^2}\int\frac{f_S(E)\,F_A(E)}{E^4}\,dE, \tag{18.76}$$

where

$$\begin{aligned}R_{SA} &= \text{sensitizer activator distance},\\ \tau_S &= (A_{21}{}^S)^{-1},\\ Q_A &= \int\sigma_A(E)\,dE.\end{aligned}$$

The matrix element for the sensitizer can, alternatively, be derived from absorption data rather than from the data on fluorescence; we note, however, that an exact result is obtained only when the Stokes shift of the sensitizer is negligible. Using absorption data for the sensitizer, the above formula, because of (17.44), becomes

$$P_{SA}(dd) = \frac{3\hbar c^2}{4\pi^3}(Q_SQ_A)\left(\frac{1}{R_{SA}}\right)^6\frac{1}{\epsilon}\frac{g_S}{g_S'}\int\frac{f_S(E)\,F_A(E)}{E^2}dE, \tag{18.77}$$

where

$$Q_S = \int \sigma_S(E)\, dE,$$

g_S = statistical weight of the sensitizer's ground state,

g'_S = statistical weight of the sensitizer's excited state.

This expression, taking into account (17.46) and using $E_{\text{eff}} \approx E_c$, can be written as follows:

$$P_{SA}(dd) = \frac{1}{\epsilon^2}\left(\frac{3c}{8\pi^2}\right)\left(\frac{e^2}{mc^2}\right)^2 \frac{f_{21}{}^S f_{12}{}^A}{(\tilde{\nu})^2 (R_{SA})^6} \int F_A(\tilde{\nu}) f_S(\tilde{\nu})\, d\tilde{\nu}, \tag{18.78}$$

where $f_{21}{}^S$ and $f_{12}{}^A$ are now the oscillator strengths for the relevant electric dipole transitions of the sensitizer and activator, respectively, and where $\tilde{\nu} = E/hc$.

The average transfer efficiency, defined in (18.72), can now be calculated,

$$\begin{aligned} \bar{\eta}_T &= \int_0^\infty N e^{-Nv} \frac{P_{SA}\tau_S}{1 + P_{SA}\tau_S}\, dv \\ &= \int_0^\infty \frac{N e^{-Nv}}{1 + \dfrac{v^2}{\gamma^2}}\, dv = \int_0^\infty \frac{y e^{-yt}}{1 + t^2}\, dt, \end{aligned} \tag{18.79}$$

where we have put

$$\begin{aligned} P_{SA}\tau_S &= \frac{\gamma^2}{v^2}, \\ v &= \gamma t, \\ N\gamma &= y. \end{aligned} \tag{18.80}$$

The quantity y may be called *reduced density of activator ions.*

These considerations are valid for a relatively low concentration of sensitizer ions; for high concentrations an energy transfer from sensitizer to sensitizer may take place. In this case the number of the sensitized activator sites is greater than the one estimated on the basis of *S*-*A* transfer alone and the rate of the transfer process becomes dependent on the sensitizer concentration.

The *S*-*S* transfer is particularly important when the sensitizer ion is part of the host lattice (consider as an example the sensitization of Nd^{3+} fluorescence by the Ce^{3+} ions in a CeF_3 crystal). Because of the high concentration of sensitizer ions, the lattice may present a high absorption coefficient even if the corresponding transition is not of electric dipole type.

Example

Let us now consider energy transfer between an ion S and an ion A under the following conditions:

$$E = 5\text{eV} = 40{,}000 \text{ cm}^{-1}$$

$$\int f_s(E)\, f_A(E)\, dE = 0.33 \text{ eV}^{-1},$$

$$\begin{aligned} n^4 &= \epsilon^2 = 6, \\ Q_A &= 10^{-16} \text{ cm}^2 \text{ eV}, \\ \tau_s &= 10^{-8} \text{ sec}, \\ C^+ &= 2.25 \times 10^{22} \text{ cm}^{-3} = \text{density of possible activator sites.} \end{aligned}$$

By using (18.76) we find

$$P_{SA}\tau_s = \left(\frac{27}{R}\right)^6 = \frac{\gamma^2}{v^2},$$

where R is expressed in angstroms. The transfer of energy can occur if the transfer rate is comparable to τ_S^{-1}, namely, if the activator ion is about 27 Å from the sensitizer ion.

The volume around a sensitizer that contains all the activator sites for which $P_{SA}\tau_s > 1$ is given by γ. Now

$$\gamma = \tfrac{4}{3}\pi R^3 = \tfrac{4}{3}\pi(27 \times 10^{-8})^3 = 8.3 \times 10^{-20} \text{cm}^3.$$

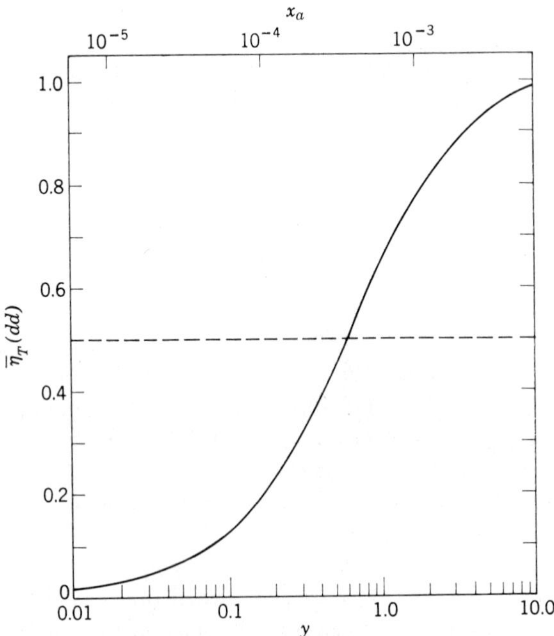

Fig. 18.5. Average transfer efficiency for dipole–dipole transfer as a function of the reduced concentration of the activator. x_a represents the values of the activator concentrations for the typical case discussed in the text (reproduced from [2] by permission of Professor Dexter).

The number of sites that can be sensitized under these conditions is given by

$$\gamma C^+ = 8.3 \times 10^{-20} \times 2.25 \times 10^{22} \approx 1870.$$

The curve in Fig. 18.5 gives us the transfer efficiency, a measurable quantity, as a function of the reduced density of activators. From this curve we can find the concentration needed in order to achieve a certain efficiency, say 50%. For $\bar{\eta}_T = 0.5$ we need $y = 0.65$ and a concentration of activators

$$\frac{N}{C^+} = \frac{y}{\gamma C^+} = \frac{0.65}{1870} = 3.5 \times 10^{-4}.$$

Electric Dipole-Electric Quadrupole Transfer. Let us now consider the case in which the relevant transitions in the sensitizer and in the activator are electric dipole and electric quadrupole, respectively. The absorption coefficient in the activator is so low that we have to use data on fluorescence in order to evaluate the relevant matrix element for the activator. Dexter [2] shows that the probability of energy transfer is given by

$$P_{SA}(dq) = \frac{135\pi\alpha\hbar^9 c^8}{4n^6 R^8 \tau_S \tau_A} \frac{g_A'}{g_A} \int \frac{f_S(E)\, F_A(E)}{E^8}\, dE, \tag{18.81}$$

where $\alpha = 1.266$. If absorption data are used for S, taking into account (17.44), the above relation becomes

$$P_{SA}(dq) = \frac{135\alpha\hbar^6 c^6}{4\pi n^4 R^8} \frac{Q_S}{\tau_A} \frac{g_A' g_S}{g_A g_S'} \int \frac{f_S(E)\, F_A(E)}{E^6}\, dE. \tag{18.82}$$

If we now consider the ratio of the probability P_{SA} of the present dq case to the probability P_{SA} of the dd case, we find, considering (18.81) and (18.76),

$$\frac{P_{SA}(dq)}{P_{SA}(dd)} = \frac{45\pi^2\alpha\hbar^5 c^4}{n^2 R^2 \tau_A(q) Q_A} \frac{g_A'}{g_A} \frac{1}{E^4} = \frac{45\alpha}{4\pi^2}\left(\frac{n\lambda}{R}\right)^2 \frac{\tau_A(d)}{\tau_A(q)}, \tag{18.83}$$

where we have again used the formula (17.44) and where $\tau_A(d)$ and $\tau_A(q)$ are the lifetimes of the activator when the relevant transitions are electric dipole and electric quadrupole, respectively.

Let us now examine the value of this ratio in some examples. In Section 7 of Chapter 14 we found that for a free atom the ratio of an electric quadrupole transition probability to an electric dipole transition probability is of the order $(a/\lambda)^2$, where a is the atomic radius; in this case the ratio $\tau_A(d)/\tau_A(q)$ is of the same order of magnitude and

$$\frac{P_{SA}(dq)}{P_{SA}(dd)} \approx \left(\frac{a}{R}\right)^2. \tag{18.84}$$

Therefore in these conditions the transfer probability in the dipole–quadrupole case is only about one order of magnitude smaller than the probability in the dipole–dipole case.

The situation is different for ions in crystals in which electric dipole transitions are often allowed by odd perturbations of the centrosymmetric environments of the ions. A typical case is that of ruby; the electric dipole transition corresponding to the R lines has an f number 3×10^{-7}. For the possible electric quadrupole transitions Tanabe and Sugano [5] estimate an f number of the order of 10^{-10}. Since the ratio of the f numbers is the inverse of the ratio of the lifetimes we have in this case

$$\frac{\tau_A(d)}{\tau_A(q)} = \frac{10^{-10}}{3 \times 10^{-7}} \simeq 3 \times 10^{-4}, \tag{18.85}$$

which is much larger than the 10^{-7} value of the free atom case and implies a larger range for the sensitizer-activator interaction in the dq case than predicted by (18.84).

We note that the expression (18.83) can also be written: [6]

$$\frac{P_{SA}(dq)}{P_{SA}(dd)} \approx \frac{1}{R^2\tilde{\nu}^2} \frac{f_A(q)}{f_A(d)}, \tag{18.86}$$

where $f_A(q)$ and $f_A(d)$ are the f number for a quadrupole and for a dipole transition in the activator, respectively.

The average transfer efficiency, defined in (18.72), can be calculated as follows:

$$\begin{aligned} \bar{\eta}_T &= \int_0^\infty Ne^{-Nv} \frac{P_{SA}\tau_S}{1 + P_{SA}\tau_S}\, dv \\ &= \int_0^\infty \frac{Ne^{-Nv}}{1 + v^{8/3}/\gamma^{8/3}}\, dv = \int_0^\infty \frac{ye^{-yt}}{1 + t^{8/3}}\, dy, \end{aligned} \tag{18.87}$$

where we have put

$$\begin{aligned} P_{SA}\tau_S &= \left(\frac{\gamma}{v}\right)^{8/3}, \\ v &= \gamma t, \\ N\gamma &= y; \end{aligned} \tag{18.88}$$

y is the reduced density of activator ions.

Example

Let us now consider energy transfer between an ion S and an ion A under the following conditions:

$$\begin{aligned} &E = 5 \text{ eV} = 40{,}000 \text{ cm}^{-1}, \\ &n^6 = 13, \\ &\tau_A = \tau_s = 0.1 \text{ sec}, \\ &\frac{g_A'}{g_A} = 5, \\ &\int f_s(E)\, F_A(E)\, dE = 0.33 \text{ eV}^{-1}, \\ &C^+ = 2.25 \times 10^{22} \text{ cm}^{-3}. \end{aligned}$$

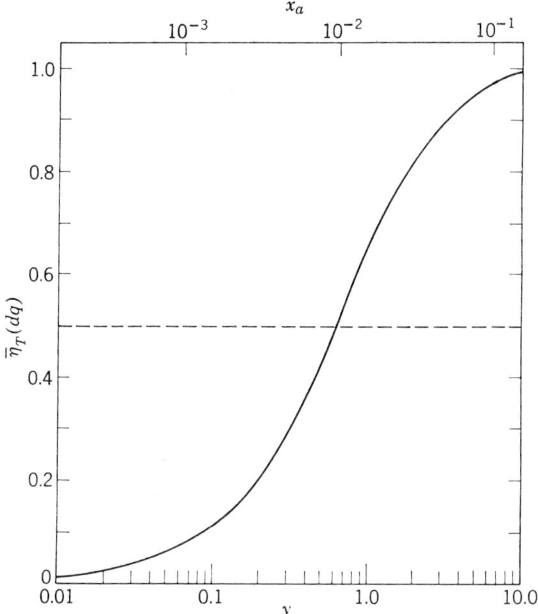

Fig. 18.6. Average transfer efficiency for dipole-quadrupole transfer as a function of the reduced concentration of the activator. x_a represents the values of the activator concentrations for the typical case discussed in the text (reproduced from [2] by permission of Professor Dexter).

We find, using (18.81),

$$P_{SA}\tau_S = \frac{\gamma^{8/3}}{v^{8/3}} = \left(\frac{3 \times 10^{-21}}{v}\right)^{8/3}.$$

Energy transfer occurs if the activator is within the volume v given by

$$\gamma = v = 3 \times 10^{-21}\,\text{cm}^3.$$

The number of sites that can be sensitized is given by

$$\gamma C^+ = 3 \times 10^{-21} \times 2.25 \times 10^{22} \approx 70.$$

The concentration needed for a $\bar{\eta}_T = 0.5$ can be derived from Fig. 18.6, which gives $y = 0.65$ and an activator concentration of

$$\frac{N}{C^+} = \frac{y}{\gamma C^+} = \frac{0.65}{70} \approx 10^{-2}.$$

Electric Quadrupole-Electric Quadrupole Transfer. In the case that the relevant transitions in the sensitizer and in the activator are both electric quadrupole in nature it may be shown that the probability for energy transfer is given by

$$P_{SA}(qq) \approx \frac{P_{SA}(dd)}{\tilde{\nu}^4 R^4} \frac{f_S(q) f_A(q)}{f_S(d) f_A(d)}. \qquad (18.89)$$

By putting estimated values for the dipole and quadrupole oscillator strengths in the expression for $P_{SA}(qq)$, Axe and Weller [6] found for this probability a value greater than that of $P_{SA}(dd)$. This fact implies that "... although quadrupole *radiative* transitions cannot favorably compete with dipolar processes, they can completely dominate nonradiative transfer in certain systems."

The average transfer efficiency is found to be given by

$$\bar{\eta}_T = \int_0^\infty Ne^{-Nv} \frac{P_{SA}\tau_S}{1 + P_{SA}\tau_S}\, dv = \int_0^\infty \frac{ye^{-yt}}{1 + t^{10/3}}, \tag{18.90}$$

where

$$\begin{aligned} P_{SA}\tau_S &= \left(\frac{\gamma}{v}\right)^{10/3}, \\ v &= \gamma t, \\ N\gamma &= y. \end{aligned} \tag{18.91}$$

Exchange Energy Transfer and Electric Dipole Magnetic Dipole Transfer. If the energy transfer is the exchange type, the relevant matrix element is given by the integral (18.66), which gives essentially the Coulombic interaction between the charge distributions $\varphi_A{}^e(\mathbf{r}_1)\, \varphi_S{}^e(\mathbf{r}_1)$ and $\varphi_S{}^o(\mathbf{r}_2)\, \varphi_A{}^o(\mathbf{r}_2)$. These charge distributions and the integral vanish if the wavefunctions of the sensitizer and of the activator do not overlap. If overlap occurs, since the wavefunctions generally decrease exponentially with the distance from the nuclei, the transfer probability varies exponentially with the *S-A* separation. Therefore the exchange process may take place only when the sensitizer-activator separation is quite small.

Another possible energy transfer process is that due to the presence of an electric dipole transition in the sensitizer and a magnetic dipole transition in the activator. Dexter [2] estimated that this type of energy transfer process is in general negligible, even in comparison to the exchange type process.

4.3 Phonon Assisted Energy Transfer [7]

The probability for energy transfer between two ions is proportional to the overlap integral

$$\int f_S(\omega) F_A(\omega)\, d\omega, \tag{18.92}$$

where $f_S(\omega)$ and $F_A(\omega)$ are the shape functions for the sensitizer and the activator, respectively. If we consider the case of two Lorentzian lines of width $\Delta\omega_S$ and $\Delta\omega_A$, centered at $\omega_S{}^e$ and $\omega_A{}^e$, respectively, we find

$$\int f_S(\omega)\, F_A(\omega)\, d\omega = \frac{1}{\pi} \frac{\Delta\omega}{(\Delta\omega)^2 + (\omega_S{}^e - \omega_A{}^e)^2}, \tag{18.93}$$

where $\Delta\omega = \Delta\omega_S + \Delta\omega_A$. For sharp and well-separated lines the value of the integral and the probability for energy transfer become negligible. At low temperatures, where the lines tend generally to be Gaussian, the value of the integral may be even smaller.

In these circumstances the energy transfer may be favored by the emission or absorption of a phonon whose energy compensates for the energy mismatch between the two transitions and ensures the conservation of energy in the transfer process.

Orbach has recently examined such process [7]. The relevant matrix element for the energy transfer process accompanied by the production of a phonon is given by

$$\frac{\langle S^e A^o| H_{OL} |S^e A^o; \hbar\omega_p\rangle \langle S^e A^o; \hbar\omega_p| H_1 |S^o A^e; \hbar\omega_p\rangle}{-\hbar\omega_p} + \frac{\langle S^e A^o| H_1 |S^o A^e\rangle \langle S^o A^e| H_{OL} |S^o A^e; \hbar\omega_p\rangle}{\hbar\omega_S{}^e - \hbar\omega_A{}^e}, \quad (18.94)$$

where H_1 is given by (18.64) and H_{OL} is the ion-vibration interaction Hamiltonian given by (15.9)

$$H_{OL} = iV_1 \sum_q \left(\frac{\hbar\omega_q}{2Mv^2}\right)^{1/2} (b_q - b_q^+). \quad (18.95)$$

The matrix element (18.94) then reduces to

$$-i\left(\frac{\hbar\omega_p}{2Mv^2}\right)^{1/2} \langle S^e A^o| H_1 |S^o A^e\rangle \left\{\frac{\langle S^e| V_1(S) |S^e\rangle + \langle A^o| V_1(A) |A^o\rangle}{-\hbar\omega_p} + \frac{\langle S^o| V_1(S) |S^o\rangle + \langle A^e| V_1(A) |A^e|}{\hbar(\omega_S{}^e - \omega_A{}^e)}\right\}(n_p + 1). \quad (18.96)$$

The density of final states is given by

$$\begin{aligned}\rho(E_f = E_i) &= \rho(E_f)\,\delta(E_f - E_i)\,dE_f = \frac{1}{\hbar}\,\delta(\omega_S{}^e - \omega_A{}^e - \omega_p)\,g(\omega_p)\,d\omega_p \\ &= \frac{1}{\hbar}\,\delta(\omega_S{}^e - \omega_A{}^e - \omega_p)\frac{3V}{2\pi^2 v^3}\,\omega_p{}^2\,d\omega_p. \end{aligned} \quad (18.97)$$

The transition probability for phonon assisted energy transfer is then given by

$$\begin{aligned} P_{SA} &= \frac{2\pi}{\hbar^2}\left|\langle S^e A^o| H_1 |S^o A^e\rangle\right|^2 \\ &\times \left\{\left|[\langle S^e| V_1 |S^e\rangle - \langle S^o| V_1 |S^o\rangle] - [\langle A^e| V_1 |A^e\rangle - \langle A^o| V_1 |A^o\rangle]\right|^2 \right. \\ &\left. \times \frac{3\omega_p}{4\pi^2\hbar\rho v^5}\begin{pmatrix} n_p + 1 \\ n_p \end{pmatrix}\right\}, \end{aligned} \quad (18.98)$$

where the factor $n_p + 1$ relates to the emission and the factor n_p to the absorption of a phonon. The expression in curly brackets is the equivalent, in the present case, of the overlap integral (18.92). We note the following:

1. The phonon assisted energy transfer process depends on the difference of the matrix elements of the ion-vibration interaction between the ground and the excited state of the sensitizer and of the activator.
2. It depends also on the difference between the matrix elements of S and of A.
3. If the energy of the sensitizer's excited state is greater than the energy of the activator's excited state, the probability for energy transfer takes place only in the direction $S \rightarrow A$ at low temperatures when there are no phonons available for absorption. In such a case the transfer probability is proportional to the energy of the emitted phonon.
4. If the probability for transfer in both $S \rightarrow A$ and $A \rightarrow S$ directions is much greater than the intrinsic decay probabilities of the sensitizer and of the activator, the phonon-assisted energy transfer mechanism can establish a Boltzmann distribution of populations in the excited states of S and A [8].

4.4 Radiative Transfer

When the transfer process is radiative, photons emitted by S are reabsorbed by A. The probability that a photon emitted by S leaves the crystal without being reabsorbed is given by [2],

$$Av \int f_S(E) e^{-C^+ x_A l \sigma_A(E)} \, dE, \tag{18.99}$$

where C^+ is the density of available activator sites, x_A is the concentration of the activator ions, and the average is performed over the dimension l. The efficiency of the process is then given by

$$\eta_T = 1 - Av \int f_S(E) e^{-C^+ x_A l \sigma_A(E)} \, dE. \tag{18.100}$$

Here we have neglected any type of S-S transfer.

The main difference between radiative and nonradiative energy transfer consists in the fact that the former depends on the size and shape of the crystal and also on the details of the overlap of the emission of the sensitizer S with the absorption of the activator. We can illustrate the second difference with an example [2]. Let us consider for simplicity $f_S(E)$ and $\sigma_A(E)$ as two rectangular functions and let us examine the following two cases:

1. $f_S(E)$ and $\sigma_A(E)$ have equal widths and overlap by $\frac{1}{3}$.
2. $\sigma_A(E)$ is three times wider than $f_S(E)$ and overlaps completely $f_S(E)$.

In both cases the integral $\int f_S(E) F_A(E) dE$ has the same value, and therefore the probability for radiationless transfer is the same. The two cases are, instead, different for radiative transfer: in the second case the complete overlap of the fluorescence band of the sensitizer by the absorption band of the activator ensures that all the radiation emitted by the sensitizer may be absorbed, whereas in the first case only one third of the emitted energy would be absorbed in the best hypothesis.

One important type of radiative coupling occurs between ions of the same type, where the energy emitted by one ion is *self absorbed* by a similar ion before it gets out of the crystal. The lines that have the best chance of being reabsorbed are those that end in the ground state, which, in general, has the largest population. (This may not be the case in a crystal under strong optical excitation. In this regard we note that no reabsorption effect occurs when the population of the excited state from which the radiation originates has the same value of the population of the ground state because the crystal is then transparent to that radiation.)

Varsanyi, Wood, and Schawlow [9] observed the selective reabsorption of the fluorescence lines of ruby split by the application of a magnetic field. They found that the relative intensities of the fluorescence lines were close to those predicted by the theory for ruby with very low concentration of Cr^{3+} ions. For ruby containing 0.05% Cr_2O_3 they observed great differences between theoretical and experimental data, with the line ending in the lowest level of the ground state manifold reduced in intensity by the greatest amount. They also found another important effect of reabsorption, the lengthening of the lifetime of the ruby metastable state. At 77°K the lifetime was found to vary from 4.3 msec for ruby powder to 15 msec for a whole boule of this material.

In general, we expect greater reabsorption effects at low temperatures at which the lines become sharper and more intense both in fluorescence and in absorption.

4.5 Self- and Cross-Quenching of Fluorescence

The presence of an additional impurity in a fluorescent system may produce the quenching of the crystals output of fluorescence. In this case the additional impurity is called a *poison* or *killer*. The transfer of energy from the fluorescent ion to the killer may take place by any of the processes already examined. Since the killer ion is not fluorescing but rather degrades its energy by radiationless processes, the net effect is a quenching of the fluorescence.

Another important effect found generally in fluorescent systems is the so-called *self-quenching* of the fluorescence. The output of fluorescence grows linearly with the ion concentration up to a certain value and then starts decreasing. Several arguments, reviewed in [3], have been brought up to explain this phenomenon.

According to one hypothesis, the quenching takes place at the site of the excited center because the nearness of other activator ions increases the probability for radiationless processes. Contrary to this, Dexter and Schulman [4] assume that the excitation energy transfers rapidly from activator to activator until it finds an *energy sink* such as an impurity or a vacancy; transfer and quenching then occur. This mechanism presupposes that the probability of radiationless processes is independent of the activator concentration and therefore is restricted to activator concentrations of less than a few percent.

5. THE FACTORS AFFECTING THE FLUORESCENCE EMISSION

The fluorescence emission of magnetic ionic systems in crystals depends on a number of factors that we shall now examine.

5.1 Absorption Bands

A broad absorption band with a strong oscillator strength is relevant to the fluorescence emission.

It has been observed experimentally that the peaks of the absorption bands of transition metal ions tend to shift as the temperature of the crystal changes and also to broaden when the temperature of the crystal is raised. Also, in addition to position and width change, changes in the integrated area of the absorption bands may take place. These effects have been examined in Chapter 17; we limit ourselves here to noting that for a certain spectral distribution of the exciting energy all these effects may have relevance with regard to the fluorescence output of a crystal.

5.2 Quantum Efficiency and Fluorescence Lifetime

The fluorescent emission of a three-level fluorescent system under continuous excitation is given by (18.15). We now define the *quantum yield of the fluorescence* by the following quantity:

$$Y = \frac{n_f}{n_a}, \tag{18.101}$$

where n_f = number of light quanta emitted per unit time in the no phonon line,

n_a = number of light quanta absorbed per unit time.

From (18.15) n_f can be written

$$n_f = \int I_f \, d\nu_f = N_0(I_a\sigma_a)\tau_F \int w_{21}(\nu_f) \, d\nu_f, \tag{18.102}$$

where the integrals are made over the purely radiative line. In the (18.102) the temperature dependence of the absorption cross section has been considered negligible; the following results are valid in this hypothesis.

We can rewrite (18.102) in the following way:

$$n_f = n_a \frac{\tau_F}{\tau_0}, \tag{18.103}$$

where

$$\tau_0^{-1} = \int w_{21}(\nu_f)\, d\nu_f = \text{radiative lifetime of the fluorescent state,}$$

$$n_a = N_0(I_a\sigma) \qquad = \text{number of photons absorbed in the unit time.}$$

From (18.101) and (18.103) we get

$$Y = \frac{n_f}{n_a} = \frac{\tau_F}{\tau_0}. \tag{18.104}$$

The quantum yield of the fluorescence is then proportional to the fluorescence lifetime.

The fluorescence lifetime is, in general, shorter than the radiative lifetime τ_0 because of the presence of decay processes other than the main radiative one for the fluorescent state. This may be expressed as follows:

$$\frac{1}{\tau_F} = \frac{1}{\tau_0} + \frac{1}{\tau_S}, \tag{18.105}$$

which indicates that the total decay probability τ_F^{-1} is equal to the sum of the purely radiative decay probability and of the probability of the competing processes τ_S^{-1}.

The radiative lifetime of a state may be determined by absorption measurements. The relation between radiative lifetime and absorption coefficients is given by the fundamental formula of absorption spectroscopy (17.39).

If the fluorescent level is connected by radiative processes to other levels besides the ground level, the intensities of the fluorescent lines are in the following relations:

$$I_1:I_2:I_3:\cdots = A_1\nu_1:A_2\nu_2:A_3\nu_3:\cdots. \tag{18.106}$$

Then, knowing the A coefficient corresponding to the transition connecting the ground state with the metastable state from absorption measurements and the ratios of the fluorescence intensities, we may calculate all the A coefficients. We can then put these values in

$$\frac{1}{\tau_0} = \sum_i A_i \tag{18.107}$$

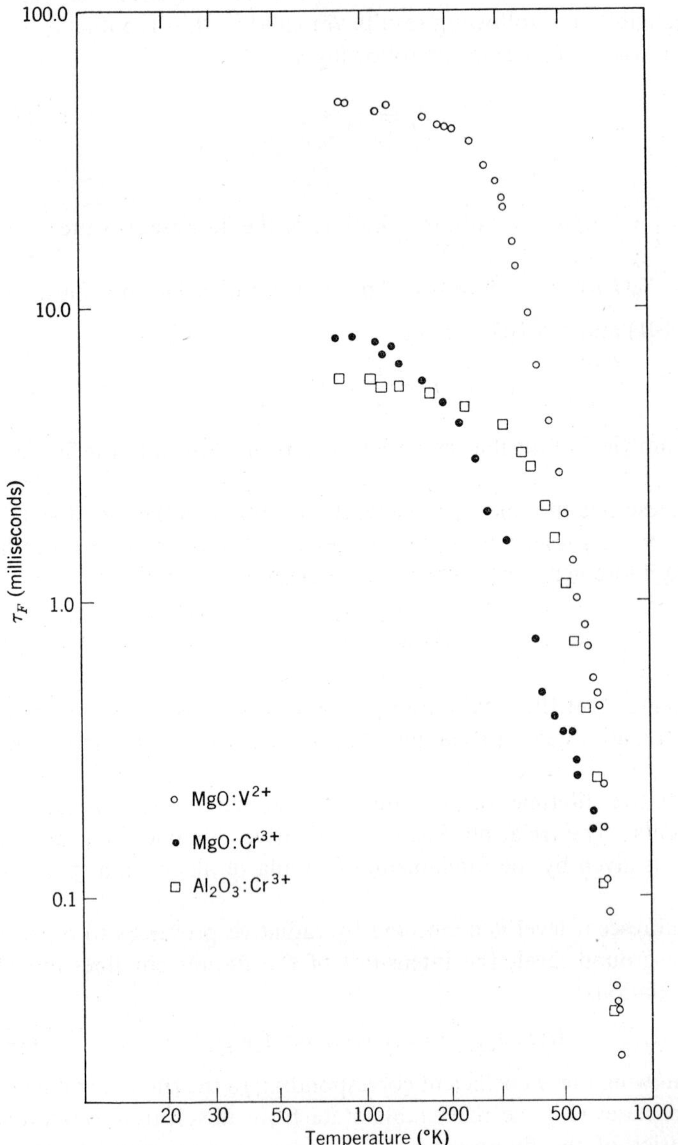

Fig. 18.7. Fluorescence lifetimes of $MgO:V^{2+}$, $MgO:Cr^{3+}$ and $Al_2O_3:Cr^{3+}$.

and get the radiative lifetime. The fluorescence lifetime may be measured by means of pulse fluorescence, exciting the fluorescent level and then switching off the exciting radiation and observing the fluorescence decay.

Once we know the radiative lifetime, we can derive from the measured value of the fluorescence lifetime the values of the secondary lifetime τ_S by using (18.105).

The decay processes competing with the purely radiative emission consist of phonon-assisted (vibronic) emission and of radiationless transitions. There is considerable evidence that when the energy gap covered by the fluorescence transition is much larger than the energy of the most energetic (Debye) phonons, the vibronic processes are mainly responsible for the thermal shortening of the lifetime [10], [11].

In Fig. 18.7 we report the temperature-dependence of the lifetimes of the fluorescence of some characteristic materials.

5.3 Fluorescence Lines

Many sharp lines are found in the absorption spectra of transition metal ions; some of these lines are also observed in fluorescence.

The sharp lines of transition metal ions present the following features:

1. The lines shift toward longer wavelengths as the temperature increases.
2. The lines broaden as the temperature increases.
3. The linewidths tend to become temperature-independent at very low temperature.
4. The line position changes even in the region in which the linewidth is constant.

In Fig. 18.8 the temperature-dependence of the position of the R line of $MgO:V^{2+}$ is reported as typical example; Fig. 18.9 shows the change of the width of the same line with temperature.

The thermal vibrations of the lattice are the cause of the thermal broadening of the lines, which appear homogeneously broadened (with Lorentzian lineshape). However, a temperature-independent, inhomogeneous contribution to the lines becomes evident at low temperatures, at which the thermal vibrations are quenched and the lines tend toward a Gaussian shape. The inhomogeneous contribution is due to microscopic strains in the crystal, which, being randomly spaced, produce a Gaussian line.

The mechanism by which the line is thermally broadened has been found to be, for several transition metal ions, the Raman scattering of phonons by the same ions [10–13]. Multiphonon or vibronic relaxation processes do not give any relevant contributions to the linewidths.

The situation is different in the rare earths, in which the crystal field produces splitting of the J levels that are smaller than kT_D (T_D = Debye

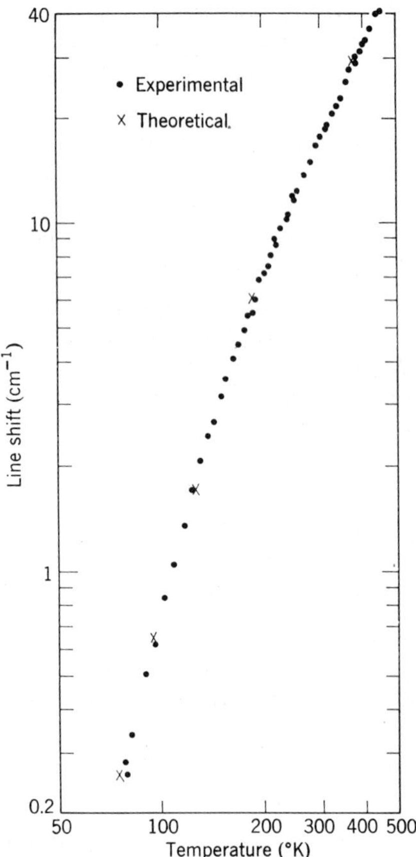

Fig. 18.8. Thermal shift of the MgO:V^{2+} R line. The theoretical points were set by using (15.144) with $\alpha = -400$ cm^{-1} and $T_D = 760$°K.

temperature). Here phonon relaxation processes from each level to lower or upper close levels are possible; they may produce a shortening of the lifetime of a certain level and give a homogeneous *lifetime broadening* contribution to a line originating or terminating on that level.

A different mechanism is responsible for the shift in the position of the lines with temperature. Here the change in position is in general due to the emission and reabsorption of virtual phonons. The interaction of the ionic system with the zero phonon field may produce an observable isotope shift [14].

Thermal effects on the $^2E \rightarrow {}^4A_2$ line of ions with a d^3 configuration in different environments (Cr^{3+} in Al_2O_3 [12], Cr^{3+} in MgO [10, 11, 13] and

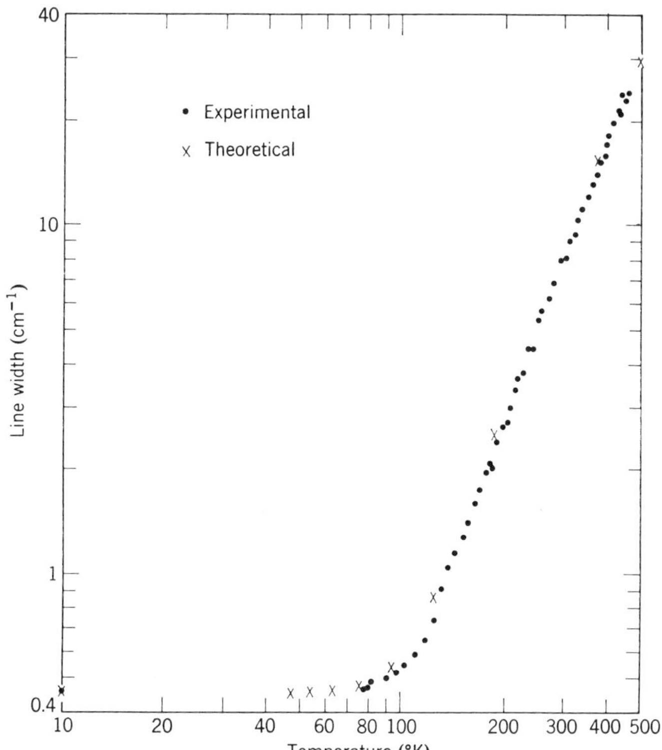

Fig. 18.9. Thermal broadening of the MgO:V^{2+} *R* line. The theoretical points were set by using (15.135) with $\beta_{ij} = 0$, $\bar{\alpha} = 377.5\ \text{cm}^{-1}$ and $T_D = 760°\text{K}$. The linewidth below ~77°K is due to strain broadening.

V^{2+} in MgO [10, 11, 13]), have been studied. The *R* line of chromium in MgO presents the same qualitative behavior as the *R* lines in ruby. The line shifts toward longer wavelengths as the temperature increases and becomes broader. The shift and width of the *R* line of Cr^{3+} in MgO are somewhat greater than the shift and width of the *R* lines in ruby. For ruby at 200°K we have for the R_1 line a shift of 6.8 cm^{-1} and a width of ~3.3 cm^{-1} and for Cr^{3+} in MgO, a shift of 9 cm^{-1} and a width of ~6 cm^{-1}.

The shift of the *R* line of V^{2+} in MgO is equal to the shift of the *R* lines of Cr^{3+} in Al_2O_3, but the linewidth is somewhat narrower: at 200°K this line presents a shift of 6.8 cm^{-1} and a width of ~2.6 cm^{-1}.

It has to be noted that the *strain linewidth* may be different for different samples of the same material.

The behavior of the sharp lines in rare earths has been studied by Yen,

Scott, and Schawlow [15] who examined trivalent praseodymium in LaF_3. The lines present the following features:

1. Most of the lines shift to the red, as the transition metal lines. For one line, however, a shift to the blue was noticed.
2. The shifts of the lines are smaller than the shift of the *R* line of a d^3 ion by $\gtrsim \frac{1}{2}$.
3. The line broadening due to Raman scattering of phonons is $\sim\frac{1}{5}$ the line broadening in transition metal ions. Relaxation processes are now relevant and give contribution to the width. The total linewidth is 1.5 to 10 times the linewidth in d^3 ions.

Recently Powell and co-workers [16] found evidence of the effects of direct phonon relaxation in the ground-state manifold on the linewidths of the so-called N_1 and N_2 lines of heavily doped ($\sim$1% Cr_2O_3) ruby. These lines (N_1 at $\sim$7041 Å and N_2 at 7009 Å) are caused by the presence of paired Cr^{3+} ions in the crystal; they originate from two different metastable states and end at two levels about 30 cm^{-1} above the ground state [16].

5.4 Vibronic Transitions [10, 11, 13, 15]

The vibronic bands that accompany the sharp fluorescence emission of magnetic ions are due to phonon-assisted transitions that involve the emission

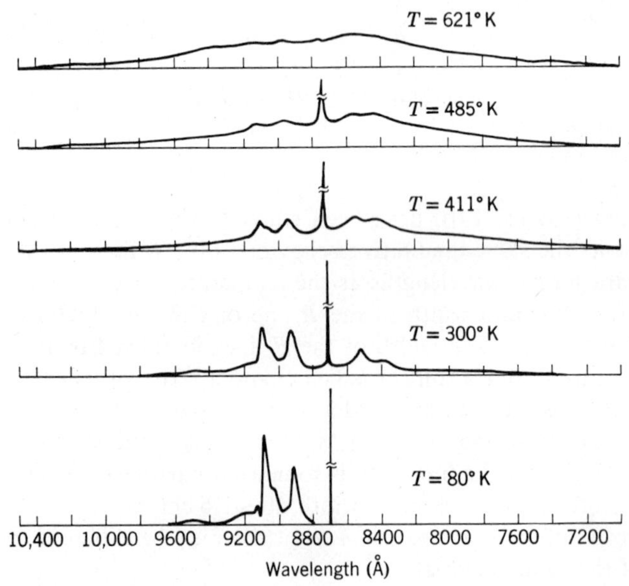

Fig. 18.10. Fluorescence spectrum of $MgO:V^{2+}$ at various temperatures showing the *R* line and the vibrational satellites.

of a phonon and the creation or annihilation of one or more phonons. Because thermal vibrations are involved, the intensities of the vibronic transitions appearing on both sides of a purely radiative (no-phonon) line are temperature-dependent.

A typical vibronic spectrum ($MgO:V^{2+}$) is reported in Fig. 18.10.

The over-all features of a vibronic spectrum are the following:

1. Certain characteristic frequencies appear.
2. As the temperature goes down, the high-energy vibronic band diminishes until it cannot be detected; simultaneously the peaks become increasingly sharp and shift with the no-phonon line.
3. With increasing temperature the continuum of the spectrum expands more and more to wavelengths farther removed from that of the no-phonon line and grows in intensity, whereas the peaks tend to smooth out and disappear.

An indication of the vibronic character of the bands accompanying a sharp line of fluorescence is given by the close fitting of the fluorescence lifetime of the bands and the lifetime of the no-phonon line.

Another indication of the vibronic character of the bands is due to the fact that the shift of the peaks of the vibronic bands is equal to the shift of the no-phonon line.

One would expect the disappearance of the high energy band because of the emission of a photon accompanied by the absorption of phonons, for at low temperatures no phonons are available to be absorbed. On the other hand, the low energy band will still exist at low temperatures, for spontaneous emission of phonons can take place even in the absence of phonons.

A correlation of the lattice frequencies derived from the vibronic spectrum and the frequencies derived from infrared, Raman, and neutron scattering data is, in principle, possible.

5.5 Energy Transfer

Energy transfer can take place when two different magnetic ions, either both rare earths or rare earth and transition metal ions, are present in a crystal. This transfer may enhance or quench the output of a fluorescent system.

Energy transfer may also affect the shape of a fluorescence line [17].

5.6 Ion Environment [18]

The strength of the bonding of the ion to the environment is expected to perturb the ion orbitals. Different environments may produce different perturbing influence and thus bear on the number of fluorescent states.

5.7 Excited State Absorption

The pumping light, used to bring the ground-state ions into the absorption bands, may produce upward transitions from the fluorescent level to higher levels. The ions in the metastable level, which are so excited, are lost to the fluorescent output if they decay directly to the ground state. Figure 18.11 shows a comparison of the excited-state absorption and ground-state absorption of ruby. The data are taken from Kushida's work [19]. It is found that the averages of the ground-state absorption (GSA) and excited-state absorption (ESA) cross sections between 15,000 and 32,500 cm^{-1} are nearly equal. In the spectral regions in which GSA and ESA overlap, ESA robs power from the pumping light that might otherwise be used to increase the metastable population; in other spectral regions in which ESA is large and GSA is small, the excited-state absorption results in additional heating of the crystal due to the radiationless decays of the ions excited from the metastable level to the upper levels. The present experimental evidence [20], however, is that excited-state absorption in ruby, when using optical pumping, does not limit the population of the ^2E state in the sense that the excited ions decay back to the metastable level and participate to the emission of fluorescence. The pumping light has a different effect on the metastable level

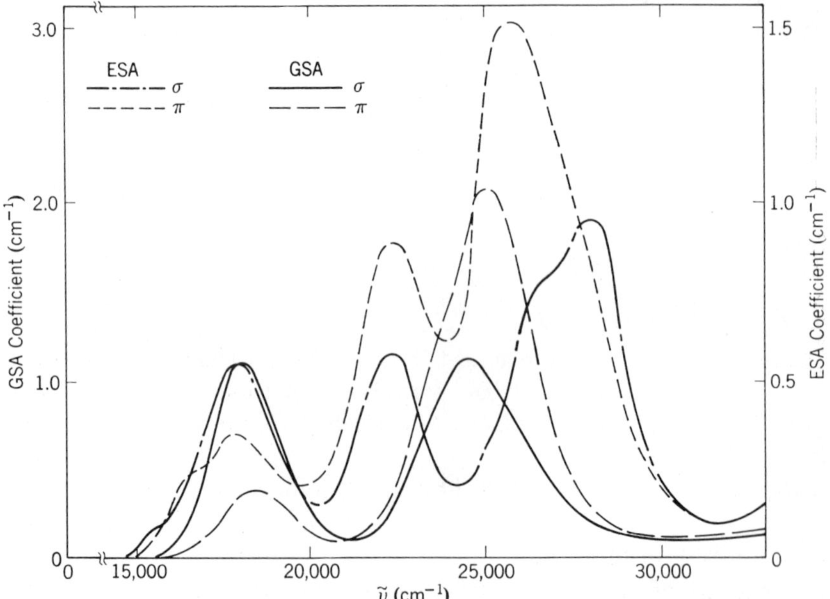

Fig. 18.11. Excited state and ground state absorptions in ruby (0.02%Cr) (adapted from [19] by permission of Dr. T. Kushida).

population when it contains radiation in the far ultraviolet. Green, Emmett, and Schawlow [21] have demonstrated that the removal of the far UV from the pumping radiation does significantly (by 30 to 40 percent) increase the efficiency of a ruby laser.

6. FLUORESCENCE OF MAGNETIC IONS IN CRYSTALS

The rare-earth ions may enter a crystal as part of a pure compound or as impurities. The pure salts of rare earths which occur in the middle of the $4f^n$ group, present strong fluorescence; among them Gd^{3+}, Tb^{3+}, and Eu^{3+} fluoresce more strongly than Dy^{3+} and Sm^{3+}. The other rare earths do not show appreciable fluorescence. Such is the case for hydrated chlorides and sulfates; the f numbers of the individual transitions are of the order of magnitude 10^{-6} and the radiative lifetimes are then of the order of 10^{-2} sec. This is actually the order of magnitude of the fluorescence lifetime found for Gd^{3+} at low temperatures. For all the rare earths other than Gd the fluorescence lifetime is shorter than 10^{-2} sec; it is reduced by 20 for Tb, 90 for Eu, and 1000 for Dy and Sm. The fluorescence of Gd^{3+} has been recognized as the brightest, the fluorescence of Tb^{3+} and Eu^{3+} as weaker, and the fluorescence of Dy^{3+} and Sm^{3+} still weaker and just sufficient [22] to allow an evaluation of the order of magnitude of the lifetime. Eu^{3+} presents two fluorescent levels, $^5D_0$ and $^5D_1$, with lifetimes in the ratio 3 to 1; the fact that radiationless processes cannot deplete the $^5D_1$ level, which is above the $^5D_0$ by only 1740 cm^{-1}, is caused by the lack of a strong ion-lattice coupling.

The rare earths may activate a luminescent solid as impurities; when they act as such, the elements near the beginning and the end of the $4f^n$ group also show fluorescence. In several cases, however, the symmetry of the crystal around the ion is not well known, and the nature of the fluorescent spectra is not easily recognizable.

A set of experiments due to Carlson and Dieke [23] has revealed the presence of strong fluorescence in anhydrous chlorides of rare earths. The crystals examined were crystals of $LaCl_3$ with concentrations of 2 percent and 0.2 percent of various rare earths; in a strict sense they were not pure crystals but mixed compounds. Strong and sharp fluorescence lines were observed for the chlorides of Pr, Nd, Sm, Eu, Gd, Tb, Dy, Er, and Tm.

In the Dieke [24] diagram (Fig. 18.12) for trivalent rare earths in anhydrous chlorides the fluorescent states are indicated. The nonfluorescent states often decay by radiationless processes. The number of fluorescent states depends on the type of salt or host lattice and also on the concentration of the ion.

Trivalent rare-earth systems are rather inefficient fluorescent materials because of the weakness of the absorption bands available for excitation.

More efficient systems may be given by divalent rare earths, such as Sm^{2+},

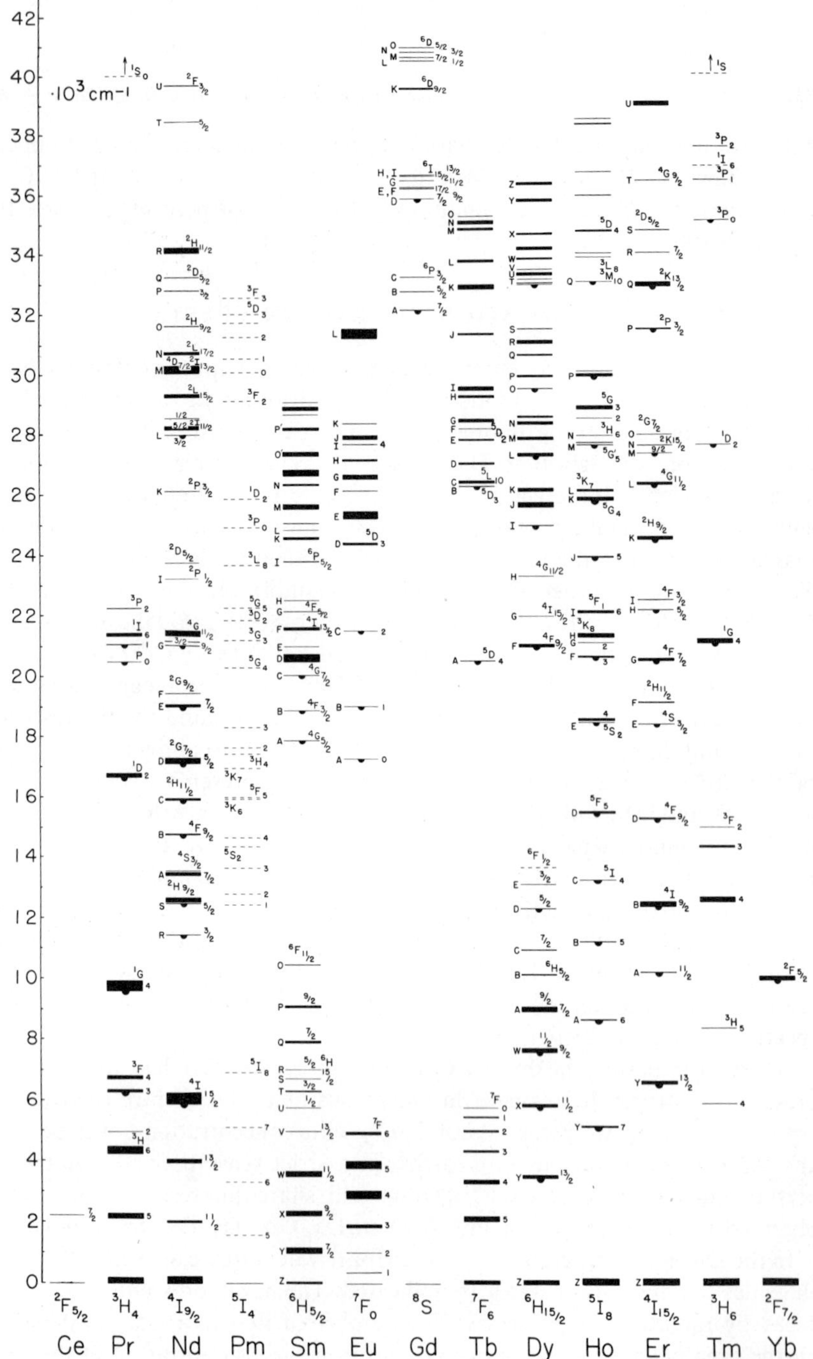

Fig. 18.12. Energy levels of trivalent rare earth ions. The width of the levels indicates the total splitting due to the crystalline field in anhydrous trichlorides. A pendant circle indicates a fluorescent state (reproduced from [24] by courtesy of Professor H. M. Crosswhite).

Eu^{2+} and Yb^{2+}, where broad and intense absorption bands are available. These bands, corresponding to $4f^{n-1}5d$ levels, may be connected to the $4f^n$ fluorescent levels by radiationless decay, determined by odd parity vibrations.

The most investigated fluorescence among transition metal ions is the fluorescence of Cr^{3+} in Al_2O_3, which occurs from the state ^2E to the ground state. Both ground state $^4A_2$ and fluorescent state ^2E belong to the crystal configuration t_2^3; their splitting is due to the electrostatic interaction and therefore is independent of the fluctuations of the crystal field. For this reason the modes of vibration cannot effectively broaden the fluorescent line and quench the fluorescence: the fluorescence lifetime of the ^2E level is in the same order of magnitude of the radiative lifetime at low temperatures. On the other hand, the big absorption bands corresponding to levels $^4T_1$ and $^4T_2$ belong to a different crystal configuration t_2^2e. The energy gaps between them and the ground level are due mainly to the crystal field and therefore they are subject to the action of crystal vibrations: this may be the reason for the broadening of these levels and for the quick radiationless processes that connect them to the fluorescent level ^2E. In general we expect fluorescence from the lowest (resonant) level, which has the same $t_2^{N-n}e^n$ configuration of the ground state. By using this criterion we may expect to find the following fluorescence transitions in transition metal ions:

Ion	Configuration	Spin Configuration	Transition
d^2	t_2^2		$^1E, {}^1T_2 \rightarrow {}^3T_1$
d^3	t_2^3		$^2E, {}^2T_1 \rightarrow {}^4A_2$
d^4	t_2^4	Low spin	$^1E, {}^1T_2 \rightarrow {}^3T_1$
d^8	$t_2^6\, e^2$		$^1E \rightarrow {}^3A_2$

d^3 ions like Cr^{3+} and V^{2+} fluoresce in different host lattices, such as Al_2O_3 and MgO. In general an Al_2O_3 crystal produces a slightly distorted octahedral environment that splits the $^2E \rightarrow {}^4A_2$ fluorescent line, whereas an MgO crystal has a relevant number of ions in a perfect cubic environment and correspondingly an unsplit fluorescent line; f numbers in the order of 10^{-8}–10^{-9} correspond to these lines, whereas the broad absorption bands have f numbers in the order 10^{-4}–10^{-3}.

Another interesting group of fluorescent ions is given by the actinides ions which in the ground state are expected to have a $5f^n$ configuration. A coupling of these ions with the lattice stronger than the ion-lattice coupling of rare earths is also expected for the likely larger radius of the $5f$ orbital with respect to the $4f$ orbital. This would allow strong absorption bands and efficient pumping. A large number of sharp lines in the visible have been reported similar to the rare-earth ion lines [25]; fluorescence has also been seen in

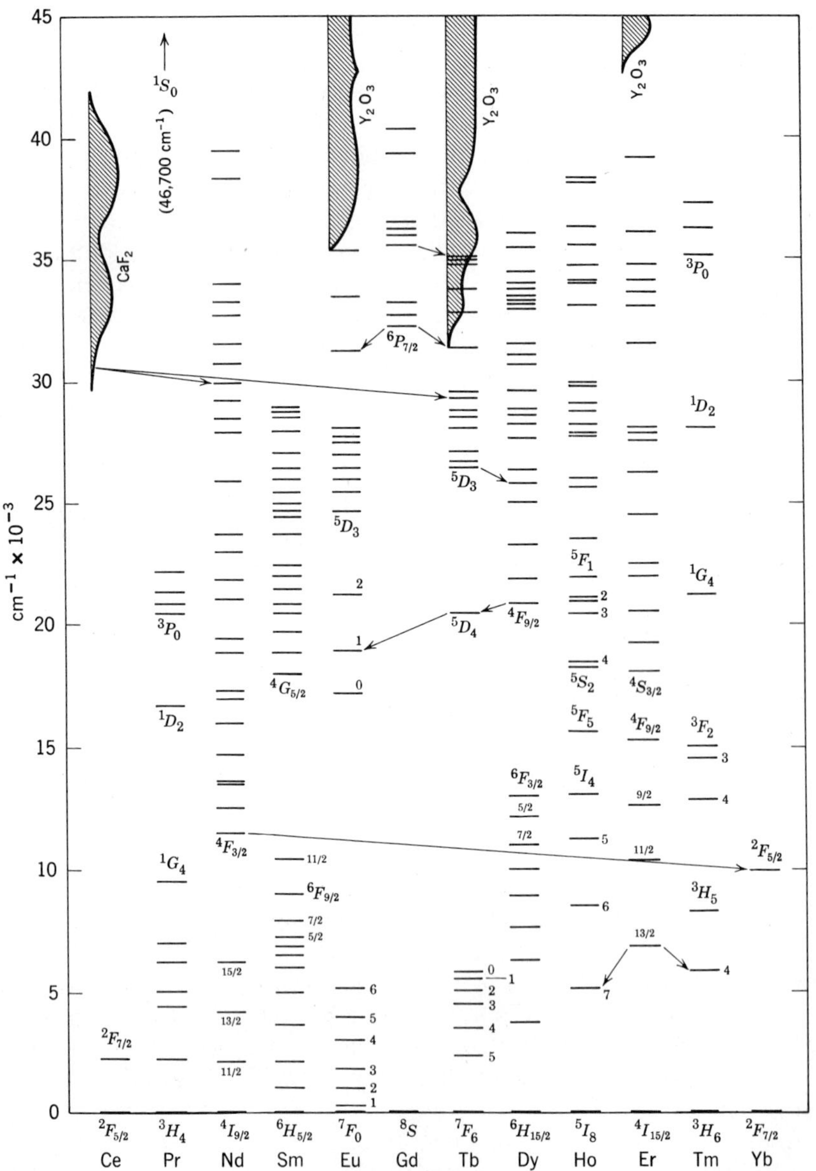

Fig. 18.13. The energy level systems of the trivalent rare earths with arrows indicating energy transfer processes resulting in sensitized fluorescence. Certain band absorption regions are indicated, together with the environment in which they were observed (reproduced from [32] by courtesy of Dr. L. G. Van Uitert and permission of the publisher).

Am^{3+} [26], Pu^{3+} [27], U^{3+}, Np^{3+}, and Cm^{3+} [28] in $LaCl_3$, Np^{3+} in $LaBr_3$ [29], and U^{3+} in CaF_2, SrF_2, and BaF_2 [30, 31].

Many combinations of magnetic ions in crystals present the phenomenon of energy transfer. In Fig. 18.13 we report the energy level diagram of the trivalent rare earths with arrows indicating known energy-transfer processes that result in sensitized emission. This figure is taken from an article by Van Uitert [32]. Also, Refs. [33] to [58] give several examples of systems found in the literature, which exhibit a fluorescence enhancement due to energy transfer.

REFERENCES

[1] D. Curie, *Luminescence in Crystals*, Methuen, London, 1963.

[2] D. L. Dexter, "A Theory of Sensitized Luminescence in Solids," *J. Chem. Phys.* **21,** 836 (1953).

[3] C. C. Klick and J. H Schulman, "Luminescence in Solids," in *Solid State Physics*, Vol. 5, F. Seitz and D. Turnbull (Eds.), Academic, New York, 1951, p. 119.

[4] D. L. Dexter and J. H. Schulman, "Theory of Concentration Quenching in Inorganic Phosphors," *J. Chem. Phys.* **22,** 1063 (1954).

[5] Y. Tanabe and S. Sugano, "On the Absorption Spectra of Complex Ions II," *J. Phys. Soc. Japan*, **9,** 766 (1954).

[6] J. D. Axe and P. F. Weller, "Fluorescence and Energy Transfer in Y_2O_3:Eu^{3+}," *J. Chem. Phys.* **40,** 3066 (1964).

[7] R. Orbach, "Phonon Sidebands and Energy Transfer," in *Optical Properties of Ions in Crystals*, H. M. Crosswhite and H. W. Moos (Eds.), Interscience, New York, 1967, p. 445.

[8] R. C. Powell, B. Di Bartolo, B. Birang, and C. S. Naiman, "Interactions of Single Ions and Pair Systems in Ruby," in *Optical Properties of Ions in Crystals*, H. M. Crosswhite and H. W. Moos (Eds.), Interscience, New York 1967, p. 207.

[9] F. Varsanyi, D. L. Wood, and A. L. Schawlow, "Self-Absorption and Trapping of Sharp Line Resonance Radiation in Ruby," *Phys. Rev. Letters* **3,** 544 (1959).

[10] B. Di Bartolo, "Fluorescence of Transition Metal Ions in Crystals," Laboratory for Insulation Research (MIT), Technical Report 190, June 1964, unpublished.

[11] B. Di Bartolo and R. Peccei, "Thermal Effects on the Fluorescence Lifetime and Spectrum of MgO:V^{2+}," *Phys. Rev.* **137,** A1770 (1965).

[12] D. E. McCumber and M. D. Sturge, "Linewidth and Temperature Shift of the R Lines in Ruby," *J. Appl. Phys.* **34,** 1682 (1963).

[13] G. F. Imbusch, W. M. Yen, A. L. Schawlow, D. E. McCumber, and M. D. Sturge, "Temperature Dependence of the Width and the Position of the $^2E \rightarrow {}^4A_2$ Fluorescence Lines of Cr^{3+} and V^{2+} in MgO," *Phys. Rev.* **133,** A1029 (1964).

[14] G. F. Imbusch, W. M. Yen, A. L. Schawlow, G. E. Devlin, and J. P. Remeika, "Isotope Shift in the R Lines of Chromium in Ruby and MgO," *Phys. Rev.* **136,** A481 (1964).

[15] W. M. Yen, W. C. Scott, and A. L. Schawlow, "Phonon-Induced Relaxation in Excited Optical States of Trivalent Praseodimium in LaF_3," *Phys. Rev.* **136,** A271 (1964).

[16] R. C. Powell, B. Di Bartolo, B. Birang, and C. S. Naiman, "Temperature Dependence of the Widths and Positions of the R and N lines in Heavily Doped Ruby," *J. Appl. Phys.*, **37,** 4973 (1966).

[17] W. M. Yen, R. L. Greene, W. C. Scott, and D. L. Huber, "Optical Linewidth and Line-Shape Studies of Energy Transfer Mechanisms Between Rare-Earth Impurity Ions," *Phys. Rev.* **140,** A1188 (1965).

[18] L. G. Van Uitert, "Factors Influencing the Luminescent Emission States of the Rare Earths," *J. Electrochem. Soc.* **107,** 803 (1960).

[19] T. Kushida, "Absorption and Emission Properties of Optically Pumped Ruby," *IEEE J. Quantum Electron.* **QE2,** 524 (1966).

[20] M. D. Galanin, V. N. Smorchkov, and Z. A. Chizhikova, "Luminescence and Absorption of Excited Ruby," *Opt. Spectr.* **19,** 168 (1965).

[21] R. L. Greene, J. L. Emmett, and A. L. Schawlow, "Effects of Ultraviolet Pumping on Ruby Laser Output," *Appl. Opt.* **5,** 350 (1966).

[22] G. H. Dieke and L. A. Hall, "Fluorescent Lifetimes of Rare Earth Salts and Ruby," *J. Chem. Phys.* **27,** 465 (1957).

[23] E. Carlson and G. H. Dieke, "Fluorescence Spectrum and Low Levels of $NdCl_3$," *J. Chem. Phys.* **29,** 229 (1958).

[24] H. M. Crosswhite and H. W. Moos (Eds.), *Optical Properties of Ions in Crystals* Interscience, New York (1967), p. vi.

[25] W. A. Runciman, "Absorption and Fluorescence Spectra of Ions in Crystals," *Repts. Progr. Phys.* **21,** 30 (1958).

[26] D. M. Gruen, J. G. Conway, R. C. McLaughlin, and B. B. Cunningham, "Fluorescence Spectrum of Am^{+3} in $LaCl_3$," *J. Chem. Phys.* **24,** 1115 (1956).

[27] B. B. Cunningham, D. M. Gruen, J. G. Conway, and R. D. McLaughlin, "Fluorescence Spectrum of Pu^{+3} in $LaCl_3$," *J. Chem. Phys.* **24,** 1275 (1956).

[28] J. G. Conway, J. C. Wallman, B. B. Cunningham, and G. V. Shalimoff, "Fluorescence Spectra of Uranium, Neptunium and Curium," *J. Chem. Phys.* **27,** 1416 (1957).

[29] W. F. Krupke and J. B. Gruber, "Energy Levels of Np^{3+} in $LaBr_3$," *J. Chem. Phys.* **46,** 542 (1967).

[30] L. N. Galkin and P. P. Feofilov, "The Luminescence of Trivalent Uranium," *Soviet Phys.—Doklady*, **2,** 255 (1957).

[31] P. P. Sorokin and M. J. Stevenson, "Stimulated Infrared Emission from Trivalent Uranium," *Phys. Rev. Letters* **5,** 557 (1960).

[32] L. G. Van Uitert, "Luminescence of Insulating Solids for Optical Masers," in *Luminescence of Inorganic Solids*, P. Goldberg (Ed.), Academic, New York, 1966, p. 465.

[33] R. Tomaschek, "Uber die Phosphoreszenzeigenschaften der Selten Erden in Erdalkaliphosphoren II," *Ann. Phys.* **75,** 561 (1924).

[34] P. J. Botden, "Transfer and Transport of Energy by Resonance Processes in Luminescent Solids," *Philips Res. Repts.* **7,** 197 (1952).

[35] Garrett and Kaiser, reported by L. G. Van Uitert in *Metallurgy of Advanced Electronic Materials*, Vol. 19, Interscience, New York, 1963.

[36] B. H. Soffer and R. H. Hoskins, "Energy Transfer and CW Laser Action in Tm^{+3}: Er_2O_3," *Appl. Phys. Letters* **6,** 200 (1965).

[37] J. R. O'Connor and W. A. Hargreaves, "Lattice Energy Transfer and Stimulated Emission from $CeF_3{:}Nd^{3+}$," *Appl. Phys. Letters* **4,** 208 (1964).

[38] G. E. Peterson and P. M. Bridenbaugh, "Application of Resonance Cooperation of Rare-Earth Ions Nd^{3+} and Yb^{3+} to Lasers ($Na_{0.5}RE_{0.5}WO_4$)," *Appl. Phys. Letters* **4,** 201 (1964).

[39] G. E. Peterson and P. M. Bridenbaugh, "Study of Relaxation Processes in Nd Using Pulsed Excitation," *J. Opt. Soc. Am.* **54,** 644 (1964).

[40] W. Heitmann, A. Moeller, and G. V. Schultz, "Fluorescence of $Nd(4f^3)$ by Irradiation

into the Chromium Absorption Bands of the System Al_2O_3:Cr, Nd," *Phys. Letters* **10,** 26 (1964).

[41] Z. J. Kiss and R. C. Duncan, "Cross-Pumped Cr^{3+}–Nd^{3+}:YAG Laser System," *Appl. Phys. Letters* **5,** 200 (1964).

[42] J. Murphy, R. C. Ohlman, and R. Mazelsky, "Energy Transfer from 3d to 4f Electrons in $LaAlO_3$:Cr, Nd," *Phys. Rev. Letters* **13,** 135 (1964).

[43] R. C. Ohlman and R. Mazelsky, "Energy Transfer from Cr^{3+} to Nd^{3+} in Solids," in *Physics of Quantum Electronics*, P. L. Kelley, B. Lax and P. E. Tannenwald (Eds.), McGraw-Hill, New York, 1966, p. 322.

[44] Z. J. Kiss, "Dynamics of Energy Transfer from 3d to 4f Electrons in $LaAlO_3$:Cr^{3+}, Nd^{3+}," *Phys. Rev. Letters* **13,** 654 (1964).

[45] L. F. Johnson, L. G. Van Uitert, J. J. Rubin, and R. A. Thomas, "Energy Transfer from Er^{3+} to Tm^{3+} and Ho^{3+} Ions in Crystals," *Phys. Rev.* **133,** A494 (1964).

[46] J. D. Kingsley, J. S. Prener, and M. Aven, "Energy Transfer from Copper and Silver to Rare-Earths in II–VI Compounds," *Phys. Rev. Letters* **14,** 136 (1965).

[47] L. F. Johnson, J. E. Geusic, and L. G. Van Uitert, "Coherent Oscillations from Tm^{3+}, Ho^{3+}, Yb^{3+} and Er^{3+} Ions in Yttrium Aluminum Garnet," *Appl. Phys. Letters* 127 (1965).

[48] L. F. Johnson, J. E. Geusic, and L. G. Van Uitert, "Efficient, High-Power Coherent Emission from Ho^{3+} Ions in Yttrium Aluminum Garnet, Assisted by Energy Transfer," *Appl. Phys. Letters* **8,** 200 (1966).

[49] Z. J. Kiss, "Energy Levels of Divalent Thulium in CaF_2," *Phys. Rev.* **127,** 718 (1962).

[50] G. E. Peterson and P. M. Bridenbaugh, "Some Studies of Relaxation Processes in Tb^{3+} Using Pulsed Excitation," *J. Opt. Soc. Am.* **53,** 1129 (1963).

[51] L. G. Van Uitert and R. R. Soden, "Enhancement of Eu^{3+} Emission by Tb^{3+}," *J. Chem. Phys.* **36,** 1289 (1962).

[52] L. G. Van Uitert, R. R. Soden, and R. C. Linares, "Enhancement of Rare-Earth Ion Fluorescence by Lattice Processes in Oxides," *J. Chem. Phys.* **36,** 1793 (1962).

[53] A. Bril and W. L. Wanmaker, "Some Properties of Europium Activated Phosphors," *J. Electrochem. Soc.* **111,** 1363 (1964).

[54] A. L. Schawlow, D. L. Wood, and A. M. Clogston "Electronic Spectra of Exchange-Coupled Ion Pairs in Crystals," *Phys. Rev. Letters* **3,** 271 (1959).

[55] G. F. Imbusch, "Energy Transfer in Ruby," *IEEE J. Quantum Electron.* **QE2,** 532 (1966); also "Energy Transfer in Ruby," *Phys. Rev.* **153,** 326 (1967).

[56] B. L. Danielson, "Saturation Effects in the Sensitized Fluorescence of CaF_2(Ce, Mn)," *Phys. Rev.* **142,** 228 (1966).

[57] R. J. Ginther, "Sensitized Luminescence of CaF_2:Ce, Mn," *J. Electrochem. Soc.* **101,** 248 (1954).

[58] R. Leach, "Energy Transfer and Sensitization in Single Crystal Phosphors," *J. Electrochem. Soc.* **105,** 27 (1958).

19

Elements of Laser Theory

1. THE BASIC CONDITIONS FOR LASER AMPLIFICATION

Consider an absorbing medium with two energy levels and a beam of light passing through it in an x direction. The component of the beam of frequency ν experiences an attenuation $e^{-k_\nu x}$. The absorption coefficient k_ν is given by[1]

$$k_\nu = \beta\left(n_1 - \frac{g_1}{g_2} n_2\right) g(\nu)$$

$$= \frac{h\nu}{v}(n_1 B_{12} - n_2 B_{21})\, g(\nu) \qquad [\text{cm}^{-1}], \tag{19.1}$$

where

$$\beta = \frac{\lambda^2}{8\pi\tau_0} \frac{g_2}{g_1}, \tag{19.2}$$

and λ = wavelength of the transition in the medium,
$g(\nu)$ = normalized line shape function,
g_1 = statistical weight of the ground state,
g_2 = statistical weight of the excited state,
$\tau_0 = A_{21}^{-1}$ = radiative lifetime of the excited state (sec),
n_1 = density of atoms in the ground state (cm^{-3}),
n_2 = density of atoms in the excited state (cm^{-3}),
$n_0 = n_1 + n_2$.

If the absorbed beam is the only cause for the excitation of atoms, for beams of low intensity we get

$$k_\nu^0 = \frac{\lambda^2}{8\pi\tau_0} \frac{g_2}{g_1} n_0\, g(\nu) = \beta n_0\, g(\nu). \tag{19.3}$$

[1] Formula 19.1 was already derived in Chapter 17, where it appears as (17.36).

If such conditions can be created in the medium that during the passage of the beam

$$\frac{n_2}{g_2} > \frac{n_1}{g_1}, \tag{19.4}$$

the absorption coefficient will become negative and the beam will experience an amplification. We shall not for the moment consider the means by which these conditions can be realized; rather, we shall examine their effects on the performance of the system.

The amplification process present in the medium when $n_2/g_2 > n_1/g_1$ is the basic feature of a *laser* system. The word *laser* is an acronym for the words *light amplification by stimulated emission of radiation.*

If (19.4) is valid, the beam is amplified by $e^{\alpha_\nu x}$, where $\alpha_\nu = -k_\nu$ and

$$\alpha_\nu = \beta\left(\frac{g_1}{g_2}\, n_2 - n_1\right) g(\nu) = \beta \frac{\Delta N}{V}\, g(\nu) = \beta n_0 n\, g(\nu) = n k_\nu^{\,0}. \tag{19.5}$$

Here

$$\Delta N = \left(\frac{g_1}{g_2}\, n_2 - n_1\right) V, \tag{19.6}$$

$$n = \frac{\Delta N}{V n_0} = \frac{\dfrac{g_1}{g_2}\, n_2 - n_1}{n_0}, \tag{19.7}$$

namely, the amplification coefficient is equal to the product of the *relative population inversion* n and the absorption coefficient of the unexcited material.

The maximum value of the amplification factor is given by

$$\alpha_m = \beta n_0 n g(\nu_0) = k_m^{\,0} n. \tag{19.8}$$

But

$$\frac{k_m^{\,0}}{n_0} = \sigma_0 = \text{maximum absorption cross section}; \tag{19.9}$$

therefore

$$\alpha_m = \sigma_0 n_0 n = \sigma_0 \frac{\Delta N}{V} = \sigma_0\left(\frac{g_1}{g_2}\, n_2 - n_1\right). \tag{19.10}$$

The gain over a length L may also be expressed in *decibels:*

$$G_{\text{db}} = 10 \log_{10} e^{\alpha_\nu L}. \tag{19.11}$$

The gain at the center frequency of the transition is given, in the case of a Lorentzian line, by

$$G_{\text{db}}(\nu_0) = 10 \log_{10}\left\{\exp\left[\frac{\lambda^2 L}{8\pi\tau_0}\left(n_2 - \frac{g_2}{g_1}\, n_1\right)\frac{2}{\pi\,\Delta\nu}\right]\right\}, \tag{19.12}$$

and in that of a Gaussian line by

$$G_{\text{db}}(\nu_0) = 10 \log_{10}\left\{\exp\left[\frac{\lambda^2 L}{8\pi\tau_0}\left(n_2 - \frac{g_2}{g_1} n_1\right)\frac{2}{\Delta\nu}\left(\frac{\ln 2}{\pi}\right)^{1/2}\right]\right\}. \quad (19.13)$$

The bandwidth of an optical amplifier, in the case of a Lorentzian line, is found to be,

$$B_L = \Delta\nu\left[\frac{3}{G_{\text{db}}(\nu_0) - 3}\right]^{1/2}, \quad (19.14)$$

and, in the case of Gaussian line,

$$B_G = \Delta\nu\left\{\frac{\log\left[G_{\text{db}}(\nu_0)/(G_{\text{db}}(\nu_0) - 3)\right]}{\log 2}\right\}^{1/2}. \quad (19.15)$$

2. NOISE CONSIDERATIONS IN A LASER AMPLIFIER

In order to consider noise in laser amplifiers we must first examine the relation between the Einstein A and B coefficients. These two coefficients are related by (14.42), which we may rewrite as follows:

$$A_{21} = B_{21} \times \frac{8\pi\nu^2}{v^3} \times h\nu$$

$$= B_{21} \times (\text{radiation modes per unit volume per unit frequency range}) \times (\text{photon energy}). \quad (19.16)$$

Therefore the probability of spontaneous emission is equal to the probability of induced emission if the number of incident photons per unit volume per unit frequency is equal to the number of radiation modes per unit volume per unit frequency range.

The probability per unit time of spontaneous emission in a single mode is equal to the probability per unit time of induced emission due to a single photon in the same mode.

Consider a beam of light going through a medium with a density of centers in the ground state n_1 and a density of centers in the excited state n_2. As the beam goes through a distance dx, the number of photons in a certain mode m increases by [1]

$$d\mathcal{N}_m = \int_S A_m(y, z)\, dy\, dz\left[\mathcal{N}_m\left(n_2 - n_1\frac{g_2}{g_1}\right) + n_2\right] g(\nu)\, dx; \quad (19.17)$$

where S is the cross section of the beam. We can rewrite this equation as follows:

$$\frac{d\mathcal{N}_m}{\mathcal{N}_m + N} = \int_S A_m\, dy\, dz\left(n_2 - n_1\frac{g_2}{g_1}\right) g(\nu)\, dx, \quad (19.18)$$

where

$$N = \frac{n_2}{n_2 - n_1 \dfrac{g_2}{g_1}}. \tag{19.19}$$

Equation 19.18 integrates to

$$\ln \frac{\mathcal{N}_m(L) + N}{\mathcal{N}_m(0) + N} = \int_S A_m \, dy \, dz \left(n_2 - n_1 \frac{g_2}{g_1}\right) g(\nu) L. \tag{19.20}$$

We can then write

$$\mathcal{N}_m(L) + N = \mathcal{N}_m(0)\, G_m + N G_m$$

or

$$\mathcal{N}_m(L) = \mathcal{N}_m(0) + N(G_m - 1), \tag{19.21}$$

where

$$G_m = \exp\left[\int A_m \, dy \, dz \left(n_2 - n_1 \frac{g_2}{g_1}\right) g(\nu) L\right]. \tag{19.22}$$

In (19.21) $\mathcal{N}_m(0)\, G_m$ represents the amplified signal and $N(G_m - 1)$ the amplified *noise* produced by the incoherent spontaneous emission. The equivalent noise at the input of the amplifier is given by

$$N\left(1 - \frac{1}{G_m}\right). \tag{19.23}$$

N is called the *noise number* of the laser amplifier.

The noise power output in the unit frequency range is given by

$$P_N = N(G_m - 1)\, h\nu. \tag{19.24}$$

We may note here that all the formulas derived above for the amplifier ($G_m > 1$) are also true for an absorbing medium ($N < 0$, $G_m < 1$).

An interesting concept, which is considered in amplifiers, is the so-called *noise temperature*. The noise temperature T_N can be interpreted by considering the actual amplifier replaced by a noiseless amplifier connected at the input to a black body at temperature T_N. In a laser amplifier this results in putting

$$N\left(1 - \frac{1}{G_m}\right) = \frac{1}{e^{h\nu/kT_N} - 1}, \tag{19.25}$$

which gives

$$T_N = \frac{h\nu}{k \ln \{[N(1 - 1/G_m)]^{-1} + 1]\}}. \tag{19.26}$$

For $G_m \gg 1$ and $N = 1$ this reduces to

$$T_N = \frac{h\nu}{k \ln 2}. \tag{19.27}$$

This noise temperature is the ultimate limitation of a laser amplifier as far as noise is concerned and it corresponds to an average of one photon per mode.

3. THE REGENERATIVE OPTICAL AMPLIFIER

An amplifier is made *regenerative* when means are provided of reporting back to the input the amplified signal.

In a laser system the regenerative coupling is provided by a pair of parallel reflecting mirrors which enclose the amplifying medium. The medium and the mirrors then constitute a Fabry–Perot interferometric cavity. The electromagnetic field inside the cavity can be approximated with plane waves that are reflected many times by the mirrors. In general, the transverse linear dimensions of the cavity are $\sim 10^4$ times the wavelength of the optical transition and the longitudinal dimension of the cavity is greater than the transverse dimension. A typical solid-state laser may consist of a cylindrical rod of material enclosed by two mirrors of radius $r = 0.5$ cm and a rod length $L = 5$ cm. For a wavelength of 10,000 Å the *Fresnel number*, defined as

$$F = \frac{r^2}{L\lambda_0}, \tag{19.28}$$

where λ_0 = wavelength in a vacuum, has a value of 500.

Fox and Li [2] have shown that transverse field distributions exist in a Fabry–Perot interferometer in the same way that modes exist in microwave cavities. The dominant mode is the TEM_{00} and it is also the mode with the lowest diffraction losses. Each transverse mode has an infinite number of resonances given by

$$\nu = n \frac{v_m}{2L}; \tag{19.29}$$

v_m, the phase velocity of mode m is given by

$$\frac{1}{v_m} = \frac{1}{c} - \frac{\phi_m(F)}{2\pi L\nu}, \tag{19.30}$$

where $\phi_m(F)$ is the "geometrical" phase shift $2\pi L/\lambda_0$ minus the total shift per transit for mode m. For large F, $\phi_m(F)$ is small and v_m is close to c.

Replacing (19.30) in (19.29), we obtain

$$\nu_n = \frac{cn}{2L} + \frac{c\phi_m}{2\pi L}, \tag{19.31}$$

and the difference in frequency between two consecutive resonances with the same transverse field distribution (same m) is given by

$$\nu_{n+1} - \nu_n = \frac{c}{2L}. \tag{19.32}$$

For $L = 5$ cm:

$$\nu_{n+1} - \nu_n = \frac{3 \times 10^{10}}{10} = 3 \times 10^9 \text{ sec}^{-1}. \tag{19.33}$$

Optical transitions in crystals have linewidths with typical values of 10 cm^{-1} at room temperature and 0.1 cm^{-1} at 77°K. Since 1 cm$^{-1} \equiv 30 \times 10^9$ sec^{-1}, this would correspond to 3×10^{11} sec^{-1} at room temperature and 3×10^9 sec^{-1} at 77°K. By comparing these values with (19.33) it is evident that several resonances may fall within the transition frequency range.

A useful concept in treating an optical cavity is the *quality factor*, or Q, of the cavity, defined as

$$Q_c = 2\pi \frac{\text{energy stored in the cavity}}{\text{energy lost in a cycle}} = 2\pi\nu_0 \frac{E}{\left|\dfrac{dE}{dt}\right|}, \tag{19.34}$$

where ν_0 = resonant frequency.

The rate at which the energy is lost is given by

$$\frac{dE}{dt} = -\frac{\omega_0 E}{Q_c} = -\frac{E}{\tau_c}. \tag{19.35}$$

Let us now calculate τ_c for a laser cavity. Starting at one point in the material, the beam of light is reflected at the two mirrors to the original point in a time $2L/v$, reduced in intensity by

$$e^{-2\gamma} \approx 1 - 2\gamma, \tag{19.36}$$

where $\gamma = -\ln R$ and R, the reflection power coefficient of the mirrors, is close to 1. R is the geometric mean of the reflection coefficients of the two mirrors:

$$R = \sqrt{R_1 R_2}. \tag{19.37}$$

The rate at which the energy is lost can then be written

$$\frac{dE}{dt} = -\frac{2\gamma E}{2L/v} = -\frac{v\gamma E}{L} = -\frac{E}{\tau_c}. \tag{19.38}$$

Therefore

$$\tau_c = \frac{L}{v\gamma} \tag{19.39}$$

and

$$Q_c = \omega_0 \tau_c = \frac{\omega_0 L}{v\gamma} \approx \frac{\omega_0 L}{v(1 - R)}. \tag{19.40}$$

For a typical laser cavity assume $L = 5$ cm, $R = 0.98$. Also $v \approx c = 3 \times 10^{10}$ cm/sec and $\lambda = 7000$ Å $= 7 \times 10^{-5}$ cm. We then obtain

$$\tau_c = \frac{L}{v(1 - R)} = \frac{5}{3 \times 10^{10} \times 0.02} = 8.3 \times 10^{-9} \text{ sec},$$

$$Q_c = \omega_0 \tau_c = \frac{2\pi c}{\lambda} \tau_c = 2.2 \times 10^7.$$

Given a certain transverse field distribution, the bandwidth associated with a certain resonance is given by

$$\Delta\nu = \frac{\nu_0}{Q_c} = \frac{\nu_0}{\omega_0 \tau_c} = \frac{1}{2\pi\tau_c} = \frac{v_m(1 - R)}{2\pi L}. \tag{19.41}$$

For this example we obtain

$$\Delta\nu = \frac{1}{2\pi\tau_c} = 1.9 \times 10^7 \text{ sec}^{-1}.$$

Now consider a plane wave incident on a Fabry–Perot laser cavity in a direction perpendicular to the mirror planes. Consider also the following parameters (see Fig. 19.1):

r_1 = reflection coefficient of the left mirror
= ratio of the amplitude reflected by the left mirror to the amplitude incident on the same,
r_2 = reflection coefficient of the right mirror,
t_1 = transmission coefficient of the left mirror
= ratio of the amplitude transmitted through the mirror to the amplitude incident on the mirror,
t_2 = transmission coefficient of the right mirror,
G_m = single pass-power gain of the active mode m; we shall assume that G_m is constant over the free spectral range $c/2L$ of the Fabry–Perot interferometer,
φ = total phase shift for a single transit from mirror to mirror,
$A^{(i)}$ = amplitude of the incident wave,
$A^{(t)}$ = amplitude of the transmitted wave,
$I^{(i)} = A^{(i)}A^{(i)*}$ = intensity of incident light,
$I^{(t)} = A^{(t)}A^{(t)*}$ = intensity of transmitted light.

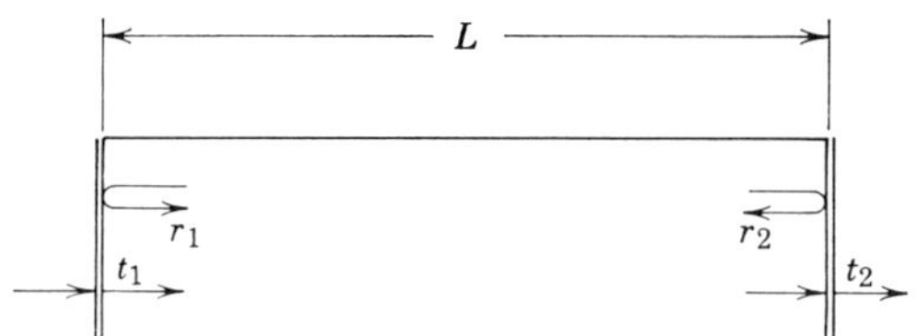

Fig. 19.1. Laser cavity with mirrors.

Also

$R_1 = r_1^2$ = power reflection coefficient of the left mirror,
$R_2 = r_2^2$ = power reflection coefficient of the right mirror,
$T_1 = t_1^2 = 1 - R_1$ = power transmission coefficient of the left mirror,
$T_2 = t_2^2 = 1 - R_2$ = power transmission coefficient of the right mirror.

The transmitted amplitude at the output of the regenerative amplifier is given by [3]

$$\begin{aligned} A^{(t)}(p) &= \sqrt{G_m}\, t_1 t_2 e^{i\varphi}[1 + G_m r_1 r_2 e^{i2\varphi} + \cdots + G_m^{p-1} r_1^{p-1} r_2^{p-1} e^{i(p-1)2\varphi}]\, A^{(i)} \\ &= \sqrt{G_m}\, t_1 t_2 e^{i\varphi} \frac{1 - r_1^p r_2^p G_m^p e^{ip2\varphi}}{1 - r_1 r_2 G_m e^{i2\varphi}} A^{(i)}, \end{aligned} \tag{19.42}$$

where the first p reflected waves have been superimposed. As $p \to \infty$, assuming $G_m r_1 r_2 < 1$, we obtain

$$A^{(t)}(\infty) = \frac{t_1 t_2 \sqrt{G_m}}{1 - r_1 r_2 G_m e^{i2\varphi}} A^{(i)}, \tag{19.43}$$

and the gain is given by [4]

$$G = \frac{I^{(t)}}{I^{(i)}} = \frac{(1 - R_1)(1 - R_2)\, G_m}{(1 - \sqrt{R_1 R_2}\, G_m)^2 + 4\sqrt{R_1 R_2}\, G_m \sin^2 \varphi}. \tag{19.44}$$

The gain G presents maxima for

$$\varphi = \frac{2\pi L \nu}{v_m} = n\pi, \tag{19.45}$$

which correspond to the values of ν for which the Fabry–Perot cavity resonates.

It is also interesting to calculate the half-width of the curve of the gain G versus ν. The gain at resonance is given by

$$G(\nu_0) = \frac{(1 - R_1)(1 - R_2)\, G_m(\nu_0)}{[1 - \sqrt{R_1 R_2}\, G_m(\nu_0)]^2}. \tag{19.46}$$

The half-width may be calculated by putting

$$\frac{1}{2}\frac{(1-R_1)(1-R_2)\,G_m(\nu_0)}{[1-\sqrt{R_1R_2}\,G_m(\nu_0)]^2} = \frac{(1-R_1)(1-R_2)\,G_m(\nu_0)}{[1-\sqrt{R_1R_2}\,G_m(\nu_0)]^2 + 4\sqrt{R_1R_2}\,G_m(\nu_0)\sin^2\varphi}, \tag{19.47}$$

where we have taken advantage of the fact that G_m is constant over the free spectral range (distance in frequency between the resonances).

According to (19.47), we must have

$$4\sqrt{R_1R_2}\,G_m(\nu_0)\sin^2\varphi = [1-\sqrt{R_1R_2}\,G_m(\nu_0)]^2 \tag{19.48}$$

or

$$\sin\varphi = \frac{1-RG_m(\nu_0)}{2\sqrt{RG_m(\nu_0)}} \tag{19.49}$$

where $R = \sqrt{R_1R_2}$. On the other hand,

$$\sin\varphi = \sin\left[\frac{2\pi(\nu_0+\delta\nu)\,L}{v_m}\right] = \sin\left(n\pi + \frac{2\pi(\delta\nu)\,L}{v_m}\right) = \sin\frac{2\pi(\delta\nu)\,L}{v_m}. \tag{19.50}$$

Therefore the bandwidth is given by

$$B = 2(\delta\nu) = \frac{v_m}{\pi L}\sin^{-1}\frac{1-RG_m(\nu_0)}{2\sqrt{RG_m(\nu_0)}}. \tag{19.51}$$

For RG_m close to 1,

$$B \simeq \frac{v_m}{2\pi L}\frac{1-RG_m(\nu_0)}{\sqrt{RG_m(\nu_0)}} = B_c\frac{1-RG_m(\nu_0)}{(1-R)\sqrt{G_m(\nu_0)}}, \tag{19.52}$$

where

$$B_c = \frac{v_m}{2\pi L}\frac{1-R}{\sqrt{R}} \tag{19.53}$$

is the bandwidth for a lossless Fabry–Perot cavity with mirror reflectivity R. B_c can be derived from (19.52) by putting $G_m(\nu_0) = 1$. For R close to 1, as assumed in (19.36), (19.53) is approximately equal to (19.41).

We note also that for $R_1 = R_2 = R$ the expression for the bandwidth (19.52), taking (19.46) into account, can be written

$$B = \frac{B_c}{\sqrt{G(\nu_0)}}, \tag{19.54}$$

which is the bandwidth-gain relation for a regenerative amplifier [1].

The output noise power per unit frequency range for a single transverse mode from one laser mirror was derived by Gordon by using an equivalent circuit analysis [5]. The output noise power per unit frequency range for a single transverse mode leaving the right mirror with reflectivity R_2 is, according to this analysis, given by

$$\begin{aligned} P_2 &= G\frac{1 + R_1G_m}{1 - R_1}\left(1 - \frac{1}{G_m}\right) Nh\nu \\ &= \frac{(1 + R_1G_m)(1 - R_2)}{(1 - RG_m)^2 + 4RG_m \sin^2 \varphi}(G_m - 1)\, Nh\nu \\ &= \frac{(1 + R_1G_m)(1 - R_2)}{(1 - RG_m)^2 + 4RG_m \sin^2 \varphi} P_N, \end{aligned} \tag{19.55}$$

where P_N, given by (19.24), is the single pass output noise power per unit frequency range. The output noise power P_1 per unit frequency range for a single mode leaving the left mirror is given by (19.55) with R_1 and R_2 interchanged.

The regenerative amplifier has two marked differences with respect to the single pass amplifier:

1. A large number of cavity resonances occur within the frequency range of the transition of the amplifying medium and therefore the gain of the regenerative amplifier varies greatly in this frequency range.
2. The regenerative amplifier has a higher noise output than the single pass amplifier.

4. CONDITIONS FOR OSCILLATION: LASER THRESHOLD

Gordon, Zeiger, and Townes [6] treated the "maser" oscillator operating in the microwave region as a regenerative amplifier driven by the thermal noise fluctuations from the cavity walls; in the microwave region the thermal noise is dominant over the noise due to the spontaneous emission process from the upper maser level. An opposite situation is found in the optical region, for here the thermal noise may be considered negligible in comparison to the spontaneous emission of the laser medium. Therefore a laser oscillator may be considered as a regenerative amplifier driven by the spontaneous emission of radiation from the laser medium.

The gain of a regenerative optical amplifier, active in a certain mode m, is expressed at resonance by

$$G(\nu_0) = \frac{(1 - R_1)(1 - R_2)\, G_m(\nu_0)}{[1 - R\, G_m(\nu_0)]^2} \tag{19.56}$$

and becomes infinite when

$$G_m(\nu_0) = \frac{1}{R}, \tag{19.57}$$

namely when the single pass gain compensates the losses.

This condition is generally considered basic to the establishment of oscillations in a regenerative amplifier. According to this point of view, the oscillator has an internal gain that exceeds its losses and is triggered by the noise fluctuations that are then amplified up to a level determined by the saturation. It is, clear, however from (19.55) and (19.54) that this condition can never be actually achieved in a steady-state situation, for an infinite noise power and a zero linewidth would result from it. In the saturation condition the gain must then remain slightly below the losses and never be equal to them.

The gain saturation in a laser system derives from the fact that stimulated emission constitutes a decay mechanism for atoms in the excited state. When the system gets close to the condition (19.57), the density of radiation starts building up and depletes the population inversion.

The *threshold* condition (19.57) can be expressed in a different way. Taking into account the two relations

$$G_m(\nu_0) = e^{\alpha_0 L}, \qquad (19.58)^2$$

$$\gamma = -\ln R, \tag{19.59}$$

(19.57) becomes

$$\alpha_0 L = \gamma. \tag{19.60}$$

This condition can also be expressed in terms of the population inversion. Assuming that the peak of the transition coincides with the resonance ν_0 of the interferometer and taking (19.10) into account, we obtain

$$\frac{\Delta N_{\text{th}}}{V} = \left(\frac{g_1}{g_2} n_2 - n_1\right)_{\text{th}} = \frac{\gamma}{\sigma_0 L}, \tag{19.61}$$

where ΔN_{th} is the population inversion at the threshold.

Let us calculate the threshold value for the population inversion for different line shapes. From Chapter 17 we derive the following expression for σ_0.

For a Lorentzian line shape [see (17.51)]:

$$\sigma_{0L} = \frac{\lambda^2 g_2/g_1}{4\pi^2(\Delta\nu)\,\tau_0}. \tag{19.62}$$

For a Gaussian line shape [see (17.54)]:

$$\sigma_{0G} = \frac{\lambda^2 g_2/g_1}{4\pi(\Delta\nu)\,\tau_0}\left(\frac{\ln 2}{\pi}\right)^{1/2}. \tag{19.63}$$

[2] Note the change of notation from α_m of (19.10) to α_0 of (19.58).

For a Voigt line shape [see (17.66)]:

$$\sigma_{0V} = \sigma_{0G} H(a, 0), \tag{19.64}$$

where

$$a = \frac{\Delta\nu_L}{\Delta\nu_G} \ln 2,$$
$$H(a, 0) = \frac{a}{\pi} \int_{-\infty}^{+\infty} \frac{e^{-y^2}}{a^2 + y^2} \, dy. \tag{19.65}$$

Equations 19.61 and 19.10 can now be expressed as follows:

Lorentzian Line

$$\frac{\Delta N_{\text{th}}}{V} = \frac{4\pi^2(\Delta\nu)\,\tau_0\gamma}{\lambda^2 L} \frac{g_1}{g_2}, \tag{19.66}$$

$$\alpha_0 = \sigma_0\left(\frac{g_1}{g_2} n_2 - n_1\right) = \frac{\lambda^2\left(n_2 - \dfrac{g_2}{g_1} n_1\right)}{4\pi^2(\Delta\nu)\,\tau_0}. \tag{19.67}$$

Gaussian Line

$$\frac{\Delta N_{\text{th}}}{V} = \frac{4\pi(\Delta\nu)\,\tau_0\gamma}{\lambda^2 L} \frac{g_1}{g_2}\left(\frac{\pi}{\ln 2}\right)^{1/2}, \tag{19.68}$$

$$\alpha_0 = \frac{\lambda^2[n_2 - (g_2/g_1)\, n_1]}{4\pi(\Delta\nu)\,\tau_0}\left(\frac{\ln 2}{\pi}\right)^{1/2}. \tag{19.69}$$

Voigt Line

$$\frac{\Delta N_{\text{th}}}{V} = \frac{\gamma}{\sigma_{0G} H(a, 0)\, L} = \frac{4\pi(\Delta\nu)\,\tau_0\gamma}{\lambda^2 L H(a, 0)} \frac{g_1}{g_2}\left(\frac{\pi}{\ln 2}\right)^{1/2}, \tag{19.70}$$

$$\alpha_0 = \frac{\lambda^2[n_2 - (g_2/g_1)\, n_1] H(a, 0)}{4\pi(\Delta\nu)\,\tau_0}\left(\frac{\ln 2}{\pi}\right)^{1/2}. \tag{19.71}$$

There are two other interesting ways of deriving this condition for oscillation.

As for the interferometric cavity, it is possible to define a quality factor for the material that accounts for the absorption and emission of radiation. The rate at which the energy is increased in the material is given by

$$\frac{dE}{dt} = E\alpha_0 v = \frac{E}{\tau_M}, \tag{19.72}$$

namely,

$$\tau_M = \frac{1}{\alpha_0 v}, \tag{19.73}$$

and

$$Q_M = \omega_0 \tau_M = \frac{\omega_0}{\alpha_0 v}. \tag{19.74}$$

The condition for oscillation is given by [7]

$$Q_c = Q_M, \tag{19.75}$$

or, taking (19.40) in account,

$$\frac{\omega_0 L}{v\gamma} = \frac{\omega_0}{\alpha_0 v}, \tag{19.76}$$

or

$$\alpha_0 L = \gamma, \tag{19.77}$$

in agreement with (19.60).

Another interesting way of deriving the laser threshold is due to Schawlow and Townes [8]. Following the considerations made at the beginning of Section 2 of this chapter, we can say that the probability of induced emission due to one photon in a certain mode is given by

$$\frac{A}{p} = \frac{1}{p\tau_0} = \frac{\text{probability of spontaneous emission}}{\text{number of effective modes}}. \tag{19.78}$$

Considering a Lorentzian line, the number of effective modes is given by the density of modes times the integrated width of the line $\frac{1}{2}\pi\Delta\nu$ times the volume:

$$p = \frac{8\pi\nu^2 V}{v^3}\frac{1}{g(\nu_0)} = \tfrac{1}{2}\pi\,\Delta\nu\,\frac{8\pi\nu^2 V}{v^3} = \frac{8\pi^2\nu^2\,\Delta\nu V}{2v^3}. \tag{19.79}$$

Therefore the probability of induced emission due to a single photon in a single mode is given by

$$\frac{A}{p} = \frac{2v^3}{8\pi^2\nu^2\,\Delta\nu V\tau_0}. \tag{19.80}$$

The net power produced by this stimulated emission is given by

$$\frac{A}{p}\left(n_2 - \frac{g_2}{g_1}n_1\right)Vh\nu \tag{19.81}$$

and the conditions for oscillations are determined by

$$\frac{A}{p}\left(n_2 - \frac{g_2}{g_1}n_1\right)Vh\nu = \frac{h\nu}{\tau_c}. \tag{19.82}$$

This gives

$$\frac{g_2}{g_1}\Delta N_{\text{th}} = V\left(n_2 - \frac{g_2}{g_1}n_1\right)_{\text{th}} = \frac{4\pi^2\nu^2(\Delta\nu)\,\tau_0 V}{v^3\tau_c} = p\frac{\tau_0}{\tau_c}, \tag{19.83}$$

which is equal to the value given by (19.66).

5. SPECTRAL CHARACTERISTICS OF THE LASER EMISSION

We shall now examine the spectral characteristics of the laser emission. The expression (19.55) for the noise power per unit frequency range can be integrated over the free spectral range

$$\nu_0 - \frac{v_m}{4L} \leq \nu \leq \nu_0 + \frac{v_m}{4L}. \tag{19.84}$$

Near the resonance the phase angle φ can be expressed as

$$\varphi = n\pi + \frac{2\pi(\nu - \nu_0)\, L}{v_m}. \tag{19.85}$$

We can then write, following Gordon [5], an expression for the total noise power, leaving the cavity in the mirror with reflection coefficient R_2:

$$P_2^t = \int_{\nu_0 - v_m/4L}^{\nu_0 + v_m/4L} \frac{NC_1\, d\nu}{C_2 + C_3 \sin^2 [2\pi(\nu - \nu_0)\, L]/v_m}, \tag{19.86}$$

where

$$C_1 = (1 + R_1 G_m)(1 - R_2)(G_1 - 1),$$

$$C_2 = (1 - RG_m)^2,$$

$$C_3 = 4RG_m.$$

If we put

$$\frac{2\pi(\nu - \nu_0)\, L}{v_m} = \theta, \tag{19.87}$$

we obtain

$$P_2^t = \frac{v_m}{2\pi L} \int_{-\pi/2}^{\pi/2} \frac{NC_1\, d\theta\, .}{C_2 + C_3 \sin^2 \theta}. \tag{19.88}$$

N, G_m, R_1, and R_2 can be considered constant over the small range of frequencies in which the integrand is large; in this approximation

$$\int_{-\pi/2}^{\pi/2} \frac{NC_1\, d\theta}{C_2 + C_3 \sin^2 \theta} = N \frac{\pi C_1}{\sqrt{C_2^2 + C_2 C_3}} \tag{19.89}$$

and

$$P_2^t = \frac{[1 + R_1 G_m(\nu_0)](1 - R_2)}{1 - R[G_m(\nu_0)]^2} [G_m(\nu_0) - 1] N \frac{v_m}{2L} h\nu$$

$$= \frac{[1 + R_1 G_m(\nu_0)](1 - R_2)}{1 - R[G_m(\nu_0)]^2} P_s, \tag{19.90}$$

where

$$P_s = [G_m(\nu_0) - 1] N h\nu \frac{v_m}{2L} \tag{19.91}$$

is the noise power that would be emitted through one of the sides of the laser medium in absence of cavity ($R_1 = R_2 = 0$) in the spectral range $v_m/2L$.

The power leaving the left mirror (which has a power reflection coefficient R_1) is given by (19.90) with R_1 and R_2 interchanged.

The total power leaving the cavity is then given by

$$P_t = P_1^t + P_2^t = 2P_s \frac{1 - R^2 G_m(\nu_0) + \frac{1}{2}[G_m(\nu_0) - 1](R_1 + R_2)}{1 - R^2[G_m(\nu_0)]^2}. \tag{19.92}$$

In order to find an approximate expression for the bandwidth, let us consider the case in which

$$R_1 = R_2 = R. \tag{19.93}$$

The total power becomes

$$P_t = 2P_s \frac{1 - R}{1 - RG_m(\nu_0)} \tag{19.94}$$

and then

$$\frac{P_s}{P_t} = 2\frac{1 - RG_m(\nu_0)}{1 - R}. \tag{19.95}$$

The bandwidth B in (19.52) can now be written

$$B = \frac{2B_c}{\sqrt{G_m(\nu_0)}} \frac{P_s}{P_t}. \tag{19.96}$$

Since the gain saturates at a value slightly below and nearly equal to the loss, we can replace $G(\nu_0)$ with $1/R$. Equation 19.96, also taking (19.91) into account, becomes

$$\begin{aligned} B &= 2\frac{B_c}{P_t}\frac{[G_m(\nu_0) - 1]Nh\nu}{\sqrt{G_m(\nu_0)}}\frac{v_m}{2L} \\ &\simeq 2\frac{B_c}{P_t}\frac{[(1/R) - 1]Nh\nu}{\sqrt{G_m(\nu_0)}}\frac{v_m}{2L} \simeq 2\frac{B_c}{P_t} h\nu N\left[\frac{1 - R}{\sqrt{R}}\frac{v_m}{2L}\right], \end{aligned} \tag{19.97}$$

Then, because of (19.53), B can be expressed as follows

$$B = 2\pi B_c^2 \frac{h\nu}{P_t} N. \tag{19.98}$$

This formula is similar to those derived by Schawlow and Townes [8], Maiman [7], Shimoda [9], and Grivet and Blaquiere [10].

It is important to note here that, as pointed out by Geusic and Scovil [4], the point at which a regenerative optical amplifier becomes an oscillator by amplifying its own spontaneous emission is not sharply defined. It is more proper to say that a regenerative amplifier is actually an oscillator whose degree of temporal coherence is described by its bandwidth, as expressed by (19.98).

Formulas (19.92) and (19.98), for the power output and the bandwidth, respectively, of a mode that has its resonance frequency at the center of the fluorescent transition, are also valid for other resonances within the fluorescence line. However, the output associated with these frequencies will be lower than the output at ν_0. The spatial coherence of the oscillator is determined by the number of transverse modes that are actively participating in the noise amplification process.

6. THE THREE-LEVEL LASER SYSTEM [7, 11–13]

In a three-level laser system the inversion of population is produced by optically pumping the atoms in the ground state to one or more (absorption) levels above the metastable (fluorescent) level. From these levels the atoms then decay nonradiatively in a very short time to the fluorescent level. When equilibrium is reached between the radiation and the laser system a population inversion is achieved, if the pumping light intensity is above a certain value.

Let us consider the three level system, as represented in Fig. 19.2 where, for simplicity, all the levels are assumed to be nondegenerate. In equilibrium the population densities are given by the equations

$$\begin{aligned} w_{13}n_1 - \alpha n_3 &= 0, \\ w_{12}n_1 - \beta n_2 + p_{32}n_3 &= 0, \\ n_1 + n_2 + n_3 &= n_0, \end{aligned} \tag{19.99}$$

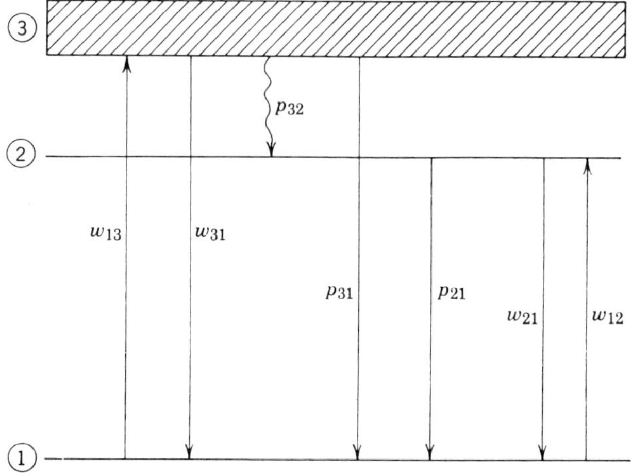

Fig. 19.2. A three-level laser system.

where

$$\alpha = w_{31} + p_{31} + p_{32}, \qquad \beta = p_{21} + w_{21}, \tag{19.100}$$

p_{ij} is the probability for spontaneous decay from level i to level j and w_{ij} are probabilities induced by the radiation. We note that $w_{ij} = w_{ji}$.

The solutions of these equations give

$$n_1 = \frac{\alpha\beta n_0}{\beta(w_{13} + \alpha) + \alpha w_{12} + p_{32}w_{13}}, \qquad n_2 = \frac{(\alpha w_{12} + p_{32}w_{13})\, n_0}{\beta(w_{13} + \alpha) + \alpha w_{12} + p_{32}w_{13}}. \tag{19.101}$$

Also

$$\frac{n_2}{n_1} = \frac{\alpha w_{12} + p_{32}w_{13}}{\alpha\beta}, \tag{19.102}$$

and

$$\begin{aligned}\frac{\Delta N}{V} &= n_2 - n_1 \\ &= \frac{\alpha w_{12} + p_{32}w_{13} - \alpha\beta}{\beta(w_{13} + \alpha) + \alpha w_{12} + p_{32}w_{13}}\, n_0 \\ &= \frac{w_{13}(\epsilon p_3 - p_{21}) - p_{21}p_3}{(w_{13} + p_3)(2w_{21} + p_{21}) + w_{13}(w_{21} + \epsilon p_3 + p_{21})}\, n_0,\end{aligned} \tag{19.103}$$

where $p_3 = p_{31} + p_{32}$,

$\epsilon = p_{32}/p_3 =$ the fraction of the atoms that decay from the absorption band to the metastable state.

We now make the following assumptions:

$$p_3 \gg p_{21}, \qquad p_{32} \gg w_{13}, \tag{19.104}$$

namely, we assume that the decay probability for an ion in the absorption band is much greater than the decay probability for an ion in the metastable state and that the pumping probability w_{13} is much smaller than the (usually radiationless) decay probability from the absorption band to the metastable state. With these assumptions we obtain

$$n_1 = \frac{p_{21} + w_{21}}{p_{21} + \epsilon w_{13} + 2w_{21}}, \qquad n_2 = \frac{p_{21} + \epsilon w_{13}}{p_{21} + \epsilon w_{13} + 2w_{21}} \tag{19.105}$$

and

$$\frac{n_2}{n_1} = \frac{w_{21} + \epsilon w_{13}}{p_{21} + w_{21}}. \tag{19.106}$$

Therefore

$$\frac{\Delta N}{V} = n_2 - n = \frac{\epsilon w_{13} - p_{21}}{p_{21} + \epsilon w_{13} + 2w_{21}} n_0. \tag{19.107}$$

The threshold condition, as expressed in (19.61), gives

$$n_{\text{th}} = \frac{\Delta N_{\text{th}}}{V n_0} = \frac{\epsilon w_{13} - p_{21}}{p_{21} + \epsilon w_{13}} = \frac{\gamma}{\sigma_{12} n_0 L}, \tag{19.108}$$

where w_{21} has been put equal to zero, since before the threshold is reached this probability is very small.

From (19.108)

$$(w_{13})_{\text{th}} = \frac{1 + n_{\text{th}}}{1 - n_{\text{th}}} \frac{p_{21}}{\epsilon} = \frac{1 + n_{\text{th}}}{1 - n_{\text{th}}} \frac{1}{\epsilon \tau_F}, \tag{19.109}$$

where $\tau_F = p_{21}^{-1}$ is the lifetime of the metastable level. In actual situations $\gamma \ll \sigma_{12} L$, and only a small excess of the population difference over zero is needed to sustain the oscillations. In these conditions,

$$(w_{13})_{\text{th}} \simeq \frac{1}{\epsilon \tau_F}. \tag{19.110}$$

It is interesting to note that a long lifetime is advantageous to ensure a low threshold.

It is important to point out that in the most general case the fluorescence lifetime τ_F is determined by all the radiative, phonon assisted (vibronic), and radiationless decay modes

$$\frac{1}{\tau_F} = \frac{1}{\tau_0} + \frac{1}{\tau_0'} + \frac{1}{\tau_{\text{vib}}} + \frac{1}{\tau_{\text{ph}}} = \frac{1}{\tau_0} + \frac{1}{\tau_s} = \frac{1}{\phi \tau_0}, \tag{19.111}$$

where τ_0 = decay time associated with the laser (radiative) transition,

τ_0' = decay time associated with radiative transitions originating from the initial laser level, and other than the laser transition,

τ_{vib} = decay time associated with vibronic transition from the initial laser level,

τ_{ph} = decay time associated with multiphonon decay,

$\phi = \dfrac{\tau_s}{\tau_0 + \tau_s}$ = fraction of atoms which decay from the metastable state by emitting radiation associated with the laser transition.

From (19.110) and (19.111) we derive

$$(w_{13})_{\text{th}} = \frac{1}{\eta \tau_0}, \tag{19.112}$$

where

$$\eta = \epsilon\phi \tag{19.113}$$

is the so called *quantum efficiency*, defined as the number of fluorescent photons emitted in the laser transition to the number of photons absorbed in the unit time.

Of the contributions from (19.111) to the fluorescent lifetime τ_F, only τ_0 enters the expression for the threshold value of the population inversion, whereas all the other contributions affect the threshold value for the pumping probability. In other words, vibronic and radiationless processes and radiative processes at frequencies other than the laser frequency do not affect the threshold for the population inversion but make it more difficult to achieve it. The presence of these processes is an undesirable feature of a laser system.

An exception to these considerations has to be made for certain laser systems in which the laser transition is a vibronic transition [14]. In this case a strong matrix element for this transition is desirable and other radiative and radiationless processes are unwanted.

7. THE FOUR-LEVEL LASER SYSTEM

Let us now consider the four-level system shown in Fig. 19.3. In this system the atoms are brought from the ground level 1 to the uppermost level 4 by the pumping radiation. From this level the atoms decay very quickly to the metastable level 3. An atom in this level can decay either directly to the

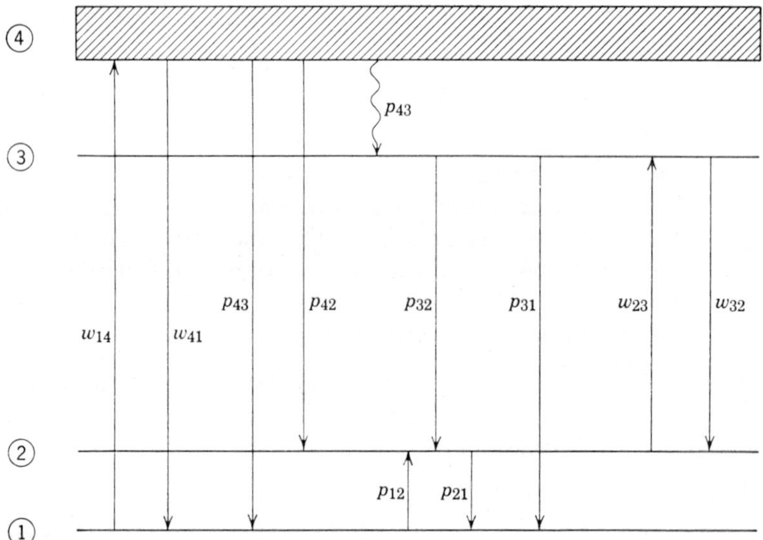

Fig. 19.3. A four-level laser system.

ground level or to the level 2 above the ground level. The transition relevant to the laser emission is the one from the metastable level 3 to the level 2.

The population densities are determined by the following equations:

$$\begin{aligned} \dot{n}_4 &= (n_1 - n_4)\, w_{14} - n_4 p_4, \\ \dot{n}_3 &= (n_2 - n_3)\, w_{32} - n_3 p_3 + n_4 p_{43}, \\ \dot{n}_2 &= n_1 p_{12} - (n_2 - n_3)\, w_{32} - n_2 p_{21} + n_3 p_{32} + n_4 p_{42}, \\ n_1 &+ n_2 + n_2 + n_4 = n_0, \end{aligned} \tag{19.114}$$

where

$$\begin{aligned} p_4 &= p_{43} + p_{42} + p_{41}, \\ p_3 &= p_{32} + p_{31}. \end{aligned}$$

We now make the following assumptions:

1. The decay probability from level 4 is much greater than the pumping probability to level 4:

$$p_4 \gg w_{14}, \tag{19.115}$$

2. The decay probability is mainly due to the $4 \to 3$ decay process:

$$\epsilon = \frac{p_{43}}{p_4} \approx 1, \tag{19.116}$$

3. The probabilities p_{12}, p_{21} are very fast because of the relaxation processes between levels 2 and 1; in particular

$$\begin{aligned} p_{12} &\gg w_{14}, \\ p_{21} &\gg w_{32}, p_{32}. \end{aligned} \tag{19.117}$$

Under these assumptions the equations in (19.114) in the steady state reduce to

$$\begin{aligned} n_2 w_{32} - n_3 \alpha + n_1 \epsilon w_{14} &= 0, \\ n_1 p_{12} - n_2 p_{21} + n_3 \beta &= 0, \\ n_1 + n_2 + n_3 &= n_0, \end{aligned} \tag{19.118}$$

where

$$\begin{aligned} \alpha &= p_3 + w_{32}, \\ \beta &= p_{32} + w_{32}. \end{aligned} \tag{19.119}$$

From this we obtain

$$\begin{aligned} \frac{n_3}{n_2} &= \frac{w_{32} p_{12} + \epsilon w_{14} p_{21}}{\alpha p_{12} + \beta \epsilon w_{14}}, \\ \frac{n_1}{n_2} &= \frac{\alpha p_{21} - \beta w_{32}}{\alpha p_{12} + \beta \epsilon w_{14}}. \end{aligned} \tag{19.120}$$

Also

$$n_3 = \frac{n_0(\alpha p_{12} + \beta\epsilon w_{14})}{\alpha p_{12} + \beta\epsilon w_{14} + \alpha p_{21} + w_{32}p_{12} + p_{21}\epsilon w_{14} - \beta w_{32}},$$

$$n_2 = \frac{n_0(w_{32}p_{12} + p_{21}\epsilon w_{14})}{\alpha p_{12} + \beta\epsilon w_{14} + \alpha p_{21} + w_{32}p_{12} + p_{21}\epsilon w_{14} - \beta w_{32}}, \tag{19.121}$$

$$n_1 = \frac{n_0(\alpha p_{21} - \beta w_{32})}{\alpha p_{12} + \beta\epsilon w_{14} + \alpha p_{21} + w_{32}p_{12} + p_{12}\epsilon w_{14} - \beta w_{32}}.$$

From this we derive

$$\frac{n_3 - n_2}{n_0} = \frac{\epsilon w_{14}(p_{21} - \beta) - p_3 p_{12}}{\epsilon w_{14}(p_{21} + \beta) + \alpha p_{21} + w_{32}(p_{21} - \beta) + \alpha p_{12}}. \tag{19.122}$$

Now, taking into account the second inequality in (19.117) and assuming that

$$\frac{p_{21}}{p_{12}} = e^{\hbar\nu_{21}/kT}, \tag{19.123}$$

we obtain

$$\frac{n_3 - n_2}{n_0} = \frac{\epsilon w_{14} - p_3 e^{-\hbar\nu_{21}/kT}}{\epsilon w_{14} + p_3 + w_{32} + [2w_{32} + p_3]e^{-\hbar\nu_{21}/kT}}. \tag{19.124}$$

For a large separation between levels 1 and 2 we obtain

$$n = \frac{n_3 - n_2}{n_0} = \frac{\epsilon w_{14}}{\epsilon w_{14} + p_3 + w_{32}}. \tag{19.125}$$

By using this formula we can express the pumping probability w_{14} in terms of the threshold value for n:

$$(w_{14})_{\text{th}} = \frac{p_3}{\epsilon}\frac{n_{\text{th}}}{1 - n_{\text{th}}} = \frac{n_{\text{th}}}{1 - n_{\text{th}}}\frac{1}{\epsilon\tau_F}, \tag{19.126}$$

where $\tau_F = p_3^{-1}$ is the lifetime of the metastable state 3.

For $\gamma \ll \sigma_{32}L$, $n_{\text{th}} \ll 1$, taking (19.66) and (19.39) into account, we obtain

$$w_{14} \simeq \frac{n_{\text{th}}}{\epsilon\tau_F} = \frac{n_{\text{th}}}{\eta\tau_0} \simeq \frac{4\pi^2(\Delta\nu)\,\gamma}{n_0\lambda^2 L\eta} = \frac{4\pi^2(\Delta\nu)\,\nu^2}{n_0 v^3\tau_c\eta}. \tag{19.127}$$

It is interesting to compare the threshold values for the pumping probability for a four level and a three level system. From (19.126) and (19.109) we obtain

$$\frac{(w_{14})_{\text{th}}}{(w_{13})_{\text{th}}} \simeq \frac{n_{\text{th}}}{1 + n_{\text{th}}}\frac{(\tau_F)_3}{(\tau_F)_4} \simeq n_{\text{th}}\frac{(\tau_F)_3}{(\tau_F)_4} = \frac{(\Delta N)_{\text{th}}}{N_0}\frac{(\tau_F)_3}{(\tau_F)_4}. \tag{19.128}$$

where

$$N_0 = n_0 V. \tag{19.129}$$

8. PARAMETERS AFFECTING THE LASER THRESHOLD

The three-level and the four-level laser systems can be compared on the basis of the formulas in (19.112) and (19.126) for very small cavity losses. We can make the following observations:

1. In a three-level laser system the threshold value for the pumping probability depends essentially on the fluorescence lifetime of the metastable level and is almost entirely insensitive to such parameters as linewidth and the quality factor of the cavity. An η factor as close to one as possible is desirable.
2. In a four-level laser system the threshold pumping probability does not depend on the radiative lifetime τ_0 but is directly proportional to the linewidth and inversely proportional to η and the cavity damping time τ_c.

On the basis of this discussion we can now list the requirements for laser systems with four levels:

1. The linewidth of the laser transition should be as small as possible.
2. The lifetime of the initial level of the laser transition should be purely radiative; that is, phonon decay processes should not be active. Also, radiative fluorescence transitions, other than the one at the laser frequency, are undesirable. Briefly, ϕ should be close to one.
3. The terminal level of the laser transition should be connected to the ground level by relaxation processes with a rate faster than the decay rate of the metastable level.
4. The laser system should present strong and wide absorption bands in the spectral region in which the light source emits. It is also desirable to ensure a uniform intensity of the pumping light throughout the crystal; for this the laser medium should be optically thin in the pumping wavelength region.
5. The ions brought to the absorption band by the pumping radiation should decay mainly to the metastable level; namely ϵ should be close to one.
6. The terminal level of the laser transition should be high in energy with respect to the ground level ($h\nu_{21} \gg kT$).
7. The photon lifetime τ_c should be long; namely the cavity losses should be small.
8. No absorption from the metastable state should take place at either the laser wavelength or the pumping wavelength.

Example

We shall now calculate the population inversion needed to achieve laser oscillations in ruby (Al_2O_3:Cr^{3+}).

Ruby crystals present two metastable levels; the $\bar{E}$ level, ~14,418 cm^{-1} above the ground state and the $2\bar{A}$ level, 29 cm^{-1} above the $\bar{E}$ level. Both levels are twofold degenerate. The ground state is $^4A_2$ and is fourfold degenerate. The $\bar{E}$ and $2\bar{A}$ levels are thermalized, and their populations are, at room temperature, in the ratio

$$\frac{n(2\bar{A})}{n(\bar{E})} = \exp\left(-\frac{\Delta E}{kT}\right) \simeq 0.87.$$

Both levels decay with a lifetime that is mainly radiative and whose value is approximately 3×10^{-3} sec.

We are concerned here with the laser line originating from the $\bar{E}$ level and terminating on the $^4A_2$ level.

The characteristics of the crystal may be summarized as follows:

$$\begin{aligned}
\nu &= 14{,}418 \text{ cm}^{-1} = 4.33 \times 10^{14} \text{ sec}^{-1},\\
\Delta\nu &= 11 \text{ cm}^{-1} = 33 \times 10^{10} \text{ sec}^{-1} \text{ (at room temperature)},\\
\tau_0 &= 3 \times 10^{-3} \text{ sec},\\
m &= 1.76 \text{ (index of refraction)},\\
g_1 &= g(^4A_2) = 4,\\
g_2 &= g(\bar{E}) = 2.
\end{aligned}$$

We now consider a ruby resonator with the following characteristics:

$$L = 7 \text{ cm},$$
$$\gamma = 0.02;$$

we find from (19.39)

$$\tau_c = \frac{Ln}{c\gamma} \simeq 2 \times 10^{-8} \text{ sec}.$$

The population inversion needed to achieve oscillations is given by

$$V\left(n_2 - n_1\frac{g_2}{g_1}\right) = \frac{4\pi^2\nu^2(\Delta\nu)n^3}{c^3}\frac{\tau_0}{\tau_c}V \simeq 10^{17}V.$$

Assuming that the density of Cr^{3+} centers is 2×10^{19} cm^{-3}, the population densities are given by the following equations:

$$n(\bar{E}) - n(^4A_2)\tfrac{1}{2} = 10^{17},$$
$$\frac{n(2\bar{A})}{n(\bar{E})} = 0.87,$$
$$n(2\bar{A}) + n(\bar{E}) + n(^4A_2) = 2 \times 10^{19},$$

from which we obtain

$$\begin{aligned}
n(2\bar{A}) &= 0.454 \times 10^{19},\\
n(\bar{E}) &= 0.522 \times 10^{19},\\
n(^4A_2) &= 1.024 \times 10^{19}.
\end{aligned}$$

By comparing the threshold value for the $\bar{E}$-level population to the threshold value for inversion 10^{17} we can see that in the case of ruby the three-level operation increases the threshold value for the population inversion by a factor of $\sim$50 with respect to the threshold value for the four-level operation.

9. OPTICAL PUMPING AND PUMPING THRESHOLD

Let us consider in a simplified manner the basic differences between three-level and four-level laser systems.

We shall assume that the initial and final states of the laser transition have equal degeneracy ($g_1 = g_2$) and that the laser transition is homogeneously broadened.

In a three-level system the number of ions that need to be brought to the metastable state in order to achieve the threshold condition is given by

$$N_{th} = \frac{N_0}{2} + \Delta N_{th}, \tag{19.130}$$

where N_0 is the total number of active ions in the crystal. ΔNth, is given, according to (19.83), by

$$\Delta N_{th} = p\frac{\tau_0}{\tau_c}. \tag{19.131}$$

In general $\Delta N_{th} \ll N_0$ and therefore (19.130) reduces to

$$N_{th} \simeq \frac{N_0}{2} \qquad \text{(3-level)}. \tag{19.132}$$

In a four-level system, if the terminal level is empty, the number of ions in the metastable state needed at the threshold is given by

$$N_{th} \simeq \Delta N_{th} = p\frac{\tau_0}{\tau_c} \qquad \text{(4-level)}. \tag{19.133}$$

We must now make a distinction between the two modes in which lasers can operate: the *pulsed* mode, in which the pumping light is provided in the form of a pulse short in comparison with the fluorescence lifetime τ_F, and the *continuous wave* (*CW*) mode, in which the pumping light is continuously exciting the ions in the crystal. We shall treat these two cases separately. The considerations derived for the *CW* mode apply also to the case in which the light pulse is long compared with τ_F.

9.1 Energy Threshold for Pulsed Lasers

When the length of the pumping pulse is much shorter than the lifetime of the metastable state, only a negligible amount of energy is lost by the laser system under the form of spontaneous emission. In this case the minimum absorbed energy required to achieve the threshold condition is given by

$$E_{min} = N_{th}\frac{h\nu_p}{\eta}, \tag{19.134}$$

where η is the quantum efficiency for the radiation at the laser frequency and ν_p is the average frequency of the absorption band.

By considering (19.132) and (19.133), we obtain the following:

$$\textit{Three-level system:} \quad E_{\min} \simeq \frac{N_0}{2\eta}(h\nu_p). \tag{19.135}$$

$$\textit{Four-level system:} \quad E_{\min} \simeq p\frac{\tau_0}{\tau_c}\frac{h\nu_p}{\eta}. \tag{19.136}$$

We note here that the energy threshold for a three-level pulsed laser depends strongly on the number of active ions and is independent of the radiative lifetime and linewidth. A reduction of this number produces a decrease of the energy threshold, provided that it is always $N_0/2 \gg \Delta N_{\text{th}}$.

The energy threshold for a four-level laser system is directly proportional to the radiative lifetime τ_0 and, through p, also to the linewidth $\Delta\nu$.

9.2 Power Threshold for CW Lasers

In order to achieve the threshold condition in a laser system we have to maintain N_{th} ions in the metastable state at all times. Because the probability for induced emission below threshold is negligible, the only decaying mechanism is represented by the fluorescent decay. The power needed to achieve the threshold condition is then given by

$$P_{\min} = N_{\text{th}}\frac{h\nu_p}{\eta\tau_F} = N_{\text{th}}\frac{h\nu_p}{\eta^2\tau_0}. \tag{19.137}$$

This specializes to the following:

$$\textit{Three-level system:} \quad P_{\min} \simeq \frac{N_0}{2\eta^2}\frac{h\nu_p}{\tau_0}. \tag{19.138}$$

$$\textit{Four-level system:} \quad P_{\min} \simeq \frac{p}{\tau_c}\frac{h\nu_p}{\eta^2}. \tag{19.139}$$

From the above we conclude that the power threshold for a *CW* three-level system is inversely proportional to the radiative lifetime τ_0, proportional to the number of active ions, and independent of the linewidth of the laser transition.

The power threshold for a *CW* four-level laser system is independent of the radiative lifetime and proportional, through p, to the linewidth $\Delta\nu$.

The light intensity necessary to achieve oscillations in a laser system, in the *CW* mode of operation, can be derived from the knowledge of the population inversion at threshold and of the optical characteristics of the crystal. Let N_{th} be the number of ions we want to maintain in the metastable state, as given by (19.132) for a three-level system and by (19.133) for a four-level system.

The quantum efficiency, as defined above, can be expressed as follows:

$$\eta = \frac{N_{\text{th}}/\tau_0}{N_0 w}, \tag{19.140}$$

where w is the pumping probability per unit time and τ_0 is the radiative lifetime, due only to the laser transition.

The number of photons absorbed in the unit time can also be expressed as

$$N_0 w = V \int \frac{I_{\lambda'} k_{\lambda'}\, d\lambda'}{h\nu'}, \tag{19.141}$$

where the integral ranges over the wavelengths of the absorption band and where

$$k_{\lambda'} = \text{absorption coefficient of the crystal (cm}^{-1}),$$
$$I_{\lambda'}\, d\lambda' = \text{energy flux incident on the crystal (erg/cm}^2\text{ sec)}.$$

Because the quantum efficiency may also be a function of λ', we may express (19.141) as

$$\frac{N_{\text{th}}}{\tau_0 V} = \int \frac{I_{\lambda'} k_{\lambda'} \lambda' \eta_{\lambda'}}{hc}\, d\lambda'. \tag{19.142}$$

Replacing $I_{\lambda'}$, $k_{\lambda'}$, and $\eta_{\lambda'}$ with their average values over the useful spectral region, we obtain

$$\frac{N_{\text{th}}}{\tau_0 V} = \frac{\bar{\lambda}' \bar{I} \bar{k} \bar{\eta}\, \Delta\lambda'}{hc}. \tag{19.143}$$

The intensity of light at threshold is then given by

$$\bar{I}\, \Delta\lambda' = \frac{h\bar{\nu}'}{\bar{k}\bar{\eta}} \frac{N_{\text{th}}}{\tau_0 V}. \tag{19.144}$$

Example[3]

Let us now consider the four-level system $CaF_2:U^{3+}$. The characteristics of such a system may be summarized as follows:

$$\lambda = 2.61 \times 10^{-4}\ \text{cm}; \qquad \nu = 3831\ \text{cm}^{-1} = 1.15 \times 10^{14}\ \text{sec}^{-1},$$
$$\tau_0 = 1.3 \times 10^{-4}\ \text{sec},$$
$$\Delta\nu = 20\ \text{cm}^{-1} = 6 \times 10^{11}\ \text{sec}^{-1},$$
$$n = \text{refractive index} = 1.4.$$

Now consider a $CaF_2:U^{3+}$ resonator with the following characteristics:

$$L = 3\ \text{cm},$$
$$\gamma = 0.05;$$

[3] This example and the following one are taken from [15] with Dr. A. Yariv's permission.

we find

$$\tau_c = \frac{Ln}{c\gamma} = \frac{3 \times 1.4}{3 \times 10^{10} \times 0.05} \simeq 2.8 \times 10^{-9} \text{ sec.}$$

The population inversion at the threshold is then given by

$$\frac{\Delta N_{\text{th}}}{V} = \frac{4\pi^2\nu^2(\Delta\nu)\, n^3}{c^3}\frac{\tau_0}{\tau_c} \simeq 1.5 \times 10^{15} \text{ cm}^{-3}.$$

This entails a minimum value for the light power density in the crystal of

$$\frac{\Delta N_{\text{th}}}{V}\frac{h\nu}{\tau_0} = \frac{1.5 \times 10^{15} \times 7.66 \times 10^{-13}}{1.3 \times 10^{-4}} = 0.9 \text{ W/cm}^3.$$

Now consider the pumping light actually needed under the following conditions:

$$\bar{k} = 2,$$
$$\bar{\eta} = 1,$$
$$\bar{\lambda}' = 0.9 \times 10^{-4} \text{ cm}; \qquad \bar{\nu}' = 11{,}100 \text{ cm}^{-1} \equiv 22 \times 10^{-13} \text{ erg}.$$

From (19.144) we derive

$$\bar{I}\,\Delta\lambda' = \frac{h\bar{\nu}'}{\bar{k}\bar{\eta}\tau_0}\frac{N_{\text{th}}}{V} = \frac{22 \times 10^{-13}}{2 \times 1.3 \times 10^{-4}} \times 1.5 \times 10^{15} \simeq 1.2 \text{ W/cm}^2,$$

which represents the light intensity needed at the surface of the crystal under threshold conditions.

Example

Let us consider the four-level system represented by $CaWO_4{:}Nd^{3+}$. The characteristics of such a system may be summarized as follows:

$$\lambda = 1.064 \times 10^{-4} \text{ cm}; \qquad \nu = 9398 \text{ cm}^{-1} = 2.81 \times 10^{14} \text{ sec}^{-1},$$
$$\tau_0 = 10^{-4} \text{ sec},$$
$$\Delta\nu = 7 \text{ cm}^{-1} = 2.1 \times 10^{11} \text{ sec}^{-1},$$
$$n = \text{refractive index} = 1.9.$$

Now consider a $CaWO_4{:}Nd^{3+}$ resonator with the following characteristics:

$$L = 3 \text{ cm},$$
$$\gamma = 0.05;$$

we find

$$\tau_c = \frac{Ln}{c\gamma} = \frac{3 \times 1.9}{3 \times 10^{10} \times 0.05} = 3.8 \times 10^{-9} \text{ sec.}$$

The population inversion at the threshold is then given by

$$\frac{\Delta N_{\text{th}}}{V} = \frac{4\pi^2\nu^2(\Delta\nu)\, n^3}{c^3}\frac{\tau_0}{\tau_c} = 4.4 \times 10^{15} \text{ cm}^{-3}.$$

This entails a minimum value for the light power density in the crystal of

$$\frac{\Delta N_{\text{th}}}{V}\frac{h\nu}{\tau_0} = \frac{4.4 \times 10^{15} \times 18.8 \times 10^{-13}}{10^{-4}} \simeq 8 \text{ W/cm}^3.$$

Now consider the pumping light actually needed under the following conditions:

$$k = 5 \text{ cm}^{-1},$$
$$\bar{\eta} = 1,$$
$$\bar{\lambda}' = 5800 \text{ Å} = 0.58 \times 10^{-4} \text{ cm}; \qquad \bar{\nu}' = 17{,}240 \text{ cm}^{-1} = 34.5 \times 10^{-13} \text{ erg}.$$

From (19.144) we derive

$$\bar{I}\,\Delta\lambda' = \frac{h\bar{\nu}'}{k\bar{\eta}}\frac{N_{\text{th}}}{\tau_0 V} = \frac{34.5 \times 10^{-13}}{5 \times 10^{-4}} \times 4.4 \times 10^{15} = 3 \text{ W/cm}^2.$$

Example [16]

Consider the four-level system $CaF_2:Sm^{2+}$ whose characteristics can be summarized as follows:

$$\lambda = 7.08 \times 10^{-5} \text{ cm},$$
$$\nu = 14{,}124 \text{ cm}^{-1} = 4.24 \times 10^{14} \text{ sec}^{-1} = 28.2 \times 10^{-13} \text{ erg},$$
$$\Delta\nu = 3.2 \text{ cm}^{-1} = 9.6 \times 10^{10} \text{ sec}^{-1},$$
$$\tau_0 = 2 \times 10^{-6} \text{ sec},$$
$$n = 1.4.$$

Consider also a $CaF_2:Sm^{2+}$ resonator with the following characteristics:

$$L = 1.2 \text{ cm},$$
$$\gamma = 0.1;$$

we find

$$\tau_c = \frac{Ln}{c\gamma} = 5.6 \times 10^{-10} \text{ sec}.$$

The population inversion is then given by

$$\frac{\Delta N_{\text{th}}}{V} = \frac{4\pi^2\nu^2(\Delta\nu)\,n^3}{c^3}\frac{\tau_0}{\tau_c} \simeq 2.5 \times 10^{14} \text{ cm}^{-3}.$$

This entails a minimum value for the light power density inside the crystal of

$$\frac{\Delta N_{\text{th}}}{V}\frac{h\nu}{\tau_0} = \frac{2.5 \times 10^{14} \times 28.2 \times 10^{-13}}{2 \times 10^{-6}} = 35 \text{ W/cm}^3.$$

Consider the pumping light actually needed to ensure oscillations under the following conditions:

$$\bar{k} = 10 \text{ cm}^{-1},$$
$$\bar{\eta} = 0.2,$$
$$\bar{\lambda}' = 6.4 \times 10^{-5} \text{ cm},$$
$$\bar{\nu}' = 15{,}625 \text{ cm}^{-1} = 4.69 \times 10^{14} \text{ sec}^{-1} = 31.25 \times 10^{-13} \text{ erg}.$$

From (19.144) we derive

$$\bar{I}\,\Delta\lambda' = \frac{h\bar{\nu}'}{\bar{k}\bar{\eta}\tau_0}\frac{N_{\text{th}}}{V} = \frac{31.25 \times 10^{-13}}{10 \times 0.2 \times 2 \times 10^{-6}} \times 2.5 \times 10^{14} \simeq 20 \text{ W/cm}^2.$$

10. CONSIDERATIONS ON THE OUTPUT OF LASER SYSTEMS [15, 17–19]

The value of the population inversion at the threshold is determined by the optical characteristics of the material and by the losses in the optical cavity. When the pumping power (or energy) exceeds the threshold value, stimulated emission overcomes the losses and tends to reduce any excess of population inversion above threshold. Any ion that is brought to the metastable level in excess of the threshold value contributes directly to the useful coherent output of the laser system. Because the population inversion does not change above threshold, the incoherent (fluorescent) emission of the system does not change when the pumping power exceeds its threshold value.

These considerations are valid for homogeneously broadened lines in which all the atoms are simultaneously under the influence of the same driving field. According to these considerations, a homogeneously broadened line should allow only single-mode oscillations; however, multimode oscillations have been found in laser systems with homogeneously broadened lines. This phenomenon has been explained as due to the fact that the standing wave patterns of the different modes are displaced in the cavity, thus causing a *spatial* inhomogeneity [20, 21].

If the line is inhomogeneously broadened, the population in the metastable (laser) level, which does not correspond to the frequency of the oscillating mode, continues to increase when the pumping is increased above threshold. When the gain at a certain frequency reaches the threshold value, the system starts oscillating at that particular frequency; in such systems the number of oscillating modes grows with the input power [22].

10.1 Energy Output of Pulsed Lasers

The number of ions brought to the metastable state by the pumping energy E_p is $E_p\eta/h\nu_p$. Of these ions N_{th} must be used to overcome the losses; we are then left with $E_p\eta/h\nu_p - N_{\text{th}}$ useful excited centers which produce the energy

$$E_0 = h\nu\left(\frac{E_p\eta}{h\nu_p} - N_{\text{th}}\right) = \eta\,\frac{\nu}{\nu_p}\left(E_p - \frac{N_{\text{th}}h\nu_p}{\eta}\right) = \eta\,\frac{\nu}{\nu_p}(E_p - E_{\text{min}}), \quad (19.145)$$

where we have made use of (19.134).

Specializing (19.145) to the three-level and four-level systems, we obtain the following:

$$\textit{Three-level systems:}\quad E_0 = \eta\,\frac{\nu}{\nu_p}\left(E_p - \frac{N_0}{2}\frac{h\nu_p}{\eta}\right). \qquad (19.146)$$

$$\textit{Four-level systems:}\quad E_0 = \eta\,\frac{\nu}{\nu_p}\left(E_p - p\,\frac{\tau_0}{\tau_c}\frac{h\nu_p}{\eta}\right). \qquad (19.147)$$

The energy output may be expressed in a different way, since

$$E_0 = \eta \frac{\nu}{\nu_p} E_{\min}\left(\frac{E_p}{E_{\min}} - 1\right)$$

$$= N_{\text{th}} h\nu \left(\frac{E_p}{E_{\min}} - 1\right). \qquad (19.148)$$

Taking (19.135) and (19.136) in account, we obtain the following:

$$\textit{Three-level systems:} \quad E_0 = \frac{N_0 h\nu}{2}\left(\frac{E_p}{E_{\min}} - 1\right). \qquad (19.149)$$

$$\textit{Four-level systems:} \quad E_0 = p \frac{\tau_0}{\tau_c} h\nu \left(\frac{E_p}{E_{\min}} - 1\right). \qquad (19.150)$$

10.2 Power Output of CW Lasers

Using considerations similar to those made for the laser systems operated in the pulsed mode, we obtain the following:

$$\textit{Three-level systems:} \quad P_0 = \frac{N_0 h\nu}{2\tau_0\eta}\left(\frac{P_p}{P_{\min}} - 1\right). \qquad (19.151)$$

$$\textit{Four-level systems:} \quad P_0 = p \frac{h\nu}{\tau_c\eta}\left(\frac{P_p}{P_{\min}} - 1\right). \qquad (19.152)$$

Yariv [17] found experimentally that the output power of the *CW* laser $CaF_2{:}U^{3+}$ at 77°K had a dependence on the pumping intensity in agreement with (19.152).

The characteristics of laser emission in three- and four-level systems are summarized in Table 19.1.

10.3 Optimum Coupling Factor

The losses of photon energy in a laser system can be divided into two main categories: (a) losses inside the cavity and (b) losses due to the transmission through the end reflecting mirrors.

The losses within the cavity include the following:

1. Absorption in the reflecting mirrors.
2. Absorption in the medium at the laser frequency due to the presence of impurities.
3. Diffraction by the mirror apertures.
4. Misalignment and geometrical imperfections in the mirrors.
5. Scattering by crystal inhomogeneities.

Table 19.1 Characteristics of Laser Emission

Laser System	Metastable State Population at Threshold	Mode of Operation	Characteristics of Laser Emission	Observations
3-Level	$N_{\text{th}} = \dfrac{N_0}{2}$ $\left(\Delta N_{\text{th}} = p\dfrac{\tau_0}{\tau_c} \ll N_0\right)$	Pulsed $\tau_p \ll \tau_F$	$E_{\min} = \dfrac{N_0}{2}\dfrac{h\nu_p}{\eta}$	$E_{\min}$ proportional to N_0, independent of τ_0 and $\Delta\nu$; $\epsilon_{\min}$ independent of N_0, τ_0, and $\Delta\nu$.
			$E_0 = \dfrac{N_0 h\nu}{2}\left(\dfrac{E_p}{E_{\min}} - 1\right)$	E_p proportional to N_0; $E_{\min}$ proportional to N_0; E_0 proportional to N_0, independent of τ_0 and $\Delta\nu$.
		CW $\tau_p \gg \tau_F$	$P_{\min} = \dfrac{N_0}{2}\dfrac{h\nu_p}{\eta^2\tau_0}$	$P_{\min}$ proportional to N_0, inversely proportional to τ_0, independent of $\Delta\nu$; $\pi_{\min}$ independent of N_0 and $\Delta\nu$, inversely proportional to τ_0.
			$P_0 = \dfrac{N_0 h\nu}{2\tau_0\eta}\left(\dfrac{P_p}{P_{\min}} - 1\right)$	P_p proportional to N_0; $P_{\min}$ proportional to N_0; P_0 proportional to N_0, and independent of $\Delta\nu$, independent of τ_0 for $P_p \gg P_{\min}$.

4-Level	$N_{th} = \Delta N_{th}$ $= p\,\dfrac{\tau_0}{\tau_c}$ $\left(p = \dfrac{4\pi^2\nu^2\,\Delta\nu V}{v^3}\right)$	Pulsed $\tau_p \ll \tau_F$	$E_{min} = p\,\dfrac{\tau_0}{\tau_c}\,\dfrac{h\nu_p}{\eta}$	E_{min} proportional to τ_0 and $\Delta\nu$, independent of N_0; ϵ_{min} proportional to τ_0 and $\Delta\nu$, inversely proportional to N_0.
			$E_0 = p\,\dfrac{\tau_0}{\tau_c}\,h\nu\left(\dfrac{E_p}{E_{min}} - 1\right)$	E_p proportional to N_0; E_{min} independent of N_0; E_0 proportional to N_0 for $E_p \gg E_{min}$, independent of τ_0 and $\Delta\nu$ for $E_p \gg E_{min}$.
		CW $\tau_p \gg \tau_F$	$P_{min} = \dfrac{p}{\tau_c}\,\dfrac{h\nu_p}{\eta^2}$	P_{min} proportional to $\Delta\nu$, independent of N_0 and τ_0; π_{min} proportional to $\Delta\nu$, independent to τ_0, inversely proportional to N_0.
			$P_0 = \dfrac{ph\nu}{\tau_c\eta}\left(\dfrac{P_p}{P_{min}} - 1\right)$	P_p proportional to N_0; P_{min} independent of N_0; P_0 proportional to N_0 for $P_p \gg P_{min}$, independent to τ_0 and $\Delta\nu$ for $P_p \gg P_{min}$.

E_{min} = minimum amount of absorbed energy necessary to achieve threshold,
E_p = amount of useful energy absorbed by the laser system from the source,
E_0 = output energy of the laser system,
ϵ_{min} = minimum energy input to the flash tube necessary to achieve threshold,
P_{min} = minimum amount of absorbed power necessary to achieve threshold,
P_p = amount of useful energy absorbed by the laser system in the unit time from the source,
P_0 = output energy emitted in the unit time,
π_{min} = minimum power input to the source,
τ_p = duration of the exciting pulse,
τ_0 = radiative lifetime,
τ_c = photon lifetime (damping time of the cavity),
η = quantum efficiency.

The mechanisms associated with the conditions 4 and 5 produce mode conversion.

The characteristic single parameter τ_c, the photon lifetime, may be expressed as follows, in analogy to the microwave cavity case [23]:

$$\frac{1}{\tau_c} = \frac{1}{\tau_R} + \frac{1}{\tau_L}, \tag{19.153}$$

where τ_R is associated with the transmission losses and τ_L with the losses inside the cavity.

We may also define a coupling coefficient as

$$S = \frac{\tau_L}{\tau_R}. \tag{19.154}$$

In an analogy of the microwave cavity case, we may refer to $S > 1$, $S < 1$, and $S = 1$ as overcoupling, undercoupling, and critical coupling, respectively.

By use of the definition of S, τ_c may be expressed as

$$\frac{1}{\tau_c} = \frac{1}{\tau_L}\left(1 + \frac{\tau_L}{\tau_R}\right) = \frac{1}{\tau_L}(1 + S). \tag{19.155}$$

The coupling coefficient expresses the ratio of the transmission of the beam per pass through the mirror to the loss per pass.

As pointed out by Yariv [17], the available laser output depends on the value of S.

We shall limit ourselves to illustrating how S_{opt} can be found in a pulsed four-level laser system. The energy output is given, according to (19.150), by

$$\begin{aligned} E_0 &= p\frac{\tau_0}{\tau_c} h\nu\left(\frac{E_p}{E_{\min}} - 1\right) \\ &= \left[\frac{E_p\eta}{p\tau_0 h\nu_p} - \frac{1}{\tau_L}(S + 1)\right] p\tau_0 h\nu. \end{aligned} \tag{19.156}$$

The available energy output can be obtained by multiplying E_0, as given in (19.156), by

$$\frac{\tau_L}{\tau_L + \tau_R} = \frac{1}{1 + S^{-1}} = \frac{S}{S + 1}. \tag{19.157}$$

Therefore we may write

$$E_{\text{av}} \propto \left[A - \frac{1}{\tau_L}(S + 1)\right]\frac{S}{S + 1} = \frac{AS}{S + 1} - \frac{S}{\tau_L}, \tag{19.158}$$

where

$$A = \frac{E_p \eta}{p\tau_0 h\nu_p}. \tag{19.159}$$

Setting

$$\frac{\partial E_{\text{av}}}{\partial S} = 0, \tag{19.160}$$

we obtain

$$S_{\text{opt}} = -1 + \sqrt{A\tau_L} = -1 + \left[\frac{E_p}{(E_{\text{min}})_{\tau_R=\infty}}\right]^{1/2}, \tag{19.161}$$

where

$$(E_{\text{min}})_{\tau_R=\infty} = p\frac{\tau_0}{\tau_L}\frac{h\nu_p}{\eta}. \tag{19.162}$$

$(E_{\text{min}})_{\tau_R=\infty}$ represents the threshold energy for zero transmittance.

Using the same approach for the *CW* case, we obtain a similar expression for S_{opt}, where E_p and E_{min} are replaced by P_p and P_{min}.

It is to be noted here that the value of the optimum coupling, contrary to the microwave case, does depend on the energy (or power) input. In the present, four-level, case, for $E_p > 4E_{\text{min}}$, the optimum condition requires an overcoupling, whereas for $E_p < 4E_{\text{min}}$ this is not necessary.

By using a similar approach S_{opt} for the three-level case may also be found [17]:

$$S_{\text{opt}} = -1 + \left[1 - \left(\frac{N_0}{(\Delta N_{\text{th}})_{\tau_R=\infty}}\right)\left(\frac{1 - E_p/E_{\text{min}}}{1 + E_p/E_{\text{min}}}\right)\right]^{1/2}. \tag{19.163}$$

S_{opt} for the *CW* three-level system may be obtained by replacing E_p and E_{min} with P_p and P_{min}, respectively.

10.4 The *Q*-Spoiled Laser

A method often used to increase the peak power output of a laser oscillator consists of the so called *Q-switching* or *Q-spoiling*. The application of this method was proposed by Hellwarth [24] and demonstrated by Hellwarth and McClung [25].

The method consists essentially in purposely degrading the *Q* of the laser cavity during the pumping pulse to prevent the system from oscillating and then allowing the population of the metastable state to build up to its maximum possible value ($N_0/2$ in three-level systems and N_0 in four-level systems). Once this condition has been achieved, the *Q* of the cavity is restored to its

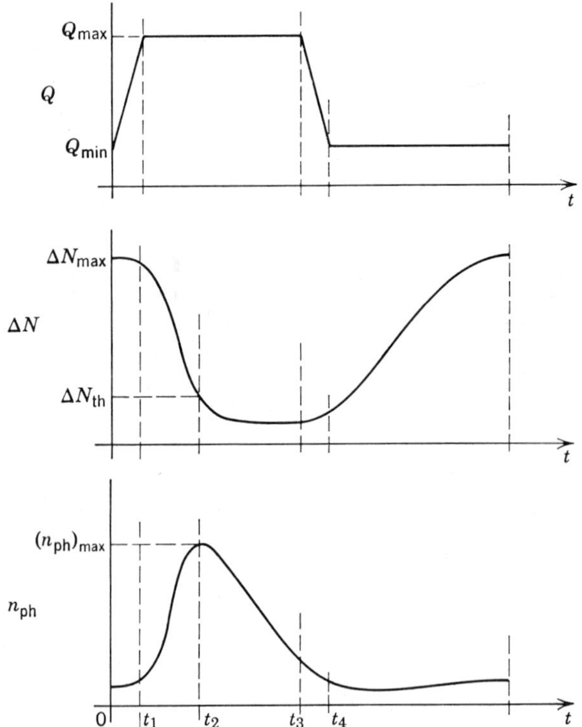

Fig. 19.4. Schematic of the Q-switching operation (reproduced from [17] by permission of Dr. A. Yariv).

original value, thus causing a great surge in stimulated emission and in radiation.

A complete cycle of the Q-switching operation is represented in Fig. 19.4 and consists of the following [17]:

1. $t = 0$. This time corresponds to the end of the pumping pulse. The Q of the cavity is still degraded, the population inversion is at its peak value, and the number of photons in the cavity n_{ph} is small.

2. $t = t_1$. The Q of the cavity is restored to its initial value. This time is of such value that only negligible changes in the population inversion and number of photons occur in the $0 < t < t_1$ interval. For typical cases $t_1 \leq 10^{-9}$ sec.

3. $t_1 < t < t_2$. In this interval of time the process of stimulated emission is greatly enhanced. At the time $t = t_2$ the excess of population inversion has almost disappeared and the number of photons in the cavity is at its maximum since $(t_2 - t_1)$ is small in comparison to τ_c.

The instantaneous power output is given by

$$P = \frac{h\nu}{\tau_c} n_{\text{ph}}. \tag{19.164}$$

The maximum power output is given by

$$P_{\max} = (n_{\text{ph}})_{\max} \frac{h\nu}{\tau_c} = \begin{cases} \dfrac{N_0}{2} \dfrac{h\nu}{\tau_c} & \text{(3-level)}, \\[2ex] N_0 \dfrac{h\nu}{\tau_c} & \text{(4-level)}. \end{cases} \tag{19.165}$$

4. $t_2 < t < t_3$. The number of photons in the cavity reduces with the characteristic time τ_c.

5. $t_3 < t < t_4$. During this time the Q of the cavity is degraded. At $t = t_4$ the pumping pulse is turned on and the population inversion starts to build up again.

The Q-switching operation has been obtained by using Kerr cells (in combination with polarizers), rotating mirrors, or bleachable solutions. For a review of these techniques [26] and [27] may be consulted.

11. PULSATIONS IN LASERS

The coherent emission of several solid state laser oscillators presents variations in its intensity or "spikes." The fact that such variations should occur can be explained considering the details of the competition between the population of the metastable level and the radiation density. As the pumping energy is switched on, the population of the metastable level starts increasing. When the threshold condition is reached the density of the radiation starts building up and with it the stimulated emission process. An increase of the radiation density is then followed by a decrease of the population inversion below its threshold value; in this situation the laser oscillations stop and the regenerative cycle starts again.

In order to study this phenomenon in more detail, we shall follow the treatment of pulsations worked out by Kaiser, Garrett and Wood [16]. According to this treatment the kinetics of the laser effect in a four level system (no population reside in the terminal level of the laser transition) is governed by the following equations:

$$\begin{aligned} \frac{dN}{dt} &= \chi I(t) - \frac{N}{\tau} - \frac{N\alpha W}{\tau}, \\ \frac{dW}{dt} &= \frac{N\alpha W}{\tau} - \beta W, \end{aligned} \tag{19.166}$$

where N = number of atoms in the metastable state;

W = number of photons in the crystal associated with the coherent excitation;

τ = lifetime of the metastable state (sec),

$$\alpha = \frac{v^3}{4\pi^2\nu^2 V\,\Delta\nu} = \frac{1}{p},$$

$$\beta = \frac{1}{\tau_c} = \left(\frac{L}{v\gamma}\right)^{-1} (\text{sec}^{-1}),$$

$$\chi = \frac{Vk}{h\nu'} \quad (\text{cm}^2/\text{erg}),$$

I = intensity of pumping light (erg/cm^2 sec).

In these equations a unit quantum efficiency has been assumed.

When the pumping light becomes time-independent, a stable solution may (or may not) exist. If such a solution exists, it is given by

$$\begin{aligned} \alpha N &= \beta\tau, \\ W &= \frac{\chi I \tau}{\alpha N} - \frac{1}{\alpha} = \frac{\chi}{\beta}\left(I - \frac{\beta}{\chi\alpha}\right). \end{aligned} \tag{19.167}$$

The second expression shows that W, the number of photons associated with the laser beam, grows linearly with $I - I_t$, where

$$I_t = \frac{\beta}{\chi\alpha} = \frac{4\pi^2\nu^2\,\Delta\nu V}{v^3}\frac{1}{\tau_c}\left(\frac{h\nu'}{kV}\right) \tag{19.168}$$

is the pumping intensity at threshold [see (19.144)]. This implies that above threshold, for every photon absorbed, a photon is added to the laser beam.

When the steady-state solutions (19.167) exist, approximate solutions of (19.166) may also represent the asymptotic behavior of the two variables as the number of photons and ions in the metastable state come close to their equilibrium values. Let us put

$$\begin{aligned} N &= \frac{\beta\tau}{\alpha} + n, \\ W &= \frac{\chi I}{\beta} - \frac{1}{\alpha} + w. \end{aligned} \tag{19.169}$$

The replacement of these expressions in (19.166) produces the following

$$\begin{aligned} \dot{n} &= -\beta w - \frac{n}{\tau}\frac{I}{I_t}, \\ \dot{w} &= \frac{n}{\tau}\left(\frac{I}{I_t} - 1\right), \end{aligned} \tag{19.170}$$

where second-order terms have been neglected. From these equations we derive

$$\ddot{w} + \frac{I}{\tau I_t}\dot{w} + \frac{\beta}{\tau}\left(\frac{I}{I_t} - 1\right)w = 0, \tag{19.171}$$

and a similar equation for n. Using as a trial solution

$$w = w_0 e^{-zt}, \tag{19.172}$$

we obtain

$$z^2 + \frac{I}{\tau I_t}z + \frac{\beta}{\tau}\left(\frac{I}{I_t} - 1\right) = 0, \tag{19.173}$$

and, assuming that $\beta/\tau \gg 1$,

$$z = -\frac{I}{2\tau I_t} \pm i\left[\left(\frac{I}{I_t} - 1\right)\frac{\beta}{\tau} - \frac{I^2}{4I_t^2\tau^2}\right]^{1/2} = -\mu \pm i\eta, \tag{19.174}$$

where

$$\mu = \frac{I}{2I_t\tau}$$
$$\eta = \left[\left(\frac{I}{I_t} - 1\right)\frac{\beta}{\tau} - \frac{I^2}{4I_t^2\tau^2}\right]^{1/2}. \tag{19.175}$$

Therefore

$$w = Ae^{-(\mu+i\eta)t} + Be^{-(\mu-i\eta)t}. \tag{19.176}$$

The solutions are damped oscillations with a frequency equal to $(\beta/\tau)^{1/2}$ and with a damping time approximately equal to τ. Now consider two laser resonators, $CaF_2{:}Sm^{2+}$ with $\tau = 2 \times 10^{-6}$ sec and $SrF_2{:}Sm^{2+}$ with $\tau = 10 \times 10^{-3}$ sec. Assuming $\beta = 1.8 \times 10^9$ for both we have:

$$CaF_2{:}Sm^{2+}{:}\ \frac{\beta}{\tau} = \frac{1.8 \times 10^9}{2 \times 10^{-6}} \simeq 10^{15}; \qquad \left(\frac{\beta}{\tau}\right)^{1/2} \simeq 3 \times 10^7\ \text{sec}^{-1},$$

$$SrF_2{:}Sm^{2+}{:}\ \frac{\beta}{\tau} = \frac{1.8 \times 10^9}{10^{-2}} \simeq 2 \times 10^{11}; \qquad \left(\frac{\beta}{\tau}\right)^{1/2} \simeq 4 \times 10^5\ \text{sec}^{-1}.$$

Actually, spiking oscillations are observed in $SrF_2{:}Sm^{2+}$ but not in $CaF_2{:}Sm^{2+}$. This is attributed to the fact that the oscillations for the latter lie beyond the limit of the frequency response of the measuring instrument [16, 28].

REFERENCES

[1] J. E. Geusic and H. E. D. Scovil, "Microwave and Optical Masers," *Rep. Progr. Phys.* **27,** 241 (1964).

[2] H. G. Fox and T. Li, "Resonant Modes in a Maser Interferometer," *Bell. System Tech. J.* **40,** 453 (1961).

[3] M. Born and E. Wolf, *Principles of Optics*, Pergamon, New York, 1959, p. 322.
[4] J. E. Geusic and H. E. D. Scovil, "A Undirectional Traveling-Wave Optical Maser," *Bell System Tech. J.* **41,** 1371 (1962).
[5] E. I. Gordon, "Optical Maser Oscillators and Noise," *Bell System Tech. J.* **43,** 507 (1963).
[6] J. P. Gordon, H. J. Zeiger and C. H. Townes, "The Maser—New Type of Microwave Amplifier, Frequency Standard and Spectrometer," *Phys. Rev.* **99,** 1264 (1955).
[7] T. H. Maiman, "Stimulated Optical Emission in Fluorescent Solids. I. Theoretical Considerations," *Phys. Rev.* **123,** 1145 (1961).
[8] A. L. Schawlow and C. H. Townes," Infrared and Optical Masers," *Phys. Rev.* **112,** 1940 (1958).
[9] K. Shimoda, "Theory of Masers for Higher Frequencies," *Inst. Phys. Chem. Res. (Tokyo)—Sci. Papers* **55,** 1 (1961).
[10] P. Grivet and A. Blaquiere, "Masers and Classical Oscillators," in *Optical Masers*, Polytechnic Press of the Polytechnic Institute of Brooklyn, New York, 1963, p. 69.
[11] T. H. Maiman, "Optical and Microwave-Optical Experiments in Ruby," *Phys. Rev. Letters* **4,** 564 (1960).
[12] T. H. Maiman, "Stimulated Optical Radiation in Ruby," *Nature* **187,** 493 (1960).
[13] T. H. Maiman, "Optical Maser Action in Ruby," *Brit. Comm. Electronics* **7,** 674 (1960).
[14] L. F. Johnson, H. J. Guggenheim and R. A. Thomas, "Phonon-Terminated Lasers," *Phys. Rev.* **149,** 179 (1966).
[15] A. Yariv and J. P. Gordon, "The Laser," *Proc. IEEE*, **51,** 4 (1963).
[16] W. Kaiser, C. G. B. Garrett and D. L. Wood, "Fluorescence and Optical Maser Effects in CaF_2:Sm^{++}," *Phys. Rev.* **123,** 766 (1961).
[17] A. Yariv, "Energy and Power Considerations in Injection and Optically Pumped Lasers," *Proc. IEEE*, **51,** 1723 (1963).
[18] A. Yariv, "Theory of Power Output and Optimum Coupling in Laser Oscillators," in *Quantum Electronics Proceedings of the Third International Congress*, edited by P. Grivet and N. Bloembergen, Columbia, New York, 1964, p. 1055.
[19] A. Yariv, *Quantum Electronics*, Wiley, New York, 1967.
[20] C. L. Tang, H. Statz, and G. De Mars, "Regular Spiking and Single-Mode Operation of Ruby Laser," *Appl. Phys. Letters* **2,** 222 (1963).
[21] C. L. Tang, H. Statz, G. De Mars, and D. T. Wilson, "Spectral Properties of a Single-Mode Ruby Laser: Evidence of Homogeneous Broadening of the Zero-Phonon Lines in Solids," *Phys. Rev.* **136,** A1 (1964).
[22] W. R. Bennett, "Gaseous Optical Masers," *Appl. Optics*, Suppl. 1, 24 (1962).
[23] C. G. Montgomery, R. H. Dicke, and E. M. Purcell, *Principles of Microwave Circuits*, McGraw Hill, New York, 1948, p. 228.
[24] R. W. Hellwarth, "Control of Fluorescent Pulsations," in *Advances in Quantum Electronics*, J. R. Singer, Ed., Columbia University Press, New York, 1961, p. 334.
[25] R. W. Hellwarth and F. J. McClung, "Giant Optical Pulsations from Ruby," *Bull. Am. Phys. Soc.* **5,** 414 (1961).
[26] B. A. Lengyel, *Introduction to Laser Physics*, Wiley, New York, 1966.
[27] W. V. Smith and P. P. Sorokin, *The Laser*, McGraw-Hill, New York, 1966.
[28] P. P. Sorokin, M. J. Stevenson, J. R. Lankard, and G. D. Pettit, "Spectroscopy and Optical Maser Action in SrF_2:Sm^{2+}," *Phys. Rev.* **127,** 503 (1962).

Appendix 1 Tables of Characteristics of Optically Pumped Solid State Lasers

Table A.1 Transition Metal Ion Lasers

Ion	Host Material	Transition	Wavelength (μ)	Fluorescence Linewidth (cm^{-1})	Fluorescence Lifetime (msec)	Energy of Terminal Level (cm^{-1})	Absorption Bands (μ)	Temperature (°K)	Lamp	Mode of Operation	Threshold	References	Comments
Cr^{3+}	Al_2O_3	${}^2E(\bar{E}) \rightarrow {}^4A_2$	0.6943	~10	3	0	0.32–0.42 0.5–0.6	300	*FT*524	*P*	>1000 J	[1, 2, 3]	
			0.6943			0		300	Hg	*CW*	840 W	[4]	70 mW obtained with 2000 W input
			0.6934	~0.1		0		77	*FT*524	*P*	~800 J	[5]	
			0.6934			0		77	Hg	*CW*	850 W	[6]	4 mW obtained with 930 W input (Arc Hanovia 941B)
		${}^2E(2\bar{A}) \rightarrow {}^4A_2$	0.6929	~0.1		0		290		*P*	>1000 J	[7]	Threshold 50% higher than for the R_1 line.
Ni^{2+}	MgF_3[1]	${}^3T_2 \rightarrow {}^3A_2$	1.623		11.5	340	0.38–0.48 0.68–0.99 1.10–1.35	77	*FT*524	*P*	150 J	[8, 9]	*CW* operation obtained at 85°K with 85 W threshold using a W lamp. For a 500 W input a 1 W output.
			1.636			390		77–82	*FT*524	*P*	160 J		
			1.674–1.676			526–533		82–100	*FT*524	*P*	160–170 J		
			1.731–1.756			723–805		100–192	*FT*524	*P*	170–570 J		
			1.785–1.797			898–935		198–240	*FT*524	*P*	570–1650 J		
	MnF_3[1]	${}^3T_2 \rightarrow {}^3A_2$	1.915		11.1	580[2]		77	*FT*524	*P*	840 J	[9]	There is evidence of energy transfer from Mn^{2+} to Ni^{2+}. The strongest pumping band for Ni^{2+} is the ${}^4T_1$ band of Mn^{2+} at 0.52μ[9].
			1.865		11.3	560		20	*FT*524	*P*	740 J		
			1.922		11.1	600		77	*FT*524	*P*	210 J		
			1.929			620		85	*FT*524	*P*			*CW* operation with a 270 W threshold using a W (*T*3*Q*) lamp.
			1.939			650		85	*FT*524	*P*			*CW* operation with a 240 W threshold using a W (*T*3*Q*) lamp.
	MgO[1]	${}^3T_3 \rightarrow {}^3A_2$	1.3144			398		77	*FT*524	*P*	230 J	[9]	
Co^{2+}	MgF_3[1]	${}^4T_2 \rightarrow {}^4T_1$	1.750		1.3	1087	0.44–0.55 0.60–0.75 1.1–1.5	77	*FT*524	*P*	690 J	[9, 10]	
			1.8035			1256		77	*FT*524	*P*	730 J		
			1.99			1780		77	*FT*524	*P*	660 J		
			2.05			1930		77	*FT*524	*P*	700 J		
	ZnF_2[1]	${}^4T_2 \rightarrow {}^4T_1$	2.165		0.4	1895		77	*FT*524	*P*	430 J	[9, 10]	
	$KMgF_3$[1]	${}^4T_2 \rightarrow {}^4T_1$	1.821		3.1	1420		77	*FT*524	*P*	530 J	[9]	
V^{2+}	MgF_2[1]	${}^4T_2 \rightarrow {}^4A_1$	1.1213		2.3	1150		77	*FT*524	*P*	1070 J	[9]	

[1] All the transitions for MgF_2:Ni^{2+}, MnF_2:Ni^{2+}, MgO:Ni^{2+}, MgF_2:Co^{2+}, ZnF_2:Co^{2+}, $KMgF_3$:Co^{2+}, and MgF_2:V^{2+} are phonon-assisted (vibronic) transitions [11]. Only the 1.750 and 1.8035 μ transitions of MgF_2Co^{2+} are purely electronic: laser emission was made possible in these two transitions only with the aid of multiple-

[2] The ground state of Ni^{2+} in MnF_2 is split into three components at 0, 123 and 235 cm^{-1} by the exchange field due to ordered Mn^{2+} spins [12]; at this temperature the metastable state is at 5927 cm^{-1}. At 77°K (above the Neèl temperature for this material) the ground state is not split by exchange magnetic interaction and the no-

REFERENCES

[1] T. H. Maiman, "Optical Maser Action in Ruby," *Brit. Commun. Electron.* **7,** 674 (1960).

[2] T. H. Maiman, "Stimulated Optical Radiation in Ruby," *Nature* **187,** 493 (1960).

[3] T. H. Maiman, "Stimulated Optical Emission in Fluorescent Solids II, Spectroscopy and Stimulated Emission in Ruby," *Phys. Rev.* **123,** 1151 (1961).

[4] V. Evtuhov and J. K. Neeland, "Continuous Operation of a Ruby Laser at Room Temperature," *Appl. Phys. Letters* **6,** 75 (1965).

[5] R. J. Collins, D. F. Nelson, A. L. Schawlow, W. Bond, C. G. B. Garrett, and W. Kaiser, "Coherence, Narrowing, Directionality and Relaxation Oscillations in the Light Emission from Ruby," *Phys. Rev. Letters* **5,** 303 (1960).

[6] D. F. Nelson, and W. S. Boyle, "A Continuously Operating Ruby Optical Maser," *Appl. Optics* **1,** 181 (1962).

[7] F. J. McClung, S. E. Schwarz, and F. J. Meyer, "R_2 Line Optical Maser Action in Ruby," *J. Appl. Phys.* **33,** 3139 (1962).

[8] L. F. Johnson, R. E. Dietz, and H. J. Guggenheim, "Optical Maser Oscillation from Ni^{2+} in MgF_2 Involving Simultaneous Emission of Phonons," *Phys. Rev. Letters* **11,** 318 (1963).

[9] L. F. Johnson, H. J. Guggenheim, and R. A. Thomas, "Phonon-Terminated Optical Masers," *Phys. Rev.* **149,** 179 (1966).

[10] L. F. Johnson, R. E. Dietz, and H. J. Guggenheim, "Spontaneous and Stimulated Emission from Co^{2+} Ions in MgF_2 and ZnF_2," *Appl. Phys. Letters* **5,** 21 (1964).

[11] D. E. McCumber, "Theory of Phonon-Termination Optical Masers," *Phys. Rev.* **134,** A299 (1964).

[12] L. F. Johnson, R. E. Dietz, and H. J. Guggenheim, "Exchange Splitting of the Ground State of Ni^{2+} Ions in Antiferromagnetic MnF_2, $KMnF_3$, and $RbMnF_3$," *Phys. Rev. Letters* **17,** 13 (1966).

Table A.2 Neodymium Lasers

Host Material	Transition	Wavelength (μ)	Fluorescence Linewidth (cm^{-1})	Fluorescence Lifetime (msec)	Energy of Terminal Level (cm^{-1})	Absorption Bands (μ)	Temperature (°K)	Lamp	Mode of Operation	Threshold	References	Comments
BaF_2	${}^4F_{3/2} \rightarrow {}^4I_{11/2}$	1.06			~2000	0.57–0.6	77	*FT*524	*P*	1600 J	[1]	
CaF_2	${}^4F_{3/2} \rightarrow {}^4I_{11/2}$	1.0457			~2000	{0.56–0.58; 0.7–0.8}	77	*FT*524	*P*	60 J	[1, 2]	
$CaMoO_4$	${}^4F_{3/2} \rightarrow {}^4I_{11/2}$	1.067			~2000	0.57–0.59	77	*FT*524	*P*	100 J	[1]	Fluorescence lines of Nd^{3+} in molybdates somewhat narrower (3.7 cm^{-1} at 77°K) than in tungstates; crystal quality of tungstates is, however, superior.
		1.0673					295	*FT*524	*P*	360 J		
$Ca(NbO_3)_2$	${}^4F_{3/2} \rightarrow {}^4I_{11/2}$	1.06	~2	0.12	~2000		77	*FT*524	*P*	2 J	[3]	Fewer prominent lines in the fluorescence than in $CaWO_4$.
$CaWO_4$[1]	${}^4F_{3/2} \rightarrow {}^4I_{11/2}$	1.065	{5.3 at 77°K; 2.6 at 20°K}	~0.1	~2000	0.57–0.6	77	*FT*524	*P*	0.8 J	[1, 4, 5, 6]	Spikes present in pulsed but not in *CW*.
							85	Hg(*AH*6)	*CW*	400 W		
		1.0652	15				295	*FT*524	*P*	3 J		
		1.0633					77	*FT*524	*P*	14 J		
		1.066					77	*FT*524	*P*	6 J		
		1.0576					77	*FT*524	*P*	80 J		
		1.0582					295	Hg(*AH*6)	*CW*			10 mW obtained with 1500 W input.
	${}^4F_{3/2} \rightarrow {}^4I_{9/2}$	0.9145	{15 at 77°K; 11 at 20°K}		471		77	*FT*524	*P*	4.6 J	[7]	
	${}^4F_{3/2} \rightarrow {}^4I_{13/2}$	1.3372			~4000		77	*FT*524	*P*	2.1 J	[7]	
		1.3392					300	*FT*524	*P*	3.6 J		
		1.345					77	*FT*524	*P*	7.6 J		
		1.387					77	*FT*524	*P*	780 J		
Gd_2O_3	${}^4F_{3/2} \rightarrow {}^4I_{11/2}$	1.0789		0.12	~2000		300		*P*	9 J	[8]	
LaF_3	${}^4F_{3/2} \rightarrow {}^4I_{11/2}$	1.0631			~2000	0.5–0.6	77	*FT*524	*P*	93 J	[1]	
		1.0633					295	*FT*524	*P*	150 J		
		1.0399					77	*FT*524	*P*	75 J		
$Na_{.5}Gd_{.5}WO_4$	${}^4F_{3/2} \rightarrow {}^4I_{11/2}$	1.06			~2000		77	*FT*91	*P*	4.5 J	[9]	
$PbMoO_4$	${}^4F_{3/2} \rightarrow {}^4I_{11/2}$	1.0586			~2000	0.57–0.59	295	*FT*524	*P*	60 J	[1]	
SrF_2	${}^4F_{3/2} \rightarrow {}^4I_{11/2}$	1.0437		{1.6 at 77°K; 1.3–1.4 at 300°K}	~2000	{0.72–0.75; 0.78–0.81}	77	*FT*524	*P*	150 J	[1, 10]	
		1.0370					295	*FT*524	*P*	480 J		

$SrMoO_4$	$^4F_{3/2} \rightarrow {}^4I_{11/2}$	1.0640	3		~2000	0.57–0.6	77	*FT*524	*P*	17 J	[1, 11]	
		1.0643	15				295	*FT*524	*P*	125 J		
		1.0652					77	*FT*524	*P*	70 J		
		1.059					77	*FT*524	*P*	150 J		
		1.0627					77	*FT*524	*P*	170 J		
		1.0611					77	*FT*524	*P*	500 J		
		1.0576					295	*FT*524	*P*	45 J		
$SrWO_4$	$^4F_{3/2} \rightarrow {}^4I_{11/2}$	1.0574			~2000	0.57–0.6	77	*FT*524	*P*	4.7 J	[1]	
		1.0627					77	*FT*524	*P*	5.1 J		
		1.063					295	*FT*524	*P*	180 J		
		1.0607					77	*FT*524	*P*	7.6 J		
$Y_3Al_5O_{12}$	$^4F_{3/2} \rightarrow {}^4I_{11/2}$	1.0612	1.6	0.23	2001		77	*FT*524	*P*	0.2 J	[12]	
		1.0648	6	0.21			300	*FT*524	*P*	1 J		
							300	Hg(*AH*6)	*CW*	700 W		
							300	W(G.E. *DWY*)	*CW*	350 W		Continuous output of 10 W achieved.
$Y_3Ga_5O_{12}$	$^4F_{3/2} \rightarrow {}^4I_{11/2}$	1.0633		0.2	~2000		300	*FT*524	*P*	250 J	[12]	
$Gd_3Ga_5O_{12}$	$^4F_{3/2} \rightarrow {}^4I_{11/2}$	1.0633		0.2	~2000		300	*FT*524	*P*	350 J	[12]	
Y_2O_3	$^4F_{3/2} \rightarrow {}^4I_{11/2}$	1.073	{3.0 at 77°K, 10 at 300°K}	{0.26 at 77 and 300°K}	~2000		77		*P*	260 J	[13]	
		1.078					77		*P*	>600 J		
YVO_4[2]	$^4F_{3/2} \rightarrow {}^4I_{11/2}$	1.069	{4.5 at 77°K, 7 at 300°K}	0.033	~2000		90	*FX*51 (3 of them)	*P*	~1 J	[14]	
Glass[3] (K–Ba–Si)	$^4F_{3/2} \rightarrow {}^4I_{11/2}$	1.06	>200	0.56	1950		300	*FX*33	*P*	50 J	[15, 16]	50 J threshold for rods doped with 6–7% Nd
Glass (Barium Crown)	$^4F_{3/2} \rightarrow {}^4I_{11/2}$	1.06		0.4			300	Hg(*AH*6)	*CW*	900 W	[17]	
Glass (La–Ba–Th–B)	$^4F_{3/2} \rightarrow {}^4I_{13/2}$	1.37			4070		300		*P*	460 J	[18]	
Glass (Na–Ca–Si)	$^4F_{3/2} \rightarrow {}^4I_{9/2}$	0.92			470		77		*P*	700 J	[19]	

[1] $CaWO_4$ doped with Nd^{3+} and Ho^{3+} may oscillate at the two corresponding laser frequencies. The same happens for $CaWO_4$ doped with Nd^{3+} and Tm^{3+} [1]. Both couples of ions have nonoverlapping absorption bands.

[2] There is evidence of energy transfer from the lattice host to Nd^{3+} at 300°K but only partly at 77°K. Pure, colorless YVO_4 emits several lines between 4800 and 5750 Å when excited with radiation in which $\lambda < 4500$ Å. Another type of YVO_4 is yellow and has broad absorption near 4200 Å.

[3] The Li–Mg–Al–Si base glass, when doped with Yb^{3+} and Nd^{3+} may lase at 77°K simultaneously at 1.015 μ and at 1.06 μ, corresponding respectively to Yb^{3+} and Nd^{3+} [20]. Also, in a Na–K–Ba–Si glass laser emission has been observed at 1.06 μ and 300°K to which both Yb^{3+} and Nd^{3+} contribute [21].

REFERENCES

[1] L. F. Johnson, "Optical Maser Characteristics of Rare-Earth Ions in Crystals," *J. Appl. Phys.* **34,** 897 (1963).

[2] L. F. Johnson, "Optical Maser Characteristics of Nd^{3+} in CaF_2," *J. Appl. Phys.* **33,** 756 (1962).

[3] A. A. Ballman, S. P. S. Porto, and A. Yariv, "Calcium Niobate—A New Laser Host Material," *J. Appl. Phys.* **34,** 3155 (1963).

[4] L. F. Johnson, "Characteristics of the $CaWO_4$:Nd^{3+} Optical Maser," in *Quantum Electronics Proceedings of the Third International Congress,* edited by P. Grivet and N. Blombergen, Columbia, New York, 1964, p. 1021.

[5] L. F. Johnson, G. D. Boyd, K. Nassau, and R. R. Soden, "Continuous Operation of a Solid State Optical Maser," *Phys. Rev.* **126,** 1406 (1962).

[6] L. F. Johnson and K. Nassau, "Infrared Fluorescence and Stimulated Emission of Nd^{3+} in $CaWO_4$," *Proc. IRE* **49,** 1704 (1961).

[7] L. F. Johnson and R. A. Thomas, "Maser Oscillations at 0.9 and 1.35 Microns in $CaWO_4$:Nd^{3+}," *Phys. Rev.* **131,** 2038 (1963).

[8] B. H. Soffer and R. H. Hoskins, "Stimulated Emission from Gd_2O_3:Nd^{3+} at Room Temperature and 77°K," *Appl. Phys. Letters* **4,** 113 (1964).

[9] G. E. Peterson and P. M. Bridenbaugh, "Laser Oscillations at 1.06 μ in the Series $Na_{0.5}Gd_{0.5-x}Nd_xWO_4$," *Appl. Phys. Letters* **4,** 173 (1964).

[10] Ya. E. Kariss and P. P. Feofilov, "Absorption, Luminescence and Laser Action of Neodymium in SrF_2 Crystals," *Opt. Spectroscopy* **14,** 89 (1963).

[11] L. F. Johnson and R. R. Soden, "Optical Maser Characteristics of Nd^{3+} in $SrMoO_4$," *J. Appl. Phys.* **33,** 757 (1962).

[12] J. E. Geusic, H. M. Marcos, and L. G. Van Uitert, "Laser Oscillations in Nd-Doped Yttrium Aluminum, Yttrium Gallium and Gadolinium Garnets," *Appl. Phys. Letters* **4,** 182 (1964).

[13] R. H. Hoskins and B. H. Soffer, "Stimulated Emission from Y_2O_3:Nd^{3+}," *Appl. Phys. Letters* **4,** 22 (1964).

[14] J. R. O'Connor, "Unusual Crystal-Field Energy Levels and Efficient Laser Properties of YVO_4:Nd," *Appl. Phys. Letters* **9,** 407 (1966).

[15] E. Snitzer, "Optical Maser Action of Nd^{3+} in a Barium Crown Glass," *Phys. Rev. Letters* **7,** 444 (1961).

[16] E. Snitzer, "Neodymium Glass Laser," in *Quantum Electronics Proceedings of the Third International Congress,* edited by P. Grivet and N. Bloembergen, Columbia, New York, 1964, p. 999.

[17] C. G. Young, "Continuous Glass Laser," *Appl. Phys. Letters* **2,** 151 (1963).

[18] P. B. Maurer, "Laser Action in Neodymium-Doped Glass at 1.37 Microns, "*Appl. Optics* **3,** 153 (1964).

[19] P. B. Maurer, "Operation of a Nd^{3+} Glass Optical Maser at 9180 Å," *Appl. Optics* **2,** 87 (1963).

[20] H. W. Gandy and R. J. Ginther, "Simultaneous Laser Action of Neodymium and Ytterbium Ions in Silicate Glass," *Proc. IRE* **50,** 2114 (1962).

[21] E. Snitzer, "Laser Emission at 1.06 μ from Nd^{3+}–Yb^{3+} Glass," *IEEE J. Quantum Electron.* **QE-2,** 562 (1966).

Table A.3 Trivalent Rare Earth Lasers

Ion	Host Material	Transition	Wavelength (μ)	Fluorescence Linewidth (cm^{-1})	Fluorescence Lifetime (msec)	Energy of Terminal Level (cm^{-1})	Absorption Bands (μ)	Temperature (°K)	Lamp	Mode of Operation	Threshold	References	Comments
Pr	$Ca(NbO_3)_2$	${}^1G_4 \to {}^3H_4$	1.04					77	*FT*524	*P*	20–25 J	[1]	
	$CaWO_4$	${}^1G_4 \to {}^3H_4$	1.0468	~10	0.05	377	0.43–0.49	90	*FT*524	*P*	20 J	[2]	About the same threshold at 77 and 20°K.
	LaF_3	${}^3P_0 \to {}^3H_6$	0.5985			~4200	0.43–0.49	77		*P*	60 J	[3]	
	$SrMoO_4$											[4]	
Eu	Y_2O_3	${}^5D_0 \to {}^7F_2$	0.6113	10.6 at 77°K 24 at 300°K	0.87	859	0.2–0.28; 0.46–0.47 0.52–0.54	220	*FX*100	*P*	85 J	[5]	
Gd	Glass (Li–Mg–Al–Si)	${}^6P_{7/2} \to {}^8S_{7/2}$	0.3125	560	4 at 77°K and 300°K	0	0.274; 0.277	78	*FT*524	*P*	4700 J	[6]	Radiative lifetime 9 msec; quantum efficiency: 0.45.
Ho	$Ca(NbO_3)_2$	${}^5I_7 \to {}^5I_8$	2.047		2.2			77	*FT*524	*P*	90 J	[1]	
	CaF_2	${}^5I_7 \to {}^5I_8$	2.092			~230	0.4–0.66	77	*FT*524	*P*	260 J	[7]	
	$CaWO_4$	${}^5I_7 \to {}^5I_8$	2.046	~10		~230	0.44–0.46	77	*FT*524	*P*	80 J	[7]	
			2.059	~10				77	*FT*524	*P*	250 J	[7, 8]	
	$Y_3Al_5O_{12}$	${}^5I_7 \to {}^5I_8$	2.0975			462		77	*FT*524	*P*	44 J	[9]	
			2.0914					77	*FT*524	*P*	1760 J		
			2.1223			518		77	*FT*524	*P*	410 J		
	Glass (Li–Mg–Al–Si)	${}^5I_7 \to {}^5I_8$	1.95		0.7	230	0.44–0.46	77	*FT*524	*P*	3600 J	[10]	
Er	CaF_2	${}^4I_{13/2} \to {}^4I_{15/2}$	1.617		20	400	0.255; 0.375; 0.52; 0.65; 0.08; 0.9	77		*P*	1000 J	[11]	
		${}^4I_{11/2} \to {}^4I_{13/2}$	2.69[1]		4.5	~6200		298		*P*		[12]	
		${}^4S_{3/2} \to {}^4I_{9/2}$	1.715		0.3 at 77°K	~12,200	0.38; 0.52		Xe	*P*	1000 J	[13]	
			1.726										
			1.696								2000 J		
		${}^4S_{3/2} \to {}^4I_{13/2}$	1.26										Oscillations at 1.26 μ obtained only at the peak of the pumping pulse.
	LaF_3	${}^4I_{13/2} \to {}^4I_{15/2}$	1.6113			400.3		77	PEK Xe	*P*	500 J	[14, 15]	Pronounced spiking present.

Table A.3 Trivalent Rare Earth Lasers (continued)

Ion	Host Material	Transition	Wave-length (μ)	Fluores-cence Linewidth (cm^{-1})	Fluores-cence Lifetime (msec)	Energy of Terminal Level (cm^{-1})	Absorption Bands (μ)	Tempera-ture (°K)	Lamp	Mode of Opera-tion	Thres-hold	Refer-ences	Comments
	$Ca(NbO_3)_2$	$^4I_{13/2} \rightarrow {}^4I_{15/2}$	1.61					77	*FT*524	*P*	800 J	[1]	
	$CaWO_4$	$^4I_{13/2} \rightarrow {}^4I_{15/2}$	1.612	~10		375	{0.38; 0.52	77		*P*	800 J	[16]	
	$Y_3A_5O_{12}$	$^4I_{13/2} \rightarrow {}^4I_{15/2}$	1.6602			525		77	*FT*524	*P*	80 J	[9]	
			1.6452			525		77	*FT*524	*P*	470 J	[9]	
Tm	$Ca(NbO_3)_2$	$^3H_4 \rightarrow {}^3H_6$	1.91					77	*FT*524	*P*	125 J	[1]	
	$CaWO_4$	$^3H_4 \rightarrow {}^3H_6$	1.911	~10		~325	{0.46–0.48; 1.7–1.8	77	*FT*524	*P*	60 J	[7, 17]	
	—		1.916	~10				77	*FT*524	*P*	73 J		
	SrF_2	$^3H_4 \rightarrow {}^3H_6$	1.972		10			77	*FT*524	*P*	1600 J	[7]	
	$Y_3Al_5O_{12}$	$^3H_4 \rightarrow {}^3H_6$	1.8834			240		77	*FT*524	*P*	590 J	[9]	
			2.0132			582		77	*FT*524	*P*	208 J		
								77	W(*T*3*Q*)	*CW*	315 W		
Yb	$Y_3Al_5O_{12}$	$^2F_{5/2} \rightarrow {}^2F_{7/2}$	1.0296	~10	~1	600	0.9–1	77	*FT*524	*P*	325 J	[9]	
	Glass (Li–Mg–Al–Si)	$^2F_{5/2} \rightarrow {}^2F_{7/2}$	1.015	~60	1.45	400	{0.31; 0.22; 0.91; 0.946; 0.976	77	*FT*403	*P*	1300 J	[18]	Going to 4°K threshold de-creases by 10%.

[1] Stimulated emission at 2.69 μ was observed at 298°K in mixed crystals of CaF_2: $x ErF_3 : y TmF_3$ with $x = 12.5, 16.5$, and 20.5 and $y = 0.05$ wt %. At $T = 100$°K, no stimulated emission occurred. For crystals with $x = 12.5, 16.5, 20.5$, and 50 and $y = 0.5$ wt % the stimulated emission shifts from 2.69 μ at 300°K corresponding to the $^4I_{11/2} \rightarrow {}^4I_{13/2}$ of Er^{3+} to 1.86 μ corresponding to the $^3H_4 \rightarrow {}^3H_6$ transition of Tm^{3+}.

REFERENCES

[1] A. A. Ballman, S. P. S. Porto, and A. Yariv, "Calcium Niobate—A New Laser Host Material," *J. Appl. Phys.* **34,** 3155 (1963).

[2] A. Yariv, S. P. S. Porto, and K. Nassau, "Optical Maser Emission from Pr^{3+} in $CaWO_4$," *J. Appl. Phys.* **33,** 2519 (1962).

[3] R. Solomon and L. Mueller, "Stimulated Emission at 5985 Å from Pr^{3+} in LaF_3," *Appl. Phys. Letters* **3,** 133 (1963).

[4] A. Yariv and J. P. Gordon, "The Laser," *Proc. IEEE* **51,** 4 (1963).

[5] N. C. Chang, "Fluorescence and Stimulated Emission from Eu^{3+} in Y_2O_3," *J. Appl. Phys.* **34,** 3500 (1963).

[6] H. W. Gandy and R. J. Ginther, "Stimulated Emission of Ultraviolet Radiation from Gadolinium Activated Glass," *Appl. Phys. Letters* **1,** 25 (1962).

[7] L. F. Johnson, "Optical Maser Characteristics of Rare-Earth Ions in Crystals," *J. Appl. Phys.* **34,** 897 (1963).

[8] L. F. Johnson, G. D. Boyd, and K. Nassau, "Optical Maser Characteristics of Ho^{3+} in $CaWO_4$," *Proc. IRE* **50,** 87 (1962).

[9] L. F. Johnson, J. E. Geusic, and L. G. Van Uitert, "Coherent Oscillations from Tm^{3+}, Ho^{3+}, Yb^{3+}, and Er^{3+} Ions in Yttrium Aluminum Garnet," *Appl. Phys. Letters* **7,** 127 (1965).

[10] H. W. Gandy and R. J. Ginther, "Stimulated Emission from Holmium-Activated Silicate Glass," *Proc. IRE* **50,** 2113 (1962).

[11] S. A. Pollack, "Stimulated Emission in CaF_2:Er^{3+}," *Proc. IEEE* **51,** 1793 (1963).

[12] M. Robinson and D. P. Devor, "Thermal Switching of Laser Emission of Er^{3+} at 2.69 μ and Tm^{3+} at 1.86 μ in Mixed Crystals of CaF_2:ErF_3:TmF_3," *Appl. Phys. Letters* **10,** 167 (1967).

[13] Yu. K. Voron'ko, G. M. Zverev, and A. M. Prokhorov, "Stimulated Emission from Er^{3+} Ions in CaF_2," *Sov. Phys. JETP* **21,** 1023 (1965).

[14] W. F. Krupke and J. B. Gruber, "Energy Levels of Er^{3+} in LaF_3 and Coherent Emission at 1.61 μ," *J. Chem. Phys.* **41,** 1225 (1964).

[15] W. F. Krupke and J. B. Gruber, "Erratum: Energy Levels of Er^{3+} in LaF_3 and Coherent Emission at 1.61 μ," *J. Chem. Phys.* **42,** 1134 (1965).

[16] Z. J. Kiss and R. C. Duncan, "Optical Maser Action in $CaWO_4$:Er^{3+}," *Proc. IRE* **50,** 1531 (1962).

[17] L. F. Johnson, G. D. Boyd, and K. Nassau, "Optical Maser Characteristics of Tm^{3+} in $CaWO_4$," *Proc. IRE* **50,** 86 (1962).

[18] H. W. Etzel, H. W. Gandy, and R. J. Ginther, "Stimulated Emission of Infrared Radiation from Ytterbium Activated Silicate Glass," *Appl. Optics* **1,** 534 (1962).

Table A.4 Divalent Rare Earth Lasers

Ion	Host Material	Transition	Wave-length (μ)	Fluores-cence Linewidth (cm^{-1})	Fluores-cence Lifetime (msec)	Energy of Terminal Level (cm^{-1})	Absorption Bands (μ)	Tempera-ture (°K)	Lamp	Mode of Opera-tion	Thres-hold	Refer-ences	Comments
Sm	CaF_2	$4f^5 5d(A_{1u}) \rightarrow {}^7F_1$	0.7085	~1	0.002	263	0.4–0.45 0.58–0.68	20	*FX*-12	*P*	<0.1 J	[1, 2]	No spikes observed. Low threshold due to short τ_F.
	SrF_2	${}^5D_0 \rightarrow {}^7F_1$	0.6967	~1	14	263		20	*FT*524	*P*	~4 J	[3]	Spikes observed.
Dy	CaF_3	${}^5I_7 \rightarrow {}^5I_8$	2.36	<0.1	12 (depends on concentration)	28.8		77	*FT*524	*P*	20 J	[4–8]	Spikes in pulsed, but not in CW operation. Lowest threshold for optically pumped CW lasers. May give 300 mW out for 800 W in at 77°K [5]. Also, threshold for CW depends on concentration [5]. The lowest CW threshold observed is 15 W with a W source [8]. The system is truly a 4 level system only at 4°K.
							0.8–1	7	Hg(*AH6*)	*CW*	600 W		
Tm	CaF_2	${}^2F_{5/2}(E_{5/2}) \rightarrow {}^2F_{7/2}(E_{5/2})$	1.116	<0.03	~4	0	0.28–0.34 0.53–0.63 0.39–0.40	4	*FX*-100	*P*	50 J	[9]	Excited state absorption at 1.189 μ prevents this system to operate as a 4 level laser.
								27	Hg(*AH6*)	*CW*	1000 W	[10]	

REFERENCES

[1] P. P. Sorokin and M. J. Stevenson, "Solid State Optical Maser Using Sm^{2+} in CaF_2," *IBM J. Res. Devel.* **5,** 56 (1961).

[2] W. Kaiser, C. G. B. Garrett, and D. L. Wood, "Fluorescence and Optical Maser Effects in CaF_2:Sm^{2+}," *Phys. Rev.* **123,** 766 (1961).

[3] P. P. Sorokin, M. J. Stevenson, J. R. Lankard, and G. D. Pettit, "Spectroscopy and Optical Maser Action in SrF_2:Sm^{2+}," *Phys. Rev.* **127,** 503 (1962).

[4] Z. J. Kiss and R. C. Duncan, "Pulsed and Continuous Optical Maser Action in CaF_2:Dy^{2+}," *Proc. IRE* **50,** 1531 (1962).

[5] A. Yariv, "Continuous Operation of a CaF_2:Dy^{2+} Optical Maser," *Proc. IRE* **50,** 1699 (1962).

[6] Z. J. Kiss, H. R. Lewis, and R. C. Duncan, "Sun-Pumped Continuous Optical Maser," *Appl. Phys. Letters* **2,** 93 (1963).

[7] L. F. Johnson, "Continuous Operation of the CaF_2:Dy^{2+} Optical Maser," *Proc. IRE* **50,** 1691 (1962).

[8] Z. J. Kiss, "The CaF_2:Tm^{2+} and the CaF_2:Dy^{2+} Optical Maser Systems," in *Quantum Electronics Proceedings of the Third International Congress*, edited by P. Grivet and N. Bloembergen, Columbia, New York, 1964, p. 805.

[9] Z. J. Kiss and R. C. Duncan, "Optical Maser Action in CaF_2:Tm^{2+}," *Proc. IRE* **50,** 1532 (1962).

[10] R. C. Duncan and Z. J. Kiss, "Continuously Operating CaF_2:Tm^{2+} Optical Maser," *Appl. Phys. Letters* **3,** 23 (1963).

Table A.5 Actinide Lasers

Ion	Host Material	Transition	Wave-length (μ)	Fluores-cence Linewidth (cm^{-1})	Fluores-cence Lifetime (msec)	Energy of Terminal Level (cm^{-1})	Absorption Bands (μ)	Tempera-ture (°K)	Lamp	Mode of Opera-tion	Thres-hold	Refer-ences	Comments
U^{3+}	BaF_2	${}^4I_{11/2} \rightarrow {}^4I_{9/2}$	2.556		0.15		1.1; 1.5	20	*FT*524	*P*	12 J	[1]	
	CaF_2[2]	${}^4I_{11/2} \rightarrow {}^4I_{9/2}$	2.613	~30	1	609	≈0.9	77	*FT*524	*P*	1.5 J[2]	[2–7]	Spikes present in pulsed, but not in *CW* operation.
								77	Hg(*AH6*)	*CW*	2000 W		
			2.57			609		300	*FT*524	*P*			
			2.24			0		77	*FT*524	*P*			
			2.51			470	≈0.6	77	*FT*524	*P*	5 J		
			2.44			398		77	*FT*524	*P*	10 J		
	SrF_2	${}^4I_{11/2} \rightarrow {}^4I_{9/2}$	2.408		0.06	334	{0.4–0.6	90	*FT*524	*P*	78 J	[8]	
					0.08		{1–1.3	77		*P*	32 J		
					0.11			20		*P*	8 J		

[1] According to Porto and Yariv [5], three types of Uranium ion can be found in CaF_2; (a) U^{3+} ions in tetragonal sites, (b) U^{4+} ions in trigonal sites, (c) U^{3+} ions in orthorombic sites. These ions are found in different percentages in different crystals. Ions of type (a) are thought to be responsible for the 2.61, 2.24, and 2.57 μ lines. Ions of type (c) are thought to be responsible for the 2.51 and 2.44 μ lines. Lifetime measurements gave the same results for tetragonal and orthorombic U^{3+}, 135 ± 15 μsec up to 77°K, 95 ± 15 μsec at 70°K, and <15 μsec at 300°K.

[2] Boyd *et al.* [4] found the following thresholds for the 2.613 μ line, using a *FT* 524 flash tube: 2 J at 20°K, 3.78 J at 77°K, 4.35 J at 90K° and 120 J at 300°K.

REFERENCES

[1] S. P. S. Porto and A. Yariv, "Optical Maser Characteristic $BaF_2:U^{3+}$," *Proc. IRE* **50,** 1542 (1962).

[2] P. P. Sorokin and M. J. Stevenson, "Stimulated Infrared Emission of Trivalent Uranium," *Phys. Rev. Letters* **5,** 557 (1960).

[3] P. P. Sorokin and M. J. Stevenson, "Stimulated Emission from $CaF_2:U^{3+}$ and $CaF_2:Sm^{2+}$" in *Advances in Quantum Electronics*, edited by J. R. Singer, Columbia New York, 1961, p. 65.

[4] G. D. Boyd, R. J. Collins, S. P. S. Porto, A. Yariv, and W. A. Hargreaves, "Excitation, Relaxation and Continuous Maser Action in the 2.613 Micron Transition of $CaF_2:U^{3+}$ Masers," *Phys. Rev. Letters* **8,** 269 (1962).

[5] S. P. S. Porto and A. Yariv, "Low Lying Energy Levels and Comparison of Laser Action of U^{3+} in CaF_2," in *Quantum Electronics Proceedings of the Third International Congress*, edited by P. Grivet and N. Bloembergen, Columbia, New York, 1964, p. 717.

[6] J. P. Wittke, Z. J. Kiss, R. C. Duncan, and J. J. McCormick, "Uranium-Doped CaF_2 as a Laser Material," *Proc. IEEE* **51,** 56 (1962).

[7] S. P. S. Porto and A. Yariv, "Trigonal Sites and 2.24 Micron Coherent Emission of U^{3+} in CaF_2," *J. Appl. Phys.* **33,** 1620 (1962).

[8] S. P. S. Porto and A. Yariv, "Excitation, Relaxation and Optical Maser Action at 2.407 Microns in $SrF_2:U^{3+}$," *Proc. IRE* **50,** 1543 (1962).

Table A.6 Cross-Pumped Lasers

Sensitizer Ion	Activator Ion	Host Material	Activator Transition	Wavelength (μ)	Fluorescence Linewidth (cm^{-1})	Activator Lifetime (msec)^1	Sensitizer Lifetime (msec)	Energy of Terminal Level (cm^{-1})	Absorption Bands (μ)	Temperature (°K)	Lamp	Mode of Operation	Threshold	References	Comments
Cr^{3+}	Cr^{3+} Ion Pair	Al_2O_3		0.701(N_2)	~2	1.1		35	{0.32–0.42; 0.5–0.6}	77	*FT*524	*P*	~3000 J	[1, 2, 3]	The single ion lifetime depends on concentration. For a 2.1% Cr^{3+}. concentration it is 0.6 msec [3].
				0.704(N_1)	~2	1.3		33		77	*FT*524	*P*	~3000 J		
Cr^{3+}	Nd^{3+}	$Y_3Al_5O_{12}$	$^4F_{3/2} \rightarrow {}^4I_{11/2}$	1.0612	~1.6	0.23	8.1; 3.5	2001	{Cr^{3+} and Nd^{3+} bands}	77	Hg(*AH*6)	*CW*	180 W	[4]	The threshold is lowered by 2 with the Hg excitation.
										77	*W*(*T*3*Q*)	*CW*	440 W		
										300	Hg(*AH*6)	*CW*	750 W		
										300	W(*T*3*Q*)	*CW*	>800 W		
										300	Xe(*FX*33)	*P*	2.1 J		
Ce^{3+}	Nd^{3+}	CeF_3	$^4F_{3/2} \rightarrow {}^4I_{11/2}$	1.06	~9	0.225		2222	<0.45	90	Xe(*FX*51)	*P*	41 J	[5]	Absorption band ($^2F_{7/2}$) at ~2000 cm^{-1} in CeF_3 helps to depopulate terminal state ($^4I_{11/2}$) of Nd^{3+}. When system pumped with 3–6 μ radiation, threshold increases.
Mn^{2+}	Nd^{3+}	Phosphate Glass	$^4F_{3/2} \rightarrow {}^4I_{11/2}$	1.06					{Nd^{3+} and Mn^{2+} Bands}		Xe(*PEK* 3-1)	*P*	~50 J	[6]	Transfer time $\leq$ 200 μsec Mn^{2+} pumping 35% as effective as Nd^{3+} pumping.
UO_2^{2+}	Nd^{3+}	Barium Crown Glass	$^4F_{3/2} \rightarrow {}^4I_{11/2}$	1.06		0.6	0.2; 0.027		Nd^{3+} bands +0.49, 0.45, 0.42, <0.35				135 J	[7]	Internal *Q* switching produced by UO_2^{2+}. Efficiency of transfer 86% for 4 weight % of Nd_2O_3.
Er^{3+}	Ho^{3+}	Er_2O_3	$^5I_7 \rightarrow {}^5I_8$	2.121		{10 for 1 at. %; 1.3 for 5 at.%}			{Er^{3+} bands (~0.49; 0.53; 0.66; 0.81 0.95; 1.5) and Ho^{3+} bands}	77		*P*	5 J	[8]	
										77		*CW*	200 W		
										145		*P*	20 J		
		$CaMoO_4$	$^5I_7 \rightarrow {}^5I_8$	2.0740	~10	1.3		~250		77	*FT*524	*P*	107 J	[9]	Threshold for Ho^{3+} oscillations reduced by 2 by energy transfer from Er^{3+}.
				2.0707	~10					77	*FT*524	*P*	170 J		
				2.0556	~10					77	*FT*524	*P*	310 J		

		$Er_{1.48}$–$Y_{1.5}$–Al_5O_{12}	$^5I_7$ - $^5I_8$	2.0979			462			*FT*524	*P*	11 J	[10]	
										Hg(*AH*6)	*CW*	600 W		
										W(*T*3*Q*)	*CW*	47 W		
				2.0917						*FT*524	*P*	390 J		
				~2.123			518			*FT*524	*P*	3800 J		
Cr^{3+}	Ho^{3+}	$Y_3Al_5O_{12}$	$^5I_7 \rightarrow {}^5I_8$	2.0975			462	Cr^{3+} and Ho^{3+} bands	77	*FT*524	*P*	25 J	[10]	
									77	W(*T*3*Q*)	*CW*	210 W		
				2.1223			518		77	*FT*524	*P*	25 J		
									77	Hg(*AH*6)	*CW*	1300 W		
									77	W(*T*3*Q*)	*CW*	250 W		
Er^{3+}, Tm^{3+}	Ho^{3+}	$Y_3Fe_5O_{12}$	$^5I_7 \rightarrow {}^5I_8$	2.086					77	*FT*524	*P*	90 J	[11]	Expected to be ½ as efficient as *CW* source as the corresponding $Y_3Al_5O_{12}$ system.
				2.09					77	*FT*524	*P*	275 J		
Er^{3+}, Yb^{3+} and Tm^{3+}	Ho^{3+}	$Y_3Al_5O_{12}$	$^5I_7 \rightarrow {}^5I_8$	2.0982			462	0.6–1.9	77		*P*		[12]	Fluorescence of Er^{3+}, Yb^{3+} and Tm^{3+} quenched because of energy transfer to Ho^{3+}.
				2.1227			518		77		*P*			
				2.1288			532		295		*P*	1240 J		
				2.1227			518		85	W	*CW*	30 W		15 W output for 300 W input; 5% efficiency. At 77°K the line at 2.098 μ has the lower threshold.
		CaF_2	$^5I_7 \rightarrow {}^5I_8$	2.06					298		*P*	100 J	[13]	At 100°K oscillations take place at 2.05 μ with 16 Joules threshold.
Yb^{3+}	Ho^{3+}	Silicate Glass	$^5I_7 \rightarrow {}^5I_8$	2.08	1.1	1.1; 0.08	300	Yb^{3+} (0.85–1.05) and Ho^{3+} Bands	80	*FT*524	*P*	150 J	[14]	
Yb^{3+}	Er^{3+}	Silicate Glass		1.5426	14		0		300		*P*	700 J	[15]	Er^{3+} lases as a three-level system in this case.
Colour Centre	Er^{3+}	CaF_2	$^4I_{13/2} \rightarrow {}^4I_{15/2}$	1.5308 1.5298	0.8^2		~30	0.36; 0.55	4		*P*	8.2 J	[16]	Laser oscillations occur only when the crystals have been subjected to γ irradiation. The colour centres are associated with the γ irradiation of oxygen impurities introduced by the oxide doping.

Table A.6 Cross-Pumped Lasers (continued)

Sensitizer Ion	Activator Ion	Host Material	Activator Transition	Wavelength (μ)	Fluorescence Linewidth (cm^{-1})	Activator Lifetime (msec)[1]	Sensitizer Lifetime (msec)	Energy of Terminal Level (cm^{-1})	Absorption Bands (μ)	Temperature (°K)	Lamp	Mode of Operation	Threshold	References	Comments
Er^{3+}	Tm^{3+}	$CaMoO_4$	$^3H_4 \rightarrow {}^3H_6$	1.9115	~10			~325	Er^{3+} and Tm^{3+} bands	77	*FT*524	*P*	19 J	[9]	Threshold for Tm^{3+} oscillations reduced by ~3 by energy transfer from Er^{3+}.
				1.9060	~10					77	*FT*524	*P*	20 J		
		$Er_{1.48}$–$Y_{1.5}$–Al_5O_{12}	$^3H_4 \rightarrow {}^3H_6$	1.880		15 at 77°K; 2.3 at 295°K		228		77	*FT*524	*P*	264 J	[10]	At room temperature $Er^{3+} \rightarrow Tm^{3+}$ transfer very inefficient.
				1.884				240		77	*FT*524	*P*	180 J		
				2.014				582		77	*FT*524	*P*	170 J		
								582		77	W(*T*3*Q*)	*CW*	520 W		
		Er_2O_3		1.934		2.9				77		*P*	<3 J	[17]	
										77	W	*CW*			
Cr^{3+}	Tm^{3+}	$Y_3Al_5O_{12}$	$^3H_4 \rightarrow {}^3H_6$	2.0132				582	Cr^{3+} and Tm^{3+} bands	77	*FT*524	*P*	30 J	[10]	
				2.0132				582		77	Hg(*AH*6)	*CW*	800 W		
				2.0132				582		77	W(*T*3*Q*)	*CW*	160 W		
				2.019				600		295	*FT*524	*P*	640 J		
Nd^{3+}	Yb^{3+}	Borate Glass		1.018		0.88			Nd^{3+} and Yb^{3+} Bands	77	Kemlite 4*HL-GH*	*P*	100 J	[18]	Same threshold at 20°K: threshold at 300°K increases by 5.

[1] When two lifetimes are given for the sensitizer ion, the first is the lifetime in the absence of the activator, the second is the lifetime in the presence of the activator.

[2] A component with 1.3 msec decay time also observed in the decay pattern.

REFERENCES

[1] A. L. Schawlow, D. L. Wood, and A. M. Clogston, "Electronic Spectra of Exchange Coupled Pairs in Crystals," *Phys. Rev. Letters* **3,** 271 (1959).

[2] A. L. Schawlow and G. E. Devlin, "Simultaneous Optical Maser Action in Two Ruby Satellite Lines," *Phys. Rev. Letters* **6,** 96 (1961).

[3] R. C. Powell, B. Di Bartolo, B. Birang, and C. S. Naiman, "Fluorescence Studies of Energy Transfer Between Single and Pair Cr^{3+} Systems in Al_2O_3," *Phys. Rev.* **155,** 296 (1967).

[4] Z. J. Kiss and R. C. Duncan, "Cross-Pumped Cr^{3+}–Nd^{3+}:YAG Laser System," *Appl. Phys. Letters* **5,** 200 (1964).

[5] J. R. O'Connor and W. A. Hargreaves, "Lattice Energy Transfer and Stimulated Emission from CeF_3:Nd^{3+}," *Appl. Phys. Letters* **4,** 208 (1964).

[6] N. T. Melamed, C. Hirayama, and E. K. Davis, "Laser Action in Neodymium Doped Glass Produced through Energy Transfer," *Appl. Phys. Letters* **7,** 170 (1965).

[7] N. T. Melamed and C. Hirayama, "Laser Action in Uranyl-Sensitized Nd-Doped Glass," *Appl. Phys. Letters* **6,** 431 (1965).

[8] B. H. Soffer and R. H. Hoskins, "Energy Transfer and CW Laser Action in Ho^{3+}: Er_2O_3," *IEEE J. Quantum Electron.* **QE-2,** 253 (1966).

[9] L. F. Johnson, L. G. Van Uitert, J. J. Rubin, and R. A. Thomas, "Energy Transfer from Er^{3+} to Tm^{3+} and Ho^{3+} in Crystals," *Phys. Rev.* **133,** A494 (1964).

[10] L. F. Johnson, J. E. Geusic, and L. G. Van Uitert, "Coherent Oscillations from Tm^{3+}, Ho^{3+}, Yb^{3+} and Er^{3+} Ions in Yttrium Aluminum Garnet," *Appl. Phys. Letters* **7,** 127 (1965).

[11] L. F. Johnson, J. P. Remeika, and J. F. Dillon, Jr., "Coherent Emission from Ho^{3+} Ions in Yttrium Iron Garnet," *Phys. Letters* **21,** 37 (1966).

[12] L. F. Johnson, J. E. Geusic, and L. G. Van Uitert, "Efficient, High Power Coherent Emission from Ho^{3+} Ions in Yttrium Aluminum Garnet, Assisted by Energy Transfer," *Appl. Phys. Letters* **8,** 200 (1966).

[13] M. Robinson and D. P. Devor, "Thermal Switching of Laser Emission of Er^{3+} at 2.69 μ and Tm^{3+} at 1.86 μ in Mixed Crystals of CaF_2:ErF_3:TmF_3," *Appl. Phys. Letters* **10,** 167 (1967).

[14] H. W. Gandy, R. J. Ginther, and J. F. Weller, "Energy Transfer and Ho^{3+} Laser Action in Silicate Glass Coactivated with Yb^{3+} and Ho^{3+}," *Appl. Phys. Letters* **6,** 237 (1965).

[15] E. Snitzer and R. Woodcock, "Yb^{3+}–Er^{3+} Laser," *Appl. Phys. Letters* **6,** 45 (1965).

[16] P. A. Forrester and D. F. Sampson, "A New Laser Line Due to Energy Transfer from Colour Centres to Erbium Ions in CaF_2," *Proc. Phys. Soc.* **88,** 199 (1966).

[17] B. H. Soffer and R. H. Hoskins, "Energy Transfer and CW Laser Action in Tm^{3+}: Er_2O_3," *Appl. Phys. Letters* **6,** 200 (1965).

[18] A. D. Pearson and S. P. S. Porto, "Nonradiative Energy Exchange and Laser Oscillation in Yb^{3+}-, Nd^{3+}-Doped Borate Glass," *Appl. Phys. Letters* **4,** 202 (1964).

Appendix 2 Bibliography on Laser Materials

[1] A. J. Bevolo and W. A. Baker, "Laser Emission Lines and Materials," *Appl. Optics* **4,** 531 (1965).

[2] L. G. Van Uitert, "Luminescence of Insulating Solids for Optical Masers," in *Luminescence of Inorganic Solids*, P. Goldberg, Ed., Academic, New York, 1966, p. 465.

[3] A. Yariv and J. P. Gordon, "The Laser," *Proc. IEEE* **51,** 4 (1963).

[4] Z. J. Kiss and R. J. Pressley, "Crystalline Solid Lasers," *Appl. Optics* **5,** 1474 (1966).

[5] E. Snitzer, "Glass Lasers," *Appl. Optics* **5,** 1487 (1966).

[6] L. F. Johnson, "Optical Characteristics of Rare-Earth Ions in Crystals," *J. Appl. Phys.* **34,** 897 (1963).

[7] Laser Focus, Characteristics of Lasers 1965, special report.

[8] K. Tomiyasu, "Laser Bibliography," *IEEE J. Quant. Electron.* **QE-1,** 133 (1965).

[9] K. Tomiyasu, "Laser Bibliography II," *IEEE J. Quant. Electron.* **QE-1,** 199 (1965).

[10] K. Tomiyasu, "Laser Bibliography III," *IEEE J. Quant. Electron.* **QE-1,** 124 (1966).

[11] K. Tomiyasu, "Laser Bibliography IV," *IEEE J. Quant. Electron.* **QE-2,** 726 (1966).

[12] K. Tomiyasu, "Laser Bibliography V," *IEEE J. Quant. Electron.* **QE-3,** 296 (1967).

[13] P. Görlich, H. Karras, G. Kötitz, and R. Lehman, "Spectroscopic Properties of Activated Laser Materials (I)," *Phys. Stat. Sol.* **5,** 437 (1964).

[14] P. Görlich, H. Karras, G. Kötitz, and R. Lehman, "Spectroscopic Properties of Activated Laser Crystals (II)," *Phys. Stat. Sol.* **6,** 277 (1964).

[15] P. Görlich, H. Karras, G. Kötitz, and R. Lehman, "Spectroscopic Properties of Activated Laser Crystals (III)," *Phys. Stat. Sol.* **8,** 835 (1965).

[16] E. V. Ashburn, "Bibliography of the Open Literature on Lasers," *J. Opt. Soc. Am.* **53,** 647 (1963).

[17] E. V. Ashburn, B. A. Lengyel, and R. W. Merry, "Bibliography on the Open Literature on Lasers II," *J. Opt. Soc. Am.* **54,** 135 (1964).

[18] E. V. Ashburn, "Bibliography on the Open Literature on Lasers III," *J. Opt. Soc. Am.* **55,** 752 (1965).

[19] E. V. Ashburn, "Bibliography on the Open Literature on Lasers IV," *J. Opt. Soc. Am.* **55,** 1040 (1965).

[20] E. V. Ashburn, "Bibliography on the Open Literature on Lasers V," *J. Opt. Soc. Am.* **56,** 263 (1966).

[21] E. V. Ashburn and B. A. Lengyel, "Bibliography on the Open Literature of Lasers VI," *J. Opt. Soc. Am.* **57,** 119 (1967).

[22] A. A. Kaminskii and V. V. Osiko, "Inorganic Laser Materials with Ionic Structure," *Inorganic Materials* (Izvestiya Akademii Naukii SSRR—Translation) **1,** 1853 (1965).

[23] G. O. Karapetyan and A. L. Reishakhrit, "Luminescent Glasses as Laser Materials," *Inorganic Materials* (Izvestiya Akademii Naukii SSRR—Translation) **3,** 190 (1967).

Author Index

Numbers in brackets indicate references.

Subject Index